Theory of Business Finance

advanced readings

Theory of Business Finance

advanced readings

J. Fred Weston and Donald H. Woods
UNIVERSITY OF CALIFORNIA, LOS ANGELES

WADSWORTH PUBLISHING COMPANY, INC., BELMONT, CALIFORNIA

L.C. Cat. Card No.: 67-19991

Printed in the United States of America

PREFACE

The articles in this book were selected on the basis of the following five criteria. First, since this book is designed for use in graduate courses in finance, it was decided that its proper focus should be on *analytical* approaches to issues in the field of business finance, rather than on the more traditional approach of descriptive and institutional material. This weighting toward analysis and measurement parallels the stress of modern professional literature in finance.

Second, articles were sought which show the relationships between financial decisions, the theory of the firm, and the operation of the economic system. The objective here is to demonstrate that the business financial decision is one segment of specific management functions. But, in addition, these decisions are also a part of the economic theory of the firm. Since business firms are one of the sets of basic units of the economic system, their relationship and interaction with the total economic system behavior should also be indicated.

A third criterion was to select articles which illustrate the application of new tools and new techniques of analysis in the finance field. Some of the important new tools and techniques have developed in response to the attempt to deal with uncertainty explicitly. This has given rise to the application of Bayesian statistics, decision theory, and the use of utility trees. Since financial decisions involve maximizing subject to some constraints, the techniques of linear and integer programming will also find increased applicability.

The fourth objective is to indicate that some fundamental issues remain unsettled in many areas of the business finance field. While tremendous advances in the finance field have taken place in the past decade, much remains to be done. For example, only a start has been made on the effective treatment of uncertainty. Analytical approaches have not yet been applied to a number of areas in business finance where descriptive and institutional materials still dominate. Thus, the reason for including some of the articles is to raise issues and to stimulate discussion. Hopefully, a stimulus for advanced research studies will also be provided.

A fifth objective is to provide examples of sound fundamental research in business finance. A number of the articles were selected for the purpose of introducing the student to research methodology and to provide examples of good fundamental research. The examples of methodology include deductive research, illustrated through the use of model building, and testing of models by empirical research. Articles demonstrating effective research methodology were selected to provide standards for further research, conceptual approaches, and guidance. Many unsettled problems still remain, and more fundamental research needs to be performed in the future.

The relevance of these articles is not necessarily limited to university graduate students for significant contributions have also been made by those actively engaged in the practice of finance. The stimulation and application of advanced methodology has taken place in business firms as well as in academia. Furthermore, the stature of the financial executive has been enhanced. His function is no longer limited to being head of a service department, or of simply performing as a staff functionary. The financial executive is presently one of the leading members of organizational management and he is often responsible for strategic planning and control of the firm's activities.

The topics covered by the book focus on fundamental questions of the finance field and are all related to the central problem of factors determining the valuation of the firm. This book includes discussion of investment decisions and financing (including mergers and acquisitions), the cost of capital and how it is affected by financial structure, and dividend policy. The final two topics concern important environmental aspects of business financial decision making: money and capital markets and international business financing.

In the Introductory Survey, we attempt to give some indication of the state of knowledge in the finance field at the present time, and to identify the accomplishments of financial theory developed in recent years, as well as to point out some of the challenges which yet remain.

We would like to thank Professors Eugene R. Lerner, Northwestern University, and Red P. Morrissey, University of California, Berkeley, who gave us invaluable advice concerning the selection of articles to be included in this book.

J. Fred Weston and Donald H. Woods

CONTENTS

Theory of Business Finance

advanced readings

PART I

Introduction

1

INTRODUCTORY SURVEY

This essay seeks to indicate the present state of knowledge in the finance field. Important advances have been made both in the methodologies applied to the subject and in the analytical concepts developed, yet important issues remain unsettled. However, a foundation for further significant progress in the development of the theory and practice of financial management has been established.

I. FINANCE AND THE PLANNING PROCESS

Financial management has now become an integral part of the over-all planning activities of the business firm. Therefore, to understand the nature of finance, it is useful to begin with a brief summary of the planning process of a business firm. It is generally recognized that there are at least five specific steps in the planning process. These are:

1. Statement of corporate goals.
2. Analysis of the present potentials of the firm.
3. A comparison of goals vs. present potentials.
4. Analysis of the firm's abilities and inabilities to close gaps between goals and present potentials.
5. Resource allocation decisions to close gaps between goals and present potentials.

In analytic terms, the goal of the enterprise is to maximize the present value of the ownership share to present stockholders. To achieve this goal, objectives are frequently expressed in terms of specific financial objectives. These would include:

1. Growth in sales equal to or greater than the growth rate of the Gross National Product.
2. A profit margin on sales of 6 percent or more after taxes.
3. A return on investment of at least 12 percent after taxes.
4. A growth in earnings per share of at least 6–8 percent per annum.
5. A price-earnings ratio for common stock of at least 20 times.
6. A growth in market price per share of at least 6–8 percent per annum.

Conventional financial analysis deals with historical data; comparisons are made either on a time trend basis or on an industry comparative basis, but basically the data are historical. What is proposed here is fundamentally different in that its orientation analyzes the firm's future prospects and compares these prospects against the goals and objectives the firm has set for itself.

The next step in assessing the firm's potential for accomplishing certain set goals involves an analysis of the firm's strengths and weaknesses. Any differences between what is required to achieve the goals in the firm's product market environment and the firm's present capabilities will require further actions on the part of the firm. These actions, to close the strategic gap faced by the firm, require an allocation of resources. Thus, the stage is set for many aspects of decision making in which finance performs a particularly important role.

II. THE NATURE OF THE FINANCE FUNCTION

The traditional definition of the finance function is the responsibility for the acquisition and utilization of cash. In recent years this traditional role, however, has been broadened in scope considerably. Now the emphasis in the finance function is on an analytical approach to firm decision making, with particular stress on value analysis. This emphasis entails a review of all factors which may influence the value or present worth of the ownership of the firm.

The role of finance has become increasingly significant and complex due to recent environmental changes. In addition to major episodic financial decisions, finance becomes involved in the day-to-day administration of the firm, which includes profit planning and control. Thus, finance participates in responsibility for the establishment of (a) over-all profit goals, (b) departmental and division goals, (c) the measuring of progress and results against standards, and (d) actions and adjustments to help the company move toward its goals and objectives.

Thus, financial decisions are focused both on asset management and on how the assets of the firm should be financed. The central questions of asset management are:

1. How large should the firm seek to be?
2. What rate of growth should the firm have as its goal in terms of sales, assets, employees, and earnings?
3. To what extent should instability in sales and profits be avoided?
4. What kinds of assets should the firm acquire and at what rate?

The traditional questions of business finance must also be considered. These are:

1. What impact will leverage have on the profitability of the firm?
2. What should the target debt to equity ratio be?
3. Should debt financing be of short or long duration?
4. What will be the impact of financial decisions on risk, income, control, and the claims of various sources of financing?
5. What options should be offered to investors in facilitating the sale of securities of the firm?

All of these questions are properly subsumed in relationship to the planning and control activities of the firm.

Financial management is concerned with all of the many aspects of financial ratio analysis used in controlling performance to achieve corporate goals and related plans. These financial ratios may be summarized as follows: (1) liquidity; (2) leverage; (3) activity; (4) profitability; (5) growth; (6) valuation.

Traditionally, finance has had the greatest responsibility with regard to liquidity and leverage. Liquidity measures the ability of the firm to meet its cash obligations as they mature. Leverage refers to the extent to which the firm employs the funds of creditors. Activity ratios measure the effectiveness with which the firm's investment in assets is turned over. Profitability measures the results of operations in terms of the difference between revenues and expenses. Growth measures the rate of progress of the firm in relationship to the economy as a whole, its industry, or past performance. Finally, valuation measures indicate the rate at which the earnings of the firm are capitalized into present values, i.e., price/earnings ratios and market to book values.

With these kinds of responsibilities, the major aspects of the finance function can be identified as embracing four major areas:

1. Fund flows.
2. Analysis of decisions to contribute to maximizing capital value.
3. Information flows.
4. Planning and control.

While a major role of financial management is the acquisition of funds at the lowest cost and under the best terms, finance is also responsible for the effective *utilization* of funds. In connection with these responsibilities, a system for reporting and analyzing fund flows is necessary.

In addition, finance is responsible for the management of capital, and this involves a management of the financing mix. Management of capital embraces the analysis of all decisions and actions affecting values, including the utilization of capital budgeting concepts. The final objective is maximization of capital values.

It is impossible to separate fund flows from information flows which provide intelligence on the flow of funds, people, and material resources. Information flows require the development of a system of accounts to guide efficient resource allocation, and this system must include prompt information on the effects of actions and decisions. It must also provide for a way to relate day-to-day operations to over-all planning goals.

Among the most important responsibilities of finance are assignments in connection with the management of the planning and control process. This process involves analysis to set standards, the formulation of alternative plans and policies, and periodic review of performance in comparison with plans. In addition to monitoring information, corrective actions and modification of plans may be required to improve performance in relation to plans. Finally, any effective system of planning and control must include an incentive system to reward successful performance and to penalize failures in order to help realize the firm's full potentials.

Thus, the finance function has come to embrace a wide range of responsibilities. A distinction should be made, in describing and explaining the nature of financial responsibilities, between process and analytical criteria. Many pages could be filled describing the many aspects of the operations of financial executives in an organizational environment. These aspects mainly concern the processes of financial planning and control, the role of finance in the total business operation, and the place of finance in the general organization and management framework. The *process* of financial administration is not developed in the articles which follow; rather, material is focused on the *analytical* criteria to be applied in carrying out the finance function.

III. FINANCIAL MANAGEMENT OF INVESTMENTS

The basic analytic criteria in finance relate to fundamental economic decision-making in the firm. In seeking to maximize capital values, the marginal efficiency of investment function for the firm is related to the cost of capital function appropriately defined. Thus, the broad area of asset management in the firm is related to investment decisions. An important evolution, the development of discounted cash flow analysis, has taken place in connection with making capital budget decisions. Under conditions of certainty, the payback technique assumes that the investment objective is to minimize the time required to make a profit. The average rate of return approach assumes that the objective is to maximize the ratio of profits plus excess terminal value to investment. Only the present value method, which recognizes the time value of money, is consistent with the enterprise goal mentioned earlier of maximizing the present value of the stockholder's investment.

Objections have been expressed to the internal rate of return method because of the problem of dual returns when additional cash outflows are required following initial inflows. While there have been no specific theoretical objections to the present value method, this method still leaves one faced with the problem of the selection of the appropriate discount rate to employ.

The preceding four criteria for capital budgeting decisions are deficient if they are related to the selection of individual assets under uncertainty, or individual projects under capital rationing and size constraints. Harry Markowitz and Martin Weingartner have made valuable contributions to this area. Harry Markowitz contributed the concept of portfolio analysis which evaluates by quadratic programming the contributions of individual projects, not only as individual projects but also in relation to other projects in the capital budget. In this way, portfolio analysis provides for the evaluation of alternative combinations of investments by taking into account the positive or negative correlations in the expected returns on individual projects. Also, in selecting combinations of expected returns and risk in portfolio decisions, the utility functions of decision makers must be clarified and taken into account.

The other significant contribution in terms of theoretical apparatus is the application of linear programming to capital budgeting and asset management decisions. Fundamentally, every type of asset management problem is an inventory type problem. Some costs increase with the size of investment or inventory while others decrease. A clear example of the type of cost that declines with the size of inventory is the amount of loss in good will caused by the unavailability of the item in the required quantity. But storage and insurance costs would rise with a larger volume of inventory or investment. Since some costs decline with volume and some rise with volume, the total cost function often is U-shaped and therefore has a minimum point.

Since capital budgeting involves indivisible projects, a problem arises if the optimal linear programming solution includes fractions of potential investments. Obviously, a decision to build only seven-tenths of an airplane is nonsense. Weingartner solves this difficulty by utilizing integer programming solutions with unique constraints.

Capital budgeting lends itself to the traditional revenue-marginal cost analysis of economics since maximizing is also involved. In addition, many financing problems can be formulated in terms of a linear programming system. Additional theoretical developments include the application of probability analysis to the data of the problem. One approach is the use of what has been called chance constraint programming. Thus, the articles in this book discuss important new developments in analytic criteria and tools of analysis.

It may be useful at this point to summarize the tools of analysis employed in financial decision making. The tools of analysis include the traditional tools of financial ratio analysis, budget systems, cash flows, and cash budgets. In addition, financial projections, forecasts, and plans will be important elements in the planning and control process. These have broadened into utilization of a wide range of techniques of modern operations analysis. These include linear programming, integer programming, quadratic programming, and chance constraint programming.

In order to make decisions and predictions involving uncertainty, the axioms of decision theory must be employed. Decision theory concepts are formulated so that the resultant choices will be consistent. The techniques of cardinal utility and Bayesian probability judgments are used in developing these decisions.

Also, the advent of the computer is of great significance. Among other things, mass data processing lends itself to the construction of a systems approach to the total firm activity. If the operations of the enterprise are viewed as a total system, the traditional specific management functions, such as production, marketing, and finance, tend to be submerged into a broader over-all framework.

It is important to recognize the distinction between the processes of financial management, the analytic criteria used in making financial decisions, and the tools of analysis which have been described and discussed in the previous section. We will now return to a discussion of analytic criteria, and relate them to the fundamental areas of financial decision making. Six major topics will be covered. These include:

1. Leverage.
2. Growth.
3. Dividend policy.
4. Share repurchase.
5. Mergers.
6. Bankruptcy.

IV. MANAGEMENT OF FINANCIAL LEVERAGE

There has been much regrettable confusion concerning the analysis of the influence of leverage on the value of the firm. A fundamental economic or linear programming situation is involved here in economic terms: for, a marginal efficiency of investment function is related to a cost of capital function.

Demand functions are characteristically negatively sloped, while supply functions at some point become positively sloped. Thus, we would expect the marginal efficiency of capital function (derived either from the traditional criteria of capital budgeting theory or from the modern developments of portfolio analysis and linear programming techniques) to be negatively sloped for the individual firm. When the cost of capital is related to the quantity of funds raised by a given firm in a well-defined time period, we would expect the cost of capital function to have a rising section. Surely, if the firm seeks to double, triple, or quadruple its quantity of funds in relation to its present asset size, it will at some point run into a rising cost of capital function.

Much of the confusion in the business finance literature, however, has arisen when the cost of capital function is related to the financing mix. Here a basic disagreement exists. One school of thought argues that the over-all cost of capital is not influenced by the financing mix. Another holds that, for a number of reasons, the cost of capital function has both a falling and a rising portion and, therefore, a point or range that represents minimum cost and optimal financial policy. Before examining the details of this basic disagreement, it is important to recognize that the analytic criteria for investment decisions will be the same no matter which point of view is adopted. The fundamental analytical principle is that the marginal efficiency of capital function is related to the cost of capital. The cost of capital is the cutoff point for accepting investment proposals. Of course, the problem is simplified if the cost of capital is a constant. If the cost of capital is a function of the quantity of capital raised and the financing mix, the problem becomes complicated from the standpoint of practical implementation. In either case, the fundamental analytical principles remain unchanged. Therefore, we may now consider the two schools of thought with regard to the nature of the cost of capital function.

Modigliani and Miller have argued that the value of the firm is determined by capitalizing its net operating income (see Proposition I in Table 1-1). They assume that personal and corporate leverage are equivalent and

Table 1–1. Basic Modigliani and Miller model.

Proposition I

(Ia) $V = \dfrac{\bar{X}}{\rho_k} = \dfrac{NOT}{\rho_k}$ Assumption

(Ib) $V \equiv D + S$ Definition

Proposition II

(IIa) $\pi \equiv \bar{X} - rD$ Definition

$\pi = \rho_k V - rD$ For $\bar{X}$ substitute $\rho_k V$

$\pi = \rho_k S + \rho_k D - rD$ For V substitute $D + S$

(IIb) $\dfrac{\pi}{S} = \rho_k + (\rho_k + r)\dfrac{D}{S}$ Divide through by S

$i = \rho_k + (\rho_k - r)\dfrac{D}{S}$

where:

V = Equilibrium current market value of the firm.
π = Expected net profits to common shareholders.
$\bar{X} = NOI$ = A firm's expected net operating income.
D = Market value of the debt of a firm.
S = Market value of the stock of a firm.
ρ_k = Capitalization rate for the expected value of uncertain, pure equity earnings streams of the type characteristic of risk class k.
r = Interest rate on debt.

interchangeable and that personal leverage is used to offset corporate leverage. They conclude, therefore, that breaking operating net income into portions paid to bondholders and portions paid to common stockholders cannot change the value of the firm.

What is called Proposition II by Modigliani and Miller is in fact Proposition I restated in a different form. It starts with a generally accepted definition of net income available to common stockholders. By substituting the two formulations of Proposition I in the initial definition, as shown in Table 1–1, the earnings-price ratio on common stock can be expressed in the form of the variables of the Modigliani and Miller Proposition I.

The resulting expression is a compact statement of the determination of a company's earnings-price ratio. The earnings-price ratio is determined by adding to the firm's overall cost of capital the difference between such cost and the cost of debt weighted by its leverage ratio. Leverage is here defined as the ratio of debt to common stock, both measured by current market values.

By making reference to two empirical studies for the oil industry and the utility industry, they found that the data were consistent with their propositions. I repeated their tests for electrical utility companies for the year 1959 and obtained similar results. However, when growth was introduced as another variable, the net effects of leverage were different. The over-all cost of capital declined with both leverage and growth. The cost of equity money also declined with growth but leverage had no significant statistical influence.

Since replication of Modigliani and Miller's empirical tests resulted in different results, their basic assumptions may be questioned. The alternative business finance formulation has asserted that risks to investors are negligible while the leverage ratio is below some critical level. Beyond this critical ratio, the cost of equity money begins to rise slowly and then continues to rise more sharply. The cost of debt money rises at some point beyond the critical leverage ratio for equity money because of the increasing risk of the senior position of creditors. While the costs of both equity money and debt money are relatively constant, the cost of capital falls with increased leverage because the lower cost debt receives greater weighting as leverage increases. At the other extreme, when the cost of equity money rises sharply and the cost of debt money also rises, the cost of capital function also begins to rise. Thus, between the declining and the rising cost of capital segments, some minimum point or range must exist which represents an optimum with respect to minimizing the cost of capital.

The discussion thus far has not dealt with the influence of taxes. Because the symbols employed in the discussion of the role of taxes are numerous and the concepts highly technical, we will begin our discussion with an illustrative income statement, Table 1–2, in order to show the numerical relations which the symbols represent.[1] The main distinction is between the concepts of earnings after taxes ($\bar{X}^t$) and tax adjusted earnings $\bar{X}(1 - t)$.

---

[1] These symbols are employed throughout the three Modigliani-Miller articles on leverage. These articles, and the basic logic behind the development of their models, are summarized in the following discussion. The original articles contain an extended formal development of the mathematical aspects of their models and a reader interested in testing his ability to work through highly formal mathematical elaboration of models from a set of abstract assumptions will find them of great interest. The articles are:

1. "The Cost of Capital, Corporation Finance and the Theory of Investments," *American Economic Review* (June 1958), pp. 261–296.

2. "Taxes and the Cost of Capital: A Correction," *American Economic Review*, LIII (June 1963), 443–443.

3. "Some Estimates of the Cost of Capital to the Electric Utility Industry," *American Economic Review*, LVI (June 1966), 333–390.

Table 1–2. Terminology for analysis of tax influence.

Income statement

Sales		$2,000
Total operating costs		1,800
Net operating income (NOI) ($EBIT$) ($\bar{X}$)		200
Interest paid with $r = 5\%$	($\bar{R}$)	20
Net income before tax (EBT)		180
Tax at 0.4	(t)	72
Net income	($\bar{\pi}^t$)	108

Illustrative relations

Taxes paid $t(\bar{X} - R) = 0.4(200 - 20) = \$72$.

$\bar{X}$ is defined as $\bar{X} = \bar{X}^t + t(\bar{X} - R)$.

$$\bar{X}^t = \bar{\pi}^t + \bar{R} \qquad \bar{X}^t = \text{earnings after taxes}$$

$$= \text{expected profits after taxes plus}$$
$$\text{interest payments}$$

$$= 108 + 20 = \$128$$
$$\bar{X} = 128 + 72 = 200$$

Tax adjusted earnings $= \bar{X}(1 - t) = \bar{X}^t - t\bar{R} = \bar{\pi}^t + \bar{R} - t\bar{R}$

$$200(0.6) = 128 - 8$$
$$\bar{X}(1 - t) = \bar{\pi}^t + (1 - t)\bar{R}$$
$$120 = 108 + 12$$

The amount of earnings after taxes ($\bar{X}^t$) is obtained by adding the total interest payments to net income after taxes and interest. The concept of tax adjusted earnings, $X(1 - t)$, takes into account the tax savings property of interest paid and adds back to net income interest less taxes shelter obtained by the interest payment.

By referring to the symbols as defined and illustrated in Table 1–2, we can summarize Modigliani and Miller's article which corrected their original presentation. The basic equation of Proposition I was expressed on an after-tax basis by dividing earnings after taxes by the value of the firm, as shown in their equation (11).

$$\frac{(\bar{X} - rD)(1 - t) + rD}{V} = \frac{\bar{X}^t}{V} = \rho^t$$

$$\frac{(200 - 20)0.6 + 20}{1,280} = \frac{108 + 20}{1,280} = 0.10 \tag{11}$$

This implies equation (4) of their 1963 "Correction" article.

$$V_L = \frac{(1 - t)\bar{X}}{\rho^t} + \frac{tR}{\rho^t} = \frac{0.6(200)}{0.10} + \frac{8}{0.10} = 1,200 + 80 = 1,280 = V \tag{4}$$

The capitalization rate to be applied to R should be the lower rate, r, since Modigliani and Miller hold the view that the interest payments have less risk associated with them than earnings available to the common stock-holders. Hence, they assert their equation (3), which appeared on page 436 of the June 1963 article.

$$V_L = \frac{(1-t)\bar{X}}{\rho^t} + \frac{tR}{r} = V_u + tD_L \tag{3}$$

Equation (3) is then employed to develop the required before-tax earnings yield. The required before-tax earnings yield had been expressed in equation (31) of the June 1958 article, on page 294.

$$\frac{\bar{X}}{V} = \frac{\rho^t}{1-t}\left[1 - \frac{tr D}{\rho^t V}\right] = \frac{0.10}{0.6}\left[1 - \frac{0.6(0.05)(400)}{0.10(1,250)}\right]$$
$$= \frac{0.10}{0.6}\left[1 - \frac{3}{32}\right] = 15.1\% \tag{31}$$

Based on (3), Modigliani and Miller modify their equation (31) to become (31c) on page 438 of the June 1963 article.

$$\frac{\bar{X}}{V} = \frac{\rho^t}{1-t}\left[1 - t\frac{D}{V}\right] = \frac{0.10}{0.6}\left[1 - 0.6\left(\frac{400}{1,280}\right)\right]$$
$$= \frac{0.10}{0.6}[1 - \tfrac{3}{16}] = 13.6\% \tag{31c}$$

Hence the required after-tax earnings yield of equation (11) above becomes equation (11c) of their "Correction."

$$\frac{\bar{X}^t}{V} = \rho^t - t(\rho^t - r)\frac{D}{V} \tag{11c}$$

The change in equation (11) is of utmost importance. Instead of the cost of capital being a constant, the cost of capital to the firm becomes a function of the tax rate and leverage, because of the tax deductibility of interest. The empirical studies which test the Modigliani and Miller model do, of course, reflect the influence of taxes. In their tax correction article Modigliani and Miller did not attempt to relate or explain the empirical data of their original article in relation to their revised after-tax formulations.

Their proposition for the required after-tax yield on equity capital is also corrected. The original statement was equation (12) of the June 1958 article.

$$\frac{\bar{\pi}^t}{S} = \rho^t + (\rho^t - r)\frac{D}{S} \tag{12}$$

This becomes equation (12c) on page 439 of the June 1963 correction.

$$\frac{\bar{\pi}^t}{S} = \rho^t + (1 - t)(\rho^t - r)\frac{D}{S} \tag{12c}$$

Again, the implications of the correction are significant. Instead of rising linearly with leverage by an amount equal to the difference between the firm's over-all cost of capital and its cost of debt, the yield on equity rises

Table 1-3. Key to symbols.

A = Total assets.
b = Average earnings retention rate.
C = Cost of capital.
D = Debts of the firm.
dA = Purchase cost of assets acquired.
dS^n = Market value of the additional securities issued to finance the investment.
dS^o = Change in value of the holdings of the original owners.
g = Compound growth rate.
$i = \frac{\frac{\% }{g}}{\frac{\pi}{S}}$ = Return to equity.
L = Target proportion of debt to the value of the firm.
P = Preferred stock.
$\overline{Pdv}$ = Expected preferred dividends.
$\bar{\pi}$ = Expected net profits to the common shareholders.
$r(MM)$ = Interest rate on debt or the market capitalization rate for sure streams.
$\rho^* = r(LC)$ = Profitability rate on new investments.
$\bar{R}$ = Expected interest payments.
$\rho_k = k$ = Market's capitalization rate for the expected value of uncertain, pure equity earnings streams of the type characteristic of risk class k.
S = The market value of the common stock.
$T = t$ = The (constant) marginal and average rate of corporate taxation.
X = The (uniform) income stream generated in perpetuity by assets presently held.
$\bar{X} = \bar{E}$ = A firm's expected total earnings.
U = Random disturbance term.
V = Equilibrium current market value.

with leverage reduced by a factor equal to $(1 - t)$. Further implications of the tax correction article of Modigliani and Miller may be seen by reviewing their 1966 article.

First we will summarize their derivation of the structural equation for measuring the influence of leverage and other factors, employing the symbols illustrated in Table 1-2 and set forth more fully in Table 1-3. Table 1-4 presents the derivation of Modigliani and Miller's equation (8) in their June 1966 article.[2] The derivation process indicated in Table 1-4 represents a

---

[2] Page 341.

Table 1–4. Miller and Modigliani derivation of the required yield.

(1)	$\bar{X} = \bar{X}^t + t(\bar{X} - R)$	Description
(1a)	$\bar{X}^t = \bar{X} - t(\bar{X} - R)$	Solving from (1)
	$= \bar{X} - t\bar{X} + tR$	
(1b)	$\bar{X} = (1 - t)\bar{X} + tR$	Substituting in (1)
(1c)	$(1 - t)\bar{X} = \bar{X}^t - tR$	
(2)	$V \equiv \dfrac{(1 - t)\bar{X}}{\rho^t}$	Definition
(3)	$V_0 \equiv \dfrac{tR}{r} = tD$	Definition
(4)	$V = \dfrac{(1 - t)\bar{X}}{\rho^t} + tD$	From (2) plus (3)
(5)	$V = \dfrac{X^t - tR}{\rho^t} + tD$	From (1c)
(6)	$V \equiv S + D + P = \dfrac{\bar{X}(1 - t)}{\rho} + tD$	Definition
(6a)	$V \equiv \dfrac{\bar{X}(1 - t)}{\rho} Dt$	Substituting in (6)
(7)	$dS^n + dP + dD = dA$	Definition from (6)
(8)	$\dfrac{dV}{dA} = \dfrac{dS^o}{dA} + \dfrac{dS^n}{dA} + \dfrac{dP}{dA} + \dfrac{dD}{dA} = \dfrac{dS^o}{dA} + 1$	From (6) and (7)
	$= \dfrac{d\bar{X}}{dA}(1 - t) \cdot \dfrac{1}{\rho} + \dfrac{tdD}{dA}$	

series of definitions and algebraic substitutions. It can readily be seen that equation (8) is equivalent to their equation (31c), previously explained in connection with their tax correction article. Miller and Modigliani's concluding statement in connection with equation (8) reemphasizes the findings of the tax correction article.

> Since the deductibility of interest payments thus makes the value of the firm a function of its financial policy, it must also make the required yield or cost of capital a function of financial policy.[3]

Equation (8) of Miller and Modigliani reflects the influence of leverage and taxes only. They next bring in the role of growth by defining C as the cost of capital in the sense of the required change in after-tax net operating earnings in response to an increase (growth) in assets. In their article Miller and Modigliani formulate an expression for the current market value of the firm "by analogy to the solution we have derived for the certainty case . . . ."[4] This is employed in equation (9d) of Table 1–5 to obtain equation (10) by "analogy."

---

[3] *Ibid.*
[4] They then make reference to their dividend article. M. H. Miller and F. Modigliani, "Dividend Policy, Growth, and the Valuation of Shares," *Journal of Business,* XXXIV (October 1961), 421–422, footnote 15.

Table 1-5. Miller and Modigliani derivation of the current market value of the firm.

(9) $C \equiv (1-t)\dfrac{d\bar{X}}{dA}$

substitute in (9) from (8)

(9a) $C\dfrac{1}{\rho} + t\dfrac{dD}{dA} = \dfrac{dS^o}{dA} + 1$

$\dfrac{dS^o}{dA} \geq 0$ if $C\dfrac{1}{\rho} + t\dfrac{dD}{dA} \geq 1$

(9b)   Therefore solve for C when the expression is equal to 1, the necessary condition for $\dfrac{dS^o}{dA} \geq 0$.

$C\dfrac{1}{\rho} + t\dfrac{dD}{dA} = 1$ (From 9a)

(9c) $C = \rho(1-t)\dfrac{dD}{dA}$ $C_s = \rho$

$= 0.10[1 - 0.4(0.4)]$ $C_D = \rho(1-t)$

$= 0.10(0.84)$

$= 8.4\%$

(9d) $V = \dfrac{\bar{X}}{\rho} + k\bar{X}\left(\dfrac{\rho^* - \rho}{\rho}\right)T$

For $\bar{X}$ substitute (4); for ρ substitute C by "analogy."

(10) $V = \dfrac{1}{\rho}\bar{X}(1-t) + tD + k\bar{X}(1-t)\left[\dfrac{\rho^* - C}{C(1+C)}\right]T$

(11) $(V - tD) = a_o + a_1\bar{X}(1-t) + a_2\overline{\Delta A} + U$
where:

    a_1 is the marginal capitalization rate for pure equity streams in the class.
    a_o is an intercept term whose size and sign will measure any effects of scale on valuation.
    a_2 is a measure of the effects of growth potential on value.
    U is a random disturbance term.

    $\overline{\Delta A} = \dfrac{\frac{1}{5}(A_t - A_{t-5})}{A_{t-5}}$.

    A_t is a linear five-year average of total assets times current total assets.

Miller and Modigliani explain the significance of their equation (10) by stating:

> ... the first two terms, as before, represent the capitalized value of the current tax-adjusted earning power plus the tax benefits on debt; and the last term is the contribution to value of the future growth potential.[5]

---

[5] "Some Estimates ... ," *op. cit.*, p. 344.

The authors then discuss a number of other factors which may potentially influence the value of the firm:

> Because of this confounding of the earnings and dividend coefficients, our approach here will be initially to omit the dividend variable entirely . . .[6]

They then state that their theory of valuation leads to the structural equation set forth in equation (11).

Modigliani and Miller make the following observation:

> Notice that since the theory implies that the coefficient of the leverage variable D is equal to the marginal tax rate t, we have so constrained it in the above equation by incorporating it with the dependent variable.[7]

In moving from equation (10) to their equation (11), Miller and Modigliani perform an interesting shift. Equation (10) was developed from a formal theoretical basis. Equation (11), however, is essentially empirical in its content. Equation (11) states that the value of a firm is a function of leverage, tax adjusted earnings, and a measure of the growth rate in the assets of the firm. Without the elaborate theoretical discussion, the essentially empirical equation (11) could readily have been set out for testing by regression analysis. Their measurement of growth is especially contrived. Growth is generally measured by reference to total earnings or to earnings per share. They choose to use assets growth. They define growth in equation (11) with a multiplier tagged on so that when they deflate by assets later, the result is the average increase in assets over a five-year period divided by initial assets.

Next Modigliani and Miller take up the problem of heteroscedasticity. They observe that the disturbance term, U, is approximately proportional to the size of the firm. They consider expressing the structural equation in its yield form, dividing through by $(V - tD)$, obtaining equation (12).

$$\frac{\bar{X}(1 - t)}{(V - tD)} = a_1' + a_0' \frac{1}{(V - tD)} + a_2' \frac{\overline{\Delta A}}{(V - tD)} + U' \tag{12}$$

But equation (12) suffers from the defect that the variable $(V - tD)$ appears in the denominator on both sides of the equation. This has the consequence of biasing the results. It would give coefficients of growth and size that would be too high and an estimate of the cost of capital that would be too low. Since Modigliani and Miller state that they have no way of determining how large such a bias is, they will use this form only to check the results obtained in other ways.

Hence, they divide the size of the firm through by the book value of total assets. This is somewhat surprising since they have repeatedly emphasized

---

[6] *Ibid.*, p. 347.
[7] *Ibid.*, p. 348.

that the book value of total assets has no meaning because it is a historical figure with no clear relation to the value of the firm. But dividing through by A, the book value of total assets, provides equation (14).

$$\frac{V - tD}{A} = a_0 \frac{1}{A} + a_1 \frac{\bar{X}(1 - t)}{A} + a_2 \frac{\overline{\Delta A}}{A} + U \tag{14}$$

When they turn to the actual empirical fitting of their structural equations they employ "an instrumental variable approach," implementing it "by means of a two-stage procedure formally equivalent to the two-stage least-squares method of Theil and Madansky."[8]

Their two stage least squares estimates for 1957 of equations (14) and (12):

$$\frac{V - tD}{A} = \frac{16.1}{(0.46)} \frac{\bar{X}^t tR}{A} - \frac{0.28}{(0.08)} \frac{10^7}{A} + \frac{1.36}{(0.23)} \frac{\Delta A}{A} \quad [R = 0.88] \tag{14}$$

$$\frac{\bar{X}^t + t\bar{R}}{V - tD} = \frac{0.0592}{(0.002)} + \frac{0.166}{(0.04)} \frac{1}{(V - tD)} - \frac{0.0516}{(0.02)} \frac{\Delta A}{(V - tD)} \tag{12}$$

Finally, by substituting sample mean values into these equations and their derived functions, Miller and Modigliani develop estimates of the cost of capital. For 1957, for example, the average tax- and leverage-adjusted total earnings yield is:

$$\frac{\bar{X}^t - t\bar{R}}{V - tD} = 0.056$$

The associated cost of equity capital is 0.062 for 1957.

The 1966 Miller and Modigliani paper is a curious combination of powerful analysis and reasoning coupled to expedient empiricism. But even their fundamental proposition is counter to observed facts. They concede that, through tax savings, leverage reduces the cost of capital. The tax benefit from leverage continues with increased leverage. Thus the higher the leverage, the lower the firm's cost of capital. Since they do not admit of a rising cost of capital function at some high level of leverage, they suggest that firms would be induced by the tax advantage to use the maximum amount of debt. But firms obviously do not use extremely high debt ratios.

Miller and Modigliani resort to the concept of a "target debt ratio" to explain the limit on increasing leverage. But a target debt ratio signifies some policy on the financing mix of debt and equity. But this is what business finance has argued and what Miller and Modigliani have denied. They state that "The determination of the optimal value of L (the firm's target debt ratio) involves many difficult issues for which no completely well-worked-out theoretical analysis is yet available."[9] They imply that L is related, but not

---

[8] Miller and Modigliani, *op. cit.*, p. 353 and references cited there to Theil and Madansky.
[9] *Ibid.*, p. 342, footnote 12.

uniformly, to the "maximum permitted by lenders." This is an imprecise way of stating that the cost of capital rises, at some point, sharply with leverage. This in turn suggests an optimal debt to equity ratio. The theoretical underpinnings of their empirical materials are misleading and inconsistent with the theory they are attempting to verify.

Under the Modigliani-Miller formulation, the influence of taxes causes the cost of capital to decline continuously with increased leverage, but their theory fails to explain why firms should not operate with extremely high leverage ratios. Thus, their theory, based on an essentially net operating income approach, fails to explain observed experience. But business finance theory, based on what can briefly be described as the net income approach, does have an explanation. Near the low range of the cost of capital function, firms would establish a target debt equity ratio. Other aspects of business finance behavior can also be explained by the modernized version of traditional business finance theory.

Another difference between the point of view of the net operating income approach and the modified net income approach is that differences in positions taken by investors reflect different expectations. Thus, there must be some rationale to explain why some investors take positions as creditors and some take positions as equity holders. Those who take positions as creditors must do so, aside from legal restrictions, on the expectation that their returns net of defaults or capital values changes will be higher than the returns received by equity holders. Or, to express the idea in terms of modern portfolio theory, the expected return-risk combination provided by the creditor position maximizes expected utility for creditors, but is inconsistent with utility maximization for equity holders. Just the reverse is true when the return-risk combination assumed by the equity position is evaluated. A priori, no one can argue that either position is better in any absolute sense. In part, realized returns to creditors vs. equity holders depend upon what actually happens in comparison with their expectations.

In their empirical studies, Professors Kessell and Alchian have found that during periods of rising price levels, net monetary debtors benefited and that during periods of falling price levels, net monetary creditors benefited. Their empirical findings imply that, on the average, investors have failed to anticipate both inflations and deflations correctly. Their empirical findings cannot be expressed as the equivalent of a general theory, however. To arrive at a general theory, they would have to demonstrate that investors always underestimate the possibility of inflation and always overestimate the possibility of deflation. In a different kind of world—for example, one in which after a long period of inflation investors begin to anticipate degrees of inflation larger than those that actually are experienced—creditors would gain during inflation and debtors would lose. Thus, the important determinant of whether creditors or debtors gain from inflation depends upon a comparison of expectations with realizations.

In this connection, modern business finance generalizes the Kessell-Alchian theory by taking into consideration the growth of the economy as a whole. If expectations of increases in sales and profits of firms are overly optimistic, the current value of equities will be bid up too high in relation to actual realizations, and the returns realized by equity holders will be lower than the basis upon which they made their decisions. As a consequence, the relative flow of funds into debt and equity positions would be altered. This process of adjustment in the total financial markets has been explained in excellent theoretical terms by James Tobin and William F. Sharpe.

It is clear that what is being discussed here is only a subset of the general theory of profits. A significant part of the financial manager's job in minimizing the cost of financing, conditional on an acceptable value function for the firm, is to formulate correct anticipations in relation to market expectations and realizations. It should be emphasized that this is not a chicanery theory of financial management. These are opportunities offered by the interplay of free market judgments and uncertainty. Economic theory, of course, predicts that the gains of some financial managers will be offset by the losses of others. Good financial managers seek to achieve net gains for their firms.

V. THE INFLUENCE OF GROWTH ON VALUATION OF THE FIRM

A number of formulations of the role of growth on value have been developed (see Table 1–6). Basically, all indicate that the value of the

Table 1–6. Growth valuation: all internal equity financing.

$$V = \frac{X(o)(1 - b)}{\rho - \rho^* b} = \frac{E_o(1 - b)}{k - g} = \frac{rA(1 - b)}{k - rb}$$

where:

X = Total earnings.
b = Retention rate.
ρ = Capitalization rate for equity.
$\rho^* = r$ = Rate of return on total assets.
A = Total assets.
$k = \rho$ = Capitalization rate for equity.
V = Value of the firm.

growth firm is determined by its dividends divided by a capitalization factor equal to the cost of capital less the firm's growth rate. These model formulations imply that the firm's cost of capital (assuming continuous growth over a long period of time) can be expressed simply as the dividend yield plus the growth rate. If firms were expected to grow on the average at least 6 percent per annum in money terms to keep pace with the over-all growth in the economy, and if dividends yields were 3–4 percent, the average cost of capital of firms in the United States would approximate 9–10 percent after taxes.

While 9–10 percent over-all cost of capital represents a useful over-all average, in many circumstances a more precise measurement is required. For high risk industries or projects, the firm's after-tax cost of capital could well be 14–15 percent or higher. On new development projects a firm may seek a 20–30 percent return on investment if it is seeking to average 10 percent return on investment over-all. The goal of a 30 percent return on individual projects may allow for the disappointment of expectations and the high error and mortality rate anticipated on new projects. In addition, the realized return on new projects must be averaged with below average returns on product activities in mature lines where excess capacity may exist and on which the market does not permit an average rate of return.

These are only rough guides at best, however, because they combine capitalization increments for both uncertainty and the time value of money. If the combination of time value of money and uncertainty differs from the mix assumed in the discount rate, then inconsistent decisions could result. A decision theory or, in special cases, a portfolio approach can be utilized if more accuracy is desired by the manager.

VI.   THE ROLE OF DIVIDEND POLICY

The growth valuation formulations shown in Table 1–6 are all internal equity financing models. They provide a transition to the discussion of dividend policy, since the formulas state that the value of a growth firm is the dividends divided by a capitalization factor.

Theoretically, under certainty and in the absence of tax advantages, it should make no difference whether a firm retains earnings or pays dividends which then can be reinvested in the firm by the stockholders. This has been demonstrated clearly by Miller and Modigliani in a formal paper which develops their analysis under the assumptions of certainty and not tax advantages to retained earnings.

The formal development of their models results in two equations which show great similarity to the equations set forth in Table 1–6. The two equations are numbered (23) and (24) in their original article.[10]

$$V(0) = \frac{X(0)}{\rho}\left[1 + \frac{k(\rho^* - \rho)}{\rho - k\rho^*}\right]$$
$$= \frac{X(0)(1 - k)}{\rho - k\rho^*} \tag{23}$$

$$D_0(0)\sum_{t=0}^{\infty}\frac{(1 + g)^t}{(1 + \rho)^{t+1}} = \frac{D(0)}{\rho - g}$$
$$= \frac{X(0)[1 - k_r]}{\rho - g} \tag{24}$$

---

[10] M. H. Miller and F. Modigliani, "Dividend Policy, Growth, and the Valuation of Shares," *Journal of Business*, XXXIV (October 1961), 421–423.

Table 1-7. Dividend policy, certainty model, all equity financing.

General symbols	*Illustrative values*
$X(0)$ = Total initial earnings of the firm.	= $1,000
$D(0)$ = Total initial dividends of the firm.	
n = Total number of shares of common stock.	= 100
$x(0)$ = Initial earnings per share.	= $10
$d(0)$ = Initial dividends per share.	
ρ = Market rate of return.	= 10%
ρ^* = Internal rate of return.	= 20%
t = Time.	
k = Ratio of investment to total earnings in time (t).	= 0.4
k_e = Investment financed from external sources.	
k_r = Investment financed from internal sources.	
ln = natural logarithm	

	1. All internal financing. $k = 0.4 \ k_e = 0 \ k_r = 0.4$	2. All external financing. $k = 0.4 \ k_e = 0.4 \ k_r = 0$	3. Mixed financing. $k = 0.4 \ k_e = 0.1 \ k_r = 0.3$
A. Total earnings.	$ln X(t) = ln X(0) + k\rho^* t$ $ln X(t) = ln \$1,000 + 0.08t$	Same as A1.	Same as A1.
B. Total dividends.	$ln D(t) = ln X(0)(1 - k_r)$ $+ k\rho^* t$ $= ln \$600 + 0.08t$	$ln D(t) = ln X(0)(1 - k_r)$ $+ k\rho^* t$ $= ln \$1,000 + 0.08t$	$ln D(t) = ln X(0)(1 - k_r)$ $+ k\rho^* t$ $= ln \$700 + 0.08t$
C. Earnings per share.	$ln x(t) = ln x(0) + gt$ $g = k\rho^*$ $ln x(t) = ln \$10 + 0.08t$	$ln x(t) = ln x(0) + gt$ $g = \dfrac{k(\rho^* - \rho)}{1 - k}$ $ln x(t) = ln \$10 + 0.067t$	$ln x(t) = ln x(0) + gt$ $g = k\rho^* \dfrac{1 - k_r}{1 - k} - k_e\rho \dfrac{1}{1 - k}$ $ln x(t) = ln \$10 + 0.076t$
D. Dividends per share.	$ln d(t) = ln x(0)(1 - k_r)$ $+ gt$ g = Same as C1 $ln d(t) = ln \$6 + 0.08t$	$ln d(t) = ln x(0)(1 - k_r)$ $+ gt$ g = Same as C2 $ln d(t) = ln \$10 + 0.067t$	$ln d(t) = ln x(0)(1 - k_r)$ $+ gt$ g = Same as C3 $ln d(t) = ln \$7 + 0.076t$
E. Value of firm.	$V(0) = \dfrac{X(0)(1 - k)}{\rho - \rho^* k}$ $= \dfrac{\$600}{0.10 - 0.08} = \dfrac{\$600}{0.02}$ $= \$30,000$	Same as E1.	Same as E1.

Source: Adapted from M. H. Miller and F. Modigliani, "Dividend Policy, Growth, and the Valuation of Shares," *Journal of Business*, XXXIV (October 1961), 423.

The symbols have the same meaning as set forth in Table 1–3, except for their symbol, k. Miller and Modigliani define k in the following statement:

> Specifically, suppose that in each period t the firm has the opportunity to invest in real assets a sum $I(t)$ that is k per cent as large as its total earnings for the period . . .[11]

Thus they express investment as a ratio of the firm's earnings. But k is composed of two parts, internal capital and external capital. This they explain in the following definitions:

> g = the rate of growth of dividends per share, or, what amounts to the same thing, the rate of growth of dividends accruing to the shares of the current holders (i.e., $D_0(t) = D_0(0)[1 + g]^t$);
>
> k_r = the fraction of total profits retained in each period (so that $D(t) = X(0)[1 - k_r]$);
>
> $k_e = k - k_r$ = the amount of external capital raised per period, expressed as a fraction of profits in the period.[12]

They assert that both equations (23) and (24) are equal to the value of the firm. Hence they state that the meaning of g can be determined by setting the two equations equal to each other and solving for g. They express the value of g in equation (25).

$$g = k\rho^* \frac{1 - k_r}{1 - k} - k_e \, \rho \, \frac{1}{1 - k} \tag{25}$$

The meaning of these formulations may be made clear by a numerical example utilizing their equations. The illustrative facts are set out at the top of Table 1–7. Utilizing the Miller and Modigliani equations (23), (24), and (25), we show the relation between earnings and dividends in the lower part of Table 1–7.

It should be observed that regardless of the financing mix employed, under the assumptions of certainty and no tax advantages, and the additional assumption that $k = 0.4$, the total earnings of the firm are the same. This is to say that given the internal profitability rate of the firm and its initial earnings, the growth rate in earnings will depend only on the ratio of investment to total earnings per period and the number of time periods.

The relations between earnings, dividends, and the value of the firm may be further clarified by graphing the equations of Table 1–7 in Fig. 1–1. Total earnings are the same. Since Fig. 1–1 is on a semi-logarithmic scale, the graph for total earnings (line A of Table 1–7) under the three assumptions of (1) all internal financing, (2) all external financing, and (3) mixed financing are all the same. Its intercept is $1,000 and grows at 8 percent per annum.

---

[11] *Ibid.*, p. 421.
[12] *Ibid.*, p. 422.

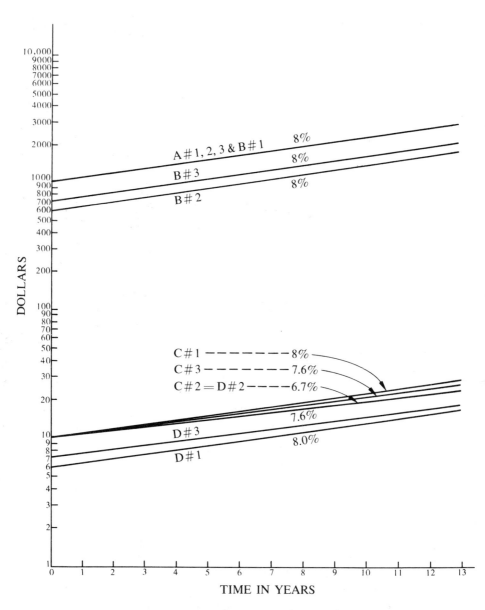

Fig. 1-1. Growth of total earnings and dividends and per share earnings and dividends. *Source:* Data of Table 1-7.

Total dividends grow at the same rate. When all financing is external, total dividends are the same as total earnings. If some or all financing is internal, the intercept of the dividend line will be lower, as shown in **B2** and **B3**.

While total dividends and earnings are less affected by the extent of external financing, dividends per share and earnings per share are greatly influenced because the extent of external equity financing determines the number of shares of stock that will be outstanding. In the all external financing case, the equations for both earnings per share and dividends per share are the same, with the lowest growth rate of all the cases, 6.7 percent per annum. The growth rate per share is highest for all internal financing, but the initial dividend is the lowest of the six cases on the per share basis.

Section E of Table 1–7 indicates that the value of the firm will be the same, independent of the method of financing under the assumptions of the model. The critical assumptions bear repeating: the amount of financing is independent of the financing mix, the amount of investment is independent of the source of financing, full certainty, and no tax advantages. But the price of the common stock per share will be influenced by the source of financing used for growth since the initial earnings or dividends per share and their respective growth rates are thereby influenced.

The Miller-Modigliani formula can be used to illustrate that dividend policy does depend upon the relation between the firm internal profitability rate and the market capitalization rate. If ρ^* is no greater than ρ, or if ρ^* is lower than ρ, the firm can increase its value by paying all of its earnings out in dividends. If ρ^* is greater than ρ, the firm will maximize its value by paying no dividends. Thus, we have demonstrated that the Miller-Modigliani formula in fact leads to the same dividend policy decisions as does the Walter formula (see Chapter 21). Indeed in all certainty and infinite period dividend models, the above implications for dividend policy will hold.

There is a fundamental flaw or internal inconsistency in the Miller-Modigliani dividend article. Their proofs depend on the assumption that investment is independent of any of the other relationships.[13] Miller and Modigliani also recognized this inconsistency, but passed over it lightly to criticize Gordon and Shapiro for a similar assumption.[14] Yet since investment is defined as a function of earnings, the financing rate is dependent on earnings. Therefore, equation (24) is logically equivalent to the Gordon and Shapiro model. Modigliani and Miller's theory that divided policy has no effect on value is not established since their proofs depend on independence of the investment rate from the earnings rate and dividend policy if constraints on external financing exist.

But all of the foregoing is based on the assumption, among others, of no tax advantages. Under such assumptions, "dividends do not matter."

---

[13] *Ibid.*, p. 414.
[14] *Ibid.*, p. 425.

However, dividends do matter when capital gains tax rates are lower than tax rates on personal income. This is particularly true when taken in conjunction with the situation of a growth firm. A growth firm has investment opportunities that promise a higher profit return than can be obtained in the market on the average. Thus, the growth firm stockholders would prefer to have their funds reinvested rather than seek alternative market opportunities. The growth firm would suffer attenuation due to tax effects if it had to pay out earnings in dividends, then had these dividends subjected to personal income tax rates in excess of 25 percent, and then had to seek to sell securities to stimulate the reinvestment of the after-tax dividends of the stockholders.[15]

Again, these basic propositions accord with the facts of real life. Growth firms have very high retention rates, typically paying out either no dividends or a dividend rate less than 20 percent of earnings. For industries and firms that grow no faster than the economy as a whole, dividends approximate a 50 percent payout range. Thus, if the firm is not a growth firm, its profit opportunities are not greater than those available to stockholders. For such firms, dividend changes are probably taken as indicators of expected changes in future earnings. The prices of these stocks probably will change in proportion to dividend changes. The higher dividend payouts of utilities which run in the 75–90 percent range is undoubtedly explained by two special factors: (1) utility commissions are reputed to give less weight to an investment base achieved by earnings retention than to one achieved by equity funds raised from the outside, (2) for a long time, investors regarded utilities as income stocks and therefore were responsive to dividend payouts.

The increased use of share repurchase merits comment in connection with dividend policy. In theory, repurchase of shares is always superior to payment of a cash dividend to shareholders. The benefit is clear if the firm's marginal profitability rate is low and the market price of its stock is depressed. If the firm's incremental internal profitability rate is high, more will be gained by reinvesting the funds than by share repurchase. But even in such circumstances, share repurchase is better than utilizing an equivalent amount of cash for dividend payment in the sense that it increases the expected market value of the firm's shares.

Corresponding to the propositions we have advanced in connection with expectations in debtor vs. equity holder position, the theory is equally applicable to the use of options. Options are in the form of rights, warrants, and convertibles. In theory, the use of rights, warrants, and convertibles

---

[15] The illustration makes clear that the combination of taxes and an internal rate of return higher than the market rate may influence the firm's rate of investment and hence its value. In the absence of taxes, the extra expenses and leakages in seeking to recapture dividends to finance further growth make it advantageous for growth firms to retain a high percentage of earnings. Conversely, firms whose internal rate is below the market rate should not reinvest below the market rate. Their dividend payout rates are likely to be high or they may be repurchasing their own shares of common stock. Hence the relation between internal rates of return and market rates of return have implications for financing rates and dividend payout rates.

cannot increase the value of the firm. They simply provide an option in the form of a call on a company's common stock. Whether the seller or buyer of the call gains depends upon the price charged for the call compared with what the future value of the call becomes.

Again the result depends on whether the market on the average is overly optimistic or overly pessimistic on the value of the call represented by the right, warrant, or convertible. If the market is overly optimistic, the call premium will not compensate for the benefit derived. If the market is overly pessimistic about the value of the call, the price of the call will be low enough so that an investor in the call will gain from buying it.

VII. DIVERSIFICATION AND MERGERS

Diversification and mergers represent still another area in which business finance policy may be expressed. In a sense, diversification and mergers represent another aspect of capital budgeting theory. However, it is a subject of special interest becase some fundamental fallacies in connection with the potentials of mergers are widely held and the range of potential enhancement of values is increased since other firms are involved.

The potential increase in values in connection with mergers and diversification can come about through synergistic or carry-over effects, in which $2 + 2 = 5$ or more. A number of forms of synergy or carry-over may occur. The clearest form is through complementarity. One firm may have a strong research organization but be weak in sales. Another firm may be strong in sales but weak in research. Combining the two would give each the benefit of the strength of the other. One firm may be in a product market area in which the needs for certain kinds of research and engineering talent have become of critical importance. Or, the combined risks of operation may be reduced by better balance in sales, or greater breadth in technological production and marketing skills. The result of such risk reduction would be a lowering of capitalization rates and therefore an increase in the market values for the merged firm.

Fallacies obtain in connection with the possible gains from merger in the area of forecast bargains. It is difficult to formulate a theoretical basis for a bargain theory of mergers. From a social standpoint, gains and losses are merely being traded. The most usual form of the bargain theory is the existence of unequal price-earnings ratios. The immediate effect of a merger in which companies of unequal price-earnings ratios trade at market prices is to increase the earnings per share of the high price-earnings ratio company and to depress the earnings per share of the low price-earnings ratio company. But if the unequal price-earnings ratios correctly forecast unequal growth rates in future earnings per share, the effects on earnings per share in the future will cancel out. In effect, present gains and losses are being traded for reverse losses and gains in the future.

The problem with the forecast bargain basis for mergers is that it is difficult to demonstrate that one firm on balance will achieve net gains. It is difficult to demonstrate that a given firm will consistently benefit from the bargaining errors of the others. For a merger to represent genuine increases in the value of the firms, some elements of true synergy must be present.

Another significant area affecting values to be achieved through financial management is the area of reorganization and bankruptcy. For too long a time, the discussion of reorganization and bankruptcy has been limited to a preoccupation with the legal and institutional rules for conducting the affairs of a firm that had encountered financial difficulties. But from an economic standpoint, reorganization and bankruptcy are legal devices for providing for a readjustment of expectations and, thus, a form of recontracting. Reorganization and bankruptcy actions change the value of the claims of the creditors and owners of the firm. Readjustment of claims may be accomplished through extension or composition. Given the time value of money, extension of the payment schedule represents a change in values of claims, while composition typically provides for a scaling down of the claims for both creditors and owners.

The existence of legal institutions for scaling down the indicated values of the firm and thus reducing the residual claims of equity holders could be expected to have economic effects. The equity holders possess the residual claims on the firm—this position could reflect either favorable or unfavorable developments for the firm. On the other hand, the creditors were presumed to have fixed claims on the firm, but reorganization and bankruptcy provide for modifying these claims. Thus, in anticipation of the possibility of such adjustments in the claims of creditors, it could be expected that the creditors would seek compensation in the form of higher promised returns, since the returns in the future are subject to recontracting and modification. It would be interesting to conduct empirical research to determine the effect of reorganization and bankruptcy on the required rates of interest paid to creditors. However, the rates of interest are subject to so many more massive and powerful influences that to isolate the influence of reorganization and bankruptcy would be difficult indeed. Students of finance, however, should be aware of the theoretical implications of these procedural and legal institutions of reorganization and bankruptcy.

VIII. AGENDA FOR THE FUTURE

This introductory material has indicated the financial management areas in which there appears to be some consensus of opinion. In many other areas, however, fundamental differences still exist. It is the purpose of the following readings to provide some insight into the theoretical foundations of the knowledge that we have achieved to date and, thus, to give a basis for continued development. In addition, an understanding of why certain disagreements continue is developed.

It is a strange paradox that as our tools of analysis and sophistication of investigative procedures have been enhanced, disagreements on some basic propositions have continued. Our increased powers of analysis and investigation have not been sufficient to eliminate the existing theoretical disagreements.

These continued disagreements are understandable in terms of the techniques of modern model building and statistical testing. A model may be developed by taking certain fundamental assumptions and building propositions on them. In terms of their theoretical validity, the propositions need only be internally consistent. In this sense, no one model is better than any other model.

When we consider the policy area, however, models must meet the test of being able to explain or predict. This implies testing models by relating them to real world data. But even here, after extensive investigation, disagreements may continue, for the same model may be tested by employing different variables. In addition, even when the same variables are employed, they may be measured in different ways and over different time periods.

These last two points are well illustrated by the cost of capital controversy. The early models by Modigliani and Miller focus on the role of leverage only. As they indicated later, their discussion of the effect of taxes on the cost of capital had to be corrected. They did not consider the influence of growth on cost of capital. Thus, discussions of the determinants of cost of capital were greatly influenced by the selection of the range of variables considered in the early discussions. Fundamental disagreements have arisen also in empirical testing of the influence of leverage on cost of capital, as to whether the book or market values of debt and equity should be employed in measurements.

Similarly, a great difficulty arises in considering the relative influence of dividends or earnings on the cost of capital for the value of the firm. Some theories hold that dividends simply provide information value as to the future expected levels of earnings. If this view is correct, are we actually measuring the influence of earnings when we measure the influence of dividends?

In the same way, alternative methods were used to measure the influence of growth on the cost of capital and the value of the firm. The growth of the firm might be measured in terms of its growth rate in sales, total assets, total earnings, earnings per share, the amount of retained earnings, the retention rate, etc. Another question is, over what time period should the duration of growth be measured? Periods of from 3–10 years have been employed. In some empirical tests greater weight is given to the most recent years. To determine some measure of growth, sometimes the first and last years are considered and a compound rate of growth measure is employed. Other problems arise in connection with growth rates that vary greatly from year to year. Some researchers would fit a regression line to all of the observations in the total period covered. Others would use regression techniques which give somewhat greater weighting to the most recent years.

Thus, even with increased sophistication and understanding of subject matter, a certain amount of disagreement persists, for a number of theoretical models may be formulated and alternative empirical measures employed to test the model. What is extremely perplexing is that rival models or theories are tested with different sets of data and procedures and, therefore, each theory is confirmed by its empirical test.

The fundamental question is, therefore, how to select the appropriate theories and tests for a given model. A basic requirement for the researcher is that he be fully familiar with the theoretical content of the relevant literature. The following readings seek to provide this familiarity. But, in addition, considerable competence in statistical and econometrical testing is necessary for developing sophistication and competence in judging between rival theories and tests. These requirements emphasize the need for the continued development of tools of empirical analysis and for the researcher's increased competence to perform empirical tests. These abilities can only be obtained in subject areas which provide the methodology for scientific research.

Over the next decade we also expect to observe rapid growth in the financial and economic studies of decision analysis and control in organizational settings. This approach differs from "decision process" aspects, and concentrates on analytical frameworks for coping with uncertainty within the constraints imposed by organizational structures, information economics, risk preferences, interdependence, and competitive behavior. We feel the most fruitful attack on organizational finance will be achieved through descriptive/prescriptive modelling for computer simulation, logical analyses, and controlled experimentation. Economic theory, decision theory (including cost/benefit analysis), game theory, portfolio theory, and systems theory all offer considerable potential for the investigation of financial decision making.

As in any scientific research endeavor, the greatest strides will be made by those who are inventive and astute enough to know where the next step is, by those whose estimate of future paths balances the over-optimistic cost of losing sight of the knowledge frontier and what is possible with the over-pessimistic cost of not going far enough and making no relevant contribution to pushing the financial knowledge frontier outward.

PART II

Capital Budgeting Theory

2

ON THE THEORY OF OPTIMAL
INVESTMENT DECISION

J. HIRSHLEIFER*

This paper has become a classic in the analysis of optimal investment decisions. It broadened the previous approach by considering consumption as an alternative to investment decisions and incorporating Fisher's contributions, which emphasized balancing consumption alternatives over time and the distinction between production opportunities and exchange opportunities.

Professor Hirshleifer considers both interest rates for borrowing and interest rates for lending. The discussion indicates the limitations of using internal rate of return for analysis of such problems, and the author develops a general framework using the present worth approach. This article is fundamental for providing a greater understanding of much of the literature on investment decisions.

This article is an attempt to solve (in the theoretical sense), through the use of isoquant analysis, the problem of optimal investment decisions (in business parlance, the problem of capital budgeting). The initial section reviews the principles laid down in Irving Fisher's justly famous works on interest[1] to see what light they shed on two competing rules of behavior currently proposed by economists to guide business investment decisions—the present-value rule and the internal-rate-of-return rule. The next concern of the paper is to show how Fisher's principles must be adapted when the perfect capital market assumed in his analysis does not exist—in particular, when borrowing and lending rates diverge, when capital can be secured only at an increasing marginal borrowing rate, and when capital is "rationed." In connection with this last situation, certain non-Fisherian views (in particular, those of Scitovsky and of the Lutzes) about the correct ultimate goal or criterion for investment decisions are examined. Section III, which presents the solution for multiperiod investments, corrects an error by Fisher which

J. Hirshleifer, "On the Theory of Optimal Investment Decision." Reprinted from *The Journal of Political Economy* (August 1958), pp. 329–352, by permission of the University of Chicago Press.

* I should like to express indebtedness to many of my colleagues, and especially to James H. Lorie and Martin J. Bailey, for valuable suggestions and criticisms.

[1] Irving Fisher, *The Theory of Interest* (New York: Macmillan Co., 1930), is most widely known. His earlier work, *The Rate of Interest* (New York: Macmillan Co., 1907), contains most of the essential ideas.

has been the source of much difficulty. The main burden of the analysis justifies the contentions of those who reject the internal rate of return as an investment criterion, and the paper attempts to show where the error in that
concept (as ordinarily defined) lies and how the internal rate must be redefined
if it is to be used as a reliable guide. On the positive side, the analysis provides
some support for the use of the present-value rule but shows that even that
rule is at best only a partial indicator of optimal investments and, in fact,
under some conditions, gives an incorrect result.

More recent works on investment decisions, I shall argue, suffer from the
neglect of Fisher's great contributions—the attainment of an optimum
through balancing consumption alternatives over time and the clear distinction between production opportunities and exchange opportunities. It is
an implication of this analysis, though it cannot be pursued here in detail,
that solutions to the problem of investment decision recently proposed by
Boulding, Samuelson, Scitovsky, and the Lutzes are at least in part erroneous.
Their common error lay in searching for a rule or formula which would
indicate optimal investment decisions *independently of consumption decisions*.
No such search can succeed, if Fisher's analysis is sound which regards investment as not an end in itself but rather a process for distributing consumption over time.

The present paper deals throughout with a highly simplified situation in
which the costs and returns of alternative individual investments are known
with certainty, the problem being to select the scale and the mix of investments
to be undertaken. To begin with, the analysis will be limited to investment
decisions relating to two time periods only. We shall see in later sections that
the two-period analysis can be translated immediately to the analysis of
investments in perpetuities. For more general fluctuating income streams,
however, additional difficulties arise whose resolution involves important new
questions of principle. The restriction of the solution to perfect-information
situations is, of course, unfortunate, since ignorance and uncertainty are of
the essence of certain important observable characteristics of investment
decision behavior. The analysis of optimal decisions under conditions of
certainty can be justified, however, as a first step toward a more complete
theory. No further apology will be offered for considering this oversimplified
problem beyond the statement that theoretical economists are in such substantial disagreement about it that a successful attempt to bring the solution
within the standard body of economic doctrine would represent a real
contribution.

I. TWO-PERIOD ANALYSIS

A. Borrowing Rate Equals Lending Rate (Fisher's Solution)

In order to establish the background for the difficult problems to be
considered later, let us first review Fisher's solution to the problem of

investment decision.[2] Consider the case in which there is a given rate at which the individual (or firm)[3] may borrow that is unaffected by the amount of his borrowings; a given rate at which he can lend that is unaffected by the amount of his loans; and in which these two rates are equal. These are the conditions used by Fisher; they represent a perfect capital market.

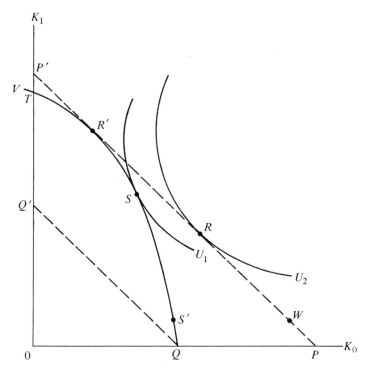

Fig. 2–1.   Fisher's solution.

In Fig. 2–1 the horizontal axis labeled K_0 represents the amount of actual or potential income (the amount consumed or available for consumption) in period 0; the vertical axis K_1 represents the amount of income in the same sense in period 1. The individual's decision problem is to choose, within the opportunities available to him, an optimum point on the graph—that is, an optimal time pattern of consumption. His starting point may conceivably be a point on either axis (initial income falling all in period 0 or all in period 1), such as points T or P, or else it may be a point in the positive quadrant

---

[2] Fisher's contributions to the theory of capital go beyond his solution of the problem discussed in this paper—optimal investment decision. He also considers the question of the equilibrium of the capital market, which balances the supplies and demands of all the decision-making agencies.

[3] This analysis does not distinguish between individuals and firms. Firms are regarded solely as agencies or instruments of individuals.

(initial income falling partly in period 0 and partly in period 1), such as points W or S'. It may even lie in the second or fourth quadrant—where his initial situation involves negative income either in period 0 or in period 1.

The individual is assumed to have a preference function relating income in periods 0 and 1. This preference function would be mapped in quite the ordinary way, and the curves U_1 and U_2 are ordinary utility-indifference curves from this map.

Finally, there are the investment opportunities open to the individual. Fisher distinguishes between "investment opportunities" and "market opportunities." The former are real productive transfers between income in one time period and in another (what we usually think of as "physical" investment, like planting a seed); the latter are transfers through borrowing or lending (which naturally are on balance off-setting in the loan market). I shall depart from Fisher's language to distinguish somewhat more clearly between "production opportunities" and "market opportunities"; the word "investment" will be used in the more general and inclusive sense to refer to both types of opportunities taken together. Thus we may invest by building a house (a sacrifice of present for future income through a production opportunity) or by lending on the money market (a sacrifice of present for future income through a market or exchange opportunity). We could, equivalently, speak of purchase and sale of capital assets instead of lending or borrowing in describing the market opportunities.

In Fig. 2–1 an investor with a starting point at Q faces a market opportunity illustrated by the dashed line QQ'. That is, starting with all his income in time 0, he can lend at some given lending rate, sacrificing present for future income, any amount until his K_0 is exhausted—receiving in exchange K_1 or income in period 1. Equivalently, we could say that he can buy capital assets—titles to future income K_1—with current income K_0. Following Fisher, I shall call QQ' a "market line."[4] The line PP', parallel to QQ' is the market line available to an individual whose starting point is P on the K_0 axis. By our assumpton that the borrowing rate is also constant and equal to the lending rate, the market line PP' is also the market opportunity to an individual whose starting point is W, within the positive quadrant.

Finally, the curve $QSTV$ shows the range of productive opportunities available to an individual with starting point Q. It is the locus of points attainable to such an individual as he sacrifices more and more of K_0 by productive investments yielding K_1 in return. This attainability locus Fisher somewhat ambiguously calls the "opportunity line"; it will be called here the "productive opportunity curve" or "productive transformation curve." Note that in its concavity to the origin the curve reveals a kind of diminishing returns to investment. More specifically, productive investment projects

---

[4] The slope of the market line is, of course, $-(1 + i)$, where i is the lending-borrowing rate. That is, when one gives up a dollar in period 0, he receives in exchange $1 + i$ dollars in period 1.

may be considered to be ranked by the expression $(\Delta K_1)/(-\Delta K_0) - 1$, which might be called the "productive rate of return."[5] Here ΔK_0 and ΔK_1 represent the changes in income of periods 0 and 1 associated with the project in question.

We may conceive of whole projects being so ranked, in which case we get the average productive rate of return for each such project. Or we may rank infinitesimal increments to projects, in which case we can deal with a marginal productive rate of return. The curve $QSTV$ will be continuous and have a continuous first derivative under certain conditions relating to absence of "lumpiness" of individual projects (or increments to projects), which we need not go into. In any case, $QSTV$ would represent a sequence of projects so arranged as to start with the one yielding the highest productive rate of return at the lower right and ending with the lowest rate of return encounterd when the last dollar of period 0 is sacrificed at the upper left.[6] It is possible to attach meaning to the portion of $QSTV$ in the second quadrant, where K_0 becomes negative. Such points could not be optimal with indifference curves as portrayed in Figure 2–1, of course, but they may enter into the determination of an optimum. (This analysis assumes that projects are independent. Where they are not, complications ensue which will be discussed in Sections E and F below.)

As to the solution itself, the investor's objective is to climb onto as high an indifference curve as possible. Moving along the productive opportunity line $QSTV$, he sees that the highest indifference curve it touches is U_1 at the point S. But this is not the best point attainable, for he can move along $QSTV$ somewhat farther to the point R', which is on the market line PP'. He can now move in the reverse direction (borrowing) along PP', and the point R on the indifference curve U_2 is seen to be the best attainable.

The investor has, therefore, a solution in two steps. The "productive" solution—the point at which the individual should stop making additional productive investments—is at R'. He may then move along his market line to a point better satisfying his time preferences, at R. That is to say, he makes the best investment from the productive point of view and then "finances" it in the loan market. A very practical example is building a house and then borrowing on it through a mortgage so as to replenish current consumption income.

We may now consider, in the light of this solution, the current debate between two competing "rules" for optimal investment behavior.[7] The first

---

[5] For the present it is best to avoid the term "internal rate of return." Fisher uses the expressions "rate of return on sacrifice" or "rate of return over cost."

[6] An individual starting at S' would also have a "disinvestment opportunity."

[7] The present-value rule is the more or less standard guide supported by a great many theorists. The internal-rate-of-return rule, in the sense used here, has also been frequently proposed (see, e.g., Joel Dean, *Capital Budgeting* [New York: Columbia University Press, 1951], pp. 17–19). Citations on the use of alternative investment criteria may be found in Friedrich and Vera Lutz, *The Theory of Investment of the Firm* (Princeton, N.J.: Princeton University Press, 1951), p. 16. The internal-rate-of-return rule which we will consider in detail (i.e., adopt all projects and

of these, the present-value rule, would have the individual or firm adopt all projects whose present value is positive at the market rate of interest. This would have the effect of maximizing the present value of the firm's position in terms of income in periods 0 and 1. Present value, under the present conditions, may be defined as $K_0 + (K_1)/(1 + i)$, income in period 1 being discounted by the factor $1 + i$, where i is the lending-borrowing rate. Since the market lines are defined by the condition that a sacrifice of one dollar in K_0 yields $1 + i$ dollars in K_1, these market lines are nothing but lines of constant present value. The equation for these lines is $K_0 + (K_1)/(1 + i) = C$, C being a parameter. The present-value rule tells us to invest until the highest such line is attained, which clearly takes place at the point R'. So far so good, but note that the rule says nothing about the "financing" (borrowing or lending) also necessary to attain the final optimum at R.

. The internal-rate-of-return rule, in the form here considered, would have the firm adopt any project whose internal rate is greater than the market rate of interest. The internal rate for a project in the general case is defined as that discounting rate ρ which reduces the stream of net returns associated with the project to a present value of zero (or, equivalently, which makes the discounted value of the associated cost stream equal to the discounted value of the receipts stream). We may write

$$0 = \Delta K_0 + \frac{\Delta K_1}{1 + \rho} + \frac{\Delta K_2}{(1 + \rho)^2} + \cdots + \frac{\Delta K_n}{(1 + \rho)^n}.$$

In the two-period case ρ is identical with the productive rate of return, $(\Delta K_1)/(-\Delta K_0) - 1$. As in the discussion above, if infinitesimal changes are permitted, we may interpret this statement in the marginal sense. The marginal (two-period) internal rate of return is measured by the slope of the productive opportunity curve minus unity. In Fig. 2–1 at each step we would compare the steepness of $QSTV$ with that of the market lines. We would move along $QSTV$ as long as, and just so long as, it is the steeper. Evidently, this rule would have us move along $QSTV$ until it beomes tangent to a market line at R'. Again, so far so good, but nothing is said about the borrowing or lending then necessary to attain the optimum.

At least for the two-period case, then, the present-value rule and the internal-rate-of-return rule lead to identical answers[8] which are the same as

increments to projects for which the internal rate of return exceeds the market rate of interest) is *not* the same as that emphasized by the Lutzes (i.e., adopt that pattern of investments maximizing the internal rate of return). The rule considered here compares the incremental or marginal rate of return with a market rate; the other would maximize the average internal rate of return, without regard to the market rate. The latter rule will be shown to be fundamentally erroneous, even in the form the Lutzes accept as their ultimate criterion (maximize the internal rate of return on the investor's owned captial). This point will be discussed in connection with capital rationing in Sec. D, below.

[8] In fact, for the two-period case the rules are identical: it is possible to show that any project (or increment to a project) of positive present value must have an internal rate of return greater than the rate of interest.

that reached by our isoquant analysis, so far as *productive* investment decisions are concerned. The rules are both silent, however, about the market exchange between K_0 and K_1, which remains necessary if an optimum is to be achieved. This second step is obviously part of the solution. Had there been no actual opportunity to borrow or lend, the point S would have been the best attainable, and the process of productive investment should not have been carried as far as R'. We cannot say that the rules are definitely wrong, however, since with no such market opportunities there would have been no market rate of interest i for calculating present values or for comparison with the marginal internal rate of return. It remains to be seen whether these rules can be restated or generalized to apply to cases where a simple market rate of interest is not available for unlimited borrowing and lending. But it should be observed that, in comparison with isoquant analysis, each of the rules leads to only a partial answer.

B.   When Borrowing and Lending Rates Differ

We may now depart from Fisher's analysis, or rather extend it, to a case he did not consider. The borrowing and lending rates are still assumed to be constant, independent of the amounts taken or supplied by the individual or firm under consideration. However, it is now assumed that these rates are not equal, the borrowing rate being higher than the lending rate.[9] In Fig. 2–2 there is the same preference map, of which only the isoquant U_1 is shown. There are now, however, two sets of market lines over the graph; the steeper (*dashed*) lines represent borrowing opportunities (note the direction of the arrows), and the flatter (*solid*) lines represent lending opportunities. The heavy solid lines show two possible sets of productive opportunities, both of which lead to solutions along U_1. Starting with amount OW of K_0, an investor with a production opportunity WVW' would move along WVW' to V, at which point he would *lend* to get to his time-preference optimum—the tangency with U_1 at V'. The curve STS' represents a much more productive possibility; starting with only OS of K_0, the investor would move along STS' to T and then *borrow* backward along the dashed line to get to T', the tangency point with U_1. Note that the total opportunity set (the points attainable through any combination of the market and productive opportunities) is WVV^* for the first opportunity, and $S'TT^*$ for the second.

More detailed analysis, however, shows that we do not yet have the full solution—there is a third possibility. An investor with a productive opportunity locus starting on the K_0 axis will never stop moving along this locus

---

[9] If the borrowing rate were lower than the lending rate, it would be possible to accumulate infinite wealth by borrowing and relending, so I shall not consider this possibility. Of course, financial institutions typically borrow at a lower average rate than that at which they lend, but they cannot expand their scale of operations indefinitely without changing this relationship.

in the direction of greater K_1 as long as the marginal productive rate of return is still above the borrowing rate—nor will he ever push along the locus beyond the point where the marginal productive rate of return falls below the lending rate. Assuming that some initial investments are available which have a higher productive rate of return than the borrowing rate, the investor

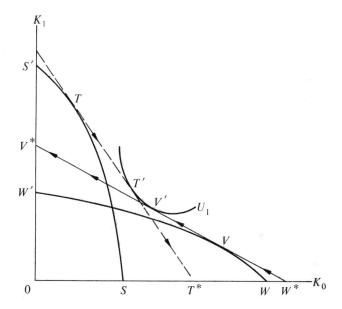

Fig. 2-2.   Extension of Fisher's solution for differing borrowing and lending rates.

should push along the locus until the borrowing rate is reached. If, at this point, it is possible to move up the utility hill by borrowing, productive investment should cease, and the borrowing should take place; the investor is at some point like T in Fig. 2-2. If borrowing decreases utility, however, more productive investment is called for. Suppose investment is then carried on until diminishing returns bring the marginal productive rate of return down to the lending rate. If lending then increases utility, productive investment should halt there, and the lending take place; the investor is at some point like V in Fig. 2-2. But suppose that now it is found that lending also decreases utility! This can only mean that a tangency of the productive opportunity locus and an indifference curve took place when the marginal productive rate of return was somewhere *between* the lending and the borrowing rates. In this case neither lending nor borrowing is called for, the optimum being reached directly in the productive investment decision by equating the marginal productive rate of return with the marginal rate of substitution (in the sense of time preference) along the utility isoquant.

These solutions are illustrated by the division of Fig. 2–3 into three zones. In Zone I the borrowing rate is relevant. Tangency solutions with the market line at the borrowing rate like that at T are carried back by borrowing to tangency with a utility isoquant at a point like T'. All such final solutions lie along the curve OB, which connects all points on the utility

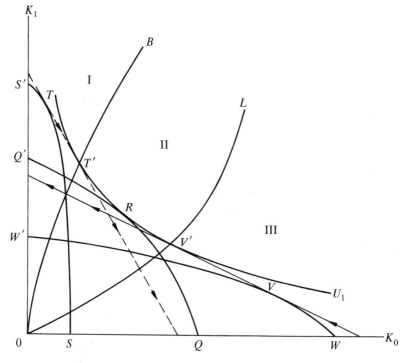

Fig. 2–3. Three solution zones for differing borrowing and lending rates.

isoquants whose slope equals that of the *borrowing* market line. Correspondingly, Zone III is that zone where the productive solution involves tangency with a lending market line (like V), which is then carried forward by lending to a final tangency optimum with a utility isoquant along the line OL at a point like V'. This line connects all points on the utility isoquants with slope equal to that of the *lending* market line. Finally, Zone II solutions occur when a productive opportunity locus like QRQ' is steeper than the lending rate throughout Zone III but flatter than the borrowing rate throughout Zone I. Therefore, such a locus must be tangent to one of the indifference curves somewhere in Zone II.

By analogy with the discussion in the previous section, we may conclude that the *borrowing* rate will lead to correct answers (to the productive investment decision, neglecting the related financing question) under the present-value rule or the internal-rate-of-return rule—when the situation involves a Zone I solution. Correspondingly, the *lending* rate will be appropriate and lead to correct investment decisions for Zone III solutions. For Zone II solutions, however, neither will be correct. There will, in fact, be some rate between the lending and the borrowing rates which would lead to the correct results. Formally speaking, we could describe this correct discount rate as the marginal productive opportunity rate,[10] which will at equilibrium equal the marginal subjective time-preference rate. In such a case neither rule is satisfactory in the sense of providing the productive solution without reference to the utility isoquants; knowledge of the comparative slopes of the utility isoquant and the productive opportunity frontier is all that is necessary, however. Of course, even when the rules in question are considered "satisfactory," they are misleading in implying that productive investment decisions can be correctly made independently of the "financing" decision.

This solution, in retrospect, may perhaps seem obvious. Where the productive opportunity, time-preference, and market (or financing) opportunities stand in such relations to one another as to require borrowing to reach the optimum, the borrowing rate is the correct rate to use in the productive investment decision. The lending rate is irrelevant because the decision on the margin involves a balancing of the cost of borrowing and the return from further productive investment, both being higher than the lending rate. The lending opportunity is indeed still available, but, the rate of return on lending being lower than the lowest marginal productive rate of return we would wish to consider in the light of the borrowing rate we must pay, lending is not a relevant alternative. Rather the relevant alternative to productive investment is a reduction in borrowing, which in terms of saving interest is more remunerative than lending. Similarly, when the balance of considerations dictates lending part of the firm's current capital funds, borrowing is not the relevant cost incurred in financing productive investment. The relevant alternative to increased productive investment is the amount of lending which must be foregone. While these considerations may be obvious, there is some disagreement in the literature as to whether the lending or the borrowing rate is *the* correct one.[11]

---

[10] The marginal productive opportunity rate, or marginal internal rate of return, measures the rate of return on the best alternative project. Assuming continuity, it is defined by the slope of QRQ' at R in Fig. 2–3. Evidently, a present-value line tangent to U_1 and QRQ' at R would, in a formal sense, make the present-value rule correct. And comparing this rate with the marginal internal rate of return as it varies along QRQ' would make the internal-rate-of-return rule also correct in the same formal sense.

[11] The borrowing rate (the "cost of capital") has been recommended by Dean and by Lorie and Savage (see Joel Dean, *Capital Budgeting* [New York: Columbia University Press, 1951], esp. pp. 43–44; James H. Lorie and Leonard J. Savage, "Three Problems in Rationing Capital," *Journal of Business*, XXVIII [October, 1955], 229–39, esp. p. 229). Roberts and the Lutzes favor the use of the lending rate (see Friedrich and Vera Lutz, *op. cit.*, esp. p. 22; Harry V. Roberts, "Current Problems in the Economics of Capital Budgeting," *Journal of Business*, XXX [January, 1957], 12–16).

C. Increasing Marginal Cost of Borrowing

While it is generally considered satisfactory to assume a constant lending rate (the investor does not drive down the loan rate as a consequence of his lendings), for practical reasons it is important to take account of the case in which increased borrowing can only take place at increasing cost. As it happens, however, this complication does not require any essential modification of principle.

Figure 2–4 shows, as before, a productive opportunity locus $QR'T$ and an indifference curve U_1. For simplicity, assume that marginal borrowing costs rise at the same rate whether the investor begins to borrow at the point R', S', or W' or at any other point along $QR'T$ (he cannot, of course, start borrowing at Q, having no K_1 to offer in exchange for more K_0). Under this assumption we can then draw market curves, now concave to the origin, like $R'R$, $S'S$, and $W'W$. The curve TE represents the total opportunity set as the

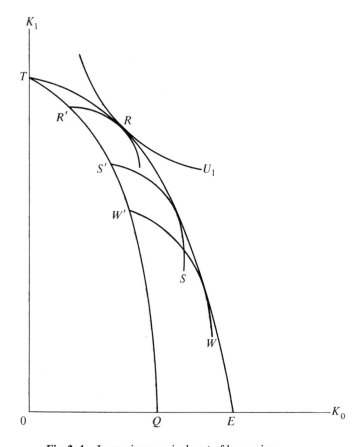

Fig. 2–4. Increasing marginal cost of borrowing.

envelope of these market curves, that is, TE connects all the points on the market curves representing the maximum K_0 attainable for any given K_1. By the nature of an envelope curve, TE will be tangent to a market curve at each such point. The optimum is then simply found where TE is tangent to the highest indifference curve attainable—here the curve U_1 at R. To reach R, the investor must exploit his productive opportunity to the point R' and then borrow back along his market curve to R.

The preceding discussion applies solely to what was called a Zone I (borrowing) solution in the previous section. Depending upon the nature of the productive opportunity, a Zone II or Zone III solution would also be possible under the assumptions of this section. With regard to the present-value and the internal-rate-of-return rules, the conclusions are unchanged for Zone II and III solutions, however. Only for Zone I solutions is there any modification.

The crucial question, as always, for these rules is what rate of discount to use. Intuition tells us that the rate representing *marginal* borrowing cost should be used as the discount rate for Zone I solutions, since productive investment will then be carried just to the point justified by the cost of the associated increment of borrowing.[12] That is, the slope of the envelope for any point on the envelope curve (for example, R), is the same as the slope of the productive opportunity curve at the corresponding point (R') connected by the market curve.[13] If this is the case, the discount rate determined by the

---

[12] I should like to thank Joel Segall for insisting on this point in discussions of the problem. Note that the rate representing marginal borrowing cost is not necessarily the borrowing rate on marginal funds—an increment of borrowing may increase the rate on infra-marginal units.

[13] While this point can be verified geometrically, it follows directly from the analytic properties of an envelope curve.

To simplify notation, in this note I shall denote K_1 of Fig. 2–4 as y and K_0 as x. The equation of the productive opportunity locus may be written

$$y_0 = f(x_0). \tag{a}$$

The family of market curves can be expressed by $y - y_0 = g(x - x_0)$, or

$$F(x, x_0) = f(x_0) + g(x - x_0). \tag{b}$$

An envelope, $y = h(x)$, is defined by the condition that any point on it must be a point of tangency with some member of the family (b). Thus we have

$$h(x) = F(x, x_0), \tag{c}$$

$$\frac{dh}{dx} = \frac{\partial F(x, x_0)}{\partial x}. \tag{d}$$

The second condition for an envelope is that the partial derivative of the function (b) with respect to the parameter must equal zero:

$$\frac{\partial F(x, x_0)}{\partial x_0} = 0. \tag{e}$$

But $$\frac{\partial F(x, x_0)}{\partial x_0} = \frac{df(x_0)}{dx_0} + (-1)\frac{dg(x - x_0)}{d(x - x_0)}$$

slope at a tangency with U_1 at a point like R will also lead to productive investment being carried to R' by the rules under consideration. Of course, this again is a purely formal statement. Operationally speaking, the rules may not be of much value, since the discount rate to be used is not known in advance independently of the utility (time-preference) function.

D. Rationing of "Capital"—A Current Controversy

The previous discussion provides the key for resolving certain current disputes over what constitutes optimal investment decision under a condition of "capital rationing" or "fixed capital budget." This condition is said to exist when the firm, or individual, or perhaps department of government under consideration cannot borrow additional "capital" but is limited instead to making the best use of the "capital" already in its possession or allocated to it.[14] In theoretical literature a closely related idea is expressed by Scitovsky, who, regarding the availability of capital (in the sense of "current capital funds") as the fixed factor limiting the size of the firm, proposes as the investment criterion the maximization of "profit per unit capital invested."[15] Lutz and Lutz, in contrast, assert as their ultimate investment criterion the maximization of the rate of return on the entrepreneur's *owned* capital, which they regard as fixed.[16]

It is of some interest to analyze these concepts in greater detail in terms of our Fisherian model. Scitovsky defines "capital" as current capital funds (our K_0) required to bridge the time lapse between factor input and product output.[17] Under this definition, however, "capital" would be fixed to the

---

Hence

$$\frac{df(x_0)}{dx_0} = \frac{dg(x - x_0)}{d(x - x_0)}.$$

Also

$$\frac{\partial F(x, x_0)}{\partial x} = \frac{dg(x - x_0)}{d(x - x_0)}.$$

So, finally,

$$\frac{df(x_0)}{dx_0} = \frac{dg(x - x_0)}{d(x - x_0)} = \frac{\partial F(x, x_0)}{dx} = \frac{dh}{dx}.$$

Thus the slope of the productive opportunity locus is the same as the slope of the envelope at points on the two curves connected by being on the same market curve.

[14] The expression "capital rationing" was used some time ago by Hart to refer to a non-price limitation on the acquisition of debt or equity financing (see A. G. Hart, "Anticipations, Business Planning, and the Cycle," *Quarterly Journal of Economics*, LI [1937], 273–97). His use of the term does not seem to imply a definitely fixed quantity available and can, in fact, be interpreted simply as indicating a rising marginal cost of capital funds. See also Joel Dean, *Managerial Economics* (Englewood Cliffs, N.J.: Prentice-Hall, Inc., 1951), pp. 586–600. In the sense of a definitely fixed quantity of funds, the term has been used by various authors discussing business or government problems. See J. Margolis, "The Discount Rate and the Benefits-Cost Justification of Federal Irrigation Investment," (Department of Economics, Stanford University-Technical Report No. 23 [Stanford, Calif., 1955]); Lorie and Savage, *op. cit.*, and R. McKean, *Efficiency in Government through Systems Analysis* (New York: John Wiley & Sons, 1958).

[15] T. Scitovsky, *Welfare and Competition* (Chicago: Richard D. Irwin, Inc., 1951), pp. 208–9.

[16] *Op. cit.*, pp. 16–48, esp. pp. 17, 20, 42.

[17] *Op. cit.*, p. 194.

firm only under rather peculiar conditions; specifically, if there is a discontinuity in the capital funds market such that the marginal borrowing rate suddenly becomes infinite at the firm's level of borrowings.[18] Without discontinuity, an infinitely high marginal borrowing rate could never represent an equilibrium position for the borrower, unless indeed his preference for present income over future income was absolute. And, of course, if the marginal borrowing rate is not infinite, current capital funds could not be said to be fixed. Nevertheless, while this case may be considered peculiar and unlikely to arise in any strict sense, it may be acceptable as a reasonable approximation of certain situations which occur in practice—especially in the short run, perhaps as a result of previous miscalculations. A division of a firm or a department of government may at times be said to face an infinite marginal borrowing rate once a budget constraint is reached—until the next meeting of the board of directors or the Congress provides more funds.

On the other hand, it is difficult to decipher the Lutzes' meaning when they speak of the firm's *owned* capital as fixed. In the Fisherian analysis, "ownership" of current or future assets is a legal form without analytical significance—to buy an asset yielding future income, with current funds, is simply to lend, while selling income is the same as borrowing. In a more fundamental sense, however, we could think of the firm as "owning" the opportunity set or at least the physical productive opportunities available to it, and this perhaps is what the Lutzes have in mind. Thus, Robinson Crusoe's house might be considered as his "owned capital"—a resource yielding consumption income in both present and future. The trouble is that the Lutzes seem to be thinking of "owned capital" as the *value* of the productive resources (in the form of capital goods) owned by the firm,[19] but owned physical capital goods cannot be converted to a capital *value* without bringing in a rate of discount for the receipts stream. But since, as we have seen, the relevant rate of discount for a firm's decisions is not (except where a perfect capital market exists) an independent entity but is itself determined by the analysis, the *capital value* cannot in general be considered to be fixed independently of the investment decision.[20]

---

[18] Scitovsky appears to leap from the acceptable argument in the earlier part of his discussion that willingness to lend and to borrow are not *unlimited* to the unacceptable position in his later discussion that current capital funds are *fixed* (*ibid.*, pp. 193–200, 208–9).

[19] Lutz and Lutz, *op. cit.*, pp. 3–13.

[20] It is possible, however, that the Lutzes had in mind only the case in which an investor starts off with current funds but no other assets. In this case no discounting problems would arise in defining owned capital, so their ultimate criterion could not be criticized on that score. The objection raised below to the Scitovsky criterion, however—that it fails to consider the *consumption* alternative, which is really the heart of the question of investment decision—would then apply to the Lutzes' rule. In addition, a rule for an investor owning solely current funds is hardly of general enough applicability to be an ultimate criterion. The Lutzes themselves recognize the case of an investor owning no "capital" but using only borrowed funds, and for this case they themselves abandon their ultimate criterion (*ibid.*, p. 42, n. 32). The most general case, of course, is that of an investor with a productive opportunity set capable of yielding him alternative combinations of present and future income.

While space does not permit a full critique of the Lutzes' important work, it is worth mentioning that—from a Fisherian point of view—it starts off on the wrong foot. They search first for an ultimate criterion or formula with which to gauge investment decision rules and settle upon "maximization of the rate of return on the investor's owned capital" on what seem to be purely intuitive grounds. The Fisherian approach, in contrast, integrates investment decision with the general theory of choice—the goal being to maximize utility subject to certain opportunities and constraints. In these terms, certain formulas can be validated as useful proximate rules for some classes of problems, as I am attempting to show here, However, the ultimate Fisherian criterion of choice—the optimal balancing of consumption alternatives over time—cannot be reduced to any of the usual formulas.

Instead of engaging in further discussion of the various senses in which "capital" may be said to be fixed to the firm, it will be more instructive to see how the Fisherian approach solves the problem of "capital rationing." I shall use as an illustration what may be called a "Scitovsky situation," in which the investor has run against a discontinuity making the marginal borrowing rate infinite. I regard this case (which I consider empirically significant only in the short run) as the model situation underlying the "capital rationing" discussion.

An infinite borrowing rate makes the dashed borrowing lines of Figs. 2–2 and 2–3 essentially vertical. In consequence, the curve OB in Fig. 2–3 shifts so far to the left as to make Zone I disappear for all practical purposes. There are then only Zone II and Zone III solutions. An investment-opportunity locus like WVW' in Fig. 2–3 becomes less steep than the lending slope in Zone III, in which case the investor will carry investment up to the point V where this occurs and then lend until a tangency solution is reached at V', which would be somewhere along the curve OL of Fig. 2–3. If an investment-opportunity locus like QRQ' in Fig. 2–3 is still steeper than the lending rate after it crosses OL, investment should be carried until tangency with an indifference curve like U_1 is attained somewhere to the left of OL, with no lending or borrowing taking place.

In terms of the present-value or internal-rate-of-return rules, under these conditions the decisions should be based on the *lending* rate (as the discounting rate or the standard of comparison) if the solution is a Zone III one. Here lending actually takes place, since movement upward and to the left still remains desirable when the last investment with a rate of return greater than the lending rate is made. If the solution is a Zone II one, the lending rate must not be used. Investments showing positive present value at the lending rate (or, equivalently, with an internal rate of return higher than the lending rate) will be nevertheless undesirable after a tangency point equating the investment-opportunity slope and the time-preference slope is reached. The correct rate, formally speaking, is the marginal opportunity rate.

The solution changes only slightly when we consider an isolated individual like Robinson Crusoe or a self-contained community like a nation under autarchy (or like the world economy as a whole). In this situation neither borrowing nor lending is possible in our sense, only productive opportunities existing. Only Zone II solutions are then possible. This case is the most extreme remove from the assumption of perfect capital markets.[21]

As in the case of the Zone II solutions arising without capital rationing, the present-value or internal-rate-of-return rules can be formally modified to apply to the Zone II solutions which are typical under capital rationing. The discount rate to be used for calculating present values or as a standard of comparison against the internal rate of project increments is the rate given by the slope of the Zone II tangency (the marginal productive rate of return); with this rate, the rules give the correct answer. But this rate cannot be discovered until the solution is attained and so is of no assistance in reaching the solution. The exception is the Zone III solution involving lending which can arise in a "Scitovsky situation." Here the lending rate should of course be used. The undetermined discount rate that gives correct results when the rules are used for Zone II solutions can, in some problems, be regarded as a kind of shadow price reflecting the productive rate of return on the best alternative opportunity not being exploited.

The reader may be curious as to why, in the Scitovsky situation, the outcome of the analysis was not Scitovsky's result—that the optimal investment decision is such as to maximize the (average) internal rate of return on the firm's present capital funds (K_0). Thus, in Fig. 2–3, for a firm starting with OQ of K_0 and faced with the productive opportunity locus QRQ', the average rate of return (K_1 received per unit of K_0 sacrificed) is a maximum for an infinitesimal movement along QRQ', since, the farther it moves, the more the marginal and average productive rates of return fall. Such a rule implies staying at Q—which is obviously the wrong decision.

How does this square with Scitovsky's intuitively plausible argument that the firm always seeks to maximize its returns on the fixed factor, present capital funds being assumed here to be fixed?[22] The answer is that this argument is applicable only for a factor "fixed" in the sense of no alternative uses. Here present capital funds K_0 are assumed to be fixed, but not in the sense Scitovsky must have had in mind. The concept here is that no additional borrowing can take place, but the possibility of *consuming* the present funds as an alternative to investing them is recognized. For Scitovsky, however, the funds *must* be invested. If in fact current income K_0 had no uses other

---

[21] We could, following the principles already laid down, work out without great difficulty the solution for the case in which borrowing is permitted but only up to a certain fixed limit. The effect of such a provision is to provide a kind of "attainability envelope" as in Fig. 2–4, but of a somewhat different shape.

[22] *Op. cit.*, p. 209.

than conversion into future income K_1 (this amounts to absolute preference for future over current income), Scitovsky's rule would correctly tell us to pick that point on the K_1 axis which is the highest.[23] Actually, our time preferences are more balanced; there *is* an alternative use (consumption) for K_0. Therefore, even in Scitovsky situations, we will balance K_0 and K_1 on the margin—and not simply accept the maximum K_1 we can get in exchange for all our "fixed" K_0.[24] The analyses of Scitovsky, the Lutzes, and many other recent writers frequently lead to incorrect solutions because of their failure to take into account the alternative consumption opportunities which Fisher integrated into his theory of investment decision.

E. Non-Independent Investment Opportunities

Up to this point, following Fisher, investment opportunities have been assumed to be independent so that it is possible to rank them in any desired way. In particular, they were ordered in Figures 2–1 through 2–4 in terms of decreasing productive rate of return; the resultant concavity produced unique tangency solutions with the utility or market curves. But suppose, now, that there are two mutually exclusive sets of such investment opportunities. Thus we may consider building a factory in the East or the West, but not both —contemplating the alternatives, the eastern opportunities may look like the locus $QV'V$, and the western opportunities like $QT'T$ in Fig. 2–5.[25]

Which is better? Actually, the solutions continue to follow directly from Fisher's principles, though too much non-independence makes for troublesome calculations in practice, and in some classes of cases, the heretofore inerrant present-value rule fails. In the simplest case, in which there is a constant borrowing-lending rate (a perfect capital market), the curve $QV'V$ is tangent to its highest attainable present-value line at V'—while the best point on $QT'T$ is T'. It is only necessary to consider these, and the one attaining the higher present-value line ($QT'T$ at T' in this case) will permit the investor to reach the highest possible indifference curve U_1 at R. In contrast, the internal-rate-of-return rule would locate the points T' and V' but could not discriminate between them. Where borrowing and lending rates differ, as in Fig. 2–2 (now interpreting the productive opportunity loci

---

[23] That is, the point Q' in Fig. 2–3. This result is of course trivial. Scitovsky may possibly have in mind choice among non-independent sets of investments (discussed in the next section), where each set may have a different intersection with the K_1 axis. Here a non-trivial choice could be made with the criterion of maximizing the average rate of return.

[24] Scitovsky may have in mind a situation in which a certain fraction of current funds K_0 are set apart from consumption (on some unknown basis) to become the "fixed" current capital funds. In this case the Scitovsky rule would lead to the correct result if it happened that just so much "fixed" capital funds were allocated to get the investor to the point R' on his productive transformation locus of Fig. 2–3.

[25] It would, of course, reduce matters to their former simplicity if one of the loci lay completely within the other, in which case it would be obviously inferior and could be dropped from consideration.

of that figure as mutually exclusive alternatives), it may be ncessary to compare, say, a lending solution at V with a borrowing solution at T. To find the *optimum optimorum*, the indifference curves must be known (in Fig. 2–2 the two solutions attain the same indifference curve). Note that present value is *not* a reliable guide here; in fact, the present value of the solution $V (= W^*)$ at the relevant discount rate for it (the lending rate) far exceeds that of the solution $T (= T^*)$ at its discount rate (the borrowing rate), when the two are actually indifferent. Assuming an increasing borrowing rate creates no new essential difficulty.

Another form of non-independence, illustrated in Fig. 2–6, is also troublesome without modifying principle. Here the projects along the productive investment locus QQ' are not entirely independent, for we are constrained to adopt some low-return ones before certain high-return ones. Again, there is a possibility of several local optima like V and T, which can be compared along the same lines as used in the previous illustration.

F. Conclusion for Two-Period Analysis

The solutions for optimal investment decisions vary according to a two-way classification of cases. The first classification refers to the way market opportunities exist for the decision-making agency; the second classification refers to the absence or presence of the complication of non-independent productive opportunities. The simplest, extreme cases for the first classification are: (*a*) a perfect capital market (market opportunities such that lending or borrowing in any amounts can take place at the same, fixed rate) and (*b*) no market opportunities whatsoever, as was true for Robinson Crusoe. Where there is a perfect capital market, the total attainable set is a triangle (considering only the first quadrant) like OPP' in Fig. 2–1, just tangent to the productive opportunity locus. Where there is no capital market at all, the total attainable set is simply the productive opportunity locus itself. It is not difficult to see how the varying forms of imperfection of the capital market fit in between these extremes.

When independence of physical (productive) opportunities holds, the opportunities may be ranked in order of descending productive rate of return. Geometrically, if the convenient (but inessential) assumption of continuity is adopted, independence means that the productive opportunity locus is everywhere concave to the origin, like $QS'TV$ in Fig. 2–1. Non-independence may take several forms (see Figs. 2–5 and 2–6), but in each case that is not trivial non-independence means that the effective productive opportunity locus is not simply concave. This is obvious in Fig. 2–6. In Fig. 2–5 each of the two alternative loci considered separately is concave, but the effective locus is the scalloped outer edge of the overlapping sets of points attainable by either—that is, the effective productive opportunity locus runs along $QT'T$ up to X and then crosses over to $QV'V$.

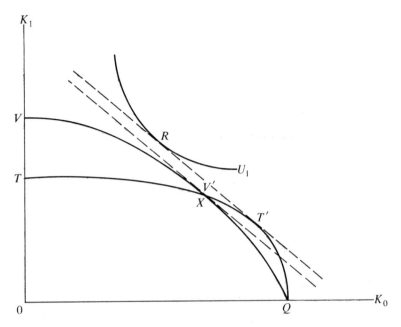

Fig. 2–5.   Non-independent investment opportunities—two alternative productive investment loci.

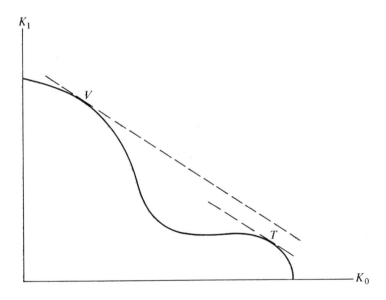

Fig. 2–6.   Non-independent investment opportunities—poorer projects prerequisite to better ones.

With this classification a detailed tabulation of the differing solutions could be presented; the following brief summary of the general principles involved should serve almost as well, however.

1. The internal-rate-of-return rule fails wherever there are multiple tangencies—the normal outcome for non-independent productive opportunities.

2. The present-value rule works whenever the other does and, in addition, correctly discriminates among multiple tangencies whenever a perfect capital market exists (or, by extension, whenever a unique discount rate can be determined for the comparison—for example when all the alternative tangencies occur in Zone I or else all in Zone III).

3. Both rules work only in a formal sense when the solution involves direct tangency between a productive opportunity locus and a utility isoquant, since the discount rate necessary for use of both rules is the marginal opportunity rate—a product of the analysis.

4. The cases when even the present-value rule fails (may actually give wrong answers) all involve the comparison of multiple tangencies arising from non-independent investments when, in addition, a perfect capital market does not exist. One important example is the comparison of a tangency involving borrowing in Zone I with another involving lending in Zone III. Only reference to the utility map can give correct answers for such cases.

5. Even when one or both rules are correct in a not merely formal sense, the answer given is the "productive solution"—only part of the way toward attainment of the utility optimum. Furthermore, this productive decision is optimal only when it can be assumed that the associated financing decision will in fact be made.

II. A BRIEF NOTE ON PERPETUITIES

A traditional way of handling the multiperiod case in capital theory has been to consider investment decisions as choices between current funds and perpetual future income flows. For many purposes this is a valuable simplifying idea. It cannot be adopted here, however, because the essence of the practical difficulties which have arisen in multiperiod investment decisions is the *reinvestment* problem—the necessity of making productive or market exchanges between incomes in future time periods. In fact, the consideration of the perpetuity case is, in a sense, only a variant of the two-period analysis, in which there is a single present and a single future. In the case of perpetuity analysis, the future is stretched out, but we cannot consider transfer between different periods of the future.

All the two-period results in Section I can easily be modified to apply to the choice between current funds and perpetuities. In the Figures, instead of income K_1 in period 1 one may speak of an annual rate of income k. Productive opportunity loci and time-preference curves will retain their familiar shapes. The lines of constant present value (borrow-lend lines) are expressed by the equation $C = K_0 + (k/i)$ instead of $C = K_0 + (K_1)/(1 + i)$. The "internal rate of return" will equal $(k)/(-\Delta K_0)$. The rest of the analysis follows directly, but, rather than trace it out, I shall turn to the consideration of the multiperiod case in a more general way.

III. MULTIPERIOD ANALYSIS

Considerable doubt prevails on how to generalize the principles of the two-period analysis to the multiperiod case. The problems which have troubled the analysis of the multiperiod case are actually the result of inappropriate generalizations of methods of solution that do lead to correct results in the simplified two-period analysis.

A. Internal Rate-of-Return Rule Versus Present-Value Rule

In the multiperiod analysis there is no formal difficulty in generalizing the indifference curves of Fig. 2–1 to indifference shells in any number of dimensions. Also the lines of constant present value or market lines become hyperplanes with the equation (in the most general form)

$$K_0 + \frac{K_1}{1 + i_1} + \frac{K_2}{(1 + i_1)(1 + i_2)} + \cdots + \frac{K_n}{(1 + i_1)(1 + i_2) \cdots (1 + i_n)} = C,$$

C being a parameter, i_1 the discount rate between income in periods 0 and 1, i_2 the discount rate between periods 1 and 2, and so forth.[26] Where $i_1 = i_2 = \cdots i_n = i$, the expression takes on the simpler and more familiar form

$$K_0 + \frac{K_1}{1 + i} + \frac{K_2}{(1 + i)^2} + \cdots + \frac{K_n}{(1 + i)^n} = C.$$

The major difficulty with the multiperiod case turns upon the third element of the solution—the description of the productive opportunities, which may be denoted by the equation $f(K_0, K_1, \ldots, K_n) = 0$. The purely theoretical specification is not too difficult, however, if the assumption is made that all investment options are independent. The problem of non-independence is not essentially different in the multiperiod case and in the two-period case, and it would enormously complicate the presentation to consider it here. Under this condition, then, and with appropriate continuity

---

[26] I shall not, in this section, consider further the possible divergences between the lending and borrowing rates studied in detail in Sec. I but shall speak simply of "the discount rate" or "the market rate." The principles involved are not essentially changed in the multiperiod case; I shall concentrate attention on certain other difficulties that appear only when more than two periods are considered. We may note that in the most general case the assumption of full information becomes rather unrealistic—e.g., that the pattern of interest rates i_1 through i_n is known today.

assumptions, the productive opportunity locus may be envisaged as a shell[27] concave to the origin in all directions. With these assumptions, between income in any two periods K_r and K_s (holding K_t for all other periods constant) there will be a two-dimensional productive opportunity locus essentially like that in Fig. 2–1.[28]

Now suppose that lending or borrowing can take place between any two successive periods r and s at the rate i_s. The theoretical solution involves finding the multidimensional analogue of the point R' (in Fig. 2–1)—that is, the point on the highest present-value hyperplane reached by the productive opportunity locus. With simple curvature and continuity assumptions, R' will be a tangency point, thus having the additional property that, between the members of any such pair of time periods, the marginal productive rate of return between K_r and K_s (holding all other K_t's constant) will be equal to the discount rate between these periods. Furthermore, if the condition is met between all pairs of successive periods, it will also be satisfied between any pairs of time periods as well.[29] Again, as in the two-period case, the final

---

[27] As in the two-period case, the locus represents not all the production opportunities but only the *boundary* of the region represented by the production opportunities. The boundary consists of those opportunities not dominated by any other; any opportunity represented by an interior point is dominated by at least one boundary point.

[28] The assumption of n-dimensional continuity is harder to swallow than two-dimensional continuity as an approximation to the nature of the real world. Nevertheless, the restriction is not essential, though it is an enormous convenience in developing the argument. One possible misinterpretation of the continuity assumption should be mentioned: it does not necessarily mean that the only investment opportunities considered are two-period options between pairs of periods in the present or future. Genuine multiperiod options are allowable—for example, the option described by cash-flows of -1, $+4$, $+2$, and $+6$ for periods 0, 1, 2, and 3, respectively. The continuity assumption means, rather, that if we choose to move from an option like this one in the direction of having more income in period 1 and less, say, in period 3, we can find other options available like -1, $+4 + e_1$, $+2$, $+6 - e_3$, where e_1 and e_3 represent infinitesimals. In other words, from any point on the locus it is possible to trade continuously between incomes in any pair of periods.

[29] Maximizing the Lagrangian expression $C - \lambda f(K_0, \ldots, K_n)$, we derive the first-order conditions

$$\begin{cases} \dfrac{\partial C}{\partial K_0} = 1 & -\lambda \dfrac{\partial f}{\partial K_0} = 0 \\[2mm] \dfrac{\partial C}{\partial K_1} = \dfrac{1}{1 + i_1} & -\lambda \dfrac{\partial f}{\partial K_1} = 0 \\[1mm] \cdots \cdots \cdots \cdots \cdots \cdots \cdots \cdots \\[1mm] \dfrac{\partial C}{\partial K_n} = \dfrac{1}{(1 + i_1)(1 + i_2) \cdots (1 + i_n)} & -\lambda \dfrac{\partial f}{\partial K_n} = 0. \end{cases}$$

Eliminating λ between any pair of successive periods:

$$\frac{\partial f / \partial K_r}{\partial f / \partial K_s} = \frac{(1 + i_1)(1 + i_2) \cdots (1 + i_r)(1 + i_s)}{(1 + i_1)(1 + i_2) \cdots (1 + i_r)}$$

$$\left. \frac{\partial K_s}{\partial K_r} \right|_{\substack{K_j \\ (j \neq r,s)}} = 1 + i_s.$$

Between non-successive periods:

$$\left. \frac{\partial K_t}{\partial K_r} \right|_{\substack{K_j \\ (j \neq r,t)}} = (1 + i_{r+1})(1 + i_{r+2}) \cdots (1 + i_{t-1})(1 + i_t).$$

solution will involve market lending or borrowing ("financing") to move along the highest present-value hyperplane attained from the intermediate productive solution R' to the true preference optimum at R. Note that, as compared with the present value or direct solution, the principle of equating the marginal productive rate of return with the discount rate requires certain continuity assumptions.

Now it is here that Fisher, who evidently understood the true nature of the solution himself, appears to have led others astray. In his *Rate of Interest* he provides a mathematical proof that the optimal investment decision involves setting what is here called the marginal productive rate of return equal to the market rate of interest *between any two periods*.[30] By obvious generalization of the result of the two-period problem, this condition is identical with that of finding the line of highest present value (the two-dimensional projection of the hyperplane of highest present value) between these time periods. Unfortunately, Fisher fails to state the qualification "between any two time-periods" consistently and at various places makes flat statements to the effect that investments will be made wherever the "rate of return on sacrifice" or "rate of return on cost" between any two options exceeds the rate of interest.[31]

Now the rate of return on sacrifice is, for two-period comparisons, equivalent to the productive rate of return. More generally, however, Fisher defines the rate of return on sacrifice in a *multiperiod* sense; that is, as that rate which reduces to a present value of zero the entire sequence of positive and negative periodic differences between the returns of any two investment options.[32] This definition is, for our purposes, equivalent to the so-called "internal rate of return."[33] This latter rate (which will be denoted ρ) will, however, be shown to lead to results which are, in general, not correct if the procedure is followed of adopting or rejecting investment options on the basis of a comparison of ρ and the market rate.[34]

---

[30] *Rate of Interest*, pp. 398–400. Actually, the proof refers only to successive periods, but this is an inessential restriction.

[31] *Ibid.*, p. 155; *Theory of Interest*, pp. 168–69.

[32] *Rate of Interest*, p. 153; *Theory of Interest*, pp. 168–69.

[33] For some purposes it is important to distinguish between the rate which sets the present value of a series of receipts from an investment equal to zero and that rate which does the same for the series of *differences* between the receipts of two alternative investment options (see A. A. Alchian, "The Rate of Interest, Fisher's Rate of Return over Cost, and Keynes' Internal Rate of Return," *American Economic Review*, XLV [December, 1955], 938–43). For present purposes there is no need to make the distinction because individual investment options are regarded as independent increments—so that the receipts of the option in question are in fact a sequence of differences over the alternative of not adopting that option.

[34] As another complication, Fisher's mathematical analysis compares the two-period marginal rates of return on sacrifice with the interest rates between those two periods, the latter not being assumed constant throughout. In the multiperiod case Fisher nowhere states how to combine the differing period-to-period interest rates into an over-all market rate for comparison with ρ. It is possible that just at this point Fisher was thinking only of a rate of interest which remained constant over time, in which case the question would not arise. The difficulty in the use of the "internal rate" when variations in the market rate over time exist will be discussed below.

B. Failure of the Generalized "Internal Rate of Return"

Recent thinking emphasizing the internal rate of return seems to be based upon the idea of finding a purely "internal" measure of the time productivity of an investment—that is, the rate of growth of capital funds invested in a project—for comparison with the market rate.[35] But the idea of rate of growth involves a ratio and cannot be uniquely defined unless one can uniquely value initial and terminal positions. Thus the investment option characterized by the annual cash-flow sequence $-1, 0, 0, 8$ clearly involves a growth rate of 100 percent (compounding annually), because it really reduces to a two-period option with intermediate compounding. Similarly, a savings deposit at 10 percent compounded annually for n years may seem to be a multiperiod option, but it is properly regarded as a series of two-period options (the "growth" will take place only if at the beginning of each period the decision is taken to reinvest the capital plus interest yielded by the investment of the previous period). A savings-account option without reinvestment would be: $-1, 0.10, 0.10, 0.10, \ldots, 1.10$ (the last element being a terminating payment); with reinvestment, the option becomes $-1, 0, 0, 0, \ldots, (1.10)^n$, n being the number of compounding periods after the initial deposit.

Consider, however, a more general investment option characterized by the sequence $-1, 2, 1$. (In general, all investment options considered here will be normalized in terms of an assumed \$1.00 of initial outlay or initial receipt.) How can a rate of growth for the initial capital outlay be determined? Unlike the savings-account opportunity, no information is provided as to the rate at which the intermediate receipt or "cash throw-off" of \$2.00 can be reinvested. If, of course, we use some external discounting rate (for example, the cost of capital or the rate of an outside lending opportunity), we will be departing from the idea of a purely *internal* growth rate. In fact, the use of an external rate will simply reduce us to a present-value evaluation of the investment option.

In an attempt to resolve this difficulty, one mathematical feature of the two-period marginal productive rate of return was selected for generalization by both Fisher and his successors. This feature is the fact that, when ρ (in the two-period case equal to the marginal productive rate of return $[\Delta K_1]/[-\Delta K_0] - 1$) is used for discounting the values in the receipt-outlay stream, the discounted value becomes zero. This concept lends itself to easy generalization: for any multiperiod stream there will be a similar discounting rate ρ which will make the discounted value equal to zero (or so it was thought). This rate seems to be purely internal, not infected by any market considerations. And, in certain simple cases, it does lead to correct answers in choosing investment projects according to the rule: Adopt the project if ρ is greater than the market rate r.

---

[35] See K. E. Boulding, *Economic Analysis* (rev. ed.; New York: Harper & Row, 1948), p. 819.

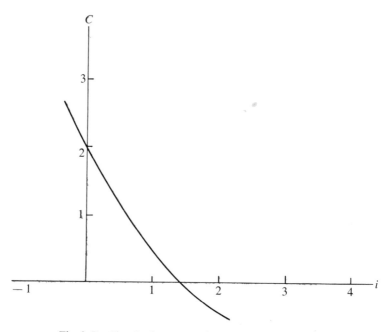

Fig. 2–7.   Sketch of present value of the option −1, 2, 1.

For the investment option −1, 2, 1 considered above, ρ is equal to $\sqrt{2}$, or 141.4 percent. And, in fact, if the borrowing rate or the rate on the best alternative opportunity (whichever is the appropriate comparison) is less than $\sqrt{2}$, the investment is desirable. Figure 2–7 plots the present value C of the option as a function of the discounting interest rate, i, assumed to be constant over the two discounting periods. Note that the present value of the option diminishes as i increases throughout the entire relevant range of i, from $i = -1$ to $i = \infty$.[36] The internal rate of return ρ is that i for which the present value curve cuts the horizontal axis. Evidently, for any $i < \rho$, present value is positive; for $i > \rho$, it is negative.

However, the fact that the use of ρ leads to the correct decision in a particular case or a particular class of cases does not mean that it is correct in principle. And, in fact, cases have been adduced where its use leads to incorrect answers. Alchian has shown that, in the comparison of two investment options which are alternatives, the choice of the one with a higher ρ is not in general correct—in fact, the decision cannot be made without knowledge of the appropriate external discounting rate.[37]   Figure 2–8

---

[36] Economic meaning may be attached to negative interest rates; these are rates of shrinkage of capital. I rule out the possibility of shrinkage rates greater than 100 percent, however.
[37] Alchian, *op. cit.*, p. 939.

illustrates two such options, I being preferable for low rates of interest and
II for high rates. The *i* at which the crossover takes place is Fisher's rate
of return on sacrifice between these two options. But II has the higher internal rate of return (that is, its present value falls to zero at a higher discounting rate) regardless of the actual rate of interest. How can we say that

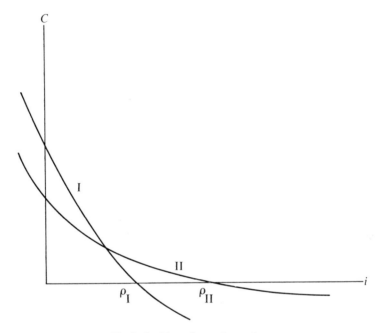

Fig. 2–8. Two alternative options.

I is preferable at low rates of interest? Because its present value is higher,
it permits the investor to move along a higher hyperplane to find the utility
optimum attained somewhere on that hyperplane. If II were adopted, the
investor would also be enabled to move along such a hyperplane, but a lower
one. Put another way, with the specified low rate of interest, the investor
adopting I could, if he chose, put himself in the position of adopting II by
appropriate borrowings and lendings together with throwing away some of
his wealth.[38]

---

[38] Some people find this so hard to believe that I shall provide a numerical example. For
investment I, we may use the annual cash-flow stream −1, 0, 4—then the internal rate of return
is 1, or 100 percent. For investment option II, we may use the option illustrated in Fig. 2–7:
−1, 2, 1. For this investment ρ is equal to $\sqrt{2}$, or 141.4 percent. So the internal rate of return
is greater for II. However, the present value for option I is greater at an interest rate of 0 percent,
and in fact it remains greater until the cross-over rate, which happens to be at 50 percent for these
two options. Now it is simple to show how, adopting I, we can get to the result II at any interest
rate lower than 50 percent—10 percent, for example. Borrowing from the final time period for
the benefit of the intermediate one, we can convert −1, 0, 4 to −1, 2.73, 1 (I have subtracted 3

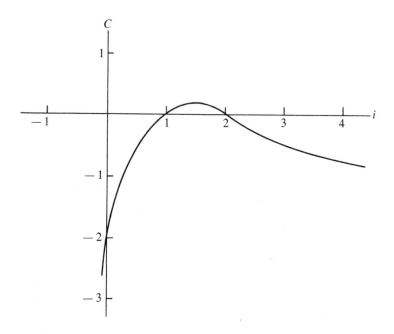

Fig. 2–9. Sketch of present value of the investment option $-1, 5, -6$.

Even more fundamentally, Lorie and Savage have shown that ρ may not be unique.[39] Consider, for example, the investment option $-1, 5, -6$. Calculation reveals that this option has a present value of zero at discounting rates of both 100 percent and 200 percent. For this investment option present value as a function of the discounting rate is sketched in Fig. 2–9. While Lorie and Savage speak only of "dual" internal rates of return, any number of zero values of the present-value function are possible in principle. The option $-1, 6, -11, 6$, illustrated in Fig. 2–10, has zero present value at the discounting rates 0 percent, 100 percent, and 200 percent, for example.[40]

---

from the final period, crediting the intermediate period with $3/1.1 = 2.73$). We can now get to option II by throwing away the 0.73, leaving us with $-1, 2, 1$. The fact that we can get to option II by throwing away some wealth demonstrates the superiority of I even though $\rho_{II} > \rho_I$, provided that borrowing and lending can take place at an interest rate less than the cross-over discounting rate of 50 percent.

[39] *Op. cit.*, pp. 236–39.

[40] The instances discussed above suggest that the alternation of signs in the receipt stream has something to do with the possibility of multiple ρ's. In fact, Descartes's rule of signs tells us that the number of solutions in the allowable range (the number of points where present value equals zero for $i > -1$) is at most equal to the number of reversals of sign in the terms of the receipts sequence. Therefore, a two-period investment option has at most a single ρ, a three-period option at most a dual ρ, and so forth. There is an interesting footnote in Fisher which suggests that he was not entirely unaware of this difficulty. Where more than a single-sign alternation takes place, he suggests the use of the present-value method rather than attempting to compute "the rate of return on sacrifice" (*Rate of Interest*, p. 155). That any number of zeros of the present value function can occur was pointed out by Paul A. Samuelson in "Some Aspects of the Pure Theory of Capital," *Quarterly Journal of Economics*, LI (1936–37), 469–96 (at p. 475).

In fact, perfectly respectable investment options may have *no* real internal rates (the present value equation has only imaginary roots). The option -1, 3, $-2\frac{1}{2}$ is an example; a plot would show that its present value is negative throughout the relevant range.[41] It is definitely not the case, however, that all options for which the internal rate cannot be calculated are bad ones. If we merely reverse the signs on the option above to get 1, -3, $2\frac{1}{2}$, we have an option with positive present value at all rates of discount.

These instances of failure of the multiperiod internal-rate-of-return rule (note that in each case the present-value rule continues to indicate the correct

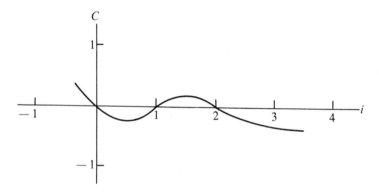

Fig. 2–10. Sketch of present value of the investment option -1, 6, -11, 6.

answer unambiguously, setting aside the question of the appropriate discounting rate which was discussed in Sec. I) are, of course, merely the symptom of an underlying erroneous conception. It is clear that the idea that ρ represents a growth rate in any simple sense cannot be true; a capital investment of $1.00 cannot grow at a rate both of 100 percent and of 200 percent. Even more fundamentally, the idea that ρ is a purely *internal* rate is not true either. Consider the option -1, 2, 1 discussed earlier, with a unique ρ equal to $\sqrt{2}$. The intermediate cash throwoff of $2.00 must clearly be reinvested externally of this option. How does the calculation of ρ handle this? This answer is that the mathematical manipulations involved in the calculation of ρ implicitly assume that all intermediate receipts, positive or

---

[41] Mathematically, the formula for the roots of a three-period option n_0, n_1, n_2 where $n_0 = -1$ is:

$$i = \frac{(n_1 - 2) \pm \sqrt{n_1^2 + 4n_2}}{2}.$$

If $-4n_2$ exceeds n_1^2, the roots will be imaginary, and an internal rate of return cannot be calculated. A necessary condition for this result is that the sum of the undiscounted cash flows be negative, but this condition should not rule out consideration of an option (note the option -1, 5, -6 in Fig. 2–9).

negative, are treated as if they could be compounded at the rate ρ being solved for.[42] The rate ρ has been characterized rather appropriately as the "solving rate" of interest. But note that this mathematical manipulation, even where it does lead to a unique answer (and, in general, it will not), is unreasonable in its economic implications. There will not normally be other investment opportunities arising for investment of intermediate cash proceeds at the rate ρ, nor is it generally true that intermediate cash inflows (if required) must be obtained by borrowing at the rate ρ. The rate ρ, arising from a mathematical manipulation, will only by rare coincidence represent relevant economic alternatives.

The preceding arguments against the use of the usual concept of the "internal rate of return" do not take any account of the possibility of non-constant interest rates over time. Martin J. Bailey has emphasized to me that it is precisely when this occurs (when there exists a known pattern of future variation of i) that the internal-rate-of-return rule fails most fundamentally. For in the use of that rule all time periods are treated on a par; the only discounting is via the solving rate defined only in terms of the sequence of cash flows. But with (a known pattern of) varying future i, shifts in the relative desirability of income in different periods are brought about. In the usual formulation the internal-rate-of-return concept can take no account of this. In fact, in such a case one might have an investment for which ρ was well defined and unique and still not be able to determine the desirability of the investment opportunity (that is, depending upon the time pattern of future interest rates, present value might be either negative or positive).

The following remarks attempt to summarize the basic principles discussed in this section.

At least in the simplest case, where we do not worry about differences between borrowing and lending rates but assume these to be equal and also constant (constant with respect to the amount borrowed or lent—not constant over time), the multidimensional solution using the present-value rule is a straightforward generalization of the two-period solution. The principle is to push productive investment to the point where the highest attainable level of present value is reached and then to "finance" this investment by borrowing or lending between time periods to achieve a time-preference optimum.

The main burden of these remarks has been to the effect that the internal-rate-of-return rule, unlike the present-value rule, does not generalize to the multiperiod case if the usual definition of the internal rate ρ is adopted—that is, as that rate which sets the present value of the discounted income stream equal to zero. I have tried to show the multiperiod generalization which *would* make the internal-rate-of-return rule still correct: between *every pair* of time periods, the marginal internal rate of return in the sense

[42] The true significance of the reinvestment assumption was brought out in Ezra Solomon, "The Arithmetic of Capital-budgeting Decisions," *Journal of Business*, XXIX (April, 1956), 124–29, esp. pp. 126–27.

of the marginal productive rate of return between those two periods, holding income in other periods constant, should be set equal to the market discount rate between those periods. That the usual interpretation of the internal-rate-of-return rule is not in general correct has been illustrated by its failure in particular cases and has been explained by exposing the implicit assumption made in the mathematical manipulation which finds p—that all intermediate cash flows are reinvested (or borrowed, if cash flows are negative) at the rate p itself. In addition, p does not allow for varying interperiod preference rates (or interest rates) over time. This generalized multiperiod internal rate of return is, therefore, not really internal, nor is the assumption implied about the external opportunities generally correct or even generally reasonable.

IV.   CONCLUDING COMMENTS

The preceding analysis has slighted a great many questions. In addition, lack of time has precluded comparative discussion of the works of other authors, however helpful this might have been.[43]

I have not attempted to generalize the results to the multiperiod case with non-independent investments or with differing or non-constant borrowing and lending rates. On the latter points intuition suggests that whether the borrowing or lending rate in calculating present value is to be used for any time period does not depend upon any characteristics of the investment option under consideration in isolation; it depends rather upon the over-all cash position after adoption of that option as an increment. If, after such adoption, time preference dictates shifting to less income in period r and more in period t, any income associated with the option in question falling in period r should be discounted back to the next earlier period at the lending rate (and that for period t at the borrowing rate). Income in any period s may then have been successively discounted at borrowing rates for a number of periods and lending rates for a number of others before being reduced to a present value.

The main positive conclusion of the paper is that the present-value rule for investment decisions is correct in a wide variety of cases (though not universally) and in a limited sense. The rule tells us to attain the highest possible level of present value, but the point at which this condition is satisfied

---

[43] I should comment, though, on the important article by Samuelson, *op. cit.* The results here are in part consistent with his, with the following main differences: (1) He limits himself to the analysis of a single investment, whereas I consider the entire investment-consumption pattern over time. (2) He concludes in favor of the present-value rule, discounting at *the* market rate of interest. I have attempted to consider explicitly the problem of what to do when the borrowing and lending rates diverge, or vary as a function of the amount borrowed, and I do not find the present-value rule to be universally valid. Of these differences, the first is really crucial. It is the heart of Fisher's message that investments *cannot* be considered in isolation but only in the context of the other investment and consumption alternatives available. Nevertheless, Samuelson's article suffices to refute a number of fallacies still current in this field of economic theory.

(that is, the distribution of incomes in various time periods) is not the final solution. It is, rather, an intermediate "productive" solution which must then be modified by borrowing or lending ("financing") to find the over-all optimum. This becomes particularly clear when we consider the case where lending and borrowing rates differ and thus enter the subcontroversy between those who favor the use of present-value discounting at the cost of capital and those who would discount at the alternative lending rate. Which is correct depends upon the financing necessary to approach the time-preference optimum. Furthermore, if a tangency takes place between the productive opportunity locus and the time-preference utility isoquant at a rate between the lending and the borrowing rates, the "productive" solution requires no financing and the present-value principle is only correct in a formal sense. The present-value rule fails to give correct answers only for certain cases which combine the difficulties of non-independent investments and absence of a perfect capital market. When a perfect capital market exists, the present-value rule is universally correct in the limited sense referred to above. With independent investments but an imperfect capital market, the present-value rule will give answers which are correct but possibly only in a formal sense (the discounting rate used is not an external opportunity but an internal shadow price which comes out of the analysis).

The main negative conclusion is that the internal-rate-of-return rule for the multiperiod case is not generally correct, if the usual definition of the internal rate is adopted as that discount rate which makes the present value of the income stream associated with an investment option equal to zero. The so-called internal rate will only give correct answers in general if restricted to two-period comparisons; I have called this two-period internal rate the productive rate of return. For multiperiod investments the usual internal-rate-of-return rule (compare ρ with the market rate r) is not generally correct; however, given certain continuity assumptions, the correct answer will be arrived at by setting the marginal productive rate of return between each *pair* of time periods equal to the discount or market rate between those periods.

More important than the specific detailed conclusions is the demonstration that the Fisherian approach—the analysis of investment decisions as a means of balancing consumption incomes over time, together with the distinction between productive and market investment opportunities—is capable of solving (in the theoretical sense) all the problems posed. This solution is, furthermore, not an excrescence upon the general economic theory of choice but entirely integrated with it, constituting another dimension, so to speak. Since Fisher, economists working in the theory of investment decision have tended to adopt a mechanical approach—some plumping for the use of this formula, some for that. From a Fisherian point of view, we can see that none of the formulas so far propounded is universally valid. Furthermore, even where the present-value rule, for example, is correct, few realize that its validity is conditional upon making certain associated financing decisions as the Fisherian analysis demonstrates. In short, the Fisherian approach permits us to define the range of applicability and the shortcomings of all the proposed formulas—thus standing over against them as the general theoretical solution to the problem of investment decision under conditions of certainty.

3

INVESTMENT AND DISCOUNT RATES UNDER CAPITAL RATIONING— A PROGRAMMING APPROACH

WILLIAM J. BAUMOL and RICHARD E. QUANDT*

In this article, Professors Baumol and Quandt develop a highly sophisticated analysis of the determination of the appropriate discount rate for investments under capital rationing. Again, the concepts of linear programming must be understood to follow the language of their presentation. The wide applicability of the analysis, particularly for allocating funds to company divisions, emphasizes the importance of their formulations

Although the capital rationing case may have an appearance of artificiality, investment decisions made under conditions which closely approximate to capital rationing are frequently encountered in practice. The investment decisions of government agencies and many company divisions are circumscribed by budgets whose magnitudes are largely beyond their control. Some companies seek to operate without recourse to the capital market, and indeed, corporate funds are often obtained preponderantly from internal sources. In times of tight money some companies are perhaps likely to find that their capital is effectively rationed by the funds market, which apparently contracts its operations by rejecting applications for funds rather than just increasing interest rates. Capital rationing is also of considerable interest to theorists, both because it serves as a limiting case to the diverging borrowing- and lending-rate problems which have recently received so much attention in the literature and because capital rationing plays an important role in a number of theoretical constructs such as Hayek's "Ricardo Effect."

This paper uses the tools of mathematical programming to explore the choice of optimal investment project combinations and shows how a number of problems left unsolved in the previous literature can be handled. In doing so, it brings together two strands of economic literature: The neo-classical theory of capital and the mathematical analysis of capital budgeting.

William J. Baumol and Richard E. Quandt, "Investment and Discount Rates Under Capital Rationing—A Programming Approach," *Economic Journal*, LXXV (June 1965), 317–329. Reprinted with permission.

* We want to express our gratitude to the National Science Foundation whose grant to our our project on the dynamics of the firm permitted the completion of this paper. We must also thank Harold W. Kuhn, Burton G. Malkiel, Edward S. Pearsall and Douglas Keare for their extremely helpful comments.

I. THE FISHER SOLUTION

The capital-rationing case poses peculiar analytical and computational difficulties which have long been recognized in the literature. Irving Fisher is justly credited with the crucial theoretical contribution. He showed (see [3], pp. 266–9) that equilibrium under capital rationing requires the investor's subjective discount rate between two periods to be equal to the marginal rate of transformation between outputs in those two periods; that is, the discount rate must equal the ratio of the marginal yields (products) of the investor's resources in those periods. This result, as Fisher showed, is simply the now commonplace requirement that in equilibrium there be tangency between the production (profit) possibility curve and an investor's indifference curve.[1]

Unfortunately, this solution, while correct, nevertheless cannot cope with a number of difficult problems:

> 1. The equilibrium conditions themselves give us no clue as to how an optimal capital budgeting decision can be made. If budgets are fixed and the firm has under consideration a sizeable set of investment projects, the number of combinations which the company can afford, and should therefore examine, is likely to be astronomical.[2] Fisher's production possibility curve cannot even be constructed until all combinations are investigated to determine which of them are "profit efficient," meaning that they constitute the north-east boundary of the graph showing their returns in the various periods.
> 2. The position of Fisher's production possibility curve, which is to be used in determining the discount rate, is itself affected by the magnitude of the discount rate. Fisher recognized this point, remarking that, "Of course the [production possibility] line cannot be drawn without the aid of valuations which involve the market principles and so involve the rate of interest . . . . Thus, strictly speaking [the production possibility] line is not to be pictured as immovable like a rock, but as subject to some slight change with every change in the [discount rate]" ([3], 278–9). But it was left to Hirshleifer to show the difficulty which that causes: "The discount rate to be used for calculating present values . . is the rate given by the slope . . . . But this rate cannot be discovered until the solution is attained, and so is of no assistance in reaching the solution" ([4], Section D). We will see later the specific form which this difficulty assumes in a programming analysis.
> 3. Strictly speaking, the Fisher solution applies only to interior maxima, i.e., to cases where investment occurs in every period and where no type of investment is totally rejected. If, for example, there is no investment in period t the ratio of the marginal product of investment in period t to that in $t - 1$ may be less than the corresponding discount rate. Though the equilibrium condition is easily amended to take this (corner maximum) possibility into account, it gives rise to fundamental computational difficulties with which only programming calculations can cope.

---

[1] Here the "production possibility curve" refers to the locus relating the yields from investment in two years, t and t'. For each possible return in year t the curve shows the maximum yield which the company can obtain in the year t' from the investment opportunities which it has available to it. Thus, it is the ordinary transformation locus between yields in periods t and t'.

[2] If, for example, it is considering some twenty projects and can finance only five of them the arithmetic of permutations and combinations tells us that 15,504 investment project combinations must be examined by the investor in order to find the most profitable among them.

II. INVESTMENT SELECTION MODELS

Quite independently of the Fisher-Hirschleifer approach to the problem there has developed a parallel line of analysis, which was better adapted to the computations necessary for the selection of investment projects. This type of investigation makes no use of the production possibility locus, and begins instead on a more fundamental level with the individual candidate investment projects and their expected streams of returns. Perhaps the first analysis in this category which makes allowance for capital constraints in more than one future period was developed by one of the present authors (see [1]). However, that study employed the Lagrange multiplier methods of the differential calculus. It was therefore unable to deal with the important corner maximum problem which has already been discussed.

Soon after that paper appeared, Lorie and Savage addressed themselves to the project selection problem in a classic article [5]. They succeeded in indicating very clearly the complexities which beset optimal decision making in the area, but their proposed selection criteria were later shown to suffer from several critical defects.[3]

Since then a number of mathematical programming models have been designed for investment project selection.[4] These have proved to be extremely powerful analytic instruments. But as we shall see, their authors have left serious gaps in these structures in failing to come to grips with the discount-rate problem. Happily, as this paper will show, it is possible to determine an appropriate set of discount rates, rates which rely heavily on the shadow prices of the dual programs. Moreover, as has so often occurred in programming studies of other subjects, the dual programme will turn out to agree with the classical theory. The Fisher analysis will be shown to come once again into its own, and the Hirschleifer paradox, too, will fall into place.

III. PROGRAMMING MODELS FOR INVESTMENT DECISIONS

The basic approach taken by the programming models of investment project selection under capital rationing involves maximization of an objective function expressing the discounted present value of the (positive and negative) future cash flows corresponding to any combination of investment projects selected. This maximization is carried out under the limitations imposed by a number of constraints. At least some of them are budget constraints which represent the distribution of the monies among competing uses available during each period in which the supply of cash is expected to be limited.

---

[3] For a discussion, see Weingartner [6].
[4] See Charnes, Cooper and Miller [2] and Weingartner [6].

A simple form which might be assumed by a model of the sort we are discussing is the following:

Maximize

$$\Pi = \sum_{i=1}^{n} \sum_{t=0}^{h} [a_{jt}/(1 + i)^t] x_j \tag{1}$$

subject to[5]

$$\sum_{j=1}^{n} b_{jt} x_j \leq M_t \qquad (t = 0, 1, \ldots, h) \tag{2}$$

$$\text{all } x_j \geq 0$$

Here

   i represents the rate of interest;
   a_{jt} represents the net cash flow obtained from a unit of project j during period t;
   b_{jt} is the net amount of cash used up by a unit of project j during period t;
   x_j is the number of units of project j constructed; and
   M_t is the amount of cash made available from outside sources during t;

so that

$$\sum_{t=0}^{n} a_{jt}/(1 + i)^t$$

is the discounted present value of the earnings of project j.

It is difficult to overstate the power and flexibility of models of this type. Their versatility is easily indicated by the following illustrative situations which, as will be indicated, are readily handled as special cases of the general programming model:

1. Cases where the funds $M_0, M_1, \ldots$, invested in the various periods must eventually be repaid can easily be handled in the constraints by taking the M values on the required repayment dates to be negative. For example, if all borrowings are to be paid with interest during the horizon period, h, and if the sum to be repaid is K dollars, we need merely set $M_h = -K$ and the model will then automatically cope with the repayment requirement.

2. Some investment project, s, may involve expenditures beginning only at some future date. Thus, suppose s represents a decision today to purchase a lathe 5 periods hence. Then to adapt the model we need merely specify $b_{0s} = b_{1s} = \cdots = b_{4s} = 0$, i.e., that the net outlays associated with project s during its first 5 periods are equal to zero. Thus, in this model, X_s may represent the number of lathes purchased during period 5 while $X_{s'}$ may represent the number of lathes bought during some other period.

3. If some project, k, is indivisible, so that X_k, the number of units of project k, cannot contain a fraction, we require as part of the programming analysis that the value of X_k be an integer. We then must employ the methods of integer programming in our calculation, but the analysis is otherwise unchanged.[6]

4. Two investment projects, a and b, may be indivisible and mutually exclusive. That is, a and b may be two alternative models of a machine so that if the investor undertakes a he will not want b and vice-versa. The analysis can take care of this specification by requiring $X_a + X_b \leq 1$. For then, since both X's will be non-negative, if project a is adopted, so that $X_a = 1$, then necessarily $X_b = 0$, i.e., project b must certainly be rejected.

---

[5] Unfortunately, the literature offers no satisfactory method for selection of the horizon period, h, and this paper has nothing to contribute on the subject.

[6] This and the following cases are systematically described by Weingartner [6] who also indicates a number of special applications.

IV. LIMITATIONS OF THE PRECEDING MODEL

A number of problems arise out of this formulation, and it is to these that this paper is addressed. Some of them are relatively minor and can be solved in straightforward fashion. One problem, however, involves difficulties so serious that the attempt to overcome them actually leads to a fairly basic reformulation of the simple model. One might say that the difficulties inherent in the simple model lead to the formulation of the "right" model.

First we may list several minor problems which can easily be taken care of: (1) there exists the possibility that funds may also be used for investment outside the firm or for personal consumption by the capitalist (the stockholder) and the model described in the preceding section has made no explicit allowance for these alternatives; (2) funds unused during period t can normally be retained for use during later periods and the model should provide for this possibility; (3) there is apparently some relationship between a_{it} and b_{it}, since whenever an investment yields a positive (or negative) cash flow it should add to (or reduce) the amount of money available during that period for use in other investments. This relationship must be discussed before we can proceed.

The M_t's are, by definition, autonomously given amounts of money which are disbursable in each period; hence the constraints are meaningful only if b_{jt} is interpreted as the net input of cash needed by project j in period t. That is, if R_{jt} and C_{jt} are defined as the total revenue generated and total cost incurred by project j in period t, $b_{jt} = C_{jt} - R_{jt}$. But the maximand is the discounted value of the net cash inflows $R_{jt} - C_{jt}$; hence[7]

$$a_{jt} = -b_{jt} \tag{3}$$

It is left as a trivial exercise for the reader to show that (3) remains valid if there are lags in the system; e.g., if the revenue earned in period $t - 1$ becomes available only in period t.

V. THE DISCOUNT RATE IN THE PROGRAMMING CAPITAL RATIONING MODEL

The most serious difficulty of all lies in the assumption that we are given an appropriate discount rate $1/(1 + i)$. So long as the firm can lend or borrow in unlimited amounts at a fixed rate of interest, i, and provided that

---

[7] Note that characteristically some of the a_{jt} will be positive and some negative, because the typical investment project will require net expenditures during some portions of its life and yield net returns during other periods. If it never involved positive net costs the project would require no financing and the corresponding programming problem—in our later formulations—will turn out to be unbounded, whereas if it never yielded net returns no one would be willing to undertake it. There are other cases in which the feasible region is unbounded, for example, where in each period some project yields enough returns to finance the others. The problem of boundedness of the feasible region is, however, no different from that arising in any other programming problem.

this is the only way in which it can acquire funds, clearly $1/(1 + i)$ is the correct discount rate. But the very nature of our model rules out these borrowing and lending possibilities. If during period t capital is in short supply and is effectively limited to the amount M_t, then, obviously, the firm cannot borrow in unlimited amounts. The firm is thereby necessarily cut off from the capital market and, as a consequence, from any external discounting criteria.

The manner in which the literature has dealt with the determination of the discount rate for such a model must be considered casual and unsatisfactory. Three of the most prominent authors in the area, Lorie and Savage and Weingartner, simply state that future earnings are discounted ". . . at the company's cost of capital." These authors are, of course, well aware that the cost of capital is an ill-defined concept which has been the subject of a great deal of controversy in the literature. Moreover, such definitions of the cost of capital as have been proposed have all been based on various market related phenomena, such as interest rates, prices at which the company can sell additional shares, etc., all of which are irrelevant for our pure capital rationing model. Thus Weingartner states that: "The choice of the appropriate rate by which future flows are to be discounted is not our primary concern. As mentioned, Lorie and Savage take this to be the cost of capital, although how this concept is to be measured is not discussed by them, and will not be discussed by us" ([6], p. 8, footnote). Clearly, this fails to meet the issue. Still less satisfactory is the statement by Miller, Charnes and Cooper that in their model future earnings are simply added together without discounting, for as they indicate, "This assumption can be interpreted as implying that an 'adequate' allotment of funds has been granted to the manager . . ." ([2], footnote 5), and indeed, it implies that the company has no other use for money (including even the purchase of government securities as a means of earning interest). But if this is so, the money constraints in the model cannot inhibit company operations, and they must be totally irrelevant for the analysis.

An alternative approach which was once employed by one of the present authors (see [1]) uses at least part of Fisher's approach and argues that in the absence of any external discounting criterion the appropriate discount rate must be determined subjectively by the decision maker in a manner which is consistent with his utility function. Although there is no logical objection to this method of resolution, care must be exercised in employing it for two reasons: (1) since no way of determining the appropriate utility function has been suggested, the proposed method of resolution may not be operational; (2) if utility is what the decision maker seeks to maximize, then the objective function will normally not take the same form as (1). Rather the objective function must be the (unspecified) utility function $U = f(x_1, \ldots, x_n)$. Since this is equivalent to abandoning the present value approach, one ought to be convinced that the latter method cannot make a contribution here.

Eventually we shall see that we are driven to a compromise which utilizes both explicit discount rates and subjective utilities and which is fully consistent with Fisher's solution.

VI.   DUAL VALUES AND IMPLICIT DISCOUNT RATES

We shall now develop a preliminary pure discount rate model. However, it will turn out that this model runs foul of Hirschleifer's problem—the difficulty of determining a discount rate when that rate is needed to construct the very model which will be used in its calculation. Our preliminary model will therefore turn out badly, but in an instructive manner which leads to a more satisfactory solution. We therefore ask for the reader's indulgence as we describe our first construct.

To determine the nature of the appropriate discount rate we must look back to the basic rationale of the discounting process. Suppose we are given either S_0 dollars at present or S_1 dollars one period hence. *If* we are indifferent between S_0 and S_1 and if $S_0 = kS_1$, then k is defined as the discount rate. In our model when will such an indifference relationship be satisfied? The present value of S_0 is the present value of the stream of earnings which it makes possible. But if the firm has available an additional dollar in period zero (if units are sufficiently small) this will add $d\Pi/dM_0$ to the capitalized present value of its earnings stream, and so the contribution of S_0 dollars must be approximately $S_0\, d\Pi/dM_0$. Similarly, the present value of having S_1 dollars available one period from now is $S_1(d\Pi)/(dM_1)$.

Since indifference between S_0 and S_1 requires that these two expressions be equal, we have

$$S_0\, d\Pi/dM_0 = S_1\, d\Pi/dM_1$$

or

$$S_0 = \left(\frac{d\Pi}{dM_1} \middle/ \frac{d\Pi}{dM_0}\right) S_1 \tag{4}$$

Therefore the expression in parentheses is the (marginal) discount rate, i.e., it is the rate corresponding to the opportunity cost of postponement of receipt of a "*small*" amount of money. Now it is well known that $d\Pi/dM_t$ is equal to the dual price corresponding to the tth constraint, i.e., to the value of the tth variable in the problem which is the dual of our linear programme. Let us designate this value by ρ_t, so that (4) becomes $S_0 = (\rho_1/\rho_0)S_1$.

By a similar argument, it can be shown that a sum S_t in period t will have the same value (during period $t - 1$) as a sum S_{t-1} available during the previous period if

$$S_{t-1} = (\rho_t/\rho_{t-1})S_t.$$

Thus, writing D_t for the corresponding (one period) discount rate, we have $D_t = \rho_t/\rho_{t-1}$, and then the present value of S_t (discounting for all t periods up to the present) is

$$S_0 = D_0 D_1 \cdots D_t S_t = (\rho_t / \rho_0) S_t.$$

This suggests immediately that the correct form of the objective function in our problem is not (1), but is rather

$$\Pi = \sum_{j=1}^{n} \sum_{t=0}^{h} (a_{jt} \rho_t / \rho_0) x_j = (1/\rho_0) \sum \sum a_{jt} \rho_t x_j \tag{5}$$

Several pecularities of this objective function and the corresponding discount rate can be observed immediately.

(a) The discount rate ρ_t / ρ_0 is independent of monetary phenomena outside the firm, as it must be in this model. It is, however, not a subjective discount rate, that is, it is an entirely objective discount rate representing the opportunity cost of postponed receipts, i.e., the marginal profit or loss incurred by postponing the receipt of money to some future date.

(b) Unlike the usual situation, there is nothing in the model as specified so far to preclude $(\rho_t / \rho_0) > 1$, i.e., one cannot rule out a case in which money in the future is *more* valuable than money today. This odd characteristic arises out of the fact that our initial model does not permit the transfer of any funds from one period to another. Hence money during period t may have a scarcity value considerably higher than money during some earlier period. However, it will be shown later than if money can be saved from one period to the next, then for any t we must have $\rho_t \leq \rho_{t-1}$, so that discount rates must, as we normally expect, take on values below unity. The reason saving restores this normal property of the discount rate is, of course, that if we were to have, say, $(\rho_{t+1} / \rho_t) > 1$, then it would pay to transfer money from period t to period $t + 1$ until the discount rate was depressed below unity by raising the marginal productivity of money in $t + 1$ and reducing its marginal yield in period t.[8]

(c) A final peculiarity of our objective function is that it cannot even be formulated until the dual problem has been solved. Since, however, the dual cannot be solved (or even specified) unless the primal problem is known, it would appear that some sort of simultaneous solution is required. We shall see presently that matters are even more difficult than this seems to suggest. Nevertheless, we may note in economic terms why the problem arises at all. The trouble simply is that in the circumstances under consideration we cannot determine a discount rate until we can calculate a marginal profit opportunity cost of postponement; but we cannot calculate profit until we have obtained our discount rate.

---

[8] A special problem arises if some of the coefficients of the period t constraint are non-positive, so that it might be possible to withdraw all funds from period t without reducing the value of ρ_{t+1}/ρ_t below unity. Otherwise such a corner maximum is precluded because if all money is withdrawn from period t we must necessarily have $x_1 = x_2 = \cdots = x_n = 0$, in accord with the tth period constraint $\sum b_{jt} x_j < M_t$.

VII. THE DUAL PROBLEM

To summarize, we may now rewrite the primal problem as follows:
Maximize

$$\frac{1}{\rho_0} \sum_j \sum_t a_{jt} \rho_t x_j$$

subject to

$$- \sum_j a_{jt} x_j \leq M_t \qquad t = 0, 1, \ldots, h$$

$$x_j \geq 0$$

Unfortunately, as we shall now see, this reformulated model collapses in our hands. The typical constraint of the corresponding dual problem is

$$- \sum_t a_{jt} \rho_t \geq \frac{1}{\rho_0} \sum_t a_{jt} \rho_t$$

that is,

$$\left(-1 - \frac{1}{\rho_0}\right) \sum_t a_{jt} \rho_t \geq 0$$

Since the dual variables are also constrained to be non-negative, this implies

$$\sum_t a_{jt} \rho_t \leq 0 \text{ for all } j$$

Because this means that the coefficients of x_j in the primal objective function must also all be non-positive, it follows that the primal objective function has an upper bound of zero which is in fact attained when $x_1 = \cdots = x_n = 0$. But even this trivial optimal solution turns out to be illusory, for it implies by virtue of the requirement that we minimize the dual objective function,

$$\sum_t M_t \rho_t, \quad \text{where} \quad M_t > 0, \quad \text{that} \quad \rho_0 = \cdots = \rho_t = 0.$$

Since ρ_0 is in the denominator of the primal objective function, that objective function is indeterminate and, in fact, no optimum exists!

What has gone wrong? It seems that our carefully laid plans to provide a genuine internal discount rate have gone seriously astray. The trouble is that there is nothing in the model to prevent the marginal contribution of an extra dollar of spendable resources in the zeroth period (ρ_0) from being arbitrarily close to zero; since discount rates are ratios of ρ's they may become indefinitely large. It seems then that we have reached an impasse: if there is capital rationing and external rates of interest are irrelevant we cannot simultaneously insist on a present value formulation of the objective function and have the relevant discount rates determined internally by our problem.[9]

---

[9] This conclusion is, of course, closely related to Hirshleifer's observation which was cited above.

Fortunately this does not mean that the capital budgeting problem cannot be formulated in a meaningful manner. This will be the task of the remaining section.

VIII. A UTILITY FORMULATION
AND THE DUAL DISCOUNT RATE

In order to arrive at a more satisfactory formulation we have to return to an argument employing a utility function. The reason for this is that for the model to possess any rationale it must yield some sort of gain to the investor. He then must be taken to wish ultimately to maximize—in some sense—his ability to consume, that is, to maximize the stream of purchasing power provided by his bundle of investments. But maximization of ability to consume directly requires us to use a utility approach as a means for evaluating the stream of earnings.

Assume for simplicity that utility is linear in money.[10] The entrepreneur plans to withdraw in the ith period ($t = 0, \ldots, h$) a sum W_t to be used for consumption.[11] In order to maximize the value to the entrepreneur of withdrawing W_0 in the zeroth period, W_1 in the next period, etc., we maximize

$$\sum_t U_t W_t$$

subject to

$$- \sum_j a_{jt} x_j + W_t \leq M_t$$

$$x_j \geq 0$$

$$W_t \geq 0$$

where U_t is the (fixed) utility of a dollar in period t. This is now an ordinary linear programming problem and has the dual[12]

minimize

$$\sum_t \rho_t M_t$$

subject to

$$- \sum_t a_{jt} \rho_t \geq 0$$

$$\rho_t \geq U_t$$

---

[10] The argument could have been made to appear far more esoteric and profound by dealing with non-linear utility functions, bringing in concave programming, the Kuhn–Tucker theorem and all the associated paraphernalia. However, as a later footnote shows, this would have added nothing to the argument.

[11] Consumption is here defined in a very broad sense; thus $W\rho$, the withdrawal in the last period, may represent the inheritance he will leave his heirs.

[12] If instead of the linear utility function we had employed the more general (concave) function $U = f(W_0, W_1, \ldots, W_h)$ the Kuhn–Tucker conditions would make the last set of constraints in the dual problem $\rho_t \geq \partial f / \partial W_t$ which has the same economic implications as the linear model. See e.g., Wolfe [5].

This shows almost immediately that our intuition was not entirely wrong in suggesting the formulation discussed in the previous sections. For consider an optimal solution and assume that W_t and $W_{t'}$ are positive in the optimal solution. Then by the duality theorems we have

$$\rho_t = U_t$$
$$\rho_{t'} = U_{t'}$$

so that

$$\frac{U_t}{U_{t'}} = \frac{\rho_t}{\rho_{t'}} \tag{6}$$

Equation (6) states that the marginal rate of substitution between withdrawals in the two periods equals the discount rate at the optimum if funds are withdrawn during both period t and period t'. On the other hand, suppose money is not withdrawn during t but it is withdrawn during t'. In that case (6) becomes

$$\frac{U_t}{U_{t'}} \leq \frac{\rho_t}{\rho_{t'}}$$

Thus the relative subjective discount (valuation) rate for period t, $U_t/U_{t'}$, must be no greater than what we might call the production opportunity discount ratio, $\rho_t/\rho_{t'}$, i.e., the rate of exchange permitted by the available investment opportunities. That is exactly what Irving Fisher's analysis would have led us to expect. It is precisely in such circumstances that it does not pay to make withdrawals during t.[13] The marriage between Fisher's analysis of the discount rate under capital rationing and the programming approach is thus complete.

The reader may feel that the discounted present value of withdrawals approach which has been employed in our last model is a rather special case and that many alternative objective functions may sometimes be more relevant. However, a little thought indicates that our objective function is really of remarkably wide applicability. For example, if instead of regular withdrawals management is interested only in the terminal (horizon) value of its investment, W_h, we need merely adjust our discount coefficients to reflect this goal. We do this by setting $U_0 = U_1 = \cdots = U_{h-1} = 0$ and $U_h = 1$ (or some other positive constant). Similarly, if the entrepreneur desires to maximize the value of the firm's earned net income, our objective function can continue to serve. For we have, by straightforward subtraction,[14] $W_t = M_t + \sum_t a_{jt}x_j$, so that our objective function can be rewritten as

$$\sum_t U_t W_t = \sum_t U_t \left(M_t + \sum_j a_{jt}x_j \right)$$

[13] The distinction between the subjective and the production opportunity discount rate throws some light on the reason for the breakdown of our preliminary model of Section IV. Only at the optimal point should these two marginal rates be equal.

[14] If $U_t > 0$ then the constraint $\sum - a_{jt}x_t + W_t \leq M_t$ must always be satisfied as an equation in an optimal solution. For then the withdrawal of any unused cash must always increase the investor's total utility.

But the discounted present value of the firm's net income is clearly $\sum_i \sum_j U_t a_{jt} x_j$, which differs only by the constant amount $\sum U_t M_t$ from the discounted present value of withdrawals, $\sum U_t W_t$.

IX. THE CARRY OVER OF FUNDS

As a final extension of our model we can amend it slightly to show how one can handle the more plausible case where funds can be carried over from one period to the next. Let the amount carried from period t to $t + 1$ be denoted by C_t. Then C_t may be interpreted as the slack variable[15] for the period t constraint and our problem becomes[16]

maximize
$$\sum U_t W_t$$
subject to
$$-\sum a_{jt} x_j + W_t + C_t - C_{t-1} \leq M_t$$
$$x_j \geq 0$$
$$W_t \geq 0$$
$$C_t \geq 0$$

with the additional requirement that $C_0 = 0$.

It is now easy to show, as was asserted earlier, that with carry over permitted, every discount rate ρ_t/ρ_0 must be no greater than unity. To prove this we need merely formulate our dual problem:

minimize
$$\sum \rho_t M_t$$
subject to
$$-\sum a_{jt} \rho_t \geq 0$$
$$\rho_t \geq U_t$$
$$\rho_0 - \rho_1 \geq 0$$
$$\rho_1 - \rho_2 \geq 0$$
$$\vdots$$
$$\rho_{t-1} - \rho_t \geq 0$$
$$\rho_t \geq 0$$

---

[15] The reader will doubtless have observed the peculiarly incestuous flavour of our models, with dual prices appearing in primal objective functions consisting of linear sums of the coefficients of the constraints, and slack variables being carried over to subsequent constraints.

[16] Though we have written our structural constraints as inequalities they must again necessarily hold as equations in an optimal solution because it will never pay to leave money unused. So long as the utility of money is positive in the current period or any future period, any funds otherwise unused will be withdrawn at once or held for future use or future withdrawal.

The last constraints show at once that the discount rates, ρ_t/ρ_0, will all necessarily be less than (or equal to) unity as was asserted.

X. CONCLUSIONS

We have constructed a model for the capital rationing case which, while it makes use of a subjective utility index, for the first time also provides an objective measure of the discount rate. We have thus made the distinction between a subjective discount rate U_t/U_0 and the objective internal production opportunity rate ρ_t/ρ_0, which is the ratio of the dual prices corresponding to the budget constraints for periods t and 0. The entire construct seems to accord fully with what economic analysis has told us about the subject and brings together the programming and the indifference curve approaches to the problem. It is also cast in a form which is usable directly in the computations required for optimal investment project selections.

The analysis may be of wider applicability than at first appears to be the case. As was indicated toward the beginning of this paper, government agencies, company divisions and a variety of other organizations operate on fixed budgets set for them by others. For such groups the choice of discount rate for investment project selection is a very real and a very practical problem toward whose solution this analysis may perhaps provide some contribution.

REFERENCES

[1] BAUMOL, W. J. "Income Effect, Substitution Effect, Ricardo Effect," in Helen Makower and W. J. Baumol, "The Analogy Between Producer and Consumer Equilibrium Analysis," *Economica*, N.S. Vol. XVII, February 1950.
[2] CHARNES, A., W. W. COOPER and M. H. MILLER, "Application of Linear Programming to Financial Budgeting and the Costing of Funds," *Journal of Business*, Vol. XXXII, January 1959, reproduced in Ezra Solomon, editor, *The Management of Corporate Capital* (Glencoe, Ill.: The Free Press, 1959).
[3] FISHER, IRVING, *The Theory of Interest* (New York: Macmillan, 1930). (Reprinted by Augustus M. Kelley, New York, 1961.)
[4] HIRSHLEIFER, J., "On the Theory of Optimal Investment Decision," *Journal of Political Economy*, August, 1958, reproduced in this volume.
[5] LORIE, J. H., and L. J. SAVAGE, "Three Problems in Rationing Capital," *Journal of Business*, Vol. XXVIII, October 1955, reproduced in Ezra Solomon, *op. cit.*
[6] WEINGARTNER, H. MARTIN, *Mathematical Programming and the Analysis of Capital Budgeting Problems* (Englewood Cliffs: Prentice-Hall, 1963).
[7] WOLFE, PHILIP, "A Duality Theorem for Nonlinear Programming," *Quarterly of Applied Mathematics*, Vol. XIX, No. 3, 1961.

4

THE RATE OF RETURN AND ASSESSMENT OF RISK

J. MORLEY ENGLISH

This article deals with the basic problem of the selection of the appropriate discount rate in the evaluation of individual investments. Professor English emphasizes that special estimates of variances of the expected returns must be independently formulated for special large projects. In addition, he suggests a method for determining the appropriate internal rate of return for the evaluation of proposed projects.

In conventional evaluation of investment alternatives some index of desirability must be established. Whether this index is a discounted cash flow, equivalent annual cost, or some other, the basic concept requires discounting future dollars at some acceptable rate of return. As a rule, the rate of return (or discount rate) is chosen arbitrarily. The same rate is presumed to be applicable for all alternatives. Often risk is considered by an arbitrary selection of a high rate of return.

One rationale for selecting a rate, and one which has gained wide-spread acceptance, is based on the "cost of capital." In principle the worthwhileness of a proposed venture is presumed to earn at least the same rate of return as the historical rate on the weighted average of its debt and equity capital. While such a rate represents the average return on the firm's past investments, it does not take account of the variance of the return from all of the separate investments. No consideration is explicitly given to the difference in the risk associated with one project in comparison with another.

In a recent issue of *The Engineering Economist* (Ref. [1]),[1] the author developed an expression for a rate of return which was proposed for use in economic comparisons. This rate of return allowed for a risk-free component, or reward for waiting, and a risk component. The rate was predicated on a measure of the investor's utility function for money. In another paper (Ref. [2]), the author suggested that the effect of preference for immediacy of return coupled with risk might be taken into account in a very simple way.

J. Morley English, "The Rate of Return and Assessment of Risk," *The Engineering Economist*, XI (Spring 1966), 1–12. Reprinted with permission.
[1] See reference list at end of this chapter.

In the latter paper it was argued that the greater the futurity of a pro-spective return on an investment the greater will be the risk. If one reflects his attitude toward risk by increasing the interest rate, then it would follow that the interest rate itself should be an increasing function of time.

The usual approach of a constant interest rate results in the familiar discount function

$$f(t) = e^{-rt} \tag{1}$$

or for discrete interest periods

$$f(t) = (1 + r)^{-t} \tag{1a}$$

where r is the rate of return and t is future time.

It was shown in Ref. [2], that where r is an increasing function of t, then a reasonable approximation for a discount function is

$$f(t) = 1 - r_0 t \tag{2}$$

where r_0 is a constant which corresponds to an equivalent rate of return for $t = 0$.

The suggested function implies a planning horizon of $T = 1/r_0$ but leaves in question the basis for evaluating the constant r_0.

In order to establish a basis for the development of this paper, the conclusions of the earlier paper will be recapitulated.

William Morris (Ref. [4]) suggests the use of an expectation-variance criterion for an investment decision rule. This corresponds to establishing a utility function for money, x. Such a function may reasonably represent the attitude of an investor toward risking a given sum of money, x_0, in anticipation of an expected amount, $\bar{x}$. Thus, the utility, $u(\bar{x})$, as developed in Ref. [1], may be expressed as

$$u(\bar{x}) = u(\bar{x}_0) + K' \sigma_x^2 \tag{3}$$

where σ_x^2 is the variance of x and K' is a constant representing the investor's risk preference.

Equation (3) may be considered valid where

(a) the utility function is monotonic and has no inflection points;
(b) the utility function is continuous within a limited region of interest.

Dividing both sides by x_0, and cancelling the investment, leads to an equiv-alent equation for rate of return rather than an absolute quantity of money. Thus, from Ref. [1]

$$E(r) = r_0 + K\sigma^2$$

where

$$E(r) = \frac{\Delta \bar{x}}{x_0}, \qquad r_0 = \frac{\Delta x_0}{x_0}$$

The constant K replacing K' now represents the investor's attitude toward risk as referenced to rate of return.

The investor will require a profit for postponing the use of his money for the time which must elapse before the outcome of the investment is determined. Thus, the investment risked in the venture would have to grow by at least Δx_0, even if no risk were associated with the proposed venture, and by Δx where there is some risk. In other words, Δx_0 is a risk-free profit and Δx is profit with risk. Therefore, equation (3) may be rewritten

$$U(x_0 + \Delta x) = U(x_0 + \Delta x_0) + K'\sigma_{\Delta x}^2 \tag{4}$$

From this it was suggested that

$$E(r) = r_0 + K\sigma_r^2 \tag{5}$$

where $E(r)$ represents the expected rate of return, $\Delta x/x_0$. It is a direct measure of the utility of the venture to include risk.

There were two implicit questions raised by the jump from equation (4) to equation (5) which will now be answered. These were (a) how size of investment will affect the required rate of return and (b) what the time relationship could be considered.

SIZE OF THE INVESTMENT

By cancelling the investment from both sides of equation (4), it becomes

$$U(\Delta \bar{x}) = U(\Delta x_0) + K\sigma_{\Delta x}^2 \tag{6}$$

Choose the reference values on a utility scale so as to make

$$U(\Delta x_0) = \Delta x_0$$

and

$$U(\Delta \bar{x}) = \Delta \bar{x}$$

then,

$$\Delta \bar{x} = \Delta x_0 + K'\sigma_{\Delta x}^2 \tag{7}$$

Dividing through by x_0

$$\frac{\Delta \bar{x}}{x_0} = \frac{\Delta x_0}{x_0} + \frac{K'}{x_0}\sigma_{\Delta x}^2$$

or an expected rate of return,

$$E(r) = r_0 + \frac{K'}{x_0}\sigma_{\Delta x}^2 \tag{8}$$

But,

$$\sigma_{\Delta x}^2 = E(\Delta x - \Delta \bar{x})^2 = x_0^2 E\left(\frac{\Delta x}{x_0} - \frac{\Delta \bar{x}}{x_0}\right)^2$$

$$= x_0^2 \sigma_r^2$$

Thus,

$$E(r) = r_0 + x_0 K\sigma_r^2 \tag{9}$$

It will be seen that equation (5) is equivalent to equation (9) where

$$K = x_0 K'$$

It will also be observed that the expected rate of return depends on the size of the investment.

Now consider that the scale of the investment, x, is chosen such that unity represents the total monetary resources of the firm. In other words, x_0 becomes a non-dimensional or proportional amount of the total business capital which is risked in a particular venture.

THE VALUE OF K'

In order for any company to remain in business, it must either pay a cash dividend or at least show a promise of a future capability of paying dividends, even if there are times when these payments may have to be interrupted. Once the dividend is paid it is no longer available for reinvestment. In this sense a dividend, insofar as the business is concerned, is equivalent to any other cash outflow, such as, for example, wages.

It may not be enough for a company just to pay a dividend. In addition a company management must plan for growth. At any time, an entire industry will be growing—as measured by its sales—to match the market demands for its products or services. For a single company to lag behind the mean growth for the industry may invite its decline and eventual collapse. Therefore, in general, a company management may be expected to choose a value for K' which reflects an optimism that the company will obtain a rate of return which will enable it to grow at least as fast as the mean for the industry.

One further consideration of the management in making an investment decision must be monetary inflation. Inflation has been a fact of life for so long that, with some degree of assurance, one may predict it will continue. Therefore, the return in dollars must be sufficient to compensate for erosion of capital value due to inflation in addition to other requirements for profit. It should be noted that, while the marketable value of an asset increases due to inflation, its replacement cost also inflates. The increment return for inflation may be considered as a maintenance of relative value.

It was suggested by the author (Ref. [3]), that the rate of growth of sales corresponds to that part of the rate of return which is represented by retained earnings, provided that a steady growth situation exists. Thus, if the business could grow without any year-to-year variance, it would need a constant rate of return, r_c, such that

$$r_c = r_G + r_I + r_D \qquad (10)$$

where the subscripts G, I, and D stand for growth, inflation and dividends. It was shown by H. M. Markowitz (Ref. [5]) that a constant rate of return to ensure a steady growth of capital is equivalent to a fluctuating rate, approximated by

$$r_c = E(r) - \tfrac{1}{2}(\sigma_r^2 + E(r)^2) \tag{11}$$

But $r_c = r_0$ since it must be considered as certain or risk-free. Also, all of the corporate capital may be conceptualized as being recommitted or reinvested each year and, hence, $x_0 = 1.0$. Therefore, from equation (9) and equation (11) the lower bound on K' to meet the foregoing conditions for healthy survival is shown in equation (12) which follows.

$$K' = \frac{1}{2}\left(1 + \frac{E(r)^2}{\sigma_r^2}\right) \tag{12}$$

If the return on any given project is perfectly correlated with the return for the business as a whole or, in other words, is statistically dependent on the business return, then equation (9), with the value of K' from equation (12), and $x_0 = 1$, provides a satisfactory internal rate of return for evaluating the efficacy of the investment in that project. However, this condition of dependence may not always hold. The income derived from an investment will be a function of both the general business success and the success of the individual project. These effects may be separated conceptually by considering that part of the return is related to the overall business environment of the project, and part is independent of it. In the first case, the variance of r is that of the variance in return on the business, and so x_0 drops out of equation (9). On the other hand, in the case of independence, only a small proportion of total capital is usually invested and $x_0 \ll 1$.

INDEPENDENT INVESTMENTS

In order to see the significance of independence, consider a highly idealized business in which the total investment is divided into $n = 1/x_0$ statistically independent and equal-sized investments. Then the variance σ_B^2, representing the business return will be

$$\sigma_B^2 = x_0\sigma_r^2 \tag{13}$$

Substituting into equation (9), and noting that x_0 cancels

$$E(r) = r_0 + K'\sigma_B^2 \tag{14}$$

Thus, for both parts of the return, the variance reduces to that for the business and the size of the project capital investment is cancelled.

Of course, such an idealized business does not exist. Both the variance and amounts of all of the separate independent investment components will vary. Thus, the true value for σ_r^2 for an independent investment would have to remain in the form of equation (9). The evaluation of σ_r^2 for large projects can be made on the basis of an independent value judgment on the part of the investor. It is observed, however, that as the size of the project reduces, the acceptable variance may—and undoubtedly does—tend to increase. If $x_0 \ll 1$ the variance, σ_r^2, while larger than σ_B^2 may not be sufficiently greater to offset the reduction in x_0, and so the risk term of equation (9) may become less significant.

A GENERALIZATION OF INDEPENDENT INVESTMENTS

The assumption of equal size of independent investment is an overidealization. An intuitively appealing, but more general, way in which independent investments may be considered is presented below. It will be shown that, from a practical standpoint, the variation in size may be neglected.

For the case of statistical independence of investments in a business, a more general expression than equation (13) is

$$\sigma_B^2 = \sum_{i=1}^{n} x_i^2 \sigma_i^2 \tag{15}$$

where σ_i^2 is the variance of return for the ith investment, and x_i is the proportion of capital invested in it. Let

$$x_i = \bar{x} + a_i \tag{16}$$

$$\sigma_i^2 = \sigma_r^2 + b_i \tag{17}$$

where a_i and b_i represent the differences from the means of x_i and σ_i^2 respectively. Thus,

$$
\begin{aligned}
\sigma_B^2 &= \sum_{i=1}^{n} (\bar{x} + a_i)^2 (\sigma_i^2 + b_i)^2 \\
&= n\bar{x}^2\sigma_i^2 + \sigma_r^2 \sum_{i=1}^{n} a_i^2 + \bar{x}^2 \sum b_i \\
&\quad + 2\bar{x}\left(\sigma_r^2 \sum_{i=1}^{n} a_i + \sum_{i=1}^{n} a_i b_i\right) + \sum_{i=1}^{n} a_i^2 b_i
\end{aligned}
\tag{18}
$$

Consider the terms of (18) separately.

   a. The number of projects is $n = 1/\bar{x}$; therefore,

$$n\bar{x}^2\sigma_r^2 = \bar{x}\sigma_r^2 \tag{19}$$

   b.
$$\sum a_i^2 = \sum (x_i - \bar{x})^2 = n\sigma_x^2$$
$$= \frac{\sigma_x^2}{\bar{x}} \tag{20}$$

   c. Now impose a restriction that the variance of the return on the project under consideration is average, then

$$\sum b_i = 0$$

Further, assume that both a and b are symmetrically distributed as well as independent. Then,

$$\sum a_i^2 b_i = 0$$

By the same reasoning, the last three terms reduce to zero. Thus,

$$\sigma_B^2 = \bar{x}\sigma_r^2 + \frac{\sigma_x^2}{\bar{x}}\sigma_r^2 \tag{21}$$

from which

$$\sigma_r^2 = \left(\frac{1}{\bar{x} + \frac{\sigma_x^2}{\bar{x}}}\right)\sigma_B^2 \tag{22}$$

substituting into (9)

$$E(r_i) = r_0 + \frac{x_i}{\left(\bar{x} + \frac{\sigma_x^2}{\bar{x}}\right)}K'\sigma_B^2 \tag{23}$$

Let $x_i = \lambda_i\bar{x}$, where λ_i represents the size of the investment relative to the average size of investment, then

$$E(r_i) = r_0 + \frac{\lambda_i K}{\left(1 + \frac{\sigma_x^2}{\bar{x}^2}\right)}\sigma_B^2 \tag{24}$$

Consider the implications of equation (24), keeping in mind the restrictions already imposed above.

   a. If the investments comprising the business were all the same size (i.e., $\sigma_x^2 = 0$), then $\lambda = 1$ and equation (24) reduces to the same function (14) as for the dependent case and, of course, is the same as developed directly in the highly idealized example.
   b. If the variance of the size of the investment is large relative to its average size, then, the term in the denominator of equation (24) would remain significant; though it might not be very large. The effect of neglecting it leads to

$$E(r_i) = r_0 + \lambda_i K'\sigma_B^2 \tag{25}$$

   and the required $E(r_i)$ would be overstated.
   c. If the size of the investment is small relative to the average size, the last term of equation (24) tends to zero. However, when this situation occurs, it is not very likely that the investment is independent of the fortunes of the rest of the business. In general, small investments are undertaken only to the extent that they are felt to further the total business objectives. Nevertheless, when such investments are independent and small, it must be concluded that $E(r_i)$ tends to approach r_0.

PARTLY CORRELATED INVESTMENTS

In the most general situation, the return on an investment will be partly correlated with the business. It is intuitively appealing to separate the returns into two components—one portion which is completely correlated, and a second which is completely independent. Thus, the net return to be used on any project will be

$$E(r) = r_0 + pK'\sigma_B{}^2 + (1 - p)\frac{\lambda}{\left(1 + \dfrac{\sigma_x{}^2}{\bar{x}^2}\right)} K'\sigma_B{}^2 \qquad (26)$$

where p is the proportion of the rate of return which is correlated with the business as a whole.

The effect of the third term is to permit a slight reduction in the rate of return used when considering small projects having some degree of independence. From a practical point of view it may be just as well to ignore such a refinement.

EXAMPLE

Consider a firm which has established a growth rate plus dividend rate at 10 percent. Its historical return on investment has exhibited a variance, $\sigma_B{}^2$ of 40 percent. Since $E(r)$ is as yet unknown, assume that it is zero for the purpose of determining a first approximation. Thus, from equation (12), K' is $\frac{1}{2}$. With this first approximation, solve for $E(r)$ in equation (9). Thus,

$$E(r) = 0.10 + \tfrac{1}{2}(0.4) = 0.30$$

Now with $E(r)$ redetermine

$$K' = \frac{1}{2}\left\{1 + \left(\frac{0.3}{0.4}\right)^2\right\} = 0.61$$

Re-substitute in (9) to obtain $E(r) = 0.34$. A second refinement is not really justified but would result in $E(r) = 0.35$ and $K' = 0.625$.

THE TIME SCALE

In the foregoing discussion, the rate of return was developed without regard to time. While r_0 was defined as the reward for waiting, the question of "For how long?" was not introduced. Implicitly this was taken as a unit time period. The acceptance of the gamble which leads to a profit presumes that one must wait for some time period in order to determine the outcome. This time period could be t years. In order to establish a standard for comparison in terms of one year, the rate would have to be adjusted to a rate of return per year (or some other agreed-upon time unit). Thus if ρ is the expected rate of return per unit time, then

$$E(r) = e^{\rho t} - 1 \qquad (27)$$

Substituting into equation (9)

$$e^{\rho t} = e^{\rho_0 t} + x_0 K \sigma_e^2 \tag{28}$$

where σ_e^2 is the variance of $e^{\rho t}$. Solving

$$\rho = \rho_0 + \frac{1}{t} \log (1 + x_0 e^{-\rho_0 t} K' \sigma_e^2) \tag{29}$$

Since K' involves a somewhat crude and largely subjective value, in any event, it is reasonable to approximate by taking the first term of the expansion for the logarithm. Hence,

$$\rho = \rho_0 + x_0 \frac{e^{-\rho_0 t}}{t} K' \sigma_e^2 \tag{30}$$

If now σ_B^2 is taken as the variance of the business rate of return ρ_B for the unit time, and suppose that

$$\sigma_e^2 = \frac{t e^{\rho_0 t}}{x_0} \sigma_B^2 \tag{31}$$

then, equation (30) becomes

$$\rho = \rho_0 + K' \sigma_B^2 \tag{32}$$

which is the same as equation (14).

The x_0 in the denominator of equation (31) implies the statistical independence of investment in the business as discussed earlier. That σ_e^2 should be an expanding function of time is reasonable. It was discussed at some length in Ref. [1]. However, in the earlier paper, a different expression was suggested to reflect the investor's estimate of variance with the length of his projection. The estimate of variance of a return in the future will increase as a function of the futurity of the prediction. Since it is largely a subjective estimate, and must remain so, the exact form of the function is not important. While equation (31) meets the requirement that it have an increasing variance, there is still a question as to rate of increase of the variance. This may be allowed for by introduction of an arbitrary constant θ in place of the risk-free interest rate ρ_0 in equation (31), and allows for a growth in the variance at a different rate than ρ_0. Certainly there is no reason for θ and ρ_0 to be related.

$$\sigma_e^2 = \frac{t e^{\theta t}}{x_0} \sigma_B^2 \tag{33}$$

Substituting in (30)

$$\rho = \rho_0 + K' e^{(\theta - \rho_0) t} \sigma_B^2 \tag{34}$$

This reduces to the basic forms of equations (9) and (32) only for the condition that $\theta = \rho_0$. When $\theta \neq \rho_0$ the rate of return becomes a function of the projection t. It is certainly more difficult to discount a projected cash flow at a rate which itself is time dependent. On the other hand, the discount function so derived represents a more realistic way in which to estimate the effect of risk. A further simplification and idealization which is extremely simple to use and which approximates equation (34) for $\theta > \rho_0$ is equation (1), referred to at the beginning of this paper, and developed independently in Ref. [2].

CONCLUSION

A general expression for an interest rate or internal rate of return for use in evaluation of a single investment, in context with the business as a whole, is provided in equations (9) and (32). This rate is a function of time, except for a special case where the variance of the projected return is the same as the required zero-risk interest. As such, it leads to the approximation suggested by the author in Ref. [2]. It provides a rational basis for selecting a suitable rate of return for each investment project to be considered.

Special estimates of variance of the return must be independently considered for special large projects which are more or less statistically independent of the main stream of the enterprise. The use of the suggested approach should afford a better method for considering risk in the business. It justifies why one rate of return may be suitable for one type of business and at the same time would be wholly inadequate for another.

By focusing the investor's attention to the specific aspects of risk as reflected in the coupling of the expectation of future cash flow with its variance, an improved method is provided for determining a suitable internal rate of return for evaluation of proposed projects.

REFERENCES

[1] ENGLISH, J. MORLEY, "Economic Comparison of Projects by Incorporating a Utility Criterion in the Rate of Return," *The Engineering Economist*, Volume 10, No. 2 (Winter, 1965), pp. 1–14.

[2] ———, "A Discount Function Comparing Economic Alternatives," *Journal of Industrial Engineering*, March–April, 1965, pp. 115–18.

[3] ———, "Corporate Growth, Capital, and the Rate of Return," contributed paper, The Institute of Management Sciences, American meeting, February 1965, San Francisco, California.

[4] MORRIS, WILLIAM T., *The Analysis of Management Decisions* (Homewood, Illinois: Richard D. Irwin, Inc., 1964).

[5] MARKOWITZ, H. M., *Portfolio Selection: Efficient Diversification of Investments* (New York: John Wiley & Sons, Inc., 1959).

5

CAPITAL BUDGETING OF INTERRELATED PROJECTS: SURVEY AND SYNTHESIS

H. MARTIN WEINGARTNER*

In considering capital rationing problems, the availability of investment opportunities over time and different patterns at which cash returns from investment come in give rise to some very difficult analytic problems. Project interrelationships and nonlinear utility structures also present significant analytical problems.

In the following paper, Professor Martin Weingartner develops some path-breaking analytical concepts in handling these types of problems. His approach involves the use of linear programming techniques. The student who has a background in the more simple formulations of linear programming can obtain an appreciation of the methodology involved even if he is unable to work through the detailed mathematics of Professor Weingartner's methods.

I. INTRODUCTION

The literature on capital budgeting generally confines itself at best to a few of the relevant aspects of the investment decision problem, omitting certain others which are nonetheless essential ingredients of the problem which managers of firms must solve. Most, though by no means all, discussions of formal decision models assume certainty. Further, they make either of two extreme assumptions: that a meaningful investment demand schedule already exists, as in the manner of Fisher's transformation function,[1] or that all investment alternatives are independent in the sense that the acceptance of any set of them does not affect the feasibility or profitability of accepting any different set. With some notable exceptions [32, 29, 11,

H. Martin Weingartner, "Capital Budgeting of Interrelated Projects: Survey and Synthesis," *Management Science*, XII (March 1966), 485–516. Reprinted by permission.

* Work on this paper was supported by the Ford Foundation's Grant to the Sloan School of Management for research in business finance. The author wishes to acknowledge this support, and also the helpful suggestions of Leon S. White, W. W. Cooper and Edwin Kuh. A part of this paper was presented at the TIMS National Meeting at San Francisco, February, 1965, and was issued as Sloan School Working Paper No. 114–65 in February, 1965.

[1] See [21]. Fisher called it the "Opportunity Line." This is not the same as Keynes' Marginal Efficiency of Capital Schedule [30] or Dean's investment demand schedule in [17]. See Alchian [2]·

46 and 45] the literature also disregards the case of capital rationing, usually on the ground that rationing ought not to exist when firms behave rationally (in the narrow economic sense). A more cogent basis for reticence, although seldom expressed, is that the appropriate criterion for the choice of investments under rationing has not been agreed upon. Nevertheless, project selections are being made all the time, even without all the theoretical niceties having been resolved, although the need for such work is recognized.

The present paper is designed to survey the techniques available to the practitioner who must decide on an investment program consisting of a potentially large number of interrelated projects, possibly also subject to constraints on capital or other sources, and who is willing to utilize the framework of certainty for making part of his analysis or who can adapt his problem to fit within the capabilities of relatively simple methods for dealing with random events. The basic outlook behind such a presentation would include the following points. First, short-run limitations on the availability of resources are a common experience. These may not be in the form of capital shortages, but rather on critical manpower or other inputs[2] which have to be accepted by the decision-maker. Second, although the theory of investment under uncertainty is not yet in an advanced state of development,[3] some progress has been made in providing aids to the decision-maker. Mathematical models are being developed by means of which the consequences of a series of complex assumptions can be followed to their conclusions, and optimization of specified objectives may be achieved.[4] Directly related is the availability of efficient computational methods, usually employing computers, which enhance or even make possible the application of formal methods. This combination of analysis and automatic calculation can then be utilized to obtain a "generalized sensitivity analysis" for the essential parameters of the problems. Thus a variety of intricate and sophisticated considerations can be brought to bear on capital budgeting decisions in such a way that the talents and energies of management may be devoted to those aspects of the problem which may benefit most from informed and experienced judgment, e.g., the data inputs.

II. THE LORIE-SAVAGE PROBLEM

A. Integer Programming

A now familiar problem, first discussed by J. H. Lorie and L. J. Savage in 1955 [32] may serve as the point of departure for our discussion. Given the net present value of a set of independent investment alternatives, and given

---

[2] See [46, Secs. 7.2 and 7.5].

[3] Witness the problem of intertemporal comparisons and aggregation of utilities, which is reflected in part in the determination of the appropriate rate for discounting.

[4] See, for example, Näslund [37].

the required outlays for the projects in each of two time periods, find the subset of projects which maximizes the total net present value of the accepted ones while simultaneously satisfying a constraint on the outlays in each of the two periods. The problem may be generalized to an arbitrary number of time periods and stated formally as an integer programming problem, using the following notation. Let b_j be the net present value of project j, when discounting is done by the appropriate rate of interest;[5] let c_{tj} be the outlay required for the jth project in the tth period; let C_t be the maximum permissible expenditure in period t. We define x_j to be the fraction of project j accepted, and require that x_j be either zero or one. The model may then be written as,

a. Maximize
$$\sum_{j=1}^{n} b_j x_j$$

b. Subject to
$$\sum_{j=1}^{n} c_{tj} x_j \leq C_t, \qquad t = 1, \ldots, T \qquad \text{(II.1)}$$

c.
$$0 \leq x_j \leq 1, \qquad j = 1, \ldots, n$$

d.
$$x_j \text{ integral.}$$

Given these data then the solution of this problem depends only upon finding a good integer programming code. Furthermore, if the c_{tj} are nonnegative the problem is bounded, and a finite optimum exists.[6] However, integer programming algorithms still perform unpredictably[7] and so it may be useful to mention alternative methods which will also be relevant for our later discussion. Before doing so it should be pointed out that the budgets expressed in constraints (II.1*b*) may refer to resources which are limited in supply in the short run, in addition or alternative to constraints on capital expenditures. An example might be drawn from a retail store chain when it is planning a sharp increase in the number of stores. A limit on its expansion could come about from the availability of managers for the new stores, a number that cannot be increased simply by bidding managers away from competitors and immediately putting them in charge of new stores. A period of time is required for the new personnel to learn the ways of the organization and thereby make possible effective communication and execution of management policies. Such an interpretation of budgets probably carries more realism than the model of capital rationing implied by the original Lorie-Savage formulation [46, pp. 126–27].

---

[5] This is usually referred to as the cost of capital. See also Baumol and Quandt [5].
[6] See [46, Chap. 4].
[7] See [36]; also the author's experience with an All-Integer code, IPM3, was that a problem of this type with three constraints (II.1*b*) and 10 projects failed to converge within 5000 iterations. However, developments in this area are coming steadily; see [8, 4, 25, and 47]. See also [22 and 23] in relation to the problems under consideration here.

A related point requires some amplification here. The example above suggests models in which the constraints also express generation or release of resources through the adoption of new projects. Thus a store might also produce future managers by training assistant managers for that duty. Basically the only change required in the formal model (II.1) would be to allow the coefficients c_{tj} to be negative as well as nonnegative. However, such changes require some more fundamental reinterpretations of the explicitly dynamic character of the process being modeled, and this falls outside the sphere of interest here. In addition, these problems have been treated at length in [46, Chaps. 8 and 9].

B. The Linear Programming Solution

The Lorie-Savage problem may also be regarded as a simple linear programming problem by dropping the requirement (II.1d) that the x_j be integers. Then, of course, some of the $x_j{}^*$, the values of x_j in the optimal solution, may turn out to be proper fractions. Fortunately it is possible to prove that there is an upper limit on the number of fractional projects given by T, the number of periods for which budget constraints exist.[8] The difficulties in the use and interpretation of the linear programming solutions may be summarized by citing the following points. First, the projects may not, in fact, be completely fixed in scale, and the budgets, designed primarily for control purposes, do permit a degree of flexibility. On the other hand, some projects are essentially discrete, as in location problems, and also the budgeted inputs may be rigidly limited. In addition, the maximum number of fractional projects increases when inter-relationships between projects must also be taken into account. Our concern in this paper is exclusively with the problem involving discrete projects, and hence we shall put aside the linear programming solution.

Before going on to alternative approaches, however, it should be pointed out that Lorie and Savage proposed a trial and error method for finding the integer solution. Their method, based on "generalized Lagrange multipliers" [19], is closely related to that discussed in the next section in relation to the dynamic programming solution. It fails to achieve the integer solution in many cases, due to the nonexistence of the desired quantities. These difficulties have been analyzed at length in the context of the duals to integer programming problems in [46];[9] however, see also below.

C. Dynamic Programming

The problem as formulated in equations (II.1) may be recognized as a special case of the knapsack or flyaway kit problem [15, 7 pp. 42–47] when

---

[8] Proofs of this and related propositions are given in [46, Sec. 3.8].

[9] See [46, Chap. 2, Secs. 3.5, 4.2 and 5.8].

the number of "budget" constraints is small. It arises, for example, when a camper must choose the number of each of n items he wishes to carry in his knapsack when the utility to him of each is given, and total volume and weight limitations are imposed by the size of the knapsack.[10] It may also be interpreted as the number of spare parts to be taken along by a submarine for which similar limitations on weight and volume exist, but for which the benefit of the spare-parts kit involves the probability that a part is needed and the cost of being without it. Leaving stochastic aspects for a later section of this paper, we may write down the dynamic programming formulation of this general problem and briefly discuss some shortcuts for the Lorie-Savage problem.

As in the dynamic programming solution to the knapsack problem, the time sequence is replaced by the sequence of projects being considered, and the ordering of the projects is arbitrary.[11] The method consists of determining the list of projects which would be accepted if the "budgets" in the T periods were $C_1', C_2', \ldots, C_T'$, and selection were restricted to the first i projects. This is done for $i = 1, \ldots, n$, and within each "stage" i, for all feasible vectors, $C' = (C_1', C_2', \ldots, C_T')$, where feasibility means that $0 \le C_t' \le C_t, t = 1, \ldots, T$. We define $f_i(C_1', C_2', \ldots, C_T')$ as the total value associated with an optimal choice among the first i projects when funds employed are as defined. The basic recurrence relationship then may be stated as

a. $f_i(C_1', C_2', \ldots, C_T') = \max_{x_i=0,1}[b_i x_i + f_{i-1}(C_1' - c_{1i}x_i,$

$$C_2' - c_{2i}x_i, \ldots, C_T' - c_{Ti}x_i)] \qquad i = 1, \ldots, n$$

for   (II.2)

b. $C_t' - c_{ti} \ge 0,$ $t = 1, \ldots, T$

and

c. $f_0(C') = 0$

where $f_i(C')$ is the total value of the optimally selected projects with projects $i + 1, i + 2, \ldots, n$ still to be considered and the unallocated funds are given by C'.

Two departures from the usual dynamic programming version of the knapsack problem may be noted.[12] First, the number of "budget" constraints is an arbitrary number T, which may be significantly greater than two. Also,

---

[10] This differs from the problem stated in (II.1) in that constraints (II.1c) are omitted, or replaced by larger right-side terms.

[11] Some preliminary screening and rearranging can help to cut computation time. See, e.g., Glover [23].

[12] An additional requirement in the dynamic programming solution to the knapsack problem is that all coefficients must be nonnegative—e.g., no negative payoff or negative resource use (resource increase). This condition may be too restrictive for certain applications, for which a more general integer programming formulation is necessary. To handle interrelations between projects we shall relax this requirement partially, in Sec. IIIB, below.

the x_j are either zero or one here, whereas in the knapsack problem they may be any integers usually up to some upper limit on each item. Dantzig regards even two budgets for the knapsack problem to be one too many,[13] and Bellman [6] suggests that a second constraint be handled by use of a Lagrangian multiplier by maximizing

$$\sum_{i=1}^{n} b_i x_i - \lambda \sum_{i=1}^{n} c_{2i} x_i \qquad (\text{II.3})$$

subject to the single constraint

$$\sum_{i=1}^{n} c_{1i} x_i \leq C_1. \qquad (\text{II.4})$$

A value of λ is assumed and the one-dimensional recurrence relation

$$f_i(C_1') = \max_{x_i = 0,1}[(b_i - \lambda c_{2i})x_i + f_{i-1}(C_1' - c_{1i}x_i)] \qquad (\text{II.5})$$

is solved as before. Bellman comments, "The value of λ is varied until the second [original] constraint is satisfied. In practice, only a few tries are required to obtain the solution in this manner" [6, p. 724]. As was pointed out in the previous section, issues of the existence of the Lagrange multipliers are involved here. It was shown in [46, Sec. 4.2 and p. 101] that it is possible to prove that Lagrange multipliers do not exist for some examples of the Lorie-Savage problem, model (II.1). It is apparent that the same technical difficulties are involved here. The work of Everett [19], partially anticipated by Lorie and Savage [32] and Bellman [6] applies this technique to arbitrary real valued functions. Everett shows, but does not emphasize, that the problem actually solved may not (and often is not) the problem originally stated.[14] Further questions have also been raised in an exchange between Charnes and Cooper and Everett [10a, 19a].

We may best illustrate the above remarks by means of an example which appeared in this journal. Joel Cord [14] utilized dynamic programming for investment project selection in exactly the way Bellman suggested, although his constraints were on total outlay and on average variance of return. We shall return to the substance of Cord's article below. For the moment we focus entirely on the computational aspects, use of the Lagrangian multiplier parametrically to reduce the problem to a one-constraint recursive optimization, as in (II.5).

Cord illustrates the model with a numerical example [14, pp. 340–41]. The solution he arrives at is not, however, the optimum, a possibility he allows for [p. 339] though he attributes it to the coarseness of the increment in the parameter λ he employed. In this he is incorrect. The optimum cannot be located by means of the Lagrangian multiplier technique, although

---

[13] "It [the dynamic programming approach to the knapsack problem] is recommended where there are only a few items and only one kind of limitation" [15, p. 275].

[14] The problem under consideration here, however, is the strict integer problem, i.e., that in which it is assumed that a solution for the *given* constraints is sought.

the value of the solution he obtained is close to that of the true optimum.[15] These conclusions were obtained by use of a program which takes advantage of the zero-one limitation on the variables, and which can handle a reasonable number of constraints without Lagrangian multipliers providing the number of projects is not excessive.[16] The computer flow chart for the program is presented in Appendix A.

Finally, a question to be resolved is the interpretation of the Lagrangian solution as opposed to the strict integer solution when these differ. It is possible to interpret the Lagrangian multiplier as the trade-off between the constrained quantity and the payoff. Thus is it possible to "cost" the projects to determine whether the payoff is sufficient in the face of consumption of resources (or other constrained quantities) whose opportunity cost may be high. The linear programming model (II.1a–c) yields a positive[17] residual for each project accepted in the optimal solution while the rejected ones have a nonpositive residual.[18] These conclusions do not necessarily apply to the strict integer optimum, whether obtained by dynamic programming or by other means. Specifically, they do not apply when the true integer optimum cannot be obtained by means of Lagrangian multipliers, either in the dynamic programming formulation or with a systematic search for these quantities as implied by Lorie and Savage. This raises the important question of the meaning of the resource constraint. If it is merely an intermediate administrative device to control the budgetary process[19] then it would be

---

[15] The true optimum, given his definition of the problem, consists of projects 8, 9, and 23, with payoff of $90,930 vs. Cord's projects 3, 8, 11, 20 with payoff of $88,460. The correct optimum was contained in Dyckman's "Communication" [18]. (It is not at all clear how Cord obtained his numerical solution even with the use of the Lagrangian multiplier in his second constraint. Attempts at reproducing his numerical results show that with the multiplier set at 1400 the solution consists of projects 3, 8, 9, 23 with average variance of .0084745, as Cord reports [p. 341]. When the multiplier is increased to 1410 the solution changes and consists of projects 1, 5, 8, 13, 20 with average variance of .0020345. This is the first solution which satisfies the variance constraint and thus would be the one which Cord was looking for, but did not find. With the multiplier set at 1410 the value of the *Lagrangian function* being maximized is $81,381.355 for {1, 5, 8, 13, 20} vs. $81,380.955 for {3, 8, 11, 20}. While small, the difference is sufficient to insure that Cord's solution will never be generated by the dynamic programming computations since it is dominated: its payoff is less (and increasingly so with larger multipliers) and its required outlay is greater by $1. It is true, though not germane, that the payoff from projects 3, 8, 11, 20 is greater than that from projects 1, 5, 8, 13, 20.)

Cord's formal statement of the problem can also be criticized, because he calculated his average variance on the basis of funds available rather than funds expended. When this correction is made, the solution 8, 9, 23 is seen to violate the variance constraint. However, the optimum then is again not Cord's solution but projects 5, 8, 12, 13, and 20, with payoff of $88,650. It is interesting to note that use of Lagrangian multipliers for both constraints in the manner suggested by Lorie and Savage also does not yield either of these additional solutions. See also Eastman [18a].

[16] The program was written to be entirely within core of a 32K memory machine, and the limitation on the number of constraints depends also on other dimensions. A sample problem with six constraints has been run. (Added in proof: subsequent to the writing of this report, further work has led to the development of programs for the solution of the "complement" problem and other devices have been employed which speed up the computations in certain numerical problems. These will be described in a forthcoming report.)

[17] More precisely, nonnegative.

[18] The residuals are defined as $b_i - \lambda_1{}^* c_{1i} - \lambda_2{}^* c_{2i}$, where $\lambda_i{}^*$ is the optimal dual to the tth constraint. See [46, Sec. 3.4] for a detailed analysis.

unreasonable to disregard the pricing information contained in the Lagrangian multipliers and to accept projects which happen to allow use of the last small amount of the budget.[20] On the other hand, some resources are only available in small amounts, and full utilization of them is at the heart of the problem. In the latter case it would probably be best to search beyond the optimum obtained through use of the Lagrangian multiplier technique, or perhaps to eschew it entirely.

III. INTERDEPENDENT PROJECTS
WITHOUT BUDGET CONSTRAINTS

Difficulties with the usual "text-book" methods of capital expenditure evaluation, e.g., internal rate of return or present value, arise when the independence assumption between projects does not hold. How strong this assumption is may be seen when one considers that alternative to almost every project is the possibility of its postponement for one or more periods, with concomitant changes in outlays and payoffs. These, of course, form a mutually-exclusive set of alternatives since it would be deemed uneconomical, if not impossible, to carry out more than one of them.[21] Mutual exclusion is by no means the only alternative to independence, even though this is the only other possibility which is usually raised in the literature. Contingent or dependent projects can arise, for instance, when "acceptance of one proposal is dependent on acceptance of one or more other proposals" [46, p. 11]. One simple example would be the purchase of an extra-long boom for a crane which would be of little value unless the crane itself were also purchased; the latter, however, may be justified on its own. When contingent projects are combined with their independent "prerequisites" we may call the combination a "compound project." Thus a compound project may be characterized by the algebraic sum of the payoffs and costs of the component projects plus, perhaps, an "interaction" term. Although contingent projects generally can be represented by sets of mutually-exclusive compound projects, in practice this is likely to prove an undesirable way of handling them, for the resulting number of compound projects may be very large. In the present section of this paper we shall take up the treatment of interdependent projects in the context of the models discussed in the previous section. We shall also take up an alternative formulation which allows a wider variety of interrelationships, omitting, for the present, consideration of budget constraints.[22]

---

[19] See [46, Chap. 6].

[20] This would imply that expenditures can be forecast with extreme accuracy, among other requirements.

[21] See, for example, Marglin's analysis of the "Myopia Rule" in [34].

[22] In this paper we omit consideration of interdependence between existing projects and new ones. Models which deal with such problems will be of the type referred to at the end of Sec. IIA, although the tools developed here will still be applicable.

A. Linear and Integer Programming

The methods of handling interrelationships of the types mentioned in the paragraph above were discussed at length elsewhere, and hence a brief summary here will suffice.[23]

Consider a set J of mutually-exclusive projects from which at most one is to be selected. This constraint may be expressed by

$$\sum_{j \in J} x_j \leq 1. \tag{III.1}$$

With the implied nonnegativity constraint on the x_j, this has the effect of limiting the sum of projects accepted from the set J to a single one. When an integer programming algorithm is utilized to solve the problem one is assured that at most one of the x_j equals unity, $j \in J$, while the remaining ones from the set are zero. Solution by linear programming leads to the possibility that several projects from the set J will be fractionally accepted. The total number of such projects will still be limited although a situation with fractional x_j^* for more than one project in the set J can arise.[24] Note that the unity upper bound constraint on the x_j individually, $j \in J$, is now superfluous.

Contingent projects may be handled in a similarly simple manner. If project r may be undertaken only if project s is accepted, but project s is an independent alternative, then we may express the relationship by

a.
$$x_r \leq x_s$$
and $\qquad\qquad\qquad\qquad\qquad\qquad\qquad\qquad\qquad\qquad$ (III.2)

b.
$$x_s \leq 1.$$

Thus, if $x_s^* = 1$, i.e., it is accepted in the optimal solution, then $x_r \leq 1$ is the effective constraint. Otherwise, $x_r \leq 0$, together with the nonnegativity requirement, forces $x_r^* = 0$. If projects u and v are mutually-exclusive alternatives, and project r is dependent on acceptance of either project u or project v, this interrelationship may be expressed by

a.
$$x_u + x_v \leq 1$$
$\qquad\qquad\qquad\qquad\qquad\qquad\qquad\qquad\qquad\qquad$ (III.3)
b.
$$x_r \leq x_u + x_v$$

Hence, if one of the pair u and v is accepted, then constraint (III.3b) becomes $x_r \leq 1$. If neither u nor v is accepted, then (III.3b) becomes $x_r \leq 0$, implying, once again, that $x_r^* = 0$. Similarly, if projects r and s are mutually-exclusive and dependent on the acceptance of either project u or v, two mutually-exclusive alternatives, the interdependence may be represented by the two constraints

a.
$$x_u + x_v \leq 1$$
$\qquad\qquad\qquad\qquad\qquad\qquad\qquad\qquad\qquad\qquad$ (III.4)
b.
$$x_r + x_s \leq x_u + x_v.$$

---

[23] See [46, pp. 10–11, 32–43], and the analysis of the duals to these constraints, [46, pp. 147–52].
[24] See [46, p. 37]. For an interpretation of this result, see also [46, p. 32].

Contingent chains can easily be built up, as when acceptance of project r is dependent on acceptance of project s, which in turn is dependent on acceptance of project u:

a. $x_u \leq 1$

b. $x_s \leq x_u$ (III.5)

c. $x_r \leq x_s$,

etc.

B. Dynamic Programming

A glance at inequality (III.1) which states the restriction on mutually-exclusive projects reveals that its algebraic form is exactly that of the budget constraints, restrictions (II.1b), i.e., the coefficients are all nonnegative. This was the only requirement necessary for applying the knapsack problem formulation, and hence solution by dynamic programming hinges only on the computational problem derived from having additional constraints. Since at most a few of the projects will be mutually-exclusive at one time, although there may be many such sets, the number of nonzero coefficients will be small. This has the effect of speeding up the calculations and keeping the "in-lists"—the lists of accepted projects—relatively small.

In principle, contingent projects can be handled as sets of mutually-exclusive compound alternatives, as was pointed out above. The difficulty with the dependency relation (III.2a) may be seen by putting both unknowns on the same side of the inequality, as in

$$x_r - x_s \leq 0. \qquad (III.6)$$

The zero right side presents no difficulty. However, the negative coefficient of x_s does. The nonnegativity condition on the coefficients of the knapsack problem derives from the requirement that the payoff function be monotonically nondecreasing in the x_i. With this condition imposed it is not possible that the space of solution vectors $(x_1, \ldots, x_n)$ becomes enlarged at one stage subsequent to the elimination of some solutions. A way for handling negative coefficients such as arise in connection with dependent projects is to preorder the projects such that the independent members of a set (with the negative coefficients) always precede the dependent ones.[25] This implies that the solution space is expanded at the start and the above difficulty is avoided. Unfortunately it is possible to construct examples in which no such preordering is possible. It seems likely, however, that these are atypical and afford no substantial obstacle to the application of dynamic programming for interrelated projects.[26]

---

[25] A program for the knapsack problem must be modified to allow violation of a "feasibility condition," e.g., (II.2b) during part of the computations.

[26] A problem was solved in which constraints (III.4) and (III.5) were applied.

C. Quadratic Integer Programming and the Generalization of Second-Order Effects

Although contrary to the teaching of the principle of "Occam's Razor," it is possible to represent the above interdependencies by means of quadratic constraints superimposed on the 0-1 integer requirement for the x_j. For two mutually-exclusive projects, r and s, the relevant restriction, in addition to nonnegativity on the unknowns, would be

$$x_r \cdot x_s = 0 \qquad (III.7)$$

which makes either $x_r{}^* = 1$ or $x_s{}^* = 1$, but not both $x_r{}^* = 1$ and $x_s{}^* = 1$. For the dependence of project r on project s, we require

$$x_r(1 - x_s) = 0. \qquad (III.8)$$

Thus, if $x_s{}^* = 1$, $x_r{}^*$ may be either zero or one and the restriction will be satisfied. However, if $x_s{}^* = 0$ then $x_r{}^* = 0$ necessarily.

A generalization to include all pair-wise second-order effects, i.e., involving interaction terms between pairs (but not larger sets) of projects has been offered by S. Reiter [40]. A triangular payoff matrix

$$B = \begin{bmatrix} b_{11} & b_{12} & b_{13} & \cdots & b_{1n} \\ 0 & b_{22} & b_{23} & \cdots & b_{2n} \\ 0 & 0 & b_{33} & \cdots & b_{3n} \\ & & \cdots & \cdots & \\ 0 & 0 & 0 & \cdots & b_{nn} \end{bmatrix} \qquad (III.9)$$

is defined for the set of n investment alternatives such that the payoff (e.g., net present value) from the acceptance of project r alone is b_{rr}, and the additional payoff from acceptance of both projects r and s is b_{rs}, apart from the payoff from acceptance of project r, b_{rr}, and project s, b_{ss}. An optimal partitioning of the set of project indices, $i = 1, \ldots, m$ into two mutually-exclusive and exhaustive subsets, $\{i_1, \ldots, i_r\}$ and its complement is sought such that the total payoff from the first subset, the "in-list," is maximum. Given any such partitioning the payoff Γ_α associated with an in-list α may be thought of as being obtained by crossing out all rows and columns of B which are not on the in-list and adding up the b_{ij} that remain. In Reiter's context such a payoff matrix represents an optimization problem only if some b_{ij} are negative, for otherwise the optimal in-list, α^*, would be the entire list of projects. However, in some of our extensions, below, this need not be the case. It is also clear that the elements below the diagonal are not needed to represent any of the interaction effects which can be handled in an $n \times n$ array.

A few examples paralleling our earlier discussion will bring out some of the features of this development. If projects r and s are mutually-exclusive, all that is necessary to prevent their simultaneous adoption is to make b_{rs} a highly negative penalty.[27] Of course, all that is required here is the value b_{rs} which makes the total $b_{rr} + b_{ss} + b_{rs}$ represent the net value of adopting both alternatives, a quantity which will certainly be smaller than either b_{rr} or b_{ss}, the value of either alternative alone. Hence, b_{rs} will be negative. Using the penalty of $-M$ we may represent a set of mutually-exclusive projects, for purposes of illustration assumed to be the first k projects, by

$$B = \begin{bmatrix} b_{11} & -M & -M & \cdots & -M \\ 0 & b_{22} & -M & \cdots & -M \\ 0 & 0 & b_{33} & \cdots & -M \\ & & \cdots & & \\ 0 & 0 & 0 & \cdots & b_{kk} \end{bmatrix} \qquad (\text{III.10})$$

A dependence of project r on project s is handled by letting b_{rr} be the cost, a negative quantity, while b_{rs} represents the benefit from having r in addition to s. b_{ss} would be the net payoff from accepting project s alone. We may finally illustrate this formulation with the situation expressed by equations (III.4a and b), in which projects u and v are mutually-exclusive, as are projects r and s, and in addition to which acceptance of project r or s is dependent on acceptance of project u or v.

$$B = \begin{bmatrix} -b_r & -M & b_{ru} & b_{rs} \\ 0 & -b_s & b_{su} & b_{sv} \\ 0 & 0 & b_{uu} & -M \\ 0 & 0 & 0 & b_{vv} \end{bmatrix} \qquad (\text{III.11})$$

Here the quantities $-b_r$ and $-b_s$ represent the cost of projects r and s, respectively; b_{uu} and b_{vv} represent the net benefit from doing project u or v alone; and $b_{ru}, b_{su}, b_{rv}, b_{sv}$ represent the additional benefits from selecting both projects r and u, s and u, r and v, and s and v, respectively. Once again the quantity $-M$ is a large penalty intended to dominate its row and column by a substantial amount.

Before presenting an outline of Reiter's method for finding the optimal partitioning of the project indices, we may show that his problem is actually an integer quadratic programming problem:

Maximize

$$XBX^t = \sum_{i=1}^{n} \sum_{j=1}^{n} b_{ij} x_i x_j \qquad (\text{III.12})$$

---

[27] This is analogous to the penalty for keeping artificial vectors out of the optimal basis of a linear programming solution. See, e.g., [10, p. 176].

where $X = (x_1, x_2, \ldots, x_n)$, X^t is its transpose, and $x_i = 0$ or 1. Thus the payoff b_{ij} is realized only if both $x_i^* = 1$ and $x_j^* = 1$. Otherwise the product $b_{ij}x_i^*x_j^* = 0$. Similarly, since the x_i are restricted to zero and unity it is unnecessary to distinguish between x_i and x_i^2. We shall return to other problems in which this formulation is of utility later on.

Reiter's method for maximizing (III.12) is not algorithmic in the usual sense. It locates a local maximum (guaranteed to exist by the finiteness of the number of projects) by a gradient method that traverses "connected in-lists." By starting at random in-lists it generates a variety of local optima which can be arranged in ascending order. Whether the global optimum is reached depends on whether an initial in-list is selected which leads to the global optimum as its local optimum. Often it is possible to estimate probabilistically the chances that the global optimum will be reached. Optimal stopping rules (based on the value of improvement vs. the computational cost of obtaining it) and optimal fixed sample-size plans have also been developed; see [41 and 42].

The method may be described as follows. Given an arbitrary in-list α, compute the corresponding payoff Γ_α. A connected in-list α' is one which differs from α either by including one project not contained in α, or by excluding one project which is included in α. The quantity $\Gamma_{\alpha'}$ is computed for each α' connected to α, and so is the gradient $G_{\alpha'} = \Gamma_{\alpha'} - \Gamma_\alpha$. The α' corresponding to the largest $G_{\alpha'}$ is selected as the starting point for the next iteration and these are continued until no α' can be found for which $G_{\alpha'} > 0$. Once this point has been reached the in-list with a local maximum has been found. (In the event of ties between $G_{\alpha'}$ along the way, a simple rule such as choosing that α' with the smallest first index [where a difference exists] can be used to break the tie.)

Having found a local optimum one seeks to choose a new starting in-list which has not already been evaluated, so as to find another local optimum. The connected in-lists constitute branches on a tree which has many starting points that lead to the top (the local maximum). The "broader" the tree having the global optimum as its local maximum, the more likely it is that the global optimum will be found. The method guarantees only that the global maximum will be found with "probability one." Unfortunately, it will not be recognized as such short of evaluating every possible in-list along the way. However, by careful use of prior information [42] and aspiration levels to indicate when the procedure should be stopped, one can arrive at "good" programs rapidly.[28] A numerical example with its tree-structure is presented in Appendix B.

One final note regarding this approach to the selection of interdependent projects is required here. Although Reiter restricts himself to a consideration of second-order interactions exclusively, there is nothing in the method which

---

[28] In any case, one would partition the matrix B into independent submatrices, if such exist, and use the method on the submatrices separately.

requires this. A generalization to k^{th} order effects requires computations involving an n^k array, for which specifying the numerical values of the parameters will be more difficult than obtaining a good solution. Increasing the dimensionality of the array does not change anything essential in the structure of the problem—the connectedness or finiteness of the iterative process for finding a local optimum—and hence only the computational problems are affected, though perhaps drastically.

IV. INTERDEPENDENT PROJECTS WITH BUDGET CONSTRAINTS

The methods outlined in the previous section, in addition to handling the interrelationships between projects, permit inclusion of budget constraints with varying degrees of difficulty. For linear and integer linear programming formulations the interrelationships are essentially like budgets, and this holds approximately for the dynamic programming formulation, as was discussed in Section III. The formulation as an integer quadratic programming problem also allows the introduction of linear restrictions such as the budget constraints, although progress toward an algorithm for such problems has not been rapid to date [31].

The only point which bears a brief discussion in this section is the introduction of side-conditions of the budget type into the Reiter format. To accomplish this end with a single restriction one may utilize a Lagrangian multiplier[29] as did Bellman in the knapsack problem. That is, the terms c_j from the constraint

$$\sum_{j=1}^{n} c_j x_j \leq C \qquad\qquad (\text{IV.1})$$

are introduced into the matrix B of (III.9) with the Lagrangian λ:

$$B = \begin{bmatrix} b_{11} - \lambda c_1 & b_{12} & b_{13} & \cdots & b_{1n} \\ 0 & b_{22} - \lambda c_2 & b_{23} & \cdots & b_{2n} \\ & & \cdots & \cdots & \\ 0 & 0 & 0 & \cdots & b_{nn} - \lambda c_n \end{bmatrix} \qquad (\text{IV.2})$$

and the optimization procedure is repeated with varying values of λ until restriction (IV.1) is met. This procedure is not without pitfalls. Suppose $\alpha^0(\lambda)$ is the in-list accepted as the best obtainable for the given aspiration level (stopping rule) and the given value of λ. Suppose, further, that $\alpha^*(\lambda)$ is the optimal in-list for this value of λ. The difference between $\Gamma_{\alpha^0}(\lambda)$ and $\Gamma_{\alpha^*}(\lambda)$ may arise (a) because larger b_{ij} are available or (b) smaller c_j are

---

[29] With the attendant qualifications indicated in Sec. IIC above.

available, or (c) both.[30] Only in case (a) are the constrained quantities c_j not involved. In both other instances, the most likely case being (c), this difference implies that the global optimum (for the given value of λ) will show a greater amount of slack or smaller surplus in constraint (IV.1) than does $\alpha^0(\lambda)$. A reasonable procedure for changing λ in the direction indicated by the presence of slack or violation of the restriction would be to begin the computations with the previous in-list α^0. The grid for such changes in λ should reflect the bias in the estimation of the optimal value of the Lagrangian multiplier.[31] It should be borne in mind, nevertheless, that feasible solutions, which satisfy the constraint (IV.1), will always be found (assuming that the constraint is consistent with the interrelationships) even though it is not guaranteed to be a global optimum.

One final observation which will be followed by a detailed discussion of a particular application below concludes this section. Given the discrete optimization technique of Reiter the cost structure may also express the whole range of second-order interactions, generalizing to the following payoff matrix:

$$B = \begin{bmatrix} b_{11} - \lambda c_{11} & b_{12} - \lambda c_{12} & b_{13} - \lambda c_{13} & \cdots & b_{1n} - \lambda c_{1n} \\ 0 & b_{22} - \lambda c_{22} & b_{23} - \lambda c_{23} & \cdots & b_{2n} - \lambda c_{2n} \\ 0 & 0 & b_{33} - \lambda c_{33} & \cdots & b_{3n} - \lambda c_{3n} \\ & & \cdots & & \\ 0 & 0 & 0 & \cdots & b_{nn} - \lambda c_{nn} \end{bmatrix} \qquad \text{(IV.3)}$$

Should the payoff matrix be partitionable into submatrices, as e.g., in

$$B = \left[\begin{array}{cc:cccc} b_{11} - \lambda c_{11} & b_{12} - \lambda c_{12} & 0 & 0 & \cdots & 0 \\ 0 & b_{22} - \lambda c_{22} & 0 & 0 & \cdots & 0 \\ \hdashline 0 & 0 & b_{33} - \lambda c_{33} & \cdots & & \\ & & & \cdots & & \end{array} \right] \qquad \text{(IV.4)}$$

the problem may be restated as

$$Z(\lambda) = \sum_{k=1}^{s} (XBX^t)_k \qquad \text{(IV.5)}$$

where each $(XBX^t)_k$ is a similar subproblem. The value of λ remains the same for all subproblems at any state since the budget constraint applies to all simultaneously.

---

[30] The c_j are nonnegative quantities, and are multiplied by the positive constant λ and then subtracted from the b_{jj}.

[31] More complete ways of handling this problem are being investigated.

V. PROBABILISTIC CONSIDERATIONS

Introduction of probability distributions into the models considered earlier cannot automatically be regarded as dealing with the problems of uncertainty. In the selection of projects whose outcomes are stochastic, it is not, in general, clear what the random variables are or how they are distributed, although some attempts at the organization of data have recently been proposed.[32] More important, it is not yet clear how such outcomes should be evaluated.[33] We shall waive these matters in order to pursue our original aim of clarifying and expanding on simple methods of analyzing the consequences from given assumptions, hopefully useful considering the current state of the art.

A. Independent Investment Projects

Even investment alternatives which are independent in the physical sense but which have probabilistic payoffs introduce a hierarchy of difficulties in the selection of an optimal set. The foremost of these is the choice of criterion function for optimization.[34] Confining ourselves, as before, to economic benefits, we first look at expected value maximization. Under this criterion, and assuming that the decision-maker is satisfied that he has defined meaningful random variables and that he knows the shapes and parameters of their distributions, we distinguish between situations where the payoffs are independently distributed and where they are not. For the present we consider the quantities subject to budget constraints to be certain.[35]

With independently distributed outcomes the problem has not been altered in any essential way.[36] The form of the original Lorie-Savage problem still applies, expected payoffs being substituted for certain ones. Integer programming or dynamic programming may be used to solve the problem, as before, or linear programming may be applied if its limitations are not important here. It should be obvious that most of the problems of uncertainty have been assumed away, although a model of this type of uncertainty has been used [3]. If the outcomes of investments are jointly distributed nothing new is introduced under expected value maximization.

The same is not the case if the conditional distribution of outcomes of a particular project, given that another is undertaken, is different from the unconditional distribution. Such is the case, for example, if the probability distribution for a manufacturing facility is affected by the decision to build

---

[32] See, for example, [26] and [27].

[33] This problem remains conspicuously unsolved in [26]. However, see also [28].

[34] We are not concerned with a general discussion of utility here.

[35] This assumption is relaxed via chance-constrained programming, in [12] and [38]. Further work following up on some of the ideas presented in this paper is being carried on by the author.

[36] In attempting to solve an explicitly dynamic problem, in which decisions are made periodically, one would also have to take into account that the decision taken at one time may affect the statistical distributions which are pertinent for later decisions.

a warehouse nearby. Such second-order effects[37] may be handled by quadratic integer programming, as in Section III.C, and solved by Reiter's method or our extension provided that no more than a single constraint is imposed. The off diagonal elements of the payoff matrix B would then express the expected value of the joint adoption of two projects while the diagonal elements are expected payoffs from acceptance of the projects by themselves. The costs would be subtracted from the diagonal elements, as in matrix (IV.2).

B. Nonlinear Utility Functions

When the stochastic nature of the outcomes is given prominence in the problem, consideration must also be given to the form of the function whose optimization is being sought. Questions of risk aversion or risk preference lead to inclusion of quantities other than expected payoffs into the criterion or utility function. The meanings of the terms "risk aversion" and "risk preference" have been sharpened considerably in a recent paper by Pratt [39], a few of whose conclusions will be referred to below. This subject, which is intertwined with the concept of uncertainty, raises such additional issues as whose utility should be optimized, as well as the effect of expectations concerning the availability of future prospects on the current decision. The latter difficulty has already been relegated to another time by omitting consideration here of sequential decision procedures. The former we leave to others, assuming that a determination can be made by the decision-maker.

As Markowitz has pointed out [35, 20] the step to the simplest nonlinear utility function can be taken directly or indirectly. First one may assume that the utility function is quadratic. Unfortunately, the quadratic is not risk-averse in Pratt's sense.[38] However, if all outcomes are normally distributed only the mean and variance of the total payoff enter into the utility function.[39]

We assume first that the outcomes are jointly normally distributed, but that the distributions are not contingent on the decisions themselves as in the preceding section. The resulting problem has a form exactly analogous to the Markowitz Portfolio Selection problem with the following exceptions. First, the projects are discrete, unlike the portfolio problem in which for a given security there are constant returns to scale. As a result, the problem is not to determine the proportion of the portfolio to be allocated to each

---

[37] I.e., again involving only interaction terms between projects, two at one time.

[38] One consequence of the quadratic utility function is that the "risk premium"—that additional amount which makes a fair gamble acceptable to a risk-averse gambler—*increases* with his initial wealth.

[39] To obtain a quadratic function requires a further simplification. In a series expansion of an arbitrary utility function, if all terms of degree higher than the second are discarded, the resulting approximation can be made to take the form of equation (V.1) by a suitable linear transformation. The utility function under discussion here (based on the von Neumann-Morgenstern postulates [33, Section 2.5]) is, in any case, unique only up to a linear transformation.

eligible security, but to determine the list of projects to be accepted. Formally, this problem may be written as

Maximize

$$\mu - \lambda\sigma^2 \equiv \sum_{i=1}^{n} \mu_i x_i - \lambda \sum_{i=1}^{n} \sum_{j=1}^{n} x_i \sigma_{ij} x_j \tag{V.1}$$

subject to

$$x_i = 0,1, \qquad i = 1, \ldots, n$$

for a preassigned value of λ, where μ is the expected value of the payoff of the accepted projects and σ^2 is the variance of the total payoff. λ may be accorded the interpretation of a measure of risk aversion—the rate of trade-off between reduction in expected value for reduction in variance. Here μ is the sum of the expected payoffs μ_i from the individual projects which are accepted. The σ_{ij} are the covariances between the outcomes of projects i and j, $i \neq j$, and $\sigma_{ii} = \sigma_i^2$ are the variances. Since we have restricted the values of x_i to zero or one, $x_i = x_i^2$, and functional (V.1) has a form similar to one treated before by Reiter's Discrete Optimization Method:

$$B = \begin{bmatrix} \mu_1 - \lambda\sigma_1^2 & -2\lambda\sigma_{12} & -2\lambda\sigma_{13} & \cdots & -2\lambda\sigma_{1n} \\ 0 & \mu_2 - \lambda\sigma_2^2 & -2\lambda\sigma_{23} & \cdots & -2\lambda\sigma_{2n} \\ 0 & 0 & \mu_3 - \lambda\sigma_3^2 & \cdots & -2\lambda\sigma_{3n} \\ & & \cdots & \cdots & \\ 0 & 0 & 0 & \cdots & \mu_n - \lambda\sigma_n^2 \end{bmatrix} \tag{V.2}$$

We may contrast this formulation with the one recently suggested by J. Cord which was referred to earlier.[40] Cord considers the problem of "optimally selecting capital investments with uncertain returns, under conditions of limited funds and a constraint on the maximum average variance allowed in the final investment package" [14, p. 335]. Although Cord's figure of merit is "interest rate of return" of a project which is multiplied by the required outlay for the project,[41] nothing essential is changed by substituting the expected present value for this quantity. Similarly, the variance of the present value may be used in place of the variance he uses.[42] Cord solves this problem by dynamic programming

---

[40] See p. 90, above.

[41] In his discussion, Cord indicated that by "interest rate of return" he means internal rate of return—that rate which equates the discounted value of inflows to the (assumed by Cord, sole) outflow. For this he was properly critized by T. R. Dyckman [18] because of the effect of project lives on total benefit. Actually, Cord's use of this quantity is not consistent with application of the internal rate of return, which he multiplies by the outlay to obtain the figure of merit used in the objective function. His model can be made consistent, however, simply by interpreting "interest rate of return" as the uniform perpetual rate of return.

[42] Cord's variance constraint is based on the variance of total funds available rather than on funds allocated to investments; i.e., in our notation, the project variances per dollar outlay are weighted by c_i/C rather than by $c_i/\sum c_i x_i^*$. The former weighting will understate the variance unless it is assumed that unallocated funds are actually maintained as cash with zero variance and

utilizing the Lagrangian multiplier technique to obtain a solution which satisfies the constraint on variance. Using the notation of the preceding paragraph and of Section IIC, above, we may restate his recurrence relation as

$$f_i(C') = \max \{[\mu_i x_i - \lambda \sigma_i^2 x_i + f_{i-1}(C' - c_i x_i)] \mid 0 \leq x_i \leq 1, 0 \leq C' \leq C\}$$

(V.3)

where C' is the unallocated budget and f_i the total value of the selected projects when C' remains to be allocated and $n - i$ projects still to be considered.

Cord explicitly assumes independence in the statistical sense between the project payoffs. Hence his total variance is the sum of the variances of the accepted projects, avoiding the quadratic terms and covariances. Although it simplifies the computations, this assumption, which he has difficulty in justifying, is not strictly necessary for application of dynamic programming. Having consciously patterned his approach after Markowitz he might also have considered Sharpe's Diagonal Model [43] which is designed to simplify the computations for obtaining optimal portfolios by allowing only a restricted covariance between the eligible securities.

Specifically, Sharpe assumes that the returns on securities are related only through a relationship with some common factor, e.g., an index of general activity. If the random variable, the return on the ith security, is denoted by p_i, and the level of the index is I, he expresses this return by

$$p_i = \mu_i + \beta_i I + w_i$$

(V.4)

where μ_i and β_i are parameters, and w_i is a random variable with mean of zero and variance of σ_i^2. Further, the level of I is given by the sum of a systematic component, μ_I, and a random part, w_I, with mean of zero and variance of σ_I^2,

$$I = \mu_I + w_I,$$

(V.5)

with w_i and σ_i^2 independent of I. Putting these relations together, with the assumption that $\text{Cov}(w_i, w_j) = 0$ he obtains

$$\text{Exp}(p_i) = \mu_i + \beta_i(\mu_I)$$
$$\text{Var}(p_i) = \sigma_i^2 + \beta_i^2 \sigma_I^2$$
$$\text{Cov}(p_i, p_j) = \beta_i \beta_j \sigma_I^2$$

(V.6)

In the portfolio problem the unknowns are the proportions of the total amount invested which are allocated to various securities. By contrast, our

---

return. On the other hand, the more reasonable second weighting makes the problem computationally more difficult since the weighting depends on the projects accepted. Dyckman [18, p. 349] suggests improving the solution by investing funds unallocated to projects in bonds at a nominal return and zero variance. This again assumes that the cash is on hand, having been procured at the cost of capital which is presumably much higher than the "nominal rate."

variables are integer-valued; $x_i = 0$ or 1. Hence we may maximize total expected investment program payoff μ subject to an expenditure ceiling of C and a variance limit of σ^2, or alternatively, maximize payoff less $\lambda\sigma^2$ subject to the budget constraint, where

$$\mu = \sum_{i=1}^{n} (\mu_i + \beta_i\mu_I)x_i \tag{V.7}$$

$$\sigma^2 = \sigma_I^2 \left(\sum_{i=1}^{n} \beta_i x_i \right)^2 + \sum_{i=1}^{n} \sigma_i^2 x_i. \tag{V.8}$$

The recurrence relation may then be written as

$$(f_i C') = \max \left\{ \mu_i x_i - \lambda x_i \left[\sigma_i^2 + \sigma_I^2 \left(\beta_i^2 + 2\beta_i \sum_{j=1}^{i-1} \beta_j x_j \right) \right] \right.$$

$$\left. + f_{i-1}(C' - c_i x_i) \,\middle|\, 0 \leqq x_i \leqq 1, 0 \leqq C' \leqq C \right\} \tag{V.9}$$

where the term enclosed in braces results from the factoring

$$\sigma^2 = \sigma_I^2 \left(\sum_{j=1}^{i} \beta_j x_j \right)^2 + \sum_{j=1}^{i} \sigma_j^2 x_j$$

$$= \sigma_I^2 \left(\sum_{j=1}^{i-1} \beta_j x_j \right)^2 + \sum_{j=1}^{i-1} \sigma_j^2 x_j + \sigma_I^2 x_i \left(\beta_i^2 + 2\beta_i \sum_{j=1}^{i-1} \beta_j x_j \right) + \sigma_i^2 x_i. \tag{V.10}$$

Contrary to Cord's viewpoint, the generalized or parametric Lagrangian multiplier formulation[43] above has the advantage here of tracing out a variety of efficient investment programs in the Markowitz sense[44] instead of requiring the decision maker to specify his tolerance for variance abstractly.

Utilization of an index to capture the major effect of covariation seems more appropriate in our context than in portfolio selection. For a single product-line firm, the payoffs from capital expenditures are apt to be related to each other mostly through a variable such as total sales. An extension of Sharpe's work to a number of uncorrelated indexes by K. J. Cohen [1] doubtlessly may be applied within this framework also.[45]

C. Interdependent Investments with Probabilistic Returns

Taking cognizance of covariance between investment payoffs may be thought of as the simplest form of interdependence, and strict independence in our original sense does not apply. However, it is still necessary to consider

---

[43] In the sense of Everett [19].
[44] I.e., one with minimum variance for given mean, or maximum mean for given variance.
[45] See also [13].

such explicit interrelationships as mutual-exclusion and dependence in order to see what these concepts imply given that outcomes are random variables.

Continuing, then, with jointly normally distributed payoffs from all investments (thus narrowing our concern to mean, variance and covariance), we observe first that the choice among mutually-exclusive investments in the absence of budget or other constraints cannot be made without reference to the whole set of alternatives. That is, if the projects within set J are mutually-exclusive, so that acceptance of more than one of them can be ruled out in advance, the quantities μ_j and σ_j, $j \in J$, are insufficient for selection of the preferred one (if any). The covariances between the mutually-exclusive project and the independent ones enter into the choice, which may be formulated once more as a quadratic integer program solved by use of Reiter's method:

$$B = \begin{bmatrix} \mu_1 - \lambda\sigma_1^2 & -M & -2\lambda\sigma_{13} & \cdots & -2\lambda\sigma_{1n} \\ 0 & \mu_2 - \lambda\sigma_2^2 & -2\lambda\sigma_{23} & \cdots & -2\lambda\sigma_{2n} \\ 0 & 0 & \mu_3 - \lambda\sigma_3^2 & \cdots & -2\lambda\sigma_{3n} \\ & & \cdots & & \\ 0 & 0 & 0 & \cdots & \mu_n - \lambda\sigma_n^2 \end{bmatrix} \quad \text{(V.11)}$$

In (V.11), projects 1 and 2 are considered mutually-exclusive, introducing the penalty $-M$ into the second column of the first row to prevent their joint acceptance. The matrix otherwise resembles (V.2).[46]

Great care must be exercised in utilizing this approach for the generalized second order effect matrix, as in (III.9). A difficulty arises around the meaning of the covariance terms, σ_{ij}, when the off-diagonal elements include expected values. Consider, for example, a machine tool for which accessories are available which increase the range of products which the machine can produce, and at the same time, increase its reliability. We can consider the tool itself project r, its accessories project s, and thus denote the random payoff from the machine tool alone by b_{rr} with expectation μ_{rr} and variance σ_{rr}; the cost of the accessories by $b_{ss} = \mu_{ss}$, with $\sigma_{ss} = 0$; and the increase in payoff due to the accessories by b_{rs} with expectation of μ_{rs}. However, we shall need σ_{rs} to denote more than the variance of b_{rs}. If we define $\pi_{rs} = b_{rr} + b_{rs} + b_{ss}$, i.e., π_{rs} is the payoff from the compound project[47] and V_{rs} is its variance, then [48]

$$V_{rs} = \sigma_{rr} + \sigma_{ss} + \sigma_{rs} = \sigma_{rr} + \sigma_{rs}$$

or   (V.12)

$$\sigma_{rs} = V_{rs} - \sigma_{rr} - \sigma_{ss} = V_{rs} - \sigma_{rr}.$$

---

[46] There is obviously no need for σ_{12} since the $-M$ will rule out $x_1^* = 1$, $x_2^* = 1$ from the optimal solution.

[47] $b_{ss} < 0$.

[48] Presumably $\sigma_{rs} < 0$, in this example.

With these definitions it is possible to treat complex interrelationships by use of Reiter's method, although the data preparation requires, in effect, computing the parameters of all possible (or likely) compound projects, which could then be handled via matrix (V.11) just as well. Using this earlier method also has the advantage of preserving the meaning of the covariance term between independent projects which would be clouded when covariances between a dependent project and unrelated independent projects are needed.

A final note regarding the quantities subject to budget constraints is needed before this section may be concluded. We have assumed that these are known with certainty. Should they also be regarded as stochastic the character of the problem would change in a significant way. One alternative would be to make compliance with the constraint less rigid, e.g., by stating only a probability less than unity with which the condition must hold. This places the problem into the realm of chance constrained programming [9]. Another would be to proceed sequentially in the allocation process, to make certain that expenditures stay within the preset ceilings.[49] The latter problem, which may be formulated as a dynamic programming problem, does take us outside the framework set for this paper and will be taken up elsewhere.

VI. R & D PROJECT SELECTION

A. Expected Value Maximization

The final section of this paper is devoted to consideration of an additional class of project interrelationships which can arise in the context of constructing a research and development program. In order to concentrate on those aspects we consider a drastically simplified problem in which the payoff from one successful development of a product or process is known with certainty (again denoted by b_i), in which the development cost, c_i, is similarly known with certainty, and in which the probability of success is believed to be p_i for a single project i.

If projects are mutually independent in all respects, acceptance is contingent only on the condition

$$p_i b_i - c_i > 0. \qquad (VI.1)$$

Where simultaneously resource limitations are also imposed, the problem has the format of the original Lorie-Savage problem, and the methods offered for this still apply. The project payoff is now given by the left side of (VI.1). This much is of little interest. Consider, however, two projects, r and s, which are mutually-exclusive in the following sense. They may

---

[49] I.e., to insure this with probability one as in linear programming under uncertainty as formulated by G. B. Dantzig [16].

represent alternative products to serve the same function, or products, e.g., chemicals or drugs, synthesized by two different methods. Then it may be that if research on both projects is undertaken and success is achieved on both, only the better project will actually be taken past the development stage. Thus, if $b_r > b_s$, p_r is the probability of success on project r independent of undertaking project s, and p_s similarly for project s, and p_{rs} is the probability of success on both projects r and s, then the payoff from undertaking research on both is given by the applicable box in the following payoff matrix:

	Success on r	Failure on r
Success on s	$b_r - c_r - c_s$	$b_s - c_r - c_s$
Failure on s	$b_r - c_r - c_s$	$- c_r - c_s$

The expected payoff then is

$$\pi_{rs} = p_r(b_r - c_r - c_s) + (p_s - p_{rs})(b_s - c_r - c_s)$$
$$+ (1 - p_r - p_s + p_{rs})(-c_r - c_s) \qquad (VI.2)$$
$$= p_r b_r + (p_s - p_{rs})b_s - (c_r + c_s)$$

and in the absence of budgets the decision to undertake both is based on a comparison of π_{rs} with the expected payoff on the better of the two projects alone, where "better" means a higher expected value of the undertaking. Thus, if

$$p_r b_r - c_r > p_s b_s - c_s \qquad (VI.3)$$

then

$$\pi_{rs} > p_r b_r - c_r$$

implies

$$(p_s - p_{rs})b_s - c_s > 0 \qquad (VI.4)$$

or

$$p_s - p_{rs} > c_s/b_s$$

and research on both should be undertaken. If the inequality (VI.3) were reversed, i.e., if research on project s were more attractive than research on project r given that only a single one were to be undertaken, even though $b_r > b_s$ (the value of success on r is greater than success on s) is assumed in (VI.2), then the comparable criterion would require

$$p_r b_r - c_r > p_{rs} b_s. \qquad (VI.5)$$

This argument may easily be generalized to an arbitrary number of alternatives. Where consideration of such mutually-exclusive alternatives is to be made alongside independent ones (to be discussed below) the matrix formulation of Reiter again suggests itself:

$$B = \begin{pmatrix} p_r b_r - c_r & -p_{rs} b_s & \cdots \\ 0 & p_s b_s - c_s & \cdots \\ 0 & 0 & \cdots \end{pmatrix} \qquad (VI.6)$$

Should both projects r and s be selected the payoff using (VI.6) is the same as in (VI.2). In the matrix formulation it is possible to add an additional term, c_{rs} (which may be positive or negative), to express an adjustment to the total development costs resulting from the joint development program. This formulation also lends itself to the simultaneous consideration of three or more projects which are mutually-exclusive in this special sense. However, for every additional project we require an additional dimension in the array, the need for which arises from a term involving $p_{ijk\ldots s}$, the joint probability of success on all such projects.[50]

Additional interrelationships can arise when the probability of success on one project is affected by the undertaking of research on a non-competing project as when, for example, the research embodies similar approaches or instrumentation. These effects may be reciprocal, though not necessarily symmetric. A project r may involve a process jointly with s, so that if both developments are undertaken the probability of success on each is enhanced. However, it may be that the joint process is only a small part of the problem involved in project s although it comprises the major component of project r. Hence, if we denote by p_{rs} the probability of success on project r given that project s is also undertaken[51] it may be that $p_{rs} \neq p_{sr}$. Hence we require a nonsymmetric matrix P:

$$P = \begin{bmatrix} p_{11} & p_{12} & p_{13} & \cdots & p_{1n} \\ p_{21} & p_{22} & p_{23} & \cdots & p_{2n} \\ & & \cdots & \cdots & \\ p_{n1} & p_{n2} & p_{n3} & \cdots & p_{nn} \end{bmatrix} \qquad (VI.7)$$

where p_{ii} represents the probability of success on project i taken by itself. This may be combined with a diagonal payoff matrix B and the triangular cost matrix C, viz.,

$$B = \begin{bmatrix} b_1 & 0 & 0 & \cdots & 0 \\ 0 & b_2 & 0 & \cdots & 0 \\ 0 & 0 & b_3 & \cdots & 0 \\ & & \cdots & & \\ 0 & 0 & 0 & \cdots & b_n \end{bmatrix} \quad C = \begin{bmatrix} c_1 & c_{12} & c_{13} & \cdots & c_{1n} \\ 0 & c_2 & c_{23} & \cdots & c_{2n} \\ 0 & 0 & c_3 & \cdots & c_{3n} \\ & & \cdots & & \\ 0 & 0 & 0 & \cdots & c_n \end{bmatrix} \qquad (VI.8)$$

in the quadratic integer programming problem[52]

Maximize $\qquad\qquad X[BP - C]X^t \qquad\qquad$ (VI.9)

---

[50] Arrays of higher dimension than two can be avoided by constructing mutually exclusive compound projects into which all the interactions have already been absorbed. This may, however, not be the preferable way of proceeding.

[51] This is a change in definition from that used above.

[52] The matrix C is still triangular since terms c_{ij} enter only once.

where X is a vector of x_i as before. The quantity in brackets is a matrix which may be solved using Reiter's method. In addition, a budget constraint may be placed on the expenditures c_{ij} by utilizing a Lagrangian multiplier, as in Section IV, which may be represented by

Maximize $$X[BP - (1 - \lambda)C]X^t \qquad \text{(VI.10)}$$

for various values of λ. We may substitute λ' for the term $(1 - \lambda)$ and solve

Maximize $$X[BP - \lambda'C]X^t \qquad \text{(VI.11)}$$

where

$$BP - \lambda'C = \begin{bmatrix} p_{11}b_1 - \lambda'c_1 & p_{12}b_1 - \lambda'c_{12} & p_{13}b_1 - \lambda'c_{13} & \cdots \\ p_{21}b_2 & p_{22}b_2 - \lambda'c_2 & p_{23}b_2 - \lambda'c_{23} & \cdots \\ p_{31}b_3 & p_{32}b_3 & p_{33}b_3 - \lambda'c_3 & \cdots \\ & & \cdots & \cdots \end{bmatrix} \qquad \text{(VI.12)}$$

Finally, the methods for handling mutually-exclusive projects and mutually independent projects may be combined. Some of the columns of (VI.12) would then be as given in matrix (VI.6), with p_{rs} as defined there, and with terms below the diagonal as defined for (VI.12).

B. Nonlinear Criterion Functions

Nonlinear utility or criterion functions give rise to a host of considerations not present when simple expected value of outcomes maximization serves as the criterion. A brief discussion of some of the issues in the context of R & D project selection will conclude this presentation. As before, we continue to regard the objective of the decision maker to select the set of projects which maximizes expected utility, but the utility function is not linear in the outcomes. For simplicity we shall illustrate our remarks by reference to a quadratic utility function,

$$U(y) = y - \alpha y^2 \qquad \text{(VI.13)}$$

recognizing that this criterion is increasingly risk averse in Pratt's sense [39]. For present purposes, however, it is adequate. (α here is a preassigned, hence known and fixed, coefficient of risk aversion.)

The first observation to be made is that the assumption of a static decision procedure, i.e., one which fails to take into account other decisions which have been made in the past and will be made in the future, is no longer tenable. Utility is defined for the entire "portfolio" of projects, including both the project being considered and those already accepted and in process of being carried out. Consider, under perfect certainty, an existing portfolio of value y and two potential projects, worth z_1 and z_2. From (VI.13) we may express the utility of a sum of two outcomes, $y + z$, by

$$U(y + z) = U(y) + U(z) - 2\alpha yz \qquad \text{(VI.14)}$$

so that, given y, the requirement for acceptance of z is an increase in total utility. Since y is not subject to reduction (unlike the securities portfolio of Markowitz) the condition for acceptability reduces to

$$U(z) > 2\alpha yz \qquad (\text{VI.15})$$

With two potential independent projects with payoffs of z_1 and z_2, the outcome of a decision procedure based on criterion (VI.15) alone could depend on the order in which the projects were considered. If project one were taken up first, acceptance of both would require

a. $\qquad\qquad U(z_1) > 2\alpha z_1 y$

$\qquad\qquad\qquad\qquad\qquad\qquad\qquad\qquad\qquad (\text{VI.16})$

b. $\qquad\qquad U(z_2) > 2\alpha z_2(y + z_1) = 2\alpha z_2 y + 2\alpha z_1 z_2$

if the first had been accepted. Alternatively, taking up the decision about the second project first requires

a. $\qquad\qquad U(z_2) > 2\alpha z_2 y$

$\qquad\qquad\qquad\qquad\qquad\qquad\qquad\qquad\qquad (\text{VI.17})$

b. $\qquad\qquad U(z_1) > 2\alpha z_1(y + z_2) = 2\alpha z_1 y + 2\alpha z_1 z_2$

if the second project had been accepted. Suppose that both projects would be acceptable if they were the only ones being considered, i.e.,

a. $\qquad\qquad\qquad\qquad U(z_1) > 2\alpha z_1 y$

$\qquad\qquad\qquad\qquad\qquad\qquad\qquad\qquad\qquad (\text{VI.18})$

b. $\qquad\qquad\qquad\qquad U(z_2) > 2\alpha z_2 y$

but that while

$$U(z_1) > 2\alpha z_1(y + z_2) \qquad (\text{VI.19})$$

also

$$U(z_2) < 2\alpha z_2(y + z_1). \qquad (\text{VI.20})$$

Given such values of z_1, z_2 and y, the second project would be accepted only if it were taken up first, while this restriction would not apply to the first project.

It is clearly undesirable for a decision procedure to depend on the order in which projects are taken up. Yet, this would be the effect with naive application of a nonlinear utility function.[53] While it is true that both projects r and s would be accepted given the condition of accepting both or neither,[54] maximization of expected utility would lead to acceptance of project r alone. This may be seen by regarding (VI.19) as an equation, and rewriting (VI.18b) as

$$U(z_2) = 2\alpha z_2 y + \epsilon, \qquad \epsilon < 2\alpha z_1 z_2. \qquad (\text{VI.21})$$

---

[53] Although these illustrations make use of a quadratic utility function, the conclusion applies to a large variety of nonlinear criterion functions, in particular also to ones which are decreasingly risk averse.

[54] $U(y + z_1 + z_2) > U(y)$.

From these one may derive

a. $U(y + z_1) \equiv U(y) + U(z_1) - 2\alpha y z_1 = U(y) + 2\alpha z_1 z_2$

b. $U(y + z_2) \equiv U(y) + U(z_2) - 2\alpha y z_2 = U(y) + \epsilon < U(y) + 2\alpha z_1 z_2$

c. $U(y + z_1 + z_2) \equiv U(y) + U(z_1) + U(z_2) - 2\alpha(y z_1 + y z_2 + z_1 z_2)$

$$= U(y) + \epsilon < U(y) + 2\alpha z_1 z_2 \qquad (VI.22)$$

leading to the stated conclusion.

An additional complication when the outcomes are random variables (as they are in the present context) is that y itself, the value of the previously accepted portfolio, is also random. This requires that the joint distribution of the outcomes of present and potential projects must enter the calculations.

In the strictly static case in which selection is to be made so as to maximize the utility of the projects being chosen without regard to past selections, we first derive the criterion for the Markowitz-type of R & D project portfolio consisting only of projects which are not interrelated in the physical sense. Statistical independence, however, is not assumed. We begin with two independent projects and generalize from there. Given two projects, r and s, with development costs (negative revenues) of $(-c_r)$ and $(-c_s)$, with net present values after successful development of b_r and b_s, and with probabilities of p_{rs} of joint success, $(p_r - p_{rs})$ and $(p_s - p_{rs})$ of success on r alone and s alone, respectively, expected utility from acceptance of both projects, U_{rs}, is given by

$$U_{rs} = p_{rs}U(b_r - c_r + b_s - c_s) + (p_r - p_{rs})U(b_r - c_r - c_s)$$
$$+ (p_s - p_{rs})U(b_s - c_s - c_r) + (1 - p_r - p_s + p_{rs})U(-c_r - c_s) \quad (VI.23)$$

which simplifies to

$$U_{rs} = U_r + U_s - 2\alpha E_{rs} \qquad (VI.24)$$

where

$$U_j = p_j U(b_j - c_j) + (1 - p_j)U(-c_j) \qquad (VI.25)$$

and[55]

$$E_{ij} = p_{ij}b_i b_j - p_i b_i c_j - p_j b_j c_i + c_i c_j. \qquad (VI.26)$$

Expression (VI.24) may be generalized to any number of independent projects, so that maximization of expected utility from acceptance of a set of projects may be written in terms parallel to model (V.1), viz.,

Maximize

$$\sum_{i=1}^{n} U_i x_i - 2\alpha \sum_{i=1}^{n} \sum_{j=i+1}^{n} x_i E_{ij} x_j \qquad (VI.27)$$

subject to

$$x_i = 0,1, \qquad i = 1, \ldots, n$$

which is once more in a form suitable for solution by Reiter's method, with

---

[55] Note that the term E_{ij} is simply the product of expected outcomes, $(p_i b_i - c_i)(p_j b_j - c_j)$ with the term $p_i p_j b_i b_j$ replaced by $p_{ij}b_i b_j$.

payoff matrix

$$B = \begin{bmatrix} U_1 & -2\alpha E_{12} & -2\alpha E_{13} & \cdots & -2\alpha E_{1n} \\ 0 & U_2 & -2\alpha E_{23} & \cdots & -2\alpha E_{2n} \\ 0 & 0 & U_3 & \cdots & -2\alpha E_{3n} \\ \cdots\cdots\cdots\cdots\cdots\cdots\cdots\cdots\cdots\cdots\cdots \\ 0 & 0 & 0 & \cdots & U_n \end{bmatrix}. \qquad \text{(VI.28)}$$

A budget constraint may be appended here by use of a Lagrangian multiplier.

Unfortunately, the relatively simple structure of (VI.28) is lost in the face of any number of the project interrelationships already discussed. We single out one of these, the situation in which if parallel research is undertaken and success is achieved on both lines of attack only the project with higher expected payoff[56] is actually carried out. For two such projects, r and s, the expression for expected utility corresponding to (VI.23) is

$$U_{rs} = p_r U(b_r - c_r - c_s) + (p_s - p_{rs})U(b_s - c_s - c_r)$$
$$+ (1 - p_r - p_s + p_{rs})U(-c_r - c_s) \quad \text{(VI.29)}$$

which reduces to

$$U_{rs} = U_r + U_s - 2\alpha E_{rs} - p_{rs}[U(b_s) - 2\alpha b_s(b_r - c_r - c_s)]. \quad \text{(VI.30)}$$

Adding an independent project, v, however, requires introduction of terms involving p_{rsv}, the probability of joint success on projects r, s and v into U_{rsv}, hence losing the important property of separability, which has been the chief characteristic of our models of capital budgeting of interrelated projects.

APPENDIX A: FLOW CHART OF THE DYNAMIC PROGRAMMING CODE FOR CAPITAL BUDGETING[57]

The program flow-charted was written in MADTRAN[58] with the exception of the strategy vectors and their manipulation. Since these consist of strings of zeros and ones, memory space and time was conserved by programming these in binary arithmetic. The program as written allows for a maximum of 2000 strategies at each stage and is able to handle ten separate constraints.[59] Cord's problem (14, p. 340) involving 25 projects was solved in 63 seconds on an IBM 7094. For a rough estimate, this compares with 12 minutes reported by Cord in his application of the Lagrangian multiplier technique, but using an IBM 7070. As pointed out in the text, Cord did not obtain the optimum, and additional time would have been required to reduce the search interval. The program was also tried out on a number of interdependencies, the total number of constraints actually utilized in any one problem was six. Three additional constraints in Cord's problem increased the time utilized to 90 seconds.

---

[56] This quantity strictly should be expected utility. However, we can make our point without opening a Pandora's Box of problems of evaluating the utility of future events today, especially without complete knowledge of the future outcomes which will obtain then.

[57] The program was written by Stanley Sachar and David Ness, making use of the time-shared computer of Project MAC, an MIT research program sponsored by the Advanced Research Projects Agency, Department of Defense under the Office of Naval Research.

[58] MADTRAN is a language almost identical with FORTRAN which, however, while compiling more rapidly, is generally slower in execution.

[59] The maximum number of strategies is variable and must be smaller when ten constraints are employed. As written the computations are entirely in core.

The program does its house-keeping on multiple constraints by lexicographically ordering the vectors of payoffs and allocated budgets, weeding out intermediate solutions which are dominated. The definitions used in the flow chart are as follows:

NN = No. of projects in problem LM = No. of constraints in problem
$N(I)$ = No. of strategies at stage I M = Maximum number of strategies permitted
b_i = payoff on project i C_j = amount of resource of type j available
c_{ij} = amount of resource of type j used by project i
$b = (b_1, b_2, \ldots b_{NN})$ $c_j = (c_{1j}, c_{2j}, \ldots, c_{NN,j})$ $C = (0, C_1, C_2, \ldots, C_{LM})$
$P(I) = (b_i, -c_{i1}, -c_{i2}, \ldots, -c_{i,LM})$
$R(I) = (b_i, C_1 - c_{i1}, C_2 - c_{i2}, \ldots, C_{LM} - c_{i,LM})$
$X(I) = (0, 0, \ldots, 0, 1, 0, \ldots, 0)$ with 1 in the ith position
$X(J) = j$th strategy, i.e., a vector of 0's and 1's with 1 in the ith position if $x_i = 1$.
$\Gamma(J), T(J) = (C^t - (-b, c_1, c_2, \ldots, c_{LM})^t[X(J)]^t)^t$, a vector of payoffs and unused resources of the jth strategy. $T(J)$ is a temporary list, $\Gamma(J)$ is the revised list.

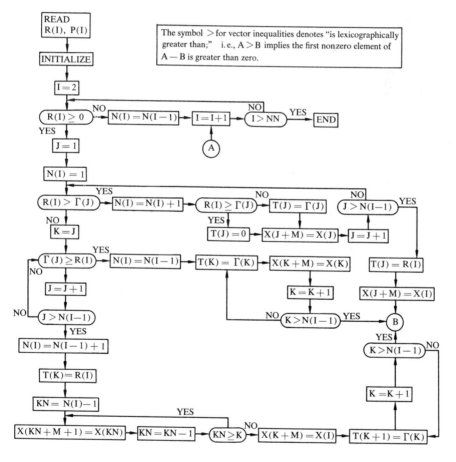

The symbol $>$ for vector inequalities denotes "is lexicographically greater than;" i.e., $A > B$ implies the first nonzero element of $A - B$ is greater than zero.

APPENDIX B: EXAMPLE USING REITER'S DISCRETE OPTIMIZING METHOD

We seek the optimal list of projects for the following payoff matrix

(B.1)
$$B = \begin{pmatrix} 3 & 0 & 2 & -1 \\ 0 & 2 & 1 & 0 \\ 0 & 0 & -1 & -3 \\ 0 & 0 & 0 & 4 \end{pmatrix}$$

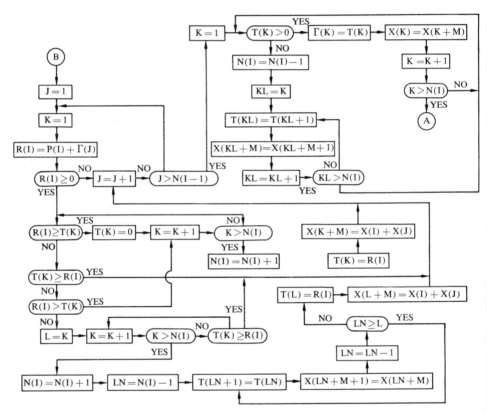

Let the (randomly or otherwise selected) starting in-list $\alpha = \{1, 3, 4\}$; i.e., we begin with a list consisting of projects 1, 3 and 4. Crossing out row 2 and column 2, we add the payoff elements not crossed out: $3 + 2 + (-1) + (-1) + (-3) + 4 = 4$. Therefore the payoff corresponding to this in-list α is $\Gamma_\alpha = 4$. In the table we give the payoffs and gradients $G_{\alpha'} = \Gamma_{\alpha'} - \Gamma_\alpha$ for all in-lists α' "connected" to α—lists which differ in only a single project index.

α'	$\Gamma_{\alpha'}$	$G_{\alpha'}$
1, 3	4	0
1, 4	6	2
3, 4	0	−4
→ 1, 2, 3, 4	7	3

The largest improvement resulting from dropping one project or adding one to the in-list $\alpha = \{1, 3, 4\}$ is 3, which is associated with $\alpha' = \{1, 2, 3, 4\}$. This forms the next starting in-list, which is once again evaluated in the table.

α'	$\Gamma_{\alpha'}$	$G_{\alpha'}$
1, 2, 3	7	0
→ 1, 2, 4	8	1
1, 3, 4	4	−3

Here the largest improvement is associated with the move to $\alpha' = \{1, 2, 4\}$, yielding a total payoff of 8. It may be seen to be a local maximum from the next table, which takes this in-list as the starting point. Only negative values for $G_{\alpha'}$ result,

α'	$\Gamma_{\alpha'}$	$G_{\alpha'}$
1, 2	5	−3
1, 4	6	−2
1, 2, 3, 4	7	−1

The local optimal list $\alpha = \{1, 2, 4\}$ turns out to be the global optimum. The tree-structure of this example is

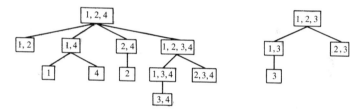

The other local optimum consists of projects 1, 2, 3 with a payoff of 7. Since the 15 possible lists are divided into two groups of 11 on the tree of the global optimum list (at left) and 4 on the tree of the local non-global optimum list (at right), the prior odds that a random starting in-list leads to the global optimum here are $\frac{11}{15} = 0.73$. For further discussion see [42].

REFERENCES

[1] ADLER, M., "The Cohen Extension to the Sharpe Diagonal Model for Portfolio Selection," unpublished paper, Carnegie Institute of Technology, May 15, 1963, revised and corrected by K. J. Cohen.

[2] ALCHIAN, A. A., "The Rate of Interest, Fisher's Rate of Return over Cost, and Keynes' Internal Rate of Return," *American Economic Review*, Dec. 1955, pp. 938–42; also in Solomon, [44].

[3] ASHER, D. T., "A Linear Programming Model for the Allocation of R and D Efforts," *IRE Transactions on Engineering Management*, Dec. 1962, pp. 154–57.

[4] BALINSKI, M. L., *On Finding Integer Solutions to Linear Programs.* Princeton: Mathematica, May 1, 1964.

[5] BAUMOL, W. J., and R. E. QUANDT, "Mathematical Programming and the Discount Rate under Capital Rationing," *Economic Journal*, June 1965, pp. 317–20.

[6] BELLMAN, R., "Comment on Dantzig's Paper on Discrete-Variable Extremum Problems," *Operations Research*, Oct. 1957, pp. 723–24.

[7] ——— and S. DREYFUS, *Applied Dynamic Programming*. Princeton: Princeton University Press, 1962.

[8] ISRAEL, A. BEN, and A. CHARNES, "On Some Problems of Diophantine Programming," *Cahiers du Centre de l'Recherche Operationelle*, 1962, pp. 215–80.

[9] CHARNES, A., and W. W. COOPER, "Chance-Constrained Programming," *Management Science*, Oct. 1959, pp. 73–79.

[10] ——— and ———, *Management Models and Industrial Applications of Linear Programming*. New York: John Wiley & Sons, 1961.

[10a] ——— and ———, "A Note on the 'Fail-Safe' Properties of the 'Generalized Lagrange Multiplier Method'," *Operations Research*, July–August 1965, pp. 673–77.

[11] ———, ———, and M. H. MILLER, "Application of Linear Programming to Financial Budgeting and the Costing of Funds," *Journal of Business*, Jan. 1959, pp. 20–46; also in Solomon, [44].

[12] ——— and S. THORE, "Planning for Liquidity in Savings and Loan Associations," ONR Research Memorandum No. 95. Evanston: Northwestern University Technological Institute, May 1964.

[13] COHEN, K. J., and B. P. FITCH, "The Average Investment Performance Index," Working Paper No. 3, Workshop on Capital Market Equilibrating Processes." Pittsburgh: Carnegie Institute of Technology, Graduate School of Industrial Administration, March 1965.

[14] CORD, J., "A Method for Allocating Funds to Investment Projects when Returns are Subject to Uncertainty," *Management Science*, Jan. 1964, pp. 335–41.

[15] DANTZIG, G., "Discrete-Variable Extremum Problems," *Operations Research*, April, 1957, pp. 266–77.

[16] DANTZIG, G. B., "Linear Programming Under Uncertainty," *Management Science*, April–July 1955, pp. 197–206.

[17] DEAN, JOEL, *Capital Budgeting*. New York: Columbia University Press, 1951.

[18] DYCKMAN, T. R., "Allocating Funds to Investment Projects when Returns are Subject to Uncertainty—A Comment," *Management Science*, Nov. 1964, pp. 348–50.

[18a] EASTMAN, W. L., "Allocating Funds to Investment Projects When Returns are Subject to Uncertainty: A Further Comment," *Management Science* (forthcoming).

[19] EVERETT, H., III, "Generalized LaGrange Multiplier Method for Solving Problems of Optimum Allocation of Resources," *Operations Research*, May–June 1963, pp. 399–417.

[19a] ———, "Comments on the Preceding Note," *Operations Research*, July–August 1965, pp. 677–78.

[20] FARRAR, D. E., *The Investment Decision Under Uncertainty*. Englewood Cliffs: Prentice-Hall, Inc., 1962.

[21] FISHER, IRVING, *The Theory of Interest*. New York: Macmillan Co., 1930.

[22] GILMORE, P. C., and R. E. GOMORY, "A Linear Programming Approach to the Cutting Stock Problem—Part II," *Operations Research*, Sept.–Oct. 1963, pp. 863–88.

[23] GLOVER, F., "The Knapsack Problem: Some Relations for an Improved Algorithm," Management Science Research Report No. 38. Pittsburgh: Carnegie Institute of Technology, Graduate School of Industrial Administration Jan. 1965.

[24] GRAVES, R., and P. WOLFE (eds.), *Recent Advances in Mathematical Programming*. New York: McGraw-Hill, 1963.

[25] HALDI, J., and L. ISAACSON, "A Linear Integer Programming Code," paper presented at the 1964 Annual Meeting of the Econometric Society, Chicago, Dec. 1964.

[26] HERTZ, D. B., "Risk Analysis in Capital Investment," *Harvard Business Review*, Jan.–Feb. 1964, pp. 95–106.

[27] HILLIER, F., "Derivation of Probabilistic Information for the Evaluation of Risky Investments," *Management Science*, April, 1963, pp. 443–57.

[28] HIRSHLEIFER, J., "Efficient Allocation of Capital in an Uncertain World," *American Economic Review*, May 1964, pp. 77–85.

[29] ———, "On the Theory of Optimal Investment," *Journal of Political Economy*, August 1958, pp. 329–52; also in Solomon, [44].

[30] KEYNES, J. M., *The General Theory of Employment, Money and Interest*. London 1936.

[31] KUNZI, H. P., and W. OETTLI, "Integer Quadratic Programming," in Graves and Wolfe, [24].

[32] LORIE, J. H., and L. J. SAVAGE, "Three Problems in Rationing Capital," *Journal of Business*, Oct. 1955, pp. 229–39; also in Solomon, [44].

[33] LUCE, D., and H. RAIFFA, *Games and Decisions*. New York: John Wiley & Sons, 1958.

[34] MARGLIN, S., *Approaches to Dynamic Investment Planning*. Amsterdam: North-Holland Publishing Company, 1963.

[35] MARKOWITZ, H. M., *Portfolio Selection*. New York: John Wiley & Sons, 1959.

[36] MARTIN, G. T., "An Accelerated Euclidean Algorithm for Integer Linear Programming," in [24], pp. 311–18.

[37] NÄSLUND, B., "A Model of Capital Budgeting Under Risk," Department of Forestry Products, Royal College of Forestry (Sweden), February 1965 (Mimeo).

[38] ———, "Decisions under Risk: Economic Applications of Chance Constrained Programming," ONR Research Memorandum No. 114, Management Sciences Research Group. Pittsburgh: Carnegie Institute of Technology, Graduate School of Industrial Administration, Nov. 1964.

[39] PRATT, J. W., "Risk Aversion in the Small and in the Large," *Econometrica*, Jan.–April 1964, pp. 122–36.

[40] REITER, S., "Choosing an Investment Program Among Interdependent Projects," *Review of Economic Studies*, Jan. 1963, pp. 32–36.

[41] ——— and G. SHERMAN, "Allocating Indivisible Resources Affording External Economies or Diseconomies," *International Economic Review*, Jan. 1962, pp. 108–35.

[42] ——— and ———, "Discrete Optimizing," Institute for Quantitative Research in Economics and Management, Paper 37, Krannert Graduate School of Industrial Administration, Purdue University.

[43] SHARPE, WILLIAM F., "A Simplified Model of Portfolio Selection," *Management Science*, Jan. 1963, pp. 277–93.

[44] SOLOMON, E. (ed.), *The Management of Corporate Capital*. Glencoe: The Free Press, 1959.

[45] WEINGARTNER, H. MARTIN, "The Excess Present Value Index—A Theoretical Basis and Critique," *Journal of Accounting Research*, Fall, 1963, pp. 213–24.

[46] ———, *Mathematical Programming and the Analysis of Capital Budgeting Problems*. Englewood Cliffs: Prentice-Hall, Inc., 1963.

[47] YOUNG, R. D., "A Primal (All-Integer) Integer Programming Algorithm: Antecedents, Description, Proof of Finiteness, Exemplification," Working Paper No. 52. Stanford: Stanford University Graduate School of Business, Dec. 1964.

PART III

Capital Budgeting
Applications

6

RELEVANT THINKING
FOR INVESTMENT DECISIONS

WILLIAM H. MECKLING

In the following brief paper Professor Meckling presents some of the practical aspects of investment decisions. He considers problems concerning the selection of the appropriate discount rate and the computation and estimation of costs.

Most business decisions are investment decisions in the sense that they have consequences which extend into the future. This article is directed to the problem of performing analyses as a basis for making major investment decisions—those that involve significant dollar amounts.

The distinctive feature of investment decisions is that they involve streams of receipts and outlays over future time—the receipts streams being generated through the sale of output, the outlay streams being generated as a consequence of costs incurred in supplying that output.

The first requirement for undertaking any analysis of an investment decision is a rule or criterion to serve as a basis for making decisions. We can, I believe, without serious distortion assert that the fundamental objective of the firm is to maximize its value. The decision rule consistent with that purpose is: "Adopt any project for which the present value of the associated stream of *net* receipts, discounted at the appropriate rate of interest, is greater than zero."[1]

The concept of present value as used here is a familiar one. Present value is defined by the equation:

$$V_0 = \frac{s_1}{1 + i} + \frac{s_2}{(1 + i)^2} + \cdots + \frac{s_n}{(1 + i)^n}$$

Or, with allowance for an immediate outlay, as

$$V_0 = -c_0 + \frac{s_1}{1 + i} + \frac{s_2}{(1 + i)^2} + \cdots + \frac{s_n}{(1 + i)^n}$$

William H. Meckling, "Relevant Thinking for Investment Decisions," *Management Accounting*, XLVII (February 1966), 8–11. Reprinted by permission.

[1] Jack Hirshleifer, James C. DeHaven and Jerome W. Milliman, *Water Supply: Economics, Technology, and Policy*, The University of Chicago Press, Chicago, Ill., 1960, p. 152.

Where V = the present value, c = the outlay at the inception of the project, s = the annual net receipts, i = the annual discount or interest rate and the subscripts and superscripts indicate the year (0 to n). The latter equation may be regarded as our basic formula for discounting net receipts streams.

The phrase "appropriate rate of interest" in our decision rule above, the i in our equation, conceals a multitude of problems. One of the most serious arises over the question of how differences in risk, that is, differences in variability of outcome among alternative investment opportunities are handled. In particular, should higher interest rates be used for higher risk investments in computing present value?

Without attempting to defend the proposition here, I shall simply assert that the correct interest rate for firms to use is the *market determined* rate for investments of *equal risk*. This means higher interest rates should be used for investments involving greater risks.

With that background on the general problem, let me turn to the specific question of the costs used for computing present value.

COMPUTING THE COST

In the first place, there is no distinction between capital costs and operating costs; any cost is simply treated as a negative item in a stream of net receipts. What is important is taking into account the timing of the outlays since the further they are into the future, the smaller is their present value.

Next, no allowance for depreciation or amortization is needed either. Since the cost of capital is fully taken into account at the time the expenditures are incurred, if we charged depreciation or interest, we would be guilty of double counting.

As a matter of fact, our net receipts stream is very similar to the accounting concept of cash flow, except when assets already in possession of a firm are used as a part of a new investment activity. Where such assets have value in alternative uses, an annual charge equal to their value in the next best alternative must also be included as a negative receipt in the present-value formula.

One further complication is the salvage value to be included as positive receipts, especially when assets which are a part of the investment decision have different useful lives—buildings versus machinery, for example. In such cases, the estimated salvage value of the longer lived assets may be a significant consideration. Estimating the useful lifetime and salvage value is, of course, a very uncertain proposition.

Frequently, in applications of our present-value equations, questions arise as to whether some item ought to be included as a cost in computing the net receipts stream. When such questions arise, the answers should be sought in fundamental economics. Costs should be measured in terms of foregone alternatives. Costs are relevant only in the context of decisions and the relevant costs are those that are incremental to the decision in question. While these concepts are obvious, in practice they are frequently ignored. The most common error is to exclude consequences of a decision which are true opportunity costs and are incremental to the decision. On the other hand, not infrequently, consequences are included as costs which are not incremental to the decision in question.

Semantically, one is less likely to err in deciding whether a cost is relevant if he thinks in terms of "avoidable costs" and "unavoidable costs" rather than "fixed" and "variable" costs. Any cost that is avoidable is relevant for the investment decision under question.

A related problem is that of joint products. The difficulty arises because there is a strong inclination to want to allocate costs among the joint products. If the costs are truly joint, however, any allocation is purely arbitrary and indefensible. From a decision standpoint, such allocations are also unnecessary.

DIFFICULTIES IN COST ESTIMATION

Let us turn now from the analytic problems encountered in providing costs for our present value equation to a brief discussion of the difficulties faced in cost estimation. The level of our uncertainty depends critically on the kind of investment under consideration. At one extreme are the routine purchases of equipment where errors in our estimates are negligible.

My own experience has largely dealt with decisions at the other end of the spectrum, where cost estimates were sometimes employed for systems that were widely different technologically from anything ever assembled.

In general, our experience with these estimates was so bad that we undertook a series of special studies of the relationship between actual and predicted costs. In retrospect, most of what we discovered seems fairly obvious. Cost estimates generally are biased downward. There are several reasons for this—not the least of which is that proponents of new things habitually are over-optimistic and must be so in order to sell their product. But there is a subtle second reason which is seldom recognized. In order to compare actual costs with estimated costs, one must use data taken from projects which are selected for completion. There are no actual costs for projects which are rejected. But the set of projects that gets selected for completion is not a random sample from the set of all projects for which cost estimates are made. Indeed, it is a biased set since projects for which costs are underestimated are more likely to be selected precisely because their costs were underestimated. Thus, the biased character of the set of projects on which data exists leads to a bias in the direction of underestimating costs.

Aside from the bias in cost estimates, there is also a great deal of variation; variation which reflects basic uncertainties. The study also revealed that both the bias and the variation were increasing functions of the stage of the development and of the size of technological advance being sought as judged by physical scientists and engineers.

While the focus of that study was on military investments, I suspect that the same general tendencies apply in other cases. Evidence from public works projects generally supports that hypothesis. Public works projects costs are almost always biased downward, with a substantial variance in the size of the error. Apparently, the estimates of residential construction costs similarly tend to be biased downward.

One reason that costs tend to be underestimated is that some resources that are required to carry out a specific investment program are completely overlooked in the analysis of the problem. For example, the introduction of new equipment involves an extensive training program, or the equipment will have to be operated in specially air-conditioned quarters. The moral here is that a determined effort to include all costs frequently has a big payoff.

Because of the enthusiasm and optimism of those who generate particular investment ideas, it is often desirable to have another group make an independent assessment of costs. Where a completely independent estimate is not possible, it frequently is possible to conduct a critical examination of the initial estimates. Open debate and discussion of cost estimates is something to be encouraged.

One important technique for dealing with uncertainty is the use of sensitivity analyses. The fundamental idea of sensitivity analyses is very simple. Where we are substantially uncertain about specific estimates, we conduct a paper experiment. We introduce different estimates into the present-value equation and see how those variations affect the estimate of present value. Thus, if we are buying a new piece of equipment and are quite uncertain about what its operating costs will be, we try a range of operating costs in our equation and determine the effect on our estimate of present value. One of the side benefits of undertaking such sensitivity analyses is simply that it forces someone to think about where the major uncertainties lie.

A final point about dealing with uncertainty is, I think, worth making. One is never forced to make an investment decision on the basis of whatever information happens to be at hand. While this is again a point which seems obvious, it also is one that is often sadly neglected. It is almost always possible to collect information which will reduce uncertainty, that is, which will on the average reduce the errors in our estimates. Of course, collecting additional information usually involves costs; but the real mark of an accomplished strategist in making investment decisions is in properly balancing the cost of additional information against the value of that information.

7

COST-BENEFIT ANALYSIS: A SURVEY

A. R. PREST and R. TURVEY*

Cost benefit analysis represents an extension of capital budgeting theory. It is a form of investment planning for project appraisal which considers near and distant effects as well as an enumeration and evaluation of relevant costs and benefits. It has emphasized attempting to quantify benefits (including nonmonetary ones) and costs which hitherto had been considered only in a general and qualitative judgmental way. The procedures, potential benefits, and limitations of this method of analysis are developed in the following survey article.

The order of discussion in this survey article will be as follows: in I we shall outline the development and scope of the subject in general terms; II will be concerned with general principles; in III we shall survey particular applications of cost-benefit techniques, examining the uses made of them in a variety of fields—water-supply projects, transport, land usage, health, education, research, etc. We shall proceed to a general summing up in IV, and conclude with a bibliography.

I. INTRODUCTION

Cost-benefit analysis[1] is a practical way of assessing the desirability of projects, where it is important to take a long view (in the sense of looking at repercussions in the further, as well as the nearer, future) and a wide view (in the sense of allowing for side-effects of many kinds on many persons, industries, regions, etc.), i.e., it implies the enumeration and evaluation of all the relevant costs and benefits. This involves drawing on a variety of traditional sections of economic study—welfare economics, public finance, resource economics—and trying to weld these components into a coherent

A. R. Prest and R. Turvey, "Cost-Benefit Analysis: A Survey," *The Economic Journal*, LXXV (December 1965), 683–735. Reprinted by permission. This represents an excerpt from a longer article which can be read in full in Volume III of *Surveys of Economic Theory*, published by Messrs. Macmillan (London) and St. Martin's Press (New York) for the American Economic Association and the Royal Economic Society, 1966. Anyone interested in the actual applications of cost-benefit analysis and in the literature of the subject should refer to the complete survey.

* This is the sixth and last of the series of surveys supported by the Rockefeller Foundation. The authors are indebted to M. E. Beesley, J. L. Carr, O. Eckstein, M. J. Farrell, M. S. Feldstein, C. D. Foster, R. N. McKean, E. Mishan, A. T. Peacock, M. H. Peston and C. S. Shoup for most valuable comments and suggestions on an earlier draft.

[1] Alternatively christened "investment planning" or "project appraisal."

whole. Although the subject of cost-benefit analysis has come into prominence among economists only in recent years, it has quite a long history, especially in France, where Dupuit's classic paper on the utility of public works, one of the most original path-breaking writings in the whole history of economics, appeared as long ago as 1844 [19]. In the present century cost-benefit analysis first came into prominence in the United States. Here, according to Hammond [32], it was "in origin an administrative device owing nothing to economic theory and adapted to a strictly limited type of Federal activity—the improvement of navigation" (*op. cit.*, p. 3).

The River and Harbor Act 1902 required a board of engineers to report on the desirability of Army Corps of Engineers' river and harbor projects, taking into account the amount of commerce benefited and the cost. Another Act further required a statement of local or special benefits as a means for charging local interests with part of the cost. So the Corps of Engineers worked out valuation techniques confined to tangible costs and benefits.

In the thirties, with the New Deal, the idea of a broader social justification for projects developed. The Flood Control Act of 1936 thus authorized Federal participation in flood-control schemes "if the benefits to whomsoever they may accrue are in excess of the estimated costs." The practice of making analyses then spread to the other agencies concerned with water-development projects. The purpose was not only to justify projects but also to help decide who should pay.

By the end of the war, agencies had broadened their approaches by:

> *a.* bringing in secondary or indirect benefits and costs;
> *b.* including intangibles.

In 1950 an inter-agency committee produced "The Green Book" [40], an attempt to codify and agree on general principles. It was noteworthy as bringing in the language of welfare economics.

Interest among economists in this technique has grown tremendously in the last few years, as can be seen from the number of references cited in the bibliography and the years in which these works appeared.[2] There seem to be several reasons for this. One has been the growth of large investment projects—absorbing a large amount of resources, having repercussions over a long period of time or substantially affecting prices and outputs of other products, etc. Another obvious reason is the growth of the public sector,

---

[2] Alternatively, one can look at earlier works to see what their authors had to say about the principles of public investment expenditures. If one selects Dalton [16] for this purpose—and in doing this one can hardly be accused of selecting someone uninterested in the subject—one finds the following kind of statement: "There is thus a large field for the intervention of public authorities to increase economic provision for the future and to create a better balance between its component elements. These two objects furnish the key to nearly all public expenditure designed to increase productive power "(*op. cit.*, p. 157). This is unexceptionable but hardly a complete guide to policy-makers.

e.g., the Central Government, local authorities and public enterprises such as nationalized industries accounted for 45% of gross fixed investment in the United Kingdom in 1963, compared with 33% in 1938. A technique which is explicitly concerned with the wide consequences of investment decisions is obviously of much more interest today than it was twenty-five years ago. Another reason for increasing interest by economists is the rapid development in recent years of such techniques as operations research, systems analysis, etc., both in the public and the private sectors of the economy. This is a point on which McKean [53] has laid particular emphasis.

It is always important, and perhaps especially so in economics, to avoid being swept off one's feet by the fashions of the moment. In the case of cost-benefit analysis, one must recognize that it is a method which can be used inappropriately as well as appropriately. There are two very clear general limitations of principle (as distinct from the many more of practice) which must be recognized at the outset. First, cost-benefit analysis as generally understood is only a technique for taking decisions within a framework which has to be decided upon in advance and which involves a wide range of considerations, many of them of a political or social character. Secondly, cost-benefit techniques as so far developed are least relevant and serviceable for what one might call large-size investment decisions. If investment decisions are so large, relative to a given economy (e.g., a major dam project in a small country), that they are likely to alter the constellation of relative outputs and prices over the whole economy, the standard technique is likely to fail us, for nothing less than some sort of general equilibrium approach would suffice in such cases. This means that the applicability of the technique to underdeveloped countries is likely to be less than is sometimes envisaged, as so many investment projects involve large structural changes in such areas. Of course, this does not rule out all applications of this technique in such countries, as a number of valuable studies (e.g., Hawkins [34], Farmer [22]) bear witness. Nor should it do so, given the shortage of capital resources in such countries. The point is simply that one must remain more acutely aware of the limitations of the technique in these cases.

So much for the general limitations of cost-benefit analysis. It must be made clear at this point that this survey has particular limitations as well. First, cost-benefit analysis has many facets and many applications[3] which we cannot hope to cover fully. There are therefore gaps in both subject matter and references. Secondly, a good deal of the material in the field lies unpublished in the files of government departments or international agencies and is therefore inaccessible. Third, there is no discussion of such maximization

---

[3] The bibliography cited by McKean [53] contains references to works on, e.g., government budgeting, capital budgeting, strategy, investment theory, welfare economics, highway pricing, operational research, staff and management control.

methods as linear and non-linear programming, simulation, game theory, etc. Finally, we shall confine ourselves to the applications of these techniques in economies which are not centrally planned and where there is a reasonable amount of recognition of the principle of consumer sovereignty. This should not be taken to mean that we think that cost-benefit analysis has no relevance at all in centrally planned economies, but simply that we are not attempting to deal with such cases.

II. GENERAL PRINCIPLES

1. Preliminary Considerations

(a) STATEMENT OF THE PROBLEM

As we have seen, cost-benefit analysis is a way of setting out the factors which need to be taken into account in making certain economic choices. Most of the choices to which it has been applied involve investment projects and decisions—whether or not a particular project is worthwhile, which is the best of several alternative projects, or when to undertake a particular project. We can, however, apply the term "project" more generally than this. Cost-benefit analysis can also be applied to proposed changes in laws or regulations, to new pricing schemes and the like. An example is furnished by proposals for regulating the traffic on urban roads. Such schemes involve making economic choices along the same lines as investment schemes. As choice involves maximization, we have to discuss what it is that decision-makers want to maximize. The formulation which, as a description, best covers most cost-benefit analyses examined in the literature we are surveying is as follows: the aim is to maximize the present value of all benefits less that of all costs, subject to specified constraints.

This formulation is very general, but it does at least enable us to set out a series of questions, the answers to which constitute the general principles of cost-benefit analysis:

    1. Which costs and which benefits are to be included?
    2. How are they to be valued?
    3. At what interest rate are they to be discounted?
    4. What are the relevant constraints?

Needless to say, there is bound to be a certain degree of arbitrariness in classifying questions under these four headings, but that cannot be helped.

(b) A GENERAL ISSUE

Before we can take these questions seriatim it is convenient to discuss an issue which involves more than one of these questions. It arises because the conditions for a welfare maximum are not likely to be fulfilled throughout the economy. If they were, and so resource allocation were optimal, the marginal social rate of time preference and the (risk-adjusted) marginal social rate of return from investment would coincide. A single rate of interest would then serve both to compare benefits and costs of different dates and to measure the opportunity cost of that private investment which is displaced by the need to provide resources for the projects in question. As things are, however, no single rate of interest will fulfill both functions simultaneously; in a non-optimal world there are two things to be measured and not one.

The problem has been discussed by a number of authors, including Eckstein [20, 21], Steiner [80], Marglin [48] and Feldstein [23, 24, 25]. They suggest that the costs and benefits of a project are the time streams of consumption foregone and provided by that project. The nature of this approach emerges clearly from Feldstein's remarks on the social opportunity cost of funds transferred from the private sector to the public sector in [25]:

> Part of the money taken from the private sector decreases consumption immediately, while the rest decreases investment and therefore future consumption. A pound transferred from consumption in a particular year has, by definition, a social value in that year of £1. But a pound transferred from private investment is worth the discounted value of the future consumption that would have occurred if the investment had been made. The original investment generates an income stream to investors and workers. Some of this income is spent on consumption and the remainder is invested. Each of these subsequent investments generates a new income stream and thus consumption and further investment. The final result is an aggregate consumption time-stream generated by the original investment. It is the current value of this aggregate that is the social opportunity cost of a one pound decrease in private investment.

The application of this approach to both costs and benefits produces a complicated expression for the present worth of a project's benefits less its costs. Nobody has as yet succeeded in quantifying such expressions, however,[4] so at present the approach can only serve as a reference-standard for judging simpler but more practicable ways of tackling the problem. Meanwhile, we note that the problem arises to the extent: (i) that a project's benefits are reinvested or create new investment opportunities, or (ii) that

---

[4] "Estimating many of the variables and parameters needed to calculate net social benefit may indeed be difficult" (Feldstein [23], p. 126).

some of the funds used for the project would otherwise have been invested or that the project renders impossible some other and mutually exclusive investment project. If neither of these conditions is fulfilled; if, in other words, benefits and costs both consist exclusively of consumption (directly provided and, respectively, precluded by the project), then these complications do not arise, and the problem is reduced to one of choosing an appropriate social time preference rate of discount.

2. The Main Questions

(a) ENUMERATION OF COSTS AND BENEFITS

(i) Definition of a Project. In most cases the scope and nature of the projects which are to be submitted to cost-benefit analysis will be clear. For the sake of completeness, however, we must make the point that if one authority is responsible for producing A goods and B goods, then in judging between A goods investment projects of different sizes it must take into account the effect of producing more A goods on its output of B goods. There are all sorts of complications here: relationships between A and B goods may be on the supply or demand side, they may be direct (in the sense of A influencing B) or indirect (in the sense of A influencing C, which influences B) and so on. One illustration is the operations of an authority responsible for a long stretch of river; if it puts a dam at a point upstream this will affect the water level, and hence the operations of existing or potential dams downstream. Construction of a fast motorway, which in itself speeds up traffic and reduces accidents, may lead to more congestion or more accidents on feeder roads if they are left unimproved. All that this amounts to saying is that where there are strong relationships on either the supply or the demand side, allowances must be made for these in cost-benefit calculations. We shall return to this point later, when discussing investment criteria.

(ii) Externalities. We now come to the wide class of costs and benefits which accrue to bodies other than the one sponsoring a project, and the equally wide issue of how far the sponsoring body should take them into account. We shall discuss the general principles at stake and then apply them to particular cases.

McKean [53, Chap. 8] discusses the distinction between technological and pecuniary *spillovers* at length. The essential points are that progenitors of public investment projects *should* take into account the external effects of their actions insofar as they alter the physical production possibilities of other producers or the satisfactions that consumers can get from given resources; they *should not* take side-effects into account if the sole effect is via prices of products or factors. One example of the first type is when the construction of a reservoir by the upstream authority of a river basin necessitates more dredging by the downstream authority. An example of the second type is when the improvement of a road leads to greater profitability of the garages and restaurants on that road, employment of more labor by them, higher rent payments to the relevant landlords, etc. In general, this will *not* be an additional benefit to be credited to the road investment, even if the extra profitability, etc., of the garages on one road is not offset by lower profitability of garages on the other, which are now less used as a result of the traffic diversion. Any net difference in profitability and any net rise in rents and land values is simply a reflection of the benefits of more journeys being undertaken, etc., than before, and it would be double counting if these were included too. In other words, we have to eliminate the purely transfer or distributional items from a cost-benefit evaluation: we are concerned with the value of the increment of output arising from a given investment and not with the increment in value of existing assets. In still other words, we measure costs and benefits on the assumption of a given set of prices, and the incidental and consequential price changes of goods and factors should be ignored.[5]

No one pretends that this distinction is a simple one to maintain in practice; there may well be results from investment which are partially technological and partially pecuniary. Nor is the task of unravelling made easier by the fact that some of the transfers occasioned by investment projects may affect the distribution of income significantly, and hence the pattern of demand. But as a general guiding principle the distinction is most valuable.

We now consider the application of this principle. First of all, an investing agency must try to take account of obvious technological spillovers, such as the effects of flood control measures or storage dams on the productivity of land at other points in the vicinity. In some cases no explicit action may be needed, e.g., these effects may be internal to different branches of the same agency, or some system of compensation may be prescribed by law. But in others there should at least be an attempt to correct for the most obvious and important repercussions. Although in principle corrections are needed whatever the relationship between the interacting organizations, it must be expected that in practice the compulsion to take side-effects into account will be much greater if similar organizations are involved, e.g., one local authority is more likely to take account of the costs it imposes on other bodies if those mainly affected are one or two local authorities than if they are a large multitude of individuals.

---

[5] Apart from allowances necessary to get a measure of the change of surplus.

(iii) Secondary Benefits. The notion that some pecuniary spillovers are properly included in benefits has appeared in a particular guise in arguments about secondary benefits. The American discussion of this matter has centred on the benefit estimation procedures used by the Bureau of Reclamation in respect of irrigation projects. In their analysis of the problem, McKean [53], Eckstein [20] and Margolis [52] all start by describing these procedures. The essential principle can be made clear by taking the case of irrigation which results in an increase in grain production, where the direct or primary benefits are measured as the value of the increase in grain output less the associated increase in farmer's costs.

The increased grain output will involve increased activity by grain merchants, transport concerns, millers, bakers and so on, and hence, it is asserted, will involve an increase in their profits. If the ratio of total profits in all these activities to the value of grain at the farm is 48 % then secondary benefits of 48 % of the value of the increase in grain output are credited to the irrigation project. These are called "stemming" secondary benefits. "Induced" secondary benefits, on the other hand, are the extra profits made from activities which sell to farmers. The profit rate here has been computed as averaging 18 % of farmers' purchases.

All the three authors mentioned are highly critical of these notions, as they were set out by the Bureau of Reclamation in 1952. We shall not give a blow-by-blow account of the arguments of each author, but instead attempt to provide our own synthesis.

Where the output of a project has a market value this value plus any consumer's surplus can be taken as the measure of the gross benefit arising from the project. But where the output either is not sold or is sold at a price fixed solely with reference to cost-sharing considerations, it is necessary to impute a value to the output. Thus, in the case of irrigation water, a value is obtained by working out what the water is worth to farmers as the excess of the value of the increased output which it makes possible over the cost of the necessary increase in all the farmers' other inputs. The question now arises whether we should not impute a value to the increased farm output just as we have imputed one to the water instead of taking the market value of that output. Thus, supposing (to simplify the argument) that wheat is the only farm output, that all the wheat is used to make flour and that all the flour is used to make bread, why should we not value the water by taking the value of the increased output of bread and deducting the increase in farmers', millers' and bakers' costs? Consumption is, after all, the end of all economic activity, so is not what matters the value of the increase in consumption of bread made possible by the irrigation project less the sacrifice of alternative consumption involved—as measured by increased farming, milling and baking costs?

The answer must be that a properly functioning price mechanism performs the function of imputing values for us. It does so not only as regards the increase in farmers' costs (as the argument implicitly assumes) but also as regards the increase in their output (as it seems to deny). The market demand for wheat is a derived demand, and so reflects the value of extra bread and the marginal costs of milling, baking, etc. Imputation of values by the analyst is thus necessary only where there is no market for a product, i.e., only for the water itself.

We conclude, therefore, that if the conditions for optimal resource allocation are fulfilled in the rest of the economy the estimate of benefits obtained by using the price of wheat and the price of farming inputs constitutes an adequate measure. Putting the matter the other way round, we need worry about secondary benefits (or, for that matter, costs) only to the extent that market prices fail to reflect marginal social costs and benefits. The real problem concerning secondary benefits (and costs) is thus a matter of second-best allocation problems.

(iv) Project Life. Estimation of length of life is clearly a highly subjective process depending on assessments of the physical length of life, technological changes, shifts in demand, emergence of competing products and so on. The effect of any error will depend on the rate of discount adopted; the higher this is, the less do errors of estimation matter. Some investigations seem to show that different assumptions about lengths of life do not affect the viability of schemes to an enormous extent (Foster and Beesley [28]). We have here, incidentally, one example of the scope for sensitivity analysis, where the calculations are repeated many times for different values of variables. This is an extremely important tool when estimates of costs and benefits are uncertain.

(b) VALUATION OF COSTS AND BENEFITS

(i) The Relevant Prices. When we are dealing with costs and benefits which can be expressed in terms of money it is generally agreed that adjustments need to be made to the expected prices of future inputs and outputs to allow for anticipated changes in relative prices of the items involved (including expected changes in interest rates over time), but not for expected changes in the *general* price level. The essential principle is that all prices must be reckoned on the same basis, and for convenience this will usually be the price-level prevailing in the initial year.[6] Future developments in output levels have also to be taken into account, e.g., it is customary in cost-benefit

---

[6] Hirshleifer [37, p. 143] argues that, since the "true" interest rate lies below the "monetary" one when prices are expected to rise, a downward adjustment should be made to market rates to allow for this.

studies of highway improvements to allow for the long-term trend of traffic growth.

(ii) Non-marginal Changes.   With the exceptions discussed below, market prices are used to value the costs and benefits of a project. Difficulties arise when investment projects are large enough to affect these prices. In the case of final products, the benefits accruing from investment cannot be measured by multiplying the additional quantum of output either by the old or the new price. The former would give an over-estimate and the latter an underestimate. What is needed, as has long been recognized (Dupuit [19]), is a measure of the addition to the area under the demand curve, which, on the assumption that the marginal utility of money remains unchanged, is an appropriate measure of the money value of the benefits provided, in the sense of assessing what the recipients would pay rather than go without them. When the demand curve is linear an unweighted average of before and after prices will suffice; but more complicated techniques are necessary for other forms of demand function—when they are known. In the case of intermediate products, the demand curve is a derived one, and so it can only be a perfect reflector of social benefit if the optimum welfare conditions are met all along the line. If this condition is satisfied the gross benefit arising from a project concerned with intermediate products is measured by the market value of sales plus any increase in consumers' and producers' surplus in respect of any final products based on the intermediate ones.

On the costs side there is a double problem, clearly distinguished in Lerner's treatment of indivisibilities [45]. First, it is necessary to adjust prices of factors so as to eliminate any rental elements, which will be measured by excesses over transfer earnings in their next best alternative use. Second, one has an exactly analogous problem to the demand side, in that as more and more of a factor is absorbed in any one line of output the price of the alternative product which it might have been making rises further and further. Therefore we are faced with the choice between valuation of factors at the original price (i.e., that ruling prior to the expansion of output of the commodity in question), the ultimate price, or some intermediate level. On the assumption of linearity, a price half-way between the original and ultimate levels will meet the bill, as on the demand side. Obviously, either or both of these two types of adjustments may be necessary at any particular time, and so to this extent the adjustments for indivisibilities on the costs side are likely to be more complex than those on the benefit side.

(iii) Market Imperfections.   Departures from Pareto-optimum situations arise when monopolistic elements or other imperfections in goods or factor markets are such as to twist relative outputs away from those which would prevail under competitive conditions. In cases of this kind investment decisions based on valuations of costs and benefits at market prices may not be appropriate; failure to correct for these distortions is likely to lead to misallocations of investment projects between different industries.

The relevance of this point for public decisions concerning investment is several-fold. First, if a public authority in a monopolistic position behaves like a private monopolist in its pricing and output policy its investment decisions will not comply with the principles of efficient allocation of resources unless the degree of monopoly is uniform throughout the economy. Secondly, complications may arise when there is monopolistic behavior at a later stage in the production process. This can be illustrated by the example of an irrigation project which enables more sugar-beet to be grown, and hence more sugar to be refined. If the refiners enjoy a monopolistic position the sugar-beet farmers' demand for irrigation water will not be a sufficient indication of the merits of the irrigation project. If the refiners were producing at the (higher) competitive level they would absorb more beet, and this would in turn react back on the demand for irrigation water.

A third illustration is in respect of factor supplies. If the wages which have to be paid to the labor engaged on an investment project include some rental element and are greater than their marginal opportunity costs, then a deduction must be made to arrive at an appropriate figure: conversely, if wages are squeezed below marginal opportunity costs by monopsony practices.

Fourthly, there may be an excess of average over marginal costs. This raises the well-known difficulty that if prices are equated to short-run marginal costs, as they must be to ensure short-period efficiency, the enterprise will run at a loss. Various ways (see, e.g., Hicks [36]) of getting over the problem have been suggested, but there are snags in all of them. Charges can be made, e.g., by means of a two-tariff, but this is likely to deter some consumers whose marginal valuation of the output exceeds its marginal cost. Various systems of discriminatory charges can be devised, but these may imply inquisitorial powers on the part of the authorities. Voluntary subscriptions can be asked for, but this runs into the Wicksell objection in respect of collective goods. If none of these solutions is acceptable one must be prepared to countenance losses. So this is still another case where investment decisions have to be divorced from accounting computations of profits. Instead, they must be based on notions of what people would be willing to pay or what the project "ought to be" worth to customers, as Hicks [36] puts it. It must be emphasized that this is not a case where prices of goods or factors are imperfect measures of benefits and costs *per se*, but where the present value of net receipts no longer measures benefits.

These are all examples of what is fundamentally the same problem: the inapplicability of investment decision rules derived from a perfectly competitive state of affairs to a world where such a competitive situation no longer holds. It should be noted that there are two possible ways of making the necessary accounting adjustments: either a correction can be made to the actual level of costs (benefits), or the costs (benefits) arising from the market can be taken as they stand but a corresponding correction has to be made to the estimation of benefits (costs). Normally, the first of these two methods would be less complicated and less liable to cause confusion.

(iv) Taxes and Controls. Imperfect competition constitutes only one case of divergence between market price and social cost or benefit. Another is that of taxes on expenditure. Most economists prefer to measure taxed inputs at their factor cost rather than at their market value, though the latter would be appropriate when the total supply of the input in question has a zero elasticity of supply, e.g., an imported item subject to a strict quota. A possible extension of this particular example relates to the cost of imported items in an economy with a fairly high level of tariff protection where it could be argued that price including duty is the best measure of social cost, because in the absence of protection the country's equilibrium exchange rate would be lower. Perhaps the most important example of a tax which it has been decided to exclude from costs is the estimation of fuel savings resulting from road improvements [14].

Public decisions may properly differ from private ones in the investment field in respect of direct tax payments too. While private profit-making decisions should allow for income and profits tax payments, this is not apposite in the public sector. What one is primarily concerned with here is a measurement of cost which corresponds to the use of real resources[7] but excludes transfer payments. Hence profits or income taxes on the income derived by a public authority from its project are irrelevant.

As an example of government controls, we may take agricultural price supports and production controls. There seem to have been cases in the past in the United States (e.g., the Missouri Basin project) where estimates of the benefits from sugar-beet production were made without taking any notice of existing sugar-beet quotas or considering whether sugar-beet production would actually be allowed to increase! Hard as it is to cope with refinements of this sort, obviously some attempt must be made to take cognizance of the more blatant discrepancies.

(v) Unemployment. A divergence of social cost from private cost which is sometimes of major importance arises when there is unemployment. When there is an excess supply at the current market price of any input that price overstates the social cost of using that input. Furthermore, when there is general unemployment, expenditure upon a project, by creating a multiplier

---

[7] Additional government expenditures necessitated by a public authority project should be included as part of its costs. But whether these expenditures are, or are not, financed by taxes on that authority is irrelevant.

When public projects are being compared with private ones there must obviously be a common standard of comparison in respect of transfers to and by government, the simplest being to ignore them.

effect, will create additional real incomes in the rest of the economy. Hence the use of market values to ascertain direct costs and benefits of a project overstates its social costs and underestimates its total benefits (by the amount of "induced benefits"). Under these conditions almost any project is better for the country than no project, so that, to achieve sub-optimization, autonomous public agencies should bring these considerations into their benefit and cost calculations, while agencies subject to central government control over their expenditure should either choose the same or be told to do so. This simple picture only holds, however, when there is but one issue to decide: shall a particular project be initiated or not? But such a choice never exists in this solitary state. The Government can choose between public works and other methods of curing unemployment. The agencies responsible for the public works can choose between a number of possible projects, some of them mutually exclusive (e.g., the choice between building a four- or six-lane motorway along a particular alignment). And it is not at all obvious that unemployment-adjusted estimates of costs and benefits constitute the right tool for making these choices.

The arguments against correcting costs for an excess of the market price of factors over the price which would clear the market for them and against including multiplier effects in benefits are largely[8] practical (cf. McKean [53]):

    a. It is easier to allow for the overpricing of labour which is to be used in constructing or operating a project than to allow for the overpricing of equipment, fuel, materials, etc., which are overpriced because they, too, include in their costs some overpriced labour. Yet if correction is made for project labour costs only, the relative social costs of project labour and of other inputs may be more poorly estimated than if no correction at all is made.

    b. Correcting future costs requires estimates of future unemployment. Government agencies are not usually equipped to make such forecasts, and governments may be reluctant to provide them on a realistic basis in view of the difficulty of keeping them out of public notice.

    c. The effect of a project upon unemployment depends not only upon the expenditure which it involves but also upon the way it is financed, and this may not be known to the people doing the cost-benefit analysis (e.g., in the case of an agency financed by government grants).

These arguments suggest that in most cases it is best for unemployment policy to be left to the central government and for the agencies responsible for public works to confine their corrections of market prices on account of under-employment (i.e., overpricing) to divergences which are local or which relate to some specialized factor of production. National unemployment, to take an example, should be no concern of the National Coal Board,

---

[8] But not entirely: it is possible to conceive of an unemployment situation in which shadow cost pricing would make a very large number of investment projects pass a cost-benefit test—in fact, a larger number than would be needed to reach full employment. The problem is to fix the shadow prices so that one can select the best projects but not so many of them that one has more than full employment.

but the alleged lack of alternative employment opportunities for miners in certain coalfields should.

(vi) Collective Goods. Market prices clearly cannot be used to value benefits which are not capable of being marketed. Thus we meet the collective goods issue (Samuelson [72, 73, 74], Musgrave [60], Head [35]). The essential point is that some goods and services supplied by Government are of a collective nature in the sense that the quantity supplied to any one member of the relevant group cannot be independently varied. For example, all members of the population benefit from defence expenditure, all the inhabitants of any given district benefit from an anti-malaria programme, and all ships in the vicinity benefit from a lighthouse. The difference between separately marketable goods and such collective goods can be shown as in Figs. 7–1

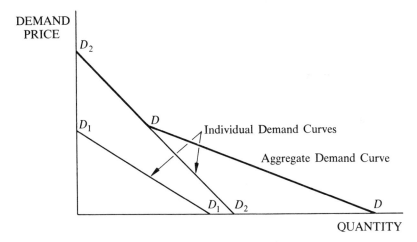

Fig. 7–1. Marketable goods.

and 7–2, following Bowen [8]. Whereas aggregation of individual demand curves is obtained by *horizontal* summation in the Fig. 7–1 case, it is obtained by *vertical* summation in the Fig. 7–2 case. This reflects the fact that though individuals may differ in their marginal valuation of a given quantity of a commodity, they all consume the same amount, in that each unit is consumed by all of them. For example, flood control afforded to different individuals is a joint product.

Ever since Wicksell, it has been recognized that any attempt to get consumers to reveal their preferences regarding collective goods founders on the rock that the rational thing for any individual consumer to do is understate his demand, in the expectation that he would thereby be relieved of part or all of his share of the cost without affecting the quantity obtained. Although a number of people (notably Lindahl) have attempted to find ways out of this impasse, it seems safe to say that no one has succeeded. In fact, the difficulties have multiplied rather than diminished. Samuelson [72, 73, 74] and Musgrave [60] have demonstrated that even if the non-revelation of preferences problem is ignored, there is still another major snag, in that there is no single best solution but rather a multiplicity of alternative optimum solutions.

The relevance of this discussion for our purposes is that where commodities are supplied at zero prices or at non-market clearing prices which bear

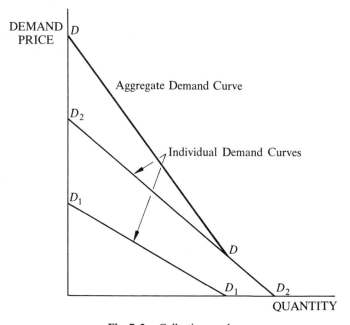

Fig. 7–2. Collective goods.

no relationship to consumer preferences, there is no basis for arriving at investment decisions by computing the present values of sales. Of course, the problem does not apply to collective goods alone; a whole range of other goods and services may be supplied free (or at nominal prices) by government for a whole variety of reasons.

(vii) Intangibles. Some costs and benefits (such as the scenic effect of building electricity transmission lines) cannot be quantified, and others, although they can be quantified, cannot be valued in any market sense (e.g., a reduction in lives lost). Such costs and benefits have been called intangible costs and benefits. They are obviously important in many cases and, equally obviously, have to be presented to the decision-maker in the prose which accompanies the cost-benefit arithmetic, since they cannot be incorporated in the arithmetic itself. It may be possible to gain some idea of their importance on the basis of consumer questionnaires, but one has to be careful of the well-known difficulties inherent in such efforts (Yates [90]).

There is one possible exception in the case of quantifiable items. Consistency requires that the net marginal cost of, say, saving an average citizen's life be the same whether it be achieved by hiring more traffic police or by having more ambulances. If there were consistency and if the marginal cost were known, then it would measure how much decision-makers were ready to pay to save a life, and hence it could be used for valuing lives saved. So the importance attached to particular "intangibles" may sometimes be inferred from private or public behaviour. Thus, one might suggest that British public standards of visual amenity are higher than the private standards manifest in most back gardens!

(c) CHOICE OF INTEREST RATE

(i) The Social Time Preference Rate. The literature on the choice of appropriate interest rates for public investment projects is voluminous, and we cannot hope to survey it in detail. But starting from the constellation of rates that one finds in the private sector, various questions have to be raised. Even if one can select a single or average risk-free long-term rate, it is not clear what significance can be attached to it. Straightaway we come up against all the old arguments about whether market rates of interest do bear any close relationship to the marginal productivity of investment and time preference or whether the relationship is so blurred as to be imperceptible. This is partly a matter of different interest theories (neo-Classical, Keynesian, Robertsonian, etc.) and partly a matter of how particular economies tick at particular times—do governments intervene in capital markets with any effectiveness, how well organized and unified is the capital market in a country, etc.? Both pure theory and imperfections in the capital market are thus involved.

Another issue is whether any market-determined interest rate would suffice for community decisions even if neo-classical theory is accepted and a perfectly functioning capital market assumed. Some writers believe that social time preference attaches more weight to the future than private time preference and that it is the former which is relevant for determining the allocation of society's current resources between investment and consumption. A number of arguments in favour of such a proposition have been produced over the years. Pigou [65], for instance, suggested that individuals were short-sighted about the future ("defective telescopic faculty") and that government intervention might be needed to give adequate weight to the welfare of unborn generations. More recently, other arguments, which seek to avoid the objection that the Pigou position is a fundamentally authoritarian one, have been put forward (Eckstein [21], Marglin [49]). One point made really relates to a special kind of externality. It is that any one individual's preference for current consumption, relatively to future consumption by himself or his successors, will be less if there is some sort of government-organized programme for imposing sacrifices on everybody—or at least on a large section of the population—than if the solution is left to the market. More generally, one might follow the lines indicated by Feldstein [24] and distinguish between: (1) market preferences; (2) preferences expressed through the ballot box; (3) what the Government in its wisdom thinks is good for this generation; and (4) what the Government thinks is good for this generation and future generations taken together.

Whatever the ultimate pros and cons of these arguments, there are two difficulties, if one tries to give effect to them. The first is actually to determine the social rate of discount. Marglin accepts that this does pose serious difficulties, but goes on to suggest that one can set about it by choosing the growth rate for an economy and thence (on the basis of the marginal capital/output ratio) determine the rate of investment; the social rate of discount must then be equated with the marginal productivity of investment. The practicability of such a procedure does not commend itself to us; but we must leave this to others to judge.

Another difficulty of operating with a social rate of discount is that we have the very awkward problem that different rates of interest would be used in the public and private sectors. There is then likely to be considerable inefficiency in the allocation of funds inside the investment sector—in the sense that if the Government is, say, responsible for electricity and the private sector for oil, inferior projects of the former kind will supplant superior projects of the latter kind.[9] This particular difficulty leads us right back to the point discussed at the beginning of Section II, i.e., that one rate of interest cannot perform two functions in a non-optimal situation. One way out of this is to recommend making the situation an optimal one. For instance, Hirshleifer [37] has suggested that the Government should take action to push down market rates of interest to the social rate, so that all investment decisions, whether in the public or private sectors, should be taken on the same basis. While applauding this idea in principle, other writers quite reasonably feel that in practice economists will still have to deal with sub-optimization problems.

(ii) The Social Opportunity Cost Rate. The government borrowing rate is a popular and easily applicable measure of costs, both because it is a financial cost in the case of government financed investment and, more academically, because it can be regarded as "the" risk-free rate of interest.[10]

---

[9] Defining "inferior" and "superior" in terms of present values of net benefits.
[10] Abstracting from uncertainty about the price level.

Yet despite the recent empirically founded recrudescence of belief in the interest elasticity of private investment, no one has demonstrated that the latter's marginal efficiency does actually equal the interest rate. A direct attempt to measure marginal rates of return on private investment is therefore required. Even if such a measure were made, however, it would be relevant only in so far as the costs being evaluated consisted exclusively of displaced private investment.

Recognizing this problem, Krutilla and Eckstein [43] assumed that the alternative to public investment would be a tax cut, considered the ways in which a likely tax cut would affect income groups, and then asked how the notional recipients would utilize their hypothetical receipts, thus finally arriving at a weighted average rate of return. An alternative postulate was that the additional public investment would be offset by tighter monetary policy; it was then asked which individuals would suffer and what sort of weighted interest rate could thence be derived. The general result from both assumptions was that Federal capital in the United States in the late 'fifties had an opportunity cost of 5–6%. Quite apart from the logical and statistical problems associated with the techniques of assigning tax cuts to the different income groups, etc., as Eckstein himself has noted [21], this approach deals with only two out of many relevant alternatives (e.g., more public investment might be met instead by less public consumption). It has also been severely criticised by Hirshleifer [37] on the grounds that the composite interest rate finally derived has an unknown allowance for a risk premium in it. Feldstein has also commented on this approach [25].

(iii) Adjustment for Uncertainty. The various ways in which uncertainty impinges upon cost-benefit analysis are discussed by Dorfman [48, Chap. 3], McKean [53, Chap. 4], Eckstein [21, Section 5], Hirshleifer [37, pp. 139–41] in their admirable surveys, and we need only add two remarks here. The first point is that there is no reason to argue that public investment projects are free of uncertainty (see, especially, Hirshleifer [37]). The second is that allowances for uncertainty can be made: (1) in the assessments of annual levels of benefits and costs; (2) in the assumptions about length of life; and (3) in the discount rate. The first is most appropriate if the risk of dispersion of outcomes (or inputs) is irregularly, rather than regularly, distributed with time. If the main risk is that there may be a sudden day of reckoning when benefits disappear or costs soar, the second type of adjustment is needed. The third correction, a premium on the discount rate, is appropriate where uncertainty is a strictly compounding function of time.

(iv) The Need for an Interest Rate. When the problem of choice involves no opportunity cost of capital—as happens when all of a fixed budget is to be spent—there is obviously no need for an opportunity-cost rate of interest. It has been argued by some authors, e.g., McKean [53], that in this case there is no need for a social discount rate of interest either. This can be generally true, however, only if the maximand is not the present worth of benefits less costs, for if it is, some rate of discount is obviously required. We shall not elaborate this point here, since one of us has already published a purely expository note on the subject [83].

(v) Principles vs. Practice.   Discussions about social rates of time preference, social opportunity cost, etc., do not cut very much ice in most empirical work, and we have not been able to discover any cases where there was any convincingly complete application of such notions.[11] Nor do ideas about allowing for future changes in interest rates seem to receive much attention. In practice, the most usual kind of procedure is to select an interest rate or rates, on the basis of observed rates ruling at the time, for calculating present values, etc. For example, Weisbrod [86] takes a rate of 10% to represent the opportunity cost of capital in the private sector (on the basis that the observed yield of 5% for corporate stocks should be grossed up to approximately double that figure to allow for the corporate profits tax)[12] and one of 4% to represent the cost of Federal Government borrowing. He then makes his present value calculations on both bases. It can obviously be said that this may give ambiguous results, e.g., that project A is preferable to project B on one basis, but project B is preferable on the other. This is indisputable; but there are also examples to show that the choice of varying discount rates does not, within the 4–8% band, make much difference to assessments of a project (Foster and Beesley [28]), though the same conclusions do not necessarily hold for a rather wider band. The truth of the matter is that, whatever one does, one is trying to unscramble an omelette, and no one has yet invented a uniquely superior way of doing this.

(d) RELEVANT CONSTRAINTS

(i) Introduction.   Eckstein [21] has provided a most helpful classification of constraints. First, there are physical constraints. The most general of these is the production function which relates the physical inputs and outputs of a project, but this enters directly into the calculation of costs and benefits. Where choice is involved between different projects or regarding the size or timing of a particular project, external physical constraints may also be relevant. Thus, one particular input may be in totally inelastic supply, or two projects may be mutually exclusive on purely technological grounds.

---

[11] Eckstein [21] concluded after several pages of discussion "thus the choice of interest rates must remain a value judgment."

[12] It might be argued that a further correction should also be made to bridge any gap between earnings yield and dividend yield. This would make for a wider spread of the rate band.

Next there are legal constraints. What is done must be within the framework of the law, which may affect matters in a multiplicity of ways, e.g., rights of access, time needed for public inquiries, regulated pricing, limits to the activities of public agencies and so on. Third, there may be administrative constraints, related to limits of what can be handled administratively. Fourth, uncertainty can be introduced by constraints, for example, by the introduction of some minimum regret requirement. Finally, there are distributional and budgetary constraints; these need more extended discussion.

(ii) Distributional Constraints. The notion that the choice between projects can be made solely on the grounds of "economic efficiency," because any unfavourable effects on income distribution can be overcome by making some of the gainers compensate some of the losers, is rarely applicable in practice.

It is perfectly possible to compensate property-owners not only for property which is expropriated but also for property which is reduced in value. Similarly, it is possible to levy a charge in respect of property which has been enhanced in value. These payments of compensation and charges, being lump sums, are not likely to have any direct effects upon resource allocation. Another way in which extra money can be raised from the beneficiaries of a project without affecting resource allocation arises where some of the project outputs are sold and intra-marginal units of these outputs can be priced at more than marginal units. (Thus electricity consumers may be charged on a two-part tariff.)

In general, however, attempts to get beneficiaries to pay more than the marginal social cost of the project outputs they consume will affect the allocation of resources. Such attempts may be made either because of a desire not to raise the real income of the beneficiaries to an extent regarded as unfair or because of a desire to raise funds to compensate a group which is made worse off by the project or simply because of a general belief that projects ought to break even. Whatever the reason, the pricing policy adopted will affect project outputs, and hence project costs. Tolls on a motorway, for instance, will affect the volume of traffic, and this may affect the appropriate width at which it should be constructed. Thus, benefits and costs are not independent of pricing policy.

This can affect cost-benefit analysis in either of two ways. The first is relevant when pricing rules have been laid down in advance in the light of political or social notions about income distribution. Here the task is to maximize the present value of benefits less costs subject to certain specified financial requirements, i.e., subject to one or more constraints. The second way in which income distribution requirements may affect cost-benefit analysis occurs when the authorities have not laid down any specific financial rules but do clearly care about income distribution. In this case it is up to the analyst to invent and present as alternatives a number of variants of a project which differ both as regards the particular people who pay (or are paid) and the prices charged and, in consequence, as regards outputs and inputs. For each alternative, the analyst will have to set out not only total costs and benefits but also the costs and benefits for those particular groups whose economic welfare is of interest to the decision-maker.

In cases like this the choice can be formalized—if the decision-maker allows it—by expressing it in terms of maximizing the excess of total benefits over total costs subject to constraints on the benefits less costs of particular groups. Alternatively, it can be expressed in terms of maximizing the net gain (or minimizing the net loss) to a particular group subject to a constraint relating to total benefits and costs. Whether or not this is helpful in practice is not known, but at least it may explain why income distribution considerations have been brought into this survey under the heading of constraints.

It should be noted that these considerations may relate to many different kinds of groups. In one context notions of "fairness" to workers may predominate, while in another it may be notions of "equity" between different geographical areas which are important. If one is taking a regional, rather than a national, viewpoint the assessment and measurement of costs and benefits may be quite markedly different. For instance, it has been argued that one of the benefits of the Morecambe Bay barrage scheme would be the attraction of more industry to the Barrow area. This would no doubt benefit Barrow; but it is perfectly conceivable that there would be equivalent or even greater losses to South Lancashire, or for that matter other regions of the United Kingdom. Therefore one gets an entirely different picture of benefits and costs, if one looks at them from the viewpoint of the Barrow area, from that prevailing for the whole of the North-west or the whole of the United Kingdom.

(iii) Budgetary Constraints. Discussions of this topic combine (and sometimes confuse) three issues: first, ought such constraints to exist; second, what form do they take; and third, how can they be incorporated into investment criteria? We shall deal with the third issue shortly when we reach the general subject of investment criteria. We do not propose to discuss the first point, but might note that Hirshleifer [37] has argued that if the budgeting authorities are worth their salt the amount allocated to the sub-budgets will take account of the productivity of the projects available to them and the costs of obtaining the necessary funds. If this is not done, it is argued, the answer is to recast the system of budget allocation rather than to go into python-like contortions at the sub-budget level. This argument, however, is rather unrealistic. For the present, at any rate, many decisions are in fact taken within the framework of a budget restraint, and the economist might as well help people to sub-optimize within this framework, even if, as a long-run proposition, he thinks in his private capacity that it should be changed.

On the second issue there is not much to be said in general terms. There may be a constraint upon total capital expenditure over one or more years, as, for instance, when the projects undertaken by a public agency have to fit within a budget framework determined in advance. The sums involved may be either maxima which do not have to be reached or amounts which are to be spent entirely.[13] In the first case, but not the second, the expenditure in question has an opportunity cost, since once the decision is made to use funds, they are effectively a bygone. There can be other kinds of constraint applying to capital expenditure, such as a prescribed percentage of self-financing, and constraints can also apply to current expenditure and/or to revenue, for example, a financial target for gross or net accounting profits.

3. Final Considerations

(a) INVESTMENT CRITERIA

We believe that the most common maximand where projects involve only costs and benefits expressed in terms of money is the present value of benefits less costs. Other maximands are possible, however, such as capital stock at a final date. We shall not attempt to argue the relative merits of different maximands, but, continuing to accept present value, now introduce the subject of investment criteria or, as they are sometimes called, decision algorithms.

Where no projects are interdependent or mutually exclusive, where starting dates are given and where no constraints are operative, the choice of projects which maximizes the present value of total benefits less total costs can be expressed in any of the following four equivalent ways:[14]

> 1. select all projects where the present value of benefits exceeds the present value of costs;

---

[13] "Maximum" or "specific" rationing to use the convenient terminology of Hirshleifer [37].
[14] Symbolically, these criteria can be summarized as follows:

Let $c_1, c_2, \ldots c_n$ = series of prospective costs in years $1, 2, \ldots n$;
        c = constant annuity with same present value as $c_1, c_2, \ldots c_n$;
$b_1, b_2, \ldots b_n$ = series of prospective benefits in years $1, 2, \ldots n$;
        b = constant annuity with same present value as $b_1, b_2, \ldots b_n$;
        s = scrap value;
        i = appropriate rate of discount for annual compounding;
        r = internal rate of return.

Then we may write the rules as follows: select projects where

$$(1) \quad \frac{b_1}{(1+i)} + \frac{b_2}{(1+i)^2} + \cdots + \frac{b_n+s}{(1+i)^n} > \frac{c_1}{(1+i)} + \frac{c_2}{(1+i)^2} + \cdots + \frac{c_n}{(1+i)^n}$$

$$(2) \quad \frac{\dfrac{b_1}{(1+i)} + \dfrac{b_2}{(1+i)^2} + \cdots + \dfrac{b_n+s}{(1+i)^n}}{\dfrac{c_1}{(1+i)} + \dfrac{c_2}{(1+i)^2} + \cdots + \dfrac{c_n}{(1+i)^n}} > 1$$

$$(3) \quad b > c$$

2. select all projects where the ratio of the present value of benefits to the present value of costs exceeds unity;
3. select all projects where the constant annuity with the same present value as benefits exceeds the constant annuity (of the same duration) with the same present value as costs;
4. select all projects where the internal rate of return exceeds the chosen rate of discount.

Once the various complications just assumed away are introduced, more complicated rules are required. We shall explain the impact of these complications in terms of the present-value approach without claiming that it is always the most convenient one. Which approach is most convenient will vary with the facts of the case. Where a rule which is not algebraically equivalent to the present value approach is used, the issue is not one of convenience, but involves either error[15] or a different maximand.

Where the costs and/or benefits of two schemes A and B are interdependent in the sense that the execution of one affects the costs or benefits of the other, they must be treated as constituting three mutually exclusive schemes, namely A and B together, A alone and B alone. Thus, if one wants to improve communications between two towns one has the choice between a road improvement, a rail improvement and a combination of road and rail improvements.

Mutual exclusivity can also arise for technological reasons. Thus, a road intersection can be built as a cross-roads, a roundabout or a flyover. Similarly, a large or a small dam, but not both, may be put in one place. Whatever the reason for mutual exclusivity, its presence must be allowed for in formulating investment rules.

Where there is a choice of starting date it must be chosen so as to maximize the present value of benefits less costs at the reference date.

Constraints cause the biggest complications, particularly when there is more than one of them and when mutual exclusivity and optimal timing are also involved. Indivisibilities also complicate matters when constraints are involved.

We shall not venture into the algebraic jungle of constructing decision algorithms. Anyone who seeks examples can turn to Marglin's discussion of income distribution and budgetary constraints in his exemplary synthesis of much of cost-benefit analysis [48] or to his monograph on dynamic investment planning [51]. A most useful discussion is also to be found in an article on capital budgeting by Dryden [18].

Finally, select projects where $r > i$, where r is given by

$$(4) \qquad \frac{b_1 - c_1}{(1 + r)} + \frac{b_2 - c_2}{(1 + r)^2} + \cdots + \frac{b_n - c_n}{(1 + r)^n} = 0$$

[15] A naïve error in early writings was the use of benefit-cost ratios to choose between two mutually exclusive projects. One project may have the lower benefit-cost ratio, yet will be preferable if the *extra* benefits exceed the *extra* costs. This is clearly brought out by McKean [53, pp. 108 ff.].

(b) SECOND-BEST MATTERS

Since cost-benefit analysis is essentially a practical tool for decision-making, it is not worth our while pursuing the second-best problem into the higher reaches of welfare economics. The non-fulfilment of the conditions for a welfare maximum elsewhere in the economy is relevant to cost-benefit analysis only insofar as it makes the market values of outputs and inputs obviously biased measures of benefits and costs. Small and remote divergences from the optimum will cause biases in these measures which fall within their margin of error, while large divergences of an unknown sort create unknowable biases which are necessarily irrelevant to action. Only those divergences which are immediate, palpable and considerable thus deserve our attention. We have discussed some of these already, and will bring in further examples in our survey of particular applications of cost-benefit analysis.

Ideally, all such divergences should be taken into account, for otherwise a sub-optimum will not be achieved. Yet it does not follow that public agencies ought always to take account of them; the ideal involves administrative costs. It has to be recognized that public agencies have defined spheres of competence and that the responsibility for wide issues lying outside these spheres rests not with them but with the Government which created them and their tasks. It is not the business of, say, the Scottish Development Department to decide whether or not the currency is overvalued, for instance, and it is not within its competence to put a shadow price upon the foreign-exchange content of proposed expenditure. Either it must value imports at their import price or it must be told to adopt a shadow rate for planning purposes by the central government, whose function it is to consider such matters. The division of labour in administration which is necessary if the public sector is to avoid monolithic sluggishness requires each part of the machine to act as if the rest were doing its job properly. After all, to continue with this example, it may be better if all government agencies value foreign exchange at a uniform but incorrect exchange rate than if they each have their own different shadow rates.

BIBLIOGRAPHY

Note: This is mainly the list of articles, books, etc., to which we have referred in the text and is, in no sense, a complete bibliography of the subject.

[1] BECKER, G. S., *Human Capital* (New York: Columbia University Press, 1964).
[2] BEESLEY, M. E., "The Value of Time Spent in Travelling: Some New Evidence," *Economica*, Vol. XXXII, May 1965.

[3] BEESLEY, M. E., and C. D. FOSTER, "The Victoria Line: Social Benefits and Finances," *Journal of the Royal Statistical Society*, Vol. 128, Part 1, 1965.

[4] BEESLEY, M. E., and J. F. KAIN, "Urban Form, Car Ownership and Public Policy: An Appraisal of Traffic in Towns," *Urban Studies*, Vol. 1, No. 2, November 1964.

[5] BLAUG, M., "The Rate of Return on Investment in Education in Great Britain," *The Manchester School*, Vol. XXXIII, No. 3, September 1965.

[6] BORUS, M. E., "A Benefit Cost Analysis of the Economic Effectiveness of Retraining the Unemployed," *Yale Economic Essays*, Vol. 4, No. 2, Fall 1964. No. 300.—VOL. LXV.

[7] BOS, H. C., and L. M. KOYCK, "The Appraisal of Road Construction Projects," *Review of Economics and Statistics*, Vol. XLIII, February 1961.

[8] BOWEN, H. R., *Toward Social Economy* (New York: Rinehart, 1948).

[9] BOWMAN, MARY J., "Social Returns to Education," *International Social Science Journal*, Vol. XIV, No. 4, 1962.

[10] British Railways Board, *The Reshaping of British Railways* (The Beeching Report) (H.M.S.O., 1963).

[11] BUCHANAN, J. M., and W. C. STUBBLEBINE, "Externality," *Economica*, Vol. XXIX, November 1962.

[12] CLAWSON, MARION, "Methods of Measuring the Demand for and Value of Outdoor Recreation," *Resources for the Future, Inc.* (Washington, D.C., 1959).

[13] COASE, R. H., "The Problem of Social Cost," *Journal of Law and Economics*, Vol. III, October 1960.

[14] COBURN, T. M., M. E. BEESLEY and D. J. REYNOLDS, *The London–Birmingham Motorway: Traffic and Economics*, Road Research Laboratory Technical Paper No. 46. D.S.I.R., H.M.S.O., 1960.

[15] CRUTCHFIELD, J. A., "Valuation of Fishery Resources," *Land Economics*, Vol. XXXVIII, May 1962.

[16] DALTON, H., *Principles of Public Finance* (4th edn. revised) (London: Routledge & Kegan Paul, 1954).

[17] DAVIS, OTTO, and ANDREW WHINSTON, "Externalities, Welfare, and the Theory of Games," *Journal of Political Economy*, Vol. LXX, June 1962.

[18] DRYDEN, M. M., "Capital Budgeting: Treatment of Uncertainty and Investment Criteria," *Scottish Journal of Political Economy*, Vol. XI, November 1964.

[19] DUPUIT, J., "On the Measurement of Utility of Public Works," *International Economic Papers*, Vol. 2 (translated from the French).

[20] ECKSTEIN, OTTO, *Water Resource Development* (Cambridge, Mass.: Harvard University Press, 1958).

[21] ECKSTEIN, OTTO, "A Survey of the Theory of Public Expenditure Criteria," in James M. Buchanan (ed.), *Public Finances: Needs, Sources and Utilization* (Princeton: Princeton University Press, 1961).

[22] FARMER, B. H., *Ceylon. A Divided Nation* (London: Oxford University Press, 1963).

[23] FELDSTEIN, M. S., "Net Social Benefit Calculation and the Public Investment Decision," *Oxford Economic Papers*, Vol. 16, March 1964.

[24] FELDSTEIN, M. S., "The Social Time Preference Discount Rate in Cost Benefit Analysis," ECONOMIC JOURNAL, Vol. LXXIV, June 1964.

[25] FELDSTEIN, M. S., "Opportunity Cost Calculations in Cost Benefit Analysis," *Public Finance*, Vol. XIX, No. 2, 1964.

[26] FISHER, I., "Report on National Vitality: Its Wastes and Conservation," *Bulletin of One Hundred on National Health*, No. 30 (Washington, 1909).

[27] FOSTER, C. D., *The Transport Problem* (London: Blackie, 1963).

[28] FOSTER, C. D., and M. E. BEESLEY, "Estimating the Social Benefit of Constructing an Underground Railway in London," *Journal of the Royal Statistical Society*, Vol. 126, Part 1, 1963.

[29] FOX, I. K., and O. C. HERFINDAHL, "Attainment of Efficiency in Satisfying Demands for Water Resources," *American Economic Review*, Vol. LIV, May 1964.

[30] FROMM, G., "Civil Aviation Expenditures," R. Dorfman (ed.) *Measuring Benefits of Government Investments* (Washington, D.C.: Brookings Institution, 1965).

[31] GRILICHES, ZVI, "Research Costs and Social Returns: Hybrid Corn and Related Innovations," *Journal of Political Economy*, Vol. LXVI, October 1958.

[32] HAMMOND, R. J., *Benefit–Cost and Water Pollution Control* (Stanford, California: Stanford University Press, 1958).

[33] HANSEN, W. L., "Total and Private Rates of Return to Investment in Schooling," *Journal of Political Economy*, Vol. LXXI, April 1963.

[34] HAWKINS, E. K., *Roads and Road Transport in an Underdeveloped Country. A Case Study of Uganda*, Colonial Office, Colonial Research Studies No. 32 (London: H.M.S.O., 1962).

[35] HEAD, J. G., "Public Goods and Public Policy," *Public Finance*, Vol. XVII, 1962.

[36] HICKS, J. R., "Economic Theory and the Evaluation of Consumers' Wants," *Journal of Business*, Chicago, Vol. 35, July 1962.

[37] HIRSHLEIFER, J., J. C. de HAVEN and J. W. MILLIMAN, *Water Supply, Economics, Technology and Policy* (Chicago: University of Chicago Press, 1960).

[38] HITCH, C. J., and R. N. McKEAN, *The Economics of Defense in the Nuclear Age* (London: Oxford University Press, 1960).

[39] HUNT, S. J., "Income Determinants for College Graduates and the Return to Educational Investment," *Yale Economic Essays*, Fall 1963.

[40] Inter-Agency River Basin Committee (Sub-Committee on Costs and Budgets), *Proposed Practices for Economic Analysis of River Basin Projects* ("The Green Book") (Washington, D.C., 1950).

[41] International Institute for Land Reclamation and Improvement, *An Assessment of Investments in Land Reclamation* (Wageningen, Holland, 1960).

[42] KLARMAN, H. E., "Syphilis Control Problems," R. Dorfman (ed.) *Measuring Benefits of Government Investments* (Washington D.C.: Brookings Institution, 1965).

[43] KRUTILLA, J. V., and OTTO ECKSTEIN, *Multiple Purpose River Development* (Baltimore: Johns Hopkins Press, 1958).

[44] KUHN, T. E., *Public Enterprise Economics and Transport Problems* (Berkeley and Los Angeles: University of California Press, 1962).

[45] LERNER, A. P., *The Economics of Control* (New York: Macmillan, 1944).

[46] LESOURNE, J., *Le Calcul Economique* (Paris: Dunod, 1964).

[47] LICHFIELD, N., *Cost Benefit Analysis in Urban Redevelopment*, Research Report, Real Estate Research Program, Institute of Business and Economic Research (Berkeley: University of California, 1962).

[48] MAASS, A., M. M. HUFSCHMIDT, R. DORFMAN, H. A. THOMAS, S. A. MARGLIN and G. M. FAIR, *Design of Water Resource Systems: New Techniques for Relating Economic Objectives, Engineering Analysis, and Governmental Planning* (London: Macmillan, 1962).

[49] MARGLIN, S. A., "The Social Rate of Discount and Optimal Rate of Investment," *Quarterly Journal of Economics*, Vol. LXXVII, February 1963.

[50] MARGLIN, S. A., "The Opportunity Costs of Public Investment," *Quarterly Journal of Economics*, Vol. LXXVII, May 1963.

[51] MARGLIN, S. A., *Approaches to Dynamic Investment Planning* (Amsterdam: North-Holland, 1963).

[52] MARGOLIS, JULIUS, "Secondary Benefits, External Economies, and the Justification of Public Investment," *Review of Economics and Statistics*, Vol. XXXIX August 1957.

[53] McKEAN, R. N., *Efficiency in Government through Systems Analysis* (New York: John Wiley & Sons, 1958).

[54] McKEAN, R. N., "Cost-benefit Analysis and British Defense Expenditure," in A. T. Peacock and D. J. Robertson (eds.), *Public Expenditure, Appraisal and Control* (Edinburgh: Oliver and Boyd, 1963).

[55] Ministry of Transport, *Panel on Road Pricing* (Smeed Report) (H.M.S.O., 1964)

[56] Ministry of Transport, *Traffic in Towns: A Study of the Long Term Problems of Traffic in Urban Areas* (Buchanan Report) (H.M.S.O., 1963).

[57] MOHRING, H., "Land Values and the Measurement of Highway Benefits," *Journal of Political Economy*, Vol. LXIX, June 1961.

[58] MOHRING, H., and N. HARWITZ, *Highway Benefits: an Analytical Framework* (Chicago: Northwestern University Press, 1962).

[59] MOSES, L. N., and H. F. WILLIAMSON, "Value of Time, Choice of Mode, and the Subsidy Issue in Urban Transportation," *Journal of Political Economy*, Vol. LXXI, June 1963.

[60] MUSGRAVE, R. A., *The Theory of Public Finance. A Study in Public Economy* (New York: McGraw-Hill, 1959).

[61] MUSGRAVE, R. A., and A. T. PEACOCK, *Classics in the Theory of Public Finance* (London: Macmillan, 1958).

[62] MUSHKIN, SELMA J., "Health as an Investment," *Journal of Political Economy*, Vol. LXX (Supplement), October 1962.

[63] National Council of Applied Economic Research (New Delhi), *Criteria for Fixation of Water Rates and Selection of Irrigation Projects* (London: Asia Publishing House, 1959).

[64] NELSON, R. R., "The Simple Economics of Basic Scientific Research," *Journal of Political Economy*, Vol. LXVII, June 1959.

[65] PIGOU, A. C., *The Economics of Welfare* (4th edn.) (London: Macmillan, 1932).

[66] PREST, A. R., and I. G. STEWART, *The National Income of Nigeria 1950–51*, Colonial Office Research Series (H.M.S.O., 1953).

[67] RAY, G. F., and R. E. CRUM, "Transport: Notes and Comments," *National Institute Economic Review*, No. 24, May 1963.

[68] RENSHAW, E. F., *Towards Responsible Government* (Chicago: Idyia Press, 1957).

[69] RENSHAW, E. F., "A Note on the Measurement of the Benefits from Public Investment in Navigation Projects," *American Economic Review*, Vol. XLVII, September 1957.

[70] REYNOLDS, D. J., "The Cost of Road Accidents," *Journal of the Royal Statistical Society*, Vol. 119, Part 4, 1956.

[71] ROTHENBERG, J., "Urban Renewal Programs," R. Dorfman (ed.) *Measuring Benefits of Government Investments* (Washington, D.C.: Brookings Institution, 1965).

[72] SAMUELSON, P. A., "The Pure Theory of Public Expenditure," *Review of Economics and Statistics*, Vol. XXXVI, November 1954.

[73] SAMUELSON, P. A., "Diagrammatic Exposition of a Theory of Public Expenditure," *Review of Economics and Statistics*, Vol. XXXVII, November 1955.

[74] SAMUELSON, P. A., "Aspects of Public Expenditure Theories," *Review of Economics and Statistics*, Vol. XL, November 1958.

[75] SCHERER, F. M., "Government Research and Development Programs," R. Dorfman (ed.) *Measuring Benefits of Government Investments* (Washington, D.C.: Brookings Institution, 1965).

[76] SCHLESINGER, J. R., "Quantitative Analysis and National Security," *World Politics*, January 1963.

[77] SEWELL, W. R. D., J. DAVIS, A. D. SCOTT and D. W. ROSS, *Guide to Benefit-Cost Analysis* (Resources for Tomorrow) (Ottawa: Queen's Printer, 1962).

[78] SMITHIES, ARTHUR, *The Budgetary Process in the United States* (Committee for Economic Development Research Study) (New York: McGraw-Hill, 1955).

[79] SOVANI, N. V., and N. RATH, *Economics of a Multiple-purpose River Dam: Report of an Inquiry into the Economic Benefits of the Hirakud Dam*, Gokhale Institute of Politics and Economics Publication No. 38 (Poona, 1960).

[80] STEINER, P. O., "Choosing Among Alternative Public Investments in the Water Resource Field," *American Economic Review*, Vol. XLIX, December 1959.

[81] THÉDIÉ, J., and C. ABRAHAM, "Economic Aspect of Road Accidents," *Traffic Engineering and Control*, Vol. II, No. 10, February 1961.

[82] TRICE, A. H., and S. E. WOOD, "Measurement of Recreation Benefits," *Land Economics*, Vol. XXXIV, August 1958.

[83] TURVEY, RALPH, "Present Value versus Internal Rate of Return—An Essay in the Theory of the Third Best," *Economic Journal*, Vol. LXXIII, March 1963.

[84] TURVEY, RALPH, "On Investment Choices in Electricity Generation," *Oxford Economic Papers*, Vol. 15, November 1963.

[85] TURVEY, RALPH, "On Divergences between Social Cost and Private Cost," *Economica*, New Series, Vol. XXX, August 1963.

[86] WEISBROD, B. A., *Economics of Public Health: Measuring the Economic Impact of Diseases* (Philadelphia: University of Pennsylvania Press, 1960).

[87] WEISBROD, B. A., "Education and Investment in Human Capital," *Journal of Political Economy*, Vol. LXX (Supplement), October, 1962.

[88] WILLIAMS, B. R., "Economics in Unwonted Places," *Economic Journal*, March 1965.

[89] WINCH, D. M., *The Economics of Highway Planning* (Toronto: Toronto University Press, 1963).

[90] YATES, F., *Sampling Methods for Censuses and Surveys* (London: Griffin, 1960).

8

THE ROLE OF COST-UTILITY
ANALYSIS IN PROGRAM BUDGETING

GENE H. FISHER

For some years new concepts of resources-allocation have been applied by the RAND Corporation to programs of the Defense Department. In 1966 the same method of analysis was extended to the remainder of the federal budget to achieve the same types of economies the methodology produced in the Defense Department. This extension was stimulated by the book from which the following selection was taken. These concepts of resources-allocation will be increasingly employed by private industry as well and they will have an important impact on business finance.

As explained in the selection, other terms also convey the same general meaning. These include systems analysis and operations research. Four important elements comprise the main characteristics of cost-utility or cost-benefit analysis:

1. Alternative courses of action are formulated and compared.

2. The evaluation emphasizes relationships of economic resource cost to benefits (gains or utility) to attain specified objectives.

3. A time horizon extending beyond one year to five, ten, or more years is involved.

4. The extended time horizon involves considerable uncertainty.

This selection describes the conceptual framework for cost-utility analysis and the construction of the appropriate model. It discusses the treatment of uncertainty and provides for validity checking.

The discussion is highly significant in that it relates quantitative analysis to qualitative analysis and indicates the relations between long-range planning and financial analysis, and planning and control.

Program budgeting as envisioned in this selection involves several essential considerations. The primary ones may be summarized under three main headings: structural (or format) aspects, analytical process considerations, and data or information system considerations to support the first two items.

The *structural* aspects of program budgeting are concerned with establishing a set of categories oriented primarily toward "end-product" or "end-objective" activities that are meaningful from a long-range-planning

---

Gene H. Fisher, "The Role of Cost-Utility Analysis in Program Budgeting." This selection is Chapter III in the book *Program Budgeting* edited by Mr. David Norvick, published by the Harvard University Press, 1965. The volume was first published as a product of the research program of the RAND Corporation of Santa Monica, California.

point of view.[1] In such a context emphasis is placed on provision for an extended time horizon—some five, even ten or more, years into the future. These characteristics are in marked contrast with conventional governmental budgeting, which stresses functional and/or object class categories and a very short time horizon.

Analytical process considerations pertain to various study activities conducted as an integral part of the program-budgeting process. The primary objective of this type of analytical effort is to examine systematically alternative courses of action in terms of utility and cost, with a view to clarifying the relevant choices (and their implications) open to the decision-makers in a certain problem area.

Information system considerations are aimed at support of the first two items. There are several senses in which this is important, the primary ones being (1) progress reporting and control and (2) providing data and information to serve as a basis for the analytical process—especially to facilitate the development of estimating relationships that will permit making estimates of benefits and costs of alternative future courses of action.

The present treatment is concerned primarily with the second of the items listed above: analytical process considerations. That an analytical effort is an important part of program budgeting (at least as practiced in the Department of Defense) is made clear in a recent statement by Secretary of Defense McNamara:

> As I have pointed out in previous appearances before this Committee, in adding to a Defense program as large as the one we now have, we soon encounter the law of diminishing returns, where each additional increment of resources used produces a proportionately smaller increment of overall defense capability. While the benefits to be gained from each additional increment cannot be measured with precision, careful cost/effectiveness analyses can greatly assist in eliminating those program proposals which clearly contribute little to our military strength in terms of the costs involved.
>
> This principle is just as applicable to qualitative improvements in weapons systems as it is to quantitative increases in our forces. The relevant question is not only "Do we want the very best for our military force?," but also, "Is the additional capability truly required and, if so, is this the least costly way of attaining it?"
>
> Let me give you one hypothetical example to illustrate the point. Suppose we have two tactical fighter aircraft which are identical in every important measure of performance, except one—Aircraft A can fly ten miles per hour faster than Aircraft B. However, Aircraft A costs $10,000 more per unit than Aircraft B. Thus, if we need about 1,000 aircraft, the total additional cost would be $10 million.
>
> If we approach this problem from the viewpoint of a given amount of resources, the additional combat effectiveness represented by the greater speed of Aircraft A would have to be weighed against the additional combat effectiveness which the same $10 million could produce if applied to other defense purposes—more Aircraft B, more or better aircraft munitions, or more ships, or even more military family housing. And if we approach the problem from the

---

[1] In many instances end products may in fact be *intermediate* products, especially from the point of view of the next higher level in the decision hierarchy.

point of view of a given amount of combat capability, we would have to determine whether that given amount could be achieved at less cost by buying, for example, more of Aircraft B or more aircraft munitions or better munitions, or perhaps surface-to-surface missiles. Thus, the fact that Aircraft A flies ten miles per hour faster than Aircraft B is not conclusive. We still have to determine whether the greater speed is worth the greater cost. *This kind of determination is the heart of the planning-programming-budgeting or resources allocation problem within the Defense Department* [italics supplied].[2]

Numerous analytical approaches may be used to support the total program budgeting process. Here we shall focus on one of them: cost-utility analysis. Before turning to this subject, however, a few of the other types of analysis should be noted briefly.

In terms of the types of problems encountered in the total program-budgeting process, one might think of a wide spectrum going all the way from major allocative decisions on the one hand to progress reporting and control on the other. Major allocative decisions involve such questions as, Should more resources be employed in national security in the future, or in national health programs, or in preservation and development of natural resources, etc.?[3]   Ideally, the decisionmakers would like to plan to allocate resources in the future so that for a given budget, for example, the estimated marginal return (or utility) in each major area of application would be equal. But this is more easily said than done; and at the current state of analytical art, no one really knows with any precision how the "grand optimum" might be attained. In the main, the analytical tools now available (particularly the quantitative ones) are just not very helpful in dealing directly with such problems. Intuition and judgment are paramount.

At the other end of the spectrum—progress reporting and control—the main problem is to keep track of programs where the major decisions have *already been made*, to try to detect impending difficulties as programs are being implemented, and to initiate remedial actions through a feedback mechanism when programs are deemed likely to get out of control in the future. Numerous techniques are available for dealing with these types of program-management problems. Examples are the following: financial and management accounting techniques;[4] network-type systems for planning, scheduling, progress reporting, and control;[5] critical-path methods (within

---

[2] From the introduction of the Statement of Secretary of Defense Robert S. McNamara before the Committee on Armed Services on the Fiscal Year 1965–1969 Defense Program and 1965 Defense Budget, January 27, 1964, *Hearings on Military Posture and H.R. 9637*, House of Representatives, 88th Cong., 2d Sess. (Washington, D.C.: U.S. Government Printing Office, 1964).

[3] For example, see Arthur Smithies, *Government Decision-Making and the Theory of Choice*, P-2960 (Santa Monica, Calif.: The RAND Corporation, October 1964).

[4] See Robert N. Anthony, *Management Accounting* (Homewood, Ill.: Richard D. Irwin, Inc., 1960), chaps. 13–15.

[5] One example is the so-called PERT system. For a description, see *USAF PERT, Volume I, PERT Time System Description Manual*, September 1963, and *USAF PERT, Volume III, PERT Cost System Description Manual*, December 1963 (Washington, D.C.: Headquarters, Air Force Systems Command, Andrews Air Force Base, 1963).

the framework of a network-type system);[6] Gantt chart techniques for program planning and control;[7] and various program management reporting and control schemes developed in recent years in the Department of Defense to help program managers in the management of complex weapon system development and production programs.[8]

The area between the ends of the spectrum is a broad and varied one, offering the opportunity for applying a variety of analytical techniques. These techniques are focused primarily toward problem areas short of dealing with determination of the "grand optimum," although they can be of real assistance in sharpening the intuition and judgement of decisionmakers in grappling with the very broad allocative questions. Technically, this is called "suboptimization," and it is here that the analytical efforts are likely to have the highest payoff.[9]

In cases where a wide range of alternative future courses of action needs to be examined in a broad suboptimization context, cost-utility analysis,[10] may well be the most useful analytical tool. However, in other cases where the suboptimization context is much narrower and a wide range of alternatives is not available, the problem may be one of examining relatively minor variations *within* an essential prescribed future course of action. The suboptimization context may be relatively narrow for numerous reasons—severe political constraints, lack of new technology to provide the basis for a wide range of alternatives, etc. Here, something akin to capital budgeting[11] techniques may be most appropriate.

In many instances the above-mentioned techniques may have to be supplemented by other methods. For example, in numerous major decision problems it is not sufficient to deal only with the *direct* economic consequences of proposed alternative future courses of action, ignoring their possible indirect or spillover effects. In such instances it may well be vitally important to consider indirect economic effects either on the economy as a whole or on

---

[6] See James E. Kelly and Morgan R. Walker, "Critical-Path Planning and Scheduling," *Proceedings of the Eastern Joint Computer Conference* (Ft. Washington, Pa.: Mauchly Associates, Inc., 1959), pp. 160–173; and F. K. Levy, G. L. Thompson, and J. D. Wiest, *Mathematical Basis of the Critical Path Method*, Office of Naval Research, Research Memorandum No. 86 (Pittsburgh, Pa.: Carnegie Institute of Technology, May 30, 1962).

[7] L. P. Alford and John R. Bangs, *Production Handbook* (New York: Ronald Press, 1947), pp. 216–229.

[8] For a good example, see *Systems Data Presentation and Reporting Procedures* (*Rainbow Report*), November 1, 1961 (with revisions as of March 9, 1962), Program Management Instruction 1–5 (Washington, D.C.: Headquarters, Air Force Systems Command, Andrews Air Force Base, 1962).

[9] For a discussion of suboptimization, see Charles Hitch, "Suboptimization in Operations Problems," *Journal of the Operations Research Society of America*, vol. 1, no. 3, May 1953, pp. 87–99; and Charles J. Hitch and Roland N. McKean, *The Economics of Defense in the Nuclear Age* (Cambridge, Mass.: Harvard University Press, 1960), pp. 396–402.

[10] Sometimes called "systems analysis"; e.g., see Roland N. McKean, *Efficiency in Government Through Systems Analysis* (New York: John Wiley & Sons, Inc., 1958).

[11] For example, see Joel Dean, *Capital Budgeting* (New York: Columbia University Press, 1951); Harold Bierman, Jr., and Seymour Smidt, *The Capital Budgeting Decision* (New York: The Macmillan Co., 1960); and Elwood S. Buffa, *Models for Production and Operations Management* (New York: John Wiley & Sons, Inc., 1963), chaps. 13 and 14.

specified regions or sectors of the total economic system. Certain transportation problems involve considerations of this type.[12] Also, in the case of certain national security and space decisions, especially in the higher echelons of the decision hierarchy, it is often necessary to consider possible regional or industry sector economic impacts associated with alternative weapon system development and procurement choices.[13] One way to deal with such problems is through the use of macroeconomic models that attempt to take into account key interactions among important components of the economic system: for example, interindustry (input-output) models for the economy as a whole[14] and various types of regional models dealing with parts of the total national economy.[15]

Thus it is clear that numerous analytical methods and techniques exist that may be used to support various facets of the total program-budgeting process. We have dealt with this point at some length to emphasize that cost-utility analysis is not the only analytical tool that might be used in program budgeting.

WHAT IS COST-UTILITY ANALYSIS?

Attempting to define cost-utility analysis poses somewhat of a semantics problem. Numerous terms in current use convey the same general meaning but have important different meanings to different people: "cost-benefit analysis," "cost-effectiveness analysis," "systems analysis," "operations research," "operations analysis," etc. Because of such terminological confusion, all these terms are rejected and "cost-utility analysis" is employed instead.

Cost-utility analysis, as envisioned here, may be distinguished by the following major characteristics:

> 1. A fundamental characteristic is the systematic examination and comparison of alternative courses of action that might be taken to achieve specified objectives for some future time period. It is important not only to systematically examine all the relevant alternatives that can be identified initially but also to *design additional ones* if those examined are found wanting.[16] Finally,

---

[12] For example, see Brian V. Martin and Charles B. Warden, "Transportation Planning in Developing Countries," *Traffic Quarterly* (January 1965), pp. 59–75.

[13] See *Convertibility of Space and Defense Resources to Civilian Needs: A Search for New Employment Potentials*, compiled for the Subcommittee on Employment and Manpower of the Committee on Labor and Public Welfare, Senate, 88th Cong., 2d Sess. (Washington, D.C.: U.S. Government Printing Office, 1964). Note especially Part III, "National Adjustments to Shifts in Defense Planning," and Part IV, "Studies in Regional Adjustment to Shifts in Defense Spending."

[14] W. W. Leontief *et al.*, *Studies in the Structure of the American Economy* (New York: Oxford University Press, 1953).

[15] For example, See Walter Isard *et al.*, *Methods of Regional Analysis: An Introduction to Regional Science* (Boston and New York: Technology Press of Massachusetts Institute of Technology and John Wiley & Sons, Inc., 1960).

[16] E. S. Quade, *Military Systems Analysis*, RM-3452-PR (Santa Monica, Calif.: The RAND Corporation, January 1963), p. 1.

the analysis, particularly if thoroughly and imaginatively done, may at times result in modifications of the initially specified objectives.

2. Critical examination of alternatives typically involves numerous consider-ations, but the two main ones are: assessment of the cost (in the sense of economic resource cost) and the utility (the benefits or gains) pertaining to each of the alternatives being compared to attain the stipulated objectives.

3. The time context is the future—often the distant future (five, ten, or more years).

4. Because of the extended time horizon, the environment is one of uncertainty—very often great uncertainty. Since uncertainty is an important facet of the problem, it should be faced and treated explicitly in the analysis. This means, among other things, that wherever possible the analyst should avoid the use of simple expected value models.

5. Usually the context in which the analysis takes place is broad (often very broad) and the environment very complex, with numerous interactions among the key variables in the problem. This means that simple, straightforward solutions are the exception rather than the rule.

6. While quantitative methods of analysis should be used as much as possible because of items 4 and 5 above,[17] purely quantitative work must often be heavily supplemented by qualitative analysis. In fact, we stress the importance of *good* qualitative work and of using an appropriate combination of quanti-tative and qualitative methods.

7. Usually the focus is on research and development and/or investment-type decision problems, although operational decisions are sometimes encountered. This does not mean, of course, that operational considerations are ignored in dealing with R & D and investment-type problems.

8. Timeliness is important. A careful, thorough analysis that comes six months after the critical time of decision may be worth essentially zero, while a less thorough (but thoughtfully done) analysis completed on time may be worth a great deal.

THE PRIMARY PURPOSE OF COST-UTILITY ANALYSIS

Let us be very clear about what is the main purpose of analysis in general, and cost-utility analysis in particular. Contrary to what some of the more enthusiastic advocates of quantitative analysis may think, we visualize cost-utility analysis as playing a somewhat modest, though very significant, role in the overall decisionmaking process. In reality, most major long-range-planning decision problems must ultimately be resolved primarily on the basis of intuition and judgment. We suggest that the main role of analysis should be to try to *sharpen* this intuition and judgment. In practically no case should it be assumed that the results of the analysis will *make* the decision. The really interesting problems are just too difficult, and there are too many intangible (e.g., political, psychological, and sociological) con-siderations that cannot be taken into account in the analytical process, especially in a quantitative sense. In sum, the analytical process should be directed toward assisting the decisionmaker in such a way that (hopefully!) his intuition and judgment are better than they would be without the results of the analysis.[18]

---

[17] Also because of inadequate data and information sources.

[18] Apparently this view is held by Alain C. Enthoven, Deputy Assistant Secretary for Systems Analysis, Department of Defense. He writes: "Where does this leave us? What is operations

Viewing the objective of cost-utility analysis in this way is likely to put the analyst in a frame of mind that will permit him to be much more useful to the decisionmaker than if he takes a more hard-core view. There are two extremes here. On the one hand, it might be argued that the types of long-range-planning decision problems considered in this selection are just too complex for the current state of analytical art to handle. Therefore, decisions must be made purely on the basis of intuition, judgment, and experience —i.e., the zero analysis position. At the other extreme are those who (naïvely) think that all problems should be tackled in a purely quantitative fashion, with a view essentially to making the decision. Such a view implies explicit (usually meaning quantitative) calculations of cost and utility for all the alternatives under consideration. This may be possible, at times, for very narrowly defined, low-level suboptimization problems; but even this is questionable.

More generally, in dealing with major decision problems of choice, if the analyst approaches his task in an inflexible hard-core frame of mind, he is likely to be in for trouble. For example, he may soon give up in complete frustration; or he may wind up with such a simplified model that the resulting calculations are essentially meaningless; or his conclusions may not be ready for presentation until two years after the critical decision time and would therefore be useless to the decisionmaker.

The viewpoint taken here is that in most cases the relevant range is between the extremes mentioned above, and that in such a context there is a wide scope of analytical effort that can be useful. Furthermore, even when only a relatively incomplete set of quantitative calculations of cost and utility can be made (probably the general situation), much can be done to assist the decisionmaker in the sense that the term "assistance" is used in this chapter. To repeat: The objective is to *sharpen* intuition and judgment. It is conceivable that even a small amount of sharpening may on occasion have a high payoff.

One other point seems relevant. In that rare circumstance when a fairly complete set of calculations of cost and utility is possible and a resulting conclusion about a preferred alternative is reached, it may well be that the

---

research or systems analysis at the Defense policy level all about? I think that it can best be described as a continuing dialogue between the policy-maker and the systems analyst, in which the policy-maker asks for alternative solutions to his problems, makes decisions to exclude some, and makes value judgments and policy decisions, while the analyst attempts to clarify the conceptual framework in which decisions must be made, to define alternative possible objectives and criteria, and to explore in as clear terms as possible (and quantitatively) the cost and effectiveness of alternative courses of action.

"The analyst at this level is not computing optimum solutions or making decisions. In fact, computation is not his most important contribution. And he is helping someone else to make decisions. His job is to ask and find answers to the questions: 'What are we trying to do?' 'What are the alternative ways of achieving it?' 'What would they cost, and how effective would they be?' 'What does the decisionmaker need to know in order to make a choice?' And to collect and organize this information for those who are responsible for deciding what the Defense program ought to be." See Alain C. Enthoven, "Decision Theory and Systems Analysis," *The Armed Forces Comptroller*, vol. IX, no. 1 (March 1964), p.39.

conclusion itself is not the most useful thing to the decisionmaker. For one thing, as pointed out earlier, the analysis usually cannot take everything into account—particularly some of the nebulous nonquantitative considerations. The decisionmaker has to allow for these himself. But more important, most high-level decisionmakers are very busy men who do not have time to structure a particular problem, think up the relevant alternatives (especially the *subtle* ones), trace out the key interactions among variables in the problem, etc. This the analyst, if he is competent, can do, and should do. And it is precisely this sort of contribution that may be most useful to the decisionmaker. The fact that the analysis reaches a firm conclusion about a preferred alternative may in many instances be of secondary importance.

SOME MAJOR CONSIDERATIONS INVOLVED IN COST-UTILITY ANALYSIS

At this point, one might logically expect the title to be "How To Do Cost-Utility Analysis"—a cookbook, so to speak. We avoid this for two main reasons: (1) If such a treatise were attempted it would take an entire book; and more important, (2) it is doubtful that even a book on the subject is possible. At the current stage of development of analytical methods, cost-utility analysis is an art rather than a science. The really significant problems to be tackled are each in a sense unique, with the result that it is not possible to give a definitive set of rules on how to do an appropriate analysis. All that can be done is to give some guidelines, principles, and illustrative examples. But books, or major parts of books, have been written on this subject.[19] Here the treatment must of necessity be more limited.

Some important guidelines to be followed in carrying out a cost-utility analysis (not necessarily in order of relative importance) are discussed in the following paragraphs.[20]

Proper Structuring of the Problem and Design of the Analysis

This is by far the most important of the guidelines. Given an incredibly complex environment, that which is relevant to the problem at hand must be included, and that which is irrelevant excluded. There are no formal rules to guide us. The experience, skill, imagination, and intuition of the analyst are paramount. It is at this point—the *design* of the analysis—that most cost-utility studies either flounder hopelessly or move ahead toward success. In sum, if we can structure the problem so that the *right questions* are being asked, we shall be well on the way toward a good analysis. This sounds

---

[19] For example, see Hitch and McKean, *The Economics of Defense*, especially Part II; and McKean, *Efficiency in Government*.

[20] Observance of these guidelines will not in itself produce a good analysis, but it will most surely help. Many of the points listed are based on Quade, *Military Systems Analysis*, pp. 8–24.

trite, but is really is not. The author has seen all too many instances of large amounts of effort being expended on an analytical exercise addressed to the wrong questions.[21]

Another point is that typically the problem and the design of the analysis may well have to be *re*structured several times. Considerations that were initially thought to be important may, after some preliminary work, turn out to be relatively unimportant, and vice versa. Finally, in the process of doing some of the analytical work, new questions and new alternatives may come to mind.

The Conceptual Framework

In general there are two principal conceptual approaches:[22]

1. *Fixed utility approach.* For a specified level of utility to be attained in the accomplishment of some given objective, the analysis attempts to determine that alternative (or feasible combination of alternatives) likely to achieve the specified level of utility at the lowest economic cost.
2. *Fixed budget approach.* For a specified budget level to be used in the attainment of some given objective, the analysis attempts to determine that alternative (or feasible combination of alternatives) likely to produce the highest utility for the given budget level.

Either (or both) of these approaches may be used, depending on the context of the problem at hand. In any event, the objective is to permit *comparisons* to be made among alternatives, and for this purpose something has to be made fixed.

At this point a comment on the use of ratios (e.g., utility to cost ratios) seems in order. Very often such ratios are used to evaluate alternatives. The use of ratios usually poses no problem as long as the analysis is conducted in the framework outlined above (i.e., with the level of either utility or cost fixed). However, the author has on occasion seen studies where this was not done, with the result that the comparisons were essentially meaningless. For example, consider the following hypothetical illustration:

Alternatives	Utility (U)	Cost (C)	U/C
A	20	10	2
B	200	100	2

If the analyst is preoccupied with ratios, the implication of the above example is a state of indifference regarding the choice between A and B. But *should* the

---

[21] Incredible as it may seem, there have been studies that started out by asking questions about which alternative would maximize gain and at the same time minimize cost—clearly an impossible situation.

[22] The fixed level of utility or budget is usually specified by someone "outside the analysis"; i.e., it is usually a datum given to the analyst. Very often the analyst will use several levels (e.g., high, medium, and low) to investigate the sensitivity of the ranking of the alternatives to the utility or budget level.

analyst be indifferent? Most probably not, because of the wide difference in scale between *A* and *B*. In fact, with such a great difference in scale, the analyst might not even be comparing relevant alternatives at all.[23]

Building the Model

Here the term "model" is used in a broad sense. Depending on the nature of the problem at hand, the model used in the analysis may be formal or informal, very mathematical or not so mathematical, heavily computerized or only moderately so, etc. However, the main point is that the model need not be highly formal and mathematical to be useful. In any event, the following are some important points to keep in mind:

1. Model building is an art, not a science.   It is often an experimental process.
2. The main thing is to try to include and highlight those factors that are relevant to the problem at hand, and to suppress (judiciously!) those that are relatively unimportant. Unless the latter is done, the model is likely to be unmanageable.
3. The main purpose in designing the model is to develop a meaningful *set of relationships* among objectives, the relevant alternatives available for attaining the objectives, the estimated cost of the alternatives, and the estimated utility for each of the alternatives.
4. Provision must be made for explicit treatment of uncertainty. (There will be more on this later.)
5. Since by definition a model is an abstraction from reality, the model must be built on a set of assumptions. These assumptions must be made *explicit*. If they are not, this is to be regarded as a defect of the model design.

Treatment of Uncertainty

Because most really interesting and important decision problems involve major elements of uncertainty, a cost-utility analysis of such problems must provide for explicit treatment of uncertainty. This may be done in numerous ways.

For purposes of discussion, two main types of uncertainty may be distinguished:

1. Uncertainty about the state of the world in the future. In a national security context, major factors are technological uncertainty, strategic uncertainty,[24] and uncertainty about the enemy and his reactions.
2. Statistical uncertainty. This type of uncertainty stems from chance elements in the real world. It would exist even if uncertainties of the first type were zero.

---

[23] For a further discussion of the possible pitfalls of using ratios, see McKean, *Efficiency in Government*, pp. 34–37, 107–113.

[24] For example: Will there be a war in the future? If so, when? General or local? With what political constraints? Who will be our enemies? Our allies? See C. J. Hitch, *An Appreciation of Systems Analysis*, P-699 (Santa Monica, Calif.: The RAND Corporation, August 18, 1955), p. 6.

Type 2 uncertainties are usually the least troublesome to handle in cost-utility studies. When necessary, Monte Carlo[25] and/or other techniques may be used to deal with statistical fluctuations; but these perturbations are usually swamped by Type 1 uncertainties, which are dominant in most long-range planning problems. The use of elaborate techniques to treat statistical uncertainties in such problems is likely to be expensive window dressing.[26]

Type 1 uncertainties are typically present in most long-range decision problems, and they are most difficult to take into account in a cost-utility analysis. Techniques that are often used are sensitivity analysis, contingency analysis, and a fortiori analysis.[27]

Sensitivity Analysis. Suppose in a given analysis there are a few key parameters about which the analyst is very uncertain. Instead of using "expected values" for these parameters, the analyst may use several values (say, high, medium, and low) in an attempt to see how sensitive the results (the ranking of the alternatives being considered) are to variations in the uncertain parameters.[28]

Contingency Analysis. This type of analysis investigates how the ranking of the alternatives under consideration holds up when a relevant change in criteria for evaluating the alternatives is postulated, or a major change in the general environment is assumed. (For example, in a military context, the enemy is assumed to be countries A and B. We might then want to investigate what would happen if C joins the A and B coalition.)

A Fortiori Analysis. Suppose that in a particular planning decision problem the generally accepted intuitive judgment strongly favors alternative X. However, the analyst feels that X might be a poor choice and that alternative Y might be preferred. In performing an analysis of X versus Y, the analyst may choose deliberately to resolve the major uncertainties in favor of X and see how Y compares under these adverse conditions. If Y still looks good, the analyst has a very strong case in favor of Y.

---

[25] For a discussion of Monte Carlo techniques, see Herman Kahn and Irwin Mann, *Monte Carlo*, P-1165 (Santa Monica, Calif.: The RAND Corporation, July 30, 1957); and E. S. Quade, *Analysis for Military Decisions*, R-387-PR (Santa Monica, Calif.: The RAND Corporation, November 1964), pp. 407–414.

[26] Hitch, *Appreciation of Systems Analysis*, p. 7.

[27] Quade, *Military Systems Analysis*, pp. 23–24.

[28] Enthoven, in "Decision Theory and Systems Analysis," pp. 16–17, talks about sensitivity analysis in the following way: "If it is a question of uncertainties about quantitative matters such as operational factors, it is generally useful to examine the available evidence and determine the bounds of the uncertainty. In many of our analyses for the Secretary of Defense, we carry three estimates through the calculations: an "optimistic," a "pessimistic," and a "best" or single most likely estimate. Although it is usually sensible to design the defense posture primarily on the basis of the best estimates, the prudent decisionmaker will keep asking himself, "Would the outcome be acceptable if the worst possible happened, i.e., if all the pessimistic estimates were borne out?" Carrying three numbers through all of the calculations can increase the workload greatly. For this reason, a certain amount of judgment has to be used as to when the best guesses are satisfactory and when the full range of uncertainty needs to be explored. If there are uncertainties about context, at least one can run the calculations on the basis of several alternative assumptions so that the decisionmaker can see how the outcome varies with the assumptions."

Creation of a New Alternative. Although the three techniques listed above may be useful in a direct analytical sense, they may also contribute indirectly. For example, through sensitivity and contingency analyses the analyst may gain a good understanding of the really critical uncertainties in a given problem area. On the basis of this knowledge he might then be able to come up with a newly designed alternative that will provide a reasonably good hedge against a *range* of the more significant uncertainties. This is often difficult to do; but when it can be accomplished, it may offer one of the best ways to compensate for uncertainty.

Treatment of Problems Associated with Time

More likely than not, the particular problem at hand will be posed in a dynamic context; or at least the problem will have some dynamic aspects to it. While a "static"-type analysis can go a long way toward providing the decisionmaker with useful information, very often this has to be supplemented by analytical work that takes time into account explicitly.

A case in point is with respect to the treatment of the estimated *costs* of the alternatives for a fixed level of utility.[29] The nature of the problem may be such that the costs have to be time-phased, resulting in cost streams through time for each of the alternatives. The question then arises whether the decisionmaker is or is not indifferent with respect to the time impact of the costs. If he is not indifferent concerning time preference, then the cost streams have to be "discounted" through time, using an appropriate rate of discount.[30] Determining specifically what rate to use can be a problem; but it is usually manageable.[31] If it is not, an upper bound rate and a lower bound rate may be used to see whether it really makes any difference in the final conclusions of the problem.

It should be pointed out that the analyst pays a price for introducing time explicitly into an analysis:[32]

1. It complicates the analysis by increasing the number of variables and hence the number of calculations. If we put time in, we may have to take something else out.
2. As implied above, it complicates the selection of a criterion for evaluating alternatives: solution X may be better for 1966 and worse for 1970; solution Y may be just the reverse.

---

[29] Maintaining a fixed level of utility *through time* is often a tricky problem in itself. We cannot go into this matter in the present limited discussion.

[30] One may raise the question regarding under what conditions the decisionmaker *would* be indifferent. Economic theorists might argue that there probably should not be any such condition. However, in practice, decisionmakers often find themselves in an institutional setting (the Department of Defense, for example) where it is customary to be indifferent regarding time preference; hence, discounting of cost streams through time is not done. This is not to say that the decisionmakers are correct in principle.

It should be emphasized that the type of discounting under discussion here is purely to equalize cost streams through time with respect to time preference—not to compensate for risk.

[31] For example, see E. B. Berman, *The Normative Interest Rate*, P-1796 (Santa Monica, Calif.: The RAND Corporation, September 15, 1959).

[32] Hitch, *Appreciation of Systems Analysis*, pp. 11–12.

Validity Checking

In the preceding paragraphs we have discussed building the analytical model, "exercising" the model (sensitivity and contingency analysis), etc. Another important consideration (often relatively neglected) is checking the validity of the model. Because the model is only a representation of reality, it is desirable to do some sort of checking to see if the analytical procedure used is a reasonably good representation, within the context of the problem at hand. This is difficult to do, especially in dealing with problems having a time horizon five, or ten, or more years into the future.

In general, we cannot test models of this type by methods of "controlled experiment." However, the analyst might try to answer the following question:[33]

1. Can the model describe known facts and situations reasonably well?
2. When the principal parameters involved are varied, do the results remain consistent and plausible?
3. Can it handle special cases in which we already have some indications as to what the outcome should be?
4. Can it assign causes to known effects?

Qualitative Supplementation

We have already stressed the importance of qualitative considerations in cost-utility analysis—particularly *supplementation* of the qualitative work. Introduction of qualitative considerations may take several forms:

1. Qualitative analysis per se as an integral part of the total analytical effort.
2. Interpretation of the quantitative work.
3. Discussion of relevant nonquantitative considerations that could not be taken into account in the "formal" analysis.

The latter item can be particularly important in presenting the results of a study of the decisionmaker. The idea is to present the results of the formal quantitative work, interpret these results, and then say that this is as far as the formal quantitative analysis per se will permit us to go. However, there are important *qualitative* considerations thay you (the decisionmaker) should try to take into account; and here they are (list them). Finally, relevant questions about each of the qualitative items can be raised and important interrelations among them discussed.

SUMMARY COMMENTS

We stress again that the discussion above pertains to a long-range-planning context, with emphasis on specifying, clarifying, and comparing the relevant alternatives. Because comparative analysis is the prime focus,

---

[33] Quade, *Military Systems Analysis*, p. 20.

it is vitally important continually to emphasize *consistency* in the analytical concepts, methods, and techniques used. That is, instead of trying for a high degree of accuracy in an *absolute* sense (which is usually unattainable anyway), the analyst should stress development and use of procedures that will treat the alternatives being considered in an unbiased, consistent manner.

The main points presented may be summarized as follows:

1. An analytical activity is an important part of the total program-budgeting process.
2. Cost-utility analysis pertains to the systematic examination and comparison of alternative courses of action that might be taken to achieve specified objectives for some future time period. Not only is it important to examine all relevant alternatives that can be identified initially but it is also important to design additional ones if those examined are found wanting.
3. The primary purpose of cost-utility analysis is usually not to *make* the decision but rather to *sharpen* the intuition and judgment of the decisionmakers. Identification of the relevant alternatives and clarification of their respective implications are of prime importance.
4. In a long-range-planning context, the following are some of the major considerations involved in doing a cost-utility analysis:
   (a) Proper structuring of the problem is all-important. The analysis must be addressed to the right questions.
   (b) In making comparisons, an appropriate analytical framework must be used. For example, for a specified level of utility to be attained in the accomplishment of some given objective, the alternatives may be compared on the basis of their estimated economic resource impact; or vice versa, for a given budget level the alternatives may be compared on the basis of their estimated utility.
   (c) It is usually necessary to construct a model (either formal or informal) to be used in the analytical process. Here the main purpose is to develop a set of relationships among objectives, the relevant alternatives available for attaining the objectives, the estimated cost of the alternatives, and the estimated utility for each of the alternatives.
   (d) Uncertainty must be faced explicitly in the analysis. Sensitivity analysis, contingency analysis, and a fortiori analysis are three possible techniques that may be used in dealing with the problem of uncertainty.
   (e) Although it complicates the analysis because of an increase in the number of variables, very often *time-phasing* of the impacts of the various alternatives is a requirement. If the decisionmakers are not indifferent with respect to time preference, the estimates of time-phased impacts must be "equalized" over time through the use of a "discounting" procedure.
   (f) Since the model is only a representation of reality, it is desirable to do some validity checking of the analytical procedure; e.g., can the model describe known facts and situations reasonably well?
   (g) Although cost-utility analysis stresses the use of quantitative methods, the analyst should not hesitate to supplement his quantitative work with appropriate *qualitative* analyses.

9

UNCERTAINTY AND ITS EFFECT ON CAPITAL INVESTMENT ANALYSIS

MARTIN B. SOLOMON, Jr.*

Many capital investment decisions, particularly for new products and new projects, involve considerable uncertainty. This article uses sensitivity analysis to analyze the effects of overestimates and underestimates on the internal rates of return. Professor Solomon finds that small errors in estimates lead to relatively large errors in discounted rates of return. He concludes that this provides a rationale for seeking alternative methods of product evaluation.

This article is concerned with one specialized aspect of capital budgeting: the usefulness of "theoretically correct" choice criteria[1] in real-world investment decisions.

There are other areas of capital budgeting that are surely much more important; but this one deserves special attention because so many recommendations, explicit and implicit, based on these criteria have bombarded the businessman.[2] Before we assail the business practitioner for his crude and unscientific methods, we should be sure that our theory will provide better total results than his unsophisticated decision rules.

There is general agreement that if investment parameters such as costs, revenues, salvage values and interest rates were amenable to accurate prediction, theoretically correct methods could be used to great advantage in most firms. But all capital investments involve uncertainty in one form or another. The contention of this article is that theoretically correct choice criteria have *limited practical value due to the uncertainty involved in the estimates required for the analysis.*

Martin B. Solomon, Jr., "Uncertainty and Its Effect on Capital Investment Analysis," *Management Science*, XII (April 1966), B-334–B-339. Reprinted by permission.

* Special thanks are due W. Warren Haynes for his help, generous comments and criticism and to the University of Kentucky Computing Center and the U.S. Small Business Administration who generously supported this work. The opinions expressed herein are not necessary those of the supporting agencies.

[1] Without entering into an unnecessary debate, present value and the discounted rate of return are simply defined for the purposes of this article as "theoretically correct" criteria.

[2] For example see Harold Bierman and Seymour Smidt, *The Capital Budgeting Decision* (New York: Macmillan Co., 1960).

A GENERAL ANALYSIS OF ESTIMATING ERRORS

Two types of investments are considered: investments with constant annual returns and investments with declining annual returns. The discussion centers on two hypothetical illustrations that have been purposely framed for easy calibration of errors. We ignore errors in salvage values.

Proposals with Constant Annual Returns

Suppose we estimate that an investment will yield $1,000 annual pre-tax returns[3] for 7 years. Assuming the supply price of the asset is $4,000, a 32 percent tax rate, straight line depreciation over the life of the asset, and no terminal salvage value, the post-tax discounted rate of return would be 11.6 percent. Now if the proposal lasts only 6 years, all else remaining equal, the discounted rate of return is 9.1 percent. This means that the actual return is 2.5 percentage points less. On the other hand if the proposal lasts for the predicted 7 years but returns $800 per year (before taxes) instead of $1,000 the discounted rate of return falls to 6.5 percent which is 5.1 percentage points less than the estimate.[4] There is a plethora of possible combinations of returns, lives and rates of return. The simplest way to illustrate these relationships is to graph them as in Fig. 9–1. Shown are lines connecting the discounted rates of return for proposals with the same life and different pre-tax annual returns. The line labeled "7 years" shows the discounted rates of return for all investments with a life of 7 years. As the pre-tax returns decrease, the discounted rate of return declines. For this reason the lines slope downward to the left.

In evaluating the effect of uncertainty, we can use Fig. 9–1 to determine the possible variations in the discounted rate of return when uncertainty exists. (The data used to construct Fig. 9–1 are shown in Table 9–1.)

How much variation then in the discounted rate of return could we expect with this amount of error? If the returns of this estimated 7 year-$1,000 per year investment are subject to an error of plus or minus 2.5 percent and plus or minus one year, the maximum and minimum rates of return are 15.6 percent and 6.5 percent (as shown in Fig. 9–1 by the X's).[5] This is a variation of about 9 percentage points. If we extended the possible error to plus or minus two years, the maximum and minimum rates are 16.8 percent and 2.8 percent, a variation of 14 percentage points. Errors in estimates of

---

[3] Returns is used here to mean the excess of revenue over out-of-pocket cost.

[4] The discounted rate of return is used instead of present value. The reason for using this criterion is that the discounted rate of return is conceptually more simple. The same conclusions hold here whether present value or discounted rate of return is used.

[5] In Fig. 9–1, −7.5% represents annual pre-tax returns of $700; −5.0% represents returns of $800; −2.5% represents returns of $900, etc. The percentage errors are percentages of the original investment ($4,000). That is,

$$(\$700-\$1,000)/\$4,000 = -7.5\%$$
$$(\$800-\$1,000)/\$4,000 = -5.0\%$$
$$(\$900-\$1,000)/\$4,000 = -2.5\%.$$

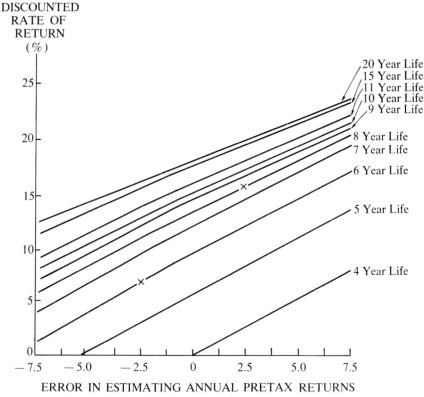

Fig. 9-1.   Constant annual pre-tax returns.

Table 9-1. The effect of estimating errors on the discounted rate of return—constant annual pre-tax returns.

Life of the proposal (years)	Annual pre-tax return												
	$700	$750	$800	$850	$900	$950	$1,000	$1,050	$1,100	$1,150	$1,200	$1,250	$1,300
20	0.122	0.132	0.142	0.151	0.161	0.170	0.180	0.189	0.198	0.207	0.216	0.225	0.234
15	0.112	0.123	0.134	0.144	0.154	0.165	0.175	0.184	0.194	0.204	0.213	0.223	0.232
11	0.092	0.104	0.116	0.127	0.139	0.150	0.161	0.172	0.182	0.193	0.203	0.213	0.223
10	0.083	0.096	0.108	0.120	0.131	0.143	0.154	0.165	0.176	0.187	0.197	0.208	0.218
9	0.072	0.085	0.097	0.110	0.122	0.134	0.145	0.156	0.168	0.179	0.190	0.200	0.211
8	0.057	0.071	0.083	0.096	0.109	0.121	0.133	0.145	0.156	0.168	0.179	0.190	0.201
7	0.037	0.051	0.065	0.078	0.091	0.103	0.116	0.128	0.140	0.152	0.163	0.175	0.186
6	0.010	0.024	0.038	0.052	0.065	0.078	0.091	0.104	0.116	0.129	0.141	0.153	0.165
5	*	*	0.010	0.015	0.028	0.042	0.055	0.068	0.081	0.094	0.107	0.119	0.131
4			*	*	*	*	0.010	0.014	0.027	0.041	0.054	0.066	0.079
3							*	*	*	*	*	*	*

* Indicates negative discounted rate of return.

these magnitudes do not appear at all unlikely.[6] This much uncertainty would seem to discourage the use of theoretically correct rationing methods for ranking investment proposals. There may be no significant difference among proposals' rates of return if they are nearly equally profitable: and if one or more proposals are obviously more profitable than the others, "alternative" methods[7] provide the same information with less cost.

Another interesting feature of Fig. 9–1 is that it provides some insight into the effect of errors in length of life versus error in returns. The relationship between annual pre-tax return and the discounted rate of return is close to linear with a slope of about 0.02 to 0.03. This means that an estimating error of about 1 percent results in an error of about 2 to 3 percentage points in the discounted rate of return. This relationship is fairly constant throughout. On the other hand, the relationship between discounted rate of return and length of life is not stable. As the life becomes shorter, an error of one year in the estimated life becomes more critical; the relationship is curvilinear. The difference in the rate of return between a life of 20 years and 15 years is only about one half of 1 percentage point when pre-tax profits = $1,000 (zero or horizontal axis). The difference of only 2 years between a life of 4 and 6 years (with $1,000 returns) results in a change of more than 6 percentage points in the discounted rate of return. Perhaps this is a good reason for businessmen being particularly cautious about making length of life estimates.

The conclusions here are that standard formulations of theoretically correct rationing methods have limited usefulness when dealing with uncertainty.

Proposal with Declining Annual Returns

To make the analysis more complete, the case of declining annual returns is included.[8]

The results are shown in Fig. 9–2. There is much similarity between Figs. 9–1 and 9–2 and most everything that has been said applies to both.

---

[6] See Martin B. Solomon, Jr., *Investment Decisions in Small Business* (Lexington, Kentucky: University of Kentucky Press, 1963).

[7] Alternative methods such as the payback period, rate of income on investment or the MAPI urgency rating.

[8] An investment's estimated pre-tax returns are: $2,500 the first year. $2,400 the second year, $2,300, $2,200, $2,100, $2,000, $1,900. The estimated life of the investment is therefore 7 years. Errors in length of life are handled the same as before, that is, if the estimated life overstates actual life by one year, the actual investment would return $2,500, $2,400, $2,300, $2,200, $2,100, $2,000, or an actual life of 6 years instead of the estimated 7 years. This estimate, although in error as far as length of the life is concerned, is correct concerning the returns (0 on the horizontal axis). Errors in pre-tax returns indicate an error in the initial annual returns. For example, a −2.5% error in estimating returns represents an investment that actually returns $2,300 the first year instead of the estimated $2,500. The annual decline in returns ($100 per year) remains constant. Thus an investment whose life was correctly estimated as 7 years but whose returns were overstated by 2.5% would return $2,300, $2,200, $2,100, $2,000, $1,900, $1,800, $1,700 (before taxes). In Fig. 9–2, zero on the horizontal axis represents an investment with an actual initial return of $2,500 and a $100 annual decline in pre-tax returns. A +3 year error in

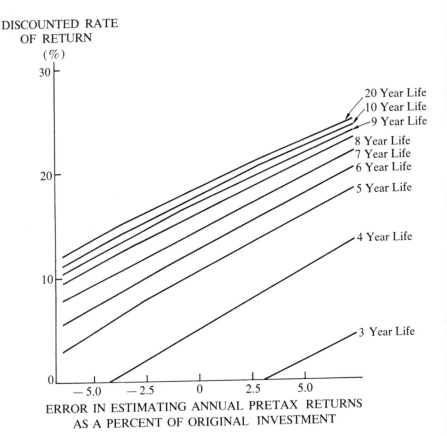

Fig. 9–2.   Declining annual pre-tax returns.

The conclusions about uncertainty seem to apply equally to both constant declining return investments.

Unless an investment will continue for a long period, a relatively small positive miscalculation in the estimate of length of life (2 to 3 years) can result in a serious overstatement of profitability.

The Effect of Technological Change

Because errors in returns are linear and errors in life are curvilinear, errors in estimating annual returns may average out over a large number of investments, whereas errors in length of life will not. Proposals that last

---

length of life (10 year life) and a −8.75% error in estimated pre-tax returns would designate an investment that actually returns $1,800 the first year, $1,700 the second year, $1,600, . . . , $1,000. The cost of the investment is $8,000, the tax rate is 32%, and straight line depreciation is used over the life of the asset with no terminal salvage value assumed. As before, errors are computed as a percentage of the original investment ($800 in this case).

less than the estimated life lower the average discounted rate of return for the firm more than proposals lasting longer than the estimated life raise the average.[9]

Today, with technological advancement so rapid and innovation so frequent, it seems logical to assume that many capital investments will be subject to extremely high rates of obsolescence. Businessmen do not usually know which of their investments will become obsolete soon; they are understandably worried about proposals that require 10 years to pay for themselves. The farther into the future one predicts, the more uncertainty of obsolescence he is subjected to and the more unsure he is of the prediction.

By insisting upon proposals that pay back quickly, or by using a higher discount rate, within the realm of feasible prediction, the businessman is providing greater flexibility for himself and, in a rough way, taking into account the effects of uncertainty. He is in a better position to maneuver and change his plans when necessary but will accept fewer projects. His hope is that those projects that are rejected (that otherwise might be accepted) will become obsolete before earning a return.

Technological change is one difficulty in estimating length of life. Businessmen can search for information about the expected annual returns from a proposal, but it is generally much more difficult to do research on the length of a proposal's life. In addition, Figs. 9–1 and 9–2 suggest that errors in length of life may be more serious. Use of the short payback period or higher discount rate tends to reduce errors of this type. The old saying about one in the hand being worth two in the bush is quite descriptive of business behavior in relation to projects in danger of obsolescence. It may be more worthwhile to invest, receiving a small quick return than to take a chance on a larger return or obsolescence.

Simple (or even simple-minded) methods of investment ranking may not be as absurd as some of the literature would lead us to believe if used in a careful way by clever people; and although no one claims superiority for a payback method, it appears that in investment decisions confounded by large amounts of uncertainty, the present value and discounted rate of return rankings are so sensitive to estimating errors that the payback criterion may provide results that are about as good as any. The main point of this paper is to point out the sensitivity in discounted rate of return results and not to recommend alternative methods.

---

[9] This curvilinear phenomenon occurs whether we plot present values or discounted rates of return. It may, however, be more apparent than real. It stems from an assumption underlying the discounted rate of return: proceeds are assumed to be reinvested at the rate of return for the original project; there is a cumulative effect of a high return project. If proceeds are not reinvested at this high rate but placed into low yield investments, this assumption does not hold and the curvilinear phenomenon is not operative.

10

STOCHASTIC DECISION TREES FOR THE ANALYSIS OF INVESTMENT DECISIONS

RICHARD F. HESPOS and PAUL A. STRASSMANN

In this paper a number of elements in modern decision theory are brought together. The authors describe the use of probability approaches, including the formulation of subjective probabilities. They illustrate how the stochastic decision tree method builds on concepts used in the risk analysis and the decision tree method of analyzing investments. Their formulation permits evaluation of all probable combinations in the decision tree, taking account of both the expected value of return and variance. Sensitivity analysis, using the model, can aid in determining the factors that are critical either because of their magnitude of influence on performance results and/or their degree of uncertainty.

Investment decisions are probably the most important and most difficult decisions that confront top management, for several reasons. First, they involve enormous amounts of money. Investments of U.S. companies in plant and equipment alone are approaching $50 billion a year. Another $50 billion or so goes into acquisition, development of new products, and other investment expenditures.

Second, investment decisions usually have long-lasting effects. They often represent a "bricks and mortar" permanence. Unlike mistakes in inventory decisions, mistakes in investment decisions cannot be worked off in a short period of time. A major investment decision often commits management to a plan of action extending over several years, and the dollar penalty for reversing the decision can be high. Third, investments are implements of strategy. They are the tools by which top management controls the direction of a corporation.

Finally, and perhaps most important, investment decisions are characterized by a high degree of uncertainty. They are always based on predictions about the future—often the distant future. And they often require judgmental estimates about future events, such as the consumer acceptance of a new product. For all of these reasons, investment decisions absorb large portions of the time and attention of top management.

Richard F. Hespos and Paul A. Strassmann, "Stochastic Decision Trees for the Analysis of Investment Decisions," *Management Science*, XI (August 1965), B-244–B-259. Reprinted by permission.

Investment decision-making has probably benefited more from the development of analytical decision-making methods than any other management area. In the past 10 or 15 years, increasingly sophisticated methods have become available for analyzing investment decisions. Perhaps the most widely known of these new developments are the analytical methods that take into account the time value of money. These include the net present value method, the discounted cash flow method, and variations on these techniques [4, 13]. Complementary to these time-oriented methods, a number of sophisticated accounting techniques have been developed for considering the tax implications of various investment proposals and the effects of investments on cash and capital position [2, 12, 16]. Considerable thought has been given to the proper methods for determining the value of money to a firm, or the cost of capital [12, 13]. The concepts of replacement theory have been applied to investment decisions on machine tools, automobile fleets, and other collections of items that must be replaced from time to time [16].

In a somewhat different direction, techniques have been developed for the selection of securities for portfolios. These techniques endeavor to select the best set of investments from a number of alternatives, each having a known expected return and a known variability [11]. In this context, the "best" selection of investments is that selection that either minimizes risk or variability for a desired level of return, or maximizes return for a specified acceptable level of risk. (In general, of course, it is not possible to minimize risk and maximize return simultaneously.) The application of these techniques to corporate capital budgeting problems is conceivable but not imminent.

In the evolution of these techniques, each advance has served to overcome certain drawbacks or weaknesses inherent in previous techniques. However, until recently, two troublesome aspects of investment decision making were not adequately treated, in a practical sense, by existing techniques. One of these problems was handling the uncertainty that exists in virtually all investment decisions. The other was analyzing separate but related investment decisions that must be made at different points in time.

Two recent and promising innovations in the methodology for analyzing investment decisions now being widely discussed are directed at these two problems. The first of these techniques is commonly known as risk analysis [6, 8]; the second involves a concept known as decision trees [9, 10, 15]. Each of these techniques has strong merits and advantages. Both are beginning to be used by several major corporations.

It is the purpose of this article to suggest and describe a new technique that combines the advantages of both the risk analysis approach and the decision tree approach. The new technique has all of the power of both antecedent techniques, but is actually simpler to use. The technique is called the stochastic decision tree approach.

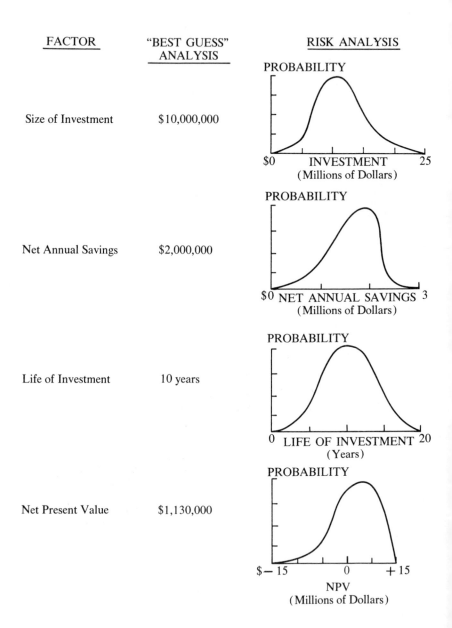

Fig. 10–1. Two analyses of an investment proposal.

To understand the stochastic decision tree approach, it is necessary to understand the two techniques from which it was developed. A review of these two techniques follows.

A REVIEW OF RISK ANALYSIS

Risk analysis consists of estimating the probability distribution of each factor affecting an investment decision, and then simulating the possible combinations of the values for each factor to determine the range of possible outcomes and the probability associated with each possible outcome. If the evaluation of an investment decision is based only on a single estimate—the "best guess"—of the value of each factor affecting the outcome, the resulting evaluation will be at best incomplete and possibly wrong. This is true especially when the investment is large and neither clearly attractive nor clearly unattractive. Risk analysis is thus an important advance over the conventional techniques. The additional information it provides can be a great aid in investment decision making.

To illustrate the benefit of the risk analysis technique, Fig. 10–1 shows the results of two analyses of an investment proposal. First, the proposal was analyzed by assigning a single, "best guess" value to each factor. The second analysis used an estimate of the probability distribution associated with each factor and a simulation to determine the probability distribution of the possible outcomes.

The best-guess analysis indicates a net present value of $1,130,000, whereas the risk analysis shows that the most likely combination of events gives the project an expected net present value of only $252,000. The conventional technique fails to take into account the skewed distributions of the various factors, the interactions between the factors, and is influenced by the subjective aspects of best guesses. Furthermore, the conventional analysis gives no indication that this investment has a 48 percent chance of losing money. Knowledge of this fact could greatly affect the decision made on this proposal, particularly if the investor is conservative and has less risky alternatives available.

The risk analysis technique can also be used for a sensitivity analysis. The purpose of a sensitivity analysis is to determine the influence of each factor on the outcome, and thus to identify the factors most critical in the investment decision because of their high leverage, high uncertainty, or both. In a sensitivity analysis, equally likely variations in the values of each factor are made systematically to determine their effect on the outcome, or net present value. Table 10–1 shows the effect of individually varying each input factor (several of which are components of the net cash inflow).

This analysis indicates that manufacturing cost is a highly critical factor, both in leverage and uncertainty. Knowing this, management may concentrate its efforts on reducing manufacturing costs or at least reducing the uncertainty in these costs.

Risk analysis is rapidly becoming an established technique in American industry. Several large corporations are now using various forms of the technique as a regular part of their investment analysis procedure [1, 3, 7, 17, 18]. A backlog of experience is being built up on the use of the technique, and advances in the state of the art are continually being made by users. For example, methods have been devised for representing complex inter-relationships among factors. Improvements are also being made in the methods of gathering subjective probability estimates, and better methods are being devised for performing sensitivity analysis.

Table 10–1. Use of sensitivity analysis to highlight critical factors.

An unfavorable change of 10 percentiles from the mean value in this factor	*Which corresponds to a percentage change of*	*Would reduce NPV by*
Annual net cash flow		
Sales level	12	17
Selling price	10	21
Manufacturing cost	18	58
Fixed cost	4	6
Amount of investment	5	12
Life of investment	12	30

One aspect of investment decisions still eludes the capabilities of this technique. This is the problem of sequential decision making—that is, the analysis of a number of highly interrelated investment decisions occurring at different points in time. Until now no extension of risk analysis has been developed that can handle this problem well.

A REVIEW OF DECISION TREES

The decision tree approach, a technique very similar to dynamic pro-gramming, is a convenient method for representing and analyzing a series of investment decisions to be made over time (see Fig. 10–2). Each decision point is represented by a numbered square at a fork or node in the decision tree. Each branch extending from a fork represents one of the alternatives that can be chosen at this decision point. At the first decision point the two alternatives in the example shown in Fig. 10–2 are "introduce product nationally" and "introduce product regionally." (It is assumed at this point that the decision has already been made to introduce the product in *some* way.)

In addition to representing management decision points, decision trees represent chance events. The forks in the tree where chance events influence the outcome are indicated by circles. The chance event forks or nodes in the example represent the various levels of demand that may appear for the product.

A node representing a chance event generally has a probability associated with each of the branches emanating from that node. This probability is the likelihood that the chance event will assume the value assigned to the particular branch. The total of such probabilities leading from a node must

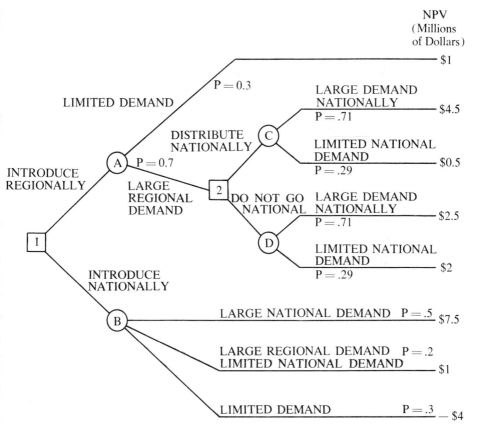

Fig. 10–2. Use of decision tree to analyze investment alternatives for a new product introduction.

equal 1. In our example, the probability of achieving a large demand in the regional introduction of the product is 0.7, shown at the branch leading from node A. Each combination of decisions and chance events has some outcome (in this case, net present value, or NPV) associated with it.

The optimal sequence of decisions in a decision tree is found by starting at the right-hand side and "rolling backward." At each node, an expected NPV must be calculated. If the node is a chance event node, the expected NPV is calculated for *all* of the branches emanating from that node. If the node is a decision point, the expected NPV is calculated for *each* branch

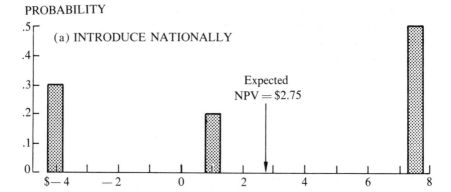

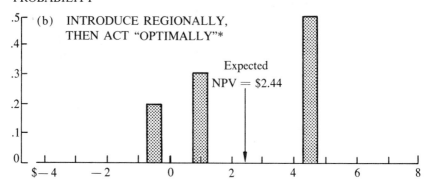

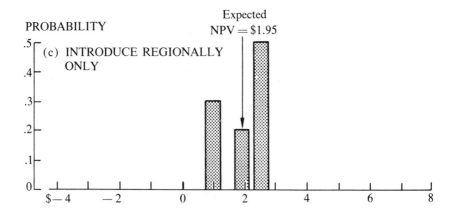

Fig. 10-3. Range of possible outcomes for each of three alternatives.

emanating from that node, and the highest is selected. In either case, the expected NPV of that node is carried back to the next chance event or decision point by multiplying it by the probabilities associated with branches that it travels over.

Thus in Fig. 10–3 the *expected* NPV of all branches emanating from chance event node C is $3.05 million ($4.5 × 0.71 + $−0.5 × 0.29). Similarly, the expected NPV at node D is $2.355 million. Now "rolling back" to the next node—decision point 2—it can be seen that the alternative with the highest NPV is "distribute nationally," with an NPV of $3.05 million. This means that, if the decision maker is ever confronted with the decision

Table 10–2. Net present value of investment alternatives for a new product introduction.

Alternative	Chance event	Probability of chance event	Net present value	Expected NPV
Introduce product nationally	Large national demand	0.5	$ 7.5⎫	
	Large regional, limited national demand	0.2	1.0⎬	$2.75
	Limited demand	0.3	−4.0⎭	
Introduce product regionally (*and distribute nationally if regional demand is large*)	Large national demand	0.5	4.5⎫	
	Large regional, limited national demand	0.2	−0.5⎬	2.44
	Limited demand	0.3	1.0⎭	
Introduce product regionally (*and do not distribute nationally*)	Large national demand	0.5	2.5⎫	
	Large regional, limited national demand	0.2	2.0⎬	1.95
	Limited demand	0.3	1.0⎭	

at node 2, he will choose to distribute nationally, and will expect an NPV of $3.05 million. In all further analysis he can ignore the other decision branch emanating from node 2 and all nodes and branches that it may lead to.

To perform further analysis, it is now necessary to carry this NPV backward in the tree. The branches emanating from chance event node A have an overall expected NPV of $2.435 million ($1 × 0.3 + $3.05 × 0.7). Similarly, the expected NPV at node B is $2.75 million. These computations, summarized in Table 10–2, show that the alternative that maximizes expected NPV of the entire decision tree is "introduce nationally" at decision point 1. (Note that in this particular case there are *no* subsequent decisions to be made.)

One drawback of the decision tree approach is that computations can quickly become unwieldy. The number of end points on the decision tree increases very rapidly as the number of decision points or chance events increases. To make this approach practical, it is necessary to limit the number of branches emanating from chance event nodes to a very small number. This means that the probability distribution of chance events at each node must be represented by a very few point estimates.

As a result, the answers obtained from a decision tree analysis are often inadequate. The single answer obtained (say, net present value) is usually close to the expectation of the probability distribution of all possible NPVs. However, it may vary somewhat from the expected NPV, depending on how the point estimates were selected from the underlying distributions and on the sensitivity of the NPV to this selection process. Furthermore, the decision tree approach gives *no* information on the range of possible outcomes from the investment or the probabilities associated with those outcomes. This can be a serious drawback.

In the example in Fig. 10–2 and Table 10–2, the decision tree approach indicated that introducing the product nationally at once would be the optimal strategy for maximizing expected NPV. However, the NPV of $2.75 million is simply the mean of three possible values of NPV, which are themselves representative of an entire range of possible values, as shown in Fig. 10–3. Comparing the range of NPVs possible under each possible set of decisions shows a vastly different view of the outcome. (See Fig. 10–3.)

Although the first alternative has the highest expected NPV, a rational manager could easily prefer one of the other two. The choice would depend on the utility function or the aversion to risk of the manager or his organization. A manager with a linear utility function would choose the first alternative, as shown in Fig. 10–4a. However, it is probably true that *most* managers would *not* choose the first alternative because of the high chance of loss, and the higher utility value that they would assign to a loss, as shown in Fig. 10–4b. This conservatism in management is, to a large extent, the result of the system of rewards and punishments that exists in many large

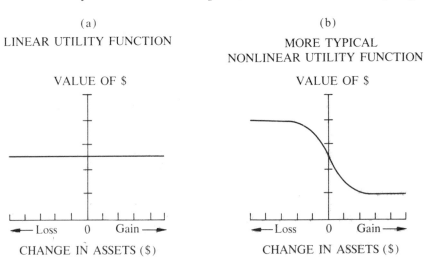

(a)

LINEAR UTILITY FUNCTION

VALUE OF $

Loss   0   Gain

CHANGE IN ASSETS ($)

(b)

MORE TYPICAL
NONLINEAR UTILITY FUNCTION

VALUE OF $

Loss   0   Gain

CHANGE IN ASSETS ($)

Fig. 10–4. Examples of utility functions.

corporations today. Whether it is good or bad is a complex question, not discussed here.

In spite of these shortcomings, the decision tree approach is a very useful analytical tool. It is particularly useful for *conceptualizing* investment planning and for controlling and monitoring an investment that stretches out over time. For these reasons, the decision tree approach has been, and will continue to be an important tool for the analysis of investment decisions.

COMBINING THESE APPROACHES: STOCHASTIC DECISION TREES

The complementary advantages and disadvantages of risk analysis and decision trees suggest that a new technique might be developed that would combine the good points of each and eliminate the disadvantages. The concept of stochastic decision trees, introduced in the remainder of this article, is intended to be such a combination.

The stochastic decision tree approach is similar to the conventional decision tree approach, except that it also has the following features:

1. All quantities and factors, including chance events, can be represented by continuous, empirical probability distributions.
2. The information about the results from any or all possible combinations of decisions made at sequential points in time can be obtained in a probabilistic form.
3. The probability distribution of possible results from any particular combination of decisions can be analyzed using the concepts of utility and risk.

A discussion of each of these features follows.

Replacement of Chance Event Nodes by Probability Distributions

The inclusion of probability distributions for the values associated with chance events is analogous to adding an arbitrarily large number of branches at each chance event node. In a conventional decision tree, the addition of a large number of branches can serve to represent any empirical probability distribution. Thus in the previous example, chance event node B can be made to approximate more closely the desired continuous probability distribution by increasing the number of branches, as shown in Fig. 10–5a and b. However, this approach makes the tree very complex, and computation very quickly becomes burdensome or impractical. Therefore, two or three branches are usually used as a coarse approximation of the actual continuous probability distribution.

Since the stochastic decision tree is to be based on *simulation*, it is not necessary to add a great many branches at the chance event nodes. In fact, it is possible to reduce the number of branches at the chance event nodes to *one*. (See Fig. 10–5c.) Thus, in effect, the chance event node can be *eliminated*. Instead, at the point where the chance event node occurred, a random selection

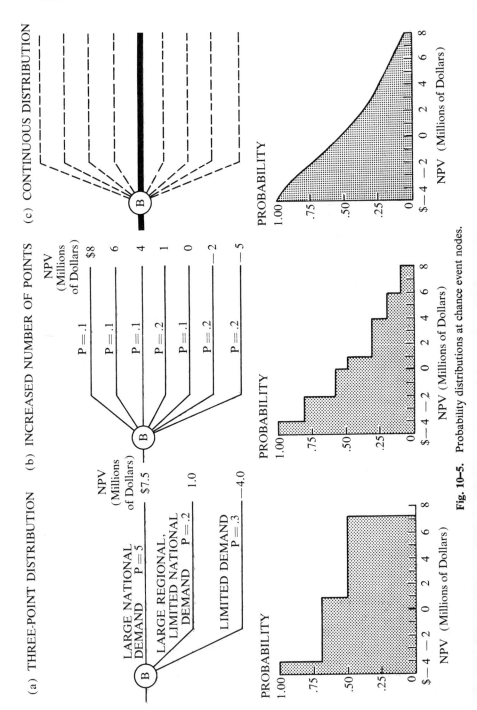

Fig. 10-5. Probability distributions at chance event nodes.

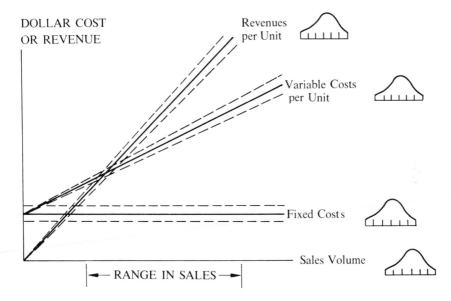

Fig. 10–6. Typical probabilistic economic model used to select values of factors at chance event nodes.

is made on each iteration from the appropriate probabilistic economic model such as the break-even chart shown in Fig. 10–6 and the value selected is used to calculate the NPV for that particular iteration. The single branch emanating from this simplified node then extends onward to the next management decision point, or to the end of the tree. This results in a drastic streamlining of the decision tree as illustrated in Fig. 10–7.

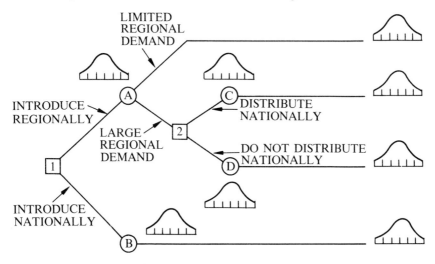

Fig. 10–7. Simplified decision tree.

Replacement of All Specific Values by Probability Distributions

In a conventional decision tree, factors such as the size of the investment in a new plant facility are often assigned specific values. Usually these values are expressed as single numbers, even though these numbers are often not known with certainty.

If the values of these factors could be represented instead of probability distributions, the degree of uncertainty characterizing each value could be expressed. The stochastic decision tree approach makes it possible to do this. Since the approach is basically a simulation, any or all specific values in the investment analysis can be represented by probability distributions. On each iteration in the simulation, a value for each factor is randomly selected from the appropriate frequency distribution and used in the computation. Thus, in the example, NPV can be calculated from not only empirical distributions of demand, but also probabilistic estimates of investment, cost, price, and other factors.

Evaluating All Possible Combinations of Decisions

Since this stochastic decision tree approach greatly simplifies the structure of the decision tree, it is often possible to evaluate by complete enumeration all of the possible paths through the tree. For example, if there are five sequential decisions in an analysis and each decision offers two alternatives, there are at most 32 possible paths through the decision tree. This number of paths is quite manageable computationally. And since most decision points are two-sided ("build" or "don't build," for example), or at worst have a very small number of alternatives, it is often feasible and convenient to evaluate all possible paths through a decision tree when the stochastic decision tree approach is used.

Why is it sometimes desirable to evaluate all possible paths through a decision tree? As the inquiry into the risk analysis approach showed, decisions cannot always be made correctly solely on the basis of a single expected value for each factor. The roll-back technique of the conventional decision tree necessarily deals only with expected values. It evaluates decisions (more exactly, sets of decisions) by comparing their expectations and selects the largest as the best, in all cases.

However, the stochastic decision tree approach produces *probabilistic* results for each possible set of decisions. These probability distributions, associated with each possible path through the decision tree, can be compared on the basis of their expectations alone, if this is considered to be sufficient. But alternative sets of decisions can *also* be evaluated by comparing the probability distributions associated with each set of decisions, in a manner exactly analogous to risk analysis. (The details of this technique are discussed in the next section.) Thus, the stochastic decision tree approach makes it possible to evaluate a series of interrelated decisions spread over time by the same kinds of risk and uncertainty criteria that one would use in a conventional risk analysis.

In a large decision tree problem, even with the simplifications afforded by the stochastic decision tree approach, complete enumeration of all possible paths through the tree could become computationally impractical, or the comparison of the probability distributions associated with all possible paths might be too laborious and costly.

In such a case, two simplifications are possible. First, a *modified* version of the roll-back technique might be used. This modified roll-back would take account of the probabilistic nature of the information being handled. Branches of the tree would be eliminated on the basis of *dominance* rather than simple expected value [7]. For example, a branch could be eliminated if it had both a lower expected return and a higher variance than an alternative branch. A number of possible sets of decisions could be eliminated this way without being completely evaluated, leaving an efficient set of decision sequences to evaluate in more detail.

Computation could also be reduced by making decision rules before the simulation, such that if, on any iteration, the value of a chance event exceeds some criterion, the resulting decision would not be considered at all. This has been done in the example shown in Fig. 10–2. If a limited demand appears at node A, national introduction of the product will not be evaluated. In the simulation, if demand were below some specified value, the simulation would not proceed to the decision point 2. This technique only saves computation effort—it does not simplify the structure of the tree, and if the criterion is chosen properly, it will not affect the final outcome.

Recording Results in the Form of Probability Distributions

It has already been shown that probability distributions are more useful than single numbers as measures of the value of a particular set of decisions. The simulation approach to the analysis permits one to get these probability distributions relatively easily. It is true that the method smacks of brute force. However, the brute force required is entirely on the part of the computer and not at all on the part of the analyst.

The technique is simply this: On each iteration or path through the decision tree, when the computer encounters a binary decision point node, it is instructed to "split itself in two" and perform the appropriate calculations along *both* branches of the tree emanating from the decision node. (The same logic applies to a node with three or more branches emanating from it.) Thus, when the computer completes a single iteration, an NPV will have been calculated for each possible path through the decision tree. These NPVs are accumulated in separate probability distributions. This simulation concept is illustrated in Fig. 10–8.

At the completion of a suitable number of iterations, there will be a probability distribution of the NPV associated with each set of decisions that it is possible to make in passing through the tree. These different sets of decisions can then be compared, one against the other, in the usual risk analysis matter, as if they were alternative investment decisions (which in fact they are). That is, they can be compared by taking into account not only the expected return, but also the shape of each probability distribution and the effects of utility and risk. On the basis of this, one can select the single best set of decisions, or a small number of possibly acceptable sets.

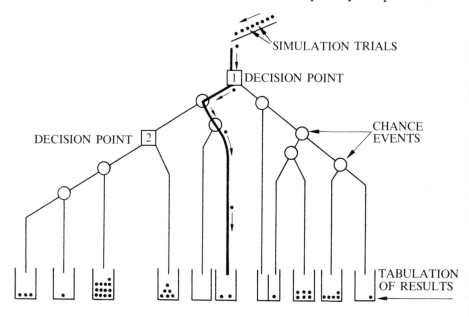

Fig. 10–8. The GPSS concept of decision trees with risk simulation.

These sets of sequential decisions can then be evaluated and a decision whether or not to undertake the investment can be made by comparing it to alternative investments elsewhere in the corporation or against alternative uses for the money.

An Example

To illustrate the kinds of results that can be expected from a stochastic decision tree analysis, the new product introduction problem described earlier has been solved using this method. The results are shown in Fig. 10–9.

The differences in the expected values of the outcomes can now be seen in proper perspective, since the results show the relationship of the expected

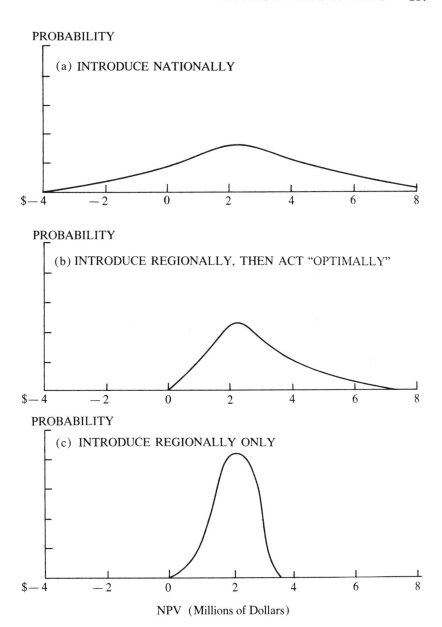

Fig. 10-9. Results of stochastic decision-tree analysis.

values to the entire distribution of possible outcomes. Moreover, the expected values of these distributions will not necessarily be identical with expectations resulting from the conventional decision tree approach, because:

1. The interdependencies among the variables were not accounted for by the conventional approach.
2. The small number of point estimates used to approximate an entire distribution under the conventional approach did not utilize all the available information.

With the three alternatives presented in this form, it is easier to understand why a rational manager might choose an alternative other than the one with the highest expected value. Presented with the full range of possible outcomes related to each alternative, he can select that alternative most consistent with his personal utility and willingness to take risk.

USING THE STOCHASTIC DECISION TREE APPROACH

Stochastic decision trees described here combine the best features of both risk analysis and conventional decision trees and are actually simpler to construct and use than either of these. The steps for collecting data and conceptualizing the problem are the same for the stochastic decision tree approach as they are for the risk analysis approach. These steps are:

1. Gather subjective probability estimates of the appropriate factors affecting the investment.
2. Define and describe any significant interdependencies among factors.
3. Specify the probable timing of future sequential investment decisions to be made.
4. Specify the model to be used to evaluate the investment.

The stochastic decision tree approach is ideally suited to the computer language known as General Purpose Systems Simulator (GPSS). [5, 14]. Although this language is not now capable of handling very complex interdependencies without certain modifications, it permits the solution of a very wide range of investment problems.

The structuring and solving of several sample problems have indicated that the stochastic decision tree approach is both easy to use and useful. The example in Table 10–2, Figs. 10–3 and 10–4 shows emphatically how the stochastic decision tree approach can detect and display the probable outcomes of an investment strategy that would be deemed optimal by the conventional decision tree approach, but that many managements would definitely regard as undesirable. Other work is being done on both sample problems and real world problems, and on the development and standardization (to a limited extent) of the computer programs for performing this analysis.

SUMMARY

The stochastic decision tree approach to analyzing investment decisions is an evolutionary improvement over previous methods of analyzing investments. It combines the advantages of several earlier approaches, eliminates several disadvantages, and is easier to apply.

REFERENCES

[1] ANDERSON, S. L., and H. G. HAIGHT, "A Two-by-Two Decision Problem," *Chemical Engineering Progress*, Vol. 57, No. 5, May 1961.

[2] ANTHONY, ROBERT N. (Editor), *Papers on Return on Investment*, Harvard Business School, Boston, 1959.

[3] "Chance Factors Meaning and Use," Atlantic Refining Company, Producing Department, July 1962.

[4] DEAN, JOEL, *Capital Budgeting*, New York, Columbia University Press, 1951.

[5] GORDON, G., "A General Purpose Systems Simulator," *IBM Systems Journal*, Vol. I., September 1962.

[6] HERTZ, DAVID B., "Risk Analysis in Capital Investment," *Harvard Business Review*, January–February, 1964.

[7] HESS, SIDNEY W., and HARRY A. QUIGLEY, "Analysis of Risk in Investments Using Monte Carlo Technique," Chemical Engineering Progress Symposium Series No. 42, Vol. 59.

[8] HILLIER, FREDERICK, S., Stanford University, "The Derivation of Probabilistic Information for the Evaluation of Risky Investments," *Management Science*, April, 1963.

[9] MAGEE, JOHN F., "Decision Trees for Decision Making," *Harvard Business Review*, July–August, 1964.

[10] MAGEE, JOHN F., "How to Use Decision Trees in Capital Investment," *Harvard Business Review*, September–October, 1964.

[11] MARKOWITZ, HARRY, *Portfolio Selection, Efficient Diversification of Investments*, New York, John Wiley and Sons, 1959.

[12] MASSE, PIERRE, *Optimal Investment Decisions*, Prentice-Hall, 1962.

[13] McLEAN, JOHN G., "How to Evaluate New Capital Investments," *Harvard Business Review*, November-December, 1958.

[14] Reference Manual General Purpose Systems Simulator II, IBM, 1963.

[15] SCHLAIFER, ROBERT, *Probability and Statistics for Business Decisions*, McGraw-Hill, 1959.

[16] TERBORGH, GEORGE, *Business Investment Policy*, Machinery and Allied Products Institute, Washington, D.C., 1958.

[17] THORNE, H. C., and D. C. WISE, American Oil Company, "Computers in Economic Evaluation," *Chemical Engineering*, April 29, 1963.

[18] "Venture Analysis," Chemical Engineering Progress Technical Manual, American Institute of Chemical Engineers.

PART IV

Intermediate and Long
Term Financing

11

THE VALUATION OF CONVERTIBLE
SECURITIES

RICHARD E. QUANDT, BURTON G. MALKIEL, and
WILLIAM J. BAUMOL*

The use of securities with options has taken on increased importance in a world of increased economic uncertainty. The use of convertible bonds and preferred stocks has become increasingly important. Convertible securities usually sell at a premium over the value of equivalent securities without the convertibility feature. The premium consists of at least two parts, the premium over the issue's bond value and the premium over the issue's stock value. In this article the determination of the value of the convertible is analyzed in terms of two components—the expected value of the security and the insurance value of the convertibility feature.

I. INTRODUCTION

This paper addresses itself to the valuation of convertible securities, those issues which may be exchanged at the option of the holder for other securities of the issuing company. We shall focus on convertible bonds, although the techniques developed here are also applicable to other convertible instruments, such as convertible preferred stock, etc. The convertible bonds treated are debenture bonds convertible into the common stock of the issuing company at a specified rate of exchange and within a limited time period. As is well known, convertible debentures normally sell at a premium over the value of otherwise equivalent bonds that are divested of the convertibility feature. They also often sell at a price higher than the debenture's conversion value, the value of the common stocks into which the bond is convertible. The former premium we shall call the premium over the issue's bond value, the latter, the premium over the issue's stock value. The purpose of this analysis is to describe the determination of these premiums

Reprinted by permission of the publishers from William J. Baumol, Burton G. Malkiel, and Richard E. Quandt: *Quarterly Journal of Economics.* Cambridge, Mass.: Harvard University Press, Copyright, 1966, by the President and Fellows of Harvard College.

* The authors are indebted to Professors Charles C. Holt and Donald E. Farrar for very valuable comments and to the National Science Foundation and the Ford Foundation whose grants helped in the completion of this paper. Our work on this subject was begun under the auspices of MATHEMATICA.

as a function of the characteristics of the common stock of the issuing company.

The model we present asserts that the value of a convertible can be divided into two parts. The first is the present worth of the security itself, representing the discounted stream of future coupon payments and the expected value of the security at the end of a specified horizon period. The second is the insurance value of the convertibility feature which enables the holder of the security to treat it either as a stock or a bond. Suppose an investor had bought the convertible on a certain date and planned to sell it three years later, expecting, because there was a rising trend in the market value of the shares of company X, that he would finally sell it at a value governed largely by its stock equivalent. This privilege is worth something to him in and of itself as that value will essentially be based on the anticipated (higher) price of the stock at the date of the sale. But our security holder also knows (assuming he has not actually converted his security in the interim) that if it turns out that his forecast was mistaken in that the stock price has in fact fallen sharply, he has the option of disposing of a security whose market price will be largely governed by its value as a bond rather than a stock. Thus the "bond value" of the convertible may provide a cushion limiting the risk assumed by the convertible holder vis-à-vis the outright owner of common shares. Consequently, the determination of the value of a convertible comes down to the analysis of the values of these two components—the expected value of the security and the insurance value of the convertibility feature.

We shall proceed as follows: We begin by presenting a first approximation of a convertible valuation model. In the preliminary application of the model we assert that investors' subjective probability distributions of future common stock prices can be treated as being wholly determined by past distributions of stock prices. Moreover, we abstract from interest payments, dividends, risk factors, and we do not employ a discounting procedure. We then test the preliminary model statistically. We offer sample calculations for seven convertible bonds and compare the normative valuations with actual market prices. Next, the implications of altering several of the assumptions of the analysis are examined. Finally, we indicate how such modifications might be incorporated into the basic model and we offer suggestions for further work.

II. A PRELIMINARY MODEL FOR THE VALUATION OF CONVERTIBLE BONDS

Consider an investor who is contemplating the purchase of a convertible security. Let us see how much he should be willing to pay for it in terms of the value of the common stock into which it can be converted and in terms of its value as an ordinary bond.

Let

C   represent the value of the convertible
B   represent the convertible's bond equivalent value (its bond value)
S   represent the number of shares of common stock into which the convertible
can be exchanged
$P(t)$ the price per common share at date t so that $P(t)S$ represents the convertible's
stock equivalent value (its stock value)
$i(t)$ a price-relative of a share at date t and let t_0 be the date on which the
convertible is being evaluated.

Therefore, by definition,

$$P(t) = i(t)P(t_0) \qquad \text{for any date, } t. \tag{1}$$

Now, suppose our investor expects to sell his convertible at the end of an as yet unspecified horizon period.

We assume for any future date t that there exists a subjective probability distribution of the price-relative $i(t)$ which expresses the purchaser's views on the likelihood of different stock values. This distribution is given by the density function $f(i, t_0)$ where the presence of the t_0 in the function indicates that the shape of the distribution may be affected by the date at which the convertible is valued.

As has been stated, the convertible is going to be worth at least as much as the contract equivalent stock (which sells for $P(t_0)S$) plus the insurance value, V, of having the option of selling the security at its bond value rather than stock value, should the stock value be below the bond value when the security is sold. Thus we have (where for the sake of simplicity we use the abbreviation P for $P(t_0)$)

$$C \geq P(t_0)S + V = PS + V. \tag{2}$$

But V refers to the possibility that the bond value, B, will in the future exceed the value of the equivalent stock, $P(t)S = i(t)PS$. For any value of $i(t)$ the difference between the bond and stock values will be $B - i(t)PS$, and this will occur with probability $f(i, t_0)\,di(t)$, Hence the expected value, V, of all circumstances in which the bond value will be worth more than the stock value will be the sum (integral) of the excesses of the bond over the stock values, each multiplied by its probability of occurring, i.e., we have, assuming B to be a constant, $\bar{B}$,

$$V = \int_0^{\bar{B}/PS} f(i, t_0)[\bar{B} - i(t)PS]\,di(t). \tag{3}$$

Here the limits of integration, $i(t) = 0$ and $i(t) = \bar{B}/PS$, are arrived at as follows: The maximum value of i for which the stock value is no greater than the bond value is that i which makes the stocks and the bonds equal in value so that $\bar{B} = i(t)PS$ or $i(t) = \bar{B}/PS$. This, then, is the upper limit of integration. And, since stock prices will not fall below zero, $i(t) = 0$ is the lower limit of integration.

Now, substituting from (3) into (2) and writing C_s for the right-hand expression (2) we obtain

$$C \geq C_s = PS + \int_0^{\bar{B}/PS} f(i, t_0)[\bar{B} - i(t)PS] \, di(t). \tag{4}$$

In exactly the same way we obtain the analogous relationship between the value of the convertible and its bond value, $\bar{B}$

$$C \geq C_b = \bar{B} + \int_{\bar{B}/PS}^{\infty} f(i, t_0)[i(t)PS - \bar{B}] \, di(t) \tag{5}$$

where the expression involving the integral represents the value of the option of having a call on the common stock of the company.

Moreover, as already explained, the value of the convertible will be equal to the greater of the values of the two expressions given on the right-hand side of (4) and (5), that is

$$C = \max (C_s, C_b). \tag{6}$$

Our final relationships (4), (5) and (6) can now be used to evaluate a convertible security in terms of the expected performance of the values of the bond and stock equivalents.[1]

It should be noted that the behavior of our model is in agreement with the observation that the difference between the value of the convertible and the value of the equivalent stocks, $C - PS$ (given by V in (3)), will tend to disappear when stock prices increase. Since the date, t_0, is the date at which our convertible is being evaluated, the price of the stock $P(t_0) = P$ will vary with the date chosen for evaluation. Suppose that the stock price P is high at t_0; then, other things being equal, the upper limit of integration, $i(t) = \bar{B}/PS$ will be low; thus the probability of an $i(t)$ less than this value will be very small. Moreover, if we choose evaluation dates involving higher and higher values of P the upper limit of integration will approach zero and, therefore, V will also approach zero. Hence the difference between C and PS will approach zero, i.e., the premium over stock value will disappear.

III. STATISTICAL IMPLEMENTATION OF THE MODEL

The basic problem in applying the model statistically was the derivation of a distribution of price relatives for stock prices. As a preliminary step we may assume that investors form a subjective probability distribution of future stock prices wholly on the basis of the past behavior of stock prices.

---

[1] It has been argued that certain economic quantities such as speculative prices have the Pareto distribution which, for appropriate values of its parameters, does not even possess a finite first moment. See B. Mandelbrot, "The Variation of Certain Speculative Prices," *Journal of Business*, XXXVI (Oct. 1963), 394–419. If that were the case any approach based on expected values would be invalid. The evidence, however, that stock prices have a Pareto distribution with Pareto α less than unity is inconclusive, at least so far.

Specifically, assuming that the bond values remain (relatively) fixed, we may proceed by choosing an earlier date, t_b, and fitting an empirical distribution of price relatives $f(i, t_b)$ which can then be substituted into our relationships.

The choice of the base date, t_b, will affect the resulting empirical distribution in two major ways: (1) through factors peculiar to the security under consideration; and (2) through factors relevant to the entire market. On the assumption that the past distribution of stock prices offers an indication of what may be expected in the future, we may use historical distributions except insofar as the sequence of price relatives contains strong cyclical elements. It was our hope that the period of seven years prior to the date of valuation from which we derived empirical distributions was long enough to wash out the effect of cycles.[2] The price relatives would then reflect only the general trend of the market and factors peculiar to the security in question, both of which are relevant for purposes of extrapolation.

We further assume that investors anticipate selling their convertible securities at the end of a fixed horizon period. Specifically, we posit that these investors are concerned only with making predictions for a period two or three years from now and that their subjective probability distribution of price relatives is based on an empirical distribution of relative prices over intervals two and three years apart. Our incorporation of a fixed horizon into the model naturally leads to a floating base date for the purposes of calculating the price relatives. Monthly closing prices for seven years were taken for each security and price relatives were derived by taking each price and dividing it by the price at some specified earlier time. In accordance with our specific assumption concerning investors' horizon periods, two approaches were used:

(a)
$$i(t) = \frac{P_t}{P_{t-24}},$$

and

(b)
$$i(t) = \frac{P_t}{P_{t-36}}$$

where t measures time in months. Arbitrarily, the observations were then grouped into seven or six intervals respectively, depending on whether (a) or (b) above was used. The frequency of observations in each interval was used to estimate the required probabilities. Formulas (4) and (5) were then applied in straightforward manner, except as indicated below:

> a. Since we do not have continuous probability distributions, summations appear in the formulas actually used instead of integrals.
> b. The estimated probabilities corresponding to each interval on the $i(t)$ axis were multiplied by the *midpoint* of that interval.

---

[2] If, for example, the period over which we calculate price relatives encompassed one half of a cycle and began at the cyclical trough, obviously all the calculated i values would tend to be high.

c. The value $\bar{B}$ used in the formulas was the most recent value of B.
d. The value P used in the formulas was the most recent value of P.
e. Whenever the quantity $\bar{B}/PS$ falls within an interval on the $i(t)$ scale (rather than on the boundary of such an interval) the associated frequency of observations in it are deemed to have been divided in the same proportion as the interval itself, with the left-hand part of this divided interval contributing to formula (4) and the right-hand part to formula (5).

Seven bonds were chosen to test the model. The criteria used in selecting the bonds were that: (1) the bonds be of homogeneous (medium) quality as evidenced by the appraisal of professional rating agencies; (2) they be convertible at a fixed price for a period of at least seven years; (3) the quantity of bonds outstanding be sufficiently large to insure that the quotations

Table 11–1

Issue	*Actual market price* 6/18/62*	*Rank*	*Predicted market price* (2-yr.) horizon*	*Rank*	*Predicted market price* (3-yr.) horizon*	*Rank*
Homestake Mining	$136\frac{3}{4}$	1	$160\frac{7}{8}$	1	$167\frac{3}{8}$	2
Northrop Aircraft	$120\frac{1}{4}$	2	$150\frac{1}{4}$	2	$176\frac{1}{8}$	1
Burroughs	115	3	$101\frac{5}{8}$	4	$102\frac{3}{8}$	3
Smith-Corona Marchant	108	4	$93\frac{5}{8}$	5	$94\frac{5}{8}$	5
Rohr Aircraft	106	5	$103\frac{5}{8}$	3	$101\frac{1}{2}$	4
Allegheny Ludlum	$99\frac{1}{4}$	6	$90\frac{3}{4}$	7	$89\frac{1}{8}$	7
Food Fair	$98\frac{7}{8}$	7	$92\frac{1}{8}$	6	$90\frac{1}{8}$	6

* All market prices expressed as a percent of par value.

for the bonds are good estimates of true market prices; and (4) the common stock of the issuing company have been traded publicly for at least seven years to permit the calculation of a distribution of price relatives over a long period. Table 11–1 above presents the market prices predicted by the valuation model on the basis of two- and three-year horizons. They are compared with actual market prices as of mid-1962, the date for which the calculation was made.

Needless to say, the version of the model tested is only a very crude and overly simplified representation of the basic apparatus. We shall indicate in the next section some of the more glaring deficiencies and how they may be rectified. Nevertheless, the results are, in some respects, fairly encouraging. The model has at least been able to do a reasonably good job of ranking the issues. The rank correlation coefficients turn out to be 0.86 for the two-year horizon and 0.89 for the three-year horizon. We notice that, for the higher-priced issues, our normative valuations tend to be higher than actual market prices, whereas for the lower-priced issues our valuations tend systematically to understate market prices. We shall note below how our computational shortcuts have contributed to such a result.

IV. ALTERING THE ASSUMPTIONS

We turn now to an examination of the more important assumptions implicit and explicit in the model. We shall indicate as we proceed what modifications seem necessary to our first approximation and the direction in which they will tend to alter our results.

A. Utilizing Expected Rather than Current Stock Prices

In equation (2) we suggested that the convertible should be worth at least as much as the (current) stock equivalent plus the insurance value V of the security's bond value which sets a floor under an investor's possible losses. An alternative formulation utilizing the expected value of the stock equivalent at the end of the horizon period would appear at least equally plausible. In this formulation the current price of the convertible is determined by its expected future stock value plus the actuarial insurance value of having the option of disposing of the security at its bond value rather than its stock value, should the latter fall below the former. Such a formulation has an important computational advantage inasmuch as equations (4) and (5) then become identical.[3] Thus equation (5) alone can be used to determine the value of a convertible.

There is one difficulty with this alternative formulation, however, which must be dealt with. We have no assurance that the calculated convertible value will exceed the *current* stock equivalent value *PS*. Such a possibility must be ruled out since, if any differential existed, an arbitrageur could always make the convertible equal its stock equivalent by simultaneously buying the convertible and selling short S shares of common. The arbitrageur would then convert his bond into common and deliver these shares to cover his short contract. Consequently, the alternative formulation of the model must become

$$C = \max (C_b, PS). \tag{7}$$

Utilizing the alternative formulation for the seven bonds in Table 11–1 we find only slight differences in calculated market prices and insignificant differences in rankings.

---

[3] Proof: Substituting the expected value of *PS* for *PS* in the right-hand side of (4) we have

$$C_s = \int_0^\infty i(t)PSf(i, t_0)\, di(t) + \int_0^{B/PS} f(i, t_0)[\bar{B} - i(t)PS]\, di(t) \tag{4a}$$

or, rearranging terms,

$$C_s = \int_{B/PS}^\infty i(t)PSf(i, t_0)\, di(t) + \bar{B} \int_0^{B/PS} f(i, t_0)\, di(t).$$

But, rewriting the right-hand side of (5), we have

$$C_b = \int_{B/PS}^\infty i(t)PSf(i, t_0)\, di(t) + \bar{B} \int_0^{B/PS} f(i, t_0)\, di(t), \tag{5a}$$

which is identical to (4a).

B. Modifications for Interest Payments and Appropriate Discounting

Recall that in the basic model we neglected the interest payments received by the bondholder. Moreover, we did not discount our final convertible value to present worth despite the fact that the value was found by calculating the actuarial value of the security two and three years hence. To remedy matters we may write instead of (7)

$$C \geq \frac{R}{\left(1 + \frac{\rho}{2}\right)} + \frac{R}{\left(1 + \frac{\rho}{2}\right)^2} + \cdots + \frac{R}{\left(1 + \frac{\rho}{2}\right)^{2N}} + \frac{C_b}{\left(1 + \frac{\rho}{2}\right)^{2N}}, \qquad (8)$$

and $C \geq PS$, where R represents the periodic coupon payment of the bond (made semi-annually), ρ is the appropriate (annual) discount rate, N is the number of years in the investors' horizon, and C_b represents the actuarial value of the security at the end of the horizon period. Summing the geometric progression we have

$$C \geq \frac{2R}{\rho} \left[1 - \frac{1}{\left(1 + \frac{\rho}{2}\right)^{2N}} \right] + \frac{C_b}{\left(1 + \frac{\rho}{2}\right)^{2N}}. \qquad (9)$$

An obvious choice of an appropriate discount rate presents itself in at least two cases. When the convertible sells at zero premium over its bond value (i.e., the expected value of the call privilege on the common stock is nil), the appropriate discount rate is clearly the yield of the bond itself (the capitalization rate for a debt stream of that risk class). If, on the other hand, the convertible sells at a zero premium over its stock equivalent, it would appear that for a good approximation we could employ the discount rate applicable to an equity in that risk class. Presumably for a convertible selling at a premium above both its stock and bond values we would be justified in interpolating between the two discount rates in proportion to the magnitudes of these premiums.

The employment of a discounting technique such as that just described would have brought our convertible value estimates closer to those actually observed as existing market prices. In particular, discounting tends to reduce our calculated valuations of convertibles selling at relatively high prices while leaving low-priced convertibles unaffected. This is so because high-priced convertibles tend to have a low current yield (annual coupon payment divided by market price) relative to the appropriate discount rate. Thus the addition of interest payments and discounting tends to reduce the value of the convertible. For low-priced convertibles the two factors tend nearly to cancel out.[4] To illustrate the effect of discounting we have

---

[4] When the convertible sells at its bond value, the two factors would exactly cancel by definition.

calculated the discounted present worth for Homestake Mining on the basis of a three-year horizon. The discounted present worth of the stream of interest payments plus the present worth of the calculated convertible price (167$\frac{3}{8}$) is found to be 156$\frac{5}{8}$. The discount rate employed was the bond-value yield obtained from the rating services. Were an appropriately higher rate used (i.e., the interpolated stock-bond rate suggested by the argument above) the present worth would have been even lower.

C. Altering the Horizon Period

In the statistical test of the model we assumed that investors would hold the convertible bond for a period of exactly two or three years. Such a procedure is arbitrary and lacks any theoretical justification. This is so because the price was calculated on the basis of probabilities assigned to a series of possible stock values without allowing for the possibility of any premiums over these values. But is it not reasonable to suppose that two years hence a convertible whose conversion feature has not expired may still command a premium over the value of otherwise equivalent bonds and stocks? Our fixed-horizon method ignores the fact that the market may take into account the probable longer-run behavior of the stock.

This difficulty is easily remedied in theory by extending the horizon period until the conversion feature expires. In this case the bond will be converted into common stock if $P(t)S > B$ and will remain outstanding as a straight debt instrument if $B > P(t)S$. We might then say that the convertible is worth the maximum value over every horizon period from the date of valuation up to the date of the expiration of the conversion privilege. It would be possible that some convertibles attain a maximum value when valued on the basis of a short horizon period. This would be the case, for example, if the stock price were expected to rise in the near future (and the convertible would be expected to rise to its stock value) but where the long-term trend was unfavorable. On the other hand, if the long-term trend of the stock price was favorable, presumably the convertible would attain its maximum value when the horizon was extended until the expiration of the option privilege.

D. The Nature of the Subjective Probability Distribution of Stock Prices

We suggested earlier a simple method by which investors' subjective probability distributions of future stock prices could be quantified. We hypothesized that investors formed expectations of future price changes as if they believed that past distributions could be extrapolated into the future directly. Thus, if the common stock in question had enjoyed a rising trend over the period during which the index values were calculated, we assumed that investors would, in effect, project this trend into the future. It was this assumption that contributed to the high valuations obtained for Homestake Mining and Northrop Aircraft, since the common stocks of both companies rose sharply over the period used in calculating the price relatives.

This assumption leaves much to be desired as a theoretical basis for equity valuation. Surely, if investors actually expected a continuation of rising earnings and dividends for the equity in question, such expectations would be reflected in the current price of the issue. If any sense is to be made of the structure of equity prices existing at any moment in time, it must be assumed that such diverse expectations for the prospects of different companies are already incorporated in present market prices. A stock-valuation model accounting for such expectations has been developed by one of us.[5] In that model, all equities of the same risk class are assumed to sell at prices that equalize their net yields. The net yield (discount rate) turns out to be the sum of the dividend yield of the security and the anticipated growth rate of the shares. For standard industrial securities as a group it was asserted that a good empirical approximation to the appropriate discount rate can be obtained by adding the dividend rate of the standard market averages to the long-term growth rate of earnings. Thus, at any moment of time we could calculate an "apparent marginal efficiency" for equities in general. If we assume that the seven sample companies belong (roughly) to the same risk class as the representative standard share, we can actually calculate the expected growth rate of the shares over the horizon period. This will equal the total apparent marginal efficiency less the dividend yield on the shares.[6]

This line of argument leads to an interesting conclusion. It asserts that if a company pays no dividend, it can be assumed that the market expects the growth rate of the price of the shares to equal the appropriate discount rate. On the other hand, if the shares are expected to provide a dividend yield equal to the discount rate, then no growth in the price of the shares is expected.

Given the discount rate and the dividend yield, we can always determine the expected growth rate of the price of the shares. Consequently, the valuation model gives an alternative method of projecting the expected value of the shares into the future. It appears that if our techniques were modified to account for this extra information, our predicted market prices would be closer to the prevailing prices. In particular, we note that our largest underestimation of the market worth of the convertible occurred in the case of Smith-Corona Marchant. Our low estimate of the issue's investment value resulted from the downward trend of the stock price over the period used in constructing the price relatives. Had we taken into account the observation that, at the time of our valuation, investors apparently expected a rising trend in the price of the common (the dividend yield on the shares was zero)

---

[5] Burton G. Malkiel, "Equity Yields, Growth, and the Structure of Share Prices," *American Economic Review*, LIII (Dec. 1963), 1004–31. (Also, Chapter 14 of this book.)

[6] *Ibid.*, p. 1014 n.

our calculated valuation would have been raised. On the other hand, the dividend yield on Northrop Aircraft and Homestake Mining (where we over-estimated the convertible's value) tended to be relatively high, suggesting that investors anticipated a lower growth rate in the price of the shares (according to the model). In this case the appropriate adjustment would have been to reduce our calculated valuations. Thus we conjecture that an adjustment of our probability distribution of future stock prices, in the manner required by the stock valuation model just discussed, would have tended to improve our results.

This suggests a method of procedure to guide us in further work in the valuation of convertibles. We could attempt to project the mean of the sub-jective probability distribution of common stock prices on the basis of the equity valuation model referred to above. To determine the variance of the distribution, we could simply extrapolate this information from our record of price relatives over a period in the past. Thus we would be arguing that the past behavior of a common stock indicates its future prospects only with respect to the volatility of the shares, not their expected value.

V. SUMMARY COMMENT

Our analytic model for the valuation of convertible securities seems to promise to be serviceable in two respects. It may help us to understand the logic of the security valuation process, and it may enable us to offer some reasonable predictions of security prices. This may be particularly useful to firms involved in the flotation of new issues who must set prices on these issues before they have been evaluated by the market. We, at least, were somewhat surprised by the relative success of the predictions undertaken with the aid of our crude model. The fact that the most obvious and apparently most appropriate modifications of the model all increase its success as a predictor is perhaps even more encouraging.

12

ANOTHER LOOK AT LEASING

HENRY G. HAMEL and G. CLARK THOMPSON

This report on the survey of company attitudes toward leasing reflects the authors' considerable company experience with leasing practices. Hamel and Thompson conducted a survey of leasing for the National Industrial Conference Board. They received responses from 220 manufacturing firms, 186 of which reported that they were leasing some type of equipment or facility. The authors note some further leasing trends that had taken place since a survey made five years earlier. They also observe that the longer duration of experience within leasing had increased understanding of its advantages and disadvantages.

Increased leasing of business facilities and equipment during the past five years is reported by about one third of the 220 manufacturing companies participating in the Board's latest *Survey of Business Opinion and Experience.* But, as in 1958, when the Board last surveyed industry leasing practices,[1] responding companies continue to approach leasing cautiously. Expensive office equipment, automobiles, and trucks—the items most favored for leasing at the time of the prior study—account for most of the over-all increase in leasing activity. On the other hand, cooperators report a tapering off in leasing of such long-term facilities as office buildings, warehouses, and tankers.

In the past five years many companies have changed their opinion about the rationale for leasing. It was once popular to cite the conservation of working capital as a major benefit; very few companies now do so, and many regard leasing as an expensive form of borrowing. But experience has demonstrated that leasing rather than buying certain types of equipment brings the company certain operating advantages, such as specialized services from lessors and avoidance of the risk of obsolescence.

Not only are more respondents leasing facilities and equipment from others than did so five years ago, but in turn more are leasing products to their customers, largely because they have found that offering lease arrangements is a helpful sales tool. But only a minority of cooperating companies

[1] "A Cautious Trend Toward Leasing," *The Conference Board Business Record*, November, 1958.

follow this practice, and even in those companies leases generally account for only a small part of product and equipment distribution.

The net outlook of participants is that in the future (1) they will lease from others more of the type of equipment they now lease and (2) the practice of leasing products to their customers will also grow. But in each case the increase is expected to be of modest proportions. Yet many companies believe that, as a result of the entry of commerical banks into the equipment- and facility-leasing business, leasing by industry as a whole will become considerably more widespread, especially among smaller companies.

LEASING'S CURRENT STATUS

One hundred and eighty-six of the 220 participating companies are currently leasing some type of equipment or facility. Of these 186 companies, 91 report no significant change in the type of equipment they lease or the extent of their leasing over the past five years; 74 companies report increases; and 21 report decreases. Thus, one in three of the 220 participating companies is leasing more than in 1958, while only one in ten is leasing less. This trend is comparable to the one reported for the years 1954–1958 in the Board's 1958 survey.

In terms of numbers of companies involved, leasing of data-processing equipment and automotive equipment shows the greatest net gains over the past five years (see Table 12–2). Leasing of other office equipment, machinery and industrial equipment has also had a net growth, but a considerably smaller one. On the other hand, very few companies report increased leasing of long-term facilities.

Reasons for Increased Leasing

Although increases in leasing are commonly attributed to the general growth of business activity, many specific reasons are also cited. Those

Table 12–1. Over-all trends in leasing practices in 220 companies.

	Trends during past 5 years		Expected trends in next 10 years	
	No. of Co's.	% of Total	No. of Co's.	% of Total
Increases in over-all leasing	74	34%	43	20%
Decreases in over-all leasing	21	10	15	7
No change	91	41	98	44
Have not leased in past five years	34	15	—	—
Do not expect to lease in future	—	—	39*	18
Undecided	—	—	25	11
Total	220	100%	220	100%

* Includes five companies that discontinued leasing in the past five years.

Table 12–2. Analysis of changes in leasing practices, by type of equipment or facilities.

Experiences and predictions reported by 220 companies	Trends during past 5 years				Expected trends in next 10 years			
	Increase		Decrease		Increase		Decrease	
	No. of Co's	% of Total	No. of Co's	% of Total	No. of Co's	% of Total	No. of Co's	% of Total
No. of companies reporting:								
A. Changes in over-all leasing activity	74	34%	21	10%	43	20%	15	7%
B. Changes by type of equipment or facilities								
Autos and trucks	36	16.4	7	3.2	15	6.8	4	1.8
Data-processing equipment	42	19.1	5	2.3	19	8.6	1	0.5
Other office equipment	8	3.6	2	0.9	6	2.7	—	—
Machinery and industrial equipment	12	5.5	5	2.3	6	2.7	1	0.5
Plants and factories	4	1.8	—	—	1	0.5	—	—
Warehouses	3	1.4	—	—	—	—	1	0.5
Buildings (office and retail)	3	1.4	1	0.5	—	—	1	0.5
Tankers and ships	2	0.9	2	0.9	—	—	—	—
Other, or not specified	4	1.8	5	2.3	9	4.1	8	3.6

most frequently mentioned are: protecting the company against the risk of obsolescence; eliminating maintenance, service, and administrative problems; and obtaining needed equipment when no other financing is available.

While these advantages were also reported in the 1958 survey, much greater emphasis is being placed on them today as a result of further experience with leasing and more critical examination by companies of the leasing concept.

Avoiding Obsolescence. Companies that need high-priced electronic data-processing equipment regard leasing as an insurance against heavy losses that could arise as a result of rapid obsolescence. Many executives of such companies are concerned not only that improved models might make their existing EDP equipment relatively expensive to operate, but also that this equipment might well become totally unsuitable for future needs. Thus they feel they cannot afford to gamble on the heavy potential loss to their companies that purchase of EDP equipment might entail. "The risk of obsolescence is so great," says the treasurer of an industrial machinery company, "that the added cost of leasing seems to be logical."

Several companies, however, have concluded that this risk is not so great as it was five years ago, and are accordingly reexamining their position. For example, another top executive reports: "Close attention is being paid to this matter, and when we feel reasonably confident of design stability we will give strong consideration to buying the equipment we are now renting."

Avoiding Maintenance, Service, and Administrative Problems. A number of companies with large fleets of automobiles and trucks have increased their leasing in an attempt to avoid maintenance, service, and administrative problems. By leasing motor vehicles a company can pass these problems on to the lessor as well as take advantage of the latter's purchasing power in acquiring new cars and skill in disposing of old ones. In recent years, quite a few cooperators have closely examined the financial implications and other costs involved in having lessors assume the burdens of maintenance and service of vehicles. Many of these companies have found automotive leasing to be more economical than either owning cars or paying mileage allowances to salesmen.

No Other Financing Available.   Several companies say they have resorted to leasing because they have had no other practical means of financing needed equipment. They have found that when conventional lines of credit are used up, or when an existing loan indenture restricts further direct borrowing, the lease route is still open. Under such circumstances, these companies say the relatively higher costs involved in lease financing can be justified.

Why Growth Has Been Modest

Two thirds of the 220 cooperating companies have never leased any equipment, or are doing less leasing now than they did five years ago or have not appreciably changed, since 1958, the amount of leasing they do. Respondents give several reasons for the modest extent of the inroads leasing has been making on more traditional means of financing equipment and facilities. A few companies say they do not engage in leasing simply because they always have adequate or surplus working funds. A much more common reason for not leasing, or not leasing more extensively, is the necessarily high interest cost implicit in lease contracts. Many companies that can borrow at prime rates of interest report that they find outright purchase and ownership to be a less costly way of securing the facilities they need. As an office equipment manufacturer observes: "Certainly the lessor has to make a profit over and beyond the cost of his doing business, with something added for the risks involved, and this we believe we can save by purchasing rather than by leasing."

Another, and related, drawback of leasing cited by several respondents is that once a lease has expired the residual value of the leased asset is commonly forfeited to the lessor, even though the latter has fully recouped his original investment. Some lease agreements, to be sure, include an option for the lessee to purchase the equipment during or after the time of the lease; but respondents comment that very often the price called for in purchase options is excessive.[2]

The financial costs of leasing—higher interest charges, and either loss of residual value of the asset or high purchase option prices—have caused some

---

[2] One company that enjoys prime interest rates in its conventional borrowing is able to protect itself against such losses by negotiating leases that are not only based on "appropriate" rates but are structured to permit purchase of the leased assets at a reasonable price. This company's vice president explains: "We insist on purchase options that avoid a premium of any kind to the lessor. He is entitled to the complete return of his capital through lease rentals plus interest on the unamortized portion of his investment, and that is all."

companies to cut back on their leasing. For example, a construction materials company executive reports:

> We are not interested in leasing as a substitute for direct financing . . . as we were five years ago . . . because we can borrow money cheaper than we can 'lease' it and receive the proceeds from the sale of the asset when we are through with it too. This change reflects our decision that the only time leasing is worthwhile to us is when the lessor brings a special talent or ability to the transaction which helps reduce the cost.

And a petroleum company executive states:

> Proportionately we are leasing fewer facilities than in 1958. We have reduced the number of such leases—primarily tanker charters—because of the expense connected with them with respect to the actual or imputed interest cost that they bear, which is in excess of what the company can do through direct financing.

A few respondents challenge the importance of one of the operating advantages cited by proponents of leasing, namely, that it frees management from burdensome administrative and servicing problems. For example, the treasurer of a chemical company that purchases rather than leases its fleet of automobiles says:

> We do not find the argument that it is important to be relieved of all the administrative details very important to us. We have a large fleet of cars and trucks. Our sales service manager and a clerk spend part time in supervising the over-all setup. Replacement of cars is handled by our field people who get three local bids (working from a policy statement as to eligible cars and equipment) and recommend their choice to our purchasing department. As to maintenance, we have well-defined procedures, and because of delegation and decentralization, it does not become a big job.

A number of companies say they are either opposed to or lukewarm about leasing because of their disenchantment with one of the chief advantages claimed for leasing in its early days: the improvement in financial ratios resulting from keeping the debt equivalent of lease obligations off the balance sheet. "You cannot cover lease obligations with balance sheet ratios," cautions the financial vice president of a paper company. "Ability to pay either rent or debt service is the important test, since it takes dollars to cover either of these obligations."

Disclosure of Lease Obligations

The growing recognition that leasing is primarily a financing device, and the inclination of bankers, accountants, credit analysts and institutional investors to regard all long-term leasing as equivalent to long-term debt have produced a gradual trend toward making some disclosure of lease obligations in published financial statements.

Over half of the participating companies indicate that they have some outstanding lease obligations that extend three years or more into the future. Of these companies, one in three makes disclosure of its lease commitments in published financial statments. However, two out of three do not consider their lease commitments to be sufficiently significant or material to require public disclosure.

A common method of complete disclosure is described in the following statement from an aircraft company: "Our company's long-term lease obligations are disclosed in the annual report in the form of a balance sheet footnote. We define long-term leases as those which have an expiration date longer than three years from the date of the report. We indicate the anticipated annual rental and lease payments for the following year and the total aggregate payments due on all long-term leases to expiration."

In a few cases, public disclosure is limited to a note in the text of the annual report describing the nature of facilities or equipment leased but not giving a dollar amount.

Although lease obligations must be reported annually to the SEC, there is no uniform legal requirement governing the disclosure of such obligations in published financial statements. Companies commenting on the question generally say they are guided by the advice of their public accountants as to whether outstanding lease commitments are considered "material" within the meaning of the formal recommendations of the American Institute of Accountants. Several respondents report that they are discussing the question of "materiality" with their auditors and when the total obligations become a little larger they will be disclosed.

None of the participating companies report capitalizing lease commitments and showing the equivalent asset value and long-term debt on the balance sheet in the manner suggested by some financial analysts. However, several respondents say they see a need to give recognition to the asset value and long-term debt equivalent of leases in their own financial planning procedures. The following comment of a corporate treasurer is illustrative:

> For internal purposes, the company is now considering the adoption of a policy to include lease obligations in the computation of return on investment in order to avoid distortions of comparisons between operations which use these facilities and those which use company-owned facilities.

Another executive points out that companies using medium- or long-term leasing as a means of financing should watch the relation of lease commitments to capital just as they would watch the relation of debt to capital in direct financing.

Leasing Equipment to Others

Over two thirds of the cooperating companies do not lease to customers. Many, of course, do not make products suitable for leasing. Among the

62 firms that lease products or equipment to customers either directly or through leasing companies, more (19) have recorded increases in such leasing during the last five years than have recorded decreases (five). The other 38 report no significant change in customer leasing since 1958.

The consensus of the 62 companies is that much of their customer rental activity is sporadic. With very few exceptions, it accounts for only a small portion of the total product distribution of the companies concerned.

The reason commonly cited for offering customers an opportunity to lease rather than to buy is that this is a way of securing business that could not be obtained through direct sales. Thus an aircraft chairman reports:

> During the past five years we have, for the first time, leased some of our products to our customers. This has not been of our own choice, however, but has been at the urging of the customers, principally because some of them have found it difficult to obtain other means of financing purchases of the equipment.

Some companies, however, are more enthusiastic about the value of leasing as a business-getting device. For example, one chief executive comments:

> Approximately a year and a half ago we formed our own financial company to offer both leasing and financing to the customers of our companies. The financial company has had a moderate growth, and we feel has aided the distribution of certain equipment produced by our companies. There has been about a fifty-fifty split between leasing and conventional forms of customer financing.

The few companies that do less leasing to customers now than they did five years ago offer several reasons for the decline. One company says its customers can buy outright more advantageously than they can lease. Another observes that "customers who formerly leased equipment are now willing to buy." And the president of a motor vehicles company says his firm has discontinued leasing simply because it has surplus funds and prefers to carry its customers on their own open accounts.

CROSS CURRENTS IN PROJECTIONS

Fewer companies are planning to increase their leasing activity in the next ten years than actually increased it during the past five. Only 20% expect to increase their leasing activity during the next ten years; 34% reported increases over the past five years. However, approximately 11% of the companies are still uncertain as to the future trend of their companies' leasing activity. About 7% expect an over-all decline.

The items most frequently leased during the past five years—EDP equipment and motor vehicles—will continue to be widely leased during the next decade. Companies anticipating increased leasing of these items outnumber those expecting decreased leasing by almost seven to one. Leasing of machinery and other office equipment is also forecast to rise, but at a slower pace. Leasing of long-term facilities, plants and factories, warehouses, office buildings, and tankers will be virtually unchanged.

The Tax Impact

In the Board's 1958 survey of leasing practices, a number of respondents pointed out that accelerated depreciation allowances increased the tax benefits gained by owning capital equipment and correspondingly reduced the incentive for leasing. The viewpoint of some of the companies participating in the current survey is that recently liberalized depreciation guidelines and the 7% investment allowance make ownership even more attractive. This is why, for instance, one corporate financial vice president states: "We lean much more strongly than we did a few years back to outright ownership." Other executives say, however, that some lessor organizations have offered to pass all or part of these increased tax benefits along to the lessee.

In commenting on the tax aspects of leasing, several cooperators point out that very high rentals called for in the early years of some lease agreements might not qualify for full tax credits. They say that the tax status of a prospective lease should be clearly resolved before it is entered into, for it has a direct bearing on the after-tax net rental cost.

Rentals to Customers

On balance the cooperators that now lease to customers believe this practice will continue its gradual upward trend, because they feel such leases will help bring in business. As an office equipment manufacturer puts it: "Experience has indicated that the sales offices with the highest percentage of their business in leasing are generally among the sales leaders."

Quite a few respondents foresee no change in rentals of their products, and a handful expect a decline in such rentals. An industrial machinery company treasurer expresses this opinion:

> It might be of interest to mention that in the past 18 months there has been evidence of an increasing number of cases where our customers were able to obtain financing through their local banks, both for the purchase of new equipment and the prepayment of obligations under conditional sales contracts. With respect to the future, it would be my opinion that there will be fewer deals through leasing and more financing going to local banks.

The 143 respondents that do not lease to customers now have no plans to do so in the future. Many members of this group share the view of an instruments company president who feels that leasing would be relatively expensive for his company's customers. He writes:

> We have made extensive studies from time to time regarding the economy of leasing vs. the sale of our product. Our products are all in the capital durable goods category. Several finance companies have offered leasing plans to our

customers. Through banks and finance companies, including our own finance subsidiary, our customers have ample resources for buying our equipment on extended deferred payment terms. Such deferred payment contracts may run for as long as seven years. Our studies indicate that with such plans available our customers will be better off purchasing on long-term credit plans than leasing.

BANKS TO STIMULATE LEASING

Although the respondents expect only a modest growth in their own roles as lessees and lessors, they believe that leasing in industry will become considerably more widespread if commercial banks follow the lead of the Bank of America and enter the leasing business. This expected development should stimulate leasing by:

> Making it available at lower cost.
> Making it more convenient.
> Enhancing its respectability.
> Giving it greater publicity.

Quite a few of the cooperating companies think that smaller companies, which often have occasion to borrow funds at higher-than-prime-interest rates, will be the most promising market for bank-sponsored leasing services. Practically all cooperators agree that bank participation in the leasing field will lead to a better understanding of the pros and cons of leasing throughout industry.

Lower Costs

A number of companies think that leasing costs will be reduced if banks enter the leasing business. The direct bank-lessee relationship should entail lower rental charges on leased equipment; for by analyzing each prospective lessee's financial structure on an individual basis, banks could probably offer many companies lower rates than they can obtain from leasing companies, which often find it necessary to set blanket rates for all classes of customers. Several respondents say that in the long run banks will tend to set the interest cost component of the rental payment at a level corresponding to the lessee's credit rating. As for leasing companies, it is felt that they will meet competition from banks with lower rates of their own. As several respondents put it: "More competitive deals can be expected."

One-Stop Service

Some managements find the prospect of banks becoming lessors especially attractive, as it may mean they will no longer have to arrange leasing with one party and direct financing with another. "I believe that the entry of commercial banks into the leasing business will definitely accelerate the movement of more firms into leasing," observes one executive. "Leasing is very close to the entire field of financing and as such can become part of a package that is normally offered by a good commercial bank."

Other respondents speak of the desirability, from the standpoint of financial planning, of coordinating leasing with other forms of financing and thus obtaining the banker's advice on all matters relating to providing operating facilities. Still others say that the long-standing and close relationship companies usually enjoy with their banks causes them to prefer these institutions to leasing firms. Thus, in a direct lease with its own bank, a company could expect maximum consideration and understanding, especially in the event that an unexpected business decline should compel it to ask for a rescheduling of rental payments. The treasurer of an industrial machinery company that is interested in distributing its equipment through a lessor organization comments as follows:

> It is my feeling that users of our equipment would much prefer to deal with their local bankers, with whom they have a close business relationship, than with leasing companies. I feel that the local banker is much better qualified to judge the business potential of the lessee; he is familiar with the lessee's business practices and standing in the community. For these reasons I would think that the participation of commercial banks in the leasing business could possibly have a favorable effect on the growth of leasing in industry.

Prestige

The prestige of the banking house will also help attract new leasing customers, according to several respondents. They say that this prestige will give leasing a new dignity and status, and, in the words of one observer, "It will at the same time bring clearly into focus the fact that leasing is essentially a matter of borrowing money—a function of banks."

The wider availability of leasing, and the greater publicity it will presumably be given through bank advertising, are likewise expected to bring this form of financing to the attention of more potential customers.

Some Doubts Expressed

Although most of the cooperating executives think that the entry of banks into the leasing field will result in a decided over-all expansion of leasing, some have their doubts. Among them is an office equipment executive who opines:

> This is an open question, but it may well be that the entry of commercial banks into the leasing field will not materially change the potential for lease financing. To some extent, this development could increase competition, but the banks' captive finance subsidiaries will probably face the same operating problems and capital requirements as other leasing companies.

Several other executives think that the difficulties banks may encounter in crossing state lines and handling repossessions and depreciation losses will put a check on their drive into the leasing field. One respondent holds the view that growing recognition of the high service costs entailed in leasing and the alternative benefits that a company can obtain by owning its facilities will tend to limit expansion of leasing despite bank participation in this area of business.

The advantages and disadvantages of leasing, according to many cooperating companies, have been brought into sharper focus in recent years as a result of experience in leasing practices and the development of improved evaluation methods. Accordingly, despite mixed opinions on the practicality of leasing in their own businesses, most respondents believe that it has become established as an important, growing business activity.

13

A LINEAR-PROGRAMMING APPROACH TO EVALUATING RESTRICTIONS UNDER A BOND INDENTURE OR LOAN AGREEMENT

JAMES VAN HORNE

In this article, the author formulates an analytic approach to the contents of bond indenture or loan agreements. Using a linear-programming model, he evaluates proposed changes in the protective-covenant restrictions through sensitivity analysis, thus indicating the opportunity costs of restrictions. Such knowledge would be particularly useful to management when entering the initial stages of negotiation.

When a company enters into a bond indenture or loan agreement, certain restrictions usually are placed on it. These restrictions, known as protective covenants, may have a significant influence on profitability, making the bargaining strategy of the company very important. But to bargain effectively over the restrictiveness of the protective covenants, management must know the impact that the covenants have on profitability.

This paper proposes a method for determining the opportunity costs of the restrictions imposed under the indenture or agreement. These opportunity costs represent the additional profit a company could make if a restriction were relaxed. The framework for analysis is a linear-programming model for capital-budgeting and financing decisions; and an example of a hypothetical company illustrates the use of this model.[1] Sensitivity analysis is employed to determine the opportunity costs of the restrictions; the insights gained from this analysis gives management a basis by which to formulate its bargaining strategy.

From James Van Horne, "A Linear-Programming Approach to Evaluating Restrictions Under a Bond Indenture or Loan Agreement," *Journal of Financial and Quantitative Analysis,* June 1966, Vol. I, 68–83. Reprinted by permission.

[1] Other applications of mathematical programming to financial-management decision making include A. Charnes, W. W. Cooper, and M. H. Miller, "Application of Linear Programming to Financial Budgeting and the Costing of Funds," *Journal of Business,* XXXII (January 1959), pp. 20–46; Y. Ijiri, F. K. Levy and R. C. Lyon, "A Linear Programming Model for Budgeting and Financial Planning," *Journal of Accounting Research,* I (Autumn 1963), pp. 198–212; A. A. Robichek, D. Teichroew and J. M. Jones, "Optimal Short Term Financing Decision," *Management Science,* XII (September 1965), pp. 1–36; and H. Martin Weingartner, *Mathematical Programming and the Analysis of Capital Budgeting Decisions* (Englewood Cliffs, N.J.: Prentice-Hall, Inc., 1963).

PROTECTIVE COVENANTS

When a bond issue is floated or a term loan undertaken, the borrowing company has use of funds for an extended period of time, during which much can happen to its financial condition. Normally, the lender relies upon payment of its loan from operations of the borrower and resulting cash flow rather than from liquidation of assets or refunding.[2] When the lender deems it desirable to safeguard the borrowing company's ability to pay a loan, the company usually will be required to maintain its financial condition and, in particular, its current position at a level at least as favorable as that which prevailed when the loan was made. The provisions for protection are contained in the indenture or loan agreement and usually are called covenants.[3] The more important covenants include a minimum working-capital requirement, a restriction on cash dividends and acquisition of capital stock, a limitation on capital expenditures, and restrictions on long-term debt. While there are numerous other provisions that might be imposed upon a borrower, the above restrictions are the most widely used.

STATEMENT OF PROBLEM

We assume that the objective of a hypothetical company is to maximize net present value arising from various investment proposals. There are, of course, many practical difficulties in forecasting the cash flows expected from an investment proposal as well as in determining the cost of capital to be used as the discount factor. We shall by-pass these problems and deal with the simplified situation, where cash flows are known with certainty and a company is able to measure accurately its cost of capital.

Assuming that all outlays are made at the time of the investment decision, net present value per dollar of investment in a proposal can be determined by the profitability index.[4] For our purposes, the profitability index is interpreted as being the net present value of all outlays and inflows, discounted at the company's existing cost of capital, divided by the amount of cash outlay.[5] Table 13–1 shows seven investment proposals available to our hypothetical

---

[2] As a matter of terminology, a lender will be interpreted as being either a bondholder, whose interests are administered by a trustee, or a direct lender, such as a bank or an insurance company. Similarly, a loan will be considered to be either the purchase of bonds by investors or a direct loan.

[3] See N. H. Jacoby and R. J. Saulnier, *Term Lending to Business* (Camden, N.J.: National Bureau of Economic Research, 1942), p. 76; and Roland I. Robinson, *The Management of Bank Funds* (New York: McGraw-Hill Book Company, Inc., 1962), pp. 253–6.

[4] It is assumed that until some terminal date, net cash benefits generated from an investment proposal are reinvested at the company's existing cost of capital. See J. Hirshleifer, "On the Theory of Optimal Investment," *Journal of Political Economy*, LXVI (August 1958), pp. 329–52; J. H. Lorie and L. J. Savage, "Three Problems in Rationing Capital," *Journal of Business*, XXVIII (October 1955), pp. 229–39; and Ezra Solomon, *The Theory of Financial Management* (New York: Columbia University Press, 1963), pp. 132–35.

[5] Robert Lindsay and Arnold W. Sametz, *Financial Management: An Analytical Approach* (Homewood, Ill.: Richard D. Irwin, Inc., 1963), p. 73. Others interpret the profitability index to be the ratio of the present value of inflows to the present value of outlays. See Robert W. Johnson, *Financial Management*, Second edition (Boston: Allyn & Bacon, Inc., 1962), p. 190.

Table 13–1. Investment proposals available.

Description	Proportion of working capital to fixed assets	Maximum amount of investment	Profitability index
Proposal #1	1:4	$350,000	0.18
Proposal #2	2:1	225,000	0.06
Proposal #3	1:1	170,000	0.13
Proposal #4	3:1	200,000	0.09
Proposal #5	1:2	150,000	0.15
Proposal #6	4:1	250,000	0.07
Proposal #7	1:3	300,000	0.08

company, all having positive profitability indexes, and involving varying proportions of working capital and fixed assets. We assume that these proposals are independent of each other and of the company's existing investment projects and that the company may invest in each proposal at any level between zero and the stated maximum.[6]

It is assumed that the size of the capital budget is limited to $800,000, financed by $400,000 in retained earnings represented by excess cash and $400,000 in debt. The debt portion may be divided between short-term and long-term borrowings. We make the additional assumption that by financing investment proposals with equal amounts of retained earnings and borrowings, the relative proportions of borrowings and equity remain unchanged. Thus, we are able to assume that the financing of investment proposals leaves the cost of capital used as a discount factor virtually unchanged.[7] The problem, as stated so far, involves weighing the alternative investment proposals in Table 13–1 so as to maximize the value of the firm. If there were no protective-covenant constraints imposed on the company, we would expect it to invest, in descending order of profitability, $350,000 in investment

---

[6] In the model, we have assumed the divisibility of investment proposals. If a proposal is non-fractional, investment must be either zero or some absolute amount, and a dichotomy exists. Problems of this sort having "either-or" conditions may be solved by integer programming. See George B. Dantzig, "On the Significance of Solving Linear Programming Problems with Some Integer Variables," *Econometrica*, XXVIII (January 1960), pp. 30–44; and Ralph E. Gomory, "Outline of an Algorithm for Integer Solutions to Linear Programs," *Bulletin of the American Mathematical Society*, LXIV (September 1958), pp. 275–78.

For example, with investment proposal #1, we could impose the condition that:

$$X_{11} + X_{12} - 350,000 - \delta(-350,000) \geq 0$$

$$-X_{11} - X_{12} - (1 - \delta)(-350,000) \geq 0,$$

where δ is an integer variable that must be 0 or 1. When $\delta = 0$, $X_{11} + X_{12}$ must be $350,000. When $\delta = 1$, $X_{11} + X_{12}$ must be zero. Consequently, we are assured that proposal #1 will not be fractional but will be either zero or $350,000.

While the direct problem is straightforward when integer-valued variables are involved, there may be complications in interpreting values for the dual variables. For exposition of the dual-variable problem in integer programming, see Ralph E. Gomory and William J. Baumol, "Integer Programming and Pricing," *Econometrica*, XXVIII (July 1960), pp. 521–50; and H. Martin Weingartner, *op. cit.*, Chap. 5.

[7] Implicitly assumed is the fact that the quality of return on the investment proposals under consideration does not differ from the quality of return on existing investments.

proposal #1, $150,000 in proposal #5, $170,000 in proposal #3, and, $130,000 in proposal #4. Investment in these proposals, totaling $800,000, would result in the maximum possible increase in net present value, namely, $119,300.

We now consider the constraints imposed by the terms of the bond indenture or loan agreement; these are the constraints that we shall evaluate later. The problem will involve a single-stage decision at a point in time to invest and to borrow, subject to liquidity and other financial constraints. In order to simplify the problem, it is assumed that the terms of the indenture or agreement are already in force and that the impact of the restrictions occurs at the time of the decision.

The first protective covenant we consider is a *minimum working-capital* constraint. If minimum working capital was $2,250,000 and existing working capital $2,500,000, investment in fixed assets (a use of working capital) could exceed long-term borrowings (a source of working capital) by only $250,000 before the working-capital covenant would be violated. A *capital-expenditures* constraint, the second covenant, involves a limitation on the amount of funds that may be invested in fixed assets. Investment in fixed assets may be limited to an absolute dollar amount, annual depreciation, or a percentage of annual depreciation. We assume that capital expenditures are limited to $500,000.

Protective covenants dealing with long-term debt may take a number of forms. We shall use only one—a *percentage limitation of long-term debt to working capital;* but additional constraints may be fashioned to fit the situation. We assume this percentage to be 80%.

The last protective-covenant constraint we consider is a *cash-dividend* restriction. This restriction is most often expressed as a percentage limitation of dividends to annual earnings on a cumulative basis. We assume that the percentage limitation is 50% in our example and that the limitation becomes effective at the time of the investment decision, there being no accumulated earnings available for dividend payments. Therefore, dividends must not exceed 50% of book earnings on existing projects plus book earnings generated from investment in the projects under consideration.

These protective covenants by no means exhaust the possible restrictions that might be imposed in a bond indenture or loan agreement. However, the covenants considered do represent some of the more widely used restrictions. In molding the above restrictions into linear-programming constraints, we use the limits imposed in the indenture or agreement. Where a constraint is binding in the final program, the company would be at the verge of violation under the specific covenant involved. It would be desirable, therefore, to allow for a margin of safety. If, for example, the minimum working-capital requirement in the indenture or loan agreement were $1,250,000, we might want to use $1,350,000 in formulating the linear-programming constraint. Other restrictions likewise can be reformulated to permit a margin of safety.

FORMULATION OF LINEAR-PROGRAMMING PROBLEM

Given the information in Table 13-1, the objective function for our hypothetical company would be:

$$\begin{aligned}
\text{Max. } Z = {} & 0.18X_{11} + 0.06X_{21} + 0.13X_{31} + 0.09X_{41} + \\
& 0.15X_{51} + 0.07X_{61} + 0.08X_{71} + 0.18X_{12} + \qquad (1a)\\
& 0.06X_{22} + 0.13X_{32} + 0.09X_{42} + 0.15X_{52} + \\
& 0.07X_{62} + 0.08X_{72},
\end{aligned}$$

where X_{11} through X_{71} represent investment in working capital for the seven proposals and X_{12} through X_{72}, investment in fixed assets. Structural constraints are introduced by virtue of the ceilings on investment, the relative proportions of working capital and fixed assets, and the need to finance the proposals with retained earnings and debt. For constraints relating to ceilings on investment, we have:

$$X_{11} + X_{12} \leq 350{,}000 \qquad (1b)$$
$$X_{21} + X_{22} \leq 225{,}000 \qquad (1c)$$
$$X_{31} + X_{32} \leq 170{,}000 \qquad (1d)$$
$$X_{41} + X_{42} \leq 200{,}000 \qquad (1e)$$
$$X_{51} + X_{52} \leq 150{,}000 \qquad (1f)$$
$$X_{61} + X_{62} \leq 175{,}000 \qquad (1g)$$
$$X_{71} + X_{72} \leq 300{,}000 \qquad (1h)$$

The structural constraints relating to proportions of working capital and fixed assets are:

$$4X_{11} - X_{12} = 0 \qquad (1i)$$
$$X_{21} - 2X_{22} = 0 \qquad (1j)$$
$$X_{31} - X_{32} = 0 \qquad (1k)$$
$$X_{41} - 3X_{42} = 0 \qquad (1l)$$
$$2X_{51} - X_{52} = 0 \qquad (1m)$$
$$X_{61} - 4X_{62} = 0 \qquad (1n)$$
$$3X_{71} - X_{72} = 0. \qquad (1o)$$

The last set of structural constraints is:

$$\sum_{i=1}^{7}\sum_{j=1}^{2} X_{ij} - \sum_{l=1}^{3} Y_l = 0 \qquad (1p)$$

$$\sum_{l=1}^{3} Y_l \leq 800{,}000 \qquad (1q)$$

$$\sum_{l=1}^{2} Y_l - Y_3 = 0, \qquad (1r)$$

where Y_1 is the amount of short-term borrowings, Y_2 the amount of long-term borrowings, and Y_3 the amount of retained earnings used to finance the investment proposals.

As taken up in the previous section, there are four protective-covenant constraints for our hypothetical example. The first, the *minimum-working-capital* constraint, may be expressed as:

$$\sum_{i=1}^{7} X_{i2} - Y_2 \leq 250{,}000, \tag{1s}$$

where \$250,000 represents existing working capital less minimum or required working capital. The *capital-expenditures* constraint may be expressed as:

$$\sum_{i=1}^{7} X_{i2} \leq 500{,}000. \tag{1t}$$

If long-term debt cannot exceed 80% of working capital under the *long-term debt to working-capital* constraint, we have:

$$W.C. - \sum_{i=1}^{7} X_{i2} + Y_2 \geq 1\tfrac{1}{4}L.T.D. + 1\tfrac{1}{4}Y_2,$$

where $W.C.$ is existing working capital and $L.T.D.$ is existing long-term debt. If existing working capital were \$2,500,000, as before, and existing long-term debt \$1,720,000, by transposing and multiplying through by -1, we obtain:

$$\sum_{i=1}^{7} X_{i2} + \tfrac{1}{4}Y_2 \leq W.C. - 1\tfrac{1}{4}L.T.D.$$
$$\leq 350{,}000. \tag{1u}$$

For the *cash dividend* restriction, dividends are limited to 50% of book earnings on existing projects and proposals under consideration. The first-year profit (or loss) per dollar of investment for the seven investment proposals under consideration is shown in the columns below.

Proposals	First-year profit (loss) per dollar of investment
#1	(0.08)
#2	(0.10)
#3	(0.04)
#4	(0.03)
#5	(0.09)
#6	(0.02)
#7	0.05

We assume that the company desires to pay at the end of the first year cash dividends totaling \$200,000 and that book first-year earnings on existing projects, exclusive of proposals under consideration, will be \$425,000. We have as a constraint:

$$0.08X_{11} - 0.10X_{21} + 0.04X_{31} + 0.03X_{41} + 0.09X_{51}$$
$$+ 0.02X_{61} - 0.05X_{71} + 0.08X_{12} - 0.10X_{22} + 0.04X_{32}$$
$$+ 0.03X_{42} + 0.09X_{52} + 0.02X_{62} - 0.05X_{72} \leq Y - 2C, \quad (1v)$$

where Y = first-year earnings on existing projects, and C = the cash dividend the company desires to pay. Thus, $Y - 2C = \$425,000 - 2(\$200,000) = \$25,000$. It would be possible to reformulate this constraint for additional years. For simplicity, we assume that book profits for all investment proposals under consideration are positive beyond the first year and that the lowest total combination of book profits in any one year is more than twice the cash dividend the company desires to pay. Consequently, the dividend restriction is of concern only in the first year.

The complete problem may be expressed as:

$$\text{Max. } Z = \sum_{i=1}^{7} \sum_{j=1}^{2} C_i X_{ij}, \quad (2)$$

subject to

$$\sum_{i=1}^{7} \sum_{j=1}^{2} A_{kij} X_{ij} + \sum_{l=1}^{3} A_{kl} Y_l \leq b_k$$

and the non-negative requirement:

$$X_{ij} \text{ and } Y_l \geq \text{ for all } ijl.$$

SOLUTION OF PROBLEM

A computer program was used to solve this problem, and optimal values of the direct-problem variables and the dual variables are shown in Table 13–2.[8] The values for the direct-problem variables tell us that we should invest \$169,500 in investment proposal #1, \$54,750 in proposal #2, \$170,000 in proposal #3, \$200,000 in proposal #4, and \$205,750 in proposal #6. Moreover, the company should borrow \$320,000 on a short-term basis and \$80,000 through long-term borrowings. Substituting into equation (1a), the increase in net present value resulting from this optimal solution is \$88,297.50.

---

[8] For each direct problem there is a dual problem that makes use of the same data as are employed in the direct problem. The dual theorem of linear programming states that the optimal solution to the direct and the dual problem is the same. For explanation of the dual method, see A. Charnes and W. W. Cooper, *Management Models and Industrial Applications of Linear Programming*, Vol. I (New York: John Wiley & Sons, Inc., 1961); Walter W. Garvin, *Introduction to Linear Programming* (New York: McGraw-Hill Book Company, Inc., 1960); G. Hadley, *Linear Programming* (Reading, Pa.: Addison-Wesley Publishing Company, Inc., 1962), or other texts dealing with linear programming.

Table 13–2. Optimal values for example problem.

Direct		Dual	
$X_{11} = 33,500$	$X_{32} = 85,000$	$W_1 = 0$	$W_{12} = 0.04671$
$X_{21} = 36,500$	$X_{42} = 50,000$	$W_2 = 0$	$W_{13} = 0.03150$
$X_{31} = 85,000$	$X_{52} = 0$	$W_3 = 0.00758$	$W_{14} = 0.09792$
$X_{41} = 150,000$	$X_{62} = 41,150$	$W_4 = 0.00954$	$W_{15} = 0.03333$
$X_{51} = 0$	$X_{72} = 0$	$W_5 = 0$	$W_{16} = 0.03333$
$X_{61} = 164,000$	$Y_1 = 320,000$	$W_6 = 0$	$W_{17} = 0$
$X_{71} = 0$	$Y_2 = 80,000$	$W_7 = 0$	$W_{18} = 0.03150$
$X_{12} = 135,600$	$Y_3 = 400,000$	$W_8 = 0.03150$	$W_{19} = 0$
$X_{22} = 18,250$		$W_9 = 0.05250$	$W_{20} = 0.12600$
		$W_{10} = 0.07875$	$W_{21} = 0.25833$
		$W_{11} = 0.03937$	

From Table 13–2 it can be seen that the optimal investment policy under the protective-covenant constraints differs considerably from that which would occur without the constraints. As mentioned previously, the latter policy would call for investment of $350,000 in investment proposal #1, $170,000 in proposal #3, $130,000 in proposal #4, and $150,000 in proposal #5; and this policy would result in a $119,300 increase in net present value. Thus, the restrictions have a marked effect on the optimal investment policy of the company. For example, under the protective-covenant restrictions, the company would invest $54,750 in the least profitable proposal, #2, while investing nothing in the second most profitable, #5. The #119,300 increase in net present value represents the limit of increase in net present value attainable with relaxation of the protective-covenant constraints. In the analysis that follows, it is useful to relate the increase in net present value arising from relaxation of an individual restriction to this limit.

EVALUATING THE PROTECTIVE-COVENANT RESTRICTIONS

The dual-variable values in Table 13–2 enable us to determine the opportunity costs of certain protective-covenant constraints imposed under the bond indenture or loan agreement. Knowledge of these costs is extremely important to management in formulating negotiation strategy. For example, what would be the effect if the minimum working capital requirement were relaxed? If this constraint is binding or critical in the final program, the dual variable for the restriction will be nonzero; if not, it will be zero. Thus, for the working capital constraint, $W_{18}{}^* = 0.0315$ signifies that if required working capital were decreased by $1, the company would be able to increase net present value $0.0315 if the dollar were optimally employed.[9] We see in Table 13–2 that the capital-expenditures limitation is

---

[9] Optimal use would involve investing an additional $0.30 in proposal #1, $0.15 in proposal #2, a $0.45 decrease in investment in proposal #6, an $0.80 increase in short-term borrowings, and an $0.80 decrease in long-term borrowings. The dual variable $W_{18} = 0.0315$ is valid only within certain limits. We can increase short-term debt and decrease long-term debt by only

not binding in the final program, for $W_{19}^* = 0$. The constraint, as formulated in inequality $(1t)$, would be critical only if investments in fixed assets increased by $170,000, bringing total investment in fixed assets to $500,000.

For the limitation of long-term debt to 80% of working capital [inequality $(1u)$], the value $W_{20}^* = 0.126$ denotes that a $1 increase in $(W.C. - 1\frac{1}{4} L.T.D.)$, if used optimally, would result in a $0.126 increase in net present value.[10] More important than the effect of changes in $W.C. - 1\frac{1}{4} L.T.D.$ is the effect that changes in the maximum percent of long-term debt to working capital have on the optimal solution. For example, what would be the effect if the percent limitation were relaxed from 80% to 100%? Inequality $(1u)$ would become:

$$\sum_{i=1}^{7} X_{i2} \leq W.C. - L.T.D., \tag{3}$$

where $W.C. - L.T.D.$ is $2,500,000 - $1,720,000 = $780,000. If optimal adjustment were made to this relaxation of the percent limitation, net present value would increase by $22,223.55 to $110,521.05.[11]

For the dividend constraint [inequality $(1l)$], $W_{21}^* = 0.25833$. If $Y - 2C$, where Y is first-year earnings on existing projects and C is the total cash dividend the company desires to pay at the end of the first year, were to increase by $1, net present value would increase $0.25833 if the $1 were employed optimally.[12] What effect does the payment of dividends have on profitability? Given the amount of the first-year earnings on existing projects and the limitation of dividends to 50% of earnings, the company may increase net present value by $0.25833 for each $0.50 decrease in total cash dividends it pays at the end of the first year. Thus, given the dividend restriction, management is able to determine the effect that the payment of dividends has on profitability.[13]

$80,000 before inequality $(1q)$ and the non-negative requirement become binding. On the other hand, investment in proposal #6 can increase by only $44,250 before inequality $(1g)$ becomes binding. Consequently, $W_{18}^* = 0.0315$ remains valid for $151,666.67 \leq (W.C. - \text{Min. } W.C.) \leq $350,000.

[10] Optimal employment of a $1 increase in the right-hand side of inequality $(1u)$ would involve a $1.20 increase in proposal #1, a $0.60 increase in proposal #2, a $1.80 decrease in proposal #6, an $0.80 decrease in short-term borrowings, and an $0.80 increase in long-term borrowings. The value $W_{20}^* = 0.126$ remains valid for $325,416.67 \leq (W.C. - 1\frac{1}{4} L.T.D.) \leq $464,305.55. At $325,416.67, inequality $(1g)$ becomes binding and precludes further investment in proposal #6, while at $464,305.55, further reductions in investment proposal #6 would not be possible.

[11] Optimal adjustment would involve increasing investment in proposal #1 by $180,500, to $350,000, an increase in investment proposal #2 of $129,460.53 to $184,210.53, elimination of investment of $200,000 in proposal #4, investment of $95,789.47 in proposal #5, elimination of investment of $205,750 in proposal #6, a decrease of $160,263.16 in short-term borrowings, and an increase of a like amount in long-term borrowings.

[12] Optimal employment would involve a $1.67 increase in proposal #1, a $7.50 decrease in proposal #2, and a $5.83 increase in proposal #6. As can be determined, $W_{21}^* - 0.25833$ remains valid for $2,300 \leq Y - 2C \leq $32,300. Below $2,300, inequality $(1c)$ becomes binding on further increases in proposal #2. Above $32,300, further decreases in proposal #2 are not possible.

[13] We ignore the problem of deviations from desired dividends having an effect on the cost of capital by assuming that the moderate changes in dividends under consideration will not affect the cost of capital.

Perhaps the more important consideration is the effect that the percent limitation has on profitability, given the dividend the company desires to pay. If the percent limitation were increased from 50% to 66⅔%, what would be the effect on net present value? The right-hand side of the constraint [inequality (1v)], would then become:

$$425,000 - 1.5(200,000) = 125,000.$$

If optimal adjustment were made to this relaxation in the dividend restriction, net present value would increase by \$18,858.33.[14]

Through sensitivity analysis, we have been able to evaluate the effect on the optimal solution of given changes in the protective-covenant constraints. The sensitivity of the optimal solution to changes in these parameters was determined without having to solve one or a series of new problems. Equipped with knowledge of the opportunity costs of the various restrictions, management is able to bargain more rationally and effectively; it is able to give ground where the restrictions involved have small or no opportunity costs and drive a hard bargain on those restrictions having high opportunity costs.

CONCLUSIONS

In this paper, a method is proposed for determining the opportunity costs of restrictions imposed on a company by the terms of a bond indenture or loan agreement. Using a linear-programming model, we evaluate proposed changes in the protective-covenant restrictions through sensitivity analysis and thereby determine the opportunity costs of these restrictions. The insight gained is important to management if there is a possibility that the covenants under an existing indenture or agreement might be relaxed through negotiation with the lender(s). Changing protective covenants is much more likely under a loan agreement, where there is only one lender or a relatively small number of lenders, than it is under a bond indenture.

Knowledge of the opportunity costs involved in various restrictions is perhaps even more valuable in the initial negotiation of protective covenants to be imposed under an indenture or agreement. Without any idea as to the effect a protective covenant has on profitability, management is not in a position to bargain rationally or effectively over the restrictiveness of these covenants. The method proposed in this paper for determining the opportunity costs of the restrictions gives management a means by which to evaluate the impact of the demands of the lender(s) and a basis for formulating a sound strategy for negotiation.

---

[14] Optimal adjustment would involve increasing investment in proposal #1 by \$12,166.67 to \$181,666.67, elimination of the \$54,750 investment in proposal #2, and increasing investment in proposal #6 by \$42,583.33 to \$248,333.33.

PART V

Financial Structure and Cost of Capital

14

EQUITY YIELDS, GROWTH, AND THE STRUCTURE OF SHARE PRICES

BURTON G. MALKIEL*

In this article, Professor Malkiel develops a logical model for valuing common stocks. He then focuses on the structure of stock prices, contrasting the prices of growth with stocks as a whole. By some simplifying assumptions, he arrives at relatively compact formulas for approximating the values of growth stocks.

The logical structure of his analysis implies some propositions about the behavior of growth stocks as compared with other stocks. After developing these propositions, Professor Malkiel tests them by reference to empirical data. This study and its results provide a foundation for our understanding of the behavior of common stock prices.

The first half of 1962 witnessed one of the most precipitous declines in stock market prices in recent history. In terms of the volume of trading and the magnitude of the daily erosion of stock values, one must look back to the crashes of 1929 and 1937 to find parallels. Moreover, the decline was not confined to U.S. stock prices, for a world-wide revaluation of equity values was transmitted from New York.

For most professional financial observers of these developments, two aspects of the decline served as the foci of their analysis. There was first the sharp drop in the *level* of share prices. Second, and perhaps more interesting, there was a marked change in the *structure* of share prices, i.e., the relationships among equities of different characteristics. We can illustrate the revaluation in the level of stock prices by noting that from December 12, 1961, the date of the pre-1962 peak level of stock prices, to June 26, 1962, the date of the 1962 trough, the Dow-Jones Industrial Average, an average of 25 very high quality shares, declined from 734 to 539, a drop of 26.6

Form Burton G. Malkiel, "Equity Yields, Growth, and the Structure of Share Prices," *The American Economic Review*, Dec. 1963, Vol. LIII, 1004–1030. Reprinted by permission.

* The author is Associate Professor of Economics at Princeton University. He is indebted to W. J. Baumol, L. V. Chandler, and R. E. Quandt who assisted through several formative drafts of this paper and made valuable suggestions which led to considerable improvements in the verbal and algebraic presentation of the argument. He has also profited from later useful criticism from F. Machlup, J. W. Land, and P. A. Tinsley as well as the members of the Princeton University Seminar on Research in Progress. Finally, acknowledgment is made to the National Science Foundation whose grant to the study "Dynamics of the Firm" helped in the completion of this paper.

percent. During the same period the Standard and Poor 425 Industrial Stock Average, a broader and more heterogeneous grouping of stocks, declined from 76.69 to 54.80, a drop of 28.5 percent. This decline of more than 25 percent we take as illustrative of the drop in the level of stock prices.

Perhaps the most interesting and conspicuous change in the structure of share prices was what the financial press called "the revaluation of 'growth stocks.' " Much steeper price declines were suffered by those companies whose extraordinary earnings growth had gained them far higher price-earnings ratios than those applied to the standard list of industrial stocks. For example, an index of five high-quality growth stocks[1] declined in the same period from 78.60 to 37.60, a drop of 52.2 percent, almost double that suffered by the standard group. Even the *ne plus ultra* of growth stocks, International Business Machines Corporation, declined in the same period from 580 to 320, a loss of 44.8 percent.

In the setting of the 1962 market adjustment, this paper will attempt to analyze the relationship of "growth stocks" to standard equities. First we will present a brief historical summary and critique of security analysis since the Great Depression. This is both necessary for explaining how the late 1961 structure of stock prices developed and useful for understanding the types of criteria long used by practical men to value common shares. Next we will construct a model designed to throw light on the "proper" relationships among equity groups that differ in their earnings and dividend growth. Several theorems from the model will be used to demonstrate the precise relationship between warranted share prices and the relevant determinants of valuation. But perhaps even more important than providing a valuation model, the analysis will serve as a conceptual scheme by which we can explain the change in the structure of share prices which occurred.

There is a remarkable similarity between the problems of building a theory of the term structure of interest rates and attempting to formulate the principles underlying the structure of equity prices with respect to issues differing in their growth characteristics. For example, we know that long-term bonds have wider price fluctuations than short issues for a given change in interest rates. Similarly, we shall find that nondividend-paying growth stocks are inherently more volatile than standard issues in response to a change in the capitalization rate applied to equities in general. Moreover, this volatility is an increasing function of the duration of growth expected. As dividends are paid on the growth stocks, however, we will find that, in response to a change in the general level of share prices, the volatility of the shares is reduced. Thus, the ingredients will be furnished for a beginning to the type of analysis based on expectations and the mathematics of price movements which I have previously [12] attempted in a study of the term

---

[1] The construction of the index, as well as the criteria for selection of the shares included, will be explained later.

structure of interest rates. Finally, we shall note that several awkward difficulties arise peculiar to the valuation of shares, and thus the limitations as well as the applications of our model will be stressed.

I. A BRIEF HISTORY OF SECURITY ANALYSIS SINCE THE GREAT DEPRESSION

After its publication in 1934, Graham and Dodd's *Security Analysis* [8] became the classic training manual and reference work for the generation of security analysts who picked over the debris left by the 1929 crash in a search for hidden earning power and hidden assets. The work was a thorough and critical survey of the existing methods and techniques of analysis and was of uniformly high quality. Many of the methods of analysis described in the text remained unexceptionable even throughout the 1950's. The central idea of the work, however, was increasingly criticized in the postwar period, and it is this, its philosophy of valuation, with which we are chiefly concerned.

The fundamental proposition of security analysis advanced by Graham and Dodd is that any common share may be valued by capitalizing its indicated "earning power" by some suitable multiple. The concept of earning power combines a statement of actual earnings shown over a period of years with the expectation that these past earnings will be approximated in the future, unless extraordinary conditions supervene [8, pp. 418–19]. It is both in the earning-power concept and in the problem of selecting an appropriate multiple of these earnings that security analysts of the fifties broke sharply with Graham and Dodd. In the first place Graham and Dodd severely admonished the analyst against unduly emphasizing the past trend in earnings of any company, particularly when the trend is upward. "It must be remembered that the automatic or normal economic forces militate against the indefinite continuance of a given trend. Competition, regulation, the law of diminishing returns, etc., are powerful foes to unlimited expansion . . ." [8, p. 422]. But, and here is the crucial distinction, even if after qualitative study the analyst is convinced that the favorable trend will continue, "the analyst's philosophy must still impel him to base his investment valuation on an assumed earning power *no larger than the company has already achieved* in some year of normal business. Investment values can be related only to demonstrated performance . . ." [8, pp. 422–23, italics mine].

Later Graham and Dodd admit that the earnings of companies which have enjoyed above-average growth may be capitalized more liberally, but the absolute maximum suggested was a multiple 20 percent higher than that accorded the securities in the Dow-Jones group [8, p. 458]. *Security Analysis* repeatedly warns against the special dangers inherent in overvaluing the earnings of growth stocks [8, pp. 388–89, 396–400, 458]. To buttress their argument they adduce the thesis of Mead and Grodinsky that all industries after a period of growth face an inexorable decline which once begun is rarely reversed [13, pp. 708–09]. Thus the security analyst who strictly followed the tenets of Graham and Dodd would view indulgently no more than a very limited premium for the earnings of a growth stock, and the entire flavor of the Graham and Dodd valuation approach would make him uneasy about even this compromise.

The opposing school of security analysis, which we shall describe as the growth-stock school, also had its beginnings in the Great Depression. It is difficult to ascribe to any one individual the credit for originating the application of the "present value" technique to growth stocks. S. Eliot Guild [9] is often given this distinction, although the classic development of the technique and particularly the nuances associated with it were worked out by John B. Williams [16] in 1938.

This theory argues that it is nonsense to claim that there must exist some arbitrarily defined maximum earnings multiple which should apply to a security no matter what its growth prospects. Surely, the warranted earnings multiple must be related to these prospects if any sense is to be made of the structure of share prices. The growth-stock approach to valuation can be illustrated by a recent variant of the approach suggested by Clendenin and Van Cleave [3]. Utilizing the basic Williams valuation formula (i.e., the present worth of a share is the summation of all dividends expected to be received from it, discounted to present value at an appropriate rate of interest) [16, p. 55], the authors have constructed tables showing the present value of a stock now paying $1.00 per share with varying assumptions concerning the growth rate and the growth period. The important point to be gained from the analysis is that, depending on the growth assumptions made, the investor may be justified in paying double or triple the price for growth shares compared with those which enjoy little or no growth [3, Table 4, p. 371]. Or to put the proposition somewhat differently, if the market values of shares corresponded roughly to the Graham and Dodd measure of central value, then an investor who purchased the shares of "growth companies" would receive an extraordinarily large effective return. Therefore, the search was on for those shares expected to enjoy above-average growth. This search and the concomitant bidding-up of the prices of such shares roughly characterized the major change in the structure of share prices in the 1950's.

While the basic idea of the growth-stock school was both correct and a necessary addition to the Graham and Dodd techniques of security analysis, there were several difficulties with the approach. In the first place, much of the theoretical valuation work focused entirely on dividend payments as the exclusive source of value. It has been argued recently [11] [14] that dividend payments may under certain assumptions be totally irrelevant. Furthermore, the search for an appropriate discount rate had led, at best, to the arbitrary choice of a single rate or, at worst, to the choice of several discount rates where dividends more distant in time are discounted at progressively higher discount rates [3, Table 5, p. 373] [6, pp. 41–43]. This type of technique is not only capricious, but it also suffers from what Miller and Modigliani call the "bird-in-the-hand fallacy."[2] In addition, an extremely long (60-year) horizon is utilized. This has the advantage of seemingly avoiding estimates of future dividend-price relationships. Unfortunately, it has the great disadvantage of resting on the unrealistic assumption that investors are actually able to make estimates for that long a period; if, indeed, it is meaningful even to speak of growth rates compounded over 60 years. Thus we must conclude that these techniques really offer no satisfactory solution to the growth-stock valuation problem.

Another difficulty is inherent in the proposition that the long-term growth rate of dividends may exceed the discount rate. This leads to a very awkward situation. Depending upon how many years one wishes to include in his horizon, one may be justified in paying any amount one wishes for the securities of those companies. Indeed, if perpetual growth at a rate greater than the discount rate is expected, the present value of the shares is infinity [3, pp. 368–69]. David Durand [5] has pointed out the remarkable analogy between this problem and the famous St. Petersburg Paradox of Bernoulli. But the common-stock buyers of the late 1950's were not troubled by the subtleties of these difficulties. Instead, it seemed logical that the investor should not worry about the price he paid for the shares of growth stocks— all that mattered was to find those securities which were experiencing the largest rates of growth. As a corollary to this "new investment maxim," the growth-stock philosophy believed that it had finally solved the age-old investment problem of timing. "The time to buy a growth stock is now. The whole purpose in such an investment is to participate in future larger earnings, so that *ipso facto* any delay in making the commitment is defeating" [2, p. 122].

Graham and Dodd's *Security Analysis*, the erstwhile bible of the security analyst, had lost touch with the realities of the new "new era" of common-stock valuation. The search for growth became the main preoccupation of the security analyst [17]. "Growth" took on an almost mystical significance, and to question the propriety of such analysis became, as in a generation past, heretical. The structure of share prices existing in late 1961 is understandable only against this background of the recrudescence of these "new-era concepts" in security analysis. This structure of prices represented the illogical extension of a procedure that was designed by Guild and Williams as simply an ancillary technique to the main body of security analysis, not its replacement.

---

[2] Miller and Modigliani [14, p. 424 n.] argue that the attempt to use a purely subjective discount rate to derive uncertainty-valuation formulas is to commit an error analogous to deriving certainty-valuation formulas for shares through the use of marginal rates of time preference.

II. THE LEVEL OF COMMON-STOCK PRICES

How then should one decide the appropriate prices for those securities which enjoy a superior rate of growth in earnings per common share? To attempt to answer this question we next begin the construction of a valuation model which, initially, will be presented in terms of perfect certainty. Later we shall introduce some elements of uncertainty into the analysis. In theory, the valuation of any common stock can be reduced to a very simple relationship. Assuming that the investor has a finite horizon, the value of any common stock can be expressed simply as the sum of the present values of both the dividends to be received over the years included in the horizon and the terminal price of the common shares at the end of the horizon period. But immediately a whole host of problems arises: how can one determine the future stream of dividends to be received? How can one solve the valuation formula without first dealing with the problem of how the common shares will be valued at the end of the horizon period? What is the appropriate discount rate to use? And so forth. We might first note that we shall set ourselves a task that will be somewhat simplified by the nature of our investigation. Our initial problem will be to deal solely with the structure of stock prices in a certainty setting where we abstract from taxes and market imperfections. The question we shall ask is what is the proper relationship between a given price level for a representative or standard security and the price of a security whose prospects for growth are above average. Then we shall seek to determine the effect of a *ceteris paribus* change in the standard price level on the price of a growth stock. But throughout the discussion we shall abstract from investor expectations concerning future movements of the prices of standard issues. Thus our first job will be to define what is meant by the level of stock prices.

When we refer to the level of stock prices, we have in mind whether equities in general seem to be high or low. In practice, financial people usually take the level of stock prices simply to be the index number associated with the popular market averages of standard securities. The difficulty with such a measure, wholly apart from the index-number problems involved, is that its information content is unsuitable for our purposes. A general price-level index can not distinguish between a change in its value that results only from a change in the earnings and dividends of standard issues and a change that reflects a difference in the capitalization rate applied to constant earnings and dividends. In this paper, which is addressed to the problem of the determination of the "real value" of a share, the appropriate measure is clearly one that deals with capitalization rates, not with absolute prices. Consequently, we shall find it useful to define the level of share prices as the price commanded by a dollar of earnings for a representative share. This "normalized" price is identical with the price-earnings-ratio concept used by financial men to describe the ratio of the price paid per share of stock (*P* to the earnings per share (E). The price-earnings multiple (ratio) for any share (m) is simply the inverse of the rate of capitalization of earnings, i.e.,

$$m \equiv \frac{P}{E}. \tag{1}$$

Our choice of this normalized price m instead of the absolute price P is also necessitated because we will want to make comparisons between the values of different securities. Clearly, the ratio of the absolute price of two stocks is a matter of the denominations in which they are issued. It is only the ratio between their price-earnings multiples which can indicate the way in which the two securities are regarded by the market.

We may now briefly outline the development of the model that follows. We shall first use the theoretical construct of a representative standard share in order to find the objective market-determined discount rate that will be employed in valuing other issues. Next we will find the relationship between the discount rate and the earnings multiple of the standard share. It will be seen that a given standard earnings multiple uniquely determines this rate. The growth-stock valuation model will then be introduced. This model will evaluate for any standard earnings multiple (and the discount rate that it implies) the warranted earnings multiple for a growth stock. Since the earnings multiples for both growth and standard shares can be considered normalized prices, we will then have determined a structure of comparable share prices for issues that differ in their earnings and dividend growth rates.

Assuming the investor could buy a share of a representative standard security, what yield would he receive if he knew with certainty the future dividends and the future valuation of the composite share? Assuming the dividend, earnings, and price per share grow at the same percentage rate, it is easy to make a marginal-efficiency-of-investment calculation and solve for the effective yield. We shall find that it equals the current dividend rate per share (i.e., the dividend payment to be received for the year expressed as a percentage of existing market price)[3] plus the percentage annual growth in earnings per share, which, by assumption, is equal to the annual growth in the dividend and the price of each share as well.

The above proposition may be demonstrated most easily if we begin with the simplest possible case and utilize the Williams' valuation formula. We define the value of the representative standard share as the present value of the dividends to be received by each share in all future periods. Since, by assumption, last year's dividend payment per representative standard share

---

[3] In financial circles this expression is often called the dividend yield. We shall use the term "rate" to avoid confusion with the total yield or marginal efficiency. It should be noted that Gordon and Shapiro [7] have previously developed an expression identical to (3) for the yield of a (standard) security, although the application made of their model is different from our own.

(D_s) is conveniently expected to grow at a constant growth rate (g_s) over time, the price per share (P_s) will equal:

$$P_s = \sum_{i=1}^{\infty} D_s \left(\frac{1 + g_s}{1 + r}\right)^i. \tag{2}$$

Summing the geometric progression and solving for r we obtain:

$$r = \frac{D_s(1 + g_s)}{P_s} + g_s, \tag{3}$$

i.e., the marginal efficiency of the investment is equal to the current year's dividend rate (the dividend to be paid at the end of the current year as a percentage of the existing market price) plus the growth rate. It can also easily be shown that the same result follows if, instead of discounting the future stream of dividends in perpetuity, we utilize a finite time period and discount back for the dividends and the price of the standard share as of any future date. Assuming that investors continue to be willing to capitalize the earnings of the share at the same rate, the price of the representative share also grows at the rate g_s, and the valuation formula becomes:

$$P_s = \sum_{i=1}^{N} D_s \left(\frac{1 + g_s}{1 + r}\right)^i + P_s \left(\frac{1 + g_s}{1 + r}\right)^N. \tag{4}$$

Summing the progression and rearranging terms we get:

$$P_s \left[1 - \left(\frac{1 + g_s}{1 + r}\right)^N\right] = \frac{D_s(1 + g_s)}{r - g_s}\left[1 - \left(\frac{1 + g_s}{1 + r}\right)^N\right]$$

which (after solving for r) reduces to (3). Thus we see that the time horizon chosen for valuing the representative security is irrelevant under the assumptions postulated.

We shall call r the "apparent marginal efficiency" of the representative standard share. Now we will demonstrate how r uniquely can be determined once the standard earnings multiple, m_s, is known. First, we will find the general relationship between the r and m_s. Let the dividend rate, d_s, be defined as:

$$d_s \equiv \frac{D_s(1 + g_s)}{P_s}. \tag{5}$$

d_s is related to r by (3), $r - g_s = d_s$. By (1), $P_s \equiv m_s E_s$. Substituting this expression into (5) and solving for m_s, we have:

$$m_s = \frac{D_s(1 + g_s)}{E_s} \Big/ d_s. \tag{6}$$

In this expression,

$$\frac{D_s(1 + g_s)}{E_s}$$

is simply the payout ratio (based on next year's dividend), which we assume to be known and constant through time, as is implied by our prior assumption that dividends and earnings would grow at the same rate. Therefore, we are able to determine the price-earnings ratio, m_s, from (6). Alternatively, we can view the price-earnings multiple as determining r. Given a fixed payout ratio for standard shares, then any m_s will uniquely determine the dividend rate (d_s). Since g_s is also taken to be a constant, we can then immediately find the apparent marginal efficiency.[4] Thus our construct describing the determination of the level of normalized share prices (i.e., the earnings multiple for a representative standard share) can provide us with a necessary building block for the construction of our valuation model. It uniquely determines an objective market rate of discount which we may then apply to the valuation of growth stocks. Moreover, we shall see that it provides both a method of capitalizing the earnings of these stocks when their period of extraordinary growth is concluded and a standard of comparison of value.

III. A MODEL FOR THE VALUATION OF GROWTH STOCKS

The term "growth stock" as used in the financial community is a term of approbation to describe those common shares which have enjoyed (or are expected to enjoy) in some sense above-average earnings growth. We shall use the term to describe any equity security that meets both of the following conditions. First,

$$d + g > d_s + g_s, \tag{7}$$

the dividend rate plus the growth rate of the growth stock (the absence of the subscript s always indicates a growth stock) must exceed the dividend plus growth rate for the representative standard share or, what is the same thing, its apparent marginal efficiency. Second, we require that

$$g > g_s, \tag{8}$$

the growth rate of the growth stock must exceed the standard growth rate. This avoids considering as growth stocks securities which merely pay unusually high dividends. In the event that the growth security pays no dividends, then the growth-stock definition simply requires:

$$g > r. \tag{9}$$

---

[4] But note that if the dividend payout ratio for the standard share is zero (i.e., no dividends are paid) then $r = g_s$, which is, of course, independent of m_s. Alternatively, we might say that the price-earnings ratio is indeterminate. This is so because, given the assumption that investors will continue to be willing to capitalize the earnings of the share at the same rate, any price-earnings ratio is consistent with (3). A, say 5 percent rate of growth in earnings will produce a 5 percent capital appreciation per year (and hence a 5 percent internal rate of return) regardless of what earnings multiple the standard share commands. Once any dividend is paid, however, this problem disappears.

Moreover, we expect that the above conditions must have been satisfied on the average, say, for the past three years and are expected to be satisfied for at least the next two years. However, we reject the possibility that a growth rate will exceed r in perpetuity.[5] This particular definition of a growth stock has been chosen to permit applicability of the model to the maximum number of shares. If these conditions are not met, the following model is not appropriate.[6]

We begin with the fundamental proposition that the "market" will tend to equalize the net yield obtainable from all securities. Since the stream of receipts from the growth stock and the representative standard issue are both expected with certainty, then we can use the apparent marginal efficiency of the standard issue as the interest rate appropriate for discounting the future stream of receipts. Let us now recapitulate the symbols to be used:

E = earnings per common share of the growth stock in the fiscal year just past. Again we remind the reader that when the subscript s appears with E, we refer to the earnings of the standard share.

D = dividends per share in the past fiscal year. Dividends are assumed to be paid out annually at the end of each fiscal year.

g = the expected growth rate of earnings per share and dividends per share over the next N years.[7]

In our valuation formula we shall assume that both the dividends and earnings per share of the growth stock grow at a rate g for a period of N years. After that period, the security enjoys only the average growth expected of the standard list of securities (and therefore is able to pay the average dividend of the standard composite security).[8] Accordingly, we postulate that the price-earnings multiple of the shares to be valued falls to that multiple which the market is applying to standard issues. This acknowledges that above-average earnings growth can continue only for a limited

---

[5] This of course would lead us into the "growth stock paradox" again. But as Modigliani and Miller point out [15, p. 644 n.] this possibility must be rejected as a curiosum devoid of economic significance. Assuming that there must be a finite value for all shares, then r (a variable in a general equilibrium setting) would have to rise to restore equilibrium to the capital markets should the rate of earnings growth of some shares be perpetually greater than r. Nevertheless, it is both possible and plausible that the rate of growth of many firms over some finite period may exceed r by a wide margin.

[6] See footnote 9.

[7] Underlying the projection of a particular growth rate are, of course, specific assumptions concerning the investment opportunities of the firm and its investment and financial policies. In my view these assumptions are better left implicit in a model which for this discussion addresses itself only to the problem of share valuation. However, in much of the recent work in this area (e.g., Gordon, and Miller and Modigliani) these assumptions are integrated explicitly into the models.

$m \equiv P/E$ = the price-earnings ratio of the share today.

$d \equiv D(1 + g)/Em$ = the dividend rate based on next year's dividend payment.

P = the present value of the future stream of receipts, i.e., the value of the common share today.

r = the apparent marginal efficiency of the representative standard share.

[8] Alternatively, the shares could grow at a rate r and retain all earnings. In fact, any combination of $g + d$ which equals r is permissible. See (A3) below.

period. Furthermore, the price-earnings ratio is expected to recede to the standard level thus avoiding the mistake of "counting the same trick twice," i.e., continuing to value growth stocks at extraordinarily high price-earnings ratios after the extraordinary rate of earnings growth has already occurred [8, pp. 459–60].[9]

Assuming that each year's dividend is paid at the end of the year and that valuation is to be made at the beginning of the year, our valuation formula becomes:

$$P = \frac{D(1 + g)}{(1 + \bar{r})} + \frac{D(1 + g)^2}{(1 + \bar{r})^2} + \cdots + \frac{D(1 + g)^N}{(1 + \bar{r})^N} + \frac{\bar{m}_s E(1 + g)^N}{(1 + \bar{r})^N}. \quad (10)$$

The numerator of the last term of (10) represents the market price of the security at the end of year N. The earnings in year N, $E(1 + g)^N$, are capitalized by applying the standard earnings multiple, m_s. This assumes that the growth stock, in effect, takes on the characteristics of a standard issue after the period of extraordinary growth is completed. Moreover, we assume that no change occurs in the standard multiple at the end of the growth period (i.e., the level of share prices remains constant). This terminal value we discount to the present and add to the sum of the present values of the stream of dividend receipts.[10] Summing (10) and dividing through by E, we can solve for the price-earnings ratio, m, of the share:

$$m = \frac{D(1 + g)}{E(\bar{r} - g)} - \frac{D(1 + g)^{N-1}}{E(\bar{r} - g)(1 + \bar{r})^N} + \frac{\bar{m}_s(1 + g)^N}{(1 + \bar{r})^N}. \quad (11)$$

It will now be useful to review three well-known theorems concerning growth stocks.[11] First, we should note that the warranted price-earnings ratio, m, that can be paid for a growth stock will always exceed the standard multiple, $\bar{m}_s$. Second, it is clear that the premium over the standard earnings multiple is an increasing function of the growth rate, g. Finally, the valuation premium is also an increasing function of the number of years that the issue continues to meet our criteria of growth. While the form of valuation equation (10) would also seem to indicate that $\partial m/\partial D > 0$, such a conclusion is not justified. Our formula omits the relationship between dividend payments per share and the ability to achieve future earnings growth per share. It could well be that $\partial m/\partial D = 0$ because, while the effect of a large dividend

---

[9] This assumption renders the model inapplicable for securities not meeting our conditions for growth. It is one thing to argue that, after a period of abnormal growth, the multiple applied to the shares will fall back to the standard ratio. It is quite another matter to invoke this condition for shares where the historical record has been substandard. In the latter case there is no reason to assume that the issue could, for example, grow at the standard rate and have the same dividend payout ratio as does the standard issue.

[10] It should be noted that the investor need not hold his security for N periods to obtain the yield r. Assuming that the standard security continues to be valued at the same rate (i.e., the level of share prices remains constant), then the investor may sell his security at any intermediate time and realize the holding yield r.

[11] Formal proof of these theorems is offered in the Appendix.

per share would tend to increase m, the lower terminal value *per share* might reduce m by an exactly equal amount.[12]

Let us turn now to the special case of the growth stock that pays no dividends at all. This case is an important one since this condition characterizes a number of securities normally considered growth stocks. Here the valuation formula reduces to:

$$P = \bar{m}_s E \frac{(1 + g)^N}{(1 + \bar{r})^N},$$ (12)

or

$$m = \bar{m}_s \frac{(1 + g)^N}{(1 + \bar{r})^N}.$$ (13)

We are thus able to express the normalized price of a nondividend-paying growth stock as some multiple of the price-earnings ratio for the representative standard share.

We shall now examine the effect of a *ceteris paribus* change in the standard price level on the normalized prices of growth stocks, that is, the effect of a change in the standard earnings multiple not associated with a change in the market's estimate of g_s or in any of the other variables of the model. Such a change might occur in response to a change in the level of interest rates.

But, while we allow for such a change to occur, we shall posit that investors have formed no expectations concerning the likelihood of the general level of equity prices moving either up or down. Thus, whatever the level of standard share prices is, the model asserts that a structure of share prices is formed which assumes the perpetuation of the present level. Given this assumption, it follows that nondividend-paying growth stocks are inherently more volatile than standard issues. Moreover, the greater the number of years for which the extraordinary growth is expected, the more widely will the shares fluctuate in price as the level of share prices changes. However, the volatility of the price-earnings ratio is invariant with respect to the *rate* of growth expected.

While formal proof is offered in the Appendix, these findings can be understood easily if one simply examines equations (12) and (13). When the level of share prices falls, the price-earnings ratio, m_s, of the standard

---

[12] Miller and Modigliani [14, p. 414], for example, have argued that when a company pays a cash dividend it simply puts in the share-owner's left-hand pocket what it has taken from his right. Given the investment decision, dividend payments to current share-holders merely reduce the value of their claim in the enterprise. This is so because additional equity shares in the business (representing an amount equal to the dividend payment) must be sold in order to finance the predetermined level of capital expenditures. The worth of the enterprise is accordingly-affected, not by "how the fruits of the earning power are 'packaged' for distribution," but only by the "real" variables of the company's earning power and investment opportunities. Looked at in this way, a cash dividend is just as irrelevant as a stock dividend. Of course, this argument abstracts, as does ours, from tax considerations, market imperfections, etc. However, for uncertainty counterarguments to the Miller-Modigliani position, see W. J. Baumol [1] and John Lintner [11].

list falls, and therefore the warranted price-earnings ratio of the shares to be valued tends to fall *pari passu* with m_s. But a falling level of share prices also implies that the dividend yield on standard shares tends to rise. Therefore, the discount rate used to convert the future value of the growth stock to present worth increases. The result is that m falls *a fortiori*. Hence, *ceteris paribus*, the price-earnings ratios of nondividend-paying growth stocks may be expected to fall by a greater percentage rate than those of ordinary shares. Furthermore, since the discount factor $(1 + r)$ is raised to the Nth power, the decline will be greater, the larger N is, i.e., the longer the period is over which the shares are expected to continue their superior growth record.

Returning to the case of dividend-paying growth stocks, the above results do not, in general, hold. The relevant elasticity expression for dividend-paying shares is, unfortunately, rather unpleasant, and I was unable to deal with it analytically. Instead I was forced to examine ranges of representative values of the function for different values of the variables to determine their effects. Specifically, the value of ϵ_m (the elasticity of the price-earnings ratio) was calculated for all the relevant ranges of m_3, D/E, g, and for N.[13] The following propositions are suggested by these calculations:

$$\frac{\partial \epsilon_m}{\partial (D/E)} < 0. \tag{14}$$

The larger is the dividend paid on the growth stock, then, *ceteris paribus*, the less volatile will it be. The computations also suggest that a necessary, but not a sufficient, condition for this elasticity to be less than unity is for the growth stock to have a payout ratio $(D/E) > (D_s/E_s)$. It also appears that

$$\frac{\partial \epsilon_m}{\partial g} > 0 \quad \text{for} \quad N \geq 2 \quad \text{and} \quad \frac{\partial \epsilon_m}{\partial g} = 0 \quad \text{for} \quad N = 1. \tag{15}$$

Thus for all horizons greater than one year, the volatility of dividend-paying growth stocks increases with the growth rate. Finally, we conjecture that

$$\frac{\partial \epsilon_m}{\partial N} > 0 \quad \text{for} \quad \epsilon_m > 1 \quad \text{when} \quad N = 1. \tag{16}$$

---

[13] The calculations were performed on the Institute for Defense Analysis CDC 1604 computer. m_s was allowed to vary from 8 to 25 in intervals of 1, D_s/E_s was set at 0.6, and g_s was held constant at 2 percent. These values were chosen as being historically relevant in accordance with the empirical analysis which follows. For each m_s (and the r it uniquely determines) a set of warranted growth-stock price-earnings ratios and corresponding elasticities was calculated. Over 17,000 hypothetical growth stocks representing all combinations of payout ratios from 0 to 100 percent, growth rates up to 40 percent, and growth horizons up to 15 years were considered in each set. It can also be shown that these volatility relationships hold (within the hypothesized range of parameters) even when m_s varies only in response to equiproportionate changes in all growth rates. I am greatly indebted to R. E. Quandt for programming the calculation.

The volatility increases with N whenever the stock is more volatile than the standard issue to begin with. Thus in the dividend-paying case the following generalization appears to be valid: a dividend payment tends *ceteris paribus* to decrease the volatility of a growth stock. Nevertheless, unless the dividend payout ratio is larger than that for standard issues, these shares will still be more volatile than standard shares and an increase in the growth horizon will, as before, increase their volatility. Finally, the volatility of dividend-paying growth stocks (in contrast to nondividend-paying shares) increases with the growth rate for all horizons longer than one year.

We conclude, then, that in one important respect growth stocks are intrinsically different from standard issues. When the level of share prices changes, the prices of growth stocks must fluctuate more than proportionately if the structure of share prices is to remain unchanged. Thus, growth stocks are inherently more volatile than standard issues. When the level of share prices drops sharply, as was the case during the first six months of 1962, a significantly larger fluctuation in the prices of growth stocks is to be expected as a normal concomitant. Thus, at least a part of the "revaluation of growth stocks" experienced in early 1962 may not have been revaluation at all, but rather a predictable result of the relevant functional relationship.

IV. APPLICATION OF THE MODEL

Before turning to the application of our model we must find some operational definition for the level of share prices and establish the conditions under which the certainty analysis may be used to approximate the world of uncertainty.[14] As the empirical counterpart to our construct of the representative standard share, we shall choose the index number associated with the Standard and Poor 425 Industrial Stock Average (425ISA).[15] This index number can be considered to be the price of a standard composite industrial share. The price-earnings ratio applicable to the composite share we will take to be the normalized price, i.e., the level of share prices.

Recall that we found by (3) that the apparent marginal efficiency of the representative standard share was composed of the sum of its dividend rate and its growth rate. If we assume that the recent rate of growth of earnings of the S & P composite share will continue at a constant rate into the future, we can, at any time, actually assign an internal rate of return to the stock average. Over the past five years (1957 through 1962) the 425ISA has achieved a compounded earnings growth of 1.9 percent per annum. By

---

[14] We shall make no attempt in this paper to develop a full uncertainty model of share valuation. However, we shall indicate in several places during the following discussion the kinds of considerations that are relevant for such an extension to uncertainty.

[15] The problems associated with any index number are well known in the economic literature. The peculiar difficulties associated with the popular market averages are particularly discouraging. Nevertheless, we know of no alternative to attempting to describe the level of share prices in terms of one of the standard lists of equities. We do assert, however, that the S & P 425ISA gives the broadest and fairest available representation of standard industrial shares.

taking different periods it is possible to find both higher and lower growth rates. If, for example, 1929 is taken as a base, the annual growth rate rises to 3.8 percent. However, if the recent high-profit year of 1955 is used, the growth rate of earnings is negligible. The growth of dividends has exceeded the growth rate of earnings in recent years, but the two have been roughly similar for longer periods. We shall use, for illustrative purposes only, the rate 2 percent as an empirical approximation to what, in the certainty analysis, would be the anticipated (with certainty) annual percentage increase in earnings and dividends per share. This rate roughly conforms to past experience as adjusted for the less favorable recent earnings performance.[16] The price-earnings ratio of the composite share and the dividend yield that it determines are, of course, matters of record. At the December 12, 1961 market peak, the 425ISA sold at a price-earnings multiple m_s of 20.3 and had an apparent marginal efficiency, r, of approximately 4.75 percent.[17] The relevant figures for the June 26, 1962 trough are $m_s = 15.5$ and $r = 5.9$ percent.

It is important to note here that in the operational counterpart to our theoretical construct, we have strayed from the protection of perfect certainty. Our empirical internal rate of return is not a "pure" yield, for it includes an allowance for the risk inherent in holding a standard industrial share. This discount rate can be applied appropriately only to growth issues for which the risk is in some sense equal to that of standard securities, for all stocks will not tend to have the same yield regardless of risk. However, we do postulate that there should be no clear risk-premium difference between growth and ordinary shares. That is, for two securities which are equally risky in all other respects, we will ignore any risk difference resulting solely from the fact that the expected yield from one may come largely from capital appreciation, whereas the yield from the second is expected to be derived largely from dividend payments.[18]

---

[16] Some support for our choice of 2 percent as the rate of anticipated earnings growth can be found by examining long-term data. Using the Cowles Commission All-Stock Index [4, p. 59], annual gains of 1.8 percent were experienced from just after the Civil War to the middle of the 1930's. Nevertheless, the choice of an appropriate growth rate is not an obvious one and the reader may wish to substitute his own. Moreover, in a world of uncertainty, the market's estimate of g_s is unlikely to remain constant for all periods.

[17] The dividend yield, based on the anticipated next year's dividend rate, was 2.75 percent, and 2 percent was the projected growth rate of earnings per share.

[18] For support of this position in the context of an argument concerning the relevancy or irrelevancy of dividend payments, see Lintner [11, p. 255] and Miller and Modigliani [14, pp. 426–32]. Their demonstration, however, is consistent with a view that growth stocks may still be more risky than standard issues. While there is undoubtedly some justification for this frequently voiced position, its importance can be overstated. It is easy to imagine cases where the risk for a company continuously investing large amounts may actually be less than the normal risk of a business doing little investing. Moreover, one can point to a large class of growth companies which derive a substantial share of their earnings from rental and service revenues. In these cases, the companies not only enjoy a stable source of revenue and profit but also grow as the result of each new sale.

Thus, it is not self-evident, when comparing issues of roughly the same quality, why the security analyst would necessarily be less confident of his forecast of earnings growth than his

There is, however, one respect in which we can say unambiguously that most growth stocks are riskier than standard securities. The former have been shown to be inherently more volatile than representative standard issues. It could be maintained that because of this greater volatility, a higher discount rate should be applied than the apparent marginal efficiency of the standard list. The investor, according to this argument, should be given a risk premium to compensate him for assuming the risks of larger price fluctuations. Thus, by a process akin to "normal backwardation" in the futures markets, growth stocks would have to sell at a discount from their certainty value, which is calculated by abstracting from changes in the level of share prices. But if one subjects this argument to careful examination, one finds a Pandora's box of difficulties. Surely, if investors expect that the level of share prices will rise, then growth stocks should be expected to sell at a premium vis-à-vis ordinary shares since they would offer greater possibilities for capital appreciation. Thus a thorough uncertainty model of share valuation would contain precisely the same considerations as make up the expectational theory of the term structure of interest rates. At times, more volatile issues should sell at a premium and at other times at a discount from their certainty valuation precisely because of their inherent mercurial qualities. While we shall not extend this discussion further, these implications may indicate a few of the considerations which need to be included in a full-uncertainty model of share valuation.

We may now proceed to apply the model to recent periods of stock market history. In particular, we shall examine the recent market "adjustment" in the United States, where both the level and the structure of share prices underwent an unusually extensive metamorphosis. Using the formulas developed above, we shall first compute the theoretically justifiable price-earnings ratios for securities with differing growth characteristics. We then may compare the "warranted" normalized prices at recent peak and trough dates with those which actually existed. Table 14–1 treats only nondividend-paying shares, and, consequently valuation formula (13) is used. The numbers enclosed in the boxes are the warranted price-earnings multiples appropriate for two different levels of share prices. They represent normative valuations, assuming that the listed rate of growth of earnings is to occur for N years.[19] After this, the security loses its extraordinary growth characteristics and

appraisal of the viability of an established yearly dividend. Indeed, any number of counter-examples may be found. Moreover, if we introduce tax considerations, most investors should be expected, if anything, to prefer growth stocks because their ultimate yield would be taxed at substantially lower rates than the shares of standard issues paying higher dividends. This is not to deny, however, that many growth companies, particularly those which invest in completely new areas of endeavor, may indeed be riskier than standard issues.

[19] Of course, the model could easily be modified to allow for a diminution in the growth rate in later years of the growth horizon or the continuation of a more moderate growth rate after the end of N years.

Table 14-1. Warranted price-earnings ratios at peak and trough levels of share prices.

Rate of growth g / No. of years ahead discounted N	7.5		15		20		25		35		Per cent decline peak to trough for all g
	Peak	Trough	Peak	Trough	Peak	Trough	Peak	Trough	Peak	Trough	
2	21.38	15.97	24.47	18.28	26.64	19.90	28.91	21.60	33.72	25.19	25.3
3	21.94	16.21	26.86	19.85	30.52	22.55	34.49	25.49	43.45	32.11	26.1
4	22.52	16.46	29.49	21.55	34.96	25.55	41.16	30.09	56.00	40.93	26.9
5	23.11	16.71	32.37	23.41	40.05	28.96	49.12	35.52	72.17	52.18	27.7
7	24.34	17.22	39.02	27.60	52.56	37.18	69.95	49.48	119.88	84.80	29.3

Peak (December 12, 1961) Equation:

$$m = 20.3 \frac{(1 + g)^N}{(1.0475)^N}$$

Trough (June 26, 1962) Equation:

$$m = 15.5 \frac{(1 + g)^N}{(1.059)^N}$$

Per Cent Decline in Standard Multiple (m_s): 23.6%.

becomes valued as a typical standard issue.[20] The greater volatility of the share compared with standard issues is immediately revealed.

We shall now look at the actual price-earnings multiples that existed for certain well-known nondividend-paying growth shares. We can then reverse the analysis. Instead of asking what the warranted earnings multiple should be, we can instead determine from our model what growth is implicitly being anticipated and is already discounted in the market prices of the shares. Then we can ask whether the past history of earnings growth of these companies suggests that the rate of growth required to justify their current prices is reasonable. What follows is perhaps a very rough and, in large measure, an impressionistic attempt to select a sample of growth stocks that are no riskier than those issues included in the standard list. We wish to insure that the apparent marginal efficiency of the standard list is the rate of return relevant for discounting. It would, of course, be impossible to formulate rigorous criteria for equal riskiness without developing a full-uncertainty valuation model. Nevertheless, we would argue that our method of choosing securities insures that our certainty model gives a good approximation to what might be considered warranted valuations.[21]

[20] A similar and independent analysis has recently been performed by Charles C. Holt [10]. However, Holt neglects the dependence of the standard yield on the earnings multiple applied to standard issues. Therefore, his analysis suggests (incorrectly) that relative earnings ratios are invariant with respect to the general level of share prices.

[21] Our five sample nondividend-paying growth stocks have been selected on the basis of the following criteria: (1) that the company has been established in business for at least ten years (we want to exclude speculative new companies without sufficient past history to indicate future prospects); (2) that the company has been profitable in each of the past five years; (3) that the company has met the requirements of the definition of a growth stock in at least four of its last five fiscal years preceding the date of valuation; and (4) that the shares be considered of "investment grade" as evidenced by ratings applied by the investment advisory services and by widespread inclusion in the portfolios of the leading investment companies specializing in common-stock investments.

Our procedure will be to compute a mean (compounded) growth rate for each company. As has become abundantly clear in much of the recent work in uncertainty analysis, it may very well be that higher moments are of very significant importance to decision-making investors. Thus our insistence on relatively consistent growth will insure that the standard deviation of the mean growth rate is very low. It is necessary that higher moments of the total expected yield for any growth security be essentially similar to those applicable for standard issues. Similarly, we require an investment grade status comparable to standard issues in order to screen out those securities whose past records would suggest that a discount rate higher than r be applied. While a full-uncertainty analysis would include several modifications of this procedure, I do not believe they would materially affect the valuation results we have derived.

We now reach the *denouement* of our story. In Table 14–2 the price-earnings ratios existing at the recent market peak and trough are compared with the growth rates and growth periods that were implicitly assumed by their prices. We find that to justify the market prices for these issues at the market peak, an investor would have to expect extraordinary rates of growth (typically larger than had ever been achieved in the past) for a very long period of years.

To appraise this finding, it is necessary to make two observations, one bordering on the obvious, the other on the metaphysical. Our first comment is simply a reminder that the maintenance of a long-run high level of compounded earnings growth implies an ever increasing arithmetic growth of earnings. If a company which has enjoyed a 25 percent annually compounded growth rate over the past five years is to continue its same rate of growth in the next five years, then it will have to triple its absolute *increase* of earnings.[22] When we consider that we are discussing earnings *per share*, it is obvious that the difficulties are increased significantly. The actual growth rate of total earnings must in most cases be even larger to overcome the dilution effects of new shares issued. Finally, we should note that most "growth companies" were able to achieve the spectacular growth rates of Table 14–2 only because of the very low earnings base from which they started. Thus we must conclude on a priori grounds that it is highly unlikely that these companies will continue such rapid rates of growth for more than perhaps one year or, at best, a very few years.

Our second comment concerns the horizon over which the valuation is based. A strong a priori case can be made for the use of a relatively short horizon. I believe that ordinarily five years should realistically be considered the maximum for the investment horizon and, for the reasons given above, growth rates of 20 percent or more should be viewed very suspiciously if

---

[22] If the company earned a dollar a share at the beginning of the first period, it must earn over three dollars at the end of the fifth year (a two-dollar increase) and over nine dollars at the end of the tenth year (a six-dollar increase over year five).

Table 14–2. Growth-stock valuations (growth rates and periods implicitly assumed).

				Market peak December 12, 1961		
			Years* of growth at historic rate needed to justify current price N	Growth rate (g) needed to justify current price		Historic growth rate g (based on past 5 years)
Growth stock	Price P	Earnings multiple† m		3-Year horizon N = 3	4-Year horizon N = 4	
	(1)	(2)	(3)	(4)	(5)	(11)
Automatic Retailers	64	98.5	8	77%	55%	28%
Howard Johnson	60	33.5	4	24%	19%	18%
Litton Industries	161	63.9	6	53%	40%	28%
Perkin-Elmer	61	54.0	4	45%	34%	37%
Varian Associates	47	64.4	5	53%	40%	31%
Average of five growth stocks	79	62.9	6	53%	39%	28%

				Market trough June 26, 1962		
			Years* of growth at historic rate needed to justify current price N	Growth rate (g) needed to justify current price		Historic growth rate g (based on past 5 years)
Growth stock	Price P	Earnings multiple† m		3-Year horizon N = 3	4-Year horizon N = 4	
	(6)	(7)	(8)	(9)	(10)	(11)
Automatic Retailers	29	25.2	2½	24%	20%	28%
Howard Johnson	32	16.4	½	8%	7%	18%
Litton Industries	78	24.8	2½	24%	19%	28%
Perkin-Elmer	26	24.5	2	23%	19%	37%
Varian Associates	23	33.8	3½	37%	29%	31%
Average of five growth stocks	38	24.9	2½	24%	19%	28%

* Rounded to nearest half-year. Thus there are minor rounding inconsistencies in the table.
† Based on latest 12-months' earnings to each period.

projected for more than three years. Usually a corporation's investment prospects can be forecast intelligently only for the shorter three-year period. The five-year period represents, to my knowledge, the maximum budgeting horizon used by corporations themselves and by financial analysts in attempting an analytical forecast of earnings. An attempt to project industrial growth rates further (except in the most unusual circumstances) seems completely unjustified.[23] But no matter how questionable, precisely these kinds of projections seem to have been made and indeed, as Table 14–2 indicates, the structure of share prices in late 1961 can be rationalized only on that basis. Thus we would argue that in the world of uncertainty, the time horizon for discounting is one of the most important variables for determining equity values. The difficulty is that while there may be a priori reasons for setting a maximum to the discounting period (and for concluding that these issues were overvalued), there is no *one* reasonable horizon. I believe there is only a *putatively reasonable horizon*, a variable characteristic of market sentiment at any time. That the putatively reasonable horizon may undergo rapid shifts is obvious when we compare columns 3 and 8 of Table 14–2. At the trough, the wheel had turned full circle. Market prices implied more moderate rates of growth (usually well below the past performance of the companies) for periods well under the five-year "maximum" horizon. Even if one argues that part of the revaluation of growth stocks represented a growing distrust of projecting the high growth rates of the past into the future, this explanation is not complete. There was also a definite reduction in the putatively reasonable horizon used by investors in the valuation process. We might also note that to the extent that one could rely on continued good rates of growth for these companies (even if more moderate than in the past), the existing structure of share prices tended to undervalue growth stocks during June 1962, just as it had overvalued them in December 1961.

Our discussion of the use of the model would be incomplete without reference to the valuation of International Business Machines' shares. No other security is so synonymous with growth in the minds of investors as is IBM. Perhaps the most salient feature of IBM's past growth is its remarkable steadiness. Computing compounded growth rates, using each of the past ten years as a basis, one finds that the growth rate in earnings per share was 20 percent, or slightly above, for each year. Despite IBM's deserved reputation as the ideal growth stock, we should nevertheless be very suspicious if the growth rate implied by the price of the shares should exceed that rate

---

[23] By utilizing a limited horizon period over which extraordinary growth may be projected, we are introducing a type of finite-horizon method for dealing with uncertainty. Economists have pointed out that this technique leaves much to be desired for, among other things, it usually ignores any prospective receipts after the cut-off date and can be shown in some circumstances to lead to rather absurd rankings of investment projects. But the growth-stock model employs a finite-horizon device that is rather less crude. If investors' horizons are limited as a practical matter to five years, this does not imply that all receipts to the shareholders after the horizon period are ignored. All that is implied is that only normal growth is projected after the cut-off period.

which has been achieved in the past decade. Indeed, as we remarked earlier, we would be surprised to see it continue, particularly considering the size of the company.[24]

Table 14–3 presents a series of valuation estimates for IBM under differing assumptions as to future growth rates and growth periods. Since IBM pays dividends, formula (11) has been used for the calculation. In addition, we have introduced one innovation into our valuation principle. We may well be accused of being too conservative in assuming that after the period of abnormal growth is completed the shares will sell at the same price-earnings ratio as do standard shares. Indeed, would it not be plausible to assume that the shares of a company such as IBM would still be able to command a premium over ordinary shares both because of its extraordinarily

Table 14–3. Valuation of IBM common stock.

	Market peak December 12, 1961				Market trough June 26, 1962			
	$g = 20\%$		$g = 15\%$		$g = 20\%$		$g = 15\%$	
Horizon	Residual earnings multiple		Residual earnings multiple		Residual earnings multiple		Residual earnings multiple	
N	20.3	30	20.3	30	15.5	23	15.5	23
3	31.5	46.1	27.5	40.3	23.6	34.5	20.5	30.1
5	42.0	61.1	33.5	49.0	31.0	45.0	24.5	35.8
7	55.7	80.8	40.7	59.4	40.4	58.4	29.3	42.7

high quality and because the company's growth prospects may still appear to be above average? To be as liberal as possible, we have made a separate calculation making the (arbitrary) assumption that the residual price-earnings multiple for the shares will be 50 percent higher than the multiple applied to standard securities. The calculations are presented below.

At the market peak, IBM shares sold at 580, a multiple of 64 times the most recent 12-months' earnings.[25] Particularly in light of our previous discussion on the implications of extending a growth rate of 20 percent for a period of seven years and beyond, we can assert unequivocally that IBM shares were overvalued relative to the standard list of securities. In the words of a favorite Wall Street aphorism "share prices were discounting not only the future but also the hereafter." At the trough, IBM shares sold at 320, a multiple of 32 times the latest 12-months' earnings. While the case for

[24] IBM's total revenues are now running at an annual rate of approximately $2 billion. To keep up a long-term 20 percent growth rate (we assume earnings and revenues must expand at the same rate) then the revenue growth from year seven to eight would equal $1.4 billion, the revenue volume of 1960. To push the argument to the absurd, if the growth rate continued for an additional 22 years, IBM's revenues would exceed the U.S. national income in 1962.
[25] As estimated by the author. Reported earnings in all cases have been adjusted to include unremitted foreign income.

considering IBM shares undervalued is not as clear-cut as the overvaluation at the December peak, it is easy to find justification for believing that the shares of IBM were probably slightly on the low side of a reasonable valuation vis-à-vis the level of share prices.[26]

V. SUMMARY AND CONCLUSION

It will be useful now to review the ground we have covered and to appraise the results we have achieved. We attempted to explain the December, 1961 peak structure of share prices as a phenomenon understandable only against a background of the history of security analysis since the Great Depression. We described the shifts in the central interest of security analysis from an analysis of balance sheet values through an emphasis on earning power and finally to the elevation of growth analysis as the *sine qua non* of profitable investment. Concomitantly, we observed that fashions of equity investment determine a structure of share prices which, at various times, has put varying degrees of premium on these values.

Next we introduced and developed a simple model by which we might determine a warranted structure of share prices on a certainty basis. In addition to demonstrating its potential usefulness in detecting cases of over- and undervaluation of growth shares, the model could serve as a conceptual scheme for analyzing the change in the structure of share prices which took place. In the first place, we showed that a part of the much larger percentage decline in growth stocks was to be expected from a stable functional relationship, just as when interest rates rise, long-term bonds can be expected to suffer a sharper decline in price. Next, we analyzed the revaluation in terms of investors' reluctance to continue to accept the plausibility of projections of past rates of growth into the future and their uneasiness with the very long horizons implicit in share prices. Moreover, we showed that precisely because some stocks were being valued on the basis of a long growth horizon, their volatility, given a change in the level of share prices, was increased. Finally, in our modification to the IBM valuation model, we suggested that the expected residual price-earnings ratio, applied to the shares at the termination of their period of extraordinary growth, could also be an important variable. In a world of uncertainty, where company prospects beyond the very immediate future become increasingly fuzzy, there may be room for a considerable range of residual valuations for the same security.

But perhaps even more important than these considerations, our analysis has at once demonstrated what an ephemeral process valuation is and underlined the very severe limitations by which any model of security valuation must necessarily be beset. There is no self-evident appropriate horizon for the projection of growth rates, only a putatively reasonable one. The history of

---

[26] Assuming a growth rate of 15 percent could be achieved for three years and that the residual multiple of earnings be a modest 23, the price-earnings multiple is (approximately) justified.

share-price behavior demonstrates ineluctably that investors are at some times willing to take a much longer view than at others. At the beginning of the present decade of the "soaring 'sixties" it did not seem unreasonable to anticipate with some degree of confidence a decade of substantial growth. At the 1962 market trough investors were unwilling to pay a substantial premium for any growth that was not expected to occur over the fairly immediate future. We have demonstrated the very large magnitude of difference in warranted prices that can result from such a change in the growth horizon. Moreover, it is enormously difficult to determine the growth rates that should be used in the valuation formulas, if, indeed, it is even admissible (except for simplification of analysis) to project compounded growth rates for earnings per share. It is very difficult to be neutral about things so uncertain as future growth rates. At times of great optimism it is easy to accept the idea that even some acceleration of past growth rates is possible, given the exorbitant claims that were made for the economy during the decade of the 'sixties. At times of great pessimism it seems implausible to believe that any but the most modest rates of growth are sustainable for companies which now must grow on a far larger base of sales and earnings than was the case in years past, when their historic growth records were made. The problem, of course, is that it is easy for investors to convince themselves of the credibility of either of these positions.

The Keynesian analogy of the newspaper contest is by now a classic statement of the problems which we face. It is immaterial to the contestant what his personal criteria of beauty may be. What is important is rather what the average opinion considers the relevant criteria to be, or rather, what the average opinion believes the popular criteria to be, etc. Similarly, it is less important in determining market values to pick, let us say, four years as the objectively proper period over which growth can be discounted, when the relevant period for discounting is determined by that period which the average opinion believes to be proper. This I believe to be at the heart of the problem of valuation. However, this is not to be construed as implying that market values are necessarily determined by the irrationality of some sort of perpetual "tulip-bulb craze." On the contrary, I am convinced that actual market values oscillate around a structure of prices that does a reasonably good job at attempting to equalize net yields, given the often very limited amount of information available to the investing community. But styles and fashions have a habit of changing drastically for considerable periods of time, so that the Keynesian admonition about the long run must always be kept in mind. Therefore, we must always accept an uncomfortably large degree of indeterminacy in economic models that attempt to determine objectively a structure of warranted stock prices. Nevertheless, it seems to me that both economists and those closest to the financial markets can benefit from this kind of conceptual scheme which, if nothing more, can describe quantitatively the market valuations that exist at any time.

APPENDIX

Theorem 1: The normalized price, m, that can be paid for a growth stock will always exceed the standard multiple, m_s.

Proof: Substituting d for $D(1 + g)/mE$ in (11) and solving for $\bar{m}_s/m$ we obtain:

$$\frac{\bar{m}_s}{m} = \frac{(1 + \bar{r})^N}{(1 + g)^N} - \frac{(1 + \bar{r})^N}{(1 + g)^N}\left(\frac{d}{\bar{r} - g}\right) + \left(\frac{d}{\bar{r} - g}\right). \tag{A1}$$

Now it can be shown that the quantity $\bar{m}_s/m < 1$ for a growth stock. Assume $g < r$. Then

$$\frac{(1 + \bar{r})^N}{(1 + g)^N} > 1 \quad \text{and} \quad \frac{d}{\bar{r} - g} > 1$$

from (7), the definition of a growth stock. It can then be seen that

$$\frac{(1 + \bar{r})^N}{(1 + g)^N}\left[1 - \left(\frac{d}{\bar{r} - g}\right)\right] < \left[1 - \left(\frac{d}{\bar{r} - g}\right)\right] \quad \text{or} \quad \frac{\bar{m}_s}{m} < 1, \tag{A2}$$

the price-earnings multiple of the growth stock is greater than the standard multiple. A similar demonstration applies to the case of $g > r$. If $g = r$, then utilizing (10) we have:

$$m - \bar{m}_s = N\left(\frac{D}{E}\right) > 0. \tag{A3}$$

But note when

$$d = r - g, \quad m = \bar{m}_s.$$

Theorem 2: The warranted price-earnings multiple for a growth stock is an increasing function of the growth rate expected.

Proof: Substituting mE for P in (10) and differentiating we obtain:

$$\frac{\partial m}{\partial g} = \frac{D}{E(1 + \bar{r})} + \frac{2D(1 + g)}{E(1 + \bar{r})^2} + \cdots + \frac{ND(1 + g)^{N-1}}{E(1 + \bar{r})^N} + \frac{N\bar{m}_s(1 + g)^{N-1}}{(1 + \bar{r})^N} > 0. \tag{A4}$$

Of course, this proposition holds even in the absence of the convenient assumption of constant growth, as the formulation of (A4) makes abundantly clear.

Theorem 3: The warranted earnings multiple is an increasing function of the number of years for which the security is expected to continue its extraordinary rate of growth.

Proof: Differentiating (11) and simplifying we obtain:

$$\frac{\partial m}{\partial N} = \ln\left[\frac{(1 + g)}{(1 + \bar{r})}\right]\left[\frac{(1 + g)}{(1 + \bar{r})}\right]^N\left[\bar{m}_s - \frac{D(1 + g)}{E(\bar{r} - g)}\right] \tag{A5}$$

If $g > \bar{r}$,

$$\ln\left[\frac{1 + g}{1 + \bar{r}}\right] > 0 \quad \text{and} \quad -\frac{D(1 + g)}{E(\bar{r} - g)} > 0 \quad \text{so that} \quad \frac{\partial m}{\partial N} > 0.$$

If $g < \bar{r}$,

$$\ln\left[\frac{1 + g}{1 + \bar{r}}\right] < 0, \quad \text{but} \quad \left[\bar{m}_s - \frac{D(1 + g)}{E(\bar{r} - g)}\right] < 0 \text{ also.}$$

To show

$$\bar{m}_s < \frac{D(1 + g)}{E(\bar{r} - g)}$$

we divide both sides by $m > 0$ and obtain

$$\frac{\overline{m}_s}{m} < \frac{d}{(\bar{r} - g)}.$$

This holds since

$$\frac{\overline{m}_s}{m} < 1 \quad \text{by (A2)} \quad \text{and} \quad \frac{d}{(\bar{r} - g)} > 1 \quad \text{by (7)}.$$

Theorem 4: Nondividend-paying growth stocks are more volatile than standard issues. For a given (percentage) change in the level of share prices, m_s, m will vary more than in proportion.

Proof: Utilizing expression (3) for r and substituting $m_s \bar{E}_s$ for P_s, we can restate (13) as

$$m = m_s \frac{(1 + g)^N}{\left[1 + \bar{g}_s + \frac{\bar{D}_s(1 + \bar{g}_s)}{m_s \bar{E}_s} \right]^N}. \tag{A6}$$

Now letting m_s vary (i.e., allowing the general level of share prices to change) and differentiating m with respect to m_s, we have:

$$\frac{\partial m}{\partial m_s} = \left[1 + \bar{g}_s + \frac{\bar{D}_s(1 + \bar{g}_s)}{m_s \bar{E}_s} \right]^N [1 + g]^N + m_s [1 + g]^N N$$

$$\frac{\times \left[1 + \bar{g}_s + \frac{\bar{D}_s(1 + \bar{g}_s)}{m_s \bar{E}_s} \right]^{N-1} \left[\frac{\bar{D}_s(1 + \bar{g}_s)}{\bar{E}_s m_s^2} \right]}{\left[1 + \bar{g}_s + \frac{\bar{D}_s(1 + \bar{g}_s)}{m_s \bar{E}_s} \right]^{2N}}. \tag{A7}$$

Multiplying through by m_s/m to convert (A7) into an elasticity formulation (where we use expression (A6) for m), we have:

$$\frac{\partial m}{\partial m_s} \cdot \frac{m_s}{m} = 1 + \frac{Nd_s}{1 + r} > 1. \tag{A8}$$

Theorem 5: The volatility of nondividend-paying growth stocks increases with the number of years included in the time horizon but is invariant with respect to the rate of growth expected.

Proof: Letting $\epsilon_m \equiv \partial m/\partial m_s \cdot m_s/m$ represent the elasticity of the price-earnings ratio and differentiating (A8), we have:

$$\frac{\partial \epsilon_m}{\partial N} = \frac{d_s}{1 + r} > 0 \tag{A9}$$

and

$$\frac{\partial \epsilon_m}{\partial g} = 0. \tag{A10}$$

REFERENCES

[1] BAUMOL, WILLIAM J., "Comment on Dividend Policy, Growth and the Valuation of Shares," *Jour. Business*, Jan. 1963, *36*, 112–15.

[2] BOHMFALK, J. F., JR., "The Growth Stock Philosophy," *Financial Analysts Jour.*, Nov.–Dec. 1960, *16*, 113–23.

[3] CLENDENIN, JOHN C., and MAURICE VAN CLEAVE, "Growth and Common Stock Values," *Jour. Finance*, Dec. 1954, *60*, 365–76.

[4] COWLES, A., et al., *Common-Stock Indexes*, 1871–1957, Cowles Commission on Research in Economics, Monograph No. 3. Bloomington 1938.

[5] DURAND, DAVID, "Growth Stocks and the St. Petersburg Paradox," *Jour. Finance*, Sept. 1957, *12*, 348–63.

[6] GORDON, MYRON J., "The Savings Investment and Valuation of a Corporation," *Rev. Econ. Stat.*, Feb. 1962, *44*, 37–51.

[7] —— and ELI SHAPIRO, "Capital Equipment Analysis: The Required Rate of Profit," *Management Science*, Oct. 1956; reprinted in Ezra Solomon, ed., *The Management of Corporate Capital*, Glencoe 1959.

[8] GRAHAM, B., and D. L. DODD with C. TATHAM, JR., *Security Analysis*. New York 1951.

[9] GUILD, S. E., *Stock Growth and Discount Tables*. Boston 1931.

[10] HOLT, C. C., "The Influence of Growth Duration on Share Prices," *Jour. Finance*, Sept. 1962, *17*, 465–75.

[11] LINTNER, JOHN, "Dividends, Earnings, Leverage, Stock Prices, and the Supply of Capital to Corporations," *Rev. Econ. Stat.*, Aug. 1962, *44*, 243–69.

[12] MALKIEL, BURTON G., "Expectations, Bond Prices and the Term Structure of Interest Rates," *Quart. Jour. Econ.*, May 1962, *76*, 197–218.

[13] MEAD, E. S., and J. GRODINSKY, *The Ebb and Flow of Investment Values*. New York 1939.

[14] MILLER, MERTON H., and FRANCO MODIGLIANI, "Dividend Policy, Growth and the Valuation of Shares," *Jour. Business*, Oct. 1961, *34*, 411–33.

[15] MODIGLIANI, FRANCO, and MERTON H. MILLER, "The Cost of Capital Corporation Finance and the Theory of Investment: Reply," *Am. Econ. Rev.*, Sept. 1959, *44*, 655–69.

[16] WILLIAMS, J. B., *The Theory of Investment Value*. Cambridge 1938.

[17] "Growth—The Hottest Word in Wall Street" (an editorial), *Financial Analysts Jour.*, Sept.–Oct. 1960, *16*, 3, 38.

15

INFLATION-CAUSED WEALTH REDISTRIBUTION: A TEST OF A HYPOTHESIS

REUBEN A. KESSEL*

Professor Kessel's work on the monetary debtor-creditor hypothesis represents a significant contribution to business finance literature. This paper focuses on the general question of whether business firms gain from inflation and the approach to the problem is expressed in the most fundamental economic terms. The author's empirical tests are sound in concept and provide useful factual data on the financial policy.

In addition, basic issues with regard to the role of expectations in financial decisions are posed and clarified, and some startling conclusions are arrived at. If both debtor and creditor classes correctly interpreted price level changes as well as changes in the level of economic activity and profits, neither creditor nor stockholders would benefit from economic changes. The difference between expectations and realizations becomes a fundamental consideration in the appraisal of all theories of financial values.

The belief that business firms gain through inflation is common among both economists and the lay public. Three independent chains of reasoning have been employed by economists to reach this conclusion. The first, most frequently encountered and the one of principal concern here is based on the hypothesis that debtors gain by inflation and the assumption that business firms are debtors. Enterprisers contract to pay fixed dollar obligations in the form of bonds or other debt instruments. Therefore depreciations in the real value of money obligations, which are the losses of creditors, are the gains of business firms.[1] This argument has become the standard textbook explanation of why business firms gain during inflation and how wealth is redistributed. In order to reveal clearly how this conclusion is obtained, an example of the following type is usually employed. Assume a business

From Reuben A. Kessel, "Inflation-Caused Wealth Redistribution: A Test of a Hypothesis," *The American Economic Review*, March 1956, Vol. XLVI, 455–466. Printed by permission.

* This paper stems from an investigation undertaken in 1952 as a doctoral dissertation at the University of Chicago. The dissertation contains all of the basic data upon which this article is based. The author is indebted to A. A. Alchian and N. Kaplan of the RAND Corporation for aid in the preparation of this paper.

[1] J. M. Keynes, *Tract on Monetary Reform* (London, 1923), p. 18; I. Fisher, *The Purchasing Power of Money* (New York, 1920), pp. 58–73, 190–91.

firm is half debt- and half equity-financed at time t_0. Between t_0 and t_1 the price level doubles. On the assumption that the volume of debt and the number of shares outstanding remains unchanged, a doubling of the price level implies a tripling of equity values. If a firm has any outstanding debts at all, its equity value can be expected to increase in real terms during inflation.[2]

Clearly the heart of this particular explanation of wealth redistribution is the assumption that interest rates fail to reflect completely price level changes during inflation. The debtor-creditor hypothesis is based on the postulate that interest rates reflect an implicit biased estimate of the future course of prices. It is because this estimate is assumed to be low that the conclusion—debtors gain and creditors lose during inflation—follows.

The second rationale for the conclusion that business firms are extraordinarily profitable during inflation is based on the assumption that inflation causes wages to lag behind prices. This lag of wage rates behind prices redistributes income from laborers to capitalists.[3]

A third argument that is relatively more popular with the public than with economists is that business firms gain during inflation because they carry inventories. These inventories are sold at prices that reflect mark-ups based on current prices rather than the lower prices at which they were in fact purchased. Therefore, on this account alone business firms are extraordinarily profitable when prices are rising.[4] Clearly in real terms there is no gain or loss, no change in the terms of trade of inventories for real resources, as a consequence of inflation for owners of inventories. Reported business profits may appear larger as a result of these "gains." However, this is purely an artifact of original cost accounting.[5]

The debtor-creditor hypothesis has two implications that will be considered explicitly. One is for absolute and the other for relative changes in real wealth positions. The absolute change implication predicts that debtors will gain and creditors lose vis-à-vis their pre-inflation wealth positions. Because it is generally believed that business firms are debtors, economists have been led to conclude that the owners of business firms are

---

[2] An example of this type may be found in L. V. Chandler, *The Economics of Money and Banking* (New York, 1948), pp. 36–37.

[3] This is essentially the argument propounded by E. J. Hamilton in "Profit Inflation and the Industrial Revolution, 1751–1800," which is found in *Enterprise and Secular Change* (London, 1953), p. 322. Hamilton argues the same thesis in a larger context in "Prices as a Factor in Business Growth," *Jour. Econ. Hist.*, Fall 1952, XII, 325. This same argument and conclusion may be found in E. M. Bernstein and I. G. Patel, "Inflation in Relation to Economic Development," *Internat. Mon. Fund Staff Papers*, Nov. 1952, p. 380. It can also be found in standard textbooks on money and banking such as Chandler, *op. cit.*, pp. 32, ff.

[4] Keynes, *op. cit.*, pp. 18–19; A. G. Hart, *Defense Without Inflation* (New York, 1951), p. 70.

[5] In order to discriminate between "gains" in wealth positions that merely reflect decreases in the purchasing power of money and true gains, *i.e.*, increases in command over real resources, the purchasing power of the dollars used to measure wealth is held constant. The wholesale price index is consistently employed for this purpose. It appears to have been somewhat less affected by price controls and therefore a somewhat more reliable indicator of true economic prices than the consumer price index.

beneficiaries of inflation. If, however, it is possible to find business firms that are creditors, then these firms should be worse off as a consequence of inflation.

The other implication is concerned with the relative magnitude of the gains among more and less extreme debtors and the corresponding relative losses among more and less extreme creditors. The debtor-creditor hypothesis suggests that inflation ought to be relatively more profitable for large debtors than small debtors and more unprofitable for large creditors than small creditors. Therefore if one found that all debtors gain but also found that modest debtors did better than extreme debtors, then one implication of this hypothesis would be confirmed while the second would be denied.

There exist two classes of evidence that have been regarded as relevant for examining the validity of the Keynes-Fisher-Hamilton belief that business firms are extraordinarily profitable during inflation. The first is provided by the investigators of particular inflations such as Bresciani-Turroni, Graham, and others.[6] Their results can be summarized into two historically observed regularities. These are that (1) banks as a class invariably lose during inflation (the real value of bank stocks seems to have gone down in every inflation studied) and (2) stock price indexes at best rise only about as much as the general level of prices and usually not as much.

The second class is studies of time series of prices and wages which indicate that real wage rates decline during inflation.[7] This has led to the conclusion that the returns to capital rise during inflation, and has been employed as evidence to buttress the more general proposition—that inflation causes wages to lag behind prices to the benefit of capitalists generally. This hypothesis implies that the more "laboristic" a firm is, the greater are its inflation-born profits.

The objectives of this paper are: (1) to evaluate the predictive content of the Keynes-Fisher hypothesis of wealth redistribution; (2) to examine some evidence pertinent for evaluating the belief that business firms gain as a consequence of inflation; and (3) to rationalize the data and conclusions of this paper with the findings of empirical investigators of inflation.

In order to achieve these goals, stock price changes, during both inflation and deflation, of large American corporations were employed as data

---

[6] Bresciani-Turroni, *Economics of Inflation* (London, 1937), pp. 253, 298; F. D. Graham, *Exchange, Prices and Production in Hyper-Inflation: Germany, 1920–23* (Princeton, 1930), pp. 74, 177; J. H. Rogers, *The Process of Inflation in France* (New York, 1929), pp. 212–13, 265; J. van Walre DeBordes, *The Austrian Crown: Its Depreciation and Stabilization* (London, 1924), p. 216; P. B. Whale, *Joint Stock Banking in Germany* (London, 1930), p. 242; D. L. Grove, "The Role of the Banking System in the Chilean Inflation," *Internat. Mon. Fund Staff Papers*, Sept. 1951, II, 55. Graham alone, of the authors cited, fails to indicate unambiguously that banks lost out. Evidently the expansion of the banking facilities in Germany during the inflation and hyperinflation led Graham to believe that the banking business must have been very profitable. See *Econ. Rev.*, Aug. 17, 1923, VIII, 136, cited by Graham, *op. cit.*, p. 74.

[7] Hamilton, "Profit Inflation," *loc cit.*, pp. 323, ff.; E. P. Lerner, "Money, Prices and Wages in the Confederacy, 1861–65," *Jour. Pol. Econ.*, Feb. 1955, LXIII, 31, ff.

reflecting capital value changes. A series of five samples, four of which were randomly drawn from the population of industrial firms listed on the New York Stock Exchange, defined the companies whose stock price changes were accepted as data. The predictive content of the Keynes-Fisher hypothesis was evaluated by employing it to forecast or explain how these stock prices ought to change, comparing these predictions with observed changes, and determining whether or not a significant relationship exists between predicted and observed stock price changes.

I. BANK SHARE PRICE CHANGES DURING THE SECOND WORLD WAR INFLATION

Before considering the first sample, which is 16 bank stocks, it is instructive to note that the Standard and Poor's index of New York bank shares increased by a mere 20 percent between the end of 1942 and 1948.[8] This represents further confirmation of the already observed regularity—that banks lose during inflation. For this sample of 16 bank shares, stock prices rose by 47 percent from the end of 1942 to the end of 1948 while the wholesale price index increased by 60 percent.[9] At first blush these results appear to contradict both the Fisher-Keynes and Hamilton hypotheses. Banks are extraordinarily large debtors in the sense that the ratio of debt to equity of banks is generally several times larger than for industrial corporations. Similarly banks are relatively laboristic enterprises. In 1941, approximately 50 percent of bank costs excluding taxes were for wages and salaries.[10] This is generally much higher than for the population of industrials.

Upon looking more closely at bank balance sheets, one is not only impressed with the volume of bank debt relative to the size of the equity of bank-stock holders, but also with the nature of bank assets. Virtually all bank assets are monetary, i.e., assets whose value is independent of the price level, such as bonds, notes, loans and discounts and deposits with other banks. Apparently the only real assets of banks, i.e., assets whose value would be expected to vary with the price level, are bank buildings and accounting machines. Therefore although it is true that banks are enormous debtors, it is not clear that banks on net balance are debtors. The answer is a function of the relative size of the bank building and accounting machine accounts, on the one hand, and the shareholders' equity, on the other.

---

[8] *Industry Survey of Banks*, Standard and Poor's Corp., New York, March 6, 1952, pp. B2-2. This index was also composed of 16 banks.

[9] This sample of 16 banking companies was drawn from the population of bank shares listed in the *New York Times*, Nov. 5, 1951. It represents virtually all of the bank stocks listed that day.

[10] *Industry Survey of Banks*, *op. cit.*, pp. B2-11. Grove, *op. cit.*, pp. 56–57, found that salaries represented from 56 to 65 percent of all costs for commercial banks in Chile between 1937 and 1950.

Are monetary assets larger than monetary liabilities? For each of these 16 banks, monetary assets exceeded monetary liabilities. Therefore these results confirm part of one implication of the debtor-creditor hypothesis, namely that the real value of creditor securities should decline during inflation. In order to examine the second implication, that more extreme creditors ought to be worse off than their less extreme fellows, the ratio of net monetary assets (the difference between monetary liabilities and monetary assets) to total assets was employed as a measure of the intensity of creditor status. The larger this ratio, the more extreme creditor status is assumed to be.[11] Therefore a ranking of these ratios represents a prediction of the relative performance of these bank shares during inflation. A second set of ratios, those of stock prices at the end of 1948 to stock prices at the end of 1942, was computed for each firm.[12] This second ranking depicts the relative stock price changes that occurred. The ranks of these two sets of ratios were then examined in an effort to detect inverse correlation. The two sets of ranks were found to be inversely correlated, assuming a 5 percent significant level, and roughly 23 percent (correlation coefficient of 0.48) of the observed variation was explained by the debtor-creditor hypothesis.[13]

II. INDUSTRIAL SHARE PRICE CHANGES DURING INFLATION

The second sample consists of 30 industrial corporations. It was obtained by random sampling from the population of the first thousand corporations, all listed on the New York Stock Exchange, reported by *The Wall Street Journal* of November 5, 1951. During the interval from the end of 1942 to the end of 1948 for which these stocks were studied, the Standard and Poor's index of 50 industrials declined in real terms by about 5 percent. The behavior of this index number obeys the historically observed regularity that stock prices at best just keep pace with the price level and generally fall behind during inflation.

In order to detect differences in the monetary positions of these 30 corporations, i.e., to distinguish debtors from creditors and subsequently to make finer distinctions within each class, the following classification system was employed to sort out the monetary from the real accounts in corporation balance sheets.

---

[11] These calculations were made from the end of 1942 blaance sheets, except for one firm whose balance sheet was drawn up in October, 1942.

[12] These stock prices, as well as all the stock prices employed in this study, were adjusted to take account of stock dividends, splits, and capital dividends.

[13] The test employed was formulated by E. G. Olds in "Distribution of Sums of Squares of Rank Difference for Small Numbers of Individuals," *Annals Math. Stat.*, June 1938, IX, 133. This test is also described by W. A. Wallis, "Rough-and-Ready Statistical Tests," *Indus. Qual. Control*, March 1952, VIII, 35–40. It should be emphasized that this test is pertinent only for relative price change implications. The use of ranks abstracts from absolute values.

Assets and Liabilities Classified as Monetary

Monetary assets	Monetary Liabilities
Cash	Accounts Payable
Marketable Securities	Notes Payable
Accounts Receivable	Tax Liability Reserve
Tax Refunds Receivable	Bonds
Notes Receivable	Preferred Stock
Prepaid Insurance	
Gold	

In general there were three difficult and important (in the sense that the size of the accounts involved were not negligible) classification problems. These were represented by preferred stock, marketable securities, and investment in other companies.

From a narrow legal point of view, nonparticipating preferred stock is an equity security. However as a corporate obligation, it is fixed in amount and yields an income stream whose size is independent of the price level. Therefore, this type of preferred stock is in substance, if not in form, a monetary obligation. This interpretation is supported by Guthman and Dougall who contend preferred stock contracts are in fact but not in name much more like bond indentures than common stock agreements.[14] Consequently, for the purposes of this study, nonconvertible and nonparticipating preferred stock were defined as debt. For convertible and participating preferred stock, there seemed to be no easy prescription to follow. Corporations that had either of these two types of preferred shares outstanding were omitted from three samples in this study. For two samples, such securities were included and assumed to be debt instruments.

To the extent that corporations own marketable securities, they act as investment companies. If these securities are debt instruments, there is no classification problem. On the other hand, if they are equities, then it is necessary to determine the net monetary position of the companies they represent in order to come to some conclusion about the expected impact of inflation upon these share values. Evidence bearing on the composition of marketable securities accounts is far from conclusive. What there is, however, suggests that in the late 'twenties a considerable proportion of marketable securities accounts consisted of stocks. In the early 'thirties, there was a switch from stocks to bonds and other forms of debt, a principal component being government securities.[15] On the basis of these bits of evidence, marketable securities were considered monetary for post-1930 years and real for all preceding years.

---

[14] H. G. Guthman and H. E. Dougall, *Corporate Financial Policy*, 2nd ed. (New York, 1948), p. 90.

[15] F. A. Lutz, *Corporate Cash Balances, 1914–1923*, Nat. Bur. of Econ. Research (New York, 1945), pp. 56 ff. 79. W. A. Chudson, *The Pattern of Corporate Financial Structure*, Nat. Bur. of Econ. Research (New York, 1945), p. 34 n.

Investment in other corporations is a second account which gives an ordinary industrial corporation an investment company cast. This account, which usually represents relatively permanent ownership in other corporations that are not consolidated with the examined corporation's balance sheet, can be evaluated only by examining the monetary structure of the company invested in. In lieu of examining the balance sheets of these companies, these investments were regarded as real, i.e., the companies represented by these accounts were considered neutrals. These are companies whose monetary assets and monetary liabilities are equal.

The second sample of 30 industrial corporations[16] yielded several interesting results. Perhaps the most interesting is the fact that 1942 year-end balance sheets indicated that this sample was evenly divided between debtors, firms whose monetary liabilities exceed their monetary assets, and creditors, firms whose monetary assets exceeded their monetary liabilities. This suggests that economists in general and Keynes and Fisher in particular may have grossly underestimated the frequency of creditors in the business population.

For this second sample, the shares of the 15 creditor corporations declined in real value by 13 percent. On the other hand, the debtor shares increased in real value by 81 percent. However before jumping to conclusions, one must ask: might this observed difference between debtor and creditor share price changes have occurred as a chance phenomenon and consequently failed to depict a characteristic of the sampled population? The answer is no; the Mann and Whitney test indicates that there exists less than a 0.0025 percent chance that a random sample with the observed properties could be drawn from a population characterized by an absence of these properties.[17] Similar results were obtained for this sample using stock prices from the end of 1939 to the end of 1948 and from the end of June 1942 to the end of June 1948.[18]

---

[16] From this sample were rejected: (a) holding and investment companies because of the costs of determining net creditor or debtor status from the balance sheets of the companies concerned, (b) corporations that issued convertible and participating preferred shares and warrants, thereby avoiding difficult problems of classification which might lead to large errors, (c) corporations that were not continuously listed between 1939 and 1948, (d) corporations whose balance sheets were not drawn up at the end of the year, (e) corporations that issued new securities to old shareholders below market prices during the time interval between the end of 1939 and the end of 1948, (f) public utilities and railroads, in order to avoid the problem of disentangling the effects of rate regulation from inflation. The rejection of corporations from this sample on account of the convertible and participating characteristics of their preferred shares tends to bias this sample in the direction of overstating the frequency of creditors in the population. On the other hand, the classification of preferred stock as debt constitutes a countervailing bias and the net effect of these two forces is not clear.

[17] H. B. Mann and D. P. Whitney, "On a Test of Whether One or Two Random Variables is Stochastically Larger than the Other," *Annals Math. Stat.*, March 1947, XVIII, 50–60. Also described in Wallis, *op. cit.*

[18] For the period from the end of June 1942 to the end of June 1948, the significance level was less than 0.0025. For the period from the end of 1939 to the end of 1948, it was less than 0.012. In real terms, the stock prices of the creditors declined by 29 percent and the stock prices of the debtors rose by 8 percent for the 1939 to 1948 experiment. On the other hand, the stock prices of both groups increased in real terms between the end of June 1942 to the end of June 1948. The stock prices of the debtors increased by a factor of 2.52 and the creditors by 13 percent.

The confirmation of the predictive content of the real-value-change implication of the debtor-creditor hypothesis suggests that the relative stock-price change implication may also have some predictive validity. In order to test this latter implication, all 30 corporations were ranked in terms of indebtedness. The ratio of the difference between monetary assets and monetary liabilities to total assets, for the end of 1942, is used to measure this property. The 15 debtors, of course, occupied the first 15 ranks. The first rank was assigned to the most extreme debtor, the fifteenth to the least extreme debtor, the sixteenth to the least extreme creditor, and the thirtieth to the most extreme creditor. If the debtor-creditor hypothesis is valid, then there ought to exist a significant correlation between this ranking and the ranking based on the observed relative change in stock prices. This is the ranking obtained by ordering the ratios of end-of-1948 to the end-of-1942 stock prices after adjusting for stock splits and capital and stock dividends. This correlation proved to be significant at the 0.002 level. It also explained about 22 percent (correlation coefficient of 0.47) of the observed variation in stock prices.[19]

These results confirm the validity of the Keynes-Fisher theorizing about the significance of debtor-creditor relations for explaining inflation-caused wealth redistribution. The predictive content of this interpretation of Keynes and Fisher constitutes at least a partial verification of what has been long suspected by many economists but never demonstrated empirically, that debtor-creditor relations are crucial for understanding the mechanism by which inflation redistributes wealth. However the frequency of debtors and creditors in this particular sample suggests that an invalid empirical assumption—that business firms are debtors—led both Keynes and Fisher to excessively sweeping conclusions about the gains of business firms during inflation.

Samples I and II were so selected that a number of biases were introduced that may have misrepresented the frequency of debtors and creditors in the population of large industrials and therefore the validity of the objection to the Keynes-Fisher assumption that business firms are debtors. Clearly the bank sample is a special case; and serious objections can be raised against the exclusion of corporations that had convertible and participating preferred outstanding. Therefore a third sample was randomly selected from the population of the last 1000 New York Stock Exchange industrials that

---

[19] For the period from the end of June 1942 to the end of June 1948, the significance level was 0.0025 percent, and 30 percent of the observed variation was explained. For the period from the end of 1939 to the end of 1948, the significance level was 0.02, and the explained portion of the observed variation was 12 percent. The Old's rank correlation test, *op. cit.*, was employed.

Incidentally, the debt-to-equity analysis, that is the debtor-creditor hypothesis if one ignores the asset side of the balance sheet (see Chandler, *op. cit.*), was found to have no independent predictive content. Partial correlation analysis of the relative price change predictions of the debt-to-equity hypothesis, using Sample II, with the changes that occurred between the end of 1942 and 1948 respectively, revealed no correlation. Therefore if the debt-to-equity hypothesis has predictive power, this can be explained by its correlation with the more general debtor-creditor hypothesis.

appeared in *The Wall Street Journal* of November 4, 1951. Convertible bonds and convertible and participating preferred shares were classified as debt, and outstanding warrants were ignored, a procedure that would tend to overstate the frequency of debtors. Those balance sheets that were closest to the end of 1942 were employed for determining the monetary status of the sampled firms.

This sample was composed of 17 debtors and 12 creditors. Stock price ratios were computed and ranked for the years between the close of 1942 and the close of 1945. These ranks were compared with the ranks reflecting predicted relative price changes. For this time interval, there existed a significant relationship between the two sets of ranks, and this relationship explained 40 percent (correlation coefficient of 0.63) of the observed variation in stock prices.[20] These results, apart from confirming previous tests of the predictive content of the debtor-creditor hypothesis, provide a somewhat firmer basis for arguing that Keynes and Fisher underestimated the frequency of creditors in the business population.

III. INDUSTRIAL SHARE PRICE CHANGES DURING DEFLATION

However, the second world war inflation may be a freak; one must avoid generalizing too broadly from tests based on predictions for one experience. The deflation that occurred during the great depression provides a second experience by which the predictive power of the debtor-creditor hypothesis can be evaluated. From the end of December 1929 to the end of June 1933, the wholesale price index declined by about one-third. Therefore it should be possible if the debtor-creditor hypothesis is valid, to observe a complete reversal of previous results. Creditor stocks should rise and debtor stocks fall in real value. Relative to one another, extreme creditors ought to have the most favorable experience followed by moderate creditors who are succeeded by moderate debtors. Extreme debtors, on the other hand, ought to have the least favorable experience.

In order to evaluate the predictive content of the debtor-creditor hypothesis for the deflation years, a fourth sample was collected by randomly sampling from the population of industrial firms that were listed on the New York Stock Exchange at the end of 1928 and that were still listed at the end of June 1933. This sample contained 12 creditors and 19 debtors.[21] The prices of the creditor shares at the end of June 1933 were 72 percent of their end-of-1928 prices. However this nominal fall conceals the real

---

[20] The Olds rank correlation test; the significance level was less than 0.005.

[21] The causes for rejection were essentially the same as those that applied to Sample II. See footnote 16 on this point. For one firm in this sample, monetary assets equaled monetary liabilities. This led to the creation of a third classification of firms—neutrals. The debtor-creditor hypothesis implies that neutral firms will neither gain nor lose as a consequence of price level changes. Only end-of-1928 balance sheets were employed both to determine the frequency of debtors and creditors and their relative indebtedness.

situation; in real terms the prices of the creditor shares rose by 6 percent. On the other hand, the corresponding real value of the debtor shares declined by 34 percent. Again statistical tests suggest that there exist valid grounds for believing that the observed difference between debtors and creditors is characteristic of the population from which the sample was drawn.[22] To test the relative price change implications of the debtor-creditor hypothesis, the firms in this sample were assigned ranks that reflected their comparative indebtedness. Indebtedness was measured, as for the first three samples, by the ratio of the difference between monetary assets and monetary liabilities to total assets. These ranks provide a basis for predicting comparative price changes for this particular set of business firms. A second ranking, based on the ratio of stock prices at the end of June 1933 to those at the end of 1928, represents the data to be predicted or explained. Therefore the observed correlation of one ranking with the other again confirms the validity of the debtor-creditor hypothesis.[23]

The demonstrated predictive content of the debtor-creditor hypothesis for such strikingly different price level movements as the inflation of the second world war and the deflation accompanying the great depression strongly supports the view that this hypothesis has a role to play as an analytical tool for explaining the wealth-redistributive consequences of price level changes. How extensive this role shall be remains to be determined by further examination of (a) the predictive power of this hypothesis for a wider range of phenomena and circumstances, for example, hyperinflations and smaller firms, and (b) the evaluation of the substantive content of alternative explanations of the same phenomenon such as the wage-lag hypothesis.

These results suggest a rationale for the uniformities reported by empirical investigators of inflation: that banks seem uniformly to lose and that stock prices in general at best just keep pace with the price level. Banks lose because they are creditors. The movements of the stock price indexes examined by these investigators were composed of both debtor and creditor securities. Consolidating the monetary positions of all the firms represented in these indexes, the stock price changes depicted by these indices represent on balance either neutral or creditor shares. Therefore either these share prices just kept pace or fall behind the increases in the price level that occurred. If these investigators had distinguished between debtors and creditors, then they would have found that some stocks more than keep pace with the price level.

Taking all four samples in total (see the accompanying tabulation)

---

[22] Using the Mann and Whitney test, the significance level was 5.4 percent. For the time interval ending with the end of 1932, the significance level was 2.2 percent. For this latter time interval, both creditors and debtors lost. In real terms, the loss of the creditors was 46 percent and the loss of the debtors was 72 percent.

[23] The Olds rank correlation test indicates a significance level of 0.03. Roughly 10 percent of the observed variation was explained. For the time period to the end of 1932, the significance level was 0.005, and 21 percent of the observed variation was explained.

provides a substantial bit of evidence on the frequency of debtors and creditors in the business population. This evidence reveals a sharp inconsistency between the Keynes-Fisher views on the indebtedness of business firms and what is apparently true of the world of observable phenomena. It may be that these data, which are for extremely large industrial and banking concerns, are not typical of small business firms. However, what evidence is available suggests that economists may have been generally laboring under a misapprehension when they assumed business firms are typically debtors.

Frequency of Debtors and Creditors

Sample	Balance sheet date	Debtors	Creditors	Neutrals
I	1942		16	
II	1942	15	15	
III	1942	17	12	
IV	1928	29	12	1

IV. SHORT-RUN FORECASTING

Thus far, the predictive power of the debtor-creditor hypothesis has been evaluated only for relatively long time intervals. This section reports the results of a series of tests of its short-run (as short as one year) predictive content for comparative stock price changes. The procedure followed for these tests is to correlate the ranking of net debtor or creditorship status, which was determined for Samples II and III with 1942 data and Sample IV with 1928 data, with the ranking of the ratios of ending to beginning stock prices for the time interval under consideration.

For Sample IV, the depression sample, statistically significant predictions were made for each of the four years. For Sample III, statistically significant predictions were made for the calendar years 1940, 1942, 1943, 1944, 1946, and for the two-year time intervals, 1943–44 and 1944–45. The hypothesis failed for the years 1941, 1945, and 1950. With Sample II, the relative stock price forecasts were evaluated for the time interval June 1941 to June 1942 and cumulatively for one, two, three, four, five and six years beyond. With the exception of the first time interval, June 1941 to June 1942, all of these forecasts proved to have real predictive value. An attempt was made to forecast for the year 1950, when there was over a 10 percent rise in the wholesale price index, with an entirely new sample. The firms in this fifth sample, composed of all 26 of the integrated oil companies listed on the New York Stock Exchange, were ranked as debtors using end-of-1950 balance sheet data. The forecast produced by these ranks failed to be statistically significant.[24]

---

[24] This sample was composed of 19 debtors and 7 creditors. It was restricted to integrated oil companies in an attempt to hold relative price effects constant. For forecasts with Sample II that were successful, significance levels were less than 5 percent. Similarly for Samples III and IV, significance levels were less than 0.06.

These results demonstrate that the debtor-creditor hypothesis also has predictive value for the short run. Clearly the observed short-run predictive failures, which seem to be concentrated about the years 1941, 1946, and 1950, argue that this hypothesis is a better long- than short-run predictor. However it may be possible that these failures are associated with causes that operate only when this country is either beginning or ending a war. If this is the case, and presumably this issue could be resolved by further investigation, then there may be some reason for believing that the debtor-creditor hypothesis is more useful for short-run predictions than one might suppose.

V. THE WAGE-LAG HYPOTHESIS

The data reported in this paper, collected primarily to test the debtor-creditor hypothesis, have some relevance for an implication of the wage-lag hypothesis. The latter hypothesis rests on the proposition that inflation causes real wage rates to decline and this loss of the laboring class is the gain of capitalists. It implies that business firms ought generally to gain as a consequence of inflation and that labor-intensive firms ought to gain more than capital-intensive firms. Converse implications ought to hold for deflation. But the implication for which pertinent evidence has been collected, that business firms should gain because of inflation and lose as a consequence of deflation, is denied. The evidence against it is: (1) banks seem invariably to lose during inflation, and (2) creditors have gained during deflation and lost during inflation. Because the debtor-creditor and wage-lag hypotheses have conflicting implications for changes in the real value of creditor shares during both inflation and deflation, evidence of such changes must inevitably deny one and confirm the other hypothesis. For both inflation and deflation, this evidence has denied the wage-lag hypothesis.

The data collected that bears on the validity of the wage-lag hypothesis is obviously fragmentary and incomplete. It is only relevant for the absolute value change implication and is of almost no value for testing the implication that labor-intensive are more profitable than capital-intensive firms during inflation.[25] Moreover, the consequences of this modicum of evidence for general acceptance of the wage-lag hypothesis must be evaluated in the context of all pertinent evidence.

The evidence that has been considered pertinent consists of time series of wages and prices during inflation.[26] These data show that real wages

---

[25] One might not want to say unequivocally that it is of no value because evidence that denies one implication of a hypothesis also lowers the probability of an untested implication being verified subsequently.

[26] Hamilton makes the strongest claims for this evidence. He argues: "This lag has benefited capitalists as a class at the expense of laborers as a class and awarded gains that dwarf into insignificance the profits from inventory appreciation and from declines in the real value of debts." Hamilton, "Prices as a Factor in Business Growth," *loc. cit.*, p. 327.

declined during some inflations. However, for the purposes of supporting the conclusion that inflation has redistributive effects from laborers to capitalists, such evidence has some serious short-comings that appear to be disqualifying. To argue that a decline in real wage rates implies a redistribution of income and or wealth from laborers to capitalists, one must show that both (a) the stock of capital did not decrease, and (b) the supply of labor did not increase. Since either of these phenomena can cause a decline in real wage rates in the absence of inflation, and the time series that have been cited in support of the wage-lag hypothesis represent periods for which there exist good *a priori* reasons for suspecting that either the stock of capital declined or the supply of labor increased, it is difficult to accept the conclusion that such evidence implies necessarily a gain for the capitalist class.

VI. CONCLUSIONS

It is apparent that the debtor-creditor hypothesis has an important role to play as an analytical tool for explaining inflation-caused wealth redistribution.[27] Its success as a predictive instrument, despite the employment of crude measures of debtor and creditor status and rudimentary statistical techniques, suggests that possibly only the surface has been scratched of what may in fact be a very rich vein.[28] Both the relative price change and the absolute value change implications of the debtor-creditor hypothesis have been confirmed by what are in substance controlled experiments.[29] These results suggest that individual monetary policy, i.e., individual policy as to holdings of monetary assets and monetary liabilities, is relatively stable during moderate inflations. This inference is confirmed by direct examination of the rankings of firms in terms of this particular property before and after inflation.[30]

---

[27] The concept of neutrality, which stems from the debtor-creditor hypothesis, ought to be of considerable value for formulating individual investment programs that provide an effective hedge against inflation. Similarly the debtor-creditor hypothesis itself should be of value to investors with particular beliefs about the future course of prices who wish to capitalize on this knowledge.

[28] Alchian has pointed out that an alternative criterion of intensity of debtor or creditor status is the difference between monetary assets and monetary liabilities taken as a ratio to total equity. Total equity is to be measured by market values. This criterion may yield better predictions because it eliminates the use of accounting valuations of real assets. This alternative and others are being explored in a larger-scale investigation, sponsored by the Merrill Foundation, of both the debtor-creditor and wage-lag hypotheses. It is expected that these results will be published.

[29] One could argue against the contention that these results confirm the real value change implications. For the two episodes studied, apparently, looking at the evidence when the episode is over and the turning point has been past and looking at portions of these episodes yield different answers. However it is surely more relevant to examine the complete episode than it is to examine portions of it for answering the question, does this theory yield correct predictions of how debtors and creditors fare as a result of inflation and deflation?

[30] For the first sample, debtor-creditor ranks at the beginning and the end of the 1942 to 1948 time interval were positively correlated. The rank correlation coefficient is 0.55 and the significance level is less than 0.005.

16

A TEST OF COST OF CAPITAL PROPOSITIONS

J. FRED WESTON*

This paper summarizes the first two propositions developed by Professors Modigliani and Miller on the use of leverage by business firms. The propositions of Modigliani and Miller are shown to be a restatement of the net operating income approach (NOI approach) to the value of the firm. The alternative approach is represented as the net income approach (NI approach).

The empirical tests of Modigliani and Miller are then exactly repeated, and the same approximate results are obtained. But when growth is introduced as an additional variable, the net regression relationships become consistent with the NI approach rather than the NOI approach of Modigliani and Miller.

Modigliani and Miller have thrown traditional concepts of cost of capital into turmoil.[1] In view of the broad implications of their propositions, this study has sought to test their propositions and underlying assumptions by further empirical analysis. While this study represents only one additional set of measurements, the findings are reported because the results differ significantly from those of Modigliani and Miller. A comparison of the empirical results illuminates the theory. In addition, measurement problems important for other empirical studies are brought to the fore.

MODIGLIANI AND MILLER PROPOSITIONS AND TRADITIONAL THEORY

The Modigliani and Miller propositions, as well as their summary of the traditional propositions, may be set forth briefly. The Modigliani-Miller

J. Fred Weston, "A Test of Cost of Capital Propositions," *The Southern Economic Journal* (Oct. 1963), Vol. XXX, 105–112. Reprinted by permission.

* I am grateful to the Bureau of Business and Economic Research, UCLA for research assistance. Louis Blumberg, Phoebe Cottingham and Roger Weiland helped gather the data upon which the analysis is based. Professor Raymond Jessen helped on a number of aspects of the statistical work. Mr. William Anderson of the Western Data Processing Center, UCLA, assisted in the use of the BIMED 06 Program for running the regressions. I also benefited from discussions with my colleagues in the Finance Area at the Graduate School of Business, UCLA.

[1] Franco Modigliani and Merton H. Miller, "The Cost of Capital, Corporation Finance, and the Theory of Investments," *The American Economic Review*, June 1958, pp. 261–96. Also see their "Reply," *The American Economic Review*, September 1959, pp. 655–69.

theory is identical with Durand's NOI approach.[2] Durand compared two theories of the valuation of the earnings of a corporation, describing one as the capitalization of net operating earnings (NOI approach) and the other as capitalization of net income (NI approach).

In the NOI approach the value of a corporation is determined by capitalizing the corporations' net operating income. The value of the company's stocks and bonds must conform to this total. In the NI approach, the cost of debt is deducted from net operating income to give net income. The appropriate capitalization rate is applied to net income available to common stock to determine the value of the company's common stock. The market value of the common stock is then added to the market value of the company's bonds to determine the total value of the company.

Durand's Net Operating Income approach and Modigliani and Miller's Proposition I are logically equivalent. Both state that the net operating income of a business firm, divided by the appropriate capitalization rate, gives the value of the enterprise to which the value of the bonds and stocks of the firm must conform. Thus, Proposition I of Modigliani and Miller can be expressed as follows: the value of a business corporation is equal to its net operating income divided by the capitalization rate appropriate for application to the leverage-free earnings of a firm in a specified risk class.[3] This NOI approach can be expressed in the symbols of Modigliani and Miller:[4]

$$V_j = (S_j + D_j) = \bar{X}_j/\rho_\kappa \equiv (\text{NOI})_j/\rho_\kappa \qquad \text{Proposition I}$$

V_j = the market value of all the firm's securities or the market value of the firm
S_j = the market value of the firm's common shares
D_j = the market value of the debts of the company
$\bar{X}_j$ = the expected return on the assets owned by the company, which equals its net operating income—NOI
ρ_κ = the capitalization rate appropriate to the risk class of the firm[5]

Proposition II is another way of stating Proposition I. Modigliani and Miller's elaborate rationalization of Proposition II is unnecessary. If Proposition I is accepted, Proposition II follows directly.

$$i_j = \frac{\bar{X}_j - rD_j}{S_j} \tag{1}$$

Definitional identity: This is equation (9) in Modigliani and Miller, *op. cit.*

---

[2] David Durand, "Costs of Debt and Equity Funds for Business: Trends and Problems of Measurement," *Conference on Research in Business Finance* (New York: National Bureau of Economic Research, Inc., 1952), p. 227.
[3] Modigliani and Miller, *op. cit.*, p. 268.
[4] *Ibid.*
[5] The analysis at this point will not take taxes into account in order to simplify the exposition. In the empirical analysis presented later, the formulations employed will be on an after-corporate-income-tax basis.

Where: i = expected yield on common stock

r = expected cost of debt

$$\bar{X}_j = \rho_\kappa V_j = \rho_\kappa (D_j + S_j) \qquad \text{Proposition I} \qquad (2)$$

$$i_j = \frac{\rho_\kappa S_j + \rho_\kappa D_j - rD_j}{S_j} \qquad (3)$$

Substituting from (2) into (1)

$$i_j = \rho_\kappa + (\rho_\kappa - r)\frac{D_j}{S_j} \qquad \text{Proposition II} \qquad (4)$$

The two propositions of Modigliani and Miller are of great significance. Proposition I states that, regardless of the degree of leverage employed by a company, its cost of capital will be the same. The cost of capital function of a firm will be unaffected by leverage.

The second proposition shows the implications of the NOI approach. Proposition II states that the earnings-price ratio on the common stock of a company in a given risk class is a linear function of leverage, the slope being the difference between the company's cost of capital and the cost of debt. It is a precise formulation for determining the earnings-price ratio of a company's stock as a function of its overall cost of capital, its cost of debt, and the degree of leverage employed.

It will be useful at this point to compare the Net Operating Income or the Modigliani and Miller theory with what Modigliani and Miller describe as the traditional approach. Modigliani and Miller point out that, in contrast to their Proposition II, "the conventional view among finance specialists is to start from the proposition that other things equal, the earnings-price ratio (or its reciprocal the times-earnings multiplier) of a firm's common stock will normally be only slightly affected by 'moderate' amounts of debt in the firm's capital structure."[6] They point out that the crucial element in the theory—that the expected earnings-price ratio of the stock is largely unaffected by leverage up to some conventional limit—"is rarely even regarded as something which requires explanation."[7]

While the traditional approach clearly disagrees with the NOI approach, it is not the NI approach in pure form. It is a modified NI theory in the following sense. It suggests that if a large corporation employs moderate amounts of leverage, the interest on debt and the capitalization factor applied to the earnings available for common stock do not rise to the same degree that risk premiums accompanying the leverage employed by individuals would increase. Thus increasing the proportion of debt employed to finance a firm would increase the expected market value of the firm up to some

---

[6] *Ibid.*, p. 276. They also cite illustrations of this position in the literature.

[7] *Ibid.*, p. 278.

critical proportion of leverage.   Beyond that point, capitalization factors rise sufficiently to offset the added earnings available to common stock, resulting in a decline in the market value of the firm.   Hence the firm's overall cost of capital would fall, then rise.

Space does not permit an exegesis of the "traditional business finance theory" by a historical survey of the literature.   The support for the traditional view rests upon the nature of the corporation and investor behavior. The corporate institution is a device which shifts a portion of financial risk from owners to creditors.   Since the risk to owners is limited to the amount which they have committed to the corporate enterprise, the owners reduce their probable loss.   While their losses are limited to the amount actually invested in the enterprise, their gains are not so restricted.   Personal leverage does not have the same limited-risk characteristic.

A related support for the assumptions of the traditional theorems is based on investment standards.   Moderate increases in leverage are not regarded as increasing risk so long as the minimum standards for debt ratios or earnings coverage of fixed charges are met.[8]

The corporate institution and investment standards make corporate leverage advantageous over personal leverage.   Since personal leverage is not a perfect substitute for corporate leverage, the arbitrage operations described by Modigliani and Miller are not possible.   The present discussion does not question their underlying assumptions;   it merely indicates the rationale of competing assumptions.   The realism of assumptions cannot be tested directly.   In a policy area such as business finance, the ultimate test of the underlying assumptions is the ability of the derived propositions to predict.   We can evaluate the rival assumptions about the behavior of investors by further empirical studies described in the following section.

EMPIRICAL TESTS OF THE INFLUENCE OF LEVERAGE ON THE COST OF CAPITAL

The essentials of two alternative models for the cost of capital have been set forth.   The choice between the two models must ultimately depend upon their conformity with the real world.   The predictive implications of the alternative theories will be tested as a basis for selecting between the two models.

As in economic theory generally, to test a model directly often involves serious inadequacies.   A very critical part of the Modigliani and Miller formulation is the concept of a risk class.   Their identification of a risk class with an industry suffers from all the problems of the non-homogeneity of

---

[8] Benjamin Graham, David L. Dodd, and Sidney Cottle, *Security Analysis* (New York: McGraw-Hill Book Co., 1962), pp. 248–9; Harry Sauvain, *Investment Management* (Englewood Cliffs, N.J.: Prentice-Hall, 1959), pp. 220–1; Douglas A. Hayes, *Investments: Analysis and Management* (New York: Macmillan Company, 1961), pp. 175–88.

"an industry." The defects are aggravated in the risk class concept because the dependent variables which they seek to explain are particularly sensitive to differences in characteristics between firms conventionally grouped in a given "industry" by government or financial agencies.

The differences between firms in the oil industry, in particular, are great. For example, in a group of 42 oil companies used by Modigliani and Miller would be found the following diversity: full-integrated oil companies, oil companies strong in refining, oil companies strong in distribution; some regional in their operations, some with heavy investments in troubled international regions; some with stable, assured or rising income from petro-chemicals or uranium or other minerals. Furthermore, lease obligations, which are common in the oil industry, are not reflected in Modigliani and Miller's data on debt. It is obviously not plausible to regard a group of companies with such wide ranging diversity in significant characteristics as a homogeneous risk class.

As a consequence, in my study the empirical tests are confined to the electrical utility industry. The utility industry is not free of the problem, but utilities are probably less heterogeneous than oils. The initial results are set forth in Table 16–1. (The symbols of Modigliani and Miller are generally followed.) The Modigliani-Miller findings for 1947–48 are compared with mine for 1959. Our findings for the earnings-price ratio are almost identical in form. The intercept is somewhat lower, and the slope is somewhat smaller, which is consistent with the change in equity markets

Table 16–1. Cost of capital calculations, electric utilities, 1959.

Year	M & M 1947–1948	Weston 1959
A. Earnings to price ratio	$z = 6.6 + 0.017h$ (± 0.004) $r = 0.53$	$z = 4.91 + 0.014h$ (± 0.004) $r = 0.43$
B. Cost of capital (investor view-point)	$x = 5.3 + 0.006d$ (± 0.008) $r = 0.12$ $n = 43$	$x = 4.27 + 0.027d$ (± 0.007) $r = 0.46$ $n = 55$
C. Cost of capital (financial manager view-point)		$x = 5.07 - 0.010d$ (± 0.007) $r = -0.193$
D. Cost of capital (risk measure of leverage)		$x = 5.25 - 0.017d^*$ (± 0.008) $r = -0.283$

Where:
  z = Yield on common stock.
  h = Market value of senior securities divided by market value of common stocks.
  x = Cost of capital equals total earnings after taxes divided by market value of all securities.
  d = Market value of senior securities divided by market value of all securities.
  d^* = Market value of debt divided by market value of all securities.

between the two periods of time. The correlation coefficient is somewhat smaller, but almost of equal significance in view of the fact that my sample size is approximately 30 percent larger.

The significant contrast occurs, however, when the cost of capital function is calculated. Three measures of the cost of capital are set forth. Equation B takes the investor viewpoint (as did Modigliani and Miller) in which the cost of debt is taken at its full value into the weighted cost of capital calculations. The second method, under part C of the Table, takes the financial manager's viewpoint in which the cost of debt is on an after-tax basis.[9] A third concept of cost of capital takes the financial manager's viewpoint, but removes preferred stock from the numerator of the leverage measure. Only fixed charges on debt carry risks of insolvency. Dividends on preferred stock do not constitute a fixed charge in this sense. It is logical therefore to measure leverage from the risk standpoint as the ratio of debt to the total market value of the company.[10]

When the investor viewpoint is taken, the cost of capital function has a positive slope. The regression coefficient is significant as well as is the correlation coefficient. This result differs fundamentally from Modigliani and Miller's findings. When the financial manager's viewpoint is taken, the cost of capital function has a negative slope, but is no longer significant. When the risk-measure of leverage is used, the negative slope of the cost of capital function becomes significant at the five percent level.

What is the explanation for the difference between my results and those of Modigliani and Miller for equation B of Table 16-1 and why does the slope of the regression equation become negative in equation C? The answer to the second part of the question provides the key to the answer to the first part. The explanation will be aided by an examination of the quantitative relations. For my study the cost of debt and the cost of equity functions are approximately:

$$r = 5 + 0.01d \tag{1}$$

$$z = 4 + 0.06d \tag{2}$$

The Modigliani-Miller procedures suggest that the weighted cost of capital is:

$$x = krd + i(1 - d) \tag{3}$$

The symbols all have the same meaning as in Table 16-1. The new symbol, k, is 1 for the investor (Modigliani and Miller) viewpoint and 0.5

---

[9] The rationale for the distinction and the circumstances under which the investor viewpoint versus the financial manager viewpoint would be taken are set forth cogently in John F. Childs, *Long-Term Financing* (Englewood Cliffs, N.J.: Prentice-Hall, 1961), Ch. X, "Profit Goals—Cost of Capital," especially pages 340–344.

[10] Of course, preferred stock (typically nonparticipating) enables a firm to trade on the equity. For an analysis of the effectiveness of trading on the equity, preferred stock would be included in senior obligations. In the present situation where we are investigating risk aspects of leverage, it is more appropriate to exclude preferred stock from senior obligations.

for the financial manager viewpoint. For the r and i functions given above, the cost of capital function may be determined.

For $\qquad k = 1, \qquad x = -0.05d^2 + 1.06d + 4 \qquad\qquad$ (4)

For $\qquad k = 0.5, \qquad x' = -0.055d^2 - 1.44d + 4 \qquad\qquad$ (5)

The value of d (a measure of leverage) in equations (4) and (5) ranges from 0.1 to under 1.0. In this range, x is positive throughout corresponding to equation B for the 1959 data in Table 16–1. Conversely, it is clear that x' would be negative throughout the range of d, consistent with equation C of Table 16–1. This analysis provides a formal explanation for the switchover from a positive slope in my results for the cost of capital function measured from an investor viewpoint and a negative slope for the cost of capital measured from the financial manager's viewpoint. This is also the key to explanation of the difference between my results and those of Modigliani and Miller in section B of Table 16–1. The full explanation is most readily seen after the influence of growth is analyzed in the following section.

INFLUENCE OF GROWTH ON THE COST OF CAPITAL

To this point my analysis has attempted to follow as closely as possible the original paper of Modigliani and Miller, including their empirical tests. Since the size of firms and the growth rate of their earnings are additional possible influences on the cost of capital, my study was broadened to include these additional variables. The investor viewpoint was used in these studies to permit direct comparison with the Modigliani and Miller data.

Table 16–2 shows that the growth in earnings per share has a significant influence on the *cost of equity financing*. However, the partial regression coefficient for the influence of leverage on equity yields is no longer significant. The influence of growth on the *total cost of capital* is also highly significant. But the sign of the leverage term is now negative, consistent with the declining segment of the cost of capital function predicted by traditional theory. Thus, when the influences on the cost of capital are partitioned through multiple regression analysis, the results are consistent with traditional theory. In view of the strong influence of growth on the cost of capital function, the relation between the cost of capital and leverage will depend on how growth is correlated with leverage. The regression equations in sections C and D of Table 16–2 show that leverage is a negative function of growth.

Thus the apparent positive correlation between leverage and equity yields observed by Modigliani and Miller actually represents the negative correlation between current equity yields and growth. The partial regression relationships show that when the influence of growth is removed, leverage is not significantly correlated with current earnings-price ratios for the range of leverage employed.

Table 16–2. Multiple regression analysis of cost of capital, electric utilities, 1959.

A. $z = 6.75 \quad - \quad 0.0029h^* \quad + \quad 0.0A \quad - \quad 0.1352E$
$\qquad\qquad\quad (\pm 0.0159) \quad + (\pm 0.0002) \quad (\pm 0.0454)$
$\qquad\qquad\qquad \beta = 0.0253 \qquad\qquad\qquad \beta = 0.4110$

$\quad R = 0.4032$

B. $x = 5.91 \quad - \quad 0.0265d^* \quad + \quad 0.0A \quad - \quad 0.0822E$
$\qquad\qquad\quad (\pm 0.0079) \quad (\pm 0.0001) \quad (\pm 0.0024)$
$\qquad\qquad\qquad \beta = 0.4333 \qquad\qquad\qquad \beta = 0.4702$

$\quad R = 0.5268$

C. $d = 51.66 \quad - \quad 1.78E \qquad\qquad r = -0.58$
$\qquad\qquad\qquad (\pm 0.34)$

D. $d^* = 39.59 \quad - \quad 1.16E \qquad\qquad r = -0.48$
$\qquad\qquad\qquad (\pm 0.29)$

Where:
$z =$ Yield on common stock.
$x =$ Cost of capital equals total earnings after taxes divided by market value of all securities.
$d =$ Market value of senior securities divided by the market value of all securities.
$h^* = d^* =$ Market value of debt divided by the market value of all securities.
$A =$ Total assets at book value.
$E =$ Compound growth rate in earnings per share per annum, 1949–1959.
$\beta =$ Beta coefficient which normalizes the regression coefficient to measure its relative influence in the dependent variable.
$R =$ Multiple correlation coefficient.

The partial regression analysis of the weighted cost of capital yields similar results. When the influence of growth is isolated, leverage is found to be negatively correlated with the cost of capital. Traditional theory suggests that firms have an aversion to debt and are likely to be operating in the range of a declining cost of capital.[11] The apparent lack of influence of leverage on the *overall cost of capital* observed by Modigliani and Miller is due to the negative correlation of leverage with earnings growth. When the net effects are measured, the cost of capital is found to be significantly negatively correlated with both leverage and growth. The reason why Modigliani and Miller found no correlation between the cost of capital and leverage is that leverage is correlated with other influences which change the gross relationship between cost of capital and leverage.[12]

The data showing the influence of growth on equity yields and the cost of capital function help explain the positive slope obtained for the cost of

---

[11] N. H. Jacoby and J. F. Weston, "Financial Policies for Regularizing Business Investment," *Regularization of Business Investment* (Princeton, N.J.: Princeton University Press, 1954), pp. 386–387.

[12] The beta coefficient for earnings growth in the regression for the yield on equity funds is much larger than the beta coefficient for leverage. In the regression for cost of capital, the two beta coefficients are approximately equal.

capital function for 1959 in Table 16–1. The empirical data utilized by Modigliani and Miller were for the late 1940's when equity prices were depressed and earnings-price ratios were high. Interest yields were low and inflexible, reflecting the support of the Government bond market by the Federal Reserve System. In contrast, my study for the year 1959 was a period of buoyant equity prices, large premiums for prospective growth, and low current earnings to current price ratios. The current cost of equity money relative to the cost of debt money was low. As shown in equations (1) and (2) of the preceding section, the intercept of the cost of debt function was higher than the intercept for the cost of equity function. In the Modigliani-Miller data, however, r is estimated at 3.5 and the intercept of the cost of equity function (shown in section A of Table 16–1) is 6.6.

The strands may now be brought together. My data show that leverage is negatively correlated with growth. Growth also lowers the (current) cost of equity money. Hence we both found that the cost of equity money was a positive function of leverage. In Modigliani and Miller's data, we observe a rising cost of equity function and a constant and lower cost of debt function. As leverage is increased, the cost of capital is pushed up by the rising cost of equity function, but is pulled down because the lower cost of debt is weighted more heavily. Modigliani and Miller's data for the late 1940's indicate that the pull of the opposing forces was about balanced so that the cost of capital function appeared not to have a significant slope.

In my data for 1959, the current cost of equity money is relatively low because current prices reflected the future growth of earnings. The cost of debt was somewhat higher. Hence in equation B of Table 16–1 where the cost of debt is taken into the measurements at its full level, the cost of capital function would rise with leverage. The rising cost of equity is offset only slightly because the cost of debt is relatively high. When the cost of debt is reduced by one-half, the greater weighting of debt cost as leverage increases, pulls down the cost of capital as shown in equation C of Table 16–1.[13]

MEASUREMENT OF THE COST OF EQUITY FUNDS WITH GROWTH

In the studies utilized by Modigliani and Miller, the ratio of current earnings to the current market price of common stock is used as a measure of the cost of equity financing. This is invalid. As their own subsequent writing has demonstrated, the cost of equity financing must add to current

---

[13] It has been observed that strong firms employ low debt ratios, but by customary financial standards could employ much higher debt ratios. Professor John P. Shelton has suggested a rationale for this. If strong firms have low equity costs, the relative gain from employing debt is small or negative. Hence it is not irrational for such firms to employ low debt ratios. This observation, as well as the discussion above, depends on a relatively low cost of equity function. But this in turn implies use of the current earnings-price ratio, rather than relating expected future earnings to the current price, to measure the cost of equity money.

yields a corrective for a growth factor in order to obtain a relevant measure of the cost of equity financing.[14] For example, in my study the average dividend yield on common stock for the year 1959 was 3.96 percent. The average compound rate of growth in either dividends or earnings per share over the eleven-year period, 1949–1959, was approximately 6 percent. The estimate of the electrical utility industry cost of equity money for 1959 is 9.96 percent, employing the Modigliani and Miller formula.[15] The current earnings-price ratio understates the cost of capital of a company with growing earnings.[16]

Thus the use of current earnings to current price would not be accurate for a measure of the cost of capital function. However, in the Modigliani-Miller studies and the present study which replicates their procedures, we are concerned not with the absolute level of the cost of capital, but how it varies with leverage and other factors. Hence the slopes of the functions and their relative levels may be little affected by using the ratio of current earnings to current price, although the absolute levels of the functions will be affected.

INDIRECT TESTS OF THE INFLUENCE OF LEVERAGE ON THE COST OF CAPITAL

In view of the measurement disputes, some broad proxy tests may be applied. We can formulate the following hypothesis. In an industry in which earnings instability is relatively small, decision-makers in different firms would be expected to view prospective risks in a similar fashion. As a consequence, traditional theory would predict a clustering of leverage ratios in a relatively narrow range for an industry or risk class in which the instability of earnings was characteristically small.

On the other hand, if we observe a wide range of variations in earnings among firms in the same industry group, we would expect decision-makers to view risks differently in view of the greater instability of earnings in the industry. The spread of leverage ratios employed would be expected to be much larger. But the Miller and Modigliani theory would predict that leverage ratios would vary randomly in both types of industries since leverage does not affect a firm's cost of capital.

---

[14] Merton H. Miller and Franco Modigliani, "Dividend Policy, Growth, and the Valuation of Shares," *Journal of Business*, October 1961, pp. 411–432.

[15] *Ibid.*, pp. 421–422.

[16] Some recent studies provide additional discussion of these problems. See Haskel Benishay, "Variability in Earnings-Price Ratios of Corporate Equities," *The American Economic Review*, March 1961, pp. 81–94; and "Reply," *The American Economic Review*, March 1962, pp. 209–216; Myron J. Gordon, *The Investment, Financing, and Valuation of the Corporation* (Homewood, Ill.: Richard D. Irwin, 1962); Myron J. Gordon, "Variability in Earnings-Price Ratios: Comment" *The American Economic Review*, March 1962, pp. 203–208; John Lintner, "Dividends, Earnings, Leverage, Stock Prices and the Supply of Capital to Corporations," *Review of Economics and Statistics*, August 1962, pp. 243–269.

A test of the influence of leverage on cost of capital is provided by the two studies used by Modigliani and Miller as well as my own. In the electrical utilities industry, which is an approximation to the first type of industry described (in which the instability of earnings is small), there is a clustering of leverage ratios within a very narrow range. The oil industry illustrates the second class of industry. It is an industry characterized by great variation among firms in earnings stability and great instability of earnings for individual firms. A wide range of leverage is employed by firms in this industry as predicted by traditional business finance theory.

Thus, the multiple regression analysis of the influence of leverage and growth on the cost of capital, as well as the broad proxy tests provided by observed differences in leverage policies followed, strongly indicate that leverage does have an influence on a firm's cost of capital. There is, thus, strong theoretical and empirical evidence that the traditional theory of business finance remains a better predictor of the real world than the Modigliani and Miller propositions.

CONCLUSIONS

This paper has shown that the Modigliani and Miller propositions are Durand's NOI approach to valuation presented in a new garb. Proposition I states that the value of a firm is obtained by capitalizing its net operating income; the sum of bond and stock values must conform to this figure. This theorem is based upon the assumption that personal leverage and corporate leverage are completely substitutable. Proposition II is an identity which is a definition of the earnings-price ratio. When Proposition I (the value of debt plus stock must total the value of the firm) is substituted in the identity, the earnings-price ratio can be expressed as a linear equation. The intercept of the equation is the firm's cost of capital; its slope is the difference between the firm's cost of capital and the cost of debt, with leverage as the independent variable.

The considerable disagreement on the NOI approach continues to surround its new appearance in the form of the Modigliani and Miller propositions. While Modigliani and Miller found two empirical studies apparently consistent with their propositions, their proof is deficient in important respects. A serious weakness of their empirical studies is the failure to investigate the nature of the relationship between leverage and other factors influencing a firm's cost of capital. The present study shows that leverage is a negative linear function of earnings growth. Thus the lack of correlation between the cost of capital and leverage is due to the counterbalancing influence of earnings growth on leverage. The partial correlation measures show that both leverage and earnings growth were significantly correlated with the cost of capital.

The apparent overwhelming empirical support of the generality of the Modigliani and Miller propositions rests upon measuring the gross influences of leverage and growth and attributing all the influence to leverage. When the influence of growth is isolated, the net influence of leverage on the cost of capital is found to be consistent with traditional business finance theory, rather than with the Modigliani and Miller propositions.

17

A NOTE ON THE EQUIVALENT RISK CLASS ASSUMPTION

RONALD F. WIPPERN

Modigliani and Miller developed their propositions about the cost of capital as applicable to groups of firms in "an equivalent risk-class." For empirical testing of their propositions, homogeneous groups of companies in a given risk-class must be identified. Professor Wippern tests the customary industry classifications to see if they can be used to represent risk-classes and his findings suggest that they cannot be so used. In addition, his results have broad implications for determining groups for the identification and application of financial ratio analysis which involves comparisons with industry composite ratios.

The assumption that firms within the same industry are subject to equivalent degrees of basic business uncertainty is widely employed in financial theory and underlies many of the approaches to valuation in the security analysis literature. The principal area in which this assumption is used, and is of major importance, is the study of the effects of capital structure on the cost of capital.

The study of Alexander Barges,[1] reviewed in *The Engineering Economist* by Richard Bower,[2] as well as the papers by Modigliani and Miller[3] and Weston,[4] included empirical tests of the relationships between capital costs and financial structure. In each of these studies, an attempt was made to hold basic business risk constant among sample firms by restricting samples to single industries. In Weston's study, the validity of this assumption was questioned but not resolved.[5]

The validity of the equivalent risk-class assumption is of critical importance in capital structure studies. The objective of these studies is to determine

Ronald F. Wippern, "A Note on the Equivalent Risk Class Assumption," *The Engineering Economist*, Vol. XI (Spring 1966), 13–22. Reprinted by permission.
[1] Alexander Barges, *The Effect of Capital Structure on the Cost of Capital* (Englewood Cliffs, N.J.: Prentice-Hall, Inc., 1963).
[2] Richard S. Bower, "Leverage and the Cost of Capital," *The Engineering Economist*, Volume 10, No. 2 (Winter, 1965), 15–36.
[3] Franco Modigliani and Merton Miller, "The Cost of Capital, Corporation Finance and the Theory of Investment," *The Management of Corporate Capital*, ed. Ezra Solomon (New York: The Free Press of Glencoe, 1959).
[4] J. Fred Weston, "A Test of Cost of Capital Propositions," *The Southern Economic Journal*, Volume XXX, No. 2 (1963), 105–12.
[5] *Ibid.*, p. 107.

the degree to which investors respond to the risks introduced by the firm's use of fixed commitment financing. If the sample firms are not homogeneous with respect to risks arising from other than financing decisions, the measurement of capital structure effects may contain important biases.

The purposes of this paper are to examine the validity of the risk-equivalency assumption and to subject this important, but previously untested, assumption to statistical analysis.

Decisions by firms and investors are typically made under conditions of uncertainty wherein the outcomes are imperfectly known, each event is unique, and the frequency distribution of outcomes cannot be objectively specified. This is in contrast to risk situations where the outcomes are, again, imperfectly known, but where each event is subject to replication and the frequency distribution of outcomes can be objectively specified.[6]

The situation of no *objective* information about the probability density functions of earnings flows is not, however, necessarily equivalent to the condition of the *complete absence* of information about these functions. It may be hypothesized that there is a high degree of similarity among decision-makers regarding the measures of standards on which judgements as to uncertainty are based. Knowledge of the behavior of past returns constitutes what is perhaps the most important basis for drawing inferences about future returns.

A measure of the cyclical variability of past earnings is the most widely-used basis from which inferences are drawn regarding the uncertainty of the receipt of future earnings.[7] The degree of variability in the earnings stream before financing charges and taxes is consistently cited as the principal determinant of the amount of fixed-charge financing that may safely be undertaken by the firm. Further, the principal undesirable effect of financial leverage referred to in the literature is that it increases the variability of the income stream to the stockholder. This study employs, therefore, as a proxy measure of uncertainty, a measure of the variability of the firm's earnings over time.

The overall uncertainty of a firm's earnings is considered to be composed of two elements: basic business or industry uncertainty, and financial uncertainty. Basic business uncertainty includes all those factors other than financing transactions which contribute to uncertainty of the receipt of the firm's income stream. Included in this category are the firm's competitive position, the determinants of demand for its products, and the structure of its costs. Financial uncertainty arises from the inclusion of fixed-commitment financing in the firm's capital structure.

The focus of this paper is on deriving objective measures of basic business

---

[6] Frank H. Knight, *Risk, Uncertainty and Profit* (Boston: Houghton Mifflin Co., 1921).

[7] See, for example: Jack Hirshleifer, "Risk, the Discount Rate, and Investment Decisions," *American Economic Review*, Papers and Proceedings (1961), p. 112. Harry Markowitz, *Portfolio Selection: Efficient Diversification of Investments* (New York: John Wiley and Sons, Inc., 1959).

uncertainty. The appropriate measure to consider, therefore, is the variability of the stream of net operating earnings, or earnings before fixed charges and taxes per share.

THE EMPIRICAL ANALYSIS

Given an appropriate proxy measure of basic business uncertainty, it is possible to test statistically the validity of the equivalent risk class assumption. The issue is: Do objectively determinable risk classes exist? And do these classes correspond to industry groups?

The Sample

In order to test the validity of the risk equivalency assumption, a sample of eight industries was selected to achieve a high degree of heterogeneity among industry characteristics such as growth trends, cost and demand patterns, expected influence of economic cycles, and the presence or absence of regulation.

The industries selected for inclusion in the study are:

Bread, Cake and Biscuit Bakers
Cement
Electric Utilities
Ethical Drugs
Industrial Machinery
Integrated Domestic Oils
Paper
Rubber

Sixty-one firms within the eight industries are included in the sample, and are listed in Appendix A.

Variability Measure

The variability of the operating earnings per share for each firm is measured by the antilog of the standard error around the logarithmic regression of annual earnings observations over the ten-year period 1954–63. The antilog of the standard error of a logarithmic regression measures percentage variations around the line. The measure of dispersion is taken around the regression of income on time to avoid the influence of earnings growth or decline on variability.

THE STATISTICAL RESULTS

The validity of the assumption that industry groups constitute equivalent risk classes was tested by an analysis of variance. Sample firms were grouped by industry and the analysis of variance was employed to determine whether the net operating income per share variability measures differ significantly among industry groups. The results of this test are shown in Table 17–1. The conventional analysis of variance lends support to the equivalent risk class assumption. The test rejects, at the one-percent level, the null hypothesis of the equality of the variability measures among industry groups. It appears from this test, that there are significant differences among industries.

This test, however, indicates nothing about the *nature* of the observed differences. The conventional analysis of variance gives no indication of whether the measure for each industry differs significantly from each other, or whether the rejection of the hypothesis is attributable to only one of two of

Table 17–1. Analysis of variance of industry mean net operating income per share variability.

	Sum of squares	Degrees of freedom	Mean square	F ratio
Means	0.3542	7	0.0506	5.5604
Within	0.4831	53	0.0091	$F_{0.99} = 3.00$
Total	0.8373	60		

the classifications. In seeking to obtain more conclusive evidence it is desirable to determine whether the proxy uncertainty measure of each industry differs significantly from that of each other industry so that the existence of distinct risk classes may be demonstrated or refuted.

In order to pursue further the investigation of the risk-class hypothesis, Scheffe's method for multiple comparisons[8] was employed to test for significant differences between each pair of sample values. In addition to yielding far more information about the relationships under consideration than the conventional analysis of variance, this test has the further advantage of being substantially unaffected if the normality and equal variance assumptions are not satisfied.[9]

With eight industries, there are twenty-eight differences to be tested. The difference matrix is shown in Table 17–2.

The differences in variability which are marked with an asterisk, a dagger, and a double dagger are those which differ significantly at the twenty-five, five, and one-percent levels, respectively. Thus, of the twenty-eight combinations, only three differed significantly at the five-percent level, and only one additional difference proved to be significant when tested at the twenty-five percent level.

[8] Henry Scheffe, *The Analysis of Variance* (New York: John Wiley and Sons, Inc., 1959), pp. 55–83. William C. Guenther, *Analysis of Variance* (Englewood Cliffs, N.J.: Prentice-Hall, Inc., 1964), pp. 50–59.

[9] Scheffe, *ibid.*, p. 58.

Table 17–2. Differences in sample means net operating income per share variability (percent).

Industry		Baking $\bar{X}_j - \bar{X}_1$	Cement $\bar{X}_j - \bar{X}_2$	Utilities $\bar{X}_j - \bar{X}_3$	Drugs $\bar{X}_j - \bar{X}_4$	Machinery $\bar{X}_j - \bar{X}_5$	Paper $\bar{X}_j - \bar{X}_6$	Oils $\bar{X}_j - \bar{X}_7$
Rubber	$\bar{X}_8$	0.008	−0.075	0.095	−0.108	−0.134	−0.018	−0.086
Oil	$\bar{X}_7$	0.094	0.011	0.181†	−0.022	−0.048	−0.068	0
Paper	$\bar{X}_6$	0.026	−0.057	0.113	−0.090	−0.116	0	
Machinery	$\bar{X}_5$	0.142	0.059	0.229*	0.026	0		
Drugs	$\bar{X}_4$	0.116	0.033	0.203†	0			
Utilities	$\bar{X}_3$	−0.087	−0.170‡	0				
Cement	$\bar{X}_2$	0.083	0					
Baking	$\bar{X}_1$	0						

* Significant difference at $F_{0.99}$.
† Significant difference at $F_{0.95}$.
‡ Significant difference at $F_{0.75}$.

The results of the multiple-comparisons test thus reveal only four significant differences, all of which are attributable to the electric utility industry. It appears that the rejection of the equal-means hypothesis in the conventional analysis of variance test was entirely due to one industry, electric utilities.

It is clear, given the validity of the proxy uncertainty variable, that differences among the variability measures for each industry are so small that the equivalent risk-class assumption is not supported by this test. The analysis of variance shows that there is, in general, as much variation within industry groups as there is among those groups. The evidence supports the view that industry classifications do not discriminate among groups of firms with approximately equivalent degrees of basic business uncertainty.

It is interesting to note that, not only were no significant differences demonstrated among the manufacturing industries, but also the electric utility measure was indistinguishable from three of the seven manufacturing industry measures. For example, from Table 17–2, the electric utility industry variability did not differ significantly from the baking, rubber and paper industry measures. The electric utility industry is one which is most frequently thought of as having a high degree of homogeneity among firms within the industry and one whose characteristics differ markedly from those of firms in other industries. Yet, on the basis of the proxy-uncertainty measure adopted, the industry risk-class assumption does not even differentiate between electric utilities and some industrials.

There are two possible reasons why a greater number of significant differences among industry variability measures were not found. The first is that the null hypothesis of no differences is, in fact, true. The second, however, is that the power of the test is not sufficient to avoid, in certain cases, accepting the null hypothesis when it is, in fact, false. This second situation may well affect the results of this test. The sample sizes of the baking, cement, and rubber industries are very small, and the power of the test to discriminate between these combinations is correspondingly low. The problem of small sample sizes is, however, one that is inherent in using industry groups as a universe from which to sample.

CONCLUSIONS

This paper represents a test of the validity of the assumption that homogeneity of basic business uncertainty can be achieved among sample firms by confining samples to single industry classifications. Given the validity of the proxy-uncertainty variable employed, the statistical analysis provides clear evidence that industry groups do not provide an adequate basis on which to insure homogeneity of basic business uncertainty.

The results of this analysis are not surprising in light of the difficulty of identifying groups of firms that are even broadly similar with regard to cost structure, demand characteristics and competitive position. The ability of a firm's management to act not only *within* but *on* the industry-determined constraints is often an important determinant of the level of uncertainty surrounding the firm's future income stream.

It is highly important, in many empirical studies, to incorporate some form of adjustment for differences in basic business uncertainty among sample firms. The results of this study, and others,[10] indicate that there is a great deal to be gained in both conceptual and statistical validity by incorporating an explicit uncertainty variable into the analysis.

APPENDIX A

List of Sample Firms

Bread, Cake and Biscuit Bakers
   Continental Baking Company
   National Biscuit Company
   Sunshine Biscuit Company
   United Biscuit Company

Cement
   Alpha Portland Cement Company
   General Portland Cement Company
   Ideal Cement Company
   Lehigh Cement Company
   Lone Star Cement Company

Electric Utilities
   Baltimore Gas and Electric
   Cincinnati Gas and Electric
   Cleveland Electric Illuminating
   Commonwealth Edison
   Consolidated Edison
   Consumer's Power
   Dayton Power and Light
   Delaware Power and Light
   Detroit Edison
   Florida Light and Power
   Illinois Power

---

[10] Haskel Benishay, "Variability in Earnings-Price Ratios of Corporate Equities," *The American Economic Review*, Vol. LI, No. 1 (March 1961), 81–94. Lawrence Fisher, "Determinants of Risk Premiums on Corporate Bonds," *Journal of Political Economy*, LXVII, No. 3 (June, 1959), 217–239. Ronald F. Wippern, "Earnings Variability, Financial Structure and the Value of the Firm," Unpublished doctoral dissertation, Graduate School of Business, Stanford University, 1964.

Indianapolis Power
Northern States Power
Pacific Gas and Electric
Public Service Electric and Gas
Southern California Edison
Virginia Electric and Power

Ethical Drugs
Abbott Laboratories
Eli Lilly
Parke, Davis
Charles Pfizer
G. D. Searle
Smith, Kline and French

Industrial Machinery
American Chain and Cable
Blaw Knox
Chain Belt
Chicago Pneumatic Tool
Ingersoll-Rand
Worthington

Integrated Domestic Oils
Atlantic Refining
Continental Oil

Phillips Petroleum
Shell Oil
Sinclair Oil
Standard Oil-Indiana
Tidewater Oil
Union Oil

Paper
Champion Paper
Crown Zellerbach
Great Northern Paper
International Paper
Kimberly-Clark Paper
Mead Paper
St. Regis Paper
Scott Paper
Union Bag-Camp
West Virginia Pulp and Paper

Rubber
Firestone
General Tire and Rubber
B. F. Goodrich
Goodyear Tire and Rubber
United States Rubber

APPENDIX B

Summary of data:
Net operating income variability
(percent)

Industry	Mean variability	Range in variability
Baking	0.133	0.063–0.296
Cement	0.216	0.123–0.276
Electric Utilities	0.046	0.024–0.066
Ethical Drugs	0.249	0.121–0.455
Machinery	0.275	0.170–0.431
Oils	0.227	0.114–0.351
Paper	0.159	0.039–0.449
Rubber	0.141	0.092–0.259

18

OPTIMAL INVESTMENT AND FINANCING POLICY

M. J. GORDON*

Professor Gordon presented this paper after publishing a number of articles on investment and financing policy. This article provides a clear exposition and summary of important aspects of his previous contributions. The derivations as well as the economic logic for the development of some basic formulas in business finance are covered, and some basic issues in connection with business financial policy are raised and discussed.

In two papers[1] and in a recent book[2] I have presented theory and evidence which lead to the conclusion that a corporation's share price (or its cost of capital) is not independent of the dividend rate. As you may know, MM (Modigliani and Miller) have the opposite view, and they argued their position at some length in a recent paper.[3] Moreover, the tone of their paper made it clear that they saw no reasonable basis on which their conclusion could be questioned. Since they were so sure of their conclusion, it would seem advisable for me to review carefully my thinking on the subject, and this appears to be a good place to do so.

I

Let us begin by examining MM's fundamental proof that the price of a share is independent of its dividend. They defined the value of a share at $t = 0$ as the present value of (i) the dividend it will pay at the end of the first period, D_1, plus (ii) the ex-dividend price of the share at the end of the period, P_1:

$$P_0 = \frac{1}{1 + k} [D_1 + P_1]. \qquad (1)$$

M. J. Gordon, "Optimal Investment and Financing Policy," *Journal of Finance* (May 1963), Vol. XVII, 264–272. Reprinted by permission.

* This paper was presented at a meeting of the American Finance Association in Pittsburgh, Pa., on December 29, 1962.

[1] "Dividends, Earnings and Stock Prices," *Review of Economics and Statistics*, May, 1959, pp. 99–105; "The Savings, Investment and Valuation of the Corporation," *ibid.*, February, 1962, pp. 37–51.

[2] *The Investment, Financing and Valuation of the Corporation* (Homewood, Ill.: R. D. Irwin, 1962).

[3] "Dividend Policy, Growth, and the Valuation of Shares," *Journal of Business*, October, 1961, pp. 411–33.

They then asked what would happen if the corporation, say, raised its dividend but kept its investment for the period constant by selling the additional number of shares needed to offset the funds lost by the dividend increase. They demonstrated that the ex-dividend price of the stock at the end of the period would go down by exactly the same amount as the increase in the dividend. Since the sum $D_1 + P_1$ remains the same, P_0 is unchanged by the change in the dividend.

I will not review their proof of the theorem in detail because I find nothing wrong with it under the assumption they made that the future is certain. However, after proving the theorem a number of times under different conditions, they withdrew the assumption of certainty and made the dramatic announcement, "our first step, alas, must be to jettison the fundamental valuation equation."[4] Under uncertainty, they continued, it is not "at all clear what meaning can be attached to the discount factor . . . ."[5] The implication which they made explicit in discussing my work is that under uncertainty we cannot represent investors as using discount rates to arrive at the present value of an expectation of future receipts.

It would seem that all is lost. But no! On the next page we are told that their "fundamental conclusion need not be modified merely because of the presence of uncertainty about the future course of profits, investment, or dividends . . . ."[6] By virtue of the postulates of "imputed rationality" and "symmetric market rationality," it remains true that "dividend policy is irrelevant for the determination of market prices."[7]

Their paper continued with a discussion of market imperfections, in which they note that the most important one, the capital gains tax, should create a preference for low payout rates. They concede that it may nevertheless be true that high payout rates sell at a premium, but they found ". . . only one way to account for it, namely as a result of systematic irrationality on the part of the investing public." They concluded with the hope that ". . . investors, however naive they may be when they enter the market, do sometimes learn from experience; and perhaps, occasionally even from reading articles such as this."[8]

It would seem that, under uncertainty, they might have been less sure of their conclusion for two reasons. First, under uncertainty, an investor need not be indifferent as to the distribution of the one-period gain on a share between the dividend and price appreciation. Since price appreciation is highly uncertain, an investor may prefer the expectation of a $5 dividend and a $50 price to a zero dividend and a $55 price without being irrational. Second, the expectation of a stock issue at $t = 1$ may have a depressing

---

[4] Miller and Modigliani, *op. cit.*, p. 426.
[5] *Ibid.*, p. 427.
[6] *Ibid.*, p. 428.
[7] *Ibid.*, p. 429.
[8] *Ibid.*, p. 432.

influence on the price at $t = 0$. What MM did was both change the dividend and change the number of new shares issued. Can we be so sure that the price of a share will not change when these two events take place?

II

Let us turn now to the proof of the MM position on the dividend rate that I presented in my papers and book. The reasons for presenting this proof will be evident shortly. Consider a corporation that earned Y_0 in the period ending at $t = 0$ and paid it all out in dividends. Further, assume that the corporation is expected to continue paying all earnings in dividends and to engage in no outside financing. Under these assumptions the company is expected to earn and pay Y_0 in every future period. If the rate of return on investment that investors require on the share is k, we may represent the valuation of the share as follows:

$$P_0 = \frac{Y_0}{(1 + k)^1} + \frac{Y_0}{(1 + k)^2} + \frac{Y_0}{(1 + k)^3} + \cdots + \frac{Y_0}{(1 + k)^t} + \cdots. \quad (2)$$

We may also say that k is the discount rate that equates the dividend expectation of Y_0 in perpetuity with the price P_0.

Next, let the corporation announce at $t = 0$ that it will retain and invest $Y_1 = Y_0$ during $t = 1$ and that it expects to earn a rate of return of $k = Y_0/P_0$ on the investment. In each subsequent period it will pay all earnings out in dividends. Share price is now given by the expression

$$P_0 = \frac{0}{(1 + k)^1} + \frac{Y_0 + kY_0}{(1 + k)^2} + \frac{Y_0 + kY_0}{(1 + k)^3} + \cdots + \frac{Y_0 + kY_0}{(1 + k)^t}. \quad (3)$$

Notice that the numerator of the first term on the right side is zero. It is the dividend and not the earnings in the period, since the investor is correctly represented as using the dividend expectation in arriving at P_0. If he were represented as looking at the earnings expectation, then as Bodenhorn[9] noted, he would be double-counting the first period's earnings.

It is evident that, as a result of the corporation's decision, the investor gives up Y_0 at the end of $t = 1$ and receives, in its place, kY_0 in perpetuity. The distribution of dividends over time has been changed. It is also evident that kY_0 in perpetuity discounted at k is exactly equal to Y_0. Hence P_0 is unchanged, and the change in the distribution over time of the dividends had no influence on share price. In general, the corporation can be expected to retain and invest any fraction of the income in any period without the share price being changed as a consequence, so long as r, the return on investment, is equal to k. If $r > k$ for any investment, P_0 will be increased, but the reason

---

[9] Diran Bodenhorn, "On the Problem of Capital Budgeting," *Journal of Finance*, December, 1959, pp. 473–92.

is the profitability of investment and not the change in the time distribution of dividends.

Assume now that when the corporation makes the announcement which changes the dividend expectation from the one given by equation (2) to the one given by equation (3), investors raise the discount rate from k to k'. For the moment let us not wonder why the discount rate is raised from k to k', i.e., why the rate of return investors require on the share is raised as a consequence of the above change in the dividend expectation. If this takes place, equation (3) becomes

$$P_0' = \frac{0}{(1 + k')^1} + \frac{Y_0 + kY_0}{(1 + k')^2} + \frac{Y_0 + kY_0}{(1 + k')^2} + \cdots + \frac{Y_0 + kY_0}{(1 + k')^4} + \cdots . \quad (3a)$$

It is clear that with $k' > k$, $P_0' < P_0$.

Let us review what happened. The dividend policy changed: the near dividend was reduced, and the distant dividends were raised. This caused a rise in the discount rate, and the result was a fall in the price of the share. I, therefore, say that the change in dividend policy changed the share's price.

In response to this argument, MM stated that I fell into "the typical confounding of dividend policy with investment policy."[10] I don't understand their reasoning. It is well known that when the rate of return on investment is set equal to the discount rate, changing the level of investment has no influence on share price. By this means, I neutralized the profitability of investment. It seems to me perfectly clear that I did not confound investment and dividend policy; I changed the discount rate. Share price changed with the dividend rate in the above example because the discount rate was changed. The issue, therefore, is whether the behavior of investors under uncertainty is correctly represented by a model in which the discount rate that equates a dividend expectation with its price is a function of the dividend rate.

I cannot categorically state that k is a function of the rate of growth in the dividend, i.e., the dividend rate, but I can present some theoretical considerations and empirical evidence in support of the theorem. It seems plausible that (i) investors have an aversion to risk or uncertainty, and (ii), given the riskiness of a corporation, the uncertainty of a dividend it is expected to pay increases with the time in the future of the dividend. It follows from these two propositions that an investor may be represented as discounting the dividend expected in period t at a rate of k_t, with k_t not independent of t. Furthermore, if aversion to risk is large enough and/or risk increases rapidly enough with time, k_t increases with t.

It is therefore possible, though not certain, that investor behavior is correctly approximated by the statement that, in arriving at the value of a

---

[10] Miller and Modigliani, *op. cit.*, p. 425.

dividend expectation, they discount it at the rates k_t, $t = 1, 2, \ldots$, with $k_t > k_{t-1}$. In this event the single discount rate we use in stock value models is an increasing function of the rate of growth in the dividend. In short, dividend policy influences share price. To illustrate the conclusion, let us rewrite equation (2):

$$P_0 = \frac{Y_0}{(1 + k_1)^1} + \frac{Y_0}{(1 + k_2)^2} + \frac{Y_0}{(1 + k_3)^3} + \cdots \frac{Y_0}{(1 + k_t)^t} + \cdots. \tag{4}$$

We now look on the k of equation (2) as an average of the k_t of equation (4) such that if the entire dividend expectation is discounted at this single rate, it results in the same share price. The discount rate k is an average of the k_t with Y_0, the weight assigned to each item.

Once again let the corporation retain $Y_1 = Y_0$ and invest it to earn kY_0 per period in perpetuity. Using the sequence of discount rates k_t, the same as that appearing in equation (4), the valuation of the new dividend expectation becomes

$$P_0' = \frac{1}{(1 + k_1)^1} + \frac{Y_0 + kY_0}{(1 + k_2)^2} + \frac{Y_0 + kY_0}{(1 + k_3)^3} + \cdots + \frac{Y_0 = kY_0}{(1 + k_t)^t} + \cdots. \tag{5}$$

The shareholder gives up Y_0 and gets $k Y_0$ in perpetuity, but the latter is now discounted at the rates k_t, $t = 2 \to \infty$, and it can be shown that kY_0 so discounted is less than Y_0. Hence $P_0' < P_0$, and dividend policy influences share price. It also can be shown that k', the new average of the same k_t, is greater than k. In general, reducing the near dividends and raising the distant dividends (lowering the dividend rate) changes the weights of the k_t and raises their average.

III

To summarize the theoretical part of my argument, I started with two assumptions: (i) aversion to risk and (ii) increase in the uncertainty of a receipt with its time in the future. From these assumptions I proceeded by deductive argument to the proposition that the single discount rate an investor is represented as using to value a share's dividend expectation is an increasing function of the rate of growth in the dividend. The consequence of the theorem is that dividend policy per se influences the value of a share. The assumptions have enough intuitive merit I believe, that the theorem may in fact be true.

Before proceeding to the empirical evidence, I would like to comment briefly on two other criticisms MM directed at my argument. First, they differentiated between my "purely subjective discount rate and the objective market-given yields" and stated: "To attempt to derive valuation formulas from these purely subjective discount factors involves, of course, an error . . . ."[11] My assumptions and empirical results may be questioned, but where is the error? Does the theorem fail to follow from the assumptions? Why, as they suggest, is it logically impossible for an investor to arrive at the value of a share by estimating its future dividends and discounting the series at a rate appropriate to its uncertainty?

The following MM criticism of my argument I find even more confusing. They stated: "Indeed if they [investors] valued shares according to the Gordon approach and thus paid a premium for higher payout ratios, then holders of the low payout shares would actually realize consistently higher returns on their investment over any stated interval of time."[12] Under this reasoning two shares cannot sell at different yields regardless of how much they differ in risk because the holders of the higher-yield share would "actually realize consistently higher returns over any stated interval of time." Do MM deny that investors have an aversion to risk?

To test the theorem empirically, I proceeded as follows. The valuation of a share may be represented by the expression

$$P_0 = \int_0^\infty D_t e^{-kt}\, dt, \tag{6}$$

where D_t is the dividend expected in period t and k is an operator on the D_t that reduces them to their present value to the investor. Equation (6) is a perfectly general statement that is not open to question. However, to use the equation in empirical work, we must specify how investors arrive at D_t from observable variables. For this, I assumed that investors expect a corporation will: (i) retain the fraction b of its income in each future period; (ii) earn a rate of return, r, on the common equity investment in each future period; (iii) maintain the existing debt-equity ratio; and (iv) undertake no new outside equity financing. Under the above assumptions the current dividend is $D_0 = (1 - b)Y_0$, and its rate of growth is br. Further, the entire dividend expectation is represented by these two variables, and equation (6) is equal to

$$P_0 = \frac{(1 - b)Y_0}{k - br}. \tag{7}$$

The above four assumptions may be criticized as being too great a simplification of reality. I have admitted their limitations, and I welcome improvement, but I know of no other empirical model that contains as rich and accurate a statement of the dividend expectation provided by a share. Most empirical work, including the published work of MM, represents the investor as expecting that the corporation will pay all earnings in dividends and engage in no outside financing. They, therefore, also ignore the influence of the

---

[11] *Ibid.*, p. 424.
[12] *Ibid.*, p. 425.

profitability of investment on share price. This model incorporates a prediction of the corporation's investment and rate of return on the investment in each future period. The expected investment in period t is the fraction b of the period's income plus the leverage on the retention that maintains the corporation's existing debt-equity ratio. Further, the influence of this retention and borrowing on the dividend expectation is incorporated in the model.

The interesting thing about the model as it stands is that it is consistent with the MM position and should provoke no objection. To see this, let us make their assumption that k is independent of b and, to neutralize the profitability of investment, let $r = k$. In this model, dividend policy is represented by b the retention rate, so that, if we take the derivative of P_0 with respect to b, we establish the relation between share price and the dividend rate. We find that $\delta P/\delta b = 0$. The value of a share is independent of the dividend rate—exactly what MM argue.

One can use this model in empirical work under the assumption that k is independent of br. I did and obtained poor results. Since I found good theoretical grounds for believing that k is an increasing function of br, it would seem reasonable to explore the hypothesis, and that is what I did. If k is an increasing function of br, we can write equation (7) as

$$P_0 = A_0[(1 - b)Y_0][1 + br]\alpha_2. \tag{8}$$

In this expression, A_0 represents the influence of all variables other than the current dividend $(1 - b)Y_0$, and its rate of growth, br. When $b = \delta$, P_0 is the multiple A_0 of Y_0. As br increases, the dividend, $(1 - b)Y_0$, falls and br rises, the former lowering price and the latter raising price. Whether P_0 rises or falls with b depends on r, the profitability of investment, and on α_2. The expression α_2 may be looked on as how much investors are willing to pay for growth. Its value depends on how fast the k_t rise with t, that is, on how fast uncertainty increases with time and on the degree of investor aversion to risk.

It should be noted that equation (8) is not merely a stock value model. Given the investor's valuation of a share, A_0 and α_2, and, given the profitability of investment, r, the model may be used to find the retention rate (equal to the investment rate under our assumptions) that maximizes the value of a share. Extensions of the model developed elsewhere[13] allow its use to find the investment and the financing, retention, debt, and new equity that maximize share price.

The empirical results I obtained with the above model have been published in detail,[14] and all I will say here is that they are very good. Although the results compare favorably with earlier work, they are not good enough to

---

[13] M. J. Gordon, *The Investment, Financing and Valuation of the Corporation* (Homewood, Ill.: R. D. Irwin, 1962).
[14] *Ibid.*

settle the question. MM[15] and Benishay[16] have pointed out that my independent variables are not free of error, and the consequence is that the parameter estimates have a downward bias. Kolin[17] has reported that his empirical work revealed no relation between dividend policy and share price. As things stand, I would say that the influence of dividend policy on share price is a question that requires further study. The axiomatic basis of the MM position is certainly not so powerful as to force the acceptance of their conclusions.

IV

I should like to close with a brief comment on the two major camps that are emerging with respect to the theory of corporation finance. In both camps optimal policy is taken as the policy that maximizes the value of the corporation. Although corporations may not make investment and financing decisions with only this objective in mind, managements are certainly not indifferent to the prices at which their corporations' securities sell. Hence the policy question posed has practical significance.

In one camp, where we find MM, it is argued that a corporation's cost of capital is a constant—i.e., independent of the method and level of financing. Optimal policy is the investment that equates the marginal return on investment with this cost of Capital. The inescapable conclusion is that financing policy is not a problem. The opposite position is that a corporation's cost of capital varies with the method and level of financing. My judgment is that the theoretical and empirical evidence we have favors this position.

However, regardless of which view prevails, the battle should be lively and productive. For a long time the position that cost of capital is a constant was held almost exclusively by economists, who were sophisticated in methods of theoretical and econometric analysis but knew little of finance. By contrast, the position that the cost of capital is a variable was held by finance men, who were familiar with their subject but not with advanced methods of theoretical and empirical research. People in each group talked only to those who agreed with them, and in consequence not much was said. The situation has changed, it will change further, and the promise is that the lively debate and active research in progress will advance our knowledge on the subject.

---

[15] Franco Modigliani and Merton Miller, "The Cost of Capital Corporation Finance, and Theory of Investment: Reply," *American Economic Review*, September 1959, pp. 655–69.

[16] Haskel Benishay, "Variability in Earnings-Price Ratios: Reply," *The American Economic Review*, March 1962, pp. 209–216.

[17] Marshall Kolin, *The Relative Price of Corporate Equity* (Boston: Harvard Business School).

19

AN INTEGRATION OF COST OF CAPITAL THEORIES

ROBERT W. JOHNSON

There are many approaches to the theory of a firm's cost of capital. In the following presentation, Professor Johnson analyzes the nature of the disagreements on the concept and measurement of the cost of capital. The author summarizes different points of view and attempts an integrated presentation on cost of capital theory and measurement. He also discusses the influence of rate of return on investments.

Cost of capital occupies a central role in engineering economics and financial management. First, it serves as a "hurdle rate" or "cutoff rate" when evaluating proposed capital expenditures using the rate-of-return approach. Alternatively, it is the discount rate in the net-present-value approach. In the latter application, an error in estimating the cost of capital may significantly change the relative attractiveness of the projects. Second, in the field of financial management the cost of capital provides a measure of the effectiveness of the design of the financial structure. For a given company at a point in time, there are likely to be some capital structures that are better than others, and, traditionally, the relative merits are measured in terms of the cost of capital. Finally, the cost of capital, and the means used to measure it, are significant to the economy as a whole. If measures of cost of capital are defective, so that cutoff rates are too high, the economy may not grow as rapidly as it might otherwise do. If some firms employ cutoff rates that are too low, resources may be diverted from more productive to less productive uses.

The widespread significance of the cost of capital is reflected in the increasingly frequent attention to the matter shown in textbooks in the fields of engineering economics, finance, accounting, and business economics. Perusal of a random sample of these books suggests that authors in each of these fields survey the writings of other authors in their own fraternity, but too seldom make forays into analyses of writers in other categories. The writings also range from descriptions of procedures for making concrete

Robert W. Johnson, "An Integration of Cost of Capital Theories," *Fourth Summer Symposium of the Engineering Economy Division of the American Society for Engineering Education*, 1966, 11–17. Reprinted by permission.

estimates of cost of capital for immediate use by management to more esoteric flights into theory which broaden our understanding of the conceptual problems; but these may not bring us much closer to providing a figure that management can use. The purpose of this paper is to locate, if possible, the common ground that may exist in the various methods of determining the cost of capital and to suggest some additional approaches. It is appropriate that this attempt be made before an audience of engineering economists, who seem to encompass a broader spectrum of academic and practical talent than other disciplines.

DEFINITION

In view of the ease of defining the cost of capital, it is disheartening to discover that it is so difficult to determine. Professor Myron Gordon[1] has provided us with an excellent definition: "The cost of capital for a firm is a discount rate with the property that an investment with a rate of profit above (below) this rate will raise (lower) the value of the firm." It is also commonly accepted by most writers that the cost of capital is not a constant, but "a function of the level of the firm's investment with the parameters of the function depending on the firm's dividend rate, debt-equity ratio, rate of return on investment, and/or other variables."[2] It should be noted that this approach implies that this function is to be matched against an array of investment opportunities whose acceptance will not change the risk class or quality of earnings of the firm.

To facilitate our analysis let us begin by separating the determination of cost capital of a firm that does not need additional external financing, from the cost of capital of a company that is growing so rapidly that it needs to borrow additional funds and/or sell more common or preferred stock. For simplicity let us refer to these cases as the static and growth models, respectively.

INTERNAL FINANCING

Depreciation

Even in the static situation there is ample room for dispute. One area of disagreement concerns the treatment of depreciation in determination of the cost of capital. Some authors assign a cost to the depreciation allowances while others combine depreciation with retained earnings, or at least treat it

---

[1] Myron J. Gordon, *The Investment, Financing and Valuation of the Corporation* (Homewood, Illinois: Richard D. Irwin, Inc., 1962), p. 218.
[2] *Ibid.*, pp. 218–219.

the same as retained earnings.[3] Thus W. T. Morris[4] argues that depreciation has a cost equal to the ratio of the estimated earnings per share, without the proposed project to the present market value per share. Other authors[5] ignore depreciation entirely and by this omission imply that it should not affect the cost of capital. Another split is between authors who make a separate evaluation of the retained earnings in the weighted cost of capital and those who weight only the common stock.[6]

Can we sort out elements of truth and fallacy in these widely differing points of view? One basic misconception relates to treatment of depreciation as a source of funds:

> Depreciation is *not*: a sum of money, dependent upon the existence of profits, or a provider of funds for the replacement of property. Depreciation is an expense to the same extent that wages, rent, insurance, etc. are expenses.[7]

Thus any cost of capital derived from a weighted average that includes bonds, stocks, retained earnings, and depreciation expense mingles, in an unusual way, several balance-sheet accounts with still another derived from the operating statement. In short, this approach mixes historical sources of funds with an expense item that is not a source of funds.

Retained Earnings

There seems to be general agreement among students of the field that retained earnings are not free. They represent direct reinvestment of funds by residual owners, similar in basic results to a fully subscribed rights offering. Since the owners had alternative uses for these funds, they are not costless. But what is the cost? In an earlier article Solomon argued that the cost of retained capital is equal to:

$$\frac{E_A(1 - T)}{P},$$

where E_A is "management's best estimate of what average future earnings would be if the proposed capital expenditure were not made," P the present

---

[3] A. J. Merrett and Allen Sykes, *The Finance and Analysis of Capital Projects* (New York: John Wiley & Sons, Inc., 1963), pp. 78–82. Ezra Solomon, "Measuring a Company's Cost of Capital" (1955) in *The Management of Corporate Capital* (Glencoe, Illinois: The Free Press of Glencoe, 1959), p. 134.

[4] William T. Morris, *Engineering Economy* (Homewood, Illinois: Richard D. Irwin, Inc., 1960), p. 64. Robert Lindsay and Arnold W. Sametz, *Financial Management: An Analytical Approach* (Homewood, Illinois: Richard D. Irwin, Inc., 1963), p. 155.

[5] J. Fred Weston, *Managerial Finance* (New York: Holt, Rinehart and Winston, Inc., 1962), pp. 230–238.

[6] Weston, for example, does not make a separate calculation for retained earnings, but Osborn does. Richard C. Osborn, *Business Finance: The Management Approach* (New York: Appleton-Century-Crofts, 1965), pp. 164–166.

[7] Charles J. Gaa, "Depreciation—The Good Provider?" *Business Topics* (Winter, 1962), pp. 7–17; reprinted in Francis J. Corrigan and Howard A. Ward's *Financial Management: Politics and Practices* (Boston: Houghton Mifflin Co., 1963), pp. 266–279.

market value per share, and T the marginal tax rate applicable to stockholders.[8]

In a more recent work Solomon argues that this is incorrect, that while this is *an* opportunity cost of retained earnings, it is not necessarily the highest or most profitable alternative. The better alternative is to invest funds in other companies or other industries, if no suitable internal investment is available. If these investments carry the same risk as the present company, the yield will be equal to E_A/P. Since this is clearly larger than the net yield after personal income taxes when dividends are paid to the shareholders, the external yield is the proper criterion for the cost of retained earnings.[9] The same principle is recognized by Grant and Ireson:[10]

> In deciding whether to invest equity funds in specific capital assets, an important question is how good an opportunity will be foregone. In other words, if the investment in the specific capital assets is not made, what return is likely to be obtainable from the same funds invested elsewhere? In principle the interest rate (minimum attractive rate of return) used in an economy study ought to be the rate of return obtainable from the opportunity foregone, as nearly as can be determined.

One of the problems with Solomon's approach to opportunity cost is determination of the estimate of average future earnings. Over what period of time is this average projected? Are all years to be weighted equally, or should earlier years receive greater weight in view of the time value of money?

Average-Weighted-Cost Approach

Other writers would determine the cost of funds in the static case by weighting the after-tax cost of each type of funds by its relative book or market values. The most common basis for assigning weights is market value. This methodology is supported on the grounds that this is what the company would have to pay were it to go out and raise those funds today. It is, in a sense, an opportunity cost; but only in a loose sense, since nobody suggests that a firm would seriously consider liquidating and then going out into the market to raise the same amount of funds in the same proportion.

Reconsideration

To examine these approaches to the cost of capital in the static case let us draw on the arguments of those who support costing depreciation and those

---

[8] Solomon (1955), *op. cit.*, pp. 130–133. Bierman and Smidt appear to have the same approach. Harold Bierman, Jr. and Seymour Smidt, *The Capital Budgeting Decision* (New York: The Macmillan Co., 1960), pp. 142–146.

[9] Ezra Solomon, *The Theory of Financial Management* (New York: Columbia University Press, 1963), pp. 53–54.

[10] Eugene L. Grant and W. Grant Ireson, *Principle of Engineering Economy*, 4th ed. (New York: Ronald Press Co., 1960), p. 140.

who assert that costs should reflect realistic opportunities foregone. Those who advocate costing depreciation perform a useful service by focusing our attention on the flow of cash available for investment (even though their devices for measuring the flow are imperfect). If depreciation is not a source of cash, what is? Quite clearly, as we sit at the beginning of a fiscal year and look ahead, we see cash flowing in through collections of accounts receivable and cash flowing out through expenditures such as wages, interest, sinking fund payments, and payments on account for materials and supplies. If the firm fails to replenish in full its accounts receivable, inventory, or fixed assets as they are drawn down, then additional cash will be generated. We should not assume that cash is automatically invested in current assets. A substantial investment in any asset, whether current or fixed, should be subjected to capital budgeting analysis. For example, a retailer who decides to offer credit, rather than sell only for cash, must decide whether the investment in accounts receivable offers an adequate rate of return in relation to his cost of capital.

Thus the financial manager of a firm will envisage a forthcoming pool of cash, net after fixed commitments, such as sinking fund payments and interest (net after taxes). What hurdle rate(s) should he demand for capital projects that will draw on this pool of cash? We have a possible answer from another source—the cost is "the rate of return obtainable from the opportunity foregone." What are the opportunities available to a financial manager as he views his anticipated pool of cash? He can invest in capital projects within the firm; he can invest in other firms: he can repay debt or retire its first cousin, preferred stock; or he can pay cash to the common stockholders via dividends or repurchase of their stock. To evaluate the desirability of various capital projects or investment in other firms, the financial manager must weigh their rates of return against the highest-yield alternative that would remove funds from the control of management— retirement of debt, or preferred stock, or payment of cash to common stockholders via dividends or repurchase.

Observe that we have not used any weighted cost of capital derived from the right-hand side of the balance sheet to determine the cost of internally generated funds. And why should we? In engineering cost analyses of make-or-buy decisions, equipment replacement, and similar problems we employ the principle of "sunk costs." These "sunk costs" are represented, in large part, by assets carried on the left-hand side of the balance sheet. But another set of "sunk costs" is shown on the right-hand side of the balance sheet. Current liabilities are not readily sunk, since they can be renegotiated within a year. But the long-term debt, preferred stock, and common stock represent contractual arrangements that were made some time in the past. These historical arrangements affect the cost of capital in the static case only insofar as they absorb some of the available cash to meet certain contractual or semi-contractual commitments.

Another way of illuminating the same point is to ask how a sophisticated investor would value the residual ownership interest. He should look first at the annual cash flow generated, net of fixed commitments. Presumably the value he placed on this net cash flow is dependent on its variability and certainty. The existence of debt does not raise the value the sophisticated investor places on the firm, even though it lowers the average weighted cost of capital. Indeed, the debt may *lower* the value he places on the expected net cash benefits because the fixed charges on the debt increase the variability of the cash flow.

A second point of departure from the traditional approach is the suggestion that the marginal cost of capital for internally generated funds is not constant, but slopes downward as more lucrative alternatives are used up.[11] Lindsay and Sametz,[12] for example, state: "That part of retained profits that arises through depreciation accounting provides funds whose cost is average current returns/market price of the stock." By this definition the marginal cost of a substantial portion of internally generated funds is constant. But if we adopt the opportunity-cost approach the opportunity cost of the first dollar of internally generated funds is quite likely to be higher than the opportunity cost of the last dollar generated. For example, assume that a corporation is paying a regular dividend of $2 per year. Studies of the effect of dividends on the market value of common stock suggest that the opportunity cost (in terms of the effect on the market value of the stock) of the first $2 per share of generated funds is a good deal higher than the opportunity cost of the next $2 per share.[13] Similarly, repurchase of 20 percent of the outstanding common stock may not enhance the market value of common stock twice as much as repurchase of 10 percent of outstanding shares.

In summary, I would argue that in the static case we are not concerned with either depreciation or the liabilities and net worth; in the one case because it does not measure the flow of funds and in the other because it does not measure the cost of existing capital. We are concerned with the marginal cost of existing capital. We are concerned with the marginal cost of internally generated funds. This cost should be based upon the ranking of the best alternative uses of these funds applied to the payment of dividends, retirement of debt or preferred stock, or repurchase of common stock, although not necessarily in that order. If this approach is valid, it appears that the marginal cost curve is initially downward sloping. For a company that faces a declining market or that has ineffective research and development

---

[11] John Lintner, "Optimal Dividends and Corporate Growth," *Quarterly Journal of Economics*, 78 (February, 1964), pp. 61–65.

[12] Lindsay and Sametz, *op. cit.*, p. 155.

[13] Irwin Friend and Marshall Puckett, "Dividends and Stock Prices," *American Economic Review*, 54 (September, 1964), pp. 680–681. John Lintner, "Distribution of Incomes of Corporations among Dividends, Retained Earnings and Taxes," *American Economic Review*, 64 (May, 1956), pp. 97–113.

programs the marginal cost curve may cut the marginal revenue "curve" before internally generated funds are fully utilized. In this case the company should consider the best of such possibilities as paying out additional dividends, retirement of debt, and so on. In more dynamic situations internally generated funds will be fully utilized before the marginal cost and revenue curves intersect.[14] Since these concerns must seek outside sources of funds, let us turn to the growth model for calculating the marginal cost of this additional capital.

EXTERNAL FINANCING

Costs of Segments of New Capital

Let us first examine the costs of raising additional long-term debt, preferred stock or common stock, leaving out for the moment the effect of each added type of security upon the overall marginal cost of capital. There seems to be general agreement that the cost of a long-term bond issue is simply the rate of interest (net after taxes) that equates the annual cash payments on interest and repayments on principal with the net amount realized at the time of issue. Interesting complexities are introduced by convertible bonds, and bonds with call privileges. The cost of preferred stock is generally held to be the annual dividend divided by the net amount realized at the time of issue. Dividends are properly regarded as a semi-contractual obligation. Complexities are again introduced by participating and convertible issues.

There is also general agreement that while equity does not have a cost in a bookkeeping sense, it does have a cost in another sense. Since management's responsibility is to existing shareholders, issue of any new shares should not force the market value of existing shares below the prices that would have prevailed without a new issue.

However, the considerable disagreement over what determines the market value of common stock results in a similar split in calculating the cost of new issues of common stock. The split rests upon whether market values are determined by the anticipated earnings on the common stock, or anticipated dividends plus a factor for growth. If k_e represents the cost of new equity; E_A, anticipated earnings, and P_n, the net price received per share after all underwriting and flotation costs, the first school maintains that $k_e = E_A/P_n$.[15]

In addition to the difficulty of estimating future earnings, this model assumes that "(1) the market appraisal is considered correct; (2) the market is expected to continue to appraise the stock at the same rate after expansion

---

[14] This would not necessarily indicate payment of no dividends. In some companies regular cash dividends may be regarded as a semi-contractual obligation. The dividends on AT&T stock are an example.

[15] Solomon (1963), *op. cit.*, pp. 38–46.

... (3) the dividend rate can be ignored; and (4) individual differences among stockholders, say tax status, can be ignored."[16]

The alternative approach is based upon the assumption that "future dividends are what the investor buys in a share."[17] On this assumption, we have the formula

$$k_e = D/P_n + g$$

where D is the current cash dividend rate and g the expected uniform annual rate of growth in dividends. The annual rate of growth is the product of the constant rate of return the corporation is expected to earn in each period, and the constant proportion of income that it is expected to retain in each period.[18] Both models involve some fairly restrictive assumptions, including an all-equity capital structure. Since there is clearly a correlation between earnings and dividends, it is very difficult to validate either approach from empirical data. At the present time there is no generally accepted model, but more sophisticated models following the logic implicit in the second formula are the most promising.[19]

Marginal Cost

Most students of the cost of capital agree that even if a new capital project is financed from a particular source, the cost of capital for the project is not equal to the after-tax cost of the source.[20] Thus if a firm simultaneously invests $5,000,000 in new plant and equipment and floats $5,000,000 issue of 6-percent debentures, it is improper to argue that the cost of capital for that investment is 3 percent (net after 50-percent taxes). While a firm does not often float issues of debt and common stock in combination, nonetheless, each issue of debt is dependent upon some equity base. An issue of debt increases the likelihood of further equity financing, either via retained earnings or new issues of stock. This "mortgage" on future equity, the increased variability in earnings per share, and the larger claim on assets in case of liquidation, explain why an increase in debt may bring about a decline in the price-earnings ratio of the common stock. To avoid a decline in the market value of the common stock, the investment must certainly earn more than 6 percent before taxes. On the other hand, an issue of common stock provides a base for additional debt, so that the cost to the firm is less than the cost of the specific source.

---

[16] David Durand, "Costs of Debt and Equity Funds for Business: Trends and Problems of Measurement," in *Conference on Research in Business Finance* (New York: National Bureau of Economic Research, 1952), p. 241.

[17] Gordon, *op. cit.*, p. 44.

[18] The formula may easily be derived from Gordon's (4.6), *ibid.*, p. 45. It is also found in Bierman and Smidt, *op. cit.*, p. 135.

[19] See Gordon, *op. cit.*, p. 52 (4.12); p. 112 (8.31).

[20] Although DeGarmo states: "In many economy studies it is clear that only borrowed capital or only owned capital will be employed. In such cases the corresponding cost of capital should be used in the calculations." E. Paul DeGarmo, *Engineering Economy* (New York: The Macmillan Co., 1960), p. 158.

Moreover, if we tried to associate each source of funds with a particular investment, we would have the chaotic situation where a machine might be purchased with a rate of return of 4 percent because it was "financed with debt" during that period, while a machine offering a 20-percent return might be rejected in the following period because it would have to be "financed by a new issue of common stock." While the cost of capital may change over time, its level at any one moment should not be dependent upon the current block of new financing.

Combined Cost of Debt and Equity

If one properly distinguishes between the cost of funds from a source and the cost of funds to the firm, it becomes necessary to combine the cost of debt and the cost of equity in some manner that recognizes the effect of leverage on the mutual or joint cost. While there are many different approaches to this problem, two seem to dominate the field at present. One is based on a weighted-average approach, with the cost of each source of funds being determined by one of the methods indicated earlier and the weights based upon the current market values of debt and equity. Because leverage changes slowly in most cases, Solomon argues that the existing capital structure can be used "regardless of how the increment of funds is financed."[21] Weston proposes an incremental cost reflecting the changes in capital structure introduced by the new issues of securities. However, given the inherent errors in such estimates, his adjustments would seldom have a significant effect upon capital budgeting decisions, although he is theoretically more accurate.[22]

The second approach involves a more sharply rising cost-of-capital function. Originally developed by Solomon,[23] the most recent version is that presented by Lindsay and Sametz.[24] A common ground is the recognition that additional amounts of debt raise both the explicit cost of debt, as the risk to bondholders rises, and the implicit cost, as the risk and variability of earnings for the common stockholders increase. However, Lindsay and Sametz introduce a time dimension (not shown in their chart) which assumes that over time a corporation introduces successive blocks of debts on the basis of annual retained earnings and occasional issues of equity. They refer to this process as "sequential marginal costing." Their analysis indicates that as companies expand, their marginal cost of capital rises fairly sharply.

---

[21] Solomon (1963), *op. cit.*, p. 88.

[22] J. Fred Weston, "The Measurement of Cost of Capital," in *Applications of Economic Evaluation in Industry*. The 1962 Summer Symposium of the Engineering Economy Division, American Society for Engineering Education (Hoboken, N.J.: The Engineering Economist, 1962), pp. 85–86.

[23] Solomon (1955), *op. cit.*, pp. 135–136.

[24] Lindsay and Sametz, *op. cit.*, pp. 158–161.

Let me suggest a possibility for integrating the approaches using a weighted cost of capital and "sequential marginal costing."[25] Consider a firm in a given risk class financed with various combinations of debt and equity (Fig. 19–1). Because of its small size, the market restricts a firm

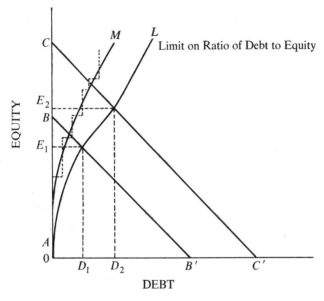

Fig. 19–1.

with only OA in total funds to an all-equity capital structure. If we draw a line at a 45-degree angle to OB, we find that a firm with a total capital structure of that size could employ up to OD_1 in debt, supported by OE_1 in equity (debt and equity at market values). A still larger concern, with total resources of OC, would be able to employ OD_2 of debt in relation to OE_2 of equity, but beyond that size firms in this risk class would not be able to increase significantly their ratios of debt to equity.

This analysis is based on the assumption that large corporations are like investment companies in that their greater diversification reduces the variance in the expected earnings before interest and taxes. With a tighter probability distribution function on expected operating income, these companies are in a position to support a larger amount of debt relative to equity than their smaller competitors.[26] This change in the acceptable ratio of debt-to-equity according to size is characteristic of finance companies, as one example.

---

[26] I am not entirely clear whether or not this should be regarded as a change in the risk class. In a given industry, such as the consumer finance business, there is no change in the basic line of business. Instead the risks are more diversified geographically. While the interest coverage may not vary significantly among firms of different size, the variance in earnings is less generally among large companies than their smaller competitors.

Now let us assume that the cost of capital is measured on a vertical axis projecting upward from the origin. If we take a cross-section of the three-dimensional function along BB', we find our rather familiar weighted-average-cost-of-capital function depicted in Fig. 19–2. At B the corporation depends entirely on equity, whereas at L, the ratio of debt to total capital might be about one to four. The minimum average cost of capital for this size of company is at OM_1.

Now if we connect the minimum costs of capital $M_1, M_2, \ldots M_n$ along each cross-section representing firms of increasing size, $AA', BB', \ldots ZZ'$,

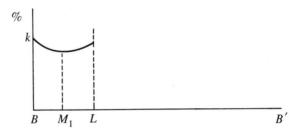

RATIO OF DEBT TO DEBT PLUS EQUITY

Fig. 19–2.

and project these points on the horizontal plane (Fig. 19–1), we define a function OAM that is a minimum financing path representing the combinations of debt and equity by size of firm that result in the minimum average cost of capital. The average cost of capital at each point along the minimum financing path is probably not a monotonic decreasing function of size; more likely it rises slightly, or at least levels off beyond some point (Fig. 19–3).[27] If there is some minimum point, OM_p, then the marginal cost curve will cut the average cost curve at that point. However, it seems likely that for large firms the average cost function is quite flat, so that the effort of estimating the marginal cost may not be worth the bother. For smaller concerns, it may be desirable to use Weston's approach to determine a marginal cost.

Now let us introduce the real-life situation that firms increase their size by issuing blocks of debt or common stock and not the neat, proportional packages suggested by OAM. This sequential marginal financing is indicated by the dotted line about OAM in Fig. 19–1. Thus at any moment of time, a firm is likely to be out of equilibrium in the sense that its mixture of debt and equity does not provide a minimum cost of capital. However, since the

[27] However, in a study of electric utilities, Weston found no influence of size on cost of capital. Rate of growth was a significant determinant. Possibly size and rate of growth were correlated, but the data suggest that the minimum average cost-of-capital function related to size is quite flat for electric utilities. However, the cost of capital would vary as successive issues of blocks of debt and equity temporarily force the utility from the optimal financing path.

firm will move around the optimal finance mix through a series of successive approximations, it seems desirable to base capital budgeting decisions on that goal, that is the marginal cost shown in Fig. 19–3.

This analysis may explain in part why empirical studies that relate the cost of capital to ratios of debt to total capital for a given industry show a relatively flat cost-of-capital function.[28] When firms of varying size in an industry attempt to achieve capital structures providing a minimum cost of capital, those minimas will occur at different ratios of debt to total capital,

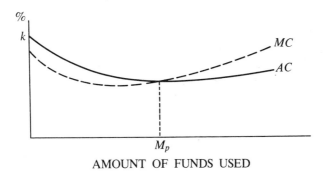

AMOUNT OF FUNDS USED

Fig. 19–3.

depending upon the size of firm. If all firms were at the optimum point for their size, an empirical study might well indicate a relatively flat cost-of-capital function, since it would reflect the function AC in Fig. 19–3. However, an empirical study of the cost of capital among firms of about the same size might show more variation of cost of capital in relation to financial leverage, since firms that are temporarily off the "optimal financing path" will pay the price in the form of a higher cost of capital.

INTERDEPENDENCE OF COST OF CAPITAL AND RATE OF RETURN

Up to this point we have been assuming that capital projects selected do not change the risk class of the firm. For small investments this is probably true. For this reason the characteristic approach has been to lower calculated rates of return, or, sometimes, to raise the hurdle rate of cost of capital to reflect any unusual risk inherent in a particular project. In general, students attempt to disassociate the prospective use of the funds from their cost.

There are certainly instances where a major investment will change the entire cost of capital function for a firm. For example, many sales finance

---

[28] Franco Modigliani and Merton H. Miller, "The Cost of Capital, Corporation Finance and the Theory of Investment," *American Economic Review*, 48 (June, 1958), pp. 281–284.

companies are diversifying into new lines of business. C.I.T. Financial Corporation has acquired firms producing X-ray equipment and greeting cards. Since the ratios of debt to equity that are suitable for a finance company are excessive (in the eyes of the market) for a manufacturer, continued diversification along these lines may materially affect the cost of capital of finance companies. As another example, a major investment in jet aircraft apparently lowered the break-even point on the airlines, with a consequent reduction in their risk class, even though they remained in the same type of business.

The basic question, then, is whether there is a cost of capital that is unique for each firm in a given risk class and independent of the project to be financed. While most cost-of-capital discussions have adopted this assumption, it does not seem to hold in important instances, While I have no ready-made solution to this problem, it appears possible that its solution must come from a series of successive approximations that will require adjustments in the long-run cost of capital to reflect the basic change in the risk class of the firm brought about by major investments. In turn, the change in cost of capital will influence the desirability of the proposed capital expenditures. As these expenditures are reduced or increased, further adjustments in the cost of capital may be required, with additional refinements to the capital-budgeting plans, and so on.[29]

My attempted integration of some of the concepts in the field of cost of capital has been deliberately non-mathematical. Hopefully, those more skilled than I am in mathematics may find thoughts here that can lead to sophisticated models. For practical operating purposes, such refinements may produce relatively slight changes in capital-budgeting decisions. The greater portion of our progress will have to come through agreement and understanding on certain basic fundamentals. That has been the objective of this paper, and even that limited objective has proved far more difficult to attain than contemplated when I accepted this assignment.

---

[29] As a possible approach see Richard S. Bower, "Finance Linkage and Capital Budgeting," *The Engineering Economist*, 7 (Winter, 1962), pp. 1–22.

20

VALUATION OF THE FIRM: EFFECTS OF UNCERTAINTY IN A MARKET CONTEXT

ALEXANDER A. ROBICHEK and STEWART C. MYERS*

Professors Robichek and Myers develop an approach to a general theory of valuation under uncertainty. They bring to bear on the approach to uncertainty in business finance recent work in portfolio analysis and in economic models of capital markets under uncertainty. They particularly utilize the materials developed by Professor Hirshleifer in his "state-preference theory." Their paper includes four dimensions relevant for the analysis of risky securities. The concept of riskiness is developed by regarding a security as a bundle of "primitive securities" each of whose contractual obligations is contingent on the occurrence of a particular state of nature.

Decisions in business finance, to the extent that they involve (*a*) the "cost of capital" as a criterion or (*b*) the value of the firm to its shareholders as an objective, depend on the valuation of the firm's securities in the market place. Yet business finance has not yet provided a theoretically satisfying, much less an empirically dependable, procedure for explaining why securities sell at certain prices but not at others.

This paper explores one important aspect of this problem: how uncertainty affects market prices of corporate securities.

The approaches to uncertainty now common in business finance are parochial. Much information latent in recent work in (*a*) portfolio analysis[1] and (*b*) economic models of capital markets under uncertainty[2] has been ignored. That this information has not been integrated with theories of business finance apparently has been because of the presumption that the applications of the theory of individual financial decision making under uncertainty to the problems of business finance remain adequate for discussion

Alexander A. Robichek and Stewart C. Myers, "Valuation of the Firm: Effects of Uncertainty in a Market Context," *Journal of Finance* (May 1966), Vol. XVI, 215–227. Reprinted by permission.

* This study was supported, in part, by funds made available by the Ford Foundation to the Graduate School of Business, Stanford University. The conclusions, opinions and other statements in this paper are those of the authors and are not necessarily those of the Ford Foundation.

[1] See Markowitz [8], Sharpe [11].

[2] Especially Sharpe [12], Arrow [1], as well as Hirshleifer's discussions of the "state-preference" framework [4, 5].

of the effects of uncertainty in a market context. A major conclusion of this paper is that this view is mistaken. Although our analysis is too eclectic to support a full-fledged theory of the market valuation of risky securities, it strongly suggests that significantly different results follow when market processes are explicitly introduced in discussions of the valuation of risky securities.

This paper is organized as follows. We first present a list of assumptions and a more nearly precise specification of what we mean by the "riskiness" of securities. We then discuss four "dimensions" relevant for analysis of the riskiness of securities in a market context. These are:

> Dimension A: Form and Dispersion of Probability Distributions of Returns;
> Dimension B: Correlation between Returns on Available Investments;
> Dimension C: Effects of Different States of Nature on the Utility Functions for Money;
> Dimension D: The Manner in which Uncertainty is Expected to be Resolved over Time.

Our analysis of these four factors suggests a number of conclusions of potential importance for business finance.

To avoid misunderstanding, we must emphasize that this paper is intended to be suggestive rather than definitive. We cheerfully admit that all flanks of our analysis cannot be defended against charges of unrealism, on the one hand, or of theoretical incompleteness, on the other. Our observations are intended to indicate (*a*) a class of problems which business finance must face if theories about the subject are to improve, and (*b*) the kinds of assumptions and procedures necessary to come to grips with these problems.

THE FRAMEWORK OF OUR DISCUSSION

The following assumptions will be made

1. A series of random variables, $\tilde{R}_1, \tilde{R}_2, \ldots, \tilde{R}_t, \ldots$, will be used to represent any stream of future returns. Any year's actual return, R_t, is defined as cash payments received by the investor on a security or portfolio, plus or minus the dollar value of capital gains or losses during the period. $\bar{R}_t$ denotes the mathematical expectation of R_t.
2. The discussion will be presented in terms of subjective probability distributions assigned by investors to the set of future states of nature. It will be assumed that these distributions are identical for all investors.[3]

---

[3] It is difficult to assess how much the argument is compromised by this assumption. When many investors approximately agree on the characteristics of a given security, it may be legitimate to speak of a "representative investor" as embodying their beliefs. For purposes of model building this is equivalent to assuming complete agreement.

However, this hypothetical investor can hardly be representative if significant differences of opinion exist. Analysis of the effects of these different opinions on market processes will have to be deferred. See, however, Lintner [7] and Berwag and Grove [2] for comments on this problem.

3. Initially, we shall assume that each investor follows a strategy with a planning horizon of one period only. That is, an investor making his portfolio decision at $t = 0$ considers (a) cash receipts in $t = 1$ and (b) the value of his portfolio at the end of $t = 1$ as a basis for assembling his portfolio. As we will note in discussing Dimension D, this does not mean that returns for later periods can be ignored. This assumption implies only that the investor expects to choose a new portfolio at the end of period $t = 1$, and that he is indifferent to the amount of trading that may be necessary in order for him to shift to his new portfolio at that time.

4. No adjustment is made for possible inflation or deflation until our discussion of Dimension C.

5. We will assume that investors are basically conservative, although not necessarily "risk-averse" in all of the many ways in which that term has been defined. The attitudes which we believe are generally regarded as conservative will be obvious in what follows.

6. We will consider how taxes may affect the analysis of this paper.

7. The possible use of short sales as a hedge against risk is not considered.

Note that we have specified the types of strategies investors are assumed to follow. Since investors' demands for particular types of securities will depend on these strategies, this is a necessary step in our analysis.[4] In a broader sense, it follows that it does not make much sense to speak of the risk of a security to an investor except with respect to his investment strategy.[5]

With this in mind, we can specify more precisely what we mean by "risk" or "riskiness."[6] We can imagine a set of possible future states of nature for each future time period, defined in such a way that specifying the state of nature which actually is to occur is equivalent to specifying the actual future values for the uncertain variables of interest to investors. In this framework, a security may be regarded as a particular bundle of contingent payments—or, in Arrow's terminology,[7] as a bundle of "primitive securities," each of which is a contract to pay one dollar contingent on the occurrence of a particular state of nature, but to pay nothing otherwise.

Given the value of payments contingent on different states of nature and given the attitudes and strategies of investors, the risk of a security is inherent in the *pattern of its returns across the various possible future states of nature*. When we refer to the risk of a security, therefore, we mean *those characteristics of this pattern which affect the value of a security to investors*.

---

[4] The one period planning horizon is chosen as a reasonable starting point. There is no presumption that the strategies considered here are necessarily optimal. In fact, the meaning of optimality is rather elusive in this context.

[5] This point may be illustrated by noting an alternative type of strategy which is apparently not unusual. "Widows and orphans" are said to be more interested in dependability of cash income over a fairly long period rather than capital gains in the near future. Their planning horizon would thus be longer than one period. If all investors had been assumed to be "widows and orphans," our analysis of risk would have had to proceed along different lines from those taken here.

[6] It should be emphasized that use of these terms here is not meant to imply Knight's [6] distinction between risk and uncertainty. According to Knight's definitions risk refers to random events subject to known probability distributions. The term uncertainty is reserved for cases where underlying probability distributions are unknown. In this sense, the world with which investors must deal is an uncertain one, since the probability distributions discussed in this paper are subjectively assessed, not objectively known.

[7] See Arrow [1].

It is important to understand the point of view embodied in this definition. Normally it is assumed that risk is something which can be defined independently of the valuation process. Thus it is often said that "risk affects value," as if the risk of a security were something that could be defined and measured *a priori*. In our view, however, risk is inseparable from valuation. When we say that one security is regarded by investors as *more risky* than another, we simply mean that the pattern of its returns across future states of nature is *less valuable* (at the margin) to a conservative investor.

Dimension A: Form and Dispersion of the Probability Distribution

We have assumed that investors agree on probabilities of occurrence of the future states of nature. Since the returns of all securities are known once the state of nature which will occur is specified, these probabilities are sufficient to derive probability distributions for the returns, $\tilde{R}_t$, of any security or portfolio of securities. These distributions are one dimension along which the risk of securities can be investigated.

In assessing the risk of the investment or portfolio yielding a random return $\tilde{R}_t$, investors will be interested in both the form of the distribution to which R_t is subject, and, given the form of the distribution, its dispersions as well. When we speak of the *form* of the distribution we will assume that this describes all its characteristics except its mean and degree of dispersion.[8]

We make this distinction in order to consider this question: how does the degree of dispersion of probability distribution assigned to expected returns affect the market values of individual securities? In our discussion we shall follow most other authors in assuming that (*a*) conservative investors attempt, other things the same, to reduce the dispersion of distributions of over-all returns on their portfolios, and (*b*) that the effects of Dimensions B, C and D (to be discussed below) can be ignored.

Our experience suggests that dispersion is normally regarded as increasing the risk of securities—i.e., making them relatively less valuable to conservative investors. This implies that the equilibrium price of securities with uncertain returns will be low enough so that investors can expect to receive a "risk premium" for investing in them.

However, the reasoning behind this conclusion is precarious unless additional assumptions are introduced. A counterargument can be made as follows. Define the expected yield on the *j*th security over the one-period planning horizon as k_j, where k_j is defined by

$$P_{j,0} = \frac{R_{j,1}}{1 + k_j}, \tag{1}$$

---

[8] In this paper we will not try to decide which type of distribution is the most appropriate. To a large extent this is an empirical question, which we could not hope to discuss adequately in a paper the conclusions of which are primarily suggestive. See, however, Fama [3].

and $P_{j,0}$ is the price of the jth security at time $t = 0$. A risk premium is said to exist if $k_j > i$, the riskless rate of interest. Suppose each investor has the opportunity to divide his portfolio without cost in any fashion among the available securities. If we assume that the returns on the various securities are uncorrelated, any investor can obtain expected future returns which are effectively certain by including enough securities in his portfolio.[9]

To show this, if x_j denotes the proportion of an individual's total investment allocated to the jth security, then $\bar{k}$, the average expected yield on the portfolio, will be given by $\sum_j x_j k_j$.

In this case, *a necessary condition for equilibrium in capital markets is that $\bar{k} = i$*, the riskless rate of interest. Otherwise, it will pay holders of riskless investments to sell riskless securities and buy the portfolio yielding $\bar{k}$. The shifts in their portfolios will tend to raise i and lower $\bar{k}$ until the equality is established. If $\bar{k} = i$, then either $k_j = i$ for *all* securities in the portfolio, or *some* securities will sell at prices such that $k_j < i$. When all possible riskless portfolios are considered, however, *the condition $k_j = i$ for each of the securities in these portfolios is necessary for equilibrium*.[10]

Obvious objections can be raised to this result. For one thing a substantial number of securities would have to be included in a portfolio in order to obtain over-all returns which are "nearly certain." At least for small investors, the higher brokerage fees of odd-lot trading would make it costly to take advantage of the law of large numbers.

Another objection to the conclusion derived above is that an insufficient number of securities with uncorrelated returns may be available to investors. It is certainly difficult to name any large number of securities with absolutely uncorrelated returns.

---

[9] We assume for the sake of this argument that securities are plentiful enough so that this result can be achieved by the law of large numbers.

[10] If, in a portfolio for which $k = i$, it happens that for some securities $k_j > i$, then $k_j < i$ for others. In this case it will pay investors to concentrate their portfolios in securities for which $k_j > i$. The operation of this motive will change prices of the securities until the equilibrium result ($k_j = i$ for all j) is achieved.

The same conclusions can also be inferred from the model recently presented by Sharpe [12]. (It should be noted that his model is based only on Dimensions A and B presented here, and assumes that the forms of the distributions of all returns are the same. Other factors, to be discussed in Dimensions C and D, are not taken into account.) The following expression can be obtained from the equilibrium conditions of Sharpe's model (by solving the last equation in footnote 22, p. 438 of Sharpe's article, for the expected yield of the security):

$$k_j = \frac{r\sigma_j}{\sigma_p}(k_p - i) + i$$

where k_p is the expected yield on the "efficient" portfolio p, which includes security j at equilibrium; σ_j and σ_p are standard deviations of the expected yields k_j and k_p; and r is the correlation coefficient between the yields on security j and the portfolio. Following the normal terminology of portfolio analysis, the portfolio p is said to be efficient if no other portfolio q exists such that either (a) $k_q \geq k_p$ and $\sigma_q < \sigma_p$ or (b) $k_q > k_p$ and $\sigma_q \leq \sigma_p$.

The risk premium of security j is, according to Sharpe's conclusions

$$\frac{r\sigma_j}{\sigma_p}(k_p - i).$$

If $r = 0$, the risk premium is zero and $k_j = i$—the conclusion we presented above.

Nevertheless, it is reasonable to predict that if some securities exist which have uncorrelated returns, there will be at least a tendency for conservative investors to regard them as relatively less risky (i.e., more valuable) than other securities, since such securities provide an opportunity to reduce the over-all risk of investors' portfolios. This would be true despite the fact that any one of these securities might be regarded as highly risky by an investor considering it independently of other securities—as would be the case if the probability distribution of its returns was transformed into a lottery on which the investor were asked to bet a substantial amount.

Dimension B: Correlation between Returns on Available Investments

In the previous section we demonstrated that under certain assumptions conservative investors will not "require" a risky premium for investing in securities which, considered individually, are risky. But it is not true, in general, that the degree of dispersion of distributions assigned to returns of individual securities does not affect their value to investors. This is so only if the returns of these securities are uncorrelated with returns of the port-folios held by investors. Dispersion of returns on individual securities is undesirable to conservative investors to the extent that positive correlation exists with respect to their portfolios; it is *desirable* to the extent that negative correlation exists.[11]

Many authors[12] have emphasized that the value of any particular security to an investor depends partly on the correlation between yearly returns on that security and the corresponding years' returns on other feasible invest-ments. An investor who is, by our definition, conservative, will attempt to reduce the over-all dispersion of returns on his portfolio; he can do so by adding to his portfolio those securities which have, for a given yield and dispersion, returns that are less positively correlated, or more negatively correlated, with returns on the investments in the original portfolio. This is the familiar argument for diversification.

Consider how an investor would evaluate a new security as a possible addition to his original portfolio. The original portfolio will offer one pattern of returns across possible future states of nature; the new security will offer another. The new security will be most effective in reducing the variability of the portfolio's pattern if the pattern of its returns is *complemen-tary* to that of the original portfolio. The term "complementary" is used to refer to a pattern which offers relatively high returns in states of nature for which returns on the original portfolio are low, and vice-versa. A pattern which is not related to the pattern of the original portfolio in any systematic way will reduce the variability of the original portfolio's pattern less than a

---

[11] Note that these conclusions are consistent with the equation given in footnote 10 above.
[12] Markowitz [8] is the leading example.

complementary one; a pattern which is similar to that of the original portfolio will have still less effect. In statistical language, securities with returns which are negatively correlated with returns of the original portfolio will tend to be preferred to securities offering returns which are uncorrelated, or positively correlated, with those of the original portfolio.

A simple example will be helpful to illustrate this. Table 20–1 shows five patterns of returns across the four *equally probable* states of nature assumed possible. Pattern 0 belongs to the original portfolio; patterns 1–4 are those of securities which our hypothetical investor is considering purchasing.

Table 20–1

| | | State | | |
Pattern	1	2	3	4
0	50	100	200	250
Security 1	5	10	20	25
Security 2	−5	5	25	35
Security 3	25	20	10	5
Security 4	35	25	5	−5

Patterns 1 and 2 are consistent with perfect positive correlation of the returns of these securities with returns on the original portfolio. Patterns 3 and 4 are consistent with perfect negative correlation.[13]

Examination of Table 20–1 reveals that the addition of one share of security 1 to the original portfolio would not change the variability of its pattern of returns—in the sense that, for each state of nature, the ratio of R_s, the contingent return for state s, to $\bar{R}$, the average return over all states, is the same for the two patterns. This is so because the *new pattern* would be uniformly *larger than* the old one by a factor of 1.1. Therefore the investor will purchase this security only if its expected yield is at least as great as the expected yield of the original portfolio. Addition of security 2, on the other hand, would increase the variability of the original portfolio—in the sense that the ratio $R_s/\bar{R}$ would vary more widely across the four states of nature for the new portfolio than for the old one. A conservative investor, therefore, would not choose security 2 unless it sold at enough of a discount relative to security 1 to offset its disadvantages in this respect.

Securities 1 and 2 thus illustrate the conclusion that a high degree of variability in the pattern of returns (i.e., a high degree of dispersion) tends to reduce the value to conservative investors of securities with patterns similar to (i.e., positively correlated with) patterns of returns on portfolios held by these investors.

The patterns of securities 3 and 4, on the other hand, are complementary to that of the original portfolio, and thus can be used to reduce the variability of its pattern. In fact, by buying ten shares of security 3, the investor could

---

[13] Two random variables are perfectly correlated if one can be predicted without error as a function of the other. In our examples, patterns 1–4 can be related to pattern 0 in this way.

obtain a portfolio with absolutely certain returns. But security 4 has a still more variable pattern of returns. The addition of only *five* shares of security 4 would suffice to give the investor a portfolio with a certain return. If securities 3 and 4 offer the same expected yield, therefore, security 4 will be preferred.

This illustrates the other side of the conclusion stated above: a high degree of variability in the pattern of returns tends to increase the value to conservative investors of securities with patterns complementary to patterns of portfolios held by these investors.

We have thus shown that our hypothetical conservative investor would rank the four securities, in descending order of desirability, 4, 3, 1, 2. That is, if all four securities could be purchased at the same price, security 4 would be preferred to security 3, and so on. We have not yet established, however, that the market prices of these four securities would conform to any particular ranking. Since not all investors hold identical portfolios at equilibrium, it does not necessarily follow that the value at the margin of a particular security will be the same to all of them.

However, if most securities have a common characteristic pattern of returns, then most portfolios will necessarily share this pattern, and our reasoning would indicate that a security offering a complementary pattern would sell at a premium in a world stocked with conservative investors. In other words, if the supply of securities with a particular type of pattern is relatively small, the value at the margin of such securities will tend to be relatively high.

In fact, securities with such complementary patterns would sell at prices high enough so that they would be expected to yield *less* than the riskless rate of interest in period $t = 1$—that is, they would offer an expected yield less than the certain yield of a government bond maturing at $t = 1$.[14] In short, "risk aversion" does not "require" that the yield on any security with uncertain returns be greater than the riskless rate.

SOME IMPLICATIONS

At least for stocks, it may not be grossly inaccurate to idealize reality in the following way:[15]

> 1. The returns of most equities are not only dependent on the characteristic pattern, but also on a "random" element unrelated to this pattern;

---

[14] Note that both securities 3 and 4 of Table 20–1 would be preferred to a riskless security if the expected yields of all three securities were the same, since the riskless security would be less effective in reducing the variability of the pattern of the investor's over-all return. Note also that this conclusion follows from the equation presented in footnote 10 above.

[15] In view of the close interdependence of the modern economy, we might expect a characteristic pattern to exist. It would not *necessarily* be closely related to the phase of the business cycle, however, even though it is tempting to think in these terms (we shall do so below for purposes of illustration). For a discussion of this idealized framework, see Sharpe [11]. See also his discussion of "systematic risk," [12], pp. 439ff.

2. For a few securities, this "random" element is so large that patterns of returns are scarcely affected by the characteristic pattern;
3. However, there are very few, if any stocks with patterns of returns which are clearly complementary to the characteristic pattern.

If these conditions hold, then there is a basis in fact for the normal view that the values of existing stocks are related to the degree of variability or dispersion of the patterns of their returns. However, if the over-all variability of the security's pattern of returns is a weighted "sum" of the variabilities of (1) the characteristic pattern and (2) a "random" element, then the risk of any stock will be less to the extent that the "random" element is predominant, since stocks with large "random" elements will be most effective in diversification.

This reasoning suggests that the cost of capital or "hurdle rate" applied by the firm as a criterion for particular investment projects should be less if the "random" element is predominant in the determination of the incremental returns of the project. For the firm's over-all cost of capital is determined, in part, by the relative weights of the characteristic pattern and the purely random variable in the firm's expected operating profits. A project with a "random" pattern of returns will have a favorable effect on this weighting. The possible implications for capital budgeting procedures are, we hope, obvious.

Dimensions A and B together form the basis for most of the discussions of risk which have advanced in the literature of finance. However, they are logically incomplete in several ways. It must be remembered, first, that analysis of the pattern of returns in terms of these dimensions does not take into account all of the information which a complete specification of the patterns would provide. The idea of the "variability" of a pattern, for instance, is simply a representation of one important characteristic of these patterns. Another important characteristic, the *forms* of the probability distributions of future returns, has not been investigated here. We shall see that still other characteristics, to be presented as Dimension C, are likely to be important, even under the assumption that in assessing demands for securities it is logically satisfactory to consider the returns for period $t = 1$ only. The implications of removing this last assumption will be investigated as Dimension D.

Dimension C: Effects of the Occurrence of Different States of Nature on the Utility of Money

In the framework used in discussing Dimensions A and B, the logic behind the portfolio decisions of investors may be generalized and idealized as follows:

1. The investor observes the prices of the given securities, which he regards as bundles of returns to be received contingent on the possible occurrence of particular states of nature one period hence.

> 2. Given the set of available securities, the investor chooses a portfolio so as to achieve that feasible distribution of returns across future states of nature which may be considered optimal—in the sense of maximizing the expected utility of these returns.

To be sure, this statement vastly simplifies the logical and computational problems of deciding what is in fact optimal. We cannot tackle these general problems here, but they can be illuminated in a limited way.

Consider the relative value of the contingent returns, R_s, one of which will be received at $t = 1$ if a certain portfolio is purchased at $t = 0$. Given a utility function of these returns, our idea of "conservative" with respect to Dimensions A and B—equivalent to "desiring to reduce the variability of the pattern of the portfolio's returns"—is implied by a monotonically increasing utility function rising at a decreasing rate (i.e., $U'(R_s) > 0$ and $U''(R_s) < 0$). Under these assumptions the same qualitative results would be reached if the analysis of Dimensions A and B were recast in terms of the expected utility of securities and portfolios to investors.[16]

However, is it sensible in general to assume that a single utility function is appropriate to express the relative value of returns in each of the states of nature under consideration? We think not, for two sorts of reasons:

> 1. Since the independent variable R_s is expressed in money terms, the utility of this return is likely to be affected by inflation or deflation, which themselves may be regarded as contingent on the occurrence of particular states of nature. If booms are inflationary and recessions deflationary, we would predict that, for a given return R^*, the purchasing power of R^*_{boom} would be less than $R^*_{\text{recession}}$ and that $U_{\text{boom}}(R^*)$ will be less than $U_{\text{recession}}(R^*)$. That is, the appropriate utility function may be contingent, in a predictable way, on the state of nature being considered.[17]
> 2. There is reason to suspect that the utility function appropriate for the evaluation of a given return R_s^* may also depend on other aspects of the economic conditions associated with state s. For instance, an investor who is conservative (in the common-sense meaning of the term) would regard a given dollar return received in a recession more highly to the extent that he would be exposed to the possibility of unemployment in recessions. Other contingent risks affecting utility functions are easy to propose.

This possibility is logically separate from our earlier conclusion that stocks with patterns of returns that are complementary to the characteristic pattern will tend to be relatively more valuable or less "risky."

The effects of this dimension on the value of securities in a market context can be traced out along the same lines taken in discussing Dimensions A and B. Whether consideration of this dimension changes the general

---

[16] Since the value or expected utility of a portfolio to an investor would still be inversely related to the "variability" of the pattern of returns across the possible states of nature in $t = 1$.

[17] It is also possible to adjust for inflation by expressing R_s in "real" terms, although this strategy may allow the analyst to dispose of the effects of possible inflation or deflation on security prices too simply. This factor is so often ignored (e.g., in discussions of the "cost of capital") that it merits much more extensive discussion in the literature. For some exploratory comments, see Robichek and Myers [11], pp. 100, 106–07.

conclusions reached earlier depends, first, on whether utility functions of different investors shift in the same manner when different states of nature are considered. If these shifts are parallel for "most investors," the utilities of, and demands for, a *given* (dollar amount of) contingent return will tend to be higher for particular states of nature, and lower for others. This would enhance the market value of securities offering relatively high returns in those states of nature for which contingent returns are relatively highly valued. In other words, the value of certain patterns of contingent returns would be increased, and securities offering such patterns would sell at higher prices, other things being equal. On the other hand, if the shifts in utility functions are not mostly in the same direction, then more detailed analysis will be needed to predict the effect of this Dimension on market value.

Supposing that investors' utility functions do shift in parallel ways when different states of nature are considered, it is still possible that patterns which are valuable from the point of view of Dimension C may not be especially valuable in terms of Dimensions A and B. This would be the case, for instance, if patterns valuable in the terms of Dimension C were similar to the characteristic pattern of returns postulated in our discussion of Dimensions A and B.[18] The opposite conclusions would follow, however, if utility functions of most investors depended on the various possible states of nature in such a way that a given dollar return was valued more highly in "recessions," and if most stocks (dominated in some degree by the characteristic pattern) paid low returns in recessions. In this case the value of securities offering relatively high returns in recessions would be doubly enhanced, and the general conclusions of our discussion of Dimensions A and B would be reinforced.

Dimension D: The Manner in Which Uncertainty is Expected to be Resolved over Time

Thus far we have assumed that investors' strategies all have one period planning horizons. Even in this simple case, of course, the characteristics of streams of returns over time have to be taken into account. For the return on any security during $t = 1$ depends in part on its price at the end of this period, which depends on the pattern of returns in $t = 2$, which in turn depends on the appropriate pattern for $t = 3$, and so on. Therefore all future returns are logically relevant, even if the investor expects to hold any given portfolio for one period only. Nevertheless, the assumed planning horizon has allowed us to concentrate on the risk of one particular outcome—the cash receipts and capital gains investors receive in $t = 1$. We have considered only one action—the choice of a portfolio in $t = 0$—and one outcome.

---

[18] In fact, Hirshleifer has pointed out that portfolios which would be inefficient if assessed in terms of Dimensions A and B might still be preferred if risk is asserted in terms of Dimension C as well. However, he does not argue that this will be the case usually . See [5], pp. 26ff.

We have not been forced to analyze explicitly the risks inherent in a *sequence* of actions and outcomes.

The analysis of value in these broader terms is very difficult. We will offer a few comments here on the special effects of uncertainty when investors' strategies include plans to hold securities for two or more periods.

The broad ideas presented above remain relevant, since we can analyze the value of a set of contingent returns for any given future period in terms of Dimensions A, B and C.[19]

If investors constantly attempt to obtain securities with "undervalued" streams of future dividends (where the effect of uncertainty on value is examined in terms of Dimensions A, B and C), then it makes sense to speak of the equilibrium market price of a security as representing the present value of the dividend stream over feasible holding periods.[20] However, the process of adjustment to equilibrium presumes that investors plan on holding securities for more than one period.[21]

In this context, however, there are other aspects of uncertainty which may affect value. We will now consider one factor: the manner in which uncertainty may be resolved over time.

As Samuelson established,[22] in a world of certainty the equilibrium prices of all securities will change in such a way that the total return on each security (cash payments plus capital gains or losses) in any given period t will be $i_t V_{t-1}$, where i_t is the (unique) short-term interest rate for period t and V_{t-1} is the market value of the security at the end of period $t-1$. Thus each security will yield exactly the same rate of return in every future period t, providing that it has some value at the end of period $t-1$. This amounts to an identical pattern of rates of return across time for all securities, as long as the securities continue to offer some return.

Can investors make a similar assumption about future rates of returns expected on risky securities? Such an assumption is, in general, not justified since the pattern of returns expected over time depends on the manner in which uncertainty is resolved over time, and securities differ in this respect. Information which affects investors' uncertainty about the future performance of securities may become available at any time. This information affects prices of the stocks, and thus the realized capital gain in any particular period.[23] The timing, amount and content of this information is, of course,

---

[19] With the qualification that the value of any particular period's dividend cannot be analyzed apart from the characteristics of the over-all dividend stream. Dividends to be received in successive periods can rarely be considered *independent* random variables. It would be formally correct, however, to regard each of the various possible sequences of dividends to be contingent on a particular (sequence of) states of nature, and to consider each of these sequences as a contingent return. The pattern of these dividend sequences across the possible (sequences of) states of nature could then be analyzed. See Markowitz, [8].

[20] Or at least to hold the security until its market price shifts into accord with the value to them of the dividend stream.

[21] We do not have to assume that *all* investors are willing to adopt this sort of strategy.

[22] See Samuelson [10]. Also Robichek and Myers [9], p. 12.

[23] For an example, see Robichek and Myers [9], 86–92.

itself uncertain, but investors nevertheless may have good reason to expect the characteristics of the flows of information about different securities to differ substantially.

With this in mind, consider a simple illustrative example. Compare two securities, A and B, which are assumed to pay only one future dividend at time $t = T$. Further, assume that, on the basis of information available at $t = 0$, investors regard both the expected dividends on the two securities *and* the subjective probability distributions of these dividends as identical. This would be the result if, say, the dividend to be paid on each security is generated by one spin of a roulette wheel. Once the wheel is spun, the return is certain. Taking this to be the case, we assume, further, that the spin determining A's dividend occurs in $t = 1$, but that the spin for B does not occur until $t = T$.

Are these sufficient conditions for the two stocks to sell at identical prices at $t = 0$? Note that this would be the prediction if the value of these securities was analyzed in the framework of Dimensions A, B and C. However, investors would value A more highly than B if they regarded the early resolution of uncertainty as valuable.

It should be noted that early resolution of uncertainty allows the investor more opportunity to adjust his personal investment decision to compensate for possibly unfavorable outcomes, or to take advantage of possible favorable outcomes. It may be, therefore, that the *length* of time within which future returns are subject to uncertainty is an important factor from the point of view of the investor. Thus the resolution of uncertainty in $t = 1$ will provide information useful to investors planning their investment strategy. We might infer from this sort of crude but suggestive reasoning that the present value of security B would be less than that of security A.

These considerations depend on investors recognizing that their future portfolio decisions may be affected by uncertainty regarding the ultimate value of security B if that security is purchased at $t = 0$. However, the investor is not compelled to continue to hold security B if at some point it becomes undesirable for him to do so. Thus the risk of security B cannot be separated from the future market value of the lottery on which it is based. If an individual's investment strategy calls for the sale of securities in some future contingencies, the degree of possible fluctuation in the prices of given securities will affect their value as marginal additions of the investor's portfolio. Moreover, the manner in which uncertainty is resolved over time affects the degree of possible fluctuation.

To see this, note that, after $t = 1$, the price of security A is uncertain only to the extent that the riskless interest rate may change. The price of B will also be affected by changes in the interest rate, but by another consideration as well. That is that the market value of the lottery on which B is based is itself uncertain, since investors' demands for marginal amounts of a given lottery depend on many factors—e.g., their wealth, their risk attitudes, the nature and price of alternative securities—which cannot, in general, be presumed to be constant over time. We would infer, therefore, that the market value of security B would be subject to greater fluctuation over time than A, and thus that A may well sell at a higher price if conservative investors predominate in the market.

Since actual securities differ in the same ways as securities A and B, we believe that Dimension D is relevant in real life. There will, of course, be many problems in generalizing the reasoning used in analyzing the simple illustrative example just presented.

CONCLUDING NOTE

It is no doubt obvious to the reader that we have only scratched the surface of the problem of developing a general theory of valuation under uncertainty. Our "dimensions" are no more than attempts to identify the most important qualitative characteristics of patterns of contingent returns across possible state-time combinations. We hope this labelling process will help improve the focus of investigations to follow, and that our exploratory analyses will indeed prove suggestive.

To conclude, we will cite three areas in which the analysis in this paper is the most incomplete:

1. What investment strategies do individuals and/or institutions actually follow? How should the risk of different securities be judged in light of these strategies?
2. What market imperfections are relevant in assessing the effects of uncertainty on valuation? For instance, do transactions costs significantly compromise the ability of investors to hedge against risk?
3. Some of the assumptions used in this paper lack realism. For example, we assumed that subjective probability distributions assigned to future states of nature are identical for all investors. How would our conclusions be changed by different assumptions about investor behavior?

REFERENCES

[1] ARROW, KENNETH J., "The Role of Securities in the Optimal Allocation of Risk Bearing," *Review of Economic Studies*, Vol. 31, 1963–1964, 91–96.
[2] BERWAG, G. O., and M. F. GROVE, "On Capital Asset Prices: Comment," *Journal of Finance*, XX, 1, March 1965, 89–93. (See also, William F. Sharpe, "Reply," *Ibid.*, 94–95.)
[3] FAMA, EUGENE J., "The Behavior of Stock Market Prices," *Journal of Business*, XXXVIII, 1, Jan. 1965, 34–105.
[4] HIRSHLEIFER, J., "Efficient Allocation of Capital in an Uncertain World," *American Economic Review*, LIV, 3 (proceedings), May 1964, 77–85.
[5] Hirshleifer, J., "Investment Decision Under Uncertainty," U.C.L.A., 1964, mimeo.

[6] KNIGHT, FRANK H., *Risk Uncertainty & Profit*, Boston & New York: Houghton Mifflin, 1921.

[7] LINTNER, J., "Dividends, Earnings, Leverage, Stock Prices and the Supply of Capital to Corporations," *Review of Economics and Statistics*, XLIV, 3, August 1962, 243–269.

[8] MARKOWITZ, HARRY, *Portfolio Selection*, Monograph 16, Cowles Foundation for Research in Economics at Yale University. New York: John Wiley & Sons, Inc., 1959.

[9] ROBICHEK, ALEXANDER, A., and STEWART C. MYERS. *Optimal Financing Decisions*, Englewood Cliffs, N. J.: Prentice-Hall, Inc., 1965.

[10] SAMUELSON, P. A., "Some Aspects of the Pure Theory of Capital," *Quarterly Journal of Economics*, LI, 3, May 1937, 469–496.

[11] SHARPE, W. F., "A Simplified Model for Portfolio Analysis," *Management Science*, Vol. 9, No. 2, Jan. 1963, 277–293.

[12] SHARPE, WILLIAM F., "Capital Asset Prices: A Theory of Market Equilibrium Under Conditions of Risk," *Journal of Finance*, XIX, 8, Sept. 1964, 425–442.

PART VI

Internal Financing and Dividend Policy

21

DIVIDEND POLICY: ITS INFLUENCE ON THE VALUE OF THE ENTERPRISE

JAMES E. WALTER

This paper provides a well-balanced summary of many of the issues concerning corporate dividend policy. The author's analysis specifies the conditions under which dividends affect the value of the firm. He then discusses the reasons why in the real world these conditions are not met. Professor Walter also makes penetrating comments on the problems of statistical testing of alternative models.

The question before the house is whether dividends are in some sense of the word weighted differently from retained earnings at the margin in the minds of marginal investors. As evidenced by the current literature on the subject, the answer is by no means self-evident.

Although the problem that confronts us can be approached in a variety of ways, our preference is to commence with net cash flows from operations and to consider the effect of additions to, and subtractions from, these flows upon stock values.[1] Not only does this starting point bypass certain measurement problems, but it also directs attention to the relevant variables in a manner that other approaches may not.

Net cash flows from operations are available for (1) the payment of interest and principal on debt or the equivalent and (2) capital expenditures and dividend payments. Operating cash flows can, of course, be supplemented in any period by debt or equity financing. Debt financing creates obligations to pay out cash in future periods and thereby reduces cash flows available for capital expenditures and dividends in those periods. Equity financing, in turn, diminishes the pro rata share of total cash flows available for dividends and reinvestment.

James E. Walter, "Dividend Policy: Its Influence on the Value of the Enterprise," *Journal of Finance* (May 1963), Vol. XVIII, 280–291. Reprinted by permission.

[1] As a point of departure, *net cash flows from operations* lie somewhat between (1) net cash flow and (2) net operating income. See, for example, Bodenhorn [1]. For an illustrative breakdown and an explanation of the manner in which net operating cash flows are derived from balance sheets and income statements, refer to Chap. 11 of Walter [12].

The stockholder shares in the operating cash flows of each period to the degree that cash dividends are declared and paid and in future cash flows insofar as they are reflected in the market price of the stock.[2] In like fashion, the purchaser of a share of stock acquires (1) a finite stream of anticipated cash dividends and (2) an anticipated market price at the end of his holding period. The market price of the stock at any time can be said to be determined by the expectations of marginal investors (as these anticipations pertain to the dividend stream and to the terminal market price) and by their system of weighting the possible outcomes per period and through time.

To focus directly upon the potential influence of variations in dividend policy in this scheme of things, it is useful, first, to draw an analogy to the stream-splitting approach to the cost of capital. Consideration is then afforded (1) the conditions under which adjustments in dividend payout exert no effect upon stock price and (2) the consequences of modifying these conditions to take account of the economic power of large corporations and other aspects of observed behavior. The final item treated in this article is that of statistical testing.

The assumptions that prevail throughout the analysis are commonplace. One is that the satisfaction which investors derive from owning stock is wholly (or almost wholly) monetary in character. A second is that investors do the best that they can; they operate, however, in a competitive capital market and are unable to stack the results.

Corporate management—we may add—is also keenly aware of the potential impact of its actions upon stock price (if only because of stock options). Management may nonetheless be confronted with such *mixed* motivations as self-preservation and avoidance of antitrust action. The consequence is that maximization of stock price need not be the sole objective.[3]

So far as uncertainty is concerned, it is supposed that—unless otherwise stated—people think whatever they think about the future. Whether this assumption is appropriate remains to be seen.

No attempt is made in this treatment of dividend policy to run the gamut from perfect foresight to generalized uncertainty. Papers by Miller and Modigliani [10] and Lintner [7]—among others—have already proceeded along these lines. Rather, the intention is to show where dividends fit into the underlying analytical scheme, to spotlight certain assumptions that underlie recent statements pertaining to the neutrality of dividend policy, and to propose extensions in the theory designed to recognize deficiencies in the perfectly competitive model.

---

[2] It almost goes without saying that an existing shareholder periodically compares the objective market price with his subjective version of anticipated dividend streams and terminal prices to determine whether to hold or liquidate. In this respect, his behavior resembles that of a prospective buyer.

[3] For justification, we have only to refer to the statistics on concentration of economic power.

ANALOGY TO COST OF CAPITAL

Before the thrust shifted to dividends, the basic issue in the cost of capital discussion was one of dividing the stream of operating cash flows (or some reconcilable variant thereof) between debt and equity in such a manner as to maximize the market value of the enterprise. Modigliani and Miller [8], it may be remembered, dramatized the stream-splitting aspect by drawing an analogy to the price effect of separating the whole milk into cream and skim milk. Their contention that, even in the face of institutional limitations, the farmer cannot gain by splitting the milk stream was subsequently subjected to empirical testing by Durand [3] and shown to be invalid.

When dividends enter the picture, the issue becomes one of dividing the stream of operating cash flows among debt, dividends, and reinvestment in such a way as to achieve the same result. The principal difference in the character of the analysis is that it may no longer be feasible to assume that the size and shape of the stream of operating cash flows is independent of the manner in which it is subdivided.[4]

Much the same as contractual interest payments and other financial outlays, the continuation of cash dividends as their prevailing (or regular) rate can be—and commonly is—assigned a priority by management.[5] In such instances, the burden of oscillations in operating cash flows is placed upon lower-priority outlays, namely, capital and related expenditures, unless management is both willing and able to compensate by adjusting the level of external financing.[6] Even if management is willing to seek funds outside the firm, moreover, the uncertainties inherent in the terms under which external financing can be obtained in the future reduce the likelihood of such action in the event of operating cash deficiencies in any period. The upshot is that current cash dividends may well be capitalized somewhat differently from anticipated future cash flows (net of current dividends, to avoid double-counting).

It may be observed that the relative instability of expenditures designed to augment future cash flows shows up even in the aggregate. The change from year to year for new plant and equipment averaged 19 percent for all manufacturing corporations in the post-war period (to 1961), as compared with 9 percent for cash dividends. The maximum declines from one year to

---

[4] Although the milk-separating analogy implies that the dimensions of the stream are unaffected by its division between debt and equity, even this need not be a fundamental difference in character. As evidenced by Donaldson [2], decisions by management to borrow or not to borrow sometimes affect growth, that is, the level of future cash flows.

[5] Cf., for example, Lintner [6], in which observed corporate behavior involves gradual adjustments of dividends to earnings and "greater reluctance to reduce than to raise dividends . . . ."

[6] The term "capital and related expenditures" refers to all outlays that affect operating cash flows over several periods. Either by reason of previous commitments or because of their importance to the continued operation of the business, certain elements of these expenditures may have priorities that equal or exceed those connected with the payment of cash dividends.

the next were 40 percent for new plant and equipment and but 2 percent for dividends.

Again, as in the case of debt versus equity, investor reactions to dividend policy changes can nullify in whole or in part their price effect. Whenever the stockholder is dissatisfied with the dividend payout, the balance between present and future income can be redressed by buying or selling shares of stock and perhaps by other means as well (for instance, by "lending" or "borrowing" on the same *risk* terms that cash dividends are paid). If dividends are deemed insufficient, the desired proportion of current income can be obtained by periodically selling part of the share owned. If current income is too high, cash dividends can be used to acquire additional shares of stock.

The one thing that shareholders cannot do through their purchase and sale transactions is to negate the consequences of investment decisions by management. If—as may well be the case—investment decisions tend to be linked with dividend policy, their neglect in the analysis of dividend effects seems inappropriate.

CONDITIONS FOR NO DIVIDEND EFFECT

The conditions under which changes in dividend payout have minimal influence upon stock values can now be stated. For the most part, they follow from the logics of stream-splitting.

1. *Condition No. 1: The level of future cash flows from operations (that is, the growth rate) is independent of the dividend-payout policy.* In essence, this condition implies that the impact of a change in dividend payout upon operating cash flows will be *exactly* offset (or negated) by a corresponding and opposite change in supplemental (or external) financing.

For those who believe that the cost of capital is unaffected by the capital structure, either debt or equity financing is a legitimate means of neutralizing dividend policy changes. For those who believe otherwise, an increase in dividends can be offset only by the sale of equity shares. In the latter instance, then, the capital structure must also be taken as independent of the dividend-payout policy.

If attention is confined to offsetting transactions in equity shares for the sake of simplicity and generality, the following result obtains: An increase in dividend payout will leave operating cash flows unchanged in the aggregate, but the share of future cash flows accruing to existing stockholders will decline, since additional stock has to be sold to finance the planned capital outlays. The existing shareholder can, of course, reconstitute this former pro rata position by purchasing shares in the market with his incremental dividends.

Implicit in these remarks is the presumption that the market completely capitalizes anticipated growth in operating cash flows. New shares are thus acquired at a price that returns new investors *only* the going market rate for the relevant class of risks. The present value of extraordinary returns from investment by the corporation goes to existing stockholders (or whoever was around at the time when the prospect of these returns was first recognized by the market), rather than to new shareholders.

To the degree that the anticipated level of operating cash flows, that is, the growth rate, is connected with the dividend payout for one reason or another, the market value of the firm may be conditioned by variations in dividend payout. The policy changes must, of course, be unexpected, and their price effect hinges at least partly upon the relation between the *internal* and *market* rates of return. If the former exceeds the latter, the present value of a dollar employed by the firm (other things being equal) will be greater than a dollar of dividends distributed and invested elsewhere. This issue was considered in my 1956 paper [11].

Condition No. 1 can readily be extended to take account of tax differentials. The amended version is that operating cash flows *net* of taxes paid thereon by shareholders are unaffected by the dividend payout. As things stand, this criterion simply does not hold; neither—it might be added—does the corresponding condition hold in the case of debt versus equity.[7]

2. *Condition No. 2: The weights employed are independent of the dividend-payout policy.* In other words, the discount factors or weights, that is, the ratios of indifference values between one period and the next, are invariant with respect to changes in dividend payout.

Gordon [4] argues that the weights employed must also be constant between periods and that such is unlikely to be the case under uncertainty. That is to say, looking forward from period zero, the ratios of the indifference values between periods 0 and 1, 1 and 2, and so on have to be all the same.

In order to evaluate this possible addition to Condition No. 2, it is pertinent to recall Condition No. 1. If the level of total operating cash flows is unaffected by the policy revision, a change in current cash dividends will alter the stockholder's stake in future cash flows. The gain or loss in current dividends will just equal the gain or loss in the present value of future cash flows (or dividends, if you wish), provided that the system of weights remains unchanged. Gordon's point is thus unacceptable because the firm has to go into the market for funds to replace those paid out in dividends and, in so doing, has to pay the market rate.

Returning to the question of the independence of the weights used from the dividend-payout policy, a change in dividend payout undoubtedly disturbs the investors in that stock to some extent unless the modification was anticipated previously. Insofar as costs of one kind or another, indivisibilities, and other factors prevent the shareholders thus activated from completely

---

[7] The price effect of tax differentials may well be less than might be supposed. For example, the marginal tax rates implied in a comparison of recent yields on tax-exempts of high quality with those on United States government securities are on the order of 15–25 percent.

reconstituting their *old* position and thereby give rise to a new and different equilibrium point, the weights employed will adjust in some measure. The role played by friction in the system is, however, well known, and there is little need to dwell upon this aspect.

More significant, perhaps, is the fact that the substitution of future cash flows for present dividends superimposes an element of market risk upon the basic uncertainty of the operating cash-flow stream. As contrasted with cash dividends in which the stockholder receives a dollar for each dollar declared, there is no telling what price the shareholder will realize in the market at any given time for his stake in future cash flows.

It is, of course, true that the corporation would confront the same market risk if it—rather than the shareholder—were forced to enter the capital market. It is also true that realized prices may average out over a period of time. The fact remains that the firm may well be better able to adjust for— as well as to assume—this class of risk.

Whether further conditions ought to be introduced is a moot point. A recent article by John Lintner [7], for example, concludes that "generalized uncertainty" is itself sufficient to insure that shareholders "will *not* be indifferent to whether cash dividends are increased (or reduced) by substituting new equity issues for retained earnings to finance given capital budgets."

As a generalization, this conclusion is suspect, for it appears to be inconsistent with a logical extension of Lintner's earlier analysis under idealized uncertainty. It is difficult to see why two or two million investors cannot be indifferent at a given price for a variety of reasons. If so, generalized uncertainty can—but perhaps need not—produce the same *surface* result as idealized uncertainty.[8]

In any event, Condition No. 2 is sufficiently broad to embrace the foregoing aspect of the uncertainty issue. To the degree that Lintner's propositon is valid, generalized uncertainty produces an effect that resembles that associated with the presence of costs and frictions in the system.

IMPERFECT COMPETITION, REGULATED ENTERPRISE, AND NON-ECONOMIC CONSIDERATIONS

That the conditions for the no dividend effect fail to hold in certain important respects has already been established here and elsewhere. At this stage, there is little point in discussing further the consequences of differences in tax treatment, new-issue and other costs associated with external financing, and uncertainty itself (although the *on balance* effect will be considered toward the end of the paper). It is nonetheless relevant—in view of their neglect in the literature—to extend the examination of dividend effects

---

[8] To add to the confusion, moreover, see n. 35 in Lintner [7].

beyond the oft-used competitive model that presupposes rational behavior in the traditional economic sense and to consider the influence of such things as management leeway, economic slack, and intramarginal pricing policies. The following remarks represent a preliminary effort in this direction.

In the bulk of corporations with which it is possible to deal statistically, management has considerable leeway in decision making. Their histories of earnings and dividends—not to mention their economic power—are such that their survival in the foreseeable future seemingly does not hinge upon single modes of behavior. The presence of generalized uncertainty implies, moreover, that there is often no best *visible* course of action.

The frequently observed association between dividend-payout policy, capital structure, and rate of growth is a useful case in point; the survival of the corporation ordinarily does not depend, in the short run at least, upon any specific rate of growth. The prime considerations affecting growth, apart from profit opportunities, are (1) the willingness of corporations to go into the public market place for additional funds and (2) their attitude toward dividends (including their willingness to return unneeded funds to the investors).

For firms that are reluctant to get involved in external financing (and there appear to be many), then, the burden of expansion rests upon residual internal sources, that is, operating cash flows *less* cash dividends and debt servicing *net* of additions to debt. Decisions to increase or decrease dividends thus condition the value of the enterprise as long as the returns on new investments differ from the market rate.

The sword cuts both ways. Wherever the available investment opportunities are unable to earn their keep, the specter of liquidating dividends or repurchase of shares or debt retirement arises. If there is no debt outstanding and if the repurchase of shares is not contemplated, the burden of liquidation falls upon dividend payout.

The fact that many of the corporations that normally constitute the statistical samples used in testing dividend hypotheses are characterized by negatively sloping demand curves is also worth noting. Suppose, for instance, that such firms do not charge what the traffic will bear in the sense of equating discounted marginal revenues with discounted marginal costs. Instead, let us assume that they employ some sort of a full-cost pricing policy.

Insofar as these companies assign priorities to the payment of dividends and regard them as a cost (that is, as an obligation of the firm that should be met if possible), the dividend-payout policy will affect stock prices. Decisions to alter the dividend payout under the full-costing approach will, sooner or later, be reflected in product prices (although the impact may be barely visible to the naked eye). If the new prices more nearly approach optimum prices from a profit-maximization standpoint, the effect is to increase stock values. If the reverse obtains, values diminish.

The foregoing consideration may be especially significant in the case of regulated companies whose prices are set by edict rather than by competitive forces. The dividends that regulatory bodies explicitly or implicitly permit to be incorporated in the elements that determine product or service prices will be reflected in stock values.

Closely connected with, but extending beyond, the matter of product or service pricing is the question of operating slack. Our experience has been that most profitable firms are able in some measure to curtail their non-operating and operating outlays without interfering with future cash flows. To the extent that a change in dividend-payout policy conditions the amount of slack in the system, the value of the firm is modified by such changes.

The impact of a revision in dividend policy need not show up immediately; it may await a softness in operating cash flows. As mentioned previously, Lintner [6] and others cite evidence that some fraction of cash dividends is commonly placed well up on the priority scale. The upshot is that managements' reactions to unanticipated reductions in operating cash flows may lead not only to the adjustment of lower-priority outlays but also to the elimination of slack from the system before dividend-payout policies (once established) are altered.

In summary, it is not our purpose to overemphasize the importance of the foregoing extension of the competitive model. The point is simply that hypothesis building in this area has barely begun to scratch the surface. With this in mind, let us turn to the important matter of statistical testing.

STATISTICAL TESTING

The woods are currently replete with statistical analyses designed to demonstrate the significance (or non-significance) of the diverse factors that may influence stock prices. While it is not our aim to add further to the mounting pile, it is meaningful to mention certain problems of a statistical nature, referred to in the recent literature, that have a bearing on the testing of most hypotheses and, in particular, on the testing of an imperfectly competitive model. Specifically, the comments that follow focus upon the notion of a random variable and collinearity.

In their 1958 article [8], Modigliani and Miller alluded to the peril of relying upon "a single year's profits as a measure of expected profits." Later [9], they argued—as have others—that investors may accept current dividends as an indirect measure of profit expectations.

The difficulties inherent in the use of a random variable to reveal expectations are well known. The realized value of a random variable in any period is ordinarily but one of several values that might have obtained; it may bear little relation—in any visible sense of the word—to the underlying expectation. With this in mind, recent studies have tended to employ averages of one kind or another for the earnings variable. Kolin [5], using an exponential weighting system, has found earnings thus measured to be superior to current dividends in explaining the relative valuation of stocks.

Notwithstanding the fact that current dividends test out more significantly than current earnings, it is important to remember that they, too, are random variables. There is on the surface (apart from their relative stability) little more to recommend current dividends as a measure of expected dividends than there is to presuppose that current earnings adequately reflect antcipated earnings.

Looking to Lintner's earlier work [6], in which dividends were said to adjust gradually to a target payout ratio, an interesting and relevant reversal of the information-content proposition comes to mind. It is entirely possible (as well as quite reasonable) for some weighted average of earnings to be a good surrogate for dividend expectations. In other words, the improved results obtained by Kolin [5] may well be entirely consistent with the *dividend* hypothesis.

In a subsequent piece [10], Miller and Modigliani remarked upon the omission of relevant variables. Pointing a critical finger at certain studies (one of mine and two of Durand's were cited!), they stipulated that "no general prediction is made (or can be made) by the theory [i.e., theirs] about what will happen to the dividend coefficient if the crucial growth term is omitted."[9] Except by oblique footnote reference to Gordon's work, however, they neglected to add that specification of the dividend coefficient may be difficult even if a growth term is included.

The issue in question is *co-linearity*. In his analysis of a linear function that includes both dividends and earnings, Gordon [4] pointed to the instability present in the coefficients whenever a strong correlation existed between two explanatory variables. His finding was: "They [i.e., the coefficients] vary over a very wide range and they cannot be used to make reliable estimates on the variation in share price with each variable." Kolin [5], in turn, referred to the danger of a "severe loss of accuracy due to near singularity of the correlation matrix of independent variables that would occur if the two highly co-linear variables were present in the same regression." His concern was with the stochastic properties that might be introduced by computer programs that treat "all digits of the words that are input to the inversion program as error free digits."

It follows that the correlation between dividend payout and growth (that is, the level of future cash flows), which seems likely to exist in many instances, contributes to the difficulty of interpreting results obtained from regression analyses. At the extreme, as Miller and Modigliani [10] affirmed, there may be "no way to distinguish between the effect of dividend policy and investment policy."

---

[9] Actually, my study should not be castigated on this score, for it incorporated variables that measure both growth and internal rate of return.

Other pitfalls to statistical testing readily come to mind. Perhaps the most significant (in the context of this paper) is the character of the sample used in relation to the hypothesis being tested. More specifically, it seems incongruous to utilize samples drawn from the universe of either regulated monopolies or very large corporations to test competitive behavior.

CONCLUSIONS

The implication of the foregoing treatment is that the choice of dividend policies almost always affects the value of the enterprise. The general conditions for neutrality are simply not satisfied in the world as we know it. The dimensions of the cash flow stream (both before and after account is taken of taxes imposed on recipients of dividends and capital gains) are conditioned by dividend-payout policy; efforts by investors to negate the effects of policy changes are frequently of limited avail; and so on.

In the real world (again, as we know it), it is insufficient to contemplate the effects of dividends under pefectly (or even purely) competitive circumstances. The fact that a great many firms exercise some control over their own destinies deserves to be recognized. Once the possibility of imperfections is admitted, the potential association between dividends and the level of future cash flows, among other things, becomes clear.

Standard objections to dividend neutrality, that is, differences in tax treatment and costs of external financing, ordinarily favor the retention of earnings. Interdependence between dividend-payout policy and capital outlays, on the other hand, can work either way; it all depends on the profitability of the enterprise.

Statistical analyses designed to support the "pure earnings" hypothesis—or any other hypothesis, for that matter—remain ambiguous. For one thing, uncertainties exist as to precisely what is being measured. For another, the closer the linkage between dividend policy and dimensions of the total stream, the less meaningful are the coefficients attached to each independent variable.

Be that as it may, we are not opposed to statistical analyses. What we do say, however, is that judgment must ultimately rest on the power of the theory generated.

REFERENCES

[1] BODENHORN, D., "On the Problem Of Capital Budgeting," *Journal of Finance*, XIV (December, 1959), 493–92.
[2] DONALDSON, G., *Corporate Debt Capacity* (Boston: Harvard Business School, 1961).

[3] DURAND, D., "The Cost of Capital in an Imperfect Market: A Reply to Modigliani and Miller," *American Economic Review*, Vol. XLIX (June, 1959).

[4] GORDON, M., *The Investment, Financing and Valuation of the Corporation* (Homewood, Ill.: R. D. Irwin, 1962).

[5] KOLIN, M., "The Relative Price of Corporate Equity with Particular Reference to Investor Valuation of Retained Earnings and Dividends" (unpublished manuscript).

[6] LINTNER, J., "Distribution of Incomes of Corporations among Dividends, Retained Earnings and Taxes," *American Economic Review*, XLVI (May, 1956), 97–113.

[7] ———. "Dividends, Earnings, Leverage, Stock Prices and the Supply of Capital to Corporations," *Review of Economics and Statistics*, XLIV (August, 1962), 243–70.

[8] MODIGLIANI, F., and M. MILLER, "The Cost of Capital, Corporation Finance and the Theory of Investment," *American Economic Review*, XLVIII (June, 1958, 261–97.

[9] ———. "The Cost of Capital. Corporation Finance and the Theory of Investment: Reply," *ibid.*, XLIV (September, 1959), 655–69.

[10] ———. "Dividend Policy, Growth, and the Valuation of Shares," *Journal of Business*, XXXIV (October, 1961), 411–33.

[11] WALTER, J., Dividend Policies and Common Stock Prices," *Journal of Finance*, XI (March, 1956), 29–41.

[12] ———. *The Investment Process* (Boston: Harvard Business School, 1962), chap. xi.

22

FINANCING DECISIONS OF THE FIRM

EUGENE M. LERNER and WILLARD T. CARLETON

In this article, Professors Lerner and Carleton make a number of significant contributions to capital budgeting and the cost of capital. The risk factor which provides a measure of the trade-off between the degree of leverage and the capitalization rate is discussed explicitly. In addition, the authors emphasize that corporate financial decisions take place within an economic environment and must be related to the prevailing conditions and the product market in which the firm sells its output and to the factor markets from which it buys its inputs. They also recognize the need for a simultaneous equation approach to empirical measurements of the firm's cost of capital.

There is general agreement among economists and financial analysts that share price (stockholder wealth) maximization is the appropriate normative model for corporate behavior.[1] However, no professional consensus has been reached about the apparatus for achieving this maximization.[2]

Eugene M. Lerner and Willard T. Carleton, "Financing Decisions of the Firm," *Journal of Finance* (May 1966), Vol. XXI, 202–214. Reprinted by permission.

[1] David Durand was the first to show that this criterion possesses different consequences and is preferable to the alternative of profit maximization. See his "Cost of Debt and Equity Funds for Business: Trends and Problems of Measurement, "*Conference on Research in Business and Finance* (New York: National Bureau of Economic Research, 1952), p. 216.

[2] Modigliani and Miller have presented a strong case that, at least in a world of no taxes and perfect capital markets (and in which stockholders are indifferent to the dividend decision) the total value of the corporation is invariant with respect to capital structure, and, as a consequence, the capital budget cut-off point is the critical financial decision. See their "The Cost of Capital, Corporation Finance, and the Theory of Investment," *American Economic Review*, June 1958, pp. 261–298; "Dividend Policy, Growth, and the Valuation of Shares," *Journal of Business*, October, 1961; and "Corporate Cost of Capital: A Correction," *American Economic Review* July, 1963, pp. 433–443.

On the other hand, M. Gordon, *The Investment, Financing, and Valuation of the Corporation* (Homewood: Richard D. Irwin, 1962) and J. Lintner, "Dividends, Earnings, Leverage, Stock Prices and the Supply of Capital to Corporations," *Review of Economics and Statistics*, August, 1962, pp. 243–269 and "Optimum Dividends and Corporate Growth Under Uncertainty," *Quarterly Journal of Economics*, February, 1964, pp. 49–95, have argued most persuasively that under realistic economic conditions the dividend and capital structure decisions are vital to stock price maximization. Theory aside, the weight of empirical evidence would appear to support Gordon and Lintner. See, for example, G. Donaldson, *Corporate Debt Capacity* (Boston: Harvard University, 1961) and J. Lintner, "Distribution of Income of Corporations Among Dividends, Retained Earnings, and Taxes," *American Economic Review*, May, 1956, pp. 97–114.

To avoid needless misunderstanding we admit at the outset that our conclusions are at variance with the several findings of Modigliani and Miller because we adopt model specifications which seem to us to be closer approximations to corporate reality than those of M and M. For a discussion of the implications of the M and M assumptions, see Lerner and Carleton, *A Theory of Financial Analysis* (New York: Harcourt, Brace and World, 1966), Chap. 10.

In a recent article, we suggested that the theoretical stalemate over the apparatus for achieving share price maximization may have arisen from the general failure to recognize explicitly that the corporate financial decisions take place within a constraint given by the prevailing conditions in the product market in which the firm sells its output and the factor market in which it buys its inputs.[3] When this constraint is recognized, it becomes transparent that corporate decision making must take place jointly on several frontiers if share prices are to be maximized.

The constrained share price maximization model that we presented, however, was incomplete, for it did not face up to the problems of corporate borrowing and uncertainty. This paper is an attempt to extend the framework of our earlier study and in so doing to gain a new perspective on some of the important issues in financial theory. Toward this end Section I sketches a purely formal framework of the corporate financial decision problem without specifying the forms of the functions involved. The classification of variables (e.g., stochastic and nonstochastic) as well as the existence and properties of any solution are discussed. Section II introduces a dividend capitalization valuation model of the sort made popular by Gordon and Lintner. Section III develops a profit opportunities schedule for the corporation for the class of investments which increase the scale rather than the diversity of the firm. Finally, in Section IV, a solution is presented to the price maximization problem for a firm facing constraints in its product and factor markets as well as in the financial market.

I. A GENERAL STATEMENT OF THE PROBLEM

Let the corporation's objective (share price) function[4] be given in terms of its potential decision variables:

$$P = P(r, b, i, L/E) \tag{I.1}$$

where: r = average rate of return on assets before interest and taxes, b = retention rate,[5] L/E = ratio of liabilities to equity, both variables measured

---

[3] Lerner and Carleton, "The Integration of Capital Budgeting and Stock Valuation," *American Economic Review*, September, 1964, pp. 683–703.

[4] We wish to thank Prof. John Bossons for pointing out a notational error in the draft presented at The American Finance Association meetings.

[5] A firm can raise additional equity through either retained earnings or the sale of additional stock. The sale of additional stock, however, usually involves a heavy transaction cost: the total cost of floating a fully underwritten public offering of securities consists of the investment banker's commission, or gross spread (the difference between the price paid by the buyer and the amount received by the issuing corporation), and the expenses incurred by the issuer, including stamp taxes, printing and engraving expenses, and registration fees. These costs can amount to as much as 10 percent of the gross proceeds realized.

If there were no transaction costs and no tax considerations, a firm would, in principle, be indifferent between retaining a portion of its earnings and distributing the rest in dividends or distributing all of its earnings as dividends and selling additional shares to raise the equity capital needs for expansion. If a corporation pursues the latter course and sells the new shares on a preemptive rights basis, that is, sells the new shares to existing shareholders in amounts proportionate to their existing holdings, the corporation in effect allows each stockholder to determine

at book value,[6] and i = the interest rate that the firm pays for borrowed funds. The form of this function will be specified in Section II.[7]

Shareholders are assumed to consider each of these variables as expected normal values, i.e., when a shareholder pays a particular price for a share of stock, he believes that the corporation will continue to earn an expected normal rate of return, r, maintain an expected normal capital structure, L/E, and so forth. The valuation of a security takes place, of course, at a moment in time. Should an unanticipated event, either favorable or unfavorable, take place, shareholders will revalue their expected normal rate of return, retention rate, capital structure, and interest rate so that the price of the security will change.

Let the corporation's profit opportunities schedule, hereinafter referred to as the LC function, be given by:

$$LC(r, b, i, L/E) = 0 \qquad (1.2)$$

where the variables are defined in the same way as they were above. The precise form of this function will be specified in Part III.[8]

Though the entire profit opportunities schedule may shift from time to time, it is assumed to be fixed at a moment in time. As the firm grows more

---

for himself the retention rate that he considers optimal. (The individual can, of course, determine his own retention rate even in the absence of subscriptions for new equity by marginal purchases and sales of stock.) Moreover, if the new stock is offered to existing stockholders at less than the market price, the right to subscribe to the new shares will have a marketable value. Since these rights can be sold, they represent, in a sense, an attempt by the corporation to give the stockholders the necessary funds to pay the personal income taxes that are incurred on the dividends received from their holdings.

It should be emphasized at this point that the ability of an individual stockholder to create his own retention rate cannot be aggregated to find the corporation's retention rate. That is, the total of funds retained or acquired for use in the firm is independent of changes in the portfolios of individual stockholders. The price of the company's stock, furthermore, will presumably reflect a balancing of such individual stockholder preferences. But this is not to deny that such an aggregate balance might take place at a different (higher or lower) share price if some other retention rate were adopted by the firm. The retention decision defined as optimal will be optimal with respect to existing and potential stockholders to avoid the non-operation conclusions that whatever is, is optimal.

Throughout this study, b, the retention rate is also defined to include both retained earnings and outside equity. Thus, let b_e be the percentage of earnings that the firm seeks to obtain by selling additional shares of stock and b_r be the percentage of earnings that are retained. Then $b = b_e + b_r$, the sum of b_e and b_r, must be less than one, other things equal, or the security will represent a net drain of funds to shareholders rather than a positive source of income. "Other things equal," it should be stressed, is an important part of this proposition since shifts in the profit opportunities schedule can give rise to shifts in stockholder growth expectations, and then to the retention rate. In such cases an historically calculated b might well exceed one.

[6] Under the assumption that a firm's entire debt is continuously refinanced, the book and market values of the debt become one and the same. Moreover, if the firm depreciates its assets at a rate such that the book value of the asset represents the present value of the asset's future stream of earnings, the book value of the equity will represent its liquidating value.

[7] In addition to these four variables, the valuation equation that will be developed in Section II utilizes three parameters. These parameters, which lie outside the range of influence of the individual corporate manager, are T, the tax rate, α, the interest rate on risk free securities and s, a market risk aversion factor.

[8] In addition to these four variables, the LC function which will be specified in Section II utilizes two parameters: γ_0, which is a function of the national income and firm's level of assets, and γ_1, which measures the change in the average rate of return that results from a change in the firm's growth rate.

rapidly, and exploits additional opportunities, it therefore moves downward along a given *LC* function. To finance this growth, the firm may either use equity (by raising *b*) or debt (by maintaining or raising the ratio of *L/E*).

By setting equation (I.2) equal to zero, we assume that the corporation is efficient, i.e., that it operates along its profit opportunities frontier. Monsen and Downs have argued that corporate managers, seeking to maximize their own lifetime earnings, may not choose to operate along the firm's maximum *LC* function.[9] Rather, they may prefer to operate along a lower (less efficient) *LC* function. The periodic movements within each corporation toward greater or lesser efficiency will be treated like any one of the several events that can cause the entire profit opportunities schedule to shift.

Finally, let the financial constraint facing a firm link the interest rate that a corporation pays for borrowed funds to its debt equity ratio:[10]

$$FC(i, L/E) = 0 \qquad (I.3)$$

The problem facing the corporation seeking to maximize the wealth of its shareholders can now be simply stated: it is to maximize the objective price equation (I.1) subject to two constraints. These constraints are, first, the *LC* function (I.2), which summarizes conditions in the firm's product and factor markets and secondly, the FC function (I.3), which summarizes conditions in the financial markets facing the firm.

In order to simplify the exposition, we specify (I.3) as

$$i = \delta L/E \qquad (I.3)'$$

and substitute into (I.1) and (I.2) to eliminate the interest rate.[11]

$$P = P(r, b, L/E) \qquad (I.1)'$$

$$LC(r, b, L/E) = 0 \qquad (I.2)'$$

The mathematics of share price maximization then become a straightforward matter assuming that second order conditions can be satisfied over some reasonable range of *r*, *b* and *L/E*.

Even at this incomplete state, a number of comments can be made about this approach to the share price valuation problem. First, while imperfect capital markets require a constraint such as (I.3) and imperfect product and factor markets require a constraint such as (I.2) whether or not a price maximization is sought, the valuation of common stocks typically has been explored with a price equation alone.

---

[9] R. Joseph Monsen, Jr. and Anthony Downs, "A Theory of Large Managerial Firms," *Journal of Political Economy*, June 1965, pp. 221–237.

[10] As was true of the valuation and *LC* functions, the financial constraint can be drawn parametric to other values. The most important of these is the interest rate that lenders can earn on government bonds.

[11] More complex forms of (I.3)' could be used which would generate similar solutions but messier mathematics. For example, $i = i_g + \delta L/E$ where i_g is the government bond rate. Inasmuch as (I.3)' is an explicit recognition of the capital market imperfections and/or lender risk aversion, it should be noted that δ will differ among corporations.

One school of practicing analysts, popularized by the writing of Arnold Bernhard[12] simply fits a multiple regression between measured stock prices and earnings, dividends, book values, lagged prices, and similar variables. In this approach the choice of the independent variables is essentially arbitrary. It might be noted that the traditional practice of security analysis can be described as the more intuitive use of this same procedure.

A second school, exemplified by Myron Gordon (*op. cit.*) utilizes an internally consistent, but inadequately constrained, valuation equation. The question as to whether a unique maximum share price exists depends upon the specification of this equation and the empirical meaning attached to the concept of uncertainty.

The only explicit recognition which we have been able to find of the effects that constraints such as (I.2) or (I.3) have upon the valuation equation is by Lintner first in 1963 and later in his 1964 article.[13]

The second comment about this approach to the valuation problem is that the existence of a binding constraint such as (I.2)' implies that when the corporation operates jointly on any two of its three decision variables, r, b, and L/E, the third is then determined. Freedom to vary all of the variables simultaneously is not possible for the system will then be overdetermined. A two-dimensional analogy to this condition can be drawn from the theory of the firm. A monopolist is free to set either his price or his output, but not both. Given a demand function, the determination of either one implies the other. Here a firm can set the values of two variables; the third is then given by the LC function.

If the firm sets any two of the three variables at an arbitrary level, however, the corporation's stock will not in general be maximized. Rather, to maximize the wealth of shareholders, the corporate managers must select the particular values of two of the values, say r and L/E so that both $\partial P/\partial r$ and $\partial P/\partial(L/E)$ are equal to zero simultaneously.

Third, each of the arguments of (I.1)' and (I.2)' is a potential decision variable and each is potentially stochastic. However because of the constraint, only two of the values can be set by the firm: the third will therefore be a stochastic variable. For example, if the firm sets both r and L/E, b is a stochastic variable; if it sets b and L/E, r is stochastic. This observation will be more fully articulated in Section III.

Finally, if a corporation's cost of capital is a function of the firm's rate of return, capital structure, retention rate or some combination of these variables, such as the growth rate, then the exact cost of capital can only be known in solution (*ex post*). Phrased differently, if the cost of capital is a

---

[12] Arnold Bernhard, "The Valuation of Listed Securities," reprinted from the *Financial Analysts Journal* in *Readings in Financial Analysis and Investment Management*, E. M. Lerner, ed. (Homewood, Ill.: Richard D. Irwin, 1963), pp. 235–245.

[13] John Lintner, "The Cost of Capital and Optimal Financing of Corporate Growth," *Journal of Finance*, May, 1963, pp. 292–310. Gordon refers to a constraint, *op. cit.*, pp. 49–50, but does not effectively integrate it into his analysis.

schedule, the precise point along this schedule where the firm operates, and hence its *ex post* cost of capital, is known only after the solution to the share price maximization problem is in hand, not before the problem is even approached.

To summarize this section then, a corporation striving to maximize shareholder wealth faces two constraints. One is in the product and factor market (*LC*), the other in the financial market (*FC*). Corporations are free to select any two of the three financial variables that influence share prices: the rate of return, the retention rate, and the capital structure. The selection of any two variables, through the constraint (I.2)' implies the third. If a lending institution, for example, dictates both the capital structure and the dividend policy (retention rate), the efficient firm is left with no degree of freedom.[14] The two variables that are fixed by the firm are nonstochastic; the remaining variable is stochastic. Finally, if the cost of capital is a function of the three financial variables, its precise value can only be known *ex post*, i.e., after the values of these variables are known.

II. THE DIVIDEND CAPITALIZATION FUNCTION

The price of a share of stock, like the price of any asset, is defined as the present value of its future return. We adopt the Gordon-Lintner definition that dividends constitute the shareholder's returns.[15] If, at time period *t*, dividends are expected to grow at a rate g[16] and are discounted at a rate k, then the capitalization model can be stated as:

$$P_0 = \int_0^\infty D_0 e^{E(g)t} e^{-kt} dt = \frac{D_0}{k - E(g)} \tag{II.1}$$

D_0, k, and $E(g)$ must now be specified so as to include the effects of corporate taxes, borrowing and the uncertainty surrounding the growth rate expectation before it can be applied to serious financial problems.

A. The Dividend Payment and the Growth Rate

The most straightforward definition of dividends is that they are expected to be a fixed percentage of after tax profits. Thus, if T = tax rate and

---

[14] This statement is strictly true only if the firm is restricted to straight debt or straight equity issues. If it has the option to sell preferred stock, convertible bonds, or other such hybrids, it has some remaining degrees of freedom.

[15] Lintner (1962) has shown that over a large class of problems, earnings and dividend capitalization models lead to equivalent results and do not require capital gains calculations. Capital gains are ignored because an infinite time horizon is postulated. If some shorter horizon is postulated, the question of what determines the price of the stock on some future date (the date of the sale) must be answered. If this future price is determined by the expected stream of dividends from that point forward, the statement that return is given by the infinite stream of dividends is equivalent to the statement that return is equal to dividends plus expected capital gain.

[16] As noted above, shareholders at a particular moment in time expect g to continue indefinitely. If some new and unanticipated development unfolds, the expected value of g will change and the new rate will then be expected to continue indefinitely.

π_t = expected profits at period t, then the corporation's expected dividend for period t, D_t, can be written as:

$$D_t = (1 - b)(1 - T)\pi_t \qquad \text{(II.2)}$$

where b is the retention rate.

Profits are defined as:

$$\pi_t = rA_t - iL_t \qquad \text{(II.3)}$$

where r and i are defined as above and A_t and L_t are book values of assets and liabilities at t respectively. In calculating book values of assets, it is assumed that accounting depreciation charges accurately reflect economic depreciation, and replacements are continually made to restore the steady state assets (steady state earning power at the equilibrium value of r).[17]

By letting r be the pre-tax rate of return on assets, the operating problem of the firm (how efficiently it manages its assets) is clearly separated from the financing problem of the firm (the sources of funds used to purchase the assets). Two firms, identical in all respects save the way in which they financed their assets would show the same r but different π_t for each time period.

Using (II.3) and the balance sheet identity, $A = L + E$, equation (II.2) can be written as:[18]

$$D_t = (1 - b)(1 - T)[r + (r - i)L/E]E_t \qquad \text{(II.4)}$$

Note that E as well as L and A are recorded at book value, not market value. Second, if the solution or equilibrium values of r, b and L/E are used in (II.4) the time subscript can be dropped. This tactic of focusing on r, b, and L/E as variables fixed in solution (or fixed in mean value) accords with both empirical practice and customary theoretical treatment,[19] and if T and $L/E = 0$, equation (II.4) collapses into expressions made familiar by Gordon and Lintner.

Finally, at least three different price equations can be derived from (II.4), depending on the kind of equilibrium model assumed. For example, if at $t = 0$, the dividend is assumed fixed, then $D_0 = D_0^*$. Alternatively, if at $t = 0$, profits are given, then $D_0 = (1 - b)(1 - T)\pi_0$. Finally, in a full equilibrium context, only E_0 is fixed and the current dividend is assumed to

---

[17] This definition of corporate asset valuation is of course consistent with a long run expected rate of return. See Modigliani and Miller, 1961, p. 434 and footnotes. Within the context of an earnings opportunities schedule, however, it can be demonstrated that all that is required to permit analysis is that the firm adopt a consistent accounting depreciation policy over time. See Lerner and Carleton, *A Theory of Financial Analysis* (New York: Harcourt, Brace and World, 1966), Chap. 4.

[18] Since $\pi = rA = iL$

$\qquad = r(E + L) - iL$

$\qquad = rE + (r - i)L$ and hence the result in the text.

[19] A. Sametz, "Trends in the Volume and Composition of Equity Finance," *Journal of Finance*, September 1964, p. 431.

reflect equilibrium values of r, b, i and L/E_0. $D = (1 - b)(1 - T)[r + (r - i)L/E]E_0$. In developing the theory, we will adopt this latter model, but a word of caution is in order: existence of a theoretical maximum price in the case of the first two models will presuppose that the LC and FC constraints and discount rate k have been appropriately specified.

It can be seen that the expected rate of growth of dividends equals the rate of growth of retained earnings:

$$E(g) = \frac{dD}{D} = \frac{dE}{E} = (1 - T)b[r + (r - i)L/E] \tag{II.5}$$

Moreover, since L/E will be fixed in solution, the rate of growth of debt as well as assets will also be at this rate.

B. The Discount Rate

The discount rate that a shareholder applies to his future stream of earnings will be specified as consisting of two components. The first, α, is the risk-free alternative open to investors.[20] The second is associated with the riskiness[21] of the growth rate and can be specified as $s \, \text{Var}(g)$ where s is a parameter reflecting the investor's risk aversion preferences.[22]

If
$$k = \alpha + s \, \text{Var}(g) \tag{II.6}$$

the denominator of the valuation equation becomes:

$$k - E(g) = \alpha + s \, \text{Var}(g) - E(g).$$

This denominator, which is the rate at which the current dividends of a corporation are discounted, can also be expressed in terms of the firm's certainty equivalent growth, $CE(g)$.

If
$$CE(g) = E(g) - s \, \text{Var}(g),$$

---

[20] To the extent that common stocks are imperfect substitutes for risk free securities (e.g., a long term government bond) α can be though of as $\alpha = (1 + M)\alpha_0$ where α_0 is the return on the government bond and M is a constant reflecting the market in which the security is traded. For example, if securities in the over the counter market are even more imperfect substitutes for government bonds than securities traded on the New York Stock Exchange, M_{otc} will be greater than M_{nyse}.

[21] In a certain world, k, the rate of discount, is a pure riskless interest rate satisfying only the investors' time preference function. In an uncertain world, several alternatives have been proposed, the most popular of which is the solution of (II.6): $k = D/P + E(g)$. Solomon for example, stresses this as a measure of the cost of capital. *The Theory of Financial Management* (New York: Columbia University Press, 1963), p. 34. Since this expression merely defines what k must be at any equilibrium share price P, uses of such a discount rate as the cost of capital for decision purposes are obviously tainted with circularity.

[22] Lintner (1964) has developed a discount function along these lines for a no-debt, no-taxes model, utilizing a hyperbolic investor utility function. Lintner's formulation possesses some advantages but we imply a quadratic utility function in our discount function on the grounds that it has better known properties. Other variants on the form of (II.6) include: (1) $\text{Var}(g) = a$ constant, in which case $k = a$ constant (the well known fixed cost of capital model); and (2) $k = \alpha + $ standard deviation (g), which under specifications to be made as to the LC function implies a discount function linear in $E(g)$. The aggregation problem is admittedly severe, whatever form and micro-justification is given to the market discount function.

the discount rate applied to a corporation's current dividend is:

$$k - E(g) = \alpha - CE(g).$$

Thus, the dividends of a common stock are discounted at the same rate as the interest stream of a risk free bond less the dividend stream's certainty equivalent growth rate.

To summarize this section then, if (II.4), (II.5), and (II.6) are substituted into (II.1), the valuation equation at period 0 becomes:

$$P_0 = \frac{\{(1 - t)[r + (r - i)L/E] - E(g)\}E_0}{\alpha + s \operatorname{Var}(g) - E(g)} \qquad \text{(II.1)}'$$

Two bounds which have to be placed on this equation are immediate: (1) $r > i$; the corporation will not borrow if there is no internal gain to leverage; and (2) $\alpha + s \operatorname{Var}(g) > E(g)$; we rule out the possibility of a growth stock paradox.

Equation (II.1)', which we believe captures most of what analysts would consider essential in a valuation equation, can be viewed as generating a family of iso-price lines. Furthermore, any given P can be obtained by an infinite number of r, b, L/E combinations. The problem that remains therefore is to specify the region of r, b, and L/E values open to the corporation. We do this in the next section.

III. THE PROFIT OPPORTUNITIES SCHEDULE

The region of obtainable r, b, and L/E values open to a corporation will be controlled by the demand and cost schedules for a company's products. Assume for the moment that the corporation produces a single product and that income, tastes, and the prices of competitive and complementary goods remain constant. Then both the price of the product and its average cost can be specified as proportionate to both the level of output and to rate of change of output.[23]

$$p_t = \alpha_0 + \alpha_1 Q_t + \alpha_2 \frac{d \ln Q}{dt} \qquad \text{(III.1)}$$

and

$$c_t = \beta_0 + \beta_1 Q_t + \beta_2 \frac{d \ln Q}{dt} \qquad \text{(III.2)}$$

where both α_1 and $\alpha_2 \leq 0$ and β_1 and $\beta_2 \geq 0$.

---

[23] The demand and cost curves are specified in this form rather than in the more conventional form because of the rather widely held belief that for the large publicly held corporations that are of concern to the shareholder, prices and costs are more sensitive to the relative changes in output than the absolute changes in output. More importantly, the stock valuation model is itself a growth model and hence the profit opportunities function must also be expressed in comparable units.

If the firm produces under perfect competition, both α_1 and α_2 equal zero. Similarly if the company purchases its inputs in competitive markets and encounters no diminishing returns as it expands output, both β_1 and β_2 equal zero. To the extent that the firms have some monopoly and monopsony power,

$$\alpha_1, \alpha_2 < 0 \quad \text{and} \quad \beta_1, \beta_2 > 0.$$

The profits of the firm at time t can be represented as:

$$\pi_t = (p_t - c_t)Q_t = (\alpha_0 - \beta_0)Q_t + (\alpha_1 - \beta_1)Q_t^2 + (\alpha_2 - \beta_2)\frac{d \ln Q}{dt}Q_t \quad \text{(III.3)}$$

If capacity is proportionate to assets,[24] and firms strive to operate at a fixed percentage of capacity,[25] then output will be proportionate to assets and the growth of output will be proportionate to the growth of assets.

$$Q_t = \lambda A_t \quad \text{(III.4)}$$

and

$$\frac{d \ln A}{dt} = \frac{d \ln Q}{dt} \quad \text{(III.5)}$$

Substitute (III.4) and (III.5) into (III.3) and divide by the level of assets:

$$r_t = \frac{\pi_t}{A_t} = (\alpha_0 - \beta_0)\lambda + (\alpha_1 - \beta_1)\lambda^2 A + (\alpha_2 - \beta_2)\frac{d \ln A}{dt}\lambda \quad \text{(III.6)}$$

The rate of return, r_t, under the assumption that national income, tastes, and the prices of competitive and complementary goods remain fixed at time t, is therefore seen to depend upon both the level of assets at time t and the rate of growth of assets. Since $(\alpha_1 - \beta_1)\lambda^2 < 0$ the average rate of return will fall from period to period as the asset base rises. If the assumptions of fixed national income and consumer tastes are relaxed, however, r need not have a secular decline. In order to focus on decisions concerning continuing growth, we assume that profits at t are a linear homogeneous function of A_t and dA/dt,

$$\pi_t = \gamma_0 A_t + \gamma_1 \frac{dA}{dt} \quad \text{(III.6)}'$$

or

$$r = \frac{\pi_t}{A_t} = \gamma_0 + \gamma_1 \frac{dA}{A} \quad \text{(III.7)}$$

---

[24] If the accounting measures of assets reflect the underlying economic value of assets, as assumed previously, this statement is a truism. To the extent that the accounting statements fail to measure economic reality, capacity will not be effectively measured by the accounting statement.

[25] Hickman has developed an imaginative measure to express excess capacity by noting the deviation of output from such a percentage. See "On a New Method of Capacity Estimation," *Journal of the American Statistical Association*, Vol. 59, No. 306, pp. 529–550.

where $\gamma_0 > 0$ reflects the effect of $(\alpha_0 - \beta_0)\lambda + (\alpha_1 - \beta_1)\lambda^2 A_t$ plus the period by period shift in the schedule to make the intercept a constant. γ_1 of course is less than zero. Under these conditions the rate of return depends upon the rate of growth of assets, and if this is set at some (to be determined) solution value we can describe a steady state r and drop the t subscript.[26]

Equation (III.7) can be readily generalized to incorporate the gross effects of changes in the output of competitive and complementary firms.[27] An obvious extension yields:

$$r = \gamma_0 + \gamma_1\left(\frac{dA}{A}\right)_1 + \gamma_2\left(\frac{dA}{A}\right)_2 + \cdots + \gamma_n\left(\frac{dA}{A}\right)_n \qquad \text{(III.8)}$$

where $\gamma_j = (\alpha_j - \beta_j)\lambda_i\lambda_j$.

Because the rate of growth of substitute and complementary firms will influence a firm's rate of return, equation (III.7) must therefore be amended to recognize its stochastic character.[28] Thus:

$$r = \gamma_0 + \gamma_1\left(\frac{dA}{A}\right) + u \qquad \text{(III.7)}'$$

Further, it is assumed that $E(u) = 0$. No bias is involved in considering the firm in isolation. The variance of u is specified as:

$$\text{Var}(u) = c\left(\frac{dA}{A}\right)^2 \qquad \text{(III.9)}$$

When a corporation is expected to grow rapidly it may, on the one hand, find new firms entering the industry and old firms expanding their output. The higher the rate of return, the more vulnerable the firm will be to vigorous competition for any given state of barriers to entry. Alternatively, firms

---

[26] An (expectationally) stationary rate of return opportunities schedule is in fact required in order to secure an exceptionally constant solution r. Functions similar to (III.7) have as a consequence been adopted by many writers. For example, see Lintner, 1964, pp. 56–58 and references cited in footnote 7 therein. We have simply demonstrated the kinds of assumptions which might be made to justify (III.7).

[27] An extension of still another sort may be made. Consider the corporation at a moment of time to possess a set of investment alternatives rather than a single option of changing the scale of activity it is presently engaged in. Such an extension forms an obvious continuity with the capital budgeting literature. Unfortunately, it introduces internal asset mix (internal portfolio) considerations which require an analysis of the internal covariance matrix, but the formulation of (III.8) would require that attention be given to a conditional covariance matrix, conditional upon the investment behavior of at least some of the firm's competitors. Rather than to broaden the analysis of this paper beyond its intended scope by considering the internal diversification problems, we restrict our attention to that class of investments which increases the scale of the firm. In this respect we follow Modigliani and Miller (1964), p. 440, footnote 15 and the reference therein to J. Hirshleifer, "Risk, the Discount Rate, and Investment Decision," *American Economic Review*, May 1961, pp. 112–120.

[28] In a general equilibrium model, r would be completely determinate. The stochastic character of r in (III.7)' is simply a reflection of the fact that a corporation's rate of return depends upon a host of "ifs" which cannot be unambiguously determined by the corporation, much less by the stockholder. Worse yet, each stockholder will consider a different set of dA/A's and subjectively assign his own values both to them and to the γ_j's. The final effect of these diverse stockholder judgments on observed share prices is moot. The simplified discount function of (II.6) assumed that the aggregate effect of such stockholder beliefs was stable in the form given.

producing complementary goods may be induced to increase their output. As a consequence, the variance of u will be specified as proportionate to the square of the growth rate itself.

IV. THE SOLUTION

For widest generality, maximization of (II.1)' subject to some form of the LC constraint should be handled by Lagrangian multipliers. This tactic would not force the choice of which variables are to be considered independent. However, the mathematical problem of maximizing share prices subject to a constraint is slightly more manageable if we proceed by elimination of b. This procedure will yield identical results. It can be justified on the following grounds: when the ratio of debt to equity is fixed by management as its solution value, the LC function can then be written either as:[29]

$$r = \frac{\gamma_0 - \gamma_1(1 - T)b \, \delta(L/E)^2 + u}{1 - \gamma_1(1 - T)b(1 + L/E)} \qquad (III.7)''$$

or

$$b = \frac{r - \gamma_0 - u}{\gamma_1(1 - T)[r + (r - i)L/E]} \qquad (III.7)'''$$

In the former case, b is considered fixable with certainty; in the latter case, r is considered fixable with certainty. Which of these two alternatives should be selected? The discount function in the valuation equation contains the term Var (g). Since Var $(g) = $ Var $\{(1 - T)b[r(1 + L/E) - \delta(L/E)^2]\}$, substituting either form of the LC function into this expression will eliminate one of the variables. In one case, Var (g) becomes a function of b and L/E; in the other, of r and L/E. We adopt the latter for it leads to a more tractable mathematical solution.[30]

Substitute (III.7)''' into (II.5),

$$g = \frac{r - \gamma_0 - \mu}{\gamma_1}$$

and

$$E(g) = \frac{r - \gamma_0}{\gamma_1} \qquad (IV.1)$$

---

[29] Recall that

$$g = \frac{dA}{A} = (1 - T)b \left[r + (r - i)\frac{L}{E} \right]$$

and that $i = \delta L/E$, (II.5) and (I.3)' respectively.

[30] If the firm's borrowing costs were stochastic, and its LC function were fixed, both the growth rate and its expected value would be different. See Lerner and Carleton, "The Corporate Structure Problem of a Regulated Public Utility," *op. cit.* To generalize the system completely, both the financial constraint and the LC function should be treated as if they were stochastic. This has not been done because we have not as yet discovered a convenient and plausible way to handle the complex problem of the covariance between the two functions.

Therefore,

$$\text{Var}\,(g) = \frac{\text{Var}\,(u)}{\gamma_1{}^2}$$

Since, Var (u) was specified in (III.9) as proportional to the square of the growth rate,

$$\text{Var}\,(g) = \frac{c}{\gamma_1{}^2}\left(\frac{r - \gamma_0}{\gamma_1}\right)^2 \qquad (IV.2)$$

By substituting (IV.1) and (IV.2) into the valuation equation, it becomes a function of only two variables.

$$P = \frac{\left\{(1 - T)[r + (r - \delta L/E)L/E]\left(\dfrac{r - \gamma_0}{\gamma_1}\right)\right\}}{\alpha + \dfrac{\psi}{\gamma_1{}^2}\left(\dfrac{r - \gamma_0}{\gamma_1}\right)^2 - \left(\dfrac{r - \gamma_0}{\gamma_1}\right)}E_0 \qquad (II.1)''$$

where s, the risk aversion coefficient and c, the factor of proportionality have been combined to form a single constant.

The maximum[31] obtainable share price is found by solving $\partial P/\partial r = 0$ and $[\partial P]/[\partial(L/E)] = 0$ for r and L/E.[32]

In Figure 22-1 a graphic solution is presented.

The vector $[\partial P]/[\partial(L/E)] = 0$ is a straight line[33] through the origin with the slope of 2δ. This vector can be interpreted as meaning that the price of the stock is maximized with respect to L/E if its L/E ratio is chosen such that the rate of return that this corporation earns on its assets is twice the interest rate it pays on borrowed funds.

The second vector $\partial P/\partial r = 0$ is a more complicated function whose position and slope will depend upon the parameters α, γ_0, γ_1, ψ, β and T. Movements along this vector can be translated as meaning that the price of the stock is maximized with respect to the rate of return if the corporation chooses (for each L/E) a rate of return regarded as optimal. The alternatives are to choose a higher (lower) rate of return, larger (smaller) present dividends, and smaller (larger) rate of growth for any capital structure that shareholders would prefer.

---

[31] It should be observed again that alternative assumptions as to forms of the discount function and as to what is controllable at $t = 0$ lead to alternative decision rules. Thus, if the numerator of (II.1)'' is fixed, then the constrained maximization of P becomes equivalent to the constrained minimization of dividend yield. Alternatively, one might regard π_0 as fixed, in which case earnings yield is minimized.

[32] Second order conditions are satisfied at this point if

$$(1 - T)(4\delta\psi + 2\psi\gamma_0 + \gamma_1 3) - \frac{4\delta\varphi}{\gamma_1} > 0.$$

This is essentially a requirement that the slope of the LC function not be too large.

[33] This result follows from specifying the financial constraint as $i = \delta L/E$. Had a different specification been used, a different result would follow. See footnote 11 above.

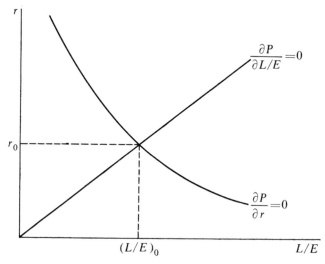

Fig. 22–1.

The only point that satisfies both conditions and thereby assures a unique maximum price is r_0 and $(L/E)_0$. Substituting these values back into the LC function assures a unique value of b, and into (II.1)″ the maximum P_0.[34]

Suboptimum cases may also be analyzed in terms of Fig. 22–1. The principal lessons remain clear however:

(1) Corporate financial decisions to maximize stockholder wealth must be made jointly, and
(2) Once the market imperfections within which the firm operates are considered as explicit constraints, these financial decisions cease to be trivial.

---

[34] While we have not drawn boundaries of the available r, L/E set in Fig. 22–1, it is assumed that r_0, $(L/E)_0$ are within limits previously established: $r \leq \gamma_0$ (for $b = 0$), $r \leq \delta L/E$, and

$$r \geq \frac{\gamma_0}{1 - \gamma_1(1 - T)}$$

(for $b \rightarrow 1$ and $L/E = 0$).

23

DIVIDENDS AND STOCK PRICES

IRWIN FRIEND and MARSHALL PUCKETT

In this empirical study of the influences of dividends on stock prices, Professors Friend and Puckett seek to structure their study to avoid a number of possible sources of statistical bias. In addition, in their actual calculations they make adjustments for "firm effects" and develop an "earnings normalization procedure." Their conclusions are very cautiously stated and indicate the need for more extensive empirical analysis.

The recent literature has been characterized by considerable controversy and confusion over the relative importance of dividends and retained earnings in determining the price-earnings ratios of common stocks.[1] The disagreement over theoretical specifications of the expected relationship seems to us to have reached a point of rapidly diminishing returns, with much of the disagreement reflecting differences in interpretation of the questions being raised. However, there do seem to be very real difficulties in the reconciliation of available empirical findings with almost any sensible theory, and in the derivation of more definitive tests to choose among different specifications. This paper, after briefly reviewing the relevant theory and earlier findings, will discuss the limitations of these findings, describe various approaches to avoiding these limitations, and present new results that seem more in accord with theoretical preconceptions.

Relative prices of different issues of stock at a point of time are presumably determined by suitable discounting of expected future returns. These returns may take the form of dividend income or capital gains, both of which, assuming rational behavior, should be estimated on an after-tax basis with a higher average tax applicable to dividend income than to capital gains.[2] The discount factor relevant to these expectations of future return

Irwin Friend and Marshall Puckett, "Dividends and Stock Prices," *American Economic Review* (September 1964), Vol. LIV, 656–682. Reprinted by permission.

[1] See Modigliani and Miller [14], Durand's "Comment" [3], and Modigliani and Miller's "Reply" [15]; Gordon [6] [7]; Fisher [4]; Benishay [1]; Miller and Modigliani [13]; Lintner [10]; and Solomon [17].

[2] The magnitude of this tax differential is difficult to evaluate, but available evidence indicates it may be smaller than commonly supposed. For instance, past yield spreads between institutional grade corporates and tax-exempt bonds are explained by an investor tax bracket of approximately 20 percent–25 percent. However, in view of the institutional forces affecting the corporate bond market, this figure is undoubtedly lower than the tax rate characterizing the marginal investor in the stock market—but we have no idea just how much lower.

is a function of both the pure rate (or rates) of interest and the degree of risk associated with a particular issue—the evaluation of risk reflecting both the subjective probability distribution of expected return on total capital of the issuer and the degree of financial leverage in the issuer's capital structure.

The fact that investors are willing to hold (or buy) a company's shares at the prevailing price implies that the rate of discount which equates their income expectation with market price constitutes a rate of return at least as high as could be obtained in alternative investments of comparable risk. Now, if these investors are willing to increase their holdings of shares at the same rate of market return, they should also be willing to forego current dividends insofar as the added equity investment yields this rate. Stated another way, investors should be indifferent if the present value of the additional future returns resulting from earnings retention equals the amount of dividends foregone. Moreover, because increases in present value (market price) are realizable as capital gains, earnings retention carries a tax advantage that lowers the rate of return on corporate investment necessary for shareholder indifference between current dividends and earnings retention.

The influence of earnings retention on share prices should therefore be a function of the profitability of corporate investment opportunities, *ceteris paribus*, in view of the fact that external equity financing is generally not a completely satisfactory substitute for internal financing. When this corporate rate of profit exceeds the minimum rate required by stockholders, price should increase as the proportion of earnings retained increases (though, since profitability is presumably a decreasing function of the amount of investment, beyond some point increased retention associated with excessive investment may depress the marginal return on investment below the required rate). Conversely, when the corporation's profit rate is less than the market rate, price should decrease with increasing earnings retention.[3]

Despite these theoretical conclusions, empirical findings indicate that, when stock prices are related to current dividends and retained earnings, higher dividend payout is usually associated with higher price-earnings ratios. This result, it might be noted, is found just about as often in highly profitable "growth" industries as it is in less profitable ones. Probably the earliest and best-known observation of this "dividend effect" was made a generation ago by Graham and Dodd [8], who went so far as to assert that a dollar of dividends has four times the average impact on price as does a dollar of

---

[3] As Miller and Modigliani [13] have shown, external equity financing destroys this relationship under conditions of costless flotation and no capital gains tax advantage, if changes in dividends are compensated by changes in external equity financing of equal magnitude and opposite direction (rate of equity investment held constant). However, flotation is not costless, capital gains tax advantages do exist, and the rate of earnings retention is in all likelihood greatly influenced by the rate of investment.

retained earnings.[4] More recent statistical studies by Myron Gordon, David Durand, and others indicate that the dividend multiplier is still several times the retained earnings multiplier, with Gordon [6] finding little change on the average in the four-to-one ratio of the two multipliers, though the ratio varies widely and inconsistently from industry to industry and from year to year. These statistical results, it might be noted, are based on a large number of cross-section studies utilizing linear and logarithmic (and occasionally even other)[5] relationships between prices and both dividends and retained earnings to explain price variations in samples of companies drawn from particular industries.

Despite the massive array of statistical results tending to confirm the existence of a strong dividend effect, many market analysts have become increasingly skeptical of their validity. With the rise in market emphasis on growth in recent years, and the presumed close relationship between growth and retention of earnings in the minds of investors and managements, it seems strange to many analysts that a dollar of retained earnings (or of total earnings) should be valued so low relative to a dollar of dividends—and even stranger that there seems to have been no substantial shift in the relationship in recent years. Moreover, these doubts are supported quite strongly by several past surveys of shareholder opinion that indicate earnings and capital gains do, in fact, weigh more heavily than dividends in evaluating the relative desirability of alternative stock investments: "Investors who say a change in corporate earnings would influence their investment decisions outnumber by three to one those who would be influenced by a change in dividends."[6]

The behavioral assumptions necessary for theoretical support of a consistently lower market valuation of retained earnings than of dividends are also quite suspect. This lower valuation could exist if any one of the following situations is present: (1) the average holder of common stock possesses, at the *margin* of his portfolio, a very strong preference for current income over future income (a situation which hardly could be expected to persist over time); (2) the expected increase in earnings arising from increased per-share investment is viewed as involving a much higher degree of risk than that attaching to earnings on existing corporate assets; (3) the profitability of incremental corporate investment, as viewed by shareholders, is extremely low relative to the competitive yield prevailing in the stock market.

Each of the first two of these assumptions implies high rates of discount on incremental investment which would result in little short-run price

---

[4] The fourth edition (1962) of this text on security analysis modifies this conclusion only moderately.

[5] See, e.g., Johnson, Shapiro, and O'Meara, Jr. [9].

[6] Friend and Parker [5]. Also see Merrill Lynch, Pierce, Fenner and Smith [12]: "Just about all surveys of shareholders in recent years show investors are primarily interested in one thing—capital gains—almost two-thirds of our customers placed this at the top of their list . . . . The emphasis on appreciation rises as income rises."

appreciation from earnings retention, even though the expected profitability of additional investment may be quite high. However, neither of these assumptions is consistent with observed behavior of the market. Contrary to what might be expected from both of these assumptions, we do not normally witness perceptible drops in the market price level when the aggregate supply of corporate stock is increased by new issues, requiring for their absorption the substitution of current for future income and potentially raising the risk premium demanded by investors; nor do we typically witness sharp drops in per-share price when the supply of an individual company's shares is increased. It is possible to infer of course that these increases in supply are precisely timed so as to be automatically offset by upward shifts in investor expectations, but this seems completely unrealistic. Thus, both of these first two assumptions can be questioned on the basis of market behavior as well as logical content.

The third assumption—that investors view the profitability of incremental investment as being quite low—also seems highly suspect. Marginal profit rates in a substantial number of industries appear to be quite high, and undue pessimism is hardly consistent with the accepted image of the average shareholder. Moreover, the generally favorable market reaction to new public stock offerings in recent years further belies the prevalence of any pessimistic beliefs about marginal profit rates.

In view of all this, it is our opinion that those statistical studies purporting to show a strong market preference for dividends are in error—especially since the analysis typically employed (described in the following section) includes as a part of the market's valuation of retained earnings the price paid for the relatively high internal rates of return which might be expected to be associated with high retention. Nonetheless, we would still not expect to find a uniform preference for dividends even if internal rates of return were held constant over the sample of companies being examined.[7] We do not, however, deny the existence of instances in which retained earnings are valued less than dividends. Certainly, some companies may be controlled by managements who knowingly do not act in the shareholder's best interest, or there may be sharp disagreement between these two groups over how that interest is defined. However, we feel that these instances are likely to be the exception rather than the rule. Moreover, we would expect that for the average firm, irrespective of investor preferences between dividends and capital gains, payout policies are such that at the margin a dollar of retained earnings should be approximately equal in market value to the dollar of dividends foregone.

---

[7] Lintner [10] maintains that under certain types of uncertainty retained earnings would be preferred to dividends if the alternative is a new stock issue to finance a given investment. If this is true, though we have some doubts, it would reinforce our argument. On the other hand, again as a result of uncertainty, Lintner argues that for firms with low leverage, investors will prefer higher dividends associated with higher corporate debt to greater retention and lower dividends.

I. POSSIBLE SOURCES OF STATISTICAL BIAS

In support of our position, we will now outline a considerable number of reasons why previous statistical studies yielded biased results. These comments are directed in particular at the following regression equation, which is the one most commonly applied to cross-section data, but most of them also apply to past variations in this equation:

$$P_{it} = a + b\,D_{it} + c\,R_{it} + e_{it}. \tag{1}$$

Reading from left to right, the variables represent per-share price, dividends, and retained earnings. The subscript i denotes the ith company in a sample of n companies selected from a particular industry, and all variables are measured in the tth time period.

Before discussing the reasons for bias in the application of this relation, we might point out that even those who believe that a higher b than c—the typical result—indicates investor preference for dividends seem nonetheless to feel that the optimum earnings payout ratio is normally less than one, which could be regarded as inconsistent with the result obtained. The implicit assumption in the above equation that optimal earnings payout—i.e., that giving rise to the highest price-earnings ratio—is either all, none, or a matter of indifference is, of course, highly questionable. However, even though this equation is quite deficient in that it does not admit of a unique optimum payout between the extremes of zero and 100 percent, it may still be quite useful for estimating price behavior within the observed range of dividend payout.

Thus, if the companies in a sample tend, *on the average*, to pay out less than the optimum, b should be greater than c; if they pay out more than the optimum, b should be less than c; and if they pay just the optimum, regardless of what that optimum is, or if the payout is a matter of indifference, b should equal c. Theory would suggest that regardless of the optimum payout for any individual company, at that optimum, \$1 of dividends would on the average have the same effect on stock price as \$1 of retained earnings.[8] Any difference between the values of b and c therefore represents either a disequilibrium payout position or a statistical limitation of the analysis employed, including most notably a correlation of dividends or retained earnings with omitted factors affecting price. Our analysis will attempt to distinguish between these two possibilities, though the persistence of the relative importance of payout on price, and its apparent invariance to such factors as the rise in market emphasis on growth through earnings retention, argues against the disequilibrium explanation even if this condition is regarded as fairly permanent.

---

[8] This conclusion does not depend on whether, under uncertainty, the relevant discount rate of investors is a function of the dividend rate.

While the linear form used does not provide measures of optimum payout, it can give useful insights into the size of such payout through examination of the residuals over the range of payout experienced. However, an adequate study of the size of optimal payout ratios under varying circumstances requires a more complex statistical analysis, allowing for many more variables than have been incorporated in the framework used in this paper, and will be deferred to a subsequent study. Our analysis in this paper is directed only to an assessment of the general rationality of company payout policy in view of the usual findings (i.e., b systematically higher than c) which imply that management typically tends to maintain too low a payout.

It will be noted that the following discussion of regression problems centers exclusively on those encountered in cross-section analysis. While it is possible to work with time-series information, and we shall do so to a limited extent, virtually all of our predecessors used cross-section data in their regression studies, and it is these studies with which we take issue.

A. Omitted Variables

The above equation assumes, among other things: (1) either that risk is held constant by restricting the sample to a particular industry or else that dividend payout is uncorrelated with risk; and (2) that expectations of growth are determined solely by the relative amount of current earnings retention or alternatively that growth from other sources is uncorrelated with the relative amount of retention.

With regard to the first of these assumptions, a typical sample of 20 or so companies drawn from industries such as foods, steels, or chemicals contains enormous variations in company size, financial structure, and product mix; therefore, it appears totally unwarranted to assume that risk variations within these industry samples are negligible. In view of what we know about managerial desire to avoid dividend cuts, it certainly seems logical to expect that companies facing greater uncertainty about future profit performance would adopt lower current dividend payout as a means of hedging the risk of being forced to cut their dividend. Thus, high risk may *result* in both low payout and low price-earnings ratios, whereas low risk may *result* in high payout and high price-earnings ratios. Consequently, omission of a risk variable from the regression equation could conceivably impart a substantial upward bias to the dividend coefficient, depending upon both the extent to which risk varies between companies and the strength of risk in determining current payout.

It might be noted that a few previous writers have incorporated a risk variable in the regression equations. However, this variable is usually measured in terms of earnings fluctuations, and is heavily influenced by cyclical factors in the company's operating performance. We are inclined to doubt that cyclical earnings variability is a good proxy measure of investor uncertainty about future long-run performance, and therefore are dubious that the problem of risk has been handled properly.

Now, the second assumption—that growth deriving from sources other than earnings retention is either nonexistent or nonbiasing—is equally questionable. Growth in per-share earnings, apart from that arising from more efficient use of existing capital, can occur through externally as well as internally financed investment, and there may be a biasing correlation within a sample of companies between internally and externally financed growth. Suppose, for instance, that some companies prefer (or in the case of public utilities are encouraged by regulatory agencies to have) low earnings retention compensated by large amounts of external financing, whereas other companies prefer high earnings retention and small amounts of external financing. This would impair the relationship between earnings retention and growth, thereby reducing the coefficient on retained earnings when the variable measuring externally financed growth is omitted.[9]

However, it is equally possible that the relationship between internal and external financing could run the other way—that is, that high rates of retention are associated with relatively heavy external financing and low rates of retention with small amounts of external financing. The inherent advantages of retained earnings undoubtedly encourage maximum use of this source of funds before resorting to the capital markets. Thus, external financing may be associated with high earnings retention for companies with abundant investment opportunities, whereas the absence of external financing may be associated with lower earnings retention for other companies. In this case the rate of earnings retention is positively correlated with external financing, and the retained earnings coefficient is biased upward by omission of any consideration of externally financed growth.

In summary, whereas the bias due to omission of a risk variable is reasonably clear in direction (but not in magnitude), the nature of the bias resulting from omission of a variable to take account of externally financed growth is not clear. Nonetheless, both of these variables are potentially too important to be omitted from the regression equation without proof of the negligibility of their influence on regression results.

B. Regression Weights

Contributing to the difficulties imposed by omitted variables is the separate but correlated problem of regression weighting. An individual

---

[9] If the objective were to arrive at the relative evaluation of dividends and retained earnings *with a given rate of return*, then the problem of bias would arise from the omission of the expected growth rate rather than from that of externally financed growth. An analysis which includes past growth rates (as proxies for expected future growth) is Benishay [1]. Gordon [7] does introduce both internally and externally financed growth, but the form of the relation he uses does not permit the isolation of dividends from retained earnings effects.

observation influences regression results according to the extent to which that observation departs from the sample average. Thus, extreme values are much more important in determining regression results than are those values centered more closely about the sample average.

Now, it is a generally accepted fact that high-quality stocks tend to be characterized by high per-share values (prices, dividends, and earnings), whereas low-quality stocks are characterized by low per-share values. Further, as discussed immediately above, high-quality stocks may tend to pay out a higher proportion of earnings than do the low-quality issues. Thus, the association between regression weights and investment quality may exaggerate whatever regression bias exists due to an association between investment quality and dividend payout. This problem of regression weights is reduced when regression variables are converted to logarithms, which was done in some earlier studies.

C. Random Variations in Income

The income reported by a corporation in any particular period is subject to a host of short-run economic and accounting factors that render it different from what would have been reported under "normal" conditions. Now if prices are related to normal rather than reported income, and if the short-run disturbances in reported earnings do not produce equiproportional disturbances in dividends, then a regression equation of the standard form will be biased in favor of dividend payout influences—a point touched upon by earlier writers but in a rather different context. To clarify, companies with above-normal earnings at a point of time will be characterized by both low price-earnings and dividend payout ratios, whereas companies reporting below-normal earnings will be characterized by both high price-earnings and high payout ratios.

The two conditions essential to the above argument are: (1) that dividends are a more stable time series than reported earnings; and (2) that the elasticity of shareholder expectations with respect to short-run income movements is less than unity. The existence of the first of these conditions has been proved quite conclusively by several studies of corporate dividend payout policy which show a rather slow adaptation of dividends to changes in reported earnings.[10] The second condition has, to our knowledge, not been proved, but in view of the great amount of background data available for the formulation of per-share income expectations, it seems reasonable to suppose that expectations are rather insensitive to those short-run movements in relative earnings which are unrelated to fundamental changes in long-run prospects for the economy, the industry, or the company.

---

[10] See especially Lintner [11], and also Darling [2].

D. Income Measurement Errors

The diversity of accounting procedures employed in estimating business earnings gives rise to consistent measurement errors that can bias regression results in favor of dividends on two counts. First, the simple fact that retained earnings are measured imprecisely exerts a downward bias on the coefficient for that variable (dividends are measured precisely, and therefore no such bias exists here). Since retained earnings are generally of the order of magnitude of one-third total earnings, and all of the probably sizable measurement error in total earnings affects the estimate of retained earnings, the downward bias in the retained earnings coefficient could be quite large.[11] Second, if both prices and dividends are geared to the economically "correct" value of earnings, then firms that employ accounting methods yielding relatively high reported earnings will be characterized by both low payout and low price-earnings ratios compared to the sample average, whereas those firms which maximize current deductions will show both high payout and high price-earnings ratios relative to the sample average. As a result, the retained earnings coefficient is again biased downward relative to the dividends coefficient.

Strictly speaking, the second of these accounting effects could logically have been discussed under the heading "omitted variables," above. However, the apparent lack of appreciation for the interrelation between accounting biases in reported earnings and the measured effect of dividends and retained earnings on share prices prompted this separate discussion as a means of drawing attention to what is potentially one of the most glaring weaknesses in those studies. In subsequent discussions of regression models and results, accounting limitations of the type described above will generally be incorporated in the "omitted variable" category.

It might be noted that the above discussion does not include accounting errors of the type that, because of fluctuations in certain costs such as write-offs, advertisement, research and development, etc., would result in random disturbances to an individual company's earnings. These are properly included in the "random income movements" category. We should also mention the problem of general over- or understatement of earnings. While the procedures we will use do adjust for differences among firms (which are consistent over time) in their reporting of earnings, they do not adjust for any general over- or understatement of earnings because of the formidable conceptual and statistical problems associated with identification and correction of this type error. We might emphasize, however, that if accounting estimates of earnings are generally less than those "estimated" by investors, the retained earnings coefficient will be biased upward.

---

[11] See, e.g., Wold [18]. On the other hand, several analyses using average dividends and average retained income as explanatory variables (e.g., see Gordon [6]) attach about the same relative importance to dividends in explaining stock prices, though this use of averages would be expected to reduce the bias in the estimated influence of retained earnings.

E. Least-Squares Bias

Assuming that management and shareholder expectations are substantially independent, it is entirely plausible that a price-earnings ratio which is regarded as high by management will result in external stock financing and high payout, while capitalization ratios regarded as low will result in heavier reliance on internal financing and consequently low payout. Moreover, a similar result would occur if management were motivated only by a desire to maintain dividend-price ratios close to the average for the industry.

If these market relationships are reflected in cross-section data, the standard regression equation will yield results biased in favor of dividend payout because it assumes one-way causality between dividends and prices. That is, the equation fails to take account of the fact that dividend payout differences are, at least in part, the result rather than the cause of differences in price-earnings ratios. Resolution of this problem of dual causality requires the use of a complete model employing both demand and supply schedules for dividends.

II. REGRESSION MODELS

The problem of omitted variables could, of course, be directly handled by expanding the regression equation to include these variables. However, measurement of such slippery concepts as subjective risk evaluation, profitability of investment opportunities, sources of expected future financing, and accounting differences is both difficult and subject to large error. Indirect approaches thus seem particularly attractive.

Theoretically speaking, continuous cross-section techniques are the most appealing of these approaches. If the separate effects on price of all omitted variables are aggregated, and this composite ("company" or "firm") effect given the designation F_i, then the basic regression equation (1) can be modified as follows:

$$P_{it} = a_t + b_t D_{it} + c_t R_{it} + F_i + e_{it}. \tag{2}$$

The assumption implicit in this equation is that firm effects, which cannot of course be measured directly, are both additive and constant over time. Such firm effects include those relevant to investor assessment of both profit prospects and risk, only some of which (e.g., size of firm and past trend and variability in book earnings) could alternatively be measured directly. Now if an identical equation is written for an earlier time period, and this last equation is then subtracted from the one above, the following result is achieved:

$$P_{it} - P_{i(t-1)} = a_t - a_{t-1} + b_t D_{it} - b_{t-1} D_{i(t-1)} + c_t R_{it} \tag{3}$$
$$- c_{t-1} R_{i(t-1)} + e_{it} - e_{i(t-1)}.$$

The F_i do not appear in this equation, so the coefficients on dividends and retained earnings ought to be free of the bias due to firm effects.

Despite its theoretical appeal, this procedure runs into two complications: (1) in this particular application the error terms in the continuous cross-section difference equation become quite large; and (2) period-to-period movements in the variables can contain random elements and serial correlations that greatly impair the meaning and reliability of the coefficients.[12] The random movements in earnings are much more likely to be reflected in retained earnings than in dividends or in stock prices, depressing the apparent influence of retained earnings on stock prices. Moreover, the firm effects are more likely to be multiplicative than additive, and continuous cross-section techniques pose special problems in the multiplicative case. Consequently we feel other approaches are more promising for our purposes, at least at this stage of development of continuous cross-section techniques. In connection with these other approaches, we will henceforth assume a multiplicative relationship for the firm effects.

Thus suppose

$$F_{it} = f_i E_{it} \qquad (4)$$

where f_i is now the firm-effect "multiplier" and E is per-share earnings. The aggregate firm effect (F_{it}) for any firm is assumed proportional to its per-share earnings, but the factor of proportionality (f_i) differs among firms. If it is tentatively assumed that earnings payout effects are negligible, then

$$P_{it} = (k_t + f_i)E_{it}, \qquad (5)$$

where k_t is the average price-earnings ratio for the sample. Making the additional assumption that the f_i are constant over any two adjacent time periods:

$$f_{it} = f_{i(t-1)} = \frac{P_{i(t-1)}}{E_{i(t-1)}} - k_{t-1} = (P/E)'_{i(t-1)}. \qquad (6)$$

Therefore, under the stated assumptions, firm effects can be held constant by introducing into the regression equation a variable $[(P/E)'_{i(t-1)}]$ which measures individual deviations from the sample average price-earnings ratio in the previous time periods, i.e.,

$$P_{it} = a + bD_{it} + cR_{it} + d(P/E)'_{i(t-1)} + e_{it}.^{13} \qquad (7)$$

---

[12] These complications can be avoided in part by the application of this type of cross-section difference equation to group rather than individual firm data, a procedure which has not been utilized previously and which we plan to experiment with.

[13] In the regressions fitted subsequently, $\left\{\frac{N}{P}\right\}_{i(t-1)}$ is used instead of $\left\{\frac{P}{E}\right\}'_{i(t-1)}$ for statistical reasons. In these regressions, annual data are used as measures of the variables involved, though it can be argued that, at least for earnings, an average over a number of years might be preferable. While this was not tested, it might be pointed out that the use of such averages in another context did not affect the results significantly (see footnote 11) and that the assumed constancy of the firm effects becomes more tenuous the longer the period covered. Another approach to holding firm effects constant is to substitute equation (6) in equation (5), which results in equation (12), except that theoretically for this purpose the $P_{i(t-1)}$ term in equation (12) should be multiplied by the ratio of E_{it} to $E_{i(t-1)}$.

In this equation (as well as in the continuous cross-section model) firm effects include the profitability of investment opportunities as assessed by the market.

The problem of least-squares bias can be handled by specifying a complete model including a dividend supply function as well as the customary price relation. For instance, let

$$P_{it} = a + bD_{it} + cR_{it} + d(P/E)'_{i(t-1)} \tag{8}$$

be the relation determining price; and let

$$D_{it} = e + fE_{it} + gD_{i(t-1)} + h(P/E)'_{i(t-1)} \tag{9}$$

be the dividend supply equation (error terms have been omitted). The dividend supply equation is developed by adding to the best type of relationship developed by previous writers[14] (which stresses the importance of past dividends on current dividends) a variable permitting the firm to adjust its current payout to past market valuation of its future earnings. The system is completed by the identity:

$$E_{it} = D_{it} + R_{it}, \tag{10}$$

where E_{it} may be considered exogenous but, of course, not D_{it} or R_{it}. Solving these equations (8), (9), and (10) we have:

$$P_{it} = [a + e(b - c)] + [c + f(b - c)]E_{it} + [g(b - c)]D_{i(t-1)} \\ + [d + h(b - c)](P/E)'_{i(t-1)}. \tag{11}$$

After obtaining the regression coefficients of equations (9) and (11) in the usual manner, the coefficients of equation (8) can be derived and are theoretically free of bias due to effects of price on dividend supply.

Turning to the problem of random income movements, the argument here, it will be recalled, implies that short-run changes in income evoke relatively small short-run changes in relative price. Thus, an equation of the form

$$P_{it} = a + bD_{it} + cR_{it} + dP_{i(t-1)} \tag{12}$$

in which previous expectations, measured by $P_{i(t-1)}$, as well as current dividend and earnings experience, are assumed to determine current price is consistent with this assumption about price behavior. The b and c coefficients in this equation measure the extent of short-run price adjustment to short-run changes in dividends and earnings retention, respectively. Long-run values of these coefficients can, after correcting d for movements in the general market price level, be obtained by dividing each through by $1 - d$, provided it can be assumed that d measures only the influence of past expectations on current expectations. One of the additional merits of this

---

[14] See Lintner [11].

equation is that lagged price to some extent also holds constant any firm effects that exist; as a result, however, long-run coefficients computed by this method may be somewhat in error.

A more direct approach to the problem of short-run earnings movements lies in the "normalization" of those earnings. Other authors have attempted this—usually by use of centered or weighted averages—but we feel that these methods are somewhat less satisfactory than available alternatives. A simple average of earnings over, say, a three-year period may still contain large short-run components (relative to future expectations) if the adjustment process is slow. The same comment also applies to weighted averages and, in view of the relatively high weight usually given to current earnings, this technique may be even less satisfactory than the use of a simple average.

Of several alternatives available for earnings normalization, an approach that seems especially promising is one in which market estimates are employed. To illustrate, assume that price and dividends are always taken as "normal," and that short-run earnings abnormalities sum to zero over the sample of companies in question (the latter being a reasonable assumption for most industries over most periods if we avoid major cyclical disturbances). Thus, the dividend-price ratio is assumed to be always normal but the earnings-price ratio is subject to short-run fluctuations. Variations about trend values of the ratio $(E/P)_{it}/(E/P)_{kt}$ are, by assumption, due solely to short-run components of the ith company's earnings, because the average earnings-price ratio for the sample $[(E/P)_{kt}]$ is defined to be free of earnings disturbances. Examination of the scatter diagrams of the time-series behavior of this "relative earnings yield" ratio failed to indicate any reason for assigning anything other than a linear equation to the underlying time trend. Therefore, on an empirical basis,

$$\frac{(E/P)_{it}}{(E/P)_{kt}} = a_i + b_i t + e_{it}. \tag{13}$$

Now normal value of company earnings-price ratios can be computed as follows (the superscript n denoting normalized value):

$$(E/P)^n_{it} = [a_i + b_i t](E/P)_{kt} \tag{14}$$

Having obtained a normalized value of the earnings-price ratio, normalized earnings are found by simply multiplying this ratio by per-share price. Normalized retained earnings are then obtained by subtracting observed dividends from normalized earnings.

The assumptions underlying this approach can, of course, be questioned —dividends do react to year-to-year fluctuations in earnings; price does contain speculative components; and earnings fluctuations may not sum to zero over the sample. However, dividends are likely to react only to fluctuations in earnings regarded as relatively permanent. Moreover, averaging price over a year should remove most relative speculative components of individual share prices since, in theory, arbitragers can be expected to hold these to short duration. Any error attaching to the assumption that sample average earnings are normal is likely to be small and thus its effect on the regression equation will also be small.[15] Nevertheless, prices, as we measure them, probably do contain individual speculative components of small magnitude. Thus normal earnings computed from measured prices will contain errors of the same relative magnitude and direction as those contained in price, so that some small bias is probably introduced in favor of the retained earnings coefficient.

All of the statistical models presented earlier can, of course, be modified to specify normalized values of those variables in which earnings fluctuations play a distorting part. The regression results presented later embody two such modifications.

Finally, the influence of dividend payout on price can be subjected to time-series analysis. For instance, the above equations relating relative earnings yield to time can be compared with regression equations of the following form,

$$\frac{(D/E)_{it}}{(D/E)_{kt}} = a_i + b_i t + e_{it}, \tag{15}$$

to ascertain if changes over time in relative earnings-price ratios are consistently associated with changes in relative dividend payout ratios—and, if so, the nature of the association. This procedure, it might be noted, involves none of the assumptions necessary for derivation of normalized earnings and, hence, constitutes an independent check on their validity. Many other time-series tests of the relative importance of dividends and retained earnings are also possible.

III.   REGRESSION RESULTS

For most of our statistical analysis we worked with five industry samples, viz., chemicals, electronics, electric utilities, foods, and steels, in each of two years, 1956 and 1958. The industries were selected to permit a distinction to be made between the results for growth and nongrowth industries and to provide a basis for comparison with results by other authors for earlier years. Both cyclical and noncyclical industries are covered. Ready accessibility of data and resource availability were also factors in both industry and year selection. An attempt was made to conform to a fairly narrow definition of the industries chosen so that the sample companies would be reasonably

---

[15] This earnings normalization procedure was developed in Mr. Puckett's forthcoming Ph.D. dissertation, and the validity of its assumptions are subjected to critical evaluation in that work. Alternative methods of earnings normalization—for instance, by derivation of a normal dividend payout ratio—are also presented.

Table 23–1. Regression equation: $P_t = a + bD_t + cR_t$.

Industry (sample size)	t	Regression coefficients (standard errors)			
		a	b	c	$\bar{R}^2$
Chemicals (n = 20)	1956	−0.86	+29.94 (3.00)	+2.91 (4.98)	0.868
	1958	−5.29	+27.72 (2.22)	+13.15 (5.65)	0.910
Electronics (n = 20)	1956	+7.32	+7.27 (9.77)	+17.87 (6.60)	0.410
	1958	+8.53	+13.56 (12.80)	+26.85 (6.57)	0.524
Electric Utilities (n = 25)	1956	+0.85	+13.86 (2.35)	+14.91 (3.42)	0.842
	1958	+1.11	+14.29 (3.36)	+18.54 (5.22)	0.772
Foods (n = 25)	1956	+0.78	+15.56 (1.70)	+5.23 (1.30)	0.834
	1958	+1.50	+17.73 (2.10)	+4.35 (1.56)	0.805
Steels (n = 20)	1956	−2.28	+17.60 (2.65)	+2.45 (1.42)	0.869
	1958	+8.55	+15.23 (1.63)	+5.98 (2.08)	0.881

Note: Per-share price (average for year), dividends, and retained earnings are represented by P, D and R, respectively; t designates year; n, size of sample; $\bar{R}^2$, coefficient of determination adjusted for degrees of freedom; and standard errors of regression coefficients are indicated under coefficients in parentheses.

homogeneous in industrial composition.[16] The periods covered include a boom year for the economy when stock prices leveled off after a substantial rise (1956) and a somewhat depressed year for the economy when stock prices, however, rose strongly (1958). Originally we had intended including several earlier years as well, but it was not feasible to do this systematically.

Table 23–1 presents the usual simple linear relationships between average prices and dividends and retained earnings to show with the data we are using the kinds of results typically obtained, and to provide a basis of comparison with alternative regression models. In this analysis, we find the customary strong dividend and relatively weak retained earnings effect in three of the five industries—i.e., chemicals, foods, and steels. In these three industries, there is little evidence of any significant shift in the relative

---

[16] A list of the corporations included may be obtained on request.

importance of retained earnings from earlier years as a result of increasing market emphasis on growth.[17] While these results may not be altogether surprising for steels and foods, they seem highly questionable for chemicals, which was probably regarded as a growth industry in this period. Even for steels and foods the magnitude of the difference between the dividend and retained earnings coefficients seems implausible.

The fact that electric utilities show fully as high a coefficient and electronics a higher coefficient for retained earnings than for dividends is in closer agreement with what might be expected. Unfortunately, we know of no earlier results for electronics that can be used as a basis of comparison.

For electric utilities, there are two earlier analyses that can be compared with our results, though the forms of the relationships used are somewhat different. The first, by Morrissey [16], relates the earnings-price and dividends-price ratios separately to the dividend payout ratios for each of the years 1950–57 and finds that the payout ratio in this industry did affect stock prices significantly in the early part of this period (with higher prices associated with higher payout) but very little in the latter part of this period. Moreover, this study found a steady reduction in the importance of the payout ratio from year to year and some evidence that the direction of its effect had changed by the end of the period, i.e., that higher payout may have been associated with lower prices for given earnings by 1957. These results are consistent with investors' changing evaluations of the growth potential of electric utilities and, for the end of the period covered, with our results in 1956 and 1958. However, the second earlier analysis referred to, which derives a logarithmic relation between the ratio of stock prices to book value and both the ratio of earnings to book value and the payout ratio, yields a different result for utilities in early 1955 showing a positive relation between the price to book ratio and payout.[18]

A recomputation of the electric utilities regressions in Table 23–1 utilizing logarithms for all the variables again points to a higher dividend than retained earnings effect, unlike the result obtained in the linear form.[19] It is not possible to choose conclusively between the linear and logarithmic results on statistical or a priori grounds. The logarithmic relations do reduce the problem of regression weights referred to earlier (with a correlation between these weights and investment quality exaggerating any regression bias due to a correlation between quality and dividend payout). However, so do both the ratio relations discussed above and the more complex linear relations in subsequent tables, all of which give the same type of results for the electric utilities as the simple linear relations. Moreover, the ratio and linear regressions, unlike the logarithmic relations, can handle satisfactorily

---

[17] See, e.g., Gordon [6] for comparable 1951 and 1954 regressions for these industries.

[18] See Durand [3]. It is not clear whether utilities other than electric are included.

[19] The only other industry regressions which were recomputed were for chemicals and here the logarithmic results were quite close to the linear results.

very small and negative retained earnings. We feel that the major difference between the logarithmic and nonlogarithmic regressions may be due to the differing degrees of bias in the regression coefficients produced by shortrun income disturbances, and we shall attempt to hold these constant in some of the following statistical analyses.

To summarize the results so far, they provide a little more evidence than has existed heretofore that in growth industries (chemicals, electronics and electric utilities) more weight relatively is given to retained earnings than in nongrowth industries (steels and foods), but the evidence is not uniform (chemicals) and for one of the two remaining industries (electric utilities) depends partly on the mathematical form of the regression used. In any event, for three of five groups including one presumably growth industry, we find again the same peculiar result obtained by our numerous predecessors using similar kinds of analysis—i.e., a predominant dividend effect.

One simple approach to holding firm effects constant (and in the process to reduce the problem of regression weights) is to add a lagged earnings-price ratio to the equations in Table 23–1. The results presented in Table 23–2

Table 23-2. Regression equation: $P_t = a + bD_t + cR_t + d(E/P)_{t-1}$.

Industry (sample size)	t	Regression coefficients (standard errors)				
		a	b	c	d	$\bar{R}^2$
Chemicals (n = 20)	1956	+58.21	+25.19 (1.69)	+13.81 (3.00)	−0.97 (0.14)	0.967
	1958	+21.75	+26.93 (1.55)	+15.20 (3.95)	−0.45 (0.10)	0.959
Electronics (n = 20)	1956	+32.83	+15.78 (7.76)	+19.14 (5.02)	−0.49 (0.13)	0.681
	1958	+54.59	+27.18 (8.14)	+28.06 (12.60)	−0.87 (1.57)	0.836
Electric Utilities (n = 25)	1956	+30.26	+12.42 (2.04)	+15.50 (2.89)	−0.41 (0.13)	0.892
	1958	+41.59	+13.12 (2.32)	+14.88 (3.65)	−0.49 (0.10)	0.897
Foods (n = 25)	1956	+15.66	+13.68 (1.44)	+7.52 (1.16)	−0.17 (0.04)	0.905
	1958	+16.93	+16.75 (6.27)	+5.68 (4.91)	−0.16 (0.07)	0.843
Steels (n = 25)	1956	−6.39	+17.85 (2.78)	+2.21 (1.55)	+0.03 (0.07)	0.870
	1958	+4.33	+15.06 (1.68)	+5.67 (2.17)	+0.05 (0.07)	0.885

Note: E represents per-share earnings. See Table 23–1 for other symbols.

again indicate that dividends have a predominant influence on stock prices in the same three out of five industries but the differences between the dividends and retained earnings coefficients are not quite so marked as in the first set of regressions. The dividends and retained earnings coefficients are closer to each other for all industries in both years except for steels in 1956, and the correlations are higher, again except for steels.

These new regressions, however, are not too satisfactory for a variety of reasons, of which the potential bias arising from short-run income

Table 23–3. Dividend supply and derived price regressions, 1958.

Dividend supply equation: $D_t = e + fE_t + gD_{t-1} + h(E/p)_{t-1}$

Industry (sample size)	Parameter estimates				$\bar{R}^2$
	e	f	g	h	
Chemicals (n = 20)	+0.0282	+0.0850 (0.0320)	+0.8334 (0.0416)	+0.0007 (0.0017)	0.995
Electric Utilities (n = 25)	−0.1163	+0.1440 (0.0326)	+0.7989 (0.0502)	+0.0024 (0.0018)	0.989
Foods (n = 25)	+0.1836	+0.0735 (0.0322)	+0.8435 (0.0579)	−0.0004 (0.0013)	0.962
Steels (n = 20)	+0.6261	+0.1456 (0.0329)	+0.6589 (0.0868)	−0.0027 (0.0020)	0.942

Derived price equation: $P_t = a + bD_t + cR_t + d(E/P)_{t-1}$

Industry (sample size)	Parameter estimates			d
	a	b	c	
Chemicals (n = 20)	+19.18	+27.02	+17.46	−0.45
Electric Utilities (n = 25)	+41.16	+11.02	+18.34	−0.46
Foods (n = 25)	+14.31	+17.65	+5.70	−0.16
Steels (n = 20)	−1.06	+22.41	+13.81	+0.07

disturbances is probably the most important. Moreover, an additional possible source of bias involves another question that was raised previously— i.e., the influence of stock price on dividend payout levels set by managements. Table 23–3 presents for four industry groups in 1958 the relevant dividend supply equations and the derived price equations obtained from the solution of the complete model, which contains three equations—the price equation (8), the dividend supply equation (9), and the identity (10). The derived price equations show no significant changes from those obtained from the single equation approach in Table 23–2, reflecting the fact that stock price, or more accurately the price-earnings ratio, does not seem to have a significant effect on dividend payout. On the other hand, it might be noted that, in three of the four cases tested, the retained earnings effect is increased relatively, with no change in the fourth case. These results suggest that price effects on dividend supply are probably not a serious source of bias in the customary derivation of dividend and retained earnings effects on stock prices, though such a bias might be masked if the disturbing effects of short-run income movements are sufficiently great.

To provide some direct evidence on the potential bias arising from short-run income movements, the standard linear equation in Table 23-1 can be

Table 23-4. Regression equation: $P_t = a + bD_t + cR_t + dP_{t-1}$.

Industry (sample size)	t	a	b	c	d	$\bar{R}^2$
			Regression coefficients (standard errors)			
Chemicals (n = 20)	1956	−1.52	−2.52 (3.78)	+6.36 (2.10)	+1.06 (0.12)	0.979
	1958	−4.06	+3.75 (3.23)	+6.45 (2.78)	+0.88 (0.11)	0.981
Electronics (n = 20)	1956	−4.92	−7.49 (3.05)	+5.18 (2.14)	+1.27 (0.09)	0.953
	1958	+0.68	−5.84 (3.02)	+9.20 (1.74)	+1.13 (0.96)	0.978
Electric Utilities (n = 25)	1956	+1.62	−8.19 (3.67)	+2.79 (2.75)	+1.30 (0.20)	0.947
	1958	+2.49	−1.36 (2.06)	+3.84 (2.59)	+1.11 (0.11)	0.963
Foods (n = 25)	1956	+1.74	+0.31 (1.84)	+2.56 (0.66)	+0.81 (0.09)	0.967
	1958	−1.15	+1.75 (2.93)	+1.43 (1.08)	+1.08 (0.18)	0.929
Steels (n = 20)	1956	+3.89	−0.17 (4.30)	+3.16 (0.98)	+0.88 (0.19)	0.943
	1958	+0.94	+7.73 (1.55)	+3.34 (1.26)	+0.55 (0.09)	0.964

modified to include a lagged price variable which allows for slow short-run adjustment in prices to current levels of income. As noted earlier, to some extent the lagged price variable also holds firm effects constant; it also minimizes the problem of regression weights. These results are presented in Table 23-4.

Examination of this table shows that retained earnings receive greater relative weight than dividends in the majority of cases. The only exceptions are steels and foods in 1958. In all three groups which would normally be considered growth industries (chemicals, electronics, and utilities) the retained earnings effect is larger than the dividend effect for both years covered. For the other two industries (steels and foods) there no longer seems to be any significant systematic differences between the retained earnings and dividend coefficients, though there is some suggestion that dividends became relatively more attractive in 1958 than in 1956, which may not be surprising in view of the possible change in outlook for these industries at that time. This set of regressions has a number of attractive features apart from eliminating the customary anomalous result for dividends and retained earnings. The correlation coefficients as a whole have been substantially improved. The regression coefficients of the constant terms are in general close to zero, which is in accord with theoretical expectations, and the magnitudes of the lagged price coefficients seem generally sensible. Interestingly also, relationships for earlier years (1949, 1950, and 1952), identical in form to those in Table 23–4, show relatively weaker retained earnings effects than in the later years, a finding fully in accord with the changing emphasis on growth characteristics of stocks in this period.[20]

However, the regressions in Table 23–4 also have numerous limitations, including the possibility that the lagged price variable may serve in part as a proxy for dividends. Perhaps as a consequence, the regressions exhibit such undesirable properties as frequently negative dividend coefficients (though these are generally insignificant) and large standard errors for both dividends and retained earnings. These regressions, nevertheless, do seem to point to the weakness of the response of price to short-run changes in earnings, and to the fact that this response is not greatly affected by whether such changes in earnings are paid out as dividends or retained. There is some indication that retained earnings are more important than dividends (particularly for growth industries) but in half the cases neither the short-run dividend nor the retained earnings coefficient is significantly different from zero.[21]

Another and independent approach to the problem of short-run income movements which was described earlier is to normalize earnings by deriving time-series regressions of the form of equation (13) for each of the i companies in the kth industry group, and obtaining normalized retained earnings by subtracting dividends from normalized earnings, i.e., from

$$[a_i + b_i t](E/P)_{kt} \cdot P_{it}.$$

This normalization procedure was based on the period 1950–61, and prices were then related to dividends and normalized retained earnings for chemicals, foods, and steels in 1956 and 1958, with the results presented in Table 23–5. Subsequently, the prior year's normalized earnings-price variable

---

[20] It was possible to derive such regressions in the earlier years for all industry samples except the electronics.

[21] Logarithmic regressions otherwise identical in form with those in Table 23–4 were computed for chemicals and electric utilities and showed very similar results to the linear relations.

Table 23–5. Regression equation: $P_t = a + bD_t + cR^n_t$.

Industry (sample size)		Regression coefficients (standard errors)			
	t	a	b	c	$\bar{R}^2$
Chemicals ($n = 20$)	1956	-6.37	$+27.84$ (2.66)	$+10.96$ (5.22)	0.89
	1958	-5.87	$+25.78$ (2.58)	$+18.82$ (7.46)	0.91
Foods ($n = 25$)	1956	$+3.00$	$+15.11$ (1.28)	$+3.83$ (1.46)	0.93
	1958	$+2.20$	$+15.96$ (1.40)	$+4.91$ (1.17)	0.94
Steels ($n = 20$)	1956	$+0.34$	$+15.36$ (1.41)	$+4.85$ (0.80)	0.98
	1958	$+6.11$	$+14.37$ (1.29)	$+8.24$ (1.93)	0.93

Note: The superscript n denotes normalized value. (See text.)

was also added to hold firm effects constant; these results are presented in Table 23–6.

A comparison of the results in Tables 23–5 and 23–6 with the corresponding regressions in Tables 23–1 and 23–2 shows the significant role of normalized earnings in eliminating part of the usual understatement of the relative importance of retained earnings, while a comparison of Tables

Table 23–6. Regression equation: $P_t = a + bD_t + cR_t^n + d(E/P)^n_{t-1}$.

Industry (sample size)		Regression coefficients (standard errors)				
	t	a	b	c	d	$\bar{R}^2$
Chemicals ($n = 20$)	1956	$+37.46$	$+25.33$ (1.77)	$+13.81$ (3.62)	-621.53 (137.11)	0.95
	1958	$+26.64$	$+24.38$ (1.95)	$+19.29$ (5.55)	-605.42 (157.64)	0.95
Foods ($n = 25$)	1956	$+21.78$	$+13.20$ (0.57)	$+9.22$ (0.80)	-241.80 (23.51)	0.98
	1958	$+23.30$	$+13.26$ (0.81)	$+8.95$ (0.81)	-227.40 (29.57)	0.97
Steels ($n = 20$)	1956	$+18.42$	$+12.10$ (0.90)	$+7.66$ (0.70)	-164.26 (34.10)	0.99
	1958	$+34.82$	$+13.59$ (0.87)	$+12.19$ (1.58)	-353.54 (79.34)	0.96

23–5 and 23–6 again indicates the similar role of a device (in this case, the normalized price-earnings ratio) holding firm effects constant. An examination of Table 23–6 shows that, for the industry groups covered, most, but not all, of the differences between dividend and retained earnings coefficients disappear when earnings are normalized and firm effects held constant. Similar regressions were not computed for the electronics sample since a sufficiently long time period for earnings normalization was not available, or for the utilities sample since a different and more satisfactory sample is

Table 23–7. Regression equations for 17 chemical companies.

$$P_t = a + bD_t + cR_t^n$$

$$P_t = a + bD_t + cR_t^n + d(E/P)_t^n$$

Regression coefficients (standard errors)

t	a	b	c	d	$\bar{R}^2$
1958	+11.12	+10.56 (4.17)	+14.64 (3.79)		0.81
1958	+6.42	+11.33 (4.28)	+16.63 (5.52)		0.79
1956	+39.12	+12.14 (2.40)	+17.23 (2.22)	−539.32 (313.11)	0.89
1958	+38.01	+12.18 (1.76)	+18.62 (2.27)	−553.87 (66.04)	0.94

being analyzed separately by one of the authors. However, it might be noted that for this somewhat different (and somewhat larger) sample of electric utilities, normalizing earnings and holding firm effects constant reduces the dividend coefficient slightly and increases the retained earnings coefficient fairly markedly.

The results of Table 23–6 seem considerably more plausible to us than the usual findings for foods and steels, suggesting that in these industries a somewhat (but not drastically) higher investor valuation may be placed on dividends than on retained earnings within the range of payout experienced so that management might be able to increase prices somewhat by raising dividends.[22] However, the regressions for chemicals in the table, though more satisfactory than those customarily obtained, do not seem quite so plausible since they imply the same type of result as for foods and steels.

A more detailed examination of our chemicals sample disclosed that the results obtained largely reflected the undue regression weighting given the three firms with prices deviating most from the average price in the sample

---

[22] In this connection, it might be noted that foods and steels are characterized by lower payout than chemicals.

of 20 firms. If these three firms are omitted, the results are changed substantially. As Table 23–7 indicates, retained earnings now become somewhat more important than dividends as a price determinant (again within the range of payout experienced).

In view of the possible bias in favor of the retained earnings coefficient that may be introduced by the earnings normalization procedure adopted, it was considered desirable to compare the time-series behavior of the relative earnings yield ratios previously discussed, i.e., equation (13), with that of relative dividend payout ratios obtained by deriving time-series regressions of the form

$$\frac{(D/E)_{it}}{(D/E)_{kt}} = a_i + b_i t$$

over the same time period. In view of resource limitations, this was done only for chemicals, which is considered the industry for which the customary results are most in question. The results in Table 23–8 show that in 12 out of 20 cases the time-slope coefficents for the relative earnings yield and relative payout regressions have the same sign, while in eight cases they are of opposite sign. This suggests that as relative payout increases, relative earnings yield increases somewhat more often than otherwise. In other words, the price-earnings ratio may have some tendency to move inversely to the payout ratio in contrast to the customary assertion of a direct relation. The correlation between the two slope coefficients is not very high but is

Table 23–8. Time-slope coefficients from relative earnings yield and relative payout regressions for companies in the chemicals industry (D/Ei).

Company	b	b'
1. Dupont	+0.014	+0.009
2. Union Carbide	+0.012	+0.015
3. Allied	+0.015	+0.016
4. Dow	+0.023	+0.019
5. American Cyanamid	+0.031	+0.036
6. Monsanto	−0.032	−0.014
7. Olin	+0.045	−0.022
8. Air Reduction	+0.026	+0.039
9. Koppers	+0.037	+0.039
10. Hercules	+0.017	−0.034
11. Texas Gulf Sulfur	−0.028	+0.012
12. Columbian Carbon	−0.038	+0.020
13. Hooker	+0.006	+0.016
14. Diamond Alkali	−0.010	+0.005
15. Pennsalt	−0.013	+0.002
16. Atlas Chem.	+0.019	−0.008
17. Commercial Solvents	−0.053	−0.072
18. Celanese	−0.128	−0.135
19. American Potash	+0.046	−0.002
20. Imperial Chem.	+0.038	+0.055

Note: b is the time-slope coefficient from the relative earnings yield regressions and b' is the corresponding coefficient from the relative payout regressions. (See text.)

significant ($\bar{R}^2 = 0.543$). This is fairly strong evidence that the customary results are invalid, since the comparison of trends in relative yield and relative payout over time largely avoids both problems of short-run income fluctuations and problems of consistent firm effects. However, it should be noted that one difficulty may remain. If relative earnings yield goes down (i.e., relative price-earnings go up) because of a higher prospective rate of return on new corporate investment, the relative payout may go down because lower payout is associated with higher profit prospects, but the decline in payout would have no causative relation to the decline in yield. On the other hand, the customary finding that investors pay a premium for dividends as against retained earnings in the market even when the profitability of corporate investment opportunities is not held constant would still be invalidated.

IV. SOME CONCLUDING REMARKS

Our analysis suggests that there is little basis for the customary view that in the stock market generally, except for unusual growth stocks, a dollar of dividends has several times the impact on price as a dollar of retained earnings. There is some indication that in nongrowth industries as a whole, a somewhat (but only moderately) higher investor valuation may be placed on dividends than on retained earnings within the range of payout experienced, but that the opposite may be true in growth industries. To the extent that this conclusion is valid, it is possible that management might be able, at least in some measure, to increase stock prices in nongrowth industries by raising dividends, and in growth industries by greater retention. However, the evidence that such possibilities exist to any important degree is rather tenuous, and there is no convincing indication of widespread management irrationality or irresponsibility in payout policy.

Unfortunately, the analysis we have carried out is limited not only in coverage of industries and time periods, but also in the linearity assumed. While the latter restriction can be justified on the grounds that a major objective was to question as expeditiously as possible the customary—and to us implausible—results obtained from similar mathematical forms, our results do not go very far in indicating what payout ratios are regarded as optimal by investors for various types of stocks with different profitability of investment opportunities, risk, sources of financing, etc., or even in indicating whether an optimal ratio exists which to some extent is independent of profit prospects. Thus it would not surprise us if investors as a rule prefer at least a small nonzero (and preferably a stable or rising) payout, even at the cost of foregoing otherwise desirable investment. However, the further study of optimal ratios, while relatively simple in theoretical terms, involves much more complicated empirical analysis than has been attempted here.

REFERENCES

[1] BENISHAY, HASKEL, "Variability in Earnings-Price Ratios of Corporate Equities," *Am. Econ. Rev.*, March 1961, *51*, 81–94.

[2] DARLING, PAUL G., "The Influence of Expectations and Liquidity on Dividend Policy," *Jour. Pol. Econ.*, June 1957, *65*, 209–24.

[3] DURAND, DAVID, "The Cost of Capital, Corporation Finance, and the Theory of Investment: Comment," *Am. Econ. Rev.*, Sept. 1959, *49*, 639–54.

[4] FISHER, G. R., "Some Factors Influencing Share Prices," *Econ. Jour.*, March 1961, *71*, 121–41.

[5] FRIEND, IRWIN, and SANFORD PARKER, "A New Slant on the Stock Market," *Fortune*, Sept. 1956.

[6] GORDON, MYRON J., "Dividends, Earnings, and Stock Prices," *Rev. Econ. Stat.*, May, 1959, *41*, 99–105.

[7] ————, *The Investment, Financing, and Valuation of the Corporation*, Homewood 1962.

[8] GRAHAM, BENJAMIN and D. L. DODD, *Security Analysis*, 1st ed. New York 1934.

[9] JOHNSON, LYLE R., ELI SHAPIRO and JOSEPH O'MEARA, JR., "Valuation of Closely-Held Stock for Federal Tax Purposes: Approach to an Objective Method," *Univ. of Penn. Law Rev.*, Nov. 1951, *100*, 166–95.

[10] LINTNER, JOHN, "Dividends, Earnings, Leverage, Stock Prices and the Supply of Capital to Corporations," *Rev. Econ. Stat.*, Aug. 1962, *44*, 243–69.

[11] ————, "Distribution of Incomes of Corporations Among Dividends, Retained Earnings, and Taxes," *Am. Econ. Rev.*, May 1956, *46*, 97–113.

[12] LYNCH, MERRILL, PIERCE, FENNER and SMITH, *Annual Report*, 1959, p. 4.

[13] MILLER, M. H. and FRANCO MODIGLIANI, "Dividend Policy, Growth, and the Valuation of Shares," *Jour. Bus.*, Oct. 1961, *34*, 411–33.

[14] MODIGLIANI, FRANCO and M. H. MILLER, "The Cost of Capital, Corporation Finance, and the Theory of Investment," *Am. Econ. Rev.*, June 1958, *48*, 261–97.

[15] ————, "The Cost of Capital, Corporation Finance, and the Theory of Investment: Reply," *Am. Econ. Rev.*, Sept. 1959, *49*, 655–69.

[16] MORRISSEY, FRED P., "Current Aspects of the Cost of Capital to Utilities," *Public Utilities Fortnightly*, April 14, 1958.

[17] SOLOMON, EZRA, *The Theory of Financial Management*, New York 1963.

[18] WOLD, HERMAN, *Demand Analysis*, New York 1953.

PART VII

Money and Capital Markets

24

PORTFOLIO SELECTION

H. MARKOWITZ*

Although this paper was first published in 1952, it is included because the underlying concepts are essential to understanding current research on analyzing uncertainty in investment situations. By taking account of covariance, Markowitz describes how risk and return expectations, measured by variance and expected return, can be combined into an undominated set of potential investments. If the investor is convinced that the mean-variance approach is a valid descriptor of both risk and willingness to assume risk, he can utilize the efficient boundary to select the combination of risk and return which maximizes his expected utility.

The process of selecting a portfolio may be divided into two stages. The first stage starts with observation and experience and ends with beliefs about the future performances of available securities. The second stage starts with the relevant beliefs about future performances and ends with the choice of portfolio. This paper is concerned with the second stage. We first consider the rule that the investor does (or should) maximize discounted expected, or anticipated, returns. This rule is rejected both as a hypothesis to explain, and as a maximum to guide investment behavior. We next consider the rule that the investor does (or should) consider expected return a desirable thing *and* variance of return an undesirable thing. This rule has many sound points, both as a maxim for, and hypothesis about, investment behavior. We illustrate geometrically relations between beliefs and choice of portfolio according to the "expected returns—variance of returns" rule.

One type of rule concerning choice of portfolio is that the investor does (or should) maximize the discounted (or capitalized) value of future returns.[1] Since the future is not known with certainty, it must be "expected" or "anticipated" returns which we discount. Variations of this type of rule can be suggested. Following Hicks, we could let "anticipated" returns include an allowance for risk.[2] Or, we could let the rate at which we capitalize the returns from particular securities vary with risk.

H. Markowitz, "Portfolio Selection," *Journal of Finance* (March 1952), pp. 77–91. Reprinted with permission.

* This paper is based on work done by the author while at the Cowles Commission for Research in Economics and with the financial assistance of the Social Science Research Council. It is reprinted as Cowles Commission Paper, New Series, No. 60.

[1] See, for example, J. B. Williams, *The Theory of Investment Value* (Cambridge, Mass.: Harvard University Press, 1938), pp. 55–75.

[2] J. R. Hicks, *Value and Capital* (New York: Oxford University Press, 1939), p. 126. Hicks applies the rule to a firm rather than a portfolio.

The hypothesis (or maxim) that the investor does (or should) maximize discounted return must be rejected. If we ignore market imperfections the foregoing rule never implies that there is a diversified portfolio which is preferable to all non-diversified portfolios. Diversification is both observed and sensible; a rule of behavior which does not imply the superiority of diversification must be rejected both as a hypothesis and as a maxim.

The foregoing rule fails to imply diversification no matter how the anticipated returns are formed; whether the same or different discount rates are used for different securities; no matter how these discount rates are decided upon or how they vary over time.[3] The hypothesis implies that the investor places all his funds in the security with the greatest discounted value. If two or more securities have the same value, then any of these or any combination of these is as good as any other.

We can see this analytically: suppose there are N securities; let r_{it} be the anticipated return (however decided upon) at time t per dollar invested in security i; let d_{it} be the rate at which the return on the ith security at time t is discounted back to the present; let X_i be the relative amount invested in security i. We exclude short sales, thus $X_i \geq 0$ for all i. Then the discounted anticipated return of the portfolio is

$$R = \sum_{t=1}^{\infty} \sum_{i=1}^{N} d_{it} r_{it} X$$

$$= \sum_{i=1}^{N} X_i \left(\sum_{t=1}^{\infty} d_{it} r_{it} \right)$$

$$R = \sum_{t=1}^{\infty} d_{it} r_{it}$$

is the discounted return of the ith security, therefore $R = \sum X_i R_i$ where R_i is independent of X_i. Since $X_i \geq 0$ for all i and $\sum X_i = 1$, R is a weighted average of R_i with the X_i as non-negative weights. To maximize R, we let $X_i = 1$ for i with maximum R_i. If several $R\alpha_a$, $a = 1, \ldots, K$ are maximum then any allocation with

$$\sum_{a=1}^{K} X\alpha_a = 1$$

maximizes R. In no case is a diversified portfolio preferred to all non-diversified portfolios.[4]

It will be convenient at this point to consider a static model. Instead of speaking of the time series of returns from the ith security $(r_{i1}, r_{i2}, \ldots, r_{it}, \ldots)$ we will speak of "the flow of returns" (r_i) from the ith security. The flow

---

[3] The results depend on the assumption that the anticipated returns and discount rates are independent of the particular investor's portfolio.

[4] If short sales were allowed, an infinite amount of money would be placed in the security with highest r.

of returns from the portfolio as a whole is $R = \sum X_i r_i$. As in the dynamic case if the investor wished to maximize "anticipated" return from the portfolio he would place all his funds in that security with maximum anticipated returns.

There is a rule which implies both that the investor should diversify and that he should maximize expected return. The rule states that the investor does (or should) diversify his funds among all those securities which give maximum expected return. The law of large numbers will insure that the actual yield of the portfolio will be almost the same as the expected yield.[5] This rule is a special case of the expected returns—variance of returns rule (to be presented below). It assumes that there is a portfolio which gives both maximum expected return and minimum variance, and it commends this portfolio to the investor.

This presumption, that the law of large numbers applies to a portfolio of securities, cannot be accepted. The returns from securities are too inter-correlated. Diversification cannot eliminate all variance.

The portfolio with maximum expected return is not necessarily the one with minimum variance. There is a rate at which the investor can gain expected return by taking on variance, or reduce variance by giving up expected return.

We saw that the expected returns or anticipated returns rule is inadequate. Let us now consider the expected returns—variance of returns (E-V) rule. It will be necessary to first present a few elementary concepts and results of mathematical statistics. We will then show some implications of the E-V rule. After this we will discuss its plausibility.

In our presentation we try to avoid complicated mathematical statements and proofs. As a consequence a price is paid in terms of rigor and generality. The chief limitations from this source are (1) we do not derive our results analytically for the n-security case; instead, we present them geometrically for the 3 and 4 security cases; (2) we assume static probability beliefs. In a general presentation we must recognize that the probability distribution of yields of the various securities is a function of time. The writer intends to present, in the future, the general, mathematical treatment which removes these limitations.

We will need the following elementary concepts and results of mathematical statistics:

Let Y be a random variable, i.e., a variable whose value is decided by chance. Suppose, for simplicity of exposition, that Y can take on a finite number of values $y_1, y_2, \ldots, y_N$. Let the probability that $Y = y_1$, be p_1; that $Y = y_2$ be p_2 etc. The expected value (or mean) of Y is defined to be

$$E = p_1 y_1 + p_2 y_2 + \cdots + p_N y_N$$

---

[5] Williams, *op. cit.*, pp. 68, 69.

The variance of Y is defined to be

$$V = p_1(y_1 - E)^2 + p_2(y_2 - E)^2 + \cdots + p_N(y_N - E)^2$$

V is the average squared deviation of Y from its expected value. V is a commonly used measure of dispersion. Other measures of dispersion, closely related to V are the standard deviation, $\sigma = \sqrt{V}$ and the coefficient of variation, σ/E.

Suppose we have a number of random variables: $R_1, \ldots, R_n$. If R is a weighted sum (linear combination) of the R_i

$$R = \alpha_1 R_1 + \alpha_2 R_2 + \cdots + \alpha_N R_n$$

then R is also a random variable. (For example R_1, may be the number which turns up on one die; R_2, that of another die, and R the sum of these numbers. In this case $n = 2$, $\alpha_1 = \alpha_2 = 1$.)

It will be important for us to know how the expected value and variance of the weighted sum (R) are related to the probability distribution of the $R_1, \ldots, R_n$. We state these relations below; we refer the reader to any standard text for proof.[6]

The expected value of a weighted sum is the weighted sum of the expected values. I.e., $E(R) = \alpha_1 E(R_1) + \alpha_2 E(R_2) + \cdots + \alpha_n E(R_n)$. The variance of a weighted sum is not as simple. To express it we must define "covariance." The covariance of R_1 and R_2 is

$$\sigma_{12} = E\{[R_1 - E(R_1)] [R_2 - E(R_2)]\}$$

i.e., the expected value of [(the deviation of R_1 from its mean) times (the deviation of R_2 from its mean)]. In general we define the covariance between R_i and R_j as

$$\sigma_{ij} = E\{[R_i - E(R_i)] [R_j - E(R_j)]\}$$

σ_{ij} may be expressed in terms of the familiar correlation coefficient (ρ_{ij}). The covariance between R_i and R_j is equal to [(their correlation) times (the standard deviation of R_i) times (the standard deviation of R_j)]:

$$\sigma_{ij} = \rho_{ij}\sigma_i\sigma_j$$

The variance of a weighted sum is

$$V(R) = \sum_{i=1}^{N} a_i^2 V(X_i) + 2\sum_{i=1}^{N} \sum_{i>1}^{N} a_i a_j \sigma_{ij}$$

If we use the fact that the variance of R_i is σ_{ii} then

$$V(R) = \sum_{i=1}^{N} \sum_{j=1}^{N} a_i a_j \sigma_{ij}$$

---

[6] E.g., J. V. Uspensky, *Introduction to Mathematical Probability* (New York: McGraw-Hill, 1937), Chap. 9, pp. 161–81.

Let R_i be the return on the ith security. Let μ_i be the expected value of R_i; σ_{ij}, be the covariance between R_i and R_j (thus σ_{ii} is the variance of R_i). Let X_i be the percentage of the investor's assets which are allocated to the ith security. The yield (R) on the portfolio as a whole is

$$R = \sum R_i X_i$$

The R_i (and consequently R) are considered to be random variables.[7] The X_i are not random variables, but are fixed by the investor. Since the X_i are percentages we have $\sum X_i = 1$. In our analysis we will exclude negative values of the X_i (i.e., short sales); therefore $X_i \geq 0$ for all i.

The return (R) on the portfolio as a whole is a weighted sum of random variables (where the investor can choose the weights). From our discussion of such weighted sums we see that the expected return E from the portfolio as a whole is

$$E = \sum_{i=1}^{N} X_i \mu_i$$

and the variance is

$$V = \sum_{i=1}^{N} \sum_{j=1}^{N} \sigma_{ij} X_i X_j$$

For fixed probability beliefs (μ_i, σ_{ij}) the investor has a choice of various combinations of E and V depending on his choice of portfolio $X_1, \ldots, X_N$. Suppose that the set of all obtainable (E, V) combinations were as in Fig. 24–1. The E-V rule states that the investor would (or should) want to select one of those portfolios which give rise to the (E, V) combinations indicated as efficient in the figure; i.e., those with minimum V for given E or more and maximum E for given V or less.

There are techniques by which we can compute the set of efficient portfolios and efficient (E, V) combinations associated with given μ_i and σ_{ij}. We will not present these techniques here. We will, however illustrate geometrically the nature of the efficient surfaces for cases in which N (the number of available securities) is small.

The calculation of efficient surfaces might possibly be of practical use. Perhaps there are ways, by combining statistical techniques and the judgment of experts, to form reasonable probability beliefs (μ_{ij}, σ_{ij}). We could use these beliefs to compute the attainable efficient combinations of (E, V).

---

[7] I.e., we assume that the investor does (and should) act as if he had probability beliefs concerning these variables. In general we would expect that the investor could tell us, for any two events (A and B), whether he personally considered A more likely than B, B more likely than A, or both equally likely. If the investor were consistent in his opinions on such matters, he would possess a system of probability beliefs. We cannot expect the investor to be consistent in every detail. We can, however, expect his probability beliefs to be roughly consistent on important matters that have been carefully considered. We should also expect that he will base his actions upon these probability beliefs—even though they be in part subjective.

This paper does not consider the difficult question of how investors do (or should) form their probability beliefs.

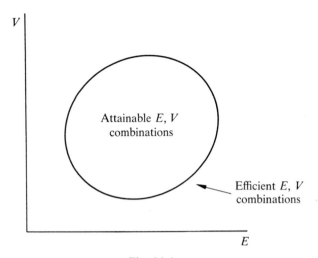

V

Attainable E, V
combinations

Efficient E, V
combinations

E

Fig. 24–1.

The investor, being informed of what (E, V) combinations were attainable, could state which he desired. We could then find the portfolio which gave this desired combination.

Two conditions—at least—must be satisfied before it would be practical to use efficient surfaces in the manner described above. First, the investor must desire to act according to the E-V maxim. Second, we must be able to arrive at reasonable μ_i and σ_{ij}. We will return to these matters later.

Let us consider the case of three securities. In the three security case our model reduces to

$$E = \sum_{i=1}^{3} X_i \mu_i \tag{1}$$

$$V = \sum_{i=1}^{3} \sum_{j=1}^{3} X_i X_j \sigma_{ij} \tag{2}$$

$$\sum_{i=1}^{3} X_i = 1 \tag{3}$$

$$X_i \geq 0 \quad \text{for} \quad i = 1, 2, 3. \tag{4}$$

From (3) we get

$$X_3 = 1 - X_1 - X_2 \tag{3'}$$

If we substitute (3') in equation (1) and (2) we get E and V as functions of X_1 and X_2. For example we find

$$E = \mu_3 + X_1(\mu_1 - \mu_3) + X_2(\mu_2 - \mu_3) \tag{1'}$$

The exact formulas are not too important here (that of V is given below).[8]

---

[8] $V = X_1^2(\sigma_{11} - 2\sigma_{13} + \sigma_{33}) + X_2^2(\sigma_{22} - 2\sigma_{23} + \sigma_{33}) + 2X_1X_2(\sigma_{12} - \sigma_{13} - \sigma_{23} + \sigma_{33}) + 2X_1(\sigma_{13} - \sigma_{33}) + 2X_2(\sigma_{23} - \sigma_{33}) + \sigma_{33}$.

We can simply write

$$E = E(X_1, X_2) \tag{a}$$

$$V = V(X_1, X_2) \tag{b}$$

$$X_1 \geq 0, X_2 \geq 0, 1 - X_1 - X_2 \geq 0 \tag{c}$$

By using relations (a), (b), (c), we can work with two dimensional geometry.

The attainable set of portfolios consists of all portfolios which satisfy constraints (c) and (3') (or equivalently (3) and (4)). The attainable combinations of X_1, X_2 are represented by the triangle abc in Figure 24–2. Any point to the left of the X_2 axis is not attainable because it violates the condition that $X_1 \geq 0$. Any point below the X_1 axis is not attainable because it violates the condition that $X_2 \geq 0$. Any point above the line $(1 - X_1 - X_2 = 0)$ is not attainable because it violates the condition that $X_3 = 1 - X_1 - X_2 \geq 0$.

We define an *isomean* curve to be the set of all points (portfolios) with a given expected return. Similarly an *isovariance* line is defined to be the set of all points (portfolios) with a given variance of return.

An examination of the formulae for E and V tells us the shapes of the isomean and isovariance curves. Specifically they tell us that typically[9] the isomean curves are a system of parallel straight lines; the isovariance curves are a system of concentric ellipses (see Fig. 24–2). For example, if $\mu_2 \neq \mu_3$ equation 1' can be written in the familiar form $X_2 = a + bX_1$; specifically (1)

$$X_2 = \frac{E - \mu_3}{\mu_2 - \mu_3} - \frac{\mu_1 - \mu_3}{\mu_2 - \mu_3} X_1.$$

Thus the slope of the isomean line associated with $E = E_0$ is $-(\mu_1 - \mu_3)/(\mu_2 - \mu_3)$; its intercept is $(E_0 - \mu_3)/(\mu_2 - \mu_3)$. If we change E we change the intercept but not the slope of the isomean line. This confirms the contention that the isomean lines form a system of parallel lines.

Similarly, by a somewhat less simple application of analytic geometry, we can confirm the contention that the isovariance lines form a family of concentric ellipses. The "center" of the system is the point which minimizes V. We will label this point X. Its expected return and variance we will label E and V. Variance increases as you move away from X. More precisely, if one isovariance curve, C_1, lies closer to X than another, C_2, then C_1 is associated with a smaller variance than C_2.

With the aid of the foregoing geometric apparatus let us seek the efficient sets.

---

[9] The isomean "curves" are as described above except when $\mu_1 = \mu_2 = \mu_3$. In the latter case all portfolios have the same expected return and the investor chooses the one with minimum variance.

As to the assumptions implicit in our description of the isovariance curves see footnote 12.

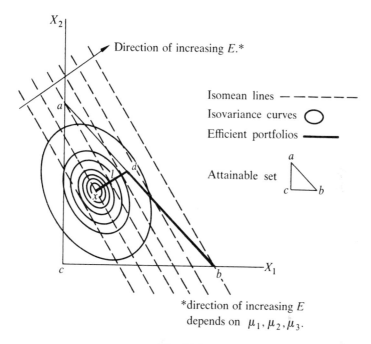

Direction of increasing E.*

Isomean lines — — — — — — —

Isovariance curves ◯

Efficient portfolios ——

Attainable set

*direction of increasing E
depends on μ_1, μ_2, μ_3.

Fig. 24–2.

X, the center of the system of isovariance ellipses, may fall either inside or outside the attainable set. Figure 24–4 illustrates a case in which X falls inside the attainable set. In this case: X is efficient. For no other portfolio has a V as low as X; therefore no portfolio can have either smaller V (with the same or greater E) or greater E with the same or smaller V. No point (portfolio) with expected return E less than E is efficient. For we have $E > E$ and $V < V$.

Consider all points with a given expected return E; i.e., all points on the isomean line associated with E. The point of the isomean line at which V takes on its least value is the point at which the isomean line is tangent to an isovariance curve. We call this point $\hat{X}(E)$. If we let E vary, $\hat{X}(E)$ traces out a curve.

Algebraic considerations (which we omit here) show us that this curve is a straight line. We will call it the critical line l. The critical line passes through X for this point minimizes V for all points with $E(X_1, X_2) = E$. As we go along l in either direction from X, V increases. The segment of the critical line from X to the point where the critical line crosses the boundary of the attainable set is part of the efficient set. The rest of the efficient set is (in the case illustrated) the segment of the $\overline{ab}$ line from d to b. b is the point of maximum attainable E. In Fig. 24–3, X lies outside the admissible area but the critical line cuts the admissible area. The efficient line begins at the

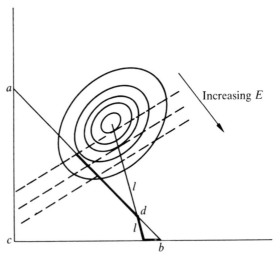

Fig. 24–3.

attainable point with minimum variance (in this case on the $\overline{ab}$ line). It moves toward b until it intersects the critical line, moves along the critical line until it intersects a boundary and finally moves along the boundary to b. The reader may wish to construct and examine the following other cases: (1) X lies outside the attainable set and the critical line does not cut the attainable set. In this case there is a security which does not enter into any efficient portfolio. (2) Two securities have the same μ_i. In this case the isomean lines are parallel to a boundary line. It may happen that the efficient portfolio with maximum E is a diversified portfolio. (3) A case wherein only one portfolio is efficient.

The efficient set in the 4 security case is, as in the 3 security and also the N security case, a series of connected line segments. At one end of the efficient set is the point of minimum variance; at the other end is a point of maximum expected return[10] (see Fig. 24–4).

---

[10] Just as we used the equation

$$\sum_{i=1}^{4} X_i = 1$$

to reduce the dimensionality in the three security case, we can use it to represent the four security case in 3 dimensional space. Eliminating X_4 we get $E = E(X_1, X_2, X_3)$, $V = V(X_1, X_2, X_3)$. The attainable set is represented in three-space, by the tetrahedron with vertices $(0, 0, 0)$, $(0, 0, 1)$, $(0, 1, 0)$, $(1, 0, 0)$, representing portfolios with, respectively, $X_4 = 1$, $X_3 = 1$, $X_2 = 1$, $X_1 = 1$.

Let s_{123} be the subspace consisting of all points with $X_4 = 0$. Similarly we can define $s_{a1}, \ldots,$ a_a to be the subspace consisting of all points with $X_i = 0$, $i \neq a_1, \ldots, a_a$. For each subspace $s_{a1}, \ldots, a_a$ we can define a *critical line* $la_1, \ldots, a_a$. This line is the locus of points P where P minimizes V for all points in $s_{a1}, \ldots, a_a$ with the same E as P. If a point 0 in $s_{a1}, \ldots, a_a$ and is efficient it must be on $la_1, \ldots, a_a$. The efficient set may be traced out by starting at the point of minimum available variance, moving continuously along various $la_1, \ldots, a_a$ according to definite rules, ending in a point which gives maximum E. As in the two dimensional case, the point with minimum available variance may be in the interior of the available set or one of its boundaries. Typically we proceed along a given critical line until either this line intersects one of a larger subspace or meets a boundary and simultaneously the critical line of a lower dimensional

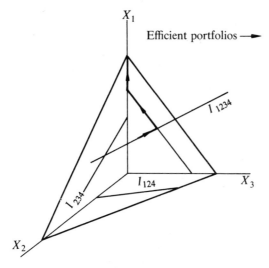

Fig. 24–4.

Now that we have seen the nature of the set of efficient portfolios, it is not difficult to see the nature of the set of efficient (E, V) combinations. In the three security case $E = a_0 + a_1X_1 + a_2X_2$ is a plane; $V = b_1 + b_1X_1 + b_2X_2 + b_{12}X_1X_2 + b_{11}X_1^2 + b_{22}X_2^2$ is a paraboloid.[11] As shown in Fig. 24-5, the section of the E-plane over the efficient portfolio set is a series of connected line segments. The section of the V-paraboloid over the efficient portfolio set is a series of connected parabola segments. If we plotted V against E for efficient portfolios we would again get a series of connected parabola segments (see Fig. 24–6). This result obtains for any number of securities.

Various reasons recommend the use of the expected return-variance of return rule, both as a hypothesis to explain well-established investment behavior and as a maxim to guide one's own action. The rule serves better, we will see, as an explanation of, and guide to, "investment" as distinguished from "speculative" behavior.

Earlier we rejected the expected returns rule on the grounds that it never implied the superiority of diversification. The expected return-variance of return rule, on the other hand, implies diversification for a wide range of μ_i, σ_{ij}. This does not mean that the E-V rule never implies the superiority of an undiversified portfolio. It is conceivable that one security might have an extremely higher yield and lower variance than all other securities; so much so that one particular undiversified portfolio would give maximum E and minimum V. But for a large, presumably representative range of μ_i, σ_{ij} the E-V rule leads to efficient portfolios almost all of which are diversified.

---

subspace). In either of these cases the efficient line turns and continues along the new line. The efficient line terminates when a point with maximum E is reached.

[11] See footnote 8.

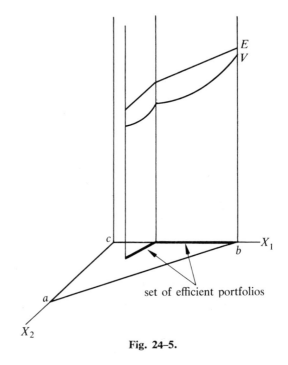

Fig. 24–5.

Not only does the *E-V* hypothesis imply diversification, it implies the "right kind" of diversification for the "right reason." The adequacy of diversification is not thought by investors to depend solely on the number of different securities held. A portfolio with sixty different railway securities, for example, would not be as well diversified as the same size portfolio with some railroad, some public utility, mining, various sort of manufacturing, etc. The reason is that it is generally more likely for firms within the same industry to do poorly at the same time than for firms in dissimilar industries.

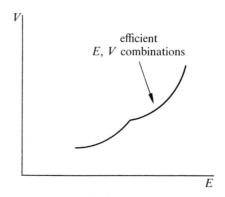

Fig. 24–6.

Similarly in trying to make variance small it is not enough to invest in many securities. It is necessary to avoid investing in securities with high covariances among themselves. We should diversify across industries because firms in different industries, especially industries with different economic characteristics, have lower covariances than firms within an industry.

The concepts "yield" and "risk" appear frequently in financial writings. Usually if the term "yield" were replaced by "expected yield" or "expected

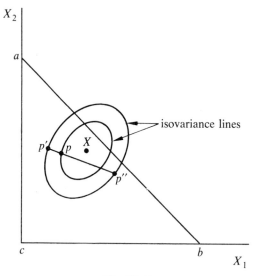

Fig. 24-7.

return," and "risk" by "variance of return," little change of apparent meaning would result.

Variance is a well-known measure of dispersion about the expected. If instead of variance the investor was concerned with standard error, $\sigma = \sqrt{V}$, or with the coefficient of dispersion, σ/E, his choice would still lie in the set of efficient portfolios.

Suppose an investor diversifies between two portfolios (i.e., if he puts some of his money in one portfolio, the rest of his money in the other. An example of diversifying among portfolios is the buying of the shares of two different investment companies). If the two original portfolios have *equal* variance then typically[12] the variance of the resulting (compound) portfolio will be less than the variance of either original portfolio. This is illustrated by Fig. 24-7. To interpret Fig. 24-7 we note that a portfolio (*P*) which is built

---

[12] In no case will variance be increased. The only case in which variance will not be decreased is if the returns from both portfolios are perfectly correlated. To draw the isovariance curves as ellipses it is both necessary and sufficient to assume that no two distinct portfolios have perfectly correlated returns.

out of two portfolios $P' = (X_1', X_2')$ and $P'' = (X_1'', X_2'')$ is of the form $P = \lambda P' + (1 - \lambda)P'' = (\lambda X_1' + (1 - \lambda)X_1'', \lambda X_2' + (1 - \lambda)X_2'')$. P is on the straight line connecting P' and P''.

The E-V principle is more plausible as a rule for investment behavior as distinguished from speculative behavior. The third moment[13] M_3 of the probability distribution of returns from the portfolio may be connected with a propensity to gamble. For example if the investor maximizes utility (U) which depends on E and $V(U = U(E, V), \partial U/\partial E > 0, \partial U/\partial E < 0)$ he will never accept an actuarially fair[14] bet. But if $U = U(E, V, M_3)$ and if $\partial U/\partial M_3 \neq 0$ then there are some fair bets which would be accepted.

Perhaps—for a great variety of investing institutions which consider yield to be a good thing; risk, a bad thing; gambling, to be avoided— E, V efficiency is reasonable as a working hypothesis and a working maxim.

Two uses of the E-V principle suggest themselves. We might use it in theoretical analyses or we might use it in the actual selection of portfolios.

In theoretical analyses we might inquire, for example, about the various effects of a change in the beliefs generally held about a firm, or a general change in preference as to expected return versus variance of return, or a change in the supply of a security. In our analyses the X_1 might represent individual securities or they might represent aggregates such as, say, bonds, stocks and real estate.[15]

To use the E-V rule in the selection of securities we must have procedures for finding reasonable μ_i and σ_{ij}. These procedures, I believe, should combine statistical techniques and the judgment of practical men. My feeling is that the statistical computations should be used to arrive at a tentative set of μ_i and σ_{ij}. Judgement should then be used in increasing or decreasing some of these μ_i and σ_{ij} on the basis of factors or nuances not taken into account by the formal computations. Using this revised set of μ_i and σ_{ij}, the set of efficient E, V combinations could be computed, the investor could select the combination he preferred, and the portfolio which gave rise to this E, V combination could be found.

One suggestion as to tentative μ_i, σ_{ij} is to use the observed μ_i, σ_{ij} for some period of the past. I believe that better methods, which take into account more information, can be found. I believe that what is needed is essentially a "probabilistic" reformulation of security analysis. I will not

---

[13] If R is a random variable that takes on a finite number of values $r_1, \ldots, r_n$ with probabilities $p_1, \ldots, p_n$ respectively, and expected value E, then

$$M_3 = \sum_{i=1}^{n} p_i(r_i - E)^3$$

[14] One in which the amount gained by winning the bet times the probability of winning is equal to the amount lost by losing the bet, times the probability of losing.

[15] Care must be used in using and interpreting relations among aggregates. We cannot deal here with the problems and pitfalls of aggregation.

pursue this subject here, for this is "another story." It is a story of which I have read only the first page of the first chapter.

In this paper we have considered the second stage in the process of selecting a portfolio. This stage starts with the relevant beliefs about the securities involved and ends with the selection of a portfolio. We have not considered the first stage: the formation of the relevant beliefs on the basis of observation.

25

CAPITAL ASSET PRICES: A THEORY OF MARKET EQUILIBRIUM UNDER CONDITIONS OF RISK

WILLIAM F. SHARPE*

Professor Sharpe's paper demonstrates the broader economic significance of portfolio decisions. The author develops the implications of portfolio decisions of individuals and proposes a theory of market equilibrium processes. The article also provides a general framework for understanding the operations of securities markets.

This study provides a clear foundation for understanding two related papers. One is by Professor John Lintner entitled, "Security Prices, Risk, and Maximal Gains from Diversification," and appears in the Journal of Finance (*December 1965*). *In a later paper, ("Security Prices, Risk, and the Maximal Gains from Diversification: Reply," Journal of Finance, December 1966) Professor Sharpe indicates that Professor Lintner has developed the basic concepts further. We present the first paper by Sharpe in order to lead the reader into the subject via a clear and relatively uncomplicated presentation. The reader then has a basis for moving on to further developments, as indicated by the following brief summary of recent developments.*

Both authors have contributed significantly toward sharpening key aspects of financial uncertainty. Assuming the bell-shaped probability distribution of normal statistical theory, the classic analytical foundation of portfolio management under uncertainty, first applied by Markowitz, serves as the point of departure. This is that the total portfolio risk can be enumerated by the sum of the calculated variance of the decision maker's assessed judgmental probability distribution of forecast returns for each security plus twice the covariance between each security. Thus, the risk of a stock is not measured simply by its variance, but also has to be assessed according to its weighted covariance with the portfolio into which it will fit. Since negatively correlated stocks have the potential of lowering the risk of the whole portfolio, they might return less than the portfolio expectation and still be acceptable in an efficient set. However, one must be cautious about assuming a negatively correlated stock will sell below the riskless rate in risk averse markets.

William F. Sharpe, "Capital Asset Prices: A Theory of Market Equilibrium Under Conditions of Risk," *Journal of Finance* (September 1964), Vol. XIX, pp. 425–442. Reprinted by permission.

* A great many people provided comments on early versions of this paper which led to major improvements in the exposition. In addition to the referees, who were most helpful, the author wishes to express his appreciation to Dr. Harry Markowitz of the RAND Corporation, Professor Jack Hirshleifer of the University of California at Los Angeles, and to Professors Yoram Barzel, George Brabb, Bruce Johnson, Walter Oi and R. Haney Scott of the University of Washington.

The utility structure for valuing uncertainty is framed according to three measures:

1. A riskless rate of return. *Unlimited investment at a certain return can be made at this rate.*
2. A market line. *This line represents the pattern of monetary trade-offs between risk and return which the market provides in equilibrium. The risk premium, or the market price for risk, is shown to increase linearly along the market line as risk increases. Its slope indicates the degree of risk aversion or conservatism present in the capital markets at a given time.*
3. Investor utility functions. *These utility functions may be different for each investor. They indicate the investor's willingness to assume risk. Once a riskless rate is assessed and a linear market line traced, a risk averse investor may tailor market opportunities to his own risk preferences by spreading his wealth between the riskless rate and an optimal stock portfolio.*

The uncertainty confronting the potential investor is described in terms of three components:

1. Systematic Risk. *The uncertainty in a projection of the level of a general economic index, such as Standard and Poor's Stock Average, is referred to as systematic risk by Professors Sharpe and Lintner. This risk is* marginally *related to the price movements of all stocks in general.*
2. Residual Risk. *This is the uncertainty remaining in individual or portfolio stock prices* conditional *on knowing the level of a general index for certain. If the general index could be forecast with certainty, then only the residual risk needs to be coped with.*
Professor Lintner refers to this component as residual risk because it remains even after all realistic steps toward efficient diversification have been taken. In an empirical situation, it is the conditional risk which will not vanish in the light of diversification. In the retrospective structure of simple linear regression analysis, it is the conditional standard error of estimate produced when individual stock portfolios are regressed on a general index.
3. Total Risk. *This is the total risk confronting the investor. It is a* joint *risk, composed of the weighted sum of the systematic and residual risk components.*

The crucial difference between the Sharpe and Lintner presentations revolves around the importance of reality in developing a theory. Sharpe's exposition dwells heavily, but not exclusively by any means, on a case where all stocks are perfectly positively correlated with an external general economic index. This completely eliminates all residual risk and the possibility of risk reduction through a diversified stock portfolio.

Lintner's concept builds on the idea that theory is simply the sum total of reality. That is, a relevant theory should be consistent with empirical observations in the capital markets. This implies that covariances between securities are nonzero and some degree of portfolio diversification is obtainable. For empirical corroboration, he indicates that the Standard and Poor's Industrial Index explains less than half of the total *variance (*total risk*) in the return of 188 out of 301 stocks in a ten year period (1954–1963). In the case of mutual fund portfolios, the residual risk (the conditional standard errors of estimate) is greater than the assessed 4 percent riskless rate in 85% of the funds studied.‡*

---

‡ See Lintner, op. cit., pp. 589–590.

This result leads to a more general model, with a unique or strong equilibrium solution. Sharpe's market adjustment process, under his special descriptive assumption, leads to a partial or weak equilibrium solution with interchangeable or equivalent risk and return combinations.

The reading of Sharpe's contribution is a necessary first step for potential portfolio experts. Those interested in greater detail and further elaboration may proceed on to Professor Lintner's fine analysis.

I. INTRODUCTION

One of the problems which has plagued those attempting to predict the behavior of capital markets is the absence of a body of positive micro-economic theory dealing with conditions of risk. Although many useful insights can be obtained from the traditional models of investment under conditions of certainty, the pervasive influence of risk in financial trans-actions has forced those working in this area to adopt models of price behavior which are little more than assertions. A typical classroom ex-planation of the determination of capital asset prices, for example, usually begins with a careful and relatively rigorous description of the process through which individual preferences and physical relationships interact to determine an equilibrium pure interest rate. This is generally followed by the assertion that somehow a market risk-premium is also determined, with the prices of assets adjusting accordingly to account for differences in their risk.

A useful representation of the view of the capital market implied in such discussions is illustrated in Fig. 25–1. In equilibrium, capital asset prices have adjusted so that the investor, if he follows rational procedures (primarily diversification), is able to attain any desired point along a

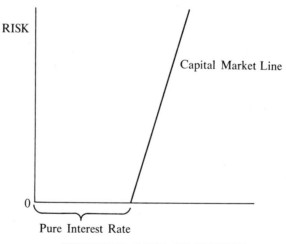

RISK

Capital Market Line

0

Pure Interest Rate

EXPECTED RATE OF RETURN

Fig. 25–1.

capital market line.[1] He may obtain a higher expected rate of return on his holdings only by incurring additional risk. In effect, the market presents him with two prices: the *price of time*, or the pure interest rate (shown by the intersection of the line with the horizontal axis) and the *price of risk*, the additional expected return per unit of risk borne (the reciprocal of the slope of the line).

At present there is no theory describing the manner in which the price of risk results from the basic influences of investor preferences, the physical attributes of capital assets, etc. Moreover, lacking such a theory, it is difficult to give any real meaning to the relationship between the price of a single asset and its risk. Through diversification, some of the risk inherent in an asset can be avoided so that its total risk is obviously not the relevant influence on its price; unfortunately little has been said concerning the particular risk component which is relevant.

In the last ten years a number of economists have developed *normative* models dealing with asset choice under conditions of risk. Markowitz[2], following Von Neumann and Morgenstern, developed an analysis based on the expected utility maxim and proposed a general solution for the portfolio selection problem. Tobin[3] showed that under certain conditions Markowitz's model implies that the process of investment choice can be broken down into two phases: first, the choice of a unique optimum combination of risky assets; and second, a separate choice concerning the allocation of funds between such a combination and a single riskless asset. Recently, Hicks[4] has used a model similar to that proposed by Tobin to derive corresponding conclusions about individual investor behavior, dealing somewhat more explicitly with the nature of the conditions under which the process of investment choice can be dichotomized. An even more detailed discussion of this process, including a rigorous proof in the context of a choice among lotteries has been presented by Gordon and Gangolli.[5]

Although all the authors cited use virtually the same model of investor behavior,[6] none has yet attempted to extend it to construct a *market*

---

[1] Although some discussions are also consistent with a non-linear (but monotonic) curve.

[2] Harry M. Markowitz, *Portfolio Selection, Efficient Diversification of Investments* (New York: John Wiley and Sons, Inc., 1959). The major elements of the theory first appeared in his article "Portfolio Selection," *The Journal of Finance*, XII (March 1952), 77–91.

[3] James Tobin, "Liquidity Preference as Behavior Towards Risk," *The Review of Economic Studies*, XXV (February, 1958), 65–86.

[4] John R. Hicks, "Liquidity," *The Economic Journal*, LXXII (December, 1962), 787–802.

[5] M. J. Gordon and Ramesh Gangolli, "Choice Among and Scale of Play on Lottery Type Alternatives," College of Business Administration, University of Rochester, 1962. For another discussion of this relationship see W. F. Sharpe, "A Simplified Model for Portfolio Analysis," *Management Science*, Vol. 9, No. 2 (January 1963), 277–293. A related discussion can be found in F. Modigliani and M. H. Miller, "The Cost of Capital, Corporation Finance, and the Theory of Investment," *The American Economic Review*, XLVIII (June 1958), 261–297.

[6] Recently Hirshleifer has suggested that the mean-variance approach used in the articles cited is best regarded as a special case of a more general formulation due to Arrow. See Hirshleifer's "Investment Decision Under Uncertainty," *Papers and Proceedings of the Seventy-Sixth Annual Meeting of the American Economic Association*, Dec. 1963, or Arrow's "Le Role des Valeurs Boursieres pour la Repartition la Meilleure des Risques," *International Colloquium on Econometrics*, 1952.

equilibrium theory of asset prices under conditions of risk.[7]   We will show that such an extension provides a theory with implications consistent with the assertions of traditional financial theory described above. Moreover, it sheds considerable light on the relationship between the price of an asset and the various components of its overall risk. For these reasons it warrants consideration as a model of the determination of capital asset prices.

Part II provides the model of individual investor behavior under conditions of risk. In Part III the equilibrium conditions for the capital market are considered and the capital market line derived. The implications for the relationship between the prices of individual capital assets and the various components of risk are described in Part IV.

II.   OPTIMAL INVESTMENT POLICY FOR THE INDIVIDUAL

The Investor's Preference Function

Assume that an individual views the outcome of any investment in probabilistic terms; that is, he thinks of the possible results in terms of some probability distribution. In assessing the desirability of a particular investment, however, he is willing to act on the basis of only two parameters of this distribution—its expected value and standard deviation.[8]   This can be represented by a total utility function of the form:

$$U = f(E_w, \sigma_w)$$

where E_w indicates expected future wealth and σ_w the predicted standard deviation of the possible divergence of actual future wealth from E_w.

Investors are assumed to prefer a higher expected future wealth to a lower value, ceteris paribus ($dU/dE_w > 0$). Moreover, they exhibit risk-aversion, choosing an investment offering a lower value of σ_w to one with a greater level, given the level of E_w ($dU/d\sigma_w < 0$). These assumptions imply that indifference curves relating E_w and σ_w will be upward-sloping.[9]

To simplify the analysis, we assume that an investor has decided to commit a given amount (W_i) of his present wealth to investment. Letting W_t be his terminal wealth and R the rate of return on his investment:

$$R \equiv \frac{W_t - W_i}{W_i},$$

---

[7] After preparing this paper the author learned that Mr. Jack L. Treynor, of Arthur D. Little, Inc., had independently developed a model similar in many respects to the one described here. Unfortunately Mr. Treynor's excellent work on this subject is, at present, unpublished.

[8] Under certain conditions the mean-variance approach can be shown to lead to unsatisfactory predictions of behavior. Markowitz suggests that a model based on the semi-variance (the average of the squared deviations below the mean) would be preferable; in light of the formidable computational problems, however, he bases his analysis on the variance and standard deviation.

[9] While only these characteristics are required for the analysis, it is generally assumed that the curves have the property of diminishing marginal rates of substitution between E_w and σ_w, as do those in our diagrams.

we have

$$W_t = R\ W_i + W_i.$$

This relationship makes it possible to express the investor's utility in terms of R, since terminal wealth is directly related to the rate of return:

$$U = g(E_R, \sigma_R).$$

Fig. 25–2 summarizes the model of investor preferences in a family of

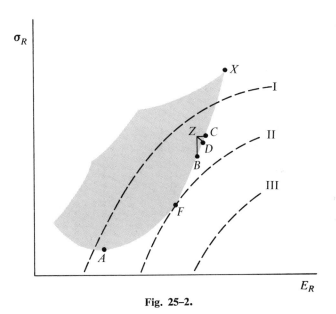

Fig. 25–2.

indifference curves; successive curves indicate higher levels of utility as one moves down and/or to the right.[10]

---

[10] Such indifference curves can also be derived by assuming that the investor wishes to maximize expected utility and that his total utility can be represented by a quadratic function of R with decreasing marginal utility. Both Markowitz and Tobin present such a derivation. A similar approach is used by Donald E. Farrar in *The Investment Decision Under Uncertainty* (Prentice-Hall, 1962). Unfortunately Farrar makes an error in his derivation; he appeals to the Von-Neumann-Morgenstern cardinal utility axioms to transform a function of the form:

$$E(U) = a + bE_R - cE_R{}^2 - c\sigma_R{}^2$$

into one of the form:

$$E(U) = k_1 E_R - k_2 \sigma_R{}^2.$$

That such a transformation is not consistent with the axioms can readily be seen in this form, since the first equation implies non-linear indifference curves in the E_R, $\sigma_R{}^2$ plane while the second implies a linear relationship. Obviously no three (different) points can lie on both a line and a non-linear curve (with a monotonic derivative). Thus the two functions must imply different orderings among alternative choices in at least some instance.

The Investment Opportunity Curve

The model of investor behavior considers the investor as choosing from a set of investment opportunities that one which maximizes his utility. Every investment plan available to him may be represented by a point in the E_R, σ_R plane. If all such plans involve some risk, the area composed of such points will have an appearance similar to that shown in Fig. 25–2. The investor will choose from among all possible plans the one placing him on

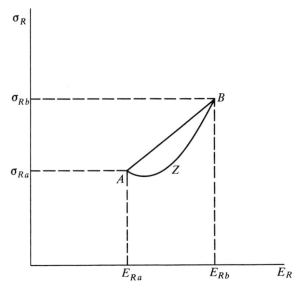

Fig. 25–3.

the indifference curve representing the highest level of utility (point F). The decision can be made in two stages: first, find the set of efficient investment plans and, second choose one from among this set. A plan is said to be efficient if (and only if) there is no alternative with either (1) the same E_R and a lower σ_R, (2) the same σ_R and a higher E_R or (3) a higher E_R and a lower σ_R. Thus investment Z is inefficient since investments B, C, and D (among others) dominate it. The only plans which would be chosen must lie along the lower right-hand boundary ($AFBDCX$)—*the investment opportunity curve.*

To understand the nature of this curve, consider two investment plans —A and B, each including one or more assets. Their predicted expected values and standard deviations of rate of return are shown in Fig. 25–3. If the proportion α of the individual's wealth is placed in plan A and the remainder $(1 - \alpha)$ in B, the expected rate of return of the combination will lie between the expected returns of the two plans:

$$E_{Rc} = \alpha E_{Ra} + (1 - \alpha)E_{Rb}$$

The predicted standard deviation of return of the combination is:

$$\sigma_{Rc} = \sqrt{\alpha^2\sigma_{Ra}{}^2 + (1 - \alpha)^2\sigma_{Rb}{}^2 + 2r_{ab}\alpha(1 - \alpha)\sigma_{Ra}\sigma_{Rb}}$$

Note that this relationship includes r_{ab}, the correlation coefficient between the predicted rates of return of the two investment plans. A value of $+1$ would indicate an investor's belief that there is a precise positive relationship between the outcomes of the two investments. A zero value would indicate a belief that the outcomes of the two investments are completely independent and -1 that the investor feels that there is a precise inverse relationship between them. In the usual case r_{ab} will have a value between 0 and $+1$.

Fig. 25–3 shows the possible values of E_{Rc} and σ_{Rc} obtainable with different combinations of A and B under two different assumptions about the value of r_{ab}. If the two investments are perfectly correlated, the combinations will lie along a straight line between the two points, since in this case both E_{Rc} and σ_{Rc} will be linearly related to the proportions invested in the two plans.[11] If they are less than perfectly positively correlated, the standard deviation of any combination must be less than that obtained with perfect correlation (since r_{ab} will be less); thus the combinations must lie along a curve below the line AB.[12] AZB shows such a curve for the case of complete independence $(r_{ab} = 0)$; with negative correlation the locus is even more U shaped.[13]

The manner in which the investment opportunity curve is formed is relatively simple conceptually, although exact solutions are usually quite difficult.[14] One first traces curves indicating E_R, σ_R values available with simple combinations of individual assets, then considers combinations of combinations of assets. The lower right-hand boundary must be either linear or increasing at an increasing rate $(d^2\sigma_R/dE_R^2 > 0)$. As suggested

---

[11]
$$E_{Rc} = \alpha E_{Ra} + (1 - \alpha)E_{Rb} = E_{Rb} + (E_{Ra} - E_{Rb})\alpha$$
$$\sigma_{Rc} = \sqrt{\alpha^2\sigma_{Ra}{}^2 + (1 - \alpha)^2\sigma_{Rb}{}^2 + 2r_{ab}\alpha(1 - \alpha)\sigma_{Ra}\sigma_{Rb}}$$

but $r_{ab} = 1$, therefore the expression under the square root sign can be factored:

$$\sigma_{Rc} = \sqrt{[\alpha\sigma_{Ra} + (1 - \alpha)\sigma_{Rb}]^2}$$
$$= \alpha\sigma_{Ra} + (1 - \alpha)\sigma_{Rb}$$
$$= \sigma_{Rb} + (\sigma_{Ra} - \sigma_{Rb})\alpha$$

[12] This curvature is, in essence, the rationale for diversification.

[13] When $r_{ab} = 0$, the slope of the curve at point A is $-(\sigma_{Ra})/(E_{Rb} - E_{Ra})$, at point B it is $(\sigma_{Rb})/(E_{Rb} - E_{Ra})$. When $r_{ab} = -1$, the curve degenerates to two straight lines to a point on the horizontal axis.

[14] Markowitz has shown that this is a problem in parametric quadratic programming. An efficient solution technique is described in his article, "The Optimization of a Quadratic Function Subject to Linear Constraints," *Naval Research Logistics Quarterly*, Vol. 3 (March and June, 1956), 111–133. A solution method for a special case is given in the author's "A Simplified Model for Portfolio Analysis," *op. cit.*

earlier, the complexity of the relationship between the characteristics of individual assets and the location of the investment opportunity curve makes it difficult to provide a simple rule for assessing the desirability of individual assets, since the effect of an asset on an investor's over-all investment opportunity curve depends not only on its expected rate of return (E_{Ri}) and risk (σ_{Ri}), but also on its correlations with the other available opportunities $(r_{i1}, r_{i2}, \ldots, r_{in})$. However, such a rule is implied by the equilibrium conditions for the model, as we will show in part IV.

The Pure Rate of Interest

We have not yet dealt with riskless assets. Let P be such an asset; its risk is zero $(\sigma_{Rp} = 0)$ and its expected rate of return, E_{Rp}, is equal (by definition) to the pure interest rate. If an investor places α of his wealth in P and the remainder in some risky asset A, he would obtain an expected rate of return:

$$E_{Rc} = \alpha E_{Rp} + (1 - \alpha)E_{Ra}.$$

The standard deviation of such a combination would be:

$$\sigma_{Rc} = \sqrt{\alpha^2\sigma_{Rp}{}^2 + (1 - \alpha)^2\sigma_{Ra}{}^2 + 2r_{pa}\alpha(1 - \alpha)\sigma_{Rp}\sigma_{Ra}}$$

but since $\sigma_{Rp} = 0$, this reduces to:

$$\sigma_{Rc} = (1 - \alpha)\sigma_{Ra}.$$

This implies that all combinations involving any risky asset or combination of assets plus the riskless asset must have values of E_{Rc} and σ_{Rc} which lie along a straight line between the points representing the two components. Thus in Fig. 25–4 all combinations of E_R and σ_R lying along the line PA are attainable if some money is loaned at the pure rate and some placed in A. Similarly, by lending at the pure rate and investing in B, combinations along PB can be attained. Of all such possibilities, however, one will dominate: that investment plan lying at the point of the original investment opportunity curve where a ray from point P is tangent to the curve. In Fig. 25–4 all investments lying along the original curve from X to ϕ are dominated by some combination of investment in ϕ and lending at the pure interest rate.

Consider next the possibility of borrowing. If the investor can borrow at the pure rate of interest, this is equivalent to disinvesting in P. The effect of borrowing to purchase more of any given investment than is possible with the given amount of wealth can be found simply by letting α take on negative values in the equations derived for the case of lending. This will obviously give points lying along the extension of line PA if borrowing is used to purchase more of A; points lying along the extension of PB if the funds are used to purchase B, etc.

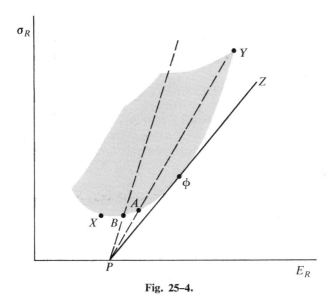

Fig. 25-4.

As in the case of lending, however, one investment plan will dominate all others when borrowing is possible. When the rate at which funds can be borrowed equals the lending rate, this plan will be the same one which is dominant if lending is to take place. Under these conditions, the investment opportunity curve becomes a line ($P\phi Z$ in Fig. 25-4). Moreover, if the original investment opportunity curve is not linear at point ϕ, the process of investment choice can be dichotomized as follows: first select the (unique) optimum combination of risky assets (point ϕ), and second borrow or lend to obtain the particular point on PZ at which an indifference curve is tangent to the line.[15]

Before proceeding with the analysis, it may be useful to consider alternative assumptions under which only a combination of assets lying at the point of tangency between the original investment opportunity curve and a ray from P can be efficient. Even if borrowing is impossible, the investor will choose ϕ (and lending) if his risk-aversion leads him to a point below ϕ on the line $P\phi$. Since a large number of investors choose to place some of their funds in relatively risk-free investments, this is not an unlikely possiblity. Alternatively, if borrowing is possible but only up to some limit, the choice

---

[15] This proof was first presented by Tobin for the case in which the pure rate of interest is zero (cash). Hicks considers the lending situation under comparable conditions but does not allow borrowing. Both authors present their analysis using maximization subject to constraints expressed as equalities. Hick's analysis assumes independence and thus insures that the solution will include no negative holdings of risky assets; Tobin's covers the general case, thus his solution would generally include negative holdings of some assets. The discussion in this paper is based on Markowitz' formulation, which includes non-negativity constraints on the holdings of all assets.

of ϕ would be made by all but those investors willing to undertake considerable risk. These alternative paths lead to the main conclusion, thus making the assumption of borrowing or lending at the pure interest rate less onerous than it might initially appear to be.

III. EQUILIBRIUM IN THE CAPITAL MARKET

In order to derive conditions for equilibrium in the capital market we invoke two assumptions. First, we assume a common pure rate of interest, with all investors able to borrow or lend funds on equal terms. Second, we assume homogeneity of investor expectations:[16] investors are assumed to agree on the prospects of various investments—the expected values, standard deviations and correlation coefficients described in Part II. Needless to say, these are highly restrictive and undoubtedly unrealistic assumptions. However, since the proper test of a theory is not the realism of its assumptions but the acceptability of its implications, and since these assumptions imply equilibrium conditions which form a major part of classical financial doctrine, it is far from clear that this formulation should be rejected—especially in view of the dearth of alternative models leading to similar results.

Under these assumptions, given some set of capital asset prices, each investor will view his alternatives in the same manner. For one set of prices the alternatives might appear as shown in Fig. 25–5. In this situation, an investor with the preferences indicated by indifference curves A_1 through A_4 would seek to lend some of his funds at the pure interest rate and to invest the remainder in the combination of assets shown by point ϕ, since this would give him the preferred over-all position A^*. An investor with the preferences indicated by curves B_1 through B_4 would seek to invest all his funds in combination ϕ, while an investor with indifference curves C_1 through C_4 would invest all his funds plus additional (borrowed) funds in combination ϕ in order to reach his preferred position (C^*). In any event, all would attempt to purchase only those risky assets which enter combination ϕ.

The attempts by investors to purchase the assets in combination ϕ and their lack of interest in holding assets not in combination ϕ would, of course, lead to a revision of prices. The prices of assets in ϕ will rise and, since an asset's expected return relates future income to present price, their expected returns will fall. This will reduce the attractiveness of combinations which include such assets; thus point ϕ (among others) will move to the left of its initial position.[17] On the other hand, the prices of assets not in ϕ will fall, causing an increase in their expected returns and a rightward movement of

---

[16] A term suggested by one of the referees.
[17] If investors consider the variability of future dollar returns unrelated to present price, both E_R and σ_R will fall; under these conditions the point representing an asset would move along a ray through the origin as its price changes.

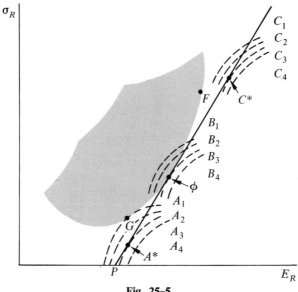

Fig. 25–5.

points representing combinations which include them. Such price changes will lead to a revision of investors' actions; some new combination or combinations will become attractive, leading to different demands and thus to further revisions in prices. As the process continues, the investment opportunity curve will tend to become more linear, with points such as ϕ moving to the left and formerly inefficient points (such as F and G) moving to the right.

Capital asset prices must, of course, continue to change until a set of prices is attained for which every asset enters at least one combination lying on the capital market line. Fig. 25–6 illustrates such an equilibrium condition.[18] All possibilities in the shaded area can be attained with combinations of risky assets, while points lying along the line PZ can be attained by borrowing or lending at the pure rate plus an investment in some combination of risky assets. Certain possibilities (those lying along PZ from point A to point B) can be obtained in either manner. For example, the E_R, σ_R values shown by point A can be obtained solely by some combination of risky assets; alternatively, the point can be reached by a combination of lending and investing in combination C of risky assets.

It is important to recognize that in the situation shown in Fig. 25–6 many alternative combinations of risky assets are efficient (i.e., lie along line PZ), and thus the theory does not imply that all investors will hold the same

---

[18] The area in Fig. 25–6 representing E_R, σ_R values attained with only risky assets has been drawn at some distance from the horizontal axis for emphasis. It is likely that a more accurate representation would place it very close to the axis.

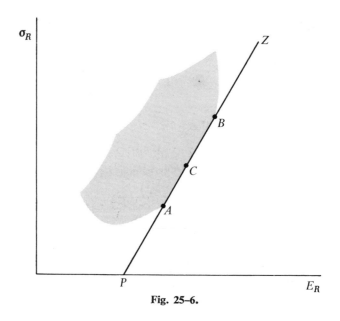

Fig. 25–6.

combination.[19] On the other hand, all such combinations must be perfectly (positively) correlated, since they lie along a linear border of the E_R, σ_R region.[20] This provides a key to the relationship between the prices of capital assets and different types of risk.

IV.   THE PRICES OF CAPITAL ASSETS

We have argued that in equilibrium there will be a simple linear relationship between the expected return and standard deviation of return for efficient combinations of risky assets. Thus far nothing has been said about such a relationship for individual assets. Typically the E_R, σ_R values associated with single assets will lie above the capital market line, reflecting the inefficiency of undiversified holdings. Moreover, such points may be scattered throughout the feasible region, with no consistent relationship between their expected return and total risk (σ_R). However, there will be a consistent

---

[19] This statement contradicts Tobin's conclusion that there will be a unique optimal combination of risky assets. Tobin's proof of a unique optimum can be shown to be incorrect for the case of perfect correlation of efficient risky investment plans if the line connecting their E_R, σ_R points would pass through point P. In the graph of this article (*op. cit.*) the constant-risk locus would, in this case, degenerate from a family of ellipses into one of straight lines parallel to the constant-return loci, thus giving multiple optima.

[20] E_R, σ_R values given by combinations of any two combinations must lie within the region and cannot plot above a straight line joining the points. In this case they cannot plot below such a straight line. But since only in the case of perfect correlation will they plot along a straight line, the two combinations must be perfectly correlated. As shown in Part IV, this does not necessarily imply that the individual securities they contain are perfectly correlated.

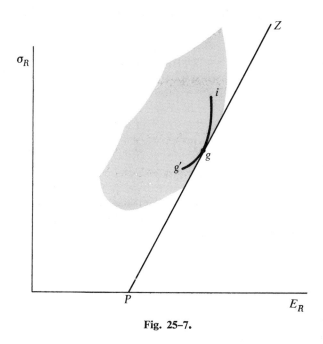

Fig. 25-7.

relationship between their expected returns and what might best be called *systematic risk*, as we will now show.

Figure 25-7 illustrates the typical relationship between a single capital asset (point *i*) and an efficient combination of assets (point *g*) of which it is a part. The curve *igg'* indicates all E_R, σ_R values which can be obtained with feasible combinations of asset *i* and combination *g*. As before, we denote such a combination in terms of a proportion α of asset *i* and (1 − α) of combination *g*. A value of α = 1 would indicate pure investment in asset *i* while α = 0 would imply investment in combination *g*. Note, however, that α = 0.5 implies a total investment of more than half the funds in asset *i*, since half would be invested in *i* itself and the other half used to purchase combination *g*, which also includes some of asset *i*. This means that a combination in which asset *i* does not appear at all must be represented by some negative value of α. Point *g'* indicates such a combination.

In Fig. 25-7 the curve *igg'* has been drawn tangent to the capital market line (*PZ*) at point *g*. This is no accident. All such curves must be tangent to the capital market line in equilibrium, since (1) they must touch it at the point representing the efficient combination and (2) they are continuous at that point.[21] Under these conditions a lack of tangency would imply that the curve intersects *PZ*. But then some feasible combination of assets would lie to the right of the capital market line, an obvious impossibility since the

---

[21] Only if $r_{ig} = -1$ will the curve be discontinuous over the range in question.

capital market line represents the efficient boundary of feasible values of E_R and σ_R.

The requirement that curves such as igg' be tangent to the capital market line can be shown to lead to a relatively simple formula which relates the expected rate of return to various elements of risk for all assets which are included in combination g.[22] Its economic meaning can best be seen if the relationship between the return of asset i and that of combination g is viewed in a manner similar to that used in regression analysis.[23] Imagine that we were given a number of (ex post) observations of the return of the two investments. The points might plot as shown in Fig. 25–8. The scatter of the R_i observations around their mean (which will approximate E_{Ri}) is, of course, evidence of the total risk of the asset—σ_{Ri}. But part of the scatter is due to an underlying relationship with the return on combination g, shown by B_{ig}, the slope of the regression line. The response of R_i to changes in R_g (and variations in R_g itself) accounts for much of the variation in R_i. It is this component of the asset's total risk which we term the *systematic* risk. The remainder,[24] being uncorrelated with R_g, is the unsystematic component. This formulation of the relationship between R_i and R_g can be employed *ex ante* as a predictive model. B_{ig} becomes the *predicted* response of R_i to changes in R_g. Then, given σ_{Rg} (the predicted risk of R_g), the systematic portion of the predicted risk of each asset can be determined.

---

[22] The standard deviation of a combination of g and i will be:

$$\sigma = \sqrt{\alpha^2\sigma_{Ri}^2 + (1-\alpha)^2\sigma_{Rg}^2 + 2r_{ig}\alpha(1-\alpha)\sigma_{Ri}\sigma_{Rg}}$$

at $\alpha = 0$:

$$\frac{d\sigma}{d\alpha} = -\frac{1}{\sigma}[\sigma_{Rg}^2 - r_{ig}\sigma_{Ri}\sigma_{Rg}]$$

but $\sigma = \sigma_{Rg}$ at $\alpha = 0$. Thus:

$$\frac{d\sigma}{d\alpha} = -[\sigma_{Rg} - r_{ig}\sigma_{Ri}].$$

The expected return of a combination will be:

$$E = \alpha E_{Ri} + (1-\alpha)E_{Rg}.$$

Thus, at all values of α:

$$\frac{dE}{d\alpha} = -[E_{Rg} - E_{Ri}]$$

and, at $\alpha = 0$:

$$\frac{d\sigma}{dE} = \frac{\sigma_{Rg} - r_{ig}\sigma_{Ri}}{E_{Rg} - E_{Ri}}.$$

Let the equation of the capital market line be:

$$\sigma_R = s(E_R - P)$$

where P is the pure interest rate. Since igg' is tangent to the line when $\alpha = 0$, and since (E_{Rg}, σ_{gR}) lies on the line:

$$\frac{\sigma_{Rg} - r_{ig}\sigma_{Ri}}{E_{Rg} - E_{Ri}} = \frac{\sigma_{Rg}}{E_{Rg} - P}$$

or:

$$\frac{r_{ig}\sigma_{Ri}}{\sigma_{Rg}} = -\left[\frac{P}{E_{Rg} - P}\right] + \left[\frac{1}{E_{Rg} - P}\right]E_{Ri}.$$

[23] This model has been called the diagonal model since its portfolio analysis solution can be facilitated by re-arranging the data so that the variance-covariance matrix becomes diagonal. The method is described in the author's article, cited earlier.

[24] ex post, the standard error.

RETURN ON
ASSET *i* (R_i)

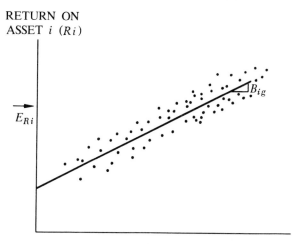

RETURN ON COMBINATION *g* (R_g)

Fig. 25–8.

This interpretation allows us to state the relationship derived from the tangency of curves such as *igg'* with the capital market line in the form shown in Fig. 25–9. All assets entering efficient combination *g* must have (predicted) B_{ig} and E_{Ri} values lying on the line *PQ*.[25] Prices will adjust so that assets which are more responsive to changes in R_g will have higher expected returns than those which are less responsive. This accords with common sense. Obviously the part of an asset's risk which is due to its correlation with the return on a combination cannot be diversified away when the asset is added to the combination. Since B_{ig} indicates the magnitude of this type of risk it should be directly related to expected return.

The relationship illustrated in Fig. 25–9 provides a partial answer to the question posed earlier concerning the relationship between an asset's risk and its expected return. But thus far we have argued only that the relationship holds for the assets which enter some particular efficient combination (*g*). Had another combination been selected, a different linear relationship would have been derived. Fortunately this limitation is easily overcome. As

---

[25]

and:

$$r_{ig} = \sqrt{\frac{B_{ig}{}^2\sigma_{Rg}{}^2}{\sigma_{Ri}{}^2}} = \frac{B_{ig}\sigma_{Rg}}{\sigma_{Ri}}$$

$$B_{ig} = \frac{r_{ig}\sigma_{Ri}}{\sigma_{Rg}}.$$

The expression on the right is the expression on the left-hand side of the last equation in footnote 22. Thus:

$$B_{ig} = -\left[\frac{P}{E_{Rg} - P}\right] + \left[\frac{1}{E_{Rg} - P}\right] E_{Ri}.$$

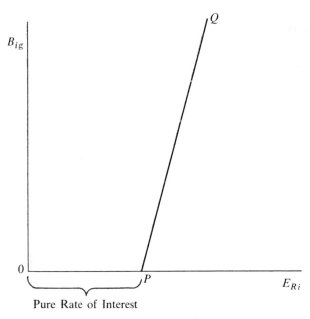

Pure Rate of Interest

Fig. 25–9.

shown in the footnote,[26] we may arbitrarily select *any* one of the efficient combinations, then measure the predicted responsiveness of *every* asset's rate of return to that of the combination selected; and these coefficients will be related to the expected rates of return of the assets in exactly the manner pictured in Fig. 25–9.

[26] Consider the two assets i and i^*, the former included in efficient combination g and the latter in combination g^*. As shown above:

$$B_{ig} = -\left[\frac{P}{E_{Rg} - P}\right] + \left[\frac{1}{E_{Rg} - P}\right] E_{Ri}$$

and:

$$B_{i^*g^*} = -\left[\frac{P}{E_{Rg^*} - P}\right] + \left[\frac{1}{E_{Rg^*} - P}\right] {}_{Ri^*}.$$

Since R_g and R_g^* are perfectly correlated:

$$r_{i^*g^*} = r_{i^*g}.$$

Thus:

$$\frac{B_{i^*g^*}\sigma_{Rg^*}}{\sigma_{Ri^*}} = \frac{B_{i^*g}\sigma_{Rg}}{\sigma_{Ri^*}}$$

and:

$$B_{i^*g^*} = B_{i^*g}\left[\frac{\sigma_{Rg}}{\sigma_{Rg^*}}\right].$$

Since both g and g^* lie on a line which intercepts the E-axis at P:

$$\frac{\sigma_{Rg}}{\sigma_{Rg^*}} = \frac{E_{Rg} - P}{E_{Rg^*} - P}$$

and:

$$B_{i^*g^*} = B_{i^*g}\left[\frac{E_{Rg} - P}{E_{Rg^*} - P}\right].$$

The fact that rates of return from all efficient combinations will be perfectly correlated provides the justification for arbitrarily selecting any one of them. Alternatively we may choose instead any variable perfectly correlated with the rate of return of such combinations. The vertical axis in Fig. 25–9 would then indicate alternative levels of a coefficient measuring the sensitivity of the rate of return of a capital asset to changes in the variable chosen.

This possibility suggests both a plausible explanation for the implication that all efficient combinations will be perfectly correlated and a useful interpretation of the relationship between an individual asset's expected return and its risk. Although the theory itself implies only that rates of return from efficient combinations will be perfectly correlated, we might expect that this would be due to their common dependence on the over-all level of economic activity. If so, diversification enables the investor to escape all but the risk resulting from swings in economic activity—this type of risk remains even in efficient combinations. And, since all other types can be avoided by diversification, only the responsiveness of an asset's rate of return to the level of economic activity is relevant in assessing its risk. Prices will adjust until there is a linear relationship between the magnitude of such responsiveness and expected return. Assets which are unaffected by changes in economic activity will return the pure interest rate; those which move with economic activity will promise appropriately higher expected rates of return.

This discussion provides an answer to the second of the two questions posed in this paper. In Part III it was shown that with respect to equilibrium conditions in the capital market as a whole, the theory leads to results consistent with classical doctrine (i.e., the capital market line). We have now shown that with regard to capital assets considered individually, it also yields implications consistent with traditional concepts: it is common practice for investment counselors to accept a lower expected return from defensive securities (those which respond little to changes in the economy) than they require from aggressive securities (which exhibit significant response). As suggested earlier, the familiarity of the implications need not be considered a drawback. The provision of a logical framework for producing some of the major elements of traditional financial theory should be a useful contribution in its own right.

Thus:

$$-\left[\frac{P}{E_{Rg}* - P}\right] + \left[\frac{1}{E_{Rg}* - P}\right] E_{Ri}* = B_i*_g \left[\frac{E_{Rg} - P}{E_{Rg}* - P}\right]$$

from which we have the desired relationship between R_i* and g:

$$B_i*_g = -\left[\frac{P}{E_{Rg} - P}\right] + \left[\frac{1}{E_{Rg} - P}\right] E_{Ri}*.$$

B_i*_g must therefore plot on the same line as does B_{ig}.

26

MERCANTILE CREDIT, MONETARY POLICY, AND SIZE OF FIRMS

ALLAN H. MELTZER*

In this article, the author discusses an aspect of the impact of tight money. He suggests that in a tight money period large firms find it easier to obtain non-bank financing than do small firms. With these funds and with liquid balances accumulated in periods of easy money, larger firms provide financing to small firms. Professor Meltzer also discusses the implications of such behavior on velocity and on monetary policy, and the possible relations between credit policy and price behavior by large firms.

In the continuing debate about the role of money, credit, and monetary policy in our society, one of the major issues centers around the specific incidence of "tight money" on individual business firms. On the one hand, leading proponents of monetary controls as a regulatory device have emphasized the general, impersonal nature of such controls. They have argued that the impact of monetary policy is determined by the reaction of individual borrowers to changed market conditions.

On the other hand, critics of general controls have suggested that institutional changes have led to discrimination by suppliers in the market for money and credit. Differences in size of firm, market structure, or type of industry, the amount of liquid assets which firms may accumulate, imperfections in the capital markets, and a variety of other institutional phenomena have been offered as reasons for the failure of monetary policy to operate as a general, impersonal, control device. Some of these institutional restrictions have been summarized under the general heading of "credit rationing."

Both conjecture and empirical observation of the structure of bank loans have suggested that credit rationing favors large firms.[1] But those who

Reprinted by permission of the publishers from Allan H. Meltzer's *The Review of Economics and Statistics* Cambridge, Mass.: Harvard University Press, Copyright, 1960, by the President and Fellows of Harvard College.

* I appreciate the assistance and helpful suggestions of my colleagues G. L. Bach, R. M. Cyert, David Granick, and Edwin Mansfield, who read earlier drafts of this paper. This research was supported by grants of the Carnegie Institute of Technology Graduate School of Industrial Administration from the School's research funds and from funds provided by the Ford Foundation for the study of organizational behavior.

[1] Professor W. L. Smith has suggested that small firms "are more dependent on the banking system than large firms are, have fewer alternative sources of funds, and seem in general to be

suggest that this is the case ignore important institutional arrangements that work in the opposite direction. Banks and financial institutions are not the only sources of credit for small firms. The existence of a large volume of interfirm (mercantile) credit makes it apparent that business firms borrow from each other.[2]

Variations in the volume and distribution of mercantile credit are important accompaniments of monetary policy changes. During the recent tight money period, for example, the increase in mercantile credit by the manufacturing sector was three times larger than the increase in the money supply (currency plus adjusted demand deposits).

We show below that, when money was tightened, firms with relatively large cash balances increased the average length of time for which credit was extended. And this extension of trade credit appears to have favored those firms against whom credit rationing is said to discriminate. Hence the credit provided by banks and financial institutions seems to have been redistributed to restore much of the general, impersonal nature of monetary controls during 1955–57. Moreover, the reduction in cash balances by liquid firms helps to explain the increase in the income velocity of money during the recent tight money period.

The following section examines the relationship between a measure of monetary tightness and the liquidity of manufacturing firms of varying size. Section II discusses the important factors influencing the allocation of trade credit. Section III points out differences in the sources and allocation of funds for large and small firms during 1955–57 and compares the importance of trade credit with that of other flows. A section discussing the limitations of this analysis and a concluding section complete the paper.

I. THE INFLUENCE OF "TIGHT MONEY" ON LIQUIDITY POSITION

The use of receivables to reallocate credit implies that some firms have access to funds which can be made available for this purpose. Information on

---

more vulnerable to the effects of tight credit." *Compendium of Papers Submitted by Panelists Before the Joint Economic Committee*, March 31, 1958, 505–506.

Over a year earlier, the Committee had summarized the situation as follows: Chairman Patman: "It is the little fellow that is hurt, and the big fellow is not hurt at all." "Monetary Policy: 1955–56," Hearing before the Subcommittee on Economic Stabilization of the Joint Economic Committee, December 10 and 11, 1956, 34–35. See also J. K. Galbraith, "Market Structure and Stabilization Policy," *Review of Economics and Statistics*, XXXIX (May 1957), 124–33.

[2] Lending by suppliers to their customers through the extension of trade credit has long been recognized as a form of interfirm relationship. Sayers and Foulke have noted that one of the prime reasons for the development of mercantile credit in the nineteenth century was the need of merchants to obtain short-term credits in circumstances under which banks did not lend. R. S. Sayers, "Central Banking in the Light of Recent British and American Experience," *Quarterly Journal of Economics*, LXIII (May 1949); R. Foulke, *Behind the Scenes of Business*, Dun and Bradstreet, 1937.

Table 26–1. Results of regression of M on L.

Size class of firms (Total assests in $ million)	1951–IV through 1957–IV		1954–I through 1957–IV	
	$b*$	r	$b*$	r
Group I Under 0.25	−0.02 (0.008)	45	−0.02 (0.006)	61
Group II 0.25–0.99	−0.06 (0.01)	74	−0.05 (0.007)	86
Group III 1.0–4.99	−0.07 (0.008)	89	−0.08 (0.006)	94
Group IV 5.0–9.99	−0.08 (0.008)	89	−0.08 (0.006)	94
Group V 10.0–49.99	−0.12 (0.01)	88	−0.12 (0.01)	94
Group VI 50.0–99.99	−0.09 (0.008)	92	−0.10 (0.006)	96
Group VII 100.0 and over	−0.09 (0.01)	91	−0.09 (0.009)	90
Total (in $ million)				

* Marginal effect of "money market" on liquidity; figures in parentheses are the standard errors obtained from the regression of M on L.

recent periods indicates that large firms were able to obtain proportionally greater access to funds than were small firms.[3] One obvious source of such funds is the commercial banking system. Others are the capital markets, insurance companies, and financial intermediaries. A further source of funds comes from the liquid assets which the lending firm holds at the time that the decision is made to increase or allow the additional extension of credit to customers.

Define liquidity position, or stock of liquidity, as the ratio of cash plus government securities to current liabilities, a variant of the "quick" or "acid test" ratio commonly used by businessmen and accountants.[4] Indications

[3] For example Table 1 of the Federal Reserve study, "Member Bank Lending to Small Business, 1955–57," shows that all but the smallest group of firms increased their loans from commercial banks but that only the groups with total assets of $25 million or more increased by more than the average for all firms. Table 4 (page VI–12) in the "Life Insurance" survey shows that large firms gained relatively in their share of the number and amount of bonds authorized as investments of life insurance companies. Cf. *Financing Small Business*, Federal Reserve Board, 1958. The FTC-SEC "blown-up" sample of manufacturing corporations indicates that both large and small manufacturing corporations gained in loans but that during 1956 and 1957 the large firms gained relatively to the small. The data suggest the importance of mercantile credit as means by which small retailers and wholesalers borrow.

[4] This definition has the advantage of being computed and published by FTC-SEC in *Quarterly Financial Report for Manufacturing Corporations*. There is no strong reason, other than common use, for preferring this definition to others. Like similar measures of stock liquidity, it ignores the possibility that some firms have open lines of credit arranged with banks.

that the average liquidity position of firms increases monotonically with size of firms have been used to suggest that large firms are not affected by changes in monetary policy. But such a proposition ignores (1) the way in which liquidity responds to changes in the money market, and (2) the way in which the larger firms may increase the extension of mercantile credit when their sales to small customers are falling. Hence, we can not assume that large size or relatively high liquidity results in firms acting as if the restriction of credit has not taken place.

The money market variable, M, is defined as the product of the rate of interest and an index of tight money.[5] Liquidity position, or stock of liquidity, L, is measured, as above, by the ratio of cash plus government securities to current liabilities.[6]

Table 26–1 shows the results obtained from a linear regression equation of the money market variable, M, on L. All groups shows that liquidity position was relatively low during periods of monetary tightness and relatively high during periods of easy money.[7]

There is some tendency for the marginal effect of M to increase with size. This is particularly true for the groups with assets less than ten million dollars. However, with the exception of Groups I and II, differences between size groups are small. Despite this indication that the marginal effect of M on L is rather independent of size, we should recall that the largest group has by far the largest absolute amount of cash, government securities, and current liabilities. The largest dollar amount of funds is therefore released by the group with assets of $100 million and over.

While the money supply increased by less than $1 billion for the tight money period, the sample as a whole shows a decrease in cash plus government securities of more than $5 billion.[8] Table 26–2 shows the relative share of total liquid assets (cash plus governments) held by different size groups on various dates during the recent tight money period.

It is unlikely that discrimination in favor of large firms and against small

---

[5] Operationally, the interest rate is measured by the end of quarter rate of interest on new issues of Treasury bills. The ratio of free reserves to total reserves in central reserve city and reserve city banks at the end of each quarter is used as a measure of the "tightness of money." Since a negative value indicates that excess reserves are borrowed from the Fed, this ratio is subtracted from 1.00 to obtain an index of monetary tightness. (Thus, negative free reserves increase quarterly observations for the rate of interest, and positive free reserves decrease them.) The seasonally adjusted value of the product of these two variables is referred to as the "money market variable" in the text. This is one of many measures which might be chosen. It has the advantage of combining both the interest rate and a measure of the availability of loans.

[6] Data used below have been obtained from the Federal Trade Commission-Securities and Exchange Commission *Quarterly Financial Report for Manufacturing Corporations*. All data have been seasonally adjusted.

[7] This result is obtained using quarterly data for two periods. The first starts approximately six months after the signing of the Federal Reserve-Treasury Accord of 1951; the second begins in 1954, a sub-period during which there has been a much-discussed use of monetary controls. The fourth quarter 1957 is the terminal date for both series.

[8] More than 80 percent of the decrease represents the experience of the group of largest firms. Groups I, II, and III do not show any relative decline in total liquid assets held. The groups of smallest firms show the largest absolute *increase* in liquid asset holdings.

Table 26-2. Percentage of total cash plus government securities held as assets, manufacturing sector only.*

Size class of firms (total assets in $ million)	1955–II	1955–IV	1957–III	1955–II to 1957–III Change in relative share	1955–II to 1957–III Dollar change ($ million)	1955–IV to 1957–III Change in relative share	1955–IV to 1957–III Dollar change ($ million)
Group I Under 0.25	2.31%	2.15%	3.15%	+0.84%	+169	+1.00%	+146
Group II 0.25–0.99	4.82	4.56	5.29	+0.47	+27	+0.73	−48
Group III 1.0–4.99	8.13	7.68	9.23	+1.10	+122	+1.55	+3
Group IV 5.0–9.99	4.78	4.60	4.37	−0.41	−200	−0.23	−298
Group V 10.0–49.99	13.16	12.92	12.92	−0.24	−323	0	−668
Group VI 50.0–99.99	7.05	7.02	7.78	+0.73	+47	+0.76	−169
Group VIII 100.0 and over	59.77	61.06	57.24	−2.53	−1841	−3.83	−4144
Total (in $ million)	27,724	30,904	25,726		−1999		−5178

* Detail may not add to total because of rounding.

firms would make the results (shown in Table 26–2) a consequence of general monetary controls. Moreover, to the extent that a reduction in liquid assets represents a significant proportion of the assets available for increasing receivables, the largest firms were in a position to allocate the assets thus released into an increase in their holdings of accounts and notes receivable.[9]

II. FACTORS INFLUENCING ALLOCATION OF TRADE CREDIT

If the suppliers of firms affected by credit rationing respond to a decrease in the demand for their product by increasing the ratio of accounts plus notes receivable to sales, a reallocation of assets and credit occurs.[10] Even if the extension of credit terms results from action initiated by the customer, the effect on the balance sheet will be the same. In either case, employees of the lending firm responsible for financial operations must make a decision: in effect they must decide to collect the outstanding receivables more aggressively and refuse to ship additional orders to delinquent accounts, or, by default, permit the average collection period to lengthen.

[9] To some extent, it may be suggested than an inability to separate industries by size of total assets weakens this conclusion. This is, of course, more likely to be the case for the intermediate groups where differences in industry group may have led to a canceling of positive and negative changes and where "large" and "small" may need redefinition in terms of the industry. Our largest group may be biased by its industrial composition, but whatever its industry composition, it is clear that such firms are large, hold a substantial proportion of the liquid assets of manufacturing corporations, and experienced a substantial reduction in such holdings during the tight money period.

[10] For the lending firm, receivables are higher and liquid assets are lower than when stated invoice terms are followed; for the borrower, payables and liquid assets are increased.

For large firms increased credit extension is a relatively inexpensive method of maintaining or increasing sales when credit rationing acts to the potential disadvantage of their customers.[11] And the lending firm may sell both to firms which do and do not borrow. Hence, extended credit terms need not be granted to all customers[12] further reducing the cost to the lender.[13]

Define the net mercantile credit position, R, of a firm or group as the ratio of the total outstanding accounts and notes receivable, r, minus the outstanding accounts and notes payable, p, shown on the quarterly balance sheet to the dollar amount of quarterly sales, s. Then we define $(r - p)/s = R$, the ratio of net receivables to sales.

Firms with the largest average liquidity position are shown by the scatter diagrams to be more likely to have relatively low liquidity position accompanying relatively high ratios of net receivables to sales.[14] Moreover,

[11] Assuming a rate of interest of twelve percent per annum as the opportunity cost of funds to the lending firm, the granting of a ninety day payment period in lieu of the "regular" thirty day terms is equivalent in cost to a 2 percent reduction in the selling price of the product. The use of interest bearing notes to finance receivables will, of course, reduce the cost to the lender.

The smaller (borrowing) firms, unable to obtain funds from banks, will value the resulting possibility of holding higher inventories at the marginal profit rate resulting from additional sales. For the borrowers, the alternative presented in this way is less costly or more flexible than other prominently available alternatives: selling accounts receivable to factoring companies, large percentage reductions in inventory, loss of control of the firm.

[12] The Robinson-Patman Act specifically prohibits differential treatment of this kind with respect to pricing practices.

[13] The extent to which the average collection period is practiced as a form of non-price competition aids in understanding the degree to which so-called "administered" prices are in fact more flexible than they appear if only announced changes in market prices are considered.

[14] For groups I, II, and III, the scatter diagrams give no evidence of a negative relationship between R and L; for the two groups of largest firms, the negative slopes of the simple regression lines which we would draw are considerably clearer.

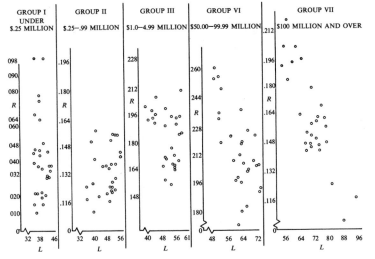

Fig. 26–1.

Table 26-3. Results obtained from regression equation (1).†

	Period: 1951-IV—1957-IV inclusive						Sub-period: 1954-I—1957-IV inclusive					
Size class (total assets in $ million)	b_1 (marginal effect of L on R)	b_2 (marginal effect of S on R)	R^* (multiple correlation coefficient)	r_1^* (partial correlation of L on R)	r_2^* (partial correlation of S on R)	S (mean of sales index)	b_1	b_2	R^*	r_1^*	r_1^*	S
Group I Under 0.25	−0.16 (0.18)	+0.03 (0.05)	0.23	0	0	0.96	−0.02 (0.02)	+0.09 (0.05)	0.50	0	41	0.96
Group II 0.25–0.99	+0.21 (0.06)	+0.16 (0.04)	0.58	58	57	0.95	+0.30 (0.10)	+0.19 (0.06)	0.57	57	57	0.97
Group III 1.0–4.99	−0.21 (0.11)	−0.12 (0.09)	0.32	32	18	0.96	−0.03 (0.07)	−0.01 (0.06)	0	0	0	0.97
Group IV 5.0–9.99	−0.26 (0.04)	−0.16 (0.06)	0.75	75	46	0.84	−0.26 (0.06)	−0.19 (0.11)	0.74	71	38	0.83
Group V 10.0–49.99	−0.20 (0.09)	−0.16 (0.15)	0.52	39	0	1.04	−0.24 (0.03)	−0.28 (0.06)	0.95	89	77	1.05
Group VI 50.0–99.99	−0.08 (0.06)	+0.10 (0.04)	0.73	12	46	1.18	−0.09 (0.05)	+0.10 (0.04)	0.87	34	51	1.23
Group VII 100.0 & over	−0.16 (0.04)	+0.03 (0.01)	0.79	60	43	1.29	−0.12 (0.04)	+0.04 (0.02)	0.86	60	47	1.43

Figures in parentheses are standard errors.
* Adjusted for degrees of freedom.
† Similar results are obtained if the ratio r/s is substituted for $(r - p)/s$.

given that they are both larger and on the average more liquid, they are less likely to have experienced credit rationing in the financial markets. A period of tight money is likely to affect them primarily through a decrease in sales to customers who cannot increase or maintain inventories.[15] Then, if high values of R result from relatively high sales obtained by granting longer credit terms, from a decrease in liquidity position, or a combination of the two, we have as a regression equation

$$R = a + b_1L + b_2S + u \qquad (1)$$

where R and L are defined as before, S is an index of seasonally adjusted sales (first quarter 1951 $= 1.00$), a and b are parameters, and u is a random variable. Obviously, once the interrelationships between firms are considered, the effects of L and S on R are no longer completely independent. However, the partial correlation coefficients show that the two effects are not closely related for all size groups. Table 26–3 presents these coefficients obtained when equation (1) was used to estimate the relationship for each of the seven size groups.[16]

Groups which experienced the largest dollar decline in liquid assets (Table 26–2) have the strongest negative relationships between L and R in Table 26–3. Of these, only Group VII shows a positive relation between S and R.[17] Thus, net receivables for this group should rise faster than sales and by a larger amount than for any other group. To the extent that a reallocation of credit takes place, it is the largest firms which should be the principal lenders.

With the exception of Group II,[18] only the two largest groups show a positive relationship between sales and net receivables during 1951–57 and 1954–57. But the positive coefficients between R and S (Table 26–3) are biased downward. When credit terms lengthen, all firms do not obtain the same terms. Credit is allocated among customers and sales are increased by financing inventories for firms which might otherwise be unable to purchase

---

[15] This effect has been previously noted in a discussion of recent British experience. H. F. Lydall; "The Impact of the Credit Squeeze on Small and Medium Sized Manufacturing Firms," *Economic Journal,* LXVII (September 1957), 428–29. However, Lydall does not consider the relationships between firms and the way in which the reduction in liquidity by the large firms may succeed in reducing the credit rationing effect of a tight money policy for the small firms. At the same time, the large firms, by lending, may limit or reverse the accompanying reduction in their sales.

[16] The use of an index of sales eliminates the direct effect of size from the regression equation. Data were obtained from the Federal Trade Commission-Securities and Exchange Commission *Quarterly Financial Report for Manufacturing Corporations.* All data have been seasonally adjusted.

[17] Group VII also showed the largest relative and absolute reduction in liquid assets and a substantial increase in the ratio R during 1955–57.

[18] The results for Group II are mixed. Sales for Group II rose during 1956–57, and equation (1) shows a positive relation between S and R. This suggests that the aggregate of Group II firms increase net receivables faster than sales when sales rise and use trade credit as a form of "nonprice competition." However, the positive coefficient for L indicates that R is low when L is low; L fell during 1956–57. But the absolute increase in receivables from high S was not sufficient to raise the ratio R, for this group during tight money.

or which might purchase smaller amounts. Since many customers will continue to observe stated invoice terms and since we know only the average net receivables-sales ratio, the increase in R shown in Table 26–3 will reflect only partially the increased lending by suppliers to their customers.

III.   CHANGES IN SOURCES AND ALLOCATION OF FUNDS

The estimates of equation (1) suggest that firms with the largest assets are more likely to increase trade credit faster than sales when increases in credit are restricted by monetary policy. Here we contrast the experience of the three groups of smallest and the two groups of largest firms to estimate the magnitude of relative and absolute changes in sales, net receivables, and other sources and allocation of funds. Consideration of the major sources of funds and the differences between groups of large and small firms indicates the extent to which interfirm "lending" reallocated credit.[19]

Date the start of the tight money period in either the second quarter or fourth quarter 1955; consider the third quarter 1957 as the end of tight money. From either second or fourth quarter 1955 to third quarter 1957, only Groups VI and VII show a larger proportion of the increase in net receivables than of the increase in sales.[20] Moreover, the increase in net receivables by Group VII was greater than the increase in short-term loans by banks to all manufacturing firms.

Clearly, changes in the amount of trade credit extended are of importance in understanding the operations of the credit system during this period. The non-manufacturing sectors were able to "borrow" $5½ billion in additional trade credit from the manufacturing sector. This amount exceeds the increase in aggregate loans (short-term plus long-term) which the manufacturing sector received from banks; moreover, it exceeds the total increase in currency plus adjusted demand deposits during these quarters (1.2 billion).

Assertions that the proportion of total bank credit which the smallest firms obtained during 1956–57 is evidence of discrimination against small firms ignore the relatively large share of such credits which the group obtained in the months immediately preceding.[21] However, the share of short-term loans from banks which Group I obtained was relatively small. But, their relatively large increase in cash plus government securities and their ability to obtain longer term credit from both banks and non-banks may be both

---

[19] References in this section are to a table of sources and allocation of funds based on the FTC-SEC *Quarterly Financial Report*.

[20] The largest firms, Group VII, increased their net receivables by nearly $3 billion, by more than the aggregate increase of all other groups. The increase by Group VII from second quarter 1955 through third quarter 1957 represented 25 percent of the stock of net receivables existing at the start of the period.

[21] From second quarter 1955 through third quarter 1957, Group I increased long-term loans from banks and nonbanks by slightly more than they increased assets or their share of the stock of assets.

an indication of their preferences during this period and a denial that monetary policy favored large firms.[22]

The principal sources of funds for the group of largest firms were the non-bank markets for long-term debt and the market for equity.[23] But the absolute increase in new funds which the group obtained from banks was less than the increase in net receivables; the "loans" extended to their customers exceeded their new borrowings from banks.[24]

Consideration of sources of funds gives little indication that the banking system discriminated sharply against the smallest firms in the manufacturing sector. In addition, the data make clear (1) that the total dollar volume of net receivables and inventory increased substantially during the period and (2) that firms with total assets of $100 million and above increased their relative and absolute share of both. Furthermore, the data indicate (3) that non-bank sources were the principal suppliers of credit to the largest firms and (4) that manufacturing corporations were important suppliers of credit to non-manufacturing firms.

When money market conditions change, a first approximation to the extent of possible differences in the effect of monetary policy on large and small firms may be obtained from an analysis of changes in the allocation of credit by the financial system. However, a more complete investigation which considers the impact of monetary controls on groups of firms stratified by size shows that the largest firms in the manufacturing sector reallocate

---

[22] The group of smallest firms emerges as the only group which increased its relative sales position and its dollar holdings of cash and government securities. During the relatively prosperous period accompanying tight money, this group substantially increased its share of sales. Though they have the smallest proportion of total sales, their increase in sales was larger than the increase for any group other than Group VII. At the same time, they increased their share of total assets. Although small firms did not increase investment very rapidly, evidence available for the earlier part of this period suggests that they wer_ able to complete investment plans which they made. See my "Comment on Market Structure and Stabilization Policy," *Review of Economics and Statistics*, XL (November 1958), 413–15.

[23] Since, on the average, these firms earned more than 63 percent of the after tax profits of all manufacturing corporations during this period, their relative success in obtaining funds from the equity markets is not surprising.

[24] The data present an example of the way in which a more than proportional increase in an asset or liability by the largest firms may be misread. Almost 81 percent of the net investment in plant and equipment was done by the firms in Group VII, almost 90 percent by Groups VI and VII combined. But, using the first quarter 1951 as a base, Groups VI and VII are the only groups whose sales increased from 1951 to 1955. The three groups of smallest firms did not reach their 1951 sales level until 1956. (Changes in price are not considered.) Undoubtedly, more of the larger firms operated close to capacity during much of this period. It is, therefore, likely that the increase in their sales led to an accelerated increase in their investment in plant and equipment. Cf. F. Modigliani, "Comment on Hickman's Capacity, Capacity Utilization, and the Acceleration Principle," *Studies in Income and Wealth*, XIX (National Bureau of Economic Research, 1957), 450–68. As noted above, much of this increase in investment was financed by increases in capital and not from a relatively large increase in the proportion of bank credit which they received.

A similar result occurs when we consider increases in inventory. For Group VII, the seasonally adjusted ratio of inventory to sales increased from 0.66 to 0.77 between second quarter 1955 and third quarter 1957. For Groups I and II, the inventory-sales ratio fell during the period. It is likely that increases in inventory by large firms were an additional source of financial aid to smaller firms. By holding larger inventories for their customers, larger firms are able to make more rapid deliveries. Faster deliveries reduce the demand to hold inventory and the demand for working capital loans by their customers.

the stock of credit made available by banks and financial institutions. The reallocation of credit and the release of previously held liquid assets appear to restore much of the general nature of monetary controls.

IV. LIMITATIONS

Certain disadvantages are inherent in the approach. There are numerous problems both with respect to reliability and comparability associated with the use of the FTC-SEC sample. There is no apparent way to separate the effects associated with type of industry or product classification from effects of size. Changes in the sample composition, which occur annually, limit confidence in comparisons over time. These differences are not unimportant and may impart biases of which we are unaware. In particular, there are sampling problems associated with the smallest group of firms which render precise interpretations difficult.[25]

A more fundamental problem occurs with respect to the inferences which may be drawn from these results. It would be desirable to know whether the initiative for the type of lending which we have described results from actions undertaken by the customer or the supplier, whether industry structure, relative size of customer liquidity position, or absolute size of lending firm is more important as a criterion for credit extension. It is extremely difficult to draw inferences from aggregate data about the way in which decisions are made by individual firms. Hence, such inferences must be regarded as an indication of the types of differences which might exist if we investigated individual firms and attempted to formulate empirically testable propositions about the way in which they behave.

Finally, there are limitations in the coverage of this study. Data are available for the manufacturing sector only. More detailed study of the behavior of firms engaged in wholesaling and retailing must be omitted. Data are not available for industry groups stratified by size. Thus, while we might infer, e.g., that the manufacturing sector as a whole extended credit to the wholesaling and retailing sectors, the size or industry classification of firms receiving these credits is unknown.

V. CONCLUSION

There has been much discussion and little investigation of the way in which changes in monetary policy influence the behavior of firms.[26] In

---

[25] This should not be construed as a critism of the FTC-SEC procedures. Users of these data are aware of the high standards set and the high percentage of response obtained.

[26] For example, Professor Baumol recently advised that he would be surprised if an investigation shows that monetary and fiscal controls "constantly favor the one group [oligopoly] against the other [competitive]." His argument is based on the proposition that "Oligopolists seek to maximize sales for some fixed profit level. The result of the 'tight money' will decrease sales and hence the reduction in the demand for his product and the increase in his cost will lead the oligopolist to reduce output." *Compendium of Papers Submitted by Panelists Before the Joint Economic Committee*, March 31, 1958, 55–56. But, for a contrary view, see also footnote 2 *supra*.

part, the controversy in this area stems from the inadequacy of the present theory of the firm to cope with the reactions of firms to changing money market conditions or to provide precise quantitative predictions of the short-run behavior of firms. Both balance sheet and income statement variables[27] must be included to obtain reasonably accurate predictions of short run behavior. Even limited use of such variables may improve social policy propositions by providing sufficient information about the units over which we aggregate.

Data for the tight money period of 1955–57 suggest that the banking system increased (the sum of short and long-term) loans to the various size groups in the manufacturing sector in rough correspondence to the share of total assets held by the group. Undoubtedly, it was easier for large firms to obtain non-bank funds. This alone would seem to indicate that a tight money policy discriminates primarily against smaller, less liquid firms. Consideration of interfirm relationships modifies this result and implies that institutional restrictions which limit the general nature of monetary controls are, at least in part, offset.

We have argued that firms which accumulate liquid balances in periods of easy money use these balances to provide trade credit during periods of tight money. (These "loans" were an important source of credit to non-manufacturing firms.) But reductions in the cash balances of the largest firms during tight money contribute to a rise in velocity. Studies of individual firm behavior may indicate that there is a level of liquidity below which such firms would prefer reduced sales to further increases in receivables and a further drop in cash balances. If such a limit can be reached, the increase in velocity which stems from this source may be slowed or stopped. If so, relatively large increases in monetary tightness would be proportionally more restrictive than small increases.

Finally, we suggest that large (relatively liquid) firms may use credit policy, as an alternative to direct price reductions, to increase sales during periods of tight money. Confirmation of these results should be of considerable interest in discussions of administered prices. Such investigation may, at the same time, indicate a way in which firms evade or avoid the restrictions imposed by the Robinson-Patman Act.

---

[27] Cf. K. E. Boulding, *A Reconstruction of Economics* (New York, 1950); W. W. Cooper, "Theory of the Firm: Some Suggestions for Revisions," *American Economic Review*, XXXIX (December 1949).

27

AN EXPOSITION OF THE STRUCTURE OF THE FLOW-OF-FUNDS ACCOUNTS

LAWRENCE S. RITTER*

Professor Ritter sets forth a clear exposition of the nature of flow-of-funds accounts and shows their relation to the national income accounts. He concludes by indicating the potential usefulness of flow-of-funds data.

I

It is now over a decade since Copeland's pioneering work set the stage for what we know today as the flows-of-funds accounts. This was followed in 1955 by the Board of Governors' first exposition of the flow of funds, and then in 1959 by the board's revised presentation. Since then the board has been disgorging statistics at an unbelievable pace, and a few economists have been having a field day discussing the host of technicalities involved.[1]

Meanwhile, the economist who is not a specialist in the capital markets has been sitting uneasily on the sidelines, wondering what all the shouting is about and growing increasingly perplexed about what he is to make of this avalanche of numbers that has descended upon him. On occasion he will righteously turn to the *Quarterly Presentation* or to *Supplement 5* and gingerly extract a number, or perhaps even a row of numbers. Other than that, he seems to find little use for the flow of funds in his research and even less use for it in the classroom. If he seeks to orient himself by first acquiring an understanding of the basic framework of the accounts, he will find little help in the literature, most of which is concerned with technical details.

And yet there is no reason why every economist, and especially those concerned with monetary matters, should not be as familiar with the flow-of-funds accounts as with the national income statistics. The reason they are

Lawerence S. Ritter, "An Exposition of the Structure of the Flow-of-Funds Accounts," *Journal of Finance*, Vol. XVIII (May 2, 1963), 219–230. Reprinted by permission.

* This paper was presented at a meeting of the American Finance Association in Pittsburgh, Pa., on December 28, 1962. The program was under the chairmanship of Roger F. Murray.

[1] See M. A. Copeland, *A Study of Moneyflows in the United States* (New York: National Bureau of Economic Research, 1952); *Flow of Funds in the United States* (Board of Governors of the Federal Reserve System, 1955); "A Quarterly Presentation of Flow of Funds, Saving, and Investment," *Federal Reserve Bulletin*, Vol. XLV, No. 8 (August, 1959); *Flow of Funds/Savings Accounts, 1946–1960 (Supplement 5)* (Board of Governors of the Federal Reserve System, 1961); and *The Flow of Funds Approach to Social Accounting* (New York: National Bureau of Economic Research, 1962).

not provides a perfect example of unbalanced growth: a vast expenditure of time and effort has gone into collecting and disseminating data and into controversy over technical details, while hardly any effort at all has been devoted to explaining the logical framework underlying the construction of the accounts. This is not a case, in other words, where entry is limited to those with prior mastery of specialized knowledge or understanding of advanced techniques. No specialized knowledge whatsoever is required, and the only techniques involved are some elementary accounting principles that are common knowledge—namely, the concept of a balance sheet and an income statement.

In brief, unfamiliarity with the structural relationships inherent in the flow-of-funds accounts has resulted in gross underutilization of a veritable mine of information; even more important, it has seriously inhibited realization of their potential usefulness as a theoretical tool. It is the purpose of this paper to attempt in some small measure to rectify this state of affairs by an exposition of the basic principles underlying the flow-of-funds accounts.

II

The flow of funds is a system of social accounting in which (*a*) the economy is divided into a number of sectors and (*b*) a "sources-and-uses-of-funds statement" is constructed for each sector. When all these sector sources-and-uses-of-funds statements are placed side by side, we obtain (*c*) the flow-of-funds matrix for the economy as a whole.[2] That is the sum and substance of the matter.

The number of sectors is a technical, rather than a fundamental, question. While there must be more than one, in order to permit transactions between sectors, the maximum practical number depends solely on such factors as the homogeneity of groups of decision-making units in the economy, the availability of raw data, and ease of handling. Too few sectors are likely to hide significant relationships, while too many are likely to become unwieldy. In the national income accounts, the Department of Commerce divides the domestic economy into three sectors: households, business firms, and governments. In the flow-of-funds accounts, the board of Governors prefers four main domestic sectors, with financial institutions added to the above three. These main sectors are in turn divided into a number of subsectors. In any case, the sectoring should be exhaustive, i.e., the entire economy should be included, if necessary by the use of a residual "all other" category. In our discussion below we confine ourselves to a closed economy throughout.

A sector "sources-and-uses-of-funds statement" is a hybrid accounting statement which combines that sector's balance sheets and income statement and is derived directly therefrom. Fundamentally, it does not involve any

---

[2] See Tables 1 and 5 in the Federal Reserve's *Quarterly Presentation* and *Supplement 5*.

concepts not already present in the balance sheet and the income statement. The construction of a model sector sources-and-uses-of-funds statement occupies most of the remainder of this paper. We proceed from the balance sheet as the first step.

A. A generalized balance sheet, applicable to any sector, would appear something like the following:

(1)

Assets	*Liabilities and net worth*
Financial assets:	Liabilities:
1. Money	1. Short-term
2. Near-monies	2. Long-term
3. Other	
Real assets	Net worth

$$\Sigma = \Sigma$$

A balance sheet similar to the above can be drawn up for each sector. The only differences between them would be in the characteristic items that would appear under each heading.

As is well known, each real asset in the economy appears on only one balance sheet, that of its owner. However, each liability, by its very nature as a debt, must necessarily imply the existence of financial assets of equal amount on some other balance sheet(s). Similarly, each financial asset, by its very definition as something due to that sector, must necessarily imply the existence of a liability of equal amount on some other balance sheet.[3] Thus, although for any one sector its liabilities are not likely to equal its financial assets, if we take all the sector balance sheets for the entire economy and consolidate them into one, the total of liabilities would conceptually equal the total of financial assets. The net worth (wealth) of the economy as a whole is therefore equal to the value of real assets in the economy.[4]

For present purposes it is helpful to rearrange and consolidate balance sheet 1 as follows:

(2)

A	*L and NW*
Real assets	Net worth
Financial assets	Liabilities
Money	

$$\Sigma = \Sigma$$

Sector balance sheet 2 is identical with 1 except for some consolidation and rearrangement of the entries. Since money is a financial asset, it should,

---

[3] See Kenneth Boulding, *Economic Analysis* (3d ed.; New York: Harper & Bros., 1955), pp. 257–61. The term "liabilities" is usually defined in the flow-of-funds accounts as including equities (stocks) as well as debt claims (bonds). This gives rise to certain problems, as pointed out by Roland Robinson in the discussion following this paper.

[4] This conclusion pleases conservatives because it implies that printing money cannot in and of itself make an economy wealthier. However, by the same token, it also implies that increasing an internally held national debt cannot in and of itself make an economy poorer.

strictly speaking, be included under that heading. However, economic theory has traditionally treated money as unique, so that it is entered separately. The entry "financial assets" must therefore be understood as standing for "financial assets other than money."

B. A balance sheet, of course, shows stocks as of a moment in time rather than flows over a period of time. However, by comparing the balance sheets of a sector at two different points in time and noting the changes that have taken place over the intervening time span, balance-sheet data can be converted from stock to flow form. Comparison of a sector's balance sheet as of December 31, 1961, with that for December 31, 1962, for example, would show the net changes that have taken place between the beginning and the end of 1962.

If we confine ourselves to financial assets and liabilities for the moment, ignoring real assets and net worth, such a comparative sector statement, indicating the net changes that have taken place between two dates in balance sheet 2, could be presented as follows:

(3)

Financial uses	*Financial sources*
Δ Financial assets Δ Money	Δ Liabilities

Such a statement is a sector *financial* sources-and-uses-of-funds statement. It need not balance, since it is derived from partial rather than complete balance sheets. A financial source of funds for a sector is, by definition, an increase in its liabilities: households, business firms, governments, and financial institutions can obtain funds by increasing their liabilities (borrowing). A financial use of funds for a sector is, by definition, an increase in its holdings of financial assets or money: households, business firms, governments, and financial institutions can utilize their funds to buy financial assets (lending) or to build up their stock of money (hoarding). Thus 3 could be re-written as follows:

(4)

Financial uses	*Financial sources*
ΔFA (lending) ΔM (hoarding)	ΔL (borrowing)

However, the above alternatives do not exhaust the possible financial sources or uses of funds. For example, another source, other than borrowing, by which a sector might acquire funds is by selling financial assets or by dishoarding. And another possible use of funds is the repayment of one's debts. These did not appear on 4 because only net changes were considered and it was assumed that these were positive.

In gross form, a sector financial sources-and-uses-of-funds statement would have slots for negative as well as positive changes:

(4′)

Financial uses	Financial sources
$\Delta FA \uparrow$ (lending)	$\Delta FA \downarrow$ (selling securities)
$\Delta M \uparrow$ (hoarding)	$\Delta M \downarrow$ (dishoarding)
$\Delta L \downarrow$ (repaying debts)	$\Delta L \uparrow$ (borrowing)

In this framework it becomes clear that lending and borrowing are not opposites, as is usually assumed. Instead, the opposite of lending, which is the purchase of a financial asset, is the sale of a financial asset. And the opposite of borrowing is the repaying of one's debts. Also evident is the similarity, in purpose and in impact on the financial markets, of borrowing and selling off financial assets; both increase the market supply of securities, the former by the sale of one's own liabilities and the latter by the sale of someone else's.

Useful analytically as 4′ is, it is difficult to collect data on a gross basis. As a result, most published data are in the form of 4, with each pair netted; by convention, if the net change in any entry turns out to be negative over a period, it is kept on the side where it presently appears in 4 but preceded by a minus sign. Net dishoarding, for example, would be recorded on the uses side but preceded by a minus sign and referred to as a negative use.

C. We have thus far ignored changes in the first pair of entries on 2, namely, changes in real assets and in net worth. This is because we have confined ourselves thus far to considering only financial sources and uses of funds. But, in addition to financial sources and uses, a sector is also likely to have "non-financial" sources and uses. These may arise from transactions on *capital* account or from *current* transactions.

Non-financial transactions on *capital* account, as in national income accounting, refer to changes in real assets and in net worth. A change in real assets over a period, the acquisition of capital goods, is usually termed real (in contrast to financial) investment. The purchase of a capital good is obviously as much a use of funds as the purchase of a bond or a stock. Investment may be reckoned on either a net or a gross basis, in the sense that depreciation may or may not be deducted from the change in the value of a sector's holdings of real assets.

The change in a sector's net worth over a period could now be derived as a residual, if one wished to do so. Net worth, by definition, is equal to total assets minus total liabilities. A change in net worth over a period must therefore equal the change in total assets minus the change in total liabilities. If we insert the change in real assets into 4, we will have accounted for all changes in assets and in liabilities and could derive the change in net worth as the difference between the two. However, this procedure might obscure the fact that the change in net worth for a sector over a period is identical with what is usually termed the "saving" of that sector during the period.

The saving of any sector is, by definition, the excess of its current receipts over its current expenditures. But an excess of current receipts over current expenditures (flows) must necessarily imply either a buildup of (stocks of) total assets or a reduction of liabilities (or some combination of the two) equal in amount to the excess of current receipts over current expenditures. Thus the saving of any sector must be equal to the change in its total assets minus the change in its liabilities, which in turn equals the change in its net worth.

The net changes for a sector between two dates in the first pair of entries on 2 can thus be presented as follows:

	Non-financial uses on capital account	*Non-financial sources on capital account*
(5)		
	Δ Real assets (investment)	Δ Net worth (saving)

Just as 4 did not have to balance, since it was derived from partial balance sheets, neither is 5 likely to balance. An individual unit or sector may invest an amount equal to its current saving, but it may also be in deficit, investing more than it saves, or in surplus, saving more than it invests. However, if 4 and 5 are combined into one, as 6, it must necessarily balance:[5]

	Uses	*Sources*
(6)		
	Δ *RA* (investment)	Δ *NW* (saving)
	Δ *FA* (lending)	Δ *L* (borrowing)
	Δ *M* (hoarding)	
	$\Sigma = \Sigma$	

Statement 6 is the most widely used form of sources-and-uses-of-funds statement and is frequently labeled that, although, strictly speaking, it is incomplete. It contains financial sources and uses of funds (4) and non-financial sources and uses on capital account (5) but does not take explicit account of current transactions. That is, it does not include current receipts as a source of funds or current expenditures as a use, except insofar as the difference between the two (saving) is included as a source of funds on capital account. Nevertheless, as it stands, 6 is useful in showing that a deficit sector, with investment greater than saving, *must* borrow, dishoard, or sell financial assets in an amount equal to its deficit, and that a surplus sector, with saving greater than investment, *must* repay debts, hoard, or lend an amount equal to its surplus.[6]

---

[5] As would also, of course, be true if 4′ and 5 were combined into one, which could be called 6′.

[6] It is also useful in providing a demonstration alternative to the usual Keynesian one that, ex post, saving must equal investment for the economy as a whole. It was noted above with respect to 1 that if all sector balance sheets were consolidated into one, the total of liabilities would equal the total of financial assets, so that the net worth of the economy as a whole must necessarily equal the value of the real assets. It follows that if all the sector-sources-and-uses statements, such as 6, were consolidated into one, the total of borrowing would equal the total of lending plus hoarding, so that, for the economy as a whole, saving must necessarily equal investment.

Although 6 is in wide use, it is difficult to recognize unless one has been forewarned. There seems to be a deep-seated aversion on the part of those who publish statistics to the establishment of consistency in either the titles or the form of the tables they issue. For example, the Department of Commerce regularly issues data in a table entitled "Sources and Uses of Corporate Funds," which is, as one would expect, statement 6 for the corporate business sector. The same department also issues data in a table entitled "Disposition of Personal Saving." This turns out to be the same thing for the household sector, although neither the titles nor the arrangements of the two tables bear any obvious relationship to each other.

D. A complete sector sources-and-uses statement, as mentioned above, must also take account of *current* transactions: receipts accruing during a period as a source of funds and expenditures as a use of funds. In other words, the income statement has thus far been neglected.[7]

A generalized income statement, applicable to any sector, would, in skeleton form, be something like the following:

(7)	*Non-financial uses on current account*	*Non-financial sources on current account*
	Current expenditures Saving (addition to *NW*)	Current receipts
	$\Sigma = \Sigma$	

The excess of current receipts over current expenditures is generally termed "saving" when it applies to the household sector, a "budget surplus" when it applies to the government sector, and "retained earnings" (or addition to net worth or to surplus) when it applies to the business sector.

As a "use" of funds on current account, saving takes the form of non-spending, of accumulation or retention. As such, it becomes available as a source of funds for capital account and represents an addition to net worth.[8] As with investment, saving may be reckoned on a net or a gross basis, in the sense that depreciation charges may or may not be deducted from the addition to net worth. It should be noted, however, that even if depreciation is deducted, so that saving is measured on a net basis, depreciation would still be a source of funds for capital account, since it represents a non-cash expense rather than an actual current outlay of funds.[9]

---

[7] Capital expenditures, which have been discussed above, do not appear on an income statement.

[8] Saving may also be negative, of course, and thereby represents a subtraction from net worth. Furthermore, net worth may also change for other reasons than those discussed in this paper, such as by revaluation of assets (capital gains or losses). This gives rise to problems closely related to those mentioned in n. 3. Again see Roland Robinson's remarks.

[9] For example, assume that a firm's current receipts exceed current expenditures by exactly the amount of depreciation charges, so that net saving (and the change in net worth) is zero. This zero change in net worth is not consistent with the fact that real assets must be written down by the amount of the depreciation; on this latter basis, net worth should be lower by the amount of depreciation. The firm must have, for example, "involuntarily" accumulated cash equal to the depreciation charges, which cash can be spent to restore real assets to their former value *or for any other purpose the firm chooses.*

E. A complete sector sources-and-uses-of-funds statement, including transactions on current and capital account, as well as financial transactions, would combine 6 and 7:[10]

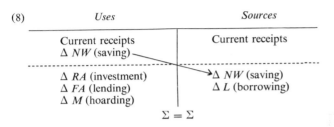

(8)

Uses	Sources
Current receipts	Current receipts
Δ NW (saving)	
Δ RA (investment)	Δ NW (saving)
Δ FA (lending)	Δ L (borrowing)
Δ M (hoarding)	

$$\Sigma = \Sigma$$

Complete sector sources-and-uses-of-funds statements, such as 8, are no longer shown explicitly in the final matrix for the economy as a whole, but they are still the basic backbone underlying the flow-of-funds accounts.[11] Since the income statement (above the dashed line) must balance, and the changes in the balance sheet (below the dashed line) must also balance, the summation of all the sources must equal the summation of all the uses of funds. Also, since saving (or the change in net worth) on the income statement must necessarily be the same as the change in net worth (or saving) on the balance sheet, saving could be deleted from both sides without disturbing the equality of total sources and total uses.[12] If this were done, the statement would simply express the logical necessity that the funds a sector receives during a period from current receipts and borrowing must necessarily be disposed of in some way and must therefore equal the sum of its current expenditures, capital expenditures, lending, and hoarding.[13]

F. As mentioned at the beginning of this section, the flow-of-funds matrix for the economy as a whole merely consists of all the sector sources-and-uses statements placed side by side. Initially, in 1955, the published matrix showed the complete sector sources-and-uses statements in the form of 8. Since the 1959 revision, however, it has consisted of only partial statements in the form of 6, i.e., only that part of 8 below the dashed line.

Assuming a total of three sectors and omitting some detail, the current presentation of the flow-of-funds matrix for a specified time period appears essentially as shown on p. 426.[14]

---

[10] Or the combination of 6' and 7 into 8'. See n. 5.

[11] See Table 4 ("Sector Statements of Sources and Uses of Funds") in either the *Quarterly Presentation* or *Supplement 5*.

[12] Thus just as the Keynesian analysis can be presented without explicit reference to the concept of saving, since it is implied once consumer spending is determined, so the flow of funds can also be presented without saving appearing explicitly.

[13] More precisely, the funds a sector receives during a period from current receipts, borrowing, selling financial assets, and dishoarding must necessarily equal the sum total of its current expenditures, capital expenditures, debt repayments, lending, and hoarding (see nn. 5 and 10).

[14] See Table 1 or 5 ("Summary of Flow of Funds Accounts") in the *Quarterly Presentation* or Table 1 in *Supplement 5*.

(9)	Sector A		Sector B		Sector C		All sectors	
	U	*S*	*U*	*S*	*U*	*S*	*U*	*S*
SAVING (ΔNW)								
INVESTMENT (ΔRA)								
LENDING (ΔFA)								
HOARDING (ΔM)								
BORROWING (ΔM)								

This complete matrix, or summary statement of the flow of funds, forms an interlocking self-contained system. It shows, for a specified time period, the balanced sources-and-uses-of-funds statements for each sector, the interrelations among the sectors, and the aggregate totals of saving, investment, lending, hoarding, and borrowing for the economy as a whole.

Any one sector may invest more or less than it saves, or borrow more or less than it lends. However, for the economy as a whole, saving must necessarily equal investment, and borrowing must equal lending plus hoarding.[15] Thus deficit sectors, which invest more than they save, necessarily imply the existence of other surplus sectors. This is not only because the economy-wide total of saving must equal investment but also because a deficit sector *must* finance its deficit by borrowing, dishoarding, or selling off securities. This implies the existence of surplus sectors to do the lending, hoarding, or buying of the securities.[16] Similarly, surplus sectors, which save more than they invest, necessarily imply the existence of other deficit sectors.

If particular types of financial instruments are specified in the flow-of-funds matrix (as government obligations or corporate bonds), as in fact they are, the financial interrelations among the individual sectors can often be observed in even greater detail, in terms of which particular surplus sectors directly or indirectly finance which particular deficit sectors.

III

It is not the purpose of this paper to delve into the technicalities involved in constructing the accounts. The literature on that is extensive and thorough (see n. 1). Nevertheless, it is worth calling attention to some of the main

---

[15] See n. 6 and the related text.

[16] The existence of deficit (or surplus) sectors in an economy thus requires a rather advanced financial structure to permit the requisite financial transactions to take place and, indeed, to facilitate them. See the lucid exposition of John G. Gurley, "Financial Institutions in the Saving-Investment Process," in *Proceedings of the 1959 Conference on Savings and Residential Financing* (U.S. Savings and Loan League 1959), especially pp. 12–17. This is reprinted in L. Ritter, *Money and Economic Activity* (2d ed.; Boston: Houghton Mifflin Co., 1961).

differences between the Federal Reserve's flow-of-funds accounts and the Department of Commerce's national income accounts. Four differences are of particular interest.

First, the national income accounts confine themselves exclusively to non-financial transactions. They contain no data on borrowing, lending, or hoarding. Second, the income accounts are designed to measure the current output of final products; so far as possible, duplicative transactions and trading in already existing assets are eliminated in order to avoid double counting. This is not true of the flow-of-funds accounts. Third, the income accounts treat all real investment, or capital expenditures, as a business activity; neither consumers nor governments, as such, can invest. In the flow-of-funds accounts, consumer purchases of durable goods are treated as investment and are shown both gross and net of depreciation. This has the effect of removing the purchase of consumer durables from the category of current expenditures and thereby greatly increasing the volume of consumer (and national) saving. Finally, the sectoring is much more detailed in the flow-of-funds accounts than in the national income statistics, making integration and reconciliation of the two a rather complicated matter. In principle, one should be able to move easily from one set of accounts to the other, but in practice the sectoring and the treatment of various transactions are so different as to make it awkward and cumbersome to do so.

The potential usefulness of the flow-of-funds accounts as a theoretical tool is still largely unrealized. In the flow of funds we now have a complete and internally consistent body of data on financial flows, interlocked with national income data. Data on the financial markets are meshed with data on the goods and services markets. However, these still consist of logical ex post identities. Upon this foundation, we need to proceed to the even more important job of testing alternative hypotheses regarding the interaction between the financial and non-financial variables, with the ultimate objective of moving from the logical identities to the construction of a set of behavior relationships possessing explanatory value.

28

THE TERM STRUCTURE OF INTEREST RATES AND HOLDING-PERIOD YIELDS ON GOVERNMENT SECURITIES

JACOB B. MICHAELSEN*

Several different theories have been used to explain the term structure of interest rates. One group of theorists has argued that long-term rates represent an average of expected future short-term rates. This is the so-called "expectations theory" of term structure. Other writers have emphasized a risk theory in which short-term rates must be lower than long-term rates because short-term holdings involve less risk than long-term holdings. Another issue is whether investor's expectations tend to be similar or diverse. Professor Michaelsen analyzes several aspects of price behavior in the default-free securities markets to provide some empirical testing of term structure theories.

The determination of the term structure of interest rates has been a subject of growing controversy in recent years. Dispute has centered chiefly on the relative importance of expectations and maturity preferences as independent determinants of the rate structure. The theoretical positions taken and the evidence offered in support of them have ranged widely.

John Culbertson[1] has virtually excluded expectations, while David Meiselman[2] has virtually excluded maturity preferences. Reuben Kessel[3]

Jacob B. Michaelsen, "The Term Structure of Interest Rates and Holding-Period Yields on Government Securities," *Journal of Finance*, Vol. XX, No. 3 (September, 1965), 444–463. Reprinted with permission.

* I am greatly indebted to Arnold Moore and George J. Benston for comments on earlier drafts of this paper. Dawson E. Brewer, David Laidler and Hyman P. Minsky made valuable comments and criticisms, as did other members of the Money and Banking Seminar of the University of California, Berkeley. The research underlying this paper was begun with assistance from the Institute of Business and Economic Research of the University of California, Berkeley, and is now part of a larger project on security price behavior supported by a grant from the National Science Foundation. A preliminary version of this paper was read at the September, 1963, meetings of the Econometric Society in Cleveland.

[1] J. M. Culbertson, "The Term Structure of Interest Rates," *Quarterly Journal of Economics*, LXXI (November 1957), pp. 485–517.

[2] David Meiselman, *The Term Structure of Interest Rates* (Englewood Cliffs, N.J.: Prentice-Hall, 1962).

[3] Reuben Kessel, *The Cyclical Behavior of the Term Structure of Interest Rates* (New York: National Bureau of Economic Research, 1965).

and Burton Malkiel[4] have taken more moderate—but by no means identical—positions, assigning important roles to both factors. The empirical work of Meiselman has done much to clarify the role of expectations, and that of Kessel and Malkiel has helped to clarify the role of maturity preferences; but the evidence offered in support of the extreme positions of both Culbertson and Meiselman has been seriously challenged.[5]

This paper presents some findings on the behavior of Treasury bill and bond holding-period yields which bear on the determination of term structure. The findings affirm the importance of both expectations and maturity preferences. They also provide evidence bearing on whether investors' expectations tend to be similar, as Kessel and Meiselman believe, or diverse, as Malkiel believes; this evidence relates only to expectations in the bill market, however, leaving open the question of longer-term expectations.

Moreover, the extensive scope of the data—nearly 12,000 U.S. Government security prices recorded during the twelve-year period from 1951 to 1962—makes possible investigation of several aspects of price behavior in the default-free security markets hitherto largely unexplored. In particular, it facilitates an analysis of the relationship between attitudes toward risk and maturity preferences which provides an alternative to the generally accepted account of the origin of maturity preferences in hedging behavior.

We shall not attempt to review in detail the work of the four investigators mentioned above, for comprehensive accounts of the theoretical and empirical issues are already available.[6] It is helpful, however, to use their theoretical positions as an expositional framework in which to interpret the findings of this paper. Part I outlines briefly the relationship each of these investigators has posited between expectations, maturity preferences, and the term structure. With the differences between the respective theories of the term structure established, Part II proceeds to show how *ex post* holding-period data can be used to distinguish among them. Part III then reports the results of the various tests this kind of data makes possible. Finally, Part IV presents an analysis of the data along lines recently developed in the portfolio selection literature,[7] which demonstrates how utility maximization (in contrast to weaknesses in the loan markets resulting from hedging behavior) can account for the kind of maturity preferences which give rise to positive liquidity premiums. Part V consists of a summary and conclusions.

---

[4] Burton G. Malkiel, "The Term Structure of Interest Rates," *American Economic Review, Papers and Proceedings*, LIV (May 1964), pp. 532–543.

[5] For a critism of Culbertson's evidence against expectations, see Meiselman, *op. cit.*, p. 12 For a critism of Meiselman's evidence against maturity preferences, see Kessel, *op. cit.*, pp. 16–17, and John H. Wood, "Expectations, Errors and the Term Structure of Interest Rates" *Journal of Political Economy*, LXXI (April 1963), pp. 160–171.

[6] For a review of these issues, see *ibid.*, and the references cited therein.

[7] Examples are Harry Markowitz, *Portfolio Selection: Efficient Diversification of Investments* (New York: John Wiley & Sons, Inc., 1959); James Tobin, "Liquidity Preference as Behavior Toward Risk," *Review of Economic Studies*, XLI (February 1959), pp. 1–11; and Donald E. Farrar, *The Investment Decision Under Uncertainty* (Englewood Cliffs, N.J.: Prentice-Hall, 1962).

I. ALTERNATIVE THEORIES OF THE TERM STRUCTURE

The following relationships between expected short-term rates and the term structure, and between yields anticipated over the same holding period on securities with different maturities, represent the cores of the four theories of the term structure cited above:

1. Uniform Expectations—No Risk Aversion

The theory of the term structure sometimes referred to as the traditional expectations theory has been advanced most recently by Meiselman:

> [it] follows from the assumptions that short- and long-term securities can be treated as if they were perfect substitutes and that transactors, indifferent to uncertainty and holding similar expectations, equate the forward rates in the market to the expected rates. As a matter of descriptive reality, individual transactors may still speculate or hedge on the basis of risk aversion, but the speculators who are indifferent to uncertainty will bulk sufficiently large to determine market rates on the basis of the mathematical expectations alone.[8]

The relationship between observable yields to maturity and expected short-term rates which these assumptions imply may be expressed as

$$(1 + R_{n_t}) = [(1 + {}_tr_{1_t})(1 + {}_{t+1}r_{1_t}) \cdots (1 + {}_{t+n}r_{1_t})]^{1/n} \qquad (1)$$

where $R_{1_t}, R_{2_t}, \ldots, R_{n_t}$ are the yields to maturity at the beginning of period t on securities maturing at the ends of periods $t, t + 1, \ldots, t + n$ and the r_{1_t} are the rates on one-period securities expected at the beginning of period t to apply during each of the periods through $t + n$.[9] Forward rates implicit in the structure of these yields to maturity may be expressed as

$$F_{n_t} = \frac{(1 + R_{n_t})^n}{(1 + R_{n-1_t})^{n-1}} - 1$$

where $F_{1_t}, F_{2_t}, \ldots, F_{n_t}$ are the forward one-period rates applicable to periods $t, t + 1, \ldots, t + n$.

The theory asserts that "forward rates, which are observable market phenomena, are unbiased estimates of expected rates";[10] that is,

$$F_{n_t} = {}_{t+n}r_{1_t} \qquad (2)$$

for all periods $t, t + 1, \ldots, t + n$. Expressed somewhat differently, over any arbitrarily defined holding period "*the expected net effective yield*

---

[8] Meiselman, *op. cit.*, p. 10.

[9] This notation follows that used by Meiselman. Capital R's represent observed yields to maturity; small r's represent expected rates. The prescript gives the period when the rate becomes applicable; the first subscript, the duration of the loan; and the second subscript, the period at the beginning of which the yield is recorded or the expectation held. While this notation is precise only if all loans are discounted notes with single lump-sum payments at maturity (e.g., Treasury bills), the modifications required for coupons are minor. For further discussion of the notation, see note 12.

[10] *Ibid.*, p. 10.

(including capital gains and losses) will be identical on all riskless securities regardless of their term."[11] An estimate of this yield, like that of future short-term rates, is implicit in the term structure and may be derived as follows:

$$H_{n_t} = \frac{(1 + R_{n_t})^n}{(1 + R_{n-1_{t+1}})^{n-1}} - 1$$

where H_{n_t} is the yield anticipated over period t on a security maturing at the end of n periods and $R_{n-1_{t+1}}$ is the yield to maturity the present term structure implies will rule on the same security one period later.[12] This expression is equivalent to

$$\frac{(1 + {}_t r_{1_t})(1 + {}_{t+1} r_{1_t}) \cdots (1 + {}_{t+n} r_{1_t})}{(1 + {}_{t+1} r_{1_{t+1}}) \cdots (1 + {}_{t+n} r_{1_{t+1}})} - 1$$

Since ${}_{t+n} r_{1_t} = {}_{t+n} r_{1_{t+1}}$ for all periods $t + 1, \ldots, t + n$, the relationship between anticipated holding-period yields on securities with different maturities is

$$H_{n_t} = H_{n-1_t} = \cdots H_{1_t} = {}_t r_{1_t} \tag{3}$$

2. Uniform Expectations—With Risk Aversion

The theory which Kessel has advanced is essentially an application to the loan market of the "normal backwardation" theory developed by Keynes and Hicks[13] concerning commodity futures markets. It assumes that all transactors are averse to risk and that none regard securities with different maturities as perfect substitutes. Aversion to risk leads borrowers to hedge long-term assets by borrowing long and leads lenders, who have few similar long-lived commitments, to prefer lending short. This "constitutional weakness" on the borrowing side of the market gives rise to a premium in long-term yields to maturity, which compensates lenders for providing protection against interest rate changes. Because speculators are also averse to risk, they do not equate forward rates to expected rates, removing this premium in the process; instead, they substitute among securities with different maturities until forward rates exceed expected rates by an equilibrium set of equalizing differentials. These differentials, or liquidity premiums, compensate speculators for the differences between securities with different maturities in "interest rate risk."

---

[11] Joseph W. Conard, *Introduction to the Theory of Interest* (Berkeley: University of California Press, 1959), p. 298. Italics in original.

[12] Certain exceptions to Meiselman's use of the second subscripts to designate the time at which yields are observed are made in this paragraph. Thus, $R_{n-1_{t+1}}$ is not an observed yield to maturity but rather one which is expected to rule in the subsequent period as inferred from the current term structure. Similarly, the ${}_{t+1} r_{1_{t+1}}$ refer to the short-term rates which will be expected at time $t + 1$ if expectations held at time t prove correct.

[13] See J. M. Keynes, *A Treatise on Money*, Vol. II (London, 1930), pp. 353–373 and J. R. Hicks, *Value and Capital*, 2nd ed. (London: Clarendon Press, 1946), pp. 135–147.

The relationship between yields to maturity and expected short-term rates in this formulation is

$$(1 + R_{n_t}) = [(1 + {}_tr_{1_t})(1 + {}_{t+1}r_{1_t} + {}_{t+1}L_{1_t}) \cdots (1 + {}_{t+n}r_{1_t} + {}_{t+n}L_{1_t})]^{1/n} \quad (4)$$

where ${}_{t+1}L_{1_t}, \ldots, {}_{t+n}L_{1_t}$ are the liquidity premiums applicable to periods $t + 1, \ldots, t + n$. This view also assumes that liquidity declines as term to maturity increases, so that ${}_{t+n}L_{1_t} > \cdots > {}_{t+1}L_{1_t}$. Forward rates comprise biased estimates of expected rates, for

$$F_{n_t} = \frac{(1 + R_{n_t})^n}{(1 + R_{n-1_t})^{n-1}} - 1 = {}_{t+n}r_{1_t} + {}_{t+n}L_{1_t} \quad (5)$$

In addition, anticipated holding-period yields on securities with different maturities are not equal as in (3); instead, these yields are

$$H_{n_t} = \frac{(1 + {}_tr_{1_t})(1 + {}_{t+1}r_{1_t} + {}_{t+1}L_{1_t}) \cdots (1 + {}_{t+n}r_{1_t} + {}_{t+n}L_{1_t})}{(1 + {}_{t+1}r_{1_{t+1}} + {}_{t+1}L_{1_{t+1}}) \cdots (1 + {}_{t+n}r_{1_{t+1}} + {}_{t+n}L_{1_{t+1}})} - 1$$

Again, ${}_{t+n}r_{1_t} = {}_{t+n}r_{1_{t+1}}$ for all periods $t + 1, \ldots, t + n$. At the end of period t, however, all securities are one period closer to maturity. Consequently, ${}_{t+n}L_{1_t} > {}_{t+n}L_{1_{t+1}}$ for all $t + n$. Therefore,

$$\frac{(1 + {}_{t+n}r_{1_t} + {}_{t+n}L_{1_{t+1}})}{(1 + {}_{t+n}r_{1_{t+1}} + {}_{t+n}L_{1_{t+1}})} > 1$$

for all $t + n$. From this it follows that

$$H_{n_t} > H_{n-1_t} > \cdots > H_{1_t} = {}_tr_{1_t} \quad (6)$$

Thus, anticipated holding-period yields on securities with different maturities are not equal but increase as the respective terms to maturity increase.

3. Diverse Expectations—With Risk Aversion

The theory recently advanced by Malkiel does not assume that speculators tend to have similar expectations about future short-term rates. Hence it is more general than either theory summarized above. Like them, however, it assumes that speculators shift among securities with different maturities until the term structure is consistent with their estimates of future rates and their attitudes toward risk which, because of a constitutional weakness on the borrowing side of the market, lead them to require positive liquidity premiums. The relationship this theory implies between yields to maturity and expected short-term rates can be expressed as

$$(1 + R_{n_t}) = [(1 + {}_t\bar{r}_{1_t})(1 + {}_{t+1}\bar{r}_{1_t} + {}_{t+1}L_{1_t}) \cdots (1 + {}_{t+n}L_{1_t})^{1/n} \quad (7)$$

where the $\bar{r}_{1_t}$ and $\bar{L}_{1_t}$ are appropriately weighted averages of the expectations and liquidity premiums of the individual market participants,[14] and forward rates are represented by

$$F_{n_t} = \frac{(1 + R_n)^n}{(1 + R_{n-1})^{n-1}} - 1 = {}_{t+n}\bar{r}_{1_t} = {}_{t+n}\bar{L}_{1_t} \tag{8}$$

This generality is not, however, without its cost. Because the *ex ante* terms in (7) and (8) represent weighted averages of diverse expectations, it is not possible to derive an expression for anticipated yields similar to (3) and (6) which has testable implications for the kind of data used in this study.

The testable implications of (3) and (6) for holding-period data flow from the consensus assumed by the uniform expectations theories. It is possible for the set of anticipated yields contained in these expressions to be realized and, when it is, the relationship between realized yields provides a basis for determining whether liquidity premiums exist. However, when such a consensus does not exist, only the holding-period yields anticipated by some speculators can, at most, be realized. Under these circumstances, realized yields cannot be related unambiguously to their anticipated counterparts; consequently, they cannot reveal whether liquidity premiums exist. Nevertheless, as will be shown in more detail below, this theory does have implications for realized holding-period yields which can reveal whether expectations exert an important influence on the term structure. These implications follow from the relationships specified in (7) and (8); changes in expectations produce changes in yields to maturity and in forward rates. The implications of all three expectational theories are quite similar in this respect and, at the same time, differ from those of the segmented markets theory.

4. Segmented Markets

The segmented markets theory advanced by Culbertson assumes that risk aversion and institutional impediments so restrict the mobility of market participants that markets for securities with different maturities are virtually independent. If they occur at all,[15] speculative shifts between markets in response to yield differentials have almost no influence in prices; hence internal supply and demand conditions in the respective markets determine yields to maturity separately. Thus, in this explanation of the term structure, expressions like those above for yields to maturity and forward rates have no operational content; and although yields to maturity and hence prices may

---

[14] For any given term structure, a set of weights could, in principle, be found which would relate the expectations and required liquidity premiums of individual transactors to observed yields to maturity. The term structure itself provides no clues to these weights, nor is there any simple means available to derive them independently.

[15] According to Culbertson (*op. cit.*, p. 497), "Speculation in debt markets will be primarily based upon short planning periods" and hence cannot exert an important influence on the term structure.

still be regarded as functions of specifiable variables, expected short-term rates are not among the arguments. Moreover, changes in prices do not result from changes in expectations, but from shifts in internal conditions in the relevant markets.

II. REALIZED HOLDING-PERIOD YIELDS UNDER ALTERNATIVE THEORIES OF THE TERM STRUCTURE

Testing these theories directly requires independent evidence on the *ex ante* variables specified in the equations presented above. Although evidence of this kind is virtually unobtainable, tests utilizing *ex post* data can be made if it can be shown how such data can reveal the influence of these *ex ante* variables. The following three hypotheses demonstrate how the behavior of the time series of realized yields I have constructed can accomplish this: (1) Realized yields closely approximate anticipated yields; (2) when (1) does not hold, realized yields primarily reflect changes in expectations; (3) realized yields primarily reflect shifts in non-expectational factors. The first two hypotheses are complementary; together, they make it possible to specify the effects of expectations both when they are realized and when they are not. The third hypothesis is an alternative to this pair; it makes it possible to specify the consequence of expectations having no influence on realized yields.

The first hypothesis may be expressed as

$$Y_{n_t} = \alpha_{n_t} + \epsilon_{n_t} \tag{9}$$

where $\alpha_{n_t} = H_{n_t}$, the anticipated holding-period yield as specified in (3) or (6), and ϵ_{n_t} is an unbiased random disturbance.[16] Time series composed of realized yields like this can be consistent with at most one of the uniform expectations theories. To determine which, it is necessary only to compare the means of a number of series having different terms to maturity. Since these means measure the average of anticipated yields on securities with corresponding terms to maturity, they can either be equal, as in (3), or rise monotonically with term to maturity as in (6), and while one or the other condition may not obtain for the realized yields in a given holding period, with a sufficiently large number of holding periods, the effects of random disturbances should "wash out."[17]

The second hypothesis may be expressed as

$$Y_{n_t} = \beta_{n_t} \tag{10}$$

---

[16] I have used this hypothesis previously in an analysis of the holding-period data presented by Culbertson (*ibid.*). See Jacob B. Michaelson, "The Term Structure of Interest Rates: Comment," *Quarterly Journal of Economics*, LXXVII (February 1963), pp. 166–174.

[17] For an interesting account of random disturbances in security prices, see George J. Stigler, "Public Regulation of Securities Markets," *Journal of Business*, XXXVII (April 1961), pp. 117–142. Although he is concerned with auction markets in equities, his main points appear applicable to dealer markets in debt.

where β_{n_t} is the change in price resulting from shifts in expected short-term rates during period t. The β_n may be positive or negative and, unlike the ϵ_n, need not "wash out" in large samples.[18] To be sure, unanticipated price changes may occur no matter which theory is correct, but, as was indicated above, it remains feasible to determine whether changes are due to shifts in expectations or in other non-expectational, factors. Because the data bear directly only on features in which the expectational theories are similar— the implications for the behavior of windfall price changes resulting from shifts in expectations and not from alterations in other factors—it seems appropriate to concentrate on the differences between them and the segmented markets theory.

The following expression for yields to maturity emphasizes the similarities of the expectational theories:

$$(1 + R_{n_t}) = [(1 + {}_tr_{1_t}) \cdots (1 + {}_{t+m}\dot{r}_{1_t}) \cdots (1 + {}_{t+n}\dot{r}_{1_t})]^{1/n} \qquad (11)$$

where the r_{1_t} represents both the r_{1_t} of (1) and (4) and the $\bar{r}_{1_t}$ of (7) and $m \leq n$. Liquidity premiums can be neglected safely if we can assume that the factors determining them (attitudes toward risk and the maturity composition of assets and liabilities, among others) change infrequently relative to the occurrence of events which produce changes in expected short-term rates. Although the tests which this simplification makes possible cannot reveal whether liquidity premiums exist nor whether expectations are uniform or diverse, they can indicate whether expectations are important determinants of the term structure.

Consider now the effect on the price of a security maturing at the end of n periods of an unanticipated shift in circumstances which causes ${}_{t+m}r_{1_t}$ to become ${}_{t+m}r_{1_t}{}'$. Abstracting from coupons and assuming a face value of unity, we may express the price before the change simply as $P_{n_t} = (1 + R_{n_t})^{-n}$. The change alters the yield to maturity so that it now becomes

$$(1 + R_{n_t}{}') = (1 + R_{n_t})\left(\frac{1 + {}_{t+m}\dot{r}_{1_t}{}'}{1 + {}_{t+m}r_{1_t}}\right)^{1/n}$$

Consequently, the price after the change is

$$P_{n_t}{}' = (1 + R_{n_t}{}')^{-n} = P_{n_t}\left(\frac{1 + {}_{t+m}\dot{r}_{1_t}}{1 + {}_{r+m}\dot{r}_{1_t}{}'}\right) \qquad (12)$$

from which it follows that the prices of securities maturing at or beyond the end of period $t + m$ all change by this same factor.

---

[18] Because these β components reflect shifts in underlying demand and supply schedules, they cannot be regarded as random disturbances in the same sense as the ϵ components. Such shifts constitute shocks to the economic system as a whole. No theoretical basis exists for expecting shocks of this kind to "cancel out," as it were, over any arbitrarily selected period of time.

It is usually assumed that unexpected shifts in circumstances—or what the literature would call shifts in *the* interest rate—produce larger windfall price changes for longer-term securities. This is not a necessary property of *the* interest rate nor of the arithmetic of yields to maturity, but is rather a consequence of the implicit empirical judgment that changes in expected short rates are positively correlated. If we assume that the r_{1_t} are positively, but not perfectly, correlated random variables subject to a distribution of shocks over time,[19] it follows that, because the number of factors (like the one in (12) relating current to previous price) is greater for longer-term securities, the absolute magnitude of windfall price changes should be positively related to term maturity.[20]

While economic theory neither predicts nor denies this empirical relationship, it is not difficult to find a rationale for it. If expectations depend on the evaluations investors make of pertinent real factors in the economy, and if the same factors typically enter into the evaluations pertaining to many periods, it seems reasonable that changes in a few, or even in one such factor often lead to revised estimates of several expected rates.[21]

The implications for the behavior of time series of realized yields which flow from this empirical judgment can, perhaps, best be made clear by an explicit statement of the relationship between windfall price changes, β components, and changes in expectations they entail. This relationship may be expressed as

$$\frac{P_{n_t}'}{P_{n_t}} = \beta_{n_t} = \left(\frac{1 + {}_{t+m}\dot{r}_{1_t}}{1 + {}_{t+m}\dot{r}_{1_t}'}\right) \cdots \left(\frac{1 + {}_{t+n}\dot{r}_{1_t}}{1 + {}_{t+n}\dot{r}_{1_t}'}\right) \tag{13}$$

It follows that the standard deviations of time series of realized yields composed principally of β components should be positively correlated with their terms to maturity, for the longer the term to maturity the greater the number of windfall terms like those in the right-hand side of (13). Moreover, the series should be positively intercorrelated, the correlation being the highest between series closest in term to maturity and hence sharing the greatest number of windfall terms. Finally, since there is no reason for successive

---

[19] This distribution need not be Gaussian. See the discussion of an alternative in Section III below.

[20] This relationship will hold only if shocks whose effects tend to be offsetting do not occur simultaneously. For example, if two disturbances occurred together, one applicable to all expected rates causing them to rise and the other applicable only to more distant rates causing them to fall, near-term security prices would fall but longer-term security prices might remain unchanged or even rise. The shorter the time period over which windfall price changes are measured, the more unlikely such an event becomes since literal simultaneity is improbable. The weekly period used in this study appears to be short enough to render this problem unimportant.

[21] Meiselman (*op. cit.*, pp. 18–21) offers a quite different explanation of this positive correlation in his error-learning model of forecasting behavior. It would appear useful to avoid forecasting models if the data can be explained without them.

windfall terms to be systematically related, the series should be serially independent.[22]

The implications of the third hypothesis—that realized yields are primarily the result of shifts in non-expectational factors specific to the separate markets—can be made clear without the use of mathematical notation. Since there is no reason to expect changes in the non-expectational factors in the separate markets to be systematically related, there is also no reason to expect the patterns of interrelationships just outlined between time series of realized yields. In addition, since speculation plays no significant role in the segmented markets theory, patterns of serial dependence in realized yields that might arise would not be exploited so that serial dependence might be observed. It is possible that some non-expectational force could, over long periods of time, act systematically on these specific market factors, thus producing the kind of systematic behavior implied by the first or second hypothesis. However, unless such a force can be plausibly rationalized, this kind of behavior should be ascribed to the influence of expectations.[23] The absence of systematic behavior would lend support to the segmented markets theory.

III. TESTS OF THE ALTERNATIVE THEORIES OF THE TERM STRUCTURE

1. The Data

Active trading in the market for U.S. Government securities provides comprehensive time series data suitable for testing these theories. Although prices are not directly observable in this market, useful approximations are: with some exceptions, dealer bid-and-ask quotations are quite firm and can be used in lieu of transaction prices.[24] My analysis uses Friday closing bid-and-ask quotations for selected Treasury bill and bond issues collected from the quotation sheets of the First Boston Corporation for the 625-week period beginning January 5, 1951 and ending December 28, 1962. Prices given for

---

[22] If these windfall terms are independent, speculative activity should make time series of realized yields behave like random walks. For a discussion of the theory of random walks and evidence from a number of speculative markets, see Paul Cootner (ed.), *The Random Character of Stock Market Prices* (Boston, Mass.: MIT Press, 1964).

[23] Since non-expectational explanations of the systematic behavior outlined above cannot be ruled out, the segmented markets theory cannot be contradicted by the data used here. However, the burden is upon those who advocate this theory to show how the findings presented here lend support to it. As in many other instances, it is cumulative weight of many pieces of evidence, no one of which is conclusive by itself, upon which a judgment must be based. As we shall see, the weight of the evidence goes against the segmented markets theory.

[24] Quotations for longer-term issues may not always be firm for the ordinary volume of transactions, although for much smaller volumes some transaction can usually be made at the stated quotations. See Allan Meltzer and Gert von der Linde, *A Study of the Dealer Market for Federal Government Securities* (Prepared for the Joint Economic Committee [Washington: U.S. Government Printing Office, 1960]), esp. pp. 15–18 and 57–66, for a discussion of the volume of trading and the meaning of quotations in this market.

Treasury bills were derived by converting the quoted bid and ask yields to dollar amounts and taking their arithmetic means.[25] Prices indicated for Treasury bonds were derived by adding the prorated coupon payment to the arithmetic mean of the quoted bid-and-ask prices.

Realized holding-period yields were derived from these prices by computing the differences in the logarithms of successive prices of individual securities as follows:

$$Y_{n_t} = ln \left[\frac{(P_{n_{t+1}} + C_{n_t})}{P_{n_t}} \right] \tag{14}$$

where Y_{n_t} is the realized yield over the tth week on the security maturing at the end of n weeks, P_{n_t} and $P_{n_{t+1}}$ are, respectively, the prices of the security at the beginning and the end of the tth week, and C_{n_t} is the coupon payment during the week, which, for weekly holding periods, is usually zero.[26] The logarithmic transformation facilitates the analysis in a number of ways. As is often the case with multiplicative relationships such as these, the logarithms tend to be normally distributed. More importantly, geometric means—as (1), (4), and (7) indicate—are the relevant average and can be computed quite easily from logarithmic data. Finally, the Y_{n_t} can be scaled up to annual percentage rates simply by multiplying them by fifty-two.

The following time series of realized holding-period yields were constructed from the data:

Bill Series. Since the Treasury issues bills weekly, it was possible to construct thirteen bill series, one for each maturity from one to thirteen weeks. Each series measures the changes in the logarithm of the price of a different n week bill as it becomes an $n - 1$ week bill for 625 successive weeks.

Bond Series. The Treasury issues bonds at irregular intervals, so the maturity of these bond series can be held only approximately constant. Four series containing 625 observations were constructed with terms to maturity of two and one-half, five, seven and one-half, and ten years. In addition, two longer-term series of variable maturity of no less than fifteen years were also constructed.[27]

Indexes. Averages of the bill and bond series were computed and indexes constructed from them as follows:

$$I_t = \Sigma (Y_{n_t}/N)$$

---

[25] Although this procedure makes no allowance for transaction costs, it does not bias the results. See note 28 below.

[26] Bonds are not simple discounted notes like bills as this treatment of coupons assumes; rather, they are portfolios of discounted notes each of which has a different term to maturity. Because the principal is large in relation to the coupons, this oversimplification does not materially affect these findings.

[27] The two longer-term series are roughly of the same maturity and hence should not differ in any important respect. They were both included in the analysis to determine whether their behavior differed in any significant way as a means of gauging the extent to which the use of one series of each maturity could be relied upon to provide adequate estimates of the various parameters of interest. As it turned out, no significant differences in behavior were discovered.

where Y_{n_t} is the measured yield in the bill or bond series with n periods to maturity during the tth week, I_t is the bill or bond index during the tth week and N is the number of bill or bond series in the index. Thus, N is thirteen for the bill index and six for the bond index.

2. The Findings

Means. The arithmetic means of thirteen bill and six bond series and of the bill and bond indexes are given in Table 28–1 for the entire 625-week period and for selected sub-periods corresponding to cyclical upturns and downturns in business activity as indicated by the NBER reference cycle turning points. Division of the series into these non-overlapping sub-periods makes it possible to determine whether the results obtained for the entire period are merely accidental or reveal a persistent relationship. In addition, these particular sub-periods make possible the detection and analysis of cyclical variations in behavior.

Table 28–1. Means of time series or realized on selected Treasury bills and bonds for the 625-week period beginning Jan. 5, 1951 and ending Dec. 28, 1962 and for selected sub-periods* (figures in annual percentages).

		Sub-periods						
Series by term to maturity (1)	Entire period 1/5/51 12/28/62 [625]† (2)	1/5/51 7/3/53 [130] T-P‡ (3)	7/3/53 8/6/54 [57] P-T (4)	8/6/54 7/5/57 [152] T-P (5)	7/5/57 4/3/58 [39] P-T (6)	4/3/58 5/13/60 [110] T-P (7)	5/13/60 2/3/61 [38] P-T (8)	2/3/61 12/28/62 [99] T-P (9)
1 week	1.69	1.24	0.79	1.70	2.37	2.12	1.69	2.03
2 week	1.84	1.53	1.01	1.85	2.44	2.15	1.69	2.16
3 week	1.95	1.60	1.07	1.93	2.60	2.29	1.94	2.31
4 week	2.03	1.64	1.15	1.97	2.75	2.46	2.02	2.42
5 week	2.16	1.69	1.32	2.06	2.98	2.63	2.30	2.52
6 week	2.29	1.76	1.38	2.14	3.22	2.82	2.56	2.66
7 week	2.30	1.79	1.43	2.14	3.16	2.87	2.63	2.63
8 week	2.34	1.79	1.51	2.17	3.22	2.90	2.81	2.68
9 week	2.40	1.82	1.52	2.16	3.41	3.02	2.94	2.72
10 week	2.49	1.84	1.54	2.21	3.59	3.25	3.17	2.77
11 week	2.40	1.78	1.54	2.13	3.64	3.07	3.00	2.66
12 week	2.38	1.78	1.57	2.12	3.69	2.92	3.00	2.70
13 week	2.52	1.88	1.71	2.29	3.94	3.10	3.37	2.67
Bill index	2.23	1.72	1.36	2.08	3.17	2.75	2.56	2.55
Bond index	2.00	0.06	7.93	−1.65	13.77	−1.64	7.64	4.02
2.5 year	2.72	1.01	5.29	1.09	8.40	1.11	6.73	3.99
5 year	2.45	0.67	6.24	−1.64	14.41	−0.47	9.42	4.74
7.5 year	1.89	0.97	6.35	−1.75	16.60	−2.67	6.67	3.54
10 year	2.25	0.15	9.15	−1.96	15.89	−1.81	8.96	4.05
Long 1§	1.25	−1.83	9.57	−2.60	12.02	−3.24	9.28	4.06
Long 2§	1.49	−0.60	10.96	−3.05	15.27	−2.78	7.30	3.73

* Sub-periods are either upturns or downturns as given by NBER reference cycle turning points. January 5, 1951 and December 28, 1962 are not turning points.
  † Number in brackets indicates number of weeks in sub-period.
  ‡ *T-P* indicates cyclical upturn; *P-T* indicates cyclical downturn (see *).
  § Maturities are variable but no less than fifteen years.

In the bill series, we can observe a clear tendency for the means to increase with term to maturity for the entire period and in each of the sub-periods.[28] Exceptions to this are the eleven- and twelve-week series, whose means exceed that of the ten-week series only in the 1957–1958 downturn (column 6). Moreover, in two periods, the 1958–1960 upturn (column 7) and the last incomplete upturn (column 9), the means of the thirteen-week series do not exceed those of the ten-week series. Apart from these anomalies, for which I have no explanation, these findings suggest that these series contain realized yields composed largely of the close approximations to anticipated yields specified in Equation (9). Hence the relationship between the means of these series supports the uniform expectations theory with risk aversion as specified in Equation (6).[29]

The means of the bond series do not display this same monotonic relationship. With the exception of the mean of the two-and-one-half-year series, the means of these series are less than that of the thirteen-week series for the period as a whole. During the complete upturns (columns 2, 4, and 6), the bond means are less than the bill means, some even being negative; during the downturns (columns 3, 5, and 7), the bond means exceed the bill means. The relatively low values of the bond means for the period as a whole are consistent with the expectational theories, for windfall gains and losses due to shifts in expectations need not "wash out" over any arbitrarily selected period of time. These low values could, however, also be consistent with the segmented markets theory if it can be assumed that the level of *the* interest rate affects the level of yields to maturity even though it does not affect their structure. During the twelve-year period the level of rates rose; this kind of secular upward movement could produce windfall losses even if the markets for bonds were segmented. But this finding does not substantiate the segmented markets theory; it merely fails to undermine it.

The segmented markets theory fares much less well with respect to the cyclical behavior of the bond means. Consider that the level of rates typically rises during upturns and falls during downturns. According to the expectational theories, windfall losses should occur during upturns and gains accrue during downturns if the extent of the rises and falls tends to be underestimated. And if changes in the level of rates over the cycles are due to parallel shifts in a large number of expected short-term rates, the windfall losses and gains should be positively associated with term to maturity—as,

---

[28] To determine whether the omission of transaction costs produced these results I estimated the impact these costs would have by assuming the beginning price to have been the ask and the ending price the bid quotation. While this reduced the means, it did not affect the ordering among them.

[29] These findings parallel Kessel's (*op. cit.*), as indeed they should since we used essentially the same data. He compared forward rates observed in the bill market to subsequent spot rates and found that, on the average, the former exceeded the latter. In the terms of this analysis this is equivalent to finding that $F_{nt} = {}_{t+n}r_{1t} + {}_{t+n}L_{1t} > {}_{t+n}r_{1t+n}$ which is another way of testing (6). Kessel did not report similar results for bonds. His procedure does not lend itself to the computation of the other statistical measures reported here.

indeed they are in our data.[30] To interpret this cyclical behavior as consistent with the responses of segmented markets to changes in the level of rates comes perilously close to admitting that expectations are important.

A cyclical pattern of windfalls is also detectable in the means of the bill series, but to a much smaller extent. Table 28–2 summarizes the pertinent information on this point. The means of the one-week and the thirteen-week series for the various periods are given in the first two rows of Table 28–2 and the differences between them appear in the third. The spreads during

Table 28–2. Summary of relationships between the means of selected time series (figures in annual percentages)

Series by term to maturity (1)	Entire period 1/5/51 12/28/62 (2)	Sub-periods						
		1/5/51 7/3/53 T-P (3)	7/3/53 8/6/54 P-T (4)	8/6/54 7/5/57 T-P (5)	7/5/57 4/3/58 P-T (6)	4/3/58 5/13/60 T-P (7)	5/13/60 2/3/61 P-T (8)	2/3/61 12/28/62 T-P (9)
1 week	1.69	1.24	0.79	1.70	2.37	2.12	1.69	2.03
13 week	2.52	1.88	1.71	2.29	3.94	3.10	3.37	2.67
13 week minus 1 week	0.83	0.64	0.92	0.59	1.57	0.98	1.68	0.64
Bond index	2.00	0.06	7.93	−1.65	13.77	−1.64	7.64	4.02

upturns (columns 3, 5, and 7) are considerably smaller than those during adjacent downturns (columns 4, 6, and 8). By comparing these spreads in the third row to the sub-period means of the bond index in the fourth, we can see that this narrowing during upturns and widening during downturns parallels the cyclical alterations in the sub-period means. At the same time, the size of the spreads is not closely correlated with the level of rates as measured by the means of the one-week series. This circumstance suggests that the presence of windfall price changes in the bill series makes it difficult to estimate the magnitude of the difference between anticipated yields, or alternatively, to estimate the magnitudes of liquidity premiums and how they vary with the level of rates and with other factors.[31]

Standard Deviations. The standard deviations of the thirteen bill and six bond series and of the bill and bond indexes for the entire 625-week period and for selected sub-periods (Table 28–3) behave largely as predicted. The standard deviations of the bill series rise monotonically with term to maturity in all of the sub-periods as well as for the entire period. For the bond series, however, although the standard deviation for the entire period increases with term to maturity, exceptions arise within the sub-periods. These variants

---

[30] With some exceptions, the means of the longer-term bond series are lower in upturns and higher in downturns than those of the shorter-term bond series. See Table 28–1.

[31] Kessel attempted to determine whether the level of liquidity premiums was systematically related to the absolute level of rates (*op. cit.*, p. 27). He did not take the effects of windfall price changes into account; since these are not negligible, his conclusions that liquidity premiums are positively related to the level of rates is open to question.

Table 28–3. Standard deviations of time series of realized yields on selected treasury bills and bonds for the 625-week period beginning Jan. 5, 1951 and ending Dec. 28, 1962 and for selected sub-periods* (figures in annual percentages)

Series by term to maturity (1)	Entire period 1/5/51 12/28/62 (625)†	Sub-periods						
		1/5/51 7/3/53 (130) T-P‡ (3)	7/3/53 8/6/54 (57) P-T (4)	8/6/54 7/5/57 (152) T-P (5)	7/5/57 4/3/58 (39) P-T (6)	4/3/58 5/13/60 (110) T-P (7)	5/13/60 2/3/61 (38) P-T (8)	2/3/61 12/28/62 (99) T-P (9)
	(2)							
1 week	0.78	0.33	0.42	0.76	0.78	0.96	0.48	0.39
2 week	0.80	0.40	0.52	0.80	0.83	1.02	0.67	0.47
3 week	0.89	0.53	0.62	0.85	0.87	1.15	0.74	0.53
4 week	1.00	0.67	0.74	0.95	1.02	1.31	0.86	0.55
5 week	1.11	0.80	0.74	1.04	1.13	1.49	0.96	0.61
6 week	1.23	0.84	0.83	1.12	1.39	1.67	1.02	0.67
7 week	1.31	0.91	0.88	1.18	1.43	1.86	1.11	0.68
8 week	1.39	0.96	0.94	1.24	1.46	2.02	1.31	0.71
9 week	1.48	1.01	0.98	1.30	1.56	2.17	1.35	0.74
10 week	1.59	1.07	1.03	1.37	1.71	2.29	1.61	0.72
11 week	1.63	1.12	1.04	1.44	1.89	2.32	1.77	0.77
12 week	1.68	1.13	1.08	1.51	1.82	2.42	1.87	0.88
13 week	1.81	1.21	1.17	1.58	2.05	2.69	2.04	0.81
Bill index	1.21	0.79	0.81	1.02	1.27	1.69	1.07	0.56
Bond index	23.24	12.88	13.36	19.86	29.80	34.40	29.84	19.52
2.5 year	11.79	5.89	8.91	10.58	13.78	15.80	13.56	12.77
5 year	23.02	8.93	12.50	17.75	28.47	34.60	36.52	20.49
7.5 year	27.95	16.09	13.13	25.20	30.99	44.08	33.68	17.60
10 year	28.53	19.47	28.70	27.68	40.50	37.68	23.81	20.76
Long 1§	32.71	19.98	23.04	24.32	39.21	46.61	41.40	34.28
Long 2§	34.12	22.43	20.80	28.11	41.05	48.62	45.38	34.20

* Sub-periods are either upturns or downturns as given by NBER reference cycle turning points. January 5, 1961 and December 28, 1962 are not turning points.
  † Number indicates number of weeks in sub-period.
  ‡ T-P indicates cyclical upturn; P-T indicates cyclical downturn (see *).
  § Maturities are variable but no less than fifteen years.

may indicate that shifts in non-expectational factors affecting only specific securities are sometimes important.[32] Expectational explanations do not rule out such shifts but assume them to be of secondary importance.

Unlike the means, the standard deviations display no cyclical patterns. Instead, they increase progressively through the fifth sub-period (column 7) and decline thereafter.[33] The theories under consideration provide no explanation of this secular trend in price variability, but all of them are consistent with it. One possible explanation is that the underlying process generating these data is not Gaussian. Recent empirical work[34] on the behavior of other kinds of speculative price series suggests that the logarithms

---

[32] This could also account for the exceptions noted in footnote 30.

[33] To determine whether this drift in the standard deviations is significant, tests for the equality of the variances of the bill index and of the bond index in the seven sub-periods were made. On the basis of the likelihood ratio test proposed by P. C. Hoel (*Introduction to Modern Statistics*, 3rd ed. [New York: John Wiley & Sons, Inc., 1962], pp. 225–227) the sub-period variances for each series are unequal.

[34] See Benoit Mandelbrot, "The Variation of Certain Speculative Prices," *Journal of Business*, XXXVI (October 1963), pp. 394–419; and Eugene F. Fama, "Mandelbrot and the Stable Paretian Hypothesis," *Journal of Business*, XXXVI (October 1963), pp. 420–429.

of successive price relatives, measures almost identical with (14), are distributed according to the "statistical law of Pareto." Since Paretian variables have infinite population variance, the variances of samples of them do not tend to a limit but are unstable. This instability could take the form of a secular drift.

The bill and bond series contain too few observations to be conclusive, but they do appear to have the "fat" tails and "peaked" middles that others

Table 28–4. Correlation coefficients between time series of realized yields on selected treasury bills and bonds for the period beginning January 5, 1951 and ending December 28, 1962.

Series by term to maturity	13 Week	2.5 Year	5 Year	7.5 Year	10 Year	Long 1	Long 2
13 week	1.000	0.333	0.291	0.277	0.251	0.260	0.217
2.5 year		1.000	0.676	0.618	0.593	0.592	0.554
5 year			1.000	0.802	0.724	0.718	0.699
7.5 year				1.000	0.809	0.720	0.735
10 year					1.000	0.726	0.721
Long 1						1.000	0.861
Long 2							1.000

have found in similar series.[35] We might therefore be faced, as Mandelbrot has suggested, with "a burden of proof that is closer to that of history and autobiography than to that of physics."[36] Thus, to say that the process is Paretian does not explain the observed secular behavior of standard deviations, but indicates that explanation in this contest requires more than the rather simplified consideration of expectations and maturity preferences presented here.

Intercorrelations. The correlation coefficients between selected bill and bond series shown in Table 28–4,[37] with the terms to maturity increasing from left to right and from top to bottom in the matrix, offer features of special interest: the coefficients in the rows tend to decrease as the difference in term to maturity between the series increases: the coefficients in the columns tend to increase as the difference in term to maturity between the series decreases; and the coefficients along the diagonals from upper left to lower right tend to increase as the terms to maturity of the series become more

[35] For example, if the series presented here were normally distributed we would expect 0.006 percent of the sample observations to lie beyond four standard deviations from the mean and 68.26 percent to lie within one standard deviation of the mean. The corresponding average proportions for the six bond series is 0.534 percent beyond four standard deviations and 78.21 percent within one standard deviation.

[36] Mandelbrot, "New Methods in Statistical Economics," *Journal of Political Economy,* LXXI (October 1963), p. 433.

[37] The pattern of intercorrelation with which we are concerned here is that produced by the windfall terms given in equation (13). Because these terms appear to be dominated by the realizations of anticipated holding period yields (the α terms) in the bill series, only the 13 week bill series is included in this Table. Much of the intercorrelation between the bill series appears to result from cyclical movements in anticipated holding period yields. The evidence on serial correlation presented below suggests that cyclical swings in the α have little influence on the bond series.

Table 28–5. Serial correlation coefficients for time series of realized yields on selected Treasury bills and bonds for the 625-week period beginning January 5, 1951 and ending December 28, 1962.

Series by term to maturity	Serial correlation coefficient		
	First-order	Second-order	Third-order
1 week	0.921	0.898	0.873
2 week	0.736	0.722	0.683
3 week	0.632	0.647	0.565
4 week	0.551	0.559	0.453
5 week	0.501	0.502	0.390
6 week	0.494	0.464	0.363
7 week	0.439	0.419	0.323
8 week	0.411	0.377	0.316
9 week	0.421	0.372	0.335
10 week	0.472	0.400	0.363
11 week	0.413	0.330	0.216
12 week	0.394	0.282	0.265
13 week	0.352	0.235	0.234
Bill index	0.520	0.473	0.413
Bond index	0.132	0.140	0.033
2.5 year	0.168	0.050	0.009
5 year	0.133	0.059	0.020
7.5 year	0.055	0.117	0.007
10 year	0.072	0.109	0.037
Long 1	0.095	0.113	0.013
Long 2	0.076	0.087	−0.018

nearly equal.[38] These systematic patterns of intercorrelation strongly suggest that unanticipated price changes are the result primarily of positively correlated changes in expected short-term rates. Thus this finding lends support to the expectational theories.

Serial Correlation. The serial correlation coefficients presented in Table 28–5 appear in part to contradict the expectational theories. The positive serial correlation in the bill series suggests the absence of speculative activity while the lack of serial correlation in the bond series suggests the presence of such activity. This seeming paradox is easily resolved. Recall that realized yields on bills often closely approximate anticipated yields. Hence cyclical swings and secular drift in anticipated holding period yields could produce the observed positive serial correlation in the bill series. Moreover, the presence of windfall price changes, the β_n of (10), would tend to mask this dependence in direct proportion to term to maturity, thus producing the observed decline in the coefficients with term to maturity of the

---

[38] This last tendency is illustrated dramatically by an apparent exception to it. Note that the correlation coefficient between the seven-and-one half-year and the ten-year series is 0.809 while the next coefficient along the diagonal, that between the ten-year and the long series, is only 0.726. This is easily explained by the fact that the seven-and-one-half-year series shares 75 percent of the windfall terms—the terms in the right-hand side of equation (13)—contained in the ten-year series, while the ten-year series shares at most only 67 percent of these terms with the long one series since the latter series has a maturity of no less than fifteen years.

series. But systematic movements of this kind provide no opportunities for speculative gain: as we have seen, anticipated yields on bills appear to be similar among speculators. This positive serial correlation is therefore consistent with the expectational theories.

In considering the absence of serial dependence in the bond series, it is pertinent to recall that realized yields on bonds, unlike those in bills, do not usually approximate anticipated yield, but appear to reflect changes in expectations. To the extent that successive shifts in the real factors leading to changes in expectations are not systematically related, speculation makes successive realized yields serially independent. But although independence is consistent with speculation, it is not inconsistent with market segmentation; the absence of speculation does not, in itself, produce systematic time patterns of behavior. Indeed, shifts in non-expectational factors in the separate markets could also be serially independent. Even so, it seems clear that no obvious speculative strategy could be devised from observation of the patterns of bond price changes alone.

IV. PORTFOLIO PLANNING HORIZONS AND MATURITY PREFERENCES

The holding-period data analyzed above also bear on the question of why liquidity premiums exist. As we have seen, the link between liquidity premiums and attitudes toward risk has been alleged to be a weakness on the borrowing side of the market which makes the maturity composition of the outstanding debt "too long." Meiselman challenged this view, arguing that because "there are many institutions which appear to be hedgers in some degree and which have strong preferences for holding long-term assets,"[39] the maturity composition of the outstanding debt could just as easily be "too short." Accepting the notion that maturity preferences depend upon the relative supply of securities with different maturities as well as attitudes toward risk, he concluded that, were such institutions to dominate the market, the constitutional weakness would be shifted to the lending side of the market and liquidity premiums would become negative.

Unfortunately, the conclusions of Meiselman and those of others who rely upon the Hicksian analysis of the debt markets as a future market in loans involve a generalization from a special and empirically unimportant class of hedging behavior. This generalization appears to stem from a confusion about the meaning of portfolio planning horizons and their relationship to hedging behavior. In the most general case, the end of a portfolio planning horizon is not a fixed point in chronological time marking the liquidation date of the portfolio: it is rather a planning dimension setting the span of time over which alternative courses of action are compared. But

---

[39] Meiselman, *op. cit.*, pp. 14–16.

under some circumstances the end of a planning horizon may be a fixed point in time; in such cases the horizon diminishes as time passes and vanishes when the fixed date arrives. The constitutional weakness rationale is based upon this special case.

A brief example can show that the kind of hedging behavior appropriate only in this special case constitutes the basis for the rationale. Consider an investor who wishes to liquidate his portfolio at some fixed date and whose planning horizon is therefore fixed. He is most certain of the liquidation value of his portfolio when the securities it contains mature exactly on the liquidation date. If his securities mature before this date, an unexpected decline in the level of short-term rates will reduce the liquidation value of his portfolio. The same will be true *mutatis mutandis*, if he holds securities which mature after this fixed date. Consequently, other things being equal, an investor with a fixed planning horizon who is averse to risk will hold securities which mature at the end of the planning horizon. If the market were dominated by investors averse to risk but with long, fixed planning horizons, and if long-term securities were in relatively short supply, negative liquidity premiums would arise.[40]

If, however, the market were dominated by investors averse to risk but with planning horizons which do not diminish with the passage of time, the constitutional weakness rationale becomes inappropriate. It would appear that most portfolios, and especially those of large institutional holders, have indeterminate rather than fixed liquidation dates, their maturity composition remaining roughly constant over time or changing in response to forces other than the passage of time. Thus, some alternative account of the factors determining liquidity premiums is necessary. While a complete account of the factors determining planning horizons and maturity preferences is outside the scope of this paper, an analysis along lines recently developed in the literature on portfolio selection under uncertainty should afford insight into the determinants of liquidity premiums.

The mean-variability approach to portfolio selection assumes that investors maximize expected utility by minimizing risk, and that this process is subject to the constraint of a utility function specifying acceptable rates of substitution between risk and anticipated yield on the portfolio as a whole. The principal method of minimizing risk is diversification of holdings among assets with relatively low intercorrelations among their distributions of possible returns. The interaction of investors diversifying in this way leads to an efficient set of portfolios in which yield and risk are positively correlated, risk being measured by the variability of possible yields on portfolios about their mean or anticipated yield. The distributions of possible yields on

---

[40] Martin J. Bailey ("Discussion," *American Economic Review, Papers and Proceedings*, May 1964, p. 554) has referred to these as "solidity premiums" required to induce investors to hold shorter-term assets than they would otherwise desire. Bailey believes that planning horizons of this kind occasionally lead to the existence of solidity premiums.

default-free securities, unlike those subject to default risk, are highly inter-correlated, so that diversification in the usual sense is ruled out. However, because of this intercorrelation, we can treat them, as a first approximation, as members of the efficient set of default-free portfolios.[41] More specifically, we can treat the bill series as efficient default-free portfolios with constant planning horizons, using their means as measures of anticipated yields and their standard derivations as measures of risk.

Seen in this way, the positive correlation between standard deviations and the means of the bill series suggests an explanation of positive liquidity premiums: the difference in their means reflects a market risk premium not basically different from similar premiums on securities subject to default risk. It is important to note that the positive correlation of terms to maturity with the means, does not, in this interpretation, result from weakness on the borrowing side of the market but from the tendency for unexpected shifts in circumstances to produce concurrent shifts in expected short-term rates. Thus, term to maturity serves as a proxy measure of risk because of the way shifts in real factors in the economy influence security prices and not because of a presumed constitutional weakness on one side of the market for loans.

The risk inherent in default-free portfolios with constant planning horizons, which the constitutional weakness rationale fails to recognize, stems from the fact that the maintenance of a constant portfolio composition entails the continuing purchase and sale of securities at prices which may turn out to have been disadvantageous. The nature of this risk is exemplified dramatically by the behavior of the bond series. The means of these series may be treated as the realized yields (not, as with the bill series, the antici-pated yields) on portfolios with relatively long planning horizons, whose maturity compositions are held constant by the replacement of securities rendered inappropriate by the passage of time by securities with longer terms to maturity. Assuming that these substitutions are made without regard to possible shifts in the level of rates or equivalently, that they are timed according to forecasts which prove no better than chance, the means indicate that the more risky portfolios performed least well over the period studied. Measured in this way, the bond means estimate the very real opportunity cost of failing to time the purchase of long-term bonds better than could be achieved by chance alone. Although these results do not measure the performance of real portfolios (some portfolio managers could be skillful speculators), they do serve as a benchmark against which actual performance can be measured.

---

[41] The standard deviation of possible yields and the anticipated yield on a portfolio is a function of the standard deviations of possible yields, anticipated yields and correlations between possible yields of the securities of which the portfolio is composed. See Markowitz, *op. cit.* In the case of default-free securities such as bills, the correlations coefficient between their distribution of possible yields may be regarded as unity. In this special case the standard deviation of possible yields and the anticipated yields on portfolios will be a linear combination of the standard deviations and anticipated yields of the components securities. The efficient set then becomes a straight line and each security becomes an efficient portfolio.

Table 28–6. Means and standard deviations of time series of realized yields simulating the yield and risk characteristics of alternative strategies for portfolios with constant planning horizons (figures in annual percentages).

Holding period (number of observations)	Strategies		Means	Standard deviations
Four weeks (156)	Short:	Four successive one-week bills	1.65	1.39
	Matching:	One four-week bill held to maturity	1.86	1.46
	Long:	One eight-week bill sold at the end of four weeks	2.26	1.83
Five weeks (125)	Short:	Five successive one-week bills	1.69	1.53
	Matching:	One five-week bill held to maturity	1.91	1.68
	Long:	One ten-week bill sold at the end of five weeks	3.38	2.26
Six weeks (104)	Short:	Six successive one-week bills	1.69	1.66
	Matching:	One six-week bill held to maturity	1.99	1.79
	Long:	One ten-week bill sold at the end of five weeks	2.40	2.48

The difference between fixed and constant planning horizons can be illustrated in yet another way with the Treasury bill price data. Consider the following alternative portfolio strategies for a planning horizon n weeks in length: a short strategy with one-week bills held for n successive weeks; a matching strategy in which bills with n weeks to maturity are held for the entire period; and a long strategy with bills with twice n weeks to maturity held to the end of the period and then sold. For a fixed planning horizon, only the comparison of possible yields over one holding period is relevant, for the portfolio is liquidated at the end of the period. As we have already seen, the matching strategy is the most certain for this program. For a constant planning horizon, the comparison of possible yields over many successive holding periods is the relevant one, for the portfolio is not liquidated. Time series of realized yields corresponding to the alternative strategies illustrate their relative risks for this latter kind of program.

The means and standard deviations of these time series are arrayed in Table 28–6 for holding periods of four, five and six weeks representing the yield and risk on short, matching and long strategies for each holding period. For all holding periods the short strategy means and standard deviations are smaller and the long strategy means and standard deviations are larger than those of the matching strategy. Assuming that most portfolios have constant planning horizons, these results lend additional support to the notion that risk aversion leads to preferences for short-term securities which, in turn, produce positive liquidity premiums and make price variability a direct measure of risk.

V. SUMMARY AND CONCLUSIONS

The findings on the behavior of holding-period yields on U.S. Government securities presented here bear upon three disputed issues in the controversy about determination of the term structure of interest rates. The evidence indicates that (1) expectations about future short-term interest rates exert an important influence on the term structure, (2) maturity preferences also exert an important influence on the term structure, and (3) investors tend to have similar expectations, at least over the relatively short planning horizon relevant for holding Treasury bills. In addition, analysis of the data in terms of recent models of portfolio selection helps explain why risk aversion leads to the kind of maturity preferences which produce positive liquidity premiums.

Because realized yields on Treasury bonds largely reflect changes in expectations, it is not possible to treat them as approximations to anticipated yields. Consequently, it is not possible to determine whether a consensus existed about short-term interest rates expected for the more distant future periods, nor whether liquidity premiums applicable to these periods were positively associated with their distance in the future. Moreover, the presence of windfall effects in the realized yields on bills presents serious problems for the estimation of the magnitude of liquidity premiums. Further investigation may lead to a method of identifying and removing these windfall effects, which may make it possible, if a tendency to consensus about all future rates does exist, to estimate anticipated holding period yields on bonds as well as bills, and on bills more accurately than at present. Such an advance would make it possible to resolve outstanding questions about the term structure, and to investigate the factors which determine the size of liquidity premiums.

29

THE UNCERTAINTY OF THE EXPECTATIONS THEORY OF THE TERM STRUCTURE OF INTEREST RATES

ALEX R. H. WEAVER*

Professor Weaver compares different approaches to the theory of the term structure of interest rates. He focuses particularly on the expectations hypothesis and argues that the theory fails to demonstrate causal relations between dependent and independent variables. He observes that it is not integrated into interest rate theory, and discusses the implications for debt management policy.

The expectations hypothesis of the term structure of interest rates has held a certain fascination for economic theorists ever since its reformulations by J. R. Hicks[1] and F. A. Lutz.[2] With the publication of David Meiselman's *The Term Structure of Interest Rates*,[3] there has been a renewed interest in the use of this approach in the analysis of the yield pattern of interest rates. In fact, John Wood in his review of Meiselman's book contends that the onus is now on those at variance with the expectations hypothesis to provide a more satisfactory explanation of term structure behavior if they are to successfully challenge the expectations hypothesis.[4] It is the contention of this paper, however, that the expectations approach as heretofore formulated presents theoretical problems that leave the theory subject to the charge of "bootstrapism" or amount to declarations of a descriptive nature; that is,

---

Alex. R. H. Weaver, "The Uncertainty of the Expectations Theory of the Term Structure of Interest Rates," *The Western Economic Journal*, Vol. IV, Spring, 1966, pp. 122–134. Reprinted with permission.

* I am indebted to Professors Earl Rolph, Benjamin Ward, and Jacob Michaelsen for their suggestions and criticisms of an earlier draft of this paper. With certainty, I accept responsibility for all errors.

[1] J. R. Hicks, *Value and Capital* (2nd ed.; Oxford: Oxford University Press, 1946), pp. 144–45.

[2] F. A. Lutz, "The Structure of Interest Rates," *Quarterly Journal of Economics*, 1940–41, vol. 60, pp. 36–63; reprinted in *Readings in the Theory of Income Distribution*, eds. William Fellner and Bernard Haley (Philadelphia: Blakiston Co., 1946), pp. 499–529.

[3] David Meiselman, *The Term Structure of Interest Rates* (Englewood Cliffs, N.J.: Prentice-Hall, 1962), pp. xii–75.

[4] J. H. Wood, "Expectations, Errors, and the Term Structure of Interest Rates," *Journal of Political Economy*, April 1963, vol. 71, p. 170.

it is not a theory in the sense of showing causal relationships between dependent and independent variables.

Section I reiterates the expectational hypothesis as it is usually characterized in the literature; the recent application of the theory by Meiselman will be discussed in Section II; Section III will point up the failure of the past literature on the subject to integrate term structure theory to "interest rate" theory; Section IV will be concerned with the implications of expectational models under conditions of certainty and under the assumption of uncertainty; and some conclusions will constitute Section V.

I

The expectations theory of the term structure of interest rates may be stated such that given expectations of future short-term rates, the yields to maturity of the securities, will tend to equal the average short-term rates expected to rule during the remaining life of the various securities involved.[5] Assume, for example, that our time horizon is the next three years and that we expect the short-term rates (the one-year rate) to be 4 percent, 2 percent, and 6 percent, respectively. The expectations theory implies that the two-year rate will be found to be 3 percent $[(4 + 2)/2]$ this year, and 4 percent $[(2 + 6)/2]$ next year; while this year's three-year rate would be equal to 4 percent $[(4 + 2 + 6)/3]$. Thus, with expectations of 4 percent, 2 percent, and 6 percent to hold in the short market, we expect to find a yield pattern of 4 percent, 3 percent, and 4 percent reflecting the yields to maturity on one-year, two-year, and three-year securities, respectively.

The above obtains in that, if it is held that the short-term rates for the next two years will be 4 percent and 2 percent, then by investing in short-term securities an investor could receive an average return of 3 percent over the two-year span. Therefore, were the two-year rate found to be above 3 percent, arbitrage would tend to drive the prices of two-year securities up (their yields down), as investors attempted to obtain the higher yields on these securities. This market reaction would tend to force the two rates back to an equality. Likewise, were the yields on these securities to lie below 3 percent, the fact that investing in short-term securities would return 3 percent on the average would result in the sale of two-year securities, thereby tending to raise their yields. While the above relates to the yields on two-year securities, it may be noted that, were an individual interested only in maximizing his investment for a single year, he could accomplish this through the purchase of any security regardless of its term to maturity. Were he to buy a two-year bond, hold it for a year, and then sell it, the effective yield would be 4 percent. This follows from our assumption that the expected short rate for this year is 4 percent. Were the nominal rate plus capital gains or minus

---

[5] For simplicity, we shall assume no compounding of interest; risk and market segmentation are also assumed away.

capital losses divided by the purchase price not equal to this rate, arbitrage would tend to equalize rates through changes in the market price. Thus, the theory implies that the net effective yield will be equal on all securities regardless of their term to maturity. In fact, the net returns on all securities must be equal, if the long rates are in fact the averages of short-term rates expected to hold over the duration of the long-term rates.

II

In his review of Meiselman's book, Wood characterizes the error-learning mechanism employed by Meiselman as showing that:

> despite the existence of institutional demands, the expectations hypothesis may constitute a valid descriptive theory of the structure of interest rates on default-free securities that are identical in all respects except term-to-maturity. He has shown that annual data taken from the 1901–54 period are consistent with the expectations hypothesis when combined with the assumption that revisions of expectations of future short-term rates are linear functions of past errors in predicting short-term rates.[6]

The error-learning mechanism itself lies outside the scope of this paper; the relevant consideration is the implications for the Federal Reserve and the U.S. Treasury, when it is understood that actions on their part will only affect the term structure of interest rates when and if they also affect expectations.

> If the Federal Reserve performs a swapping operation whereby long rates are driven upward and short rates driven downward, Meiselman's error term (p. 20) will be affected, causing a different revision of expectations than would have been the case in the absence of government activities and thereby inducing a different relation between long and short rates than would have existed had the swapping operation not occurred. Consequently, although the expectations hypothesis does not imply as great or as reliable an effect on the structure of rates due to government operations as is implied by the hedging theory, the expectations hypothesis, incorporating the error-learning mechanism by which expectations are revised, does not imply that changes in the maturity composition of outstanding debt will have no influence on the term structure of interest rates.[7]

Relating the above implications with the expectations hypothesis, we note that Wood has defined the hypothesis such that it

> · · · asserts that securities of different maturity are perfect substitutes in the eyes of a significant portion of investors, that these investors maximize the present value of expected receipts on the basis of confidently held single-valued expectations with respect to future rates of interest, and that investors operating on the basis of expectations control a sufficiently large proportion of total investible funds to bring long-term rates plus unity into equality with geometric averages of current and expected short-term rates plus unity.[8]

---

[6] Wood, *loc. cit.*
[7] *Ibid.*
[8] *Ibid.*, p. 160.

Unfortunately, this definition creates a logical impasse when it is brought to bear on Wood's statement of implications. The phrase "the Federal Reserve performs a swapping operation whereby long rates are driven upward and short rates driven downward" is inconsistent with Wood's definition of "confidently held single-valued expectations" which implies that it is impossible for Federal Reserve actions to influence the rate structure except through changes in expectations. In his conclusion, Wood has rates changing due to direct Federal Reserve purchases and sales which thereby also change expectations and the yield to maturity structure. But if the term to maturity structure is set by expectations and expectations are given, then it follows that the only way in which the term to maturity structure can change is through exogenous changes acting upon expectations. Federal Reserve operations can have no direct effect on the pattern of rates according to Wood's definition. In fact, given the validity of Wood's definition, we are forced to assume that moral suasion becomes the only effective policy instrument of the central bank. If interest rate changes are caused by changes in expectations, central bank effectiveness depends only on the extent to which it influences investor expectations. The central bank must persuade the public to hold certain views. Expectations become the transmitting devices by which real actions are resolved into real effects. Even if we say that Federal Reserve purchases and sales may influence interest rates (as Wood does), we must still discover what forces are determining interest rates. To make the expectations hypothesis operational, the exogenous variables must be distinguished from those that are endogenous to the theoretical structure. As it stands, Wood asserts that expectations determine interest rates and that open-market operations influence interest rates; one may reasonably ask what theory is being advanced. Wood cannot consistently claim that central banks can alter interest rates by open-market operations without thereby sacrificing the expectations hypothesis. What we must ascertain is whether the paradox above is primarily a semantic outgrowth which can be eliminated by definitional reworking, or whether these problems are in fact inherent to any expectational approach to the term structure of interest rates.

Turning to Meiselman, we can see how the expectational hypothesis supposedly functions.

> The real but statistically unspecified independent variable is unanticipated changes in what the literature would typically call "the interest rate." For given expectations, the entire brunt of an unanticipated change in "the interest rate" will be felt on the shortest end of the yield curve regardless of the source of the disturbance. Prices of long-term bonds cannot change much unless the disturbance alters expectations, even if the disturbance is financed completely by or associated with a change in long-term bonds outstanding. If the long-term rate were initially affected by an increase in bonds outstanding, speculation would force bond prices to return to their original positions.[9]

---

[9] Meiselman, *op. cit.*, p. 31

In this passage Meiselman shows that the expectations hypothesis is really a theory of two parts: (1) "the interest rate," an instantaneous rate, which is determined by market supply and demand forces, and (2) all other rates which are determined by "the interest rate" and expectations as to what "the interest rate" will be in future periods. Accordingly, the causality runs in only one direction: from the "interest rate" to the expectations of future short rates of interest. Meiselman presents a different hypothesis from Wood's—Wood's analysis is self-contradictory whereas Meiselman's is logically valid, given his rather strained assumptions. If we are to gain a firm understanding of the expectational approach, we must investigate both parts of this hypothesis, especially the implicit portion dealing with "the interest rate."

III

In the classic article by Lutz, it is difficult to find any causality structure at all. In reference to the implications of the system, however, we can find much to question. In his analysis of long and short rates Lutz states that:

> If the long rate is above the short, which implies an expectation that the long rate will rise, borrowers will try to borrow long in order to take advantage of the particularly low rate. The lenders, among them the banks, have an opposite interest: they prefer shorter maturities in this situation. It may therefore be difficult to float long-term securities.[10]

This is a bit surprising to read since, when he explained the concept of net effective yield, he stated:

> Thus, as long as the long-term rate expresses the average of the future short-term rates, it does not pay to borrow short and to buy long-term bonds, even though the long-term interest rate (whether this be represented by the running yield or by the yield to redemption) may be above the short-term rate.[11]

Of course, if net effective yields are equal, it matters not what security one buys or what security one sells; in this regard Lutz has evidently misplaced the concept of opportunity cost. Be this as it may, his statement that it may be difficult to float long-term securities must imply that the increase in supply of long-term securities has a direct effect on this price. But to allow this is to admit that the expectations hypothesis is not oriented to explain the term structure. A similar problem appears when the author remarks concerning central bank discount policy that "the discount rate should be altered as infrequently as possible. If this is not feasible, the central bank must try to influence the long rate directly, if they want to regulate investment."[12] But

---

[10] Lutz, *op. cit.*, p. 526.
[11] *Ibid.*, pp. 503–04.
[12] *Ibid.*, p. 525.

if the central bank can influence long rates directly then expectations no longer solely determine long rates! If the central bank cannot influence the long rate, it should not bother trying.[13] Since Lutz gives no indication as to how the term structure coordinates with "interest rate" theory, we must turn to the analysis as presented in Hicks's *Value and Capital*.

In Hicks's theory of the interest-rate structure, he takes one week as the relevant period which fixes the duration of any given short rate. Assuming simple interest with no compounding, he sets up the relationship:

$$R_1 = r_1$$

$$2R_2 = r_2 + r_1$$

$$3R_3 = r_1 + r_2 + r_3$$

therefore,

$$R_2 = \frac{r_1 + r_2}{2}$$

$$R_3 = \frac{r_1 + r_2 + r_3}{3}$$

where R_1, R_2 and R_3 are the current one-week, two-week, and three-week rates (the long rates), and r_1, r_2 and r_3 are the forward short rates.[14] The long rate is the arithmetic average among the current short rate and the relevant forward short rates. To determine "the rate of interest," Hicks posits two simplifying possibilities: (1) the spot economy where there is no long lending whatsoever, and (2) an economy where Consols are the only form of security.[15] Thus, the "only difference between them is that while we have explained the span of interest rates in terms of expectations about the future course of the short rate, here we explain in terms of expectations about the future course of the long rate."[16]

From the above it is an easy step for Hicks to launch into an analysis of a Walrasian type.[17] In the usual presentation of a Walrasian system of $n + 1$ equations, one equation is dropped to make the system determinate. Hicks says we can drop the money equation, thereby determining the supply and demand for loan funds; or we can follow Keynes and drop the purchase and sale of securities equation and have the demand and supply of money determined. However, it may be seen that Hicks does not develop any causal relationships between the various interest rates he is describing.

---

[13] It appears a little strange to hold that the central bank cannot change the price of long-term securities directly when we notice that the U.S. Treasury's main problem appears to be concern with refunding operations and the fear of price declines.

[14] Hicks, *op. cit.*, p. 145.

[15] *Ibid.*, pp. 148–51.

[16] *Ibid.*, p. 152.

[17] *Ibid.*, p. 155.

This lack of causal structuring brings up the interesting question of how Meiselman would analyze a transaction in the long end of the market if we explain the term structure by means of the long rate. Or, what if we decide to leave both the money equations in and drop the peanuts equation? Hicks has not given any justification of his choice of equations to be used, nor has he presented any causative sequence to explain how we can move from "the interest rate" to the overall system of interest rates in existence. Since letters are free and this is a general equilibrium approach, might it not be appropriate to set up one equation for each interest rather than to choose arbitrarily two polar equations? Although causality appears to be lacking in Hicks's analysis, he is aware that causality doubtlessly cannot be assuaged as a single-directional force when he notes:

> But since, in reality, there is no minimum period of borrowing and lending, and no division of trading into discontinuous "market days" (as we have conveniently supposed), those influences which we have described as working on the short rate become entangled with the speculative elements discussed previously. In practice, there is no rate so short that it may not be affected by speculative elements; there is no rate so long that it may not be affected by the advantages of the alternative use of funds in holding cash.[18]

Hicks's theory does not provide us with a specific causality structure and thus, we must assess his hypothesis as lacking in content.

IV

In this section we shall explore the expectational hypothesis and its relevancy under the polar conditions of certainty and uncertainty. For this analysis to be of significance, we must make some statement as to the likely causative relationships implicit in the term structure of interest rates. Joseph Conard states what he believes to be the causative forces implementing expected future short-term interest rates:

> These short rates do not in any sense "cause" long rates. Rather, all rates are caused by present and expected future supply and demand for funds. The long-term rates depend upon the supply and demand conditions expected to rule throughout the life of the securities involved. To say that today's long rate will equal the average of future shorts implies that today's long rate will be determined, as will today's and tomorrow's short rates, by today's and tomorrow's supplies and demands for funds.[19]

Without other information the above would appear to be a reasonable interpretation of the causative relationships we wish to analyze. Keeping the above in mind, let us consider the system under the assumption of

---

[18] *Ibid.*, p. 166.
[19] J. W. Conard, *An Introduction to the Theory of Interest* (Berkeley: University of California Press, 1959), p. 301.

certainty which for our purposes shall also include the condition of perfect foresight.[20]

With perfect foresight and rationality on the part of the market participants the "rate of interest" would be a unique single-valued number that would also be determinate. Under these conditions,

> ... the effective rate of return for a given period of time will be the same on securities of all maturities so long as capital gains and losses as well as interest income are included in this return. It is this rate which is given by "the theory of interest," whether that theory be liquidity-preference or loanable-funds.[21]

This is essentially what Hicks said in *Value and Capital*; but both statements are basically empty in that, given the conditions assumed, there is only one interest rate anyway. A clarifying assumption here is to make all securities equal in term to maturity; either Consols or of short duration. Thus, the term to maturity pattern becomes a single point. Note that under these conditions there is no risk and any market segmentation extant will have already been included in the determination of "the rate of interest." To allow for debt of varying maturity becomes an arithmetic calculation. If we assume a constant rate over time, we have a horizontal yield pattern; any other rate structure implies that the yield pattern is continually in the process of shifting as short rates are dropped and long rates picked up. Since prices of all securities are known and "the rate of interest" is known, we have a situation where all securities are perfect substitutes. When two or more commodities are perfect substitutes for each other it is usual to consider them to be the same economic good. With perfect foresight and given securities of different term to maturity, we are forced to assume that term to maturity is no longer a relevant market factor. One may ask: Why is it that there would ever be more than one term to maturity security issued under such conditions?

What can we say about the term structure in a world of certainty? Since we have been given future rates by assumption, the derived yield pattern tells us nothing about the cause-and-effect relationships which have brought this about. Returning to the numerical example used in the first section of this paper let us assume the expectations used are known with

---

[20] Two of the many connotations of the term "certainty" are brought to mind in the present context. In a causal sense, certainty is often used in reference to conditional statements, such as: if "a," then "b." The term is also used in reference to a situation or condition that is sure to happen, occur, or be present sometime in the future. Newtonian physics is an example of the former, while the phenomenon of certain religious sects holding with certainty that the world shall come to an end on a specific date exemplifies the latter. It is, of course, the nonconditional sort of certainty that is used in this paper.

The association of foresight and certainty follows from our assumption of rationality on the part of the market participants. That is, it is illogical to assume that an individual would believe with certainty what some interest rate would be in some future period, have himself proved wrong by the events of history, and then continue to orient his behavior in the future as if he were blessed with perfect certainty.

[21] Conard, *op. cit.*, pp. 298–99.

certainty. "The interest rate" will be 4 percent, 2 percent, and 6 percent in the next three years, while this year the term to maturity structure is 4 percent, 3 percent, and 4 percent, for one-year, two-year, and three-year securities, respectively. We cannot assert that the present interest rate of 4 percent, together with expectations of future rates, "caused" the term to maturity pattern to be 4 percent, 3 percent, and 4 percent, just as we cannot assert that the present term to maturity structure "causes" expectations to be what they are![22] To portray the above situation by means of a liquidity-preference model or loanable-funds model would be misleading and incorrect were anything to be implied about reality other than that these given rates do indeed exist.

In a more general sense the assumption of perfect foresight means the total absence of unknowns, thereby reducing the usual dichotomy of independent and dependent variables to an undefinable quantification. In a dynamic sense, time loses its essential significance and the fourth dimension collapses out of the system. With the future assumed to be known, one is forced to assume the existence of predestination along with full knowledge thereto.[23]

The expectations theory under conditions of less-than-perfect foresight— that is, with uncertainty—presents what may be insurmountable problems for the functional operation of the hypothesis.[24] In Conard's words:

> An important consequence for the theory of interest is that there is no longer a single rate of interest even over defined short periods of time as there was in the unmodified theory. Thus, securities of different term are no longer perfect substitutes for one another, and a rate determined by the theory of interest is no longer unambiguous.[25]

If one allows for uncertainty and market segmentation by applying certain risk premiums and other adjustment mechanisms to the basic yield structure, that is, the riskless perfect certainty model, one, of necessity, must allow for risk and uncertainty in one's rate of interest theory. Unfortunately, less than

---

[22] If equilibrium is defined as that situation wherein $a = b$, we can say very little other than that we are or are not in equilibrium. Without further information, we cannot say that a affected b and caused the equilibrium, or that b affected a and caused the equilibrium, or that a and b are directly related. In equilibrium, $MU_a = P_a$ — which does not imply that the demand side caused the equilibrium.

[23] This hypothesis has some rather peculiar ramifications: with respect to economic theorizing, the certainty assumption is not only simplifying, it is stultifying. Economics deals with the problems of choice; under certainty, there is no choice and there is no freedom. Philosophically, those individuals who espouse an almighty who is endowed with the quality of all-knowing are stopped from also espousing free will in their own actions.

[24] In Wood's definition of the expectational hypothesis, he includes the phrase "single-valued expectations." This is, of necessity, an irrational assumption or implies irrationality, since holding single-valued expectations implies certainty and perfect foresight, and these conditions are not part of the real world. This kind of oversight seems to be prevalent in the literature dealing with these matters; it may be characterized as a sort of have-your-cake-and-eat-it-too syndrome.

[25] Conard, *op. cit.*, p. 351.

perfectly competitive securities markets imply that there will be varying prices (yields) on the same securities depending upon the buyer (his knowledge, location, and so forth). Likewise, since risk is a subjective evaluation, each individual will view the market through his own eyes and give each security his own subjective expected yield evaluation. How then can we speak of a single rate of interest? In terms of the loanable-funds market there is no one rate that equates the supply and demand for securities. There are many rates that individually equate the supply and demand functions for many different markets made up of many different securities. In terms of liquidity preference, the price of money is not the same for each individual who is in the market for it. For the expectations hypothesis to have validity in a real world context, the term structure must be connected to reality through some mechanism other than "the rate of interest," or it will necessarily give incorrect implications both as to causal relationships and as to policy. On Wall Street "the rate of interest" is nonexistent.

Since we have assumed that all rates are interrelated, it follows that, in order to integrate an expectational hypothesis with "the rate of interest," all rates of interest must be known. In an appropriate Walrasian system where all markets (including the securities markets) are interdependent, all interest rates are functionally related to each other; therefore, to determine any one rate all others must be known. Multidirectional causality means that the expectations hypothesis, in any functional sense, is redundant since to make it operative the variables become parameters.

V

The expectations hypothesis under conditions of perfect certainty has been found to be valid as a descriptive statement, while being found to be lacking as a causative theory. With the condition of uncertainty, the necessary information to make the hypothesis function results in its being of little value while its causality is, of course, still suspect. Thus, we can say that the naïve-interest theory, upon which Meiselman bases his error-learning model, invalidates his analysis. One need only ask: Why it is not possible for changes in expectations about future short-term rates to have an influence directly upon the present supply and demand conditions which determine the current short rate to negate his analysis?

The value of a positive debt-management policy cannot be negated by recourse to an expectational approach to the term structure of interest rates. It may well be that securities are generally very close substitutes; but more importantly, it may be that under conditions of stress the substitution nexus breaks down, in which case debt management can take on considerable significance as a policy variable. For instance, under stress conditions central bank operations in the short end of the market, with the goal of bringing down the long rates of interest, may be ineffectual, given the need for rapid accomplishment of this policy objective. The testing of various hypotheses dealing with the substitutibility of the various securities in the debt market which indicate high correlations over time may not be a valid indication of the real significance of this substitutibility. If over a half-century there are only a few occasions when substitutibility breaks down, these times may be washed out in the statistics due to the fact that, generally, securities are somewhat close substitutes for each other. The implication is that a positive debt-management policy may only be effective at just those times when it is most needed.[26]

Although only passing discussion has been given to the relationship between certainty and uncertainty conditions in this paper, it may be worthwhile to reappraise the benefits and costs of approaching economic problems by the use of the first approximation of certainty. It may be noted that this assumption has a propensity to turn up in the analysis of just those problems where it is most deleterious to the schemata being presented; namely, problems—the interest rate, investment, and situations of a dynamic intertemporal nature—the essence of which is risk and uncertainty.

---

[26] See J. M. Culbertson, "The Term Structure of Interest Rates," *Quarterly Journal of Economics*, November 1957, vol. 71, pp. 485–517.

APPENDIX A

On page 355 of *Introduction to the Theory of Interest*, Professor Conard presents an integration of his modified-structure theory—that is, making an allowance for uncertainty and market segmentation, with the general theory of interest. He uses the following notation:

I = investment	R = two-year rate
S = saving	T = long (three-year) rate
Y = income	M_1 = funds available for active balances
r = short (one-year) rate	M_2 = funds available for idle balances.

Subscripts a, b and c indicate the year of reference: e.g., R_c equal the two-year rate in year three. Barred symbols are given data. L, f and ϕ are functional notations for the demands for money, for desired saving, and for desired investment, respectively. Subscripts 1 and 2 related to L indicate active and idle money. Q equals the current short rate that exists because of the distortions recognized by the modified theory. Symbols m and n are multiplicative co-efficients required to give the yield curve its positive bias. The symbols α, β and γ represent additive adjustments made necessary by market segmentation. They may be defined as the premium which the marginal buyer (or seller) of a security is willing to pay because of the buyer's particularized demand for a given term. The model is:

(1) $\qquad \bar{M} = M_1 + M_2$

(2) $\qquad M_1 = L_1(Y)$

(3) $\qquad M_2 = L_2(Q, R, T)$

(4) $\qquad S = f(T, Y)$

(5) $\qquad I = \phi(T, Y)$

(6) $\qquad S = I$

(7) $\qquad Q = mr_a + \alpha \qquad (1 > m > 0; \alpha \lessgtr 0)$

(8) $\qquad R = \dfrac{(1 + r_a)(1 + r_b) - 1}{(1 + r_b)} + \beta \qquad (\beta \lessgtr 0)$

(9) $\qquad T = \left[\dfrac{(1 + r_a)(1 + r_b)(1 + r_c) - 1}{(1 + r_b)(1 + r_c) + (1 + r_c) + 1}\right] n + \gamma \qquad (n > 1; \gamma \lessgtr 0).$

This three-year model is simplified in that investment and saving are considered to be dependent upon long rates of interest while the decision to hold idle funds depends upon short rates. No multiplicative coefficient is given in the equation for R, since it is assumed that two-year terms are the fulcrum about which the yield curve rotates in obtaining its positive bias. Conard states "Since equations for years b and c are not given, we must assume r_b and r_c to be known. This leaves as unknowns: M_1, M_2, Y, S, I, Q, R, T and r_a."[27] This necessity for assuming r_b and r_c to be known, I feel, justifies the first paragraph on page 459; that is, assuming interdependency of rates requires all rates to be known for the solution of the model. Knowing all rates, one can telescope this information into a compact mathematical relationship, but one cannot return the other way.

---

[27] Conard, *op. cit.*, p. 355.

APPENDIX B

David Meiselman presents his "substantive" hypothesis on page 20 of *The Term Structure of Interest Rates*, where he uses capital letters to represent actual market rates; lower-case letters to represent forward, implied, or expected rates; the first subscript, the duration of the loan; the prescript, the beginning of the period in which the rate in question becomes applicable; and the second subscript $_{1923}r_{6(1910)}$ is the forward rate on a six-year loan to commence in 1923 implied by rates at the beginning of 1910.

Thus, we can present the hypothesis that forward short-term rates change on the basis of errors made in forecasting the current short-term rate:

$$_{t+n}t_{1(t)} - {}_{t+n}r_{1(t-1)} = f(_tR_{1(t)} - {}_tr_{1(t-1)})$$

or:

$$\Delta_{t+n}r_{1(t)} = g(E_t)$$

where E is the forecasting error $(_tR_{1(t)} - {}_tr_{1(t-1)})$ the difference between the actual one-year rate and the one-year rate which had been expected to prevail. If we assume that the functional relationship is linear it may be expressed as:

$$\Delta_{t+n}r_{1(t)} = a + bE_t.$$

Since the long-term rate is an average of current and forward short-term rates, we also have the hypothesis that unanticipated changes in the long-term rate are also based on errors made in forecasting short-term rates:

$$_{t+n}R_{j(t)} - {}_{t+n}R_{j(t-1)} = h(_tR_{1(t)} - {}_tr_{1(t-1)})$$

or:

$$\Delta_{t+n}R_{j(t)} = k(E_t)$$

where n equals 0, 1, 2, 3 years, and j equals 1, 2 years. Thus, for example:

$$_tR_{30(t)} = a + bE_t$$

is the regression equation for a thirty-year rate.

Since Meiselman offers no rationale for setting up his functional relationships, might it not be possible that causation runs from errors in anticipated long-rates or even errors in anticipated medium-term rates to the other rates? For long-rate causation, we may assume the functional relation:

$$_tR_{1(t-1)} - {}_tr_{1(t-1)} = h^*(_{t+n}R_{j(t)} - {}_{t+n}R_{j(t-1)})$$

or:

$$\Delta_tR_{1(t)} = k^*(E_t)$$

In the thirty-year regression we have:

$$\Delta_tR_{1(t)} = c + dE_t$$

There are no leads or lags used in Meiselman's study and, therefore, there is no way to check causality using his statistics. On the other hand this allows the above inverse hypothesis to be substantiated to the same degree as Meiselman's hypothesis by the use of these statistics.

Limitation of the data in Meiselman's study has allowed only the most superficial lead-lag analysis. Lagging by one year the error term to the thirty-year rate and lagging the thirty-year rate to the error term and using "synchronous" to designate observations where the sign change was the same and "nonsynchronous" where signs were not consistent resulted in the following:

	$_tR_{30(t)}$ and E_t	$_tR_{30(t-1)}$ and E_t	$_tR_{30(t)}$ and E_{t-1}
Synchronous	45	30	21
Nonsynchronous	9	24	33

It may be seen that the error model of Meiselman's has much better synchronization than the other two—this would, of course, be expected when the analysis uses yearly data. However, concerning the lag between the models themselves, it may be argued that causation apparently runs from long to short rather than the opposite, as most expectational hypotheses assume. It is not meant to be argued that the alternative hypothesis presented above is in any realistic sense better than the Meiselman hypothesis, but rather that so little is known about the causative nature of interdependent interest rates that little can be said without further study. A tentative hypothesis is that causation varies over time and that, given the reaction times of market speculators, any data used that is not exceedingly short in duration (such as daily or even hourly data) will only result in nebulous statistical results.

In order to identify changes in interest rates which are primarily the result of other demand and supply conditions, we may possibly group those occasions where the dependent interest rate may have reacted primarily from changes in some other market. For instance, those times when there were large exogenous changes in Federal Reserve or U.S. Treasury purchases and where apparently there were no such similar exogenous activities in other markets may show a causal expectational linkage. The delineation of which variables are exogenous and which variables are endogenous in any given situation will, of course, be difficult, but unless this is done there is little hope for constructive theorizing about expectations and their effects.

PART VIII

International Business Financing

30

THE EURO-DOLLAR MARKET

GEOFFREY L. BELL

This article describes the development of the Euro-dollar market. The author discusses its origins in the desire of Eastern European banks to leave their dollar balances with their correspondents in France and England rather than to carry them in their own name in the United States. The correspondent banks then found that they could profit by lending the dollar balances at rates lower than those charged by traditional lending outlets in the U.S. Thus, Euro-dollar operations are a form of banking in which foreign banks accept deposits of dollar claims and in turn lend these dollar claims to their customers. The implications of the Euro-dollar market in the international structure of interest rates and on the international flow of funds is discussed.

Recently there has been discussion in the financial press devoted to the somewhat mysterious "Euro-dollar" banking market. This note describes the market, its origins, and its effects, especially on the United States balance-of-payments position. The word "mysterious," used with respect to the market, is rather apt in the sense that the statistical information on Euro-dollar operations is scanty and, consequently, it is difficult to evaluate fully the impact of the market on the U.S. balance of payments.

THE MARKET

The focus of this article is the market for dollars, although currencies such as sterling, Swiss francs, and Deutsche marks are traded in a similar fashion in what could be more generally referred to as the "Euro-currency" market. It is impossible to give a precise estimate of the size of foreign markets for dollars and other currencies, but it has been put at between $4-5 billion in mid-1962, with dollars constituting the biggest proportion of the currencies traded. Mr. Oscar Altman, Advisor, International Monetary Fund, estimates that $2\frac{1}{2}$ billion of this total was outstanding in the London market.[1]

From Geoffrey L. Bell, "The Euro-Dollar Market," *Federal Reserve Bank of St. Louis Review*, Vol. 45, No. 12, 5–8.
[1] Oscar Altman, "Recent Developments in Foreign Market for Dollars and Other Currencies," *Factors Affecting the United States Balance of Payments*. Compilation of Studies prepared for the Subcommittee on International Exchange and Payments, 1962.

Euro-dollar operations are a particular form of banking whereby foreign banks, chiefly European, accept deposits of dollar claims and, in turn, lend these dollar claims to their customers. Typically, these deposits and loans are made for short periods. The supply of funds to the market comes mainly from foreigners having dollar claims as a result of the U.S. balance-of-payments deficit. The demand for dollar claims comes from a wide range of sources, including international traders who use the dollar as the world's major trading currency and American corporations which find the Euro-dollar market a relatively cheap and convenient source of borrowed funds.

The original impetus for the development of the Euro-dollar market has been ascribed to the desire of several banks in Eastern Europe to leave their dollar balances with their correspondents in France and England rather than to carry them in their own name in the United States.[2] The correspondent banks found that, operating with only a small interest rate spread, they could make a profit by lending these dollar balances at rates lower than those charged by traditional lending outlets in the United States. Other dollar holders soon found that they also could engage in similar operations. Further impetus was given to the market when British authorities in 1957 put restrictions on the use of sterling for refinancing of foreign trade credits for nonresidents and banned sterling acceptance credits covering trade between countries outside the sterling area. British banks then offered their customers and correspondents dollar facilities to take the place of the prohibited sterling credits, obtaining requisite balances in the European dollar market. Similar selective controls in other countries have helped to stimulate the Euro-market.

The introduction of nonresident convertibility in Western Europe at the end of 1958, whereby nonresidents could exchange European currencies into dollars without restriction, aided the development of foreign exchange operations and the Euro-dollar market. European banks were then able to accept deposits in foreign currencies, exchange the foreign currencies for dollars (while at the same time "covering" the transactions by repurchasing the foreign currency for delivery at a future date), and then invest these dollars in the Euro-dollar market.

Although the introduction of convertibility and the existence of exchange and other selective controls have helped to stimulate the market, the main reason for its continuance is the existence of a spread between borrowing and lending rates in the United States market. This spread enables Euro-bankers to offer higher interest rates on dollar deposits than could be obtained in U.S. banks and at the same time to offer lower rates on dollar loans, relying on large transactions and a heavy volume of business to make their profit. This same feature characterizes the United Kingdom market and similarly has encouraged the Euro-sterling market centered in Paris.

---

[2] Alan R. Holmes and Fred M. Klopstock, "The Market for Dollar Deposits in Europe," Federal Reserve Bank of New York, *Monthly Review*, November, 1960.

It should be pointed out that the transfer of dollar deposits among European banks, or to users of dollars in the United States or elsewhere, is conducted through the transfer of ownership of dollar deposits lodged in American banks. Thus, when a European bank lends dollars to, say, a French importer who imports from the United States, the appropriate sum of dollars is first transferred (within a U.S. bank) to the account of the French importer. The importer then pays for United States' goods by drawing on that account in favor of the U.S. exporter. The U.S. exporter finally "owns" that dollar deposit. The whole complex of Euro-dollar operations is reflected in the transfer of ownership of dollar deposits within the United States banking system.

Transactions in the Euro-dollar market are typically confined to large customers and are usually denominated in terms of $1 million. The present low limit for individual transactions is probably $100,000.[3] Thus, banks engaged in the Euro-dollar market can best be regarded as "wholesaling" units which can operate on smaller margins than can banks operating in the domestic market.

Because of higher interest rates on dollar deposits in Europe, dollars coming into the hands of foreigners as a result of the U.S. deficit on current and long-term capital account can be more profitably deposited in Europe than in the United States. In addition to foreign-owned dollar deposits, U.S. corporations have been attracted to the market because of the higher interest rates and because of the availability of interest rate returns on very short-term investments, e.g., for 7 days. American funds have been placed in the market mainly through depositing with Canadian banks which have in turn loaned them to the Euro-dollar market. Nonetheless, at present most of the funds in the market come from nonresidents. According to Altman, a substantial proportion of the funds have been supplied to the market by foreign central monetary authorities.

The demand for Euro-dollars comes from a variety of sources, mostly in the private sector. The commerical banks of a large number of countries accept and employ dollar deposits for use in both international and domestic operations. A substantial amount of Euro-dollars are used to finance firms engaged in international trade. These firms use Euro-dollar finance in preference to the more normal acceptance credits because of lower interest rate charges and because of the convenience of borrowing (given both the wide range of maturities available and the ready supply of funds in the market). Japan has figured prominently in the use of Euro-dollars for international trading. The highest interest rate that a Euro-banker could charge for lending dollars would be what it would cost that borrower to raise dollars on the New York market. This does not mean, however, that

---

[3] Paul Einzig, "Has the Euro-Dollar a Future?" *The Statist*, October 11, 1963.

the effective upper limit to lending charges is the New York prime rate, as relatively few foreign borrowers would be eligible for that rate.

Perhaps most of the funds provided in the Euro-dollar market are lent in the United States. Virtually since the market began, U.S. banks, through their European branches, have been active in the borrowing side of the market. The European branches have actively bid for Euro-dollars and have then repatriated the funds to the United States. To the extent that the subsidiaries have attracted U.S. resident funds, domestic residents may have been paid, indirectly, rates on time deposits in excess of those permitted under Regulation Q.

It has been suggested that one unexpected result of higher interest rates in the United States in recent months has been that American nonbanking borrowers have appeared in the Euro-dollar market for the first time on a large scale.[4] While large American corporations still find it worthwhile to lend short-term Euro-dollar deposits, they also find it worthwhile to borrow Euro-dollars for six months or longer. The fact that corporations have come to operate both as borrowers and lenders is regarded as a landmark in the evolution of the market by Einzig. The market is now regarded as a competitor for American domestic financing. U.S. banks are now competing against Euro-bankers for both domestic and international lending.

A feature of some interest in both the evolution of the Euro-dollar market and the revival of the London international capital market was the issue of a $20 million Belgian Government loan in London during May 1963. The loan had a three-year maturity and was denominated in dollars. The subscribers were a group of British banks which, it is generally thought, financed the loan in Euro-dollars.[5] This was a departure from the normal short-term lending prevalent in the market and was the first issue handled by British banks in currencies other than sterling since the war.

Euro-dollars are also used as money market instruments by foreign commerical banks. In view of the fact that dollars can be loaned or borrowed for various periods they constitute an excellent medium for banks to adjust their liquidity positions. In these operations the market is analogous to the Federal Funds Market in the U.S. Often banks are trading on both sides of the balance sheet, both lending Euro-dollars and at the same time borrowing.

As well as loaning dollars, the Euro-bankers may use the dollars to buy other currencies and lend in foreign markets. In such a case the bank will arrange to sell its foreign currency holdings for dollars at a future date, i.e., it will hedge against the exchange risk. Occasionally, dollar deposits in European banks are used to take advantage of interest arbitrage opportunities. For example, there is likely to be a strong relationship between the

---

[4] Einzig, *Ibid.*
[5] See "All About Euro-Dollars," *The Economist*, May 25, 1963.

amount of dollars switched into sterling and loaned to the United Kingdom Local Authority Market[6] and the margin between rates of interest on Local Authority deposits (adjusted for the cost of forward cover) and the rates on Euro-dollar deposits. At times, Local Authorities have borrowed substantial short-term funds from the Euro-dollar market. Although Euro-bankers will not usually ignore an interest arbitrage possibility, the main type of transaction is that in which dollars are loaned directly.

Selling dollars for foreign currencies can be profitable either for the Euro-banker or for the borrower who wants to be financed in his own currency. In such a case, the limit would be where the cost of borrowing dollars and switching into the foreign currency and covering the transaction for exchange risk equalled the rates charged on local funds. It can be seen that Euro-dollar operations are similar to normal foreign exchange operations. Therefore, the market can best be regarded as a supplement to normal foreign exchange operations whereby foreigners having claims on the United States sell their dollars for other currencies, and others, wanting dollars, buy them through the exchanges.

It should again be emphasized that the whole complex of Euro-dollar operations is reflected in the transference of ownership of dollar deposits within the U.S. These dollar deposits will continue to be held in U.S. banks unless (1) at some stage, dollars are converted into a foreign currency, or (2) the dollars come into the hands of central banks, that, in turn, convert them into gold, or (3) the dollars are used to pay off a loan at a United States bank.

IMPLICATIONS OF THE MARKET

The growth of the Euro-dollar market has had two types of effects—on the international structure of interest rates and on international flows of funds. Since the general return to convertibility in late 1958, international movements of capital have become considerably more flexible with funds in the hands of Euro-bankers being particularly interest-rate sensitive. If interest rates in one country become out of line, after allowing for the premium or discount on forward cover, with those of other countries, Euro-bankers will be induced to switch funds into the relatively high market, and out of the relatively low market. This has tended to bring short-term interest rates (allowing for forward cover), into closer alignment. And as a result it may be somewhat more difficult for monetary authorities to carry out changes in monetary policy. An easing of credit, which may be accompanied by lower domestic interest rates, tends to lead to an outflow of funds. The converse is true if rates stand at a premium compared with Euro-dollar rates.

---

[6] The Local Authority Market is broadly similar to the Market for Municipal Bonds in the United States.

Although movements of Euro-dollars do *tend* to bring short-term interest rates into closer alignment, the effects of these flows of funds are inhibited both by the lack of suitable money market investments in various countries and by artificial barriers. If money market investments are not available in foreign markets, it follows that there will be no inflows or outflows and hence no effects on interest rates or domestic monetary policy. However, there could be indirect effects if Euro-dollar financing was used in such countries for foreign trade loans.

Altman mentions three ways in which the effects of Euro-dollar flows have been prevented by artificial constraints from exerting major effects on domestic rates. First, attempts have been made to regulate (i.e., increase) the rates of interest charged on dollar loans. Agreements by Italian banks covering minimum rates on loans in lire were supplemented in 1961 by minimum rates on dollars and other foreign currencies. Second, under the stress of competition, it has been agreed or understood by banks in some countries, e.g., Germany, that loans in foreign currency should be made to the foreign trade sector only. Third, in many European countries, the competitive effect of foreign currency loans, and, therefore, of lower interest rates, has been restricted by exchange and capital control regulations. These regulations prevent domestic residents from borrowing foreign currencies without permission of the monetary authorities. In these various fashions the foreign markets are isolated to some extent from the effects of competition by the Euro-dollar market.

In addition to the Euro-dollar market's effects on interest rates and international flows, the growth of the market has increased the use of the dollar and has reduced the cost of foreign trade financing as the Euro-bankers have undercut domestic charges. Also, the interest rates on dollar deposits have probably been influential in the decision of private foreign dollar holders to invest in dollar deposits rather than in other currencies. To the extent that private dollar holders have been willing to remain invested in dollars rather than other currencies, the amount of dollars in the hands of foreign central monetary authorities is less than it otherwise would have been. If the foreign monetary authorities have limits on their dollar holdings, the market has helped, to some extent, to finance the U.S. deficit on current and long-term capital account with smaller gold losses than would otherwise have been the case. Although foreign central monetary authorities are unlikely to determine their dollar holdings on the basis of interest rate returns, to the extent that the market has increased the willingness of some of these institutions to hold dollars, international liquidity has been also increased. In other words, the foreign central monetary authorities acquire an increase in reserves without any parallel loss to the U.S. gold stock.

On the other hand, the high dollar deposit rates have attracted some United States residents to invest in the Euro-dollar market thus adding to the outflow of dollars and to the over-all balance-of-payments deficit. There are two ways of looking at this latter point. By one view, although lending by U.S. residents to the market constitutes an outflow of dollars, the lending is generally undertaken for short periods, and hence the U.S. asset may be thought of as offsetting the liability of a short-term outflow. By this method of accounting, the existence of the Euro-dollar market would be regarded as having no effect on the over-all balance of payments. However, the alternative view is that the outflow constitutes a claim (for a given period) on the U.S. gold stock, while the asset equivalent, being private, is not available to defend the dollar against a speculative movement. Consequently, a flow of dollars from the United States to the market is regarded as adding to the over-all payments deficit.

31

THE SWAP AS A HEDGE IN FOREIGN EXCHANGE

CLAUDE McMILLAN

While the previous selection has dealt with the general market aspects of international finance, this paper focuses on aspects significant for the financial manager in a multi-national firm. Professor McMillan begins by indicating the nature of exchange fluctuations which give rise to the need for hedging foreign exchange. He briefly discusses the nature of foreign exchange operations as a hedge, and explains why the use of swaps has arisen. The author then formulates an analytical framework for evaluating the swap as a hedge, and provides some illustrations of the actual uses of swaps.

Since the early 1950's a large number of American firms with investments in Brazil have swapped currencies with the Bank of Brazil as a means of hedging foreign exchange. Swaps between private firms and the central bank of a foreign country are relatively uncommon. However, the extent to which they have been employed since the war in Brazil, Colombia, and a few other soft currency areas, and the likelihood that their use may become more prevalent elsewhere makes them worthy of some study. As employed by U.S. firms in Brazil, the swap has involved a simultaneous spot and futures contract for the exchange of dollars for cruzeiros.

The mechanics have been some modification of the following example. U.S. subsidiary XYZ in Brazil has dollar credits either with its parent company or with an affiliated creditor in the U.S.A. and needs cruzeiros for a period of perhaps one year. Subsidiary XYZ arranges with the Bank of Brazil, a private Brazilian bank which acts as fiscal agent for the Brazilian government, for delivery of its dollar credits in the United States to the Bank of Brazil, against delivery to the subsidiary in Brazil of cruzeiro credits, with a contract to reverse the process at the end of a year. Both contracts are made at the same exchange rate so that at the end of the year subsidiary XYZ presents the same number of cruzeiros to the Bank of Brazil and receives in exchange its original dollar credits in the U.S.A.

The prevalence of swapping in Brazil can be attributed to a number of factors which are common to most Latin American countries today. The

From Claude McMillan, "The Swap as a Hedge in Foreign Exchange." Reprinted from *California Management Review*, Vol. IV, Summer, 1962, 57–65.

basic factors are: (1) the U.S. foreign subsidiary's increasing dependence on foreign exchange; (2) Brazil's burgeoning industrial growth; and (3) Brazil's unfavorable balance of payments.

DEPENDENCE ON FOREIGN EXCHANGE

Increasingly United States investments abroad are in manufacturing facilities which produce for the domestic markets of the host country. In an earlier era most U.S. operations abroad were confined to the development and export of raw materials. Export operations generate or produce foreign exchange. Manufacturing operations may, in the long run, conserve foreign exchange by decreasing the host country's dependence on foreign sources of supply for manufactured products. But these operations do not produce foreign exchange.

The American manufacturer in Latin America must buy foreign exchange in the host country's exchange markets. To import equipment, components and materials, to pay royalty and technical assistance fees, to service loans, remit profits and repatriate capital, the American manufacturer must buy dollars. As American firms abroad become more dependent upon the foreign exchange markets, they become more interested in devices such as the swap for minimizing exchange risks.

BURGEONING INDUSTRIAL GROWTH

Brazil's postwar industrial growth has been too rapid to permit the financing of expansion entirely out of earnings. This growth rate, coupled with the rudimentary state of development of Brazil's capital markets, has served to create a shortage of cruzeiro investment capital in Brazil.

As a consequence, many American subsidiaries in Brazil have secured capital for expansion from or through their parent organizations in the U.S.A. Much of this has taken the form of debt capital. The obligation of the subsidiary to repay a certain sum in dollars forces it to deal with the added risk of exchange fluctuation, and makes a hedge of some sort highly desirable.

UNFAVORABLE BALANCE OF PAYMENTS

Since the depression Brazil has been plagued with a shortage of foreign exchange. Foreign credits arranged with the International Monetary Fund, the World Bank, the United States Export-Import Bank, and a host of private lending agencies have never been adequate. As a consequence the government of Brazil has relied in a number of ways on U.S. firms which have operations in Brazil, as a source of dollar credits. The swap is one of the devices employed for this purpose.

IMPACT OF EXCHANGE FLUCTUATION

For almost ten years Brazil's currency has depreciated at rates ranging from 10 percent to 35 percent per year. Thus in 1958, a typical year, the free market rate of exchange dropped from 89 cruzeiros to the dollar to 138 per dollar. The precariousness of a fixed dollar loan commitment is apparent: the 89 million cruzeiros which a one million dollar loan would have purchased in January, 1958, would have been sufficient to repurchase only $645,000 on December 31, 1958.

In the long run it might be expected that the cruzeiro investment which was made possible by a dollar loan in one period would appreciate sufficiently to permit later repurchase of the full amount of dollars to repay the loan, even at the inflated exchange rate. Where the cruzeiro funds have been invested in fixed assets this is almost never the case. Prices of fixed assets tend to lag behind the depreciation in the value of the cruzeiro. When the investment is in more liquid assets, notably inventories, the cruzeiro investment may very well appreciate, in its cruzeiro value, sufficiently to earn a profit, or at least to preserve its real value.

Even here, however, the problem persists. The difficulty is in short run discrepancies, a source of constant concern to the manager of an American subsidiary in a soft currency country. Repayment of loans, importing materials and components, internal budgetary planning and financial reporting to the parent firm all are complicated by the fact that fluctuations in the exchange rate and fluctuations in the purchasing power of the soft currency are not in phase in the short run.

In 1958, many U.S. firms had one of their best years in Brazil. But as a consequence of violent short run fluctuations, the dollar profits into which their cruzeiro earnings were converted made it one of their worst years.

FORWARD EXCHANGE AS A HEDGE

Forward exchange, the purchase and sale of exchange for future delivery, is at least 100 years old. Today almost everywhere that hard currencies are traded, an active forward exchange market can also be found. By means of forward contracts businessmen and bankers eliminate or minimize risks arising from unfavorable exchange fluctuations.

Forward contracts are particularly useful to those engaged in import-export operations, as a hedge against exchange risks. They are also valuable in minimizing exchange uncertainties and in meeting sinking fund or interest commitments. Since World War II they have been used increasingly in connection with foreign investments.

But active forward exchange markets are confined largely to dealings in hard currencies. Even here contracts beyond a year's duration generally have to be negotiated. The forward exchange contract, therefore, is either prohibitively expensive or unavailable for hedging loans of one to five years term, when a soft currency is involved.

USE OF THE SWAP

Swaps, on the other hand, are being made for longer periods. Swaps differ from forward exchange in that the swap involves both a spot and a futures contract. Thus, whereas a forward exchange contract involves no immediate outlay of funds, a swap is a simultaneous loan of one currency in exchange for a loan of another currency, both loans repayable on the same future date.

The terms and volume of swapping are not well documented in financial literature. Most forward exchange dealings seem to be clothed in secrecy and the data available are limited and not very reliable. Paul Einzig suggests that the volume of outright buying or selling of forward exchange is much smaller than that of dealings in swaps.[1] Others have questioned this.

Most swapping involves private banks, but a number of central banks have found occasion to engage in swaps. In 1927, the Bank of France did a brisk and profitable business swapping francs for dollars and sterling with private French banks. By this means the Bank of France was able to maintain its own discount rate at a high level at a time when it was experiencing a plethora of funds.[2]

In the Western hemisphere the Bank of Brazil appears to have been among the first central banks to employ swaps. As early as the 1920's Brazil swapped cruzeiros for dollars and sterling as a means of obtaining short term credits abroad. But Brazil's postwar swaps have differed from earlier European bank swaps in that the Bank of Brazil has dealt directly with foreign business enterprises, and has swapped for longer periods. The recent willingness of the Bank of Brazil to swap for long periods has provided the American subsidiary operating in Brazil with an opportunity to hedge dollar loans for periods up to and even beyond five-year terms.

EVALUATION OF SWAP AS A HEDGE

Perfect hedges are rare. To understand the potential and limitations of the swap as a hedge involving a soft currency, we might examine in some detail the swap opportunity which has been presented to the American subsidiary in Brazil in recent years. It will become apparent that one cannot evaluate the attractiveness of the Bank of Brazil's recent swap offers solely by reference to the effective interest rate which one would pay. Both the

---

[1] Paul Einzig, *Theory of Forward Exchange* (London: Macmillan and Company, Ltd., 1961), p. 18.

[2] See note 1, p. 338.

attractiveness of a swap offer and the success of a consummated swap can better be determined by comparing the subsidiary's experience in a cruzeiro investment made with swapped dollars on the one hand, and with dollars sold on the free market on the other.

To perform this comparative evaluation it will be useful to adopt symbols for the more important variables:

F = the number of cruzeiros required to buy one dollar on the free market at the beginning of the investment period

P_i = the percentage *increase* in the cruzeiro value of the cruzeiro investment, during the life of the investment

P_c = the percentage *decrease* in the dollar value of the cruzeiro on the free market, during the life of the investment

I = the annual rate of interest on the dollars employed to make the cruzeiro investment, in percentage

S = the number of cruzeiros received from the Bank of Brazil for each dollar swapped

From the above notation it follows that: $F/(100\% - P_c)$ = the number of cruzeiros required to buy one dollar on the free market at the end of the investment period.[3]

If the subsidiary does not swap its borrowed dollars, but instead converts them on the free market and, after liquidating its cruzeiro investment at the end of the investment period, again converts on the free market to recover its dollars, the dollar value of its cruzeiro investment will have appreciated by:[4]

Percentage Gain *Without* a Swap:

$$P_i(100\% - P_c) - P_c - I \tag{I}$$

If the subsidiary swaps its dollars, and makes its investment with the cruzeiros it receives in exchange for those dollars, it will have a different experience. To begin with, the subsidiary will receive only S cruzeiros for each dollar swapped. In the past, in swaps with the Bank of Brazil, S has been considerably less than the prevailing free market rate. In order to make a cruzeiro investment of one dollar value, therefore, the subsidiary will have to swap not just one dollar but instead F/S dollars, and will therefore have to pay interest at the effective rate FI/S. At the end of the investment period the dollar value of its cruzeiro investment will have appreciated by:

Percentage Gain *With* a Swap:[5]

$$P_i(100\% - P_c) - FI/S \tag{II}$$

---

[3] The spread between the spot buying and selling price for foreign exchange—that is, the broker's commission—is ignored.

[4] Whether the investment is actually liquidated, or whether the dollars are repurchased with cruzeiros obtained from another source, an evaluation of the success of the swap obliges one to liquidate the cruzeiro investment "in theory" if not in fact.

[5] Customarily the Bank of Brazil has charged interest on the cruzeiros it has swapped for dollars. However the interest charged is seldom in excess of 4 percent, and is usually less. As the cruzeiro deteriorates during the investment period the dollar value of the cruzeiro interest charge

Finally, the difference between the percentage gain (or loss) from an investment made with swapped dollars and the gain (or loss) from an investment made with free market dollars would be:

Difference Between Expressions (II) and (I):

$$P_c + I(1 - F/S) \qquad \text{(III)}$$

From Expression (II) it would appear that by swapping the subsidiary maintains intact the dollar value of the principal of its investment. Regardless of what happens to the value of the cruzeiro, the first term of Expression (II) will not be less than zero.

From Expression (I) it is apparent that without a swap a loss of principal is possible, since in Expression (I), the sum of the first two terms could easily become negative.

However, as (II) shows, by swapping the subsidiary does not eliminate all risk arising out of unfavorable exchange fluctuation. The subsidiary's swap contract entitles it to convert the *principal* into dollars at rate S, but any excess which is attributable to growth of the cruzeiro investment must be converted at the less attractive free market rate which happens to prevail at the end of the investment period.

The seriousness of the obligation to convert on the free market all the cruzeiros which are in excess of the principal is readily apparent. If the swap rate is low relative to the free market rate, that is, if the ratio S/F is small, then the effective interest rate, FI/S, will be high. If this condition is accompanied by a heavily unfavorable free market rate at the end of the investment period, the cruzeiro excess from the liquidated investment will be inadequate to pay the interest on the dollar loan.

The combined effects of a deterioration in the exchange rate and a high effective interest charge will serve to erode part of the principal. Thus it makes less sense to evaluate the swap solely by reference to the effective interest rate charged. It is more meaningful to think in terms of gains and losses with and without the hedge provided by the swap.

To limit the attractiveness of swapping, the Bank of Brazil has offered swap rates which recently have been less than $\frac{1}{3}$ of the prevailing free market rate. Thus in mid-1960, one-year swaps were being made at 58 cruzeiros per dollar when the free market rate was 200 cruzeiros per dollar. The effect of this was to oblige the American subsidiary to swap $3.45 in order to make a cruzeiro investment of $1.00 value. For its one dollar's worth of cruzeiros, therefore, the subsidiary paid 3.45 times the normal interest.[6]

shrinks. The net effect of these factors is to reduce the effective cost which can be attributed to interest charged on the cruzeiro loan to between one percent and three percent. This charge will be ignored in the development outlined in the text. Note that in both Expression (I) and (II) interest has been deducted. Expressions (I) and (II), therefore, represent *net* gain.

[6] The Bank of Brazil could have made the swap less attractive by charging a high cruzeiro interest on its cruzeiro loan. But the Bank of Brazil's chief interest in swapping is to obtain needed dollar credits for its own use; for this purpose these swap rates serve nicely.

AN EXAMPLE OF HOW SWAP WORKS

Suppose that in mid-1960, a fictitious company, Americana Limited had a 200 million cruzeiro investment opportunity which offered promise of appreciation sufficient to justify the operating risks involved. It was Americana's expectation that at the end of a year enough of the investment could be liquidated to repay the funds borrowed to make the investment possible.

Finding cruzeiro capital almost impossible to obtain in Brazil, Americana arranged to borrow dollars from the U.S.A. at five percent, with the parent company in the U.S.A. guaranteeing the loan. Americana then had to decide whether to convert its borrowed dollars on the free market or to swap them for cruzeiros with the Bank of Brazil.

If Americana converted on the free market, one million dollars was required to make its 200 million cruzeiro investment, and at five percent the interest cost was $50,000.

If Americana swapped, $(F/S) \times (\$1,000,000)$ or $3,450,000 was required to make its 200 million cruzeiro investment, and the interest cost was $172,500.

From mid-1960 to mid-1961 the dollar value of the free market cruzeiro depreciated to 286 cruzeiros per dollars (thus $P_c = 30$ percent). From Expression (I) it is apparent that without a swap, P_i, the percentage appreciation of Americana's cruzeiro investment, would have had to be 50 percent for Americana's dollar investment simply to be preserved.

From Expression (II) it is apparent that had Americana swapped, the cruzeiro value of its cruzeiro investment would have had to increase by only 24.3 percent in order for the dollar investment to be just preserved.

It would appear that the swap, from the viewpoint of security, was the wiser choice. However, by swapping and paying in effect 3.45 times the normal interest rate, Americana would have foregone a part of its gain in the event that the exchange rate did not deteriorate seriously. Thus if the value of the cruzeiro had dropped by only 10 percent, and Americana's cruzeiro investment had appreciated 50 percent, Americana's gain would have been:

    a. Gain Without a Swap: 30.0%
    b. Gain With a Swap: 27.7%

How much of its prospective gain should a firm be willing to sacrifice in exchange for some security of its principal against exchange risk? This would appear to be dependent upon: (*a*) the cost of security against an adverse exchange fluctuation; (*b*) the seriousness of the consequences of adverse fluctuations of varying magnitude; and (*c*) the probabilities of these fluctuations of varying magnitudes occurring.

Factor (*a*) above, the cost of security against adverse fluctuations, is easily calculated. It is simply the excess effective interest charge arising out of the fact that the swap rate is less than the free market rate. This cost amounts to: $R(F/S - 1)$ percent on an annual basis.

Factor (*b*) depends upon the ease with which a subsidiary can afford to sustain losses of various magnitudes. This will vary, of course, from firm to firm.

Factor (*c*) would seem to be a complete unknown since the free market rate depends not only on economic factors which are exceedingly complex and difficult to predict, but also on what the government of Brazil does or does not do to influence the free market rate. However (*c*) is not entirely unpredictable. American businessmen operating abroad can and do forecast exchange rates; they are forced to do so. They are never really operating totally in the dark. Americana Limited could have predicted with virtual certainty that the cruzeiro would not lose more than 60 percent of its value from mid-1960 to mid-1961 (that is, would not drop from around 200 cruzeiros per dollar to a low of 500 cruzeiros per dollar). But the cruzeiro might reasonably be expected to drop from 10 percent to 50 percent per year, with a drop in the neighborhood of 25 percent to 40 percent rather likely.

PAYOFF MATRIX

One might construct a payoff matrix, with a forecast probability density function for varying values of P_c. Then by evaluating the relative seriousness of the consequences of losses of various magnitudes one might make a rather judicious decision as to whether to swap. The logic employed in an analysis of this sort is undoubtedly used, in a less formal way, by American firms which have elected to swap. Assume once again, for example, that Americana Limited is confronted with the investment opportunity previously described. An appreciation in the cruzeiro value of Americana's cruzeiro investment of between 10 percent and 50 percent is regarded as a distinct likelihood.

Referring to Expression (III), it is apparent that if the dollar value of the free market cruzeiro drops by around 12 percent, Americana's dollar gain from the investment would be about the same whether or not Americana swaps. That is: If $P_i = 50$ percent, with or without the swap Americana can expect a dollar loss of about 8 percent.[7]

---

[7] Some may be tempted to quarrel with the argument embodied in this development on the grounds that it makes possible a net loss in excess of the cost of money on an investment whose principal is "guaranteed" (i.e., secured by the swap). It should be noted, however, that the percentage loss we have discussed is the percentage loss on the dollar value (i.e., the "real" value) of the cruzeiro investment. The American investor may argue that he thinks only in terms of dollars, and since his dollars are securely hedged his maximum possible percentage loss is the interest rate on his dollars. But the subsidiary in Brazil cannot think only in terms of dollars. Its investment opportunity is a "cruzeiro-generating" investment opportunity, not a "dollar-generating" investment opportunity. It is an investment for which cruzeiros, rather than dollars, might more appropriately be borrowed. For evaluating the choice between investing with borrowed cruzeiros versus cruzeiros purchased with borrowed dollars, and the choice between swapping versus not swapping the borrowed dollars, the subsidiary in Brazil, like the Brazilian national firm with which it competes, should consider the real value percentage gain or loss anticipated from its cruzeiro investment. Basically the logic is the same as that employed in estimating percentage gain from trading on the equity.

If P_c is less than 12 percent, the swap is less attractive. At $P_c = 5$ percent, Americana's gain with the swap would be about 7 percent greater than without a swap.

However, if the cruzeiro should continue to deteriorate as it has in the past, a P_c of only 12 percent is unlikely, and with each successive decrease in the value of the cruzeiro the swap becomes more attractive. With a 40 percent drop in the value of the cruzeiro, the experience from an investment with a swap is about 27.8 percent better than without a swap.

Obviously with a low ratio of S to F the swap does not provide complete protection against exchange risks. Unless P_i is at least $FI/S(1 - P_i)$, even with a swap the investor would lose part of his principal because of the high effective interest charged, and would thus sustain a net loss from the experience.

Since an annual cruzeiro depreciation in Brazil of at least 20 percent is almost a certainty, an investor should be disinterested in investing even with swapped dollars at current swap rates unless a cruzeiro growth of at least 22 percent between investment and liquidation can be expected. Undoubtedly, however, American subsidiaries in Brazil have elected to invest in Brazil with swapped dollars even when a 22 percent growth in the investment could not reasonably have been expected. Other considerations, such as a determination to hold one's share of the market, may override short-run return.

THE USE OF SWAPS IN BRAZIL

The swap analyzed above has been referred to as the conventional swap. In mid-1960 the Bank of Brazil, when the free market rate was 200 cruzeiros per dollar, was offering conventional swaps at the following rates and terms:

Term of swap	Swap rate	Interest rate on the cruzeiro loan
Up to two years	58 cruzeiros per dollar	4.0% per year
Two to three years	70 cruzeiros per dollar	3.5% per year
Three to four years	81 cruzeiros per dollar	3.0% per year
Four to five years	87 cruzeiros per dollar	2.0% per year
Five years and longer	92 cruzeiros per dollar	1.0% per year

It is apparent that as the term increases the swap rate becomes more attractive. As the free market rate changes the swap rates offered also have changed. By mid-1961 several one-year swaps were made by American firms with the Bank of Brazil at a swap rate of 185 cruzeiros per dollar when the free market rate was 286 cruzeiros per dollar.

Recent swaps with the Bank of Brazil have ranged in value from as little as $50,000 to well over $5,000,000. To date Brazil has never defaulted on a swap in spite of its own foreign exchange imbalance.

THE FINANCIAL SWAP

In addition to the conventional swap the Bank of Brazil has offered what have been termed "financial" swaps and "export" swaps. In the financial swap the American subsidiary does not exchange his cruzeiros for dollars with the Bank of Brazil at the end of the investment period, but instead he terminates the affair by selling his dollars to the Bank of Brazil permanently, at the going market rate *less* the swap rate received when the swap was initiated. The decision as to when to terminate the swap rests with the American subsidiary.

THE EXPORT SWAP

The export swap is little more than a modification of the financial swap. Strictly speaking neither the financial swap nor the export swap is a genuine swap. Both are, in reality, delayed purchases of foreign exchange.

The availability of swaps and their terms have varied as the government of Brazil's need for dollar credits has fluctuated and as foreign firms in Brazil have needed funds. These factors are heavily influenced by the timing and sales abroad of Brazil's chief export product, coffee, and also by the Brazilian government's various economic development projects as they have required dollar funding.

By October, 1959, Brazil held dollar credits in the United States amounting to some $212,000,000 which could be attributed to swaps outstanding, and some $17,000,000 in A.C.L. funds (areas of limited convertibility).[8] By mid-1960 the total had risen to about $300,000,000.[9]

According to *Conjuntura Economica*, one of Brazil's most respected economic journals, Brazil's foreign exchange deficit in 1959 was covered largely by the government's swap operations with American firms. In a rare tribute to foreign enterprise this journal observed:

> Paradoxically, at a time when foreign capital is being indiscriminately attacked, it is this very capital which offers its services for the regularizing of Brazil's transactions with the rest of the world in an obvious demonstration that, despite everything, it (foreign capital) is integrated into the spirit of economic development of our country.[10]

---

[8] As stated by the Brazilian Minister of Finance and reported in the Sao Paulo newsletter of the American Chamber of Commerce for Brazil, October 19, 1959.

[9] Summary Proceedings of the September meeting of the Board of Governors of the International Monetary Fund, Washington, D.C., 1960, p. 62.

[10] *Conjuntura Economica*, February, 1960, p. 58.